Database
Performance
Tuning
Handbook

Contributors to this book include:

Microsoft® Windows NT ™ Technical Consultant
Michael Dunham

Computer Graphics Consultant
Allan Dunham

CALCSPAC.SQL Tuning Script
Robert Walters

Vendors
Aonix

ARIS Corporation

Menlo Software

Microsoft®

Precise Software

SQLBENCH International Incorporated

Database
Performance
Tuning Handbook

Jeff Dunham

McGraw-Hill

New York   San Francisco   Washington, D.C.   Auckland   Bogotá
Caracas   Lisbon   London   Madrid   Mexico City   Milan
Montreal   New Delhi   San Juan   Singapore
Sydney   Tokyo   Toronto

Library of Congress Cataloging-in-Publication Data

Dunham, Jeff.
    Database performance tuning handbook / Jeff Dunham.
       p.   cm.
    Includes index.
    ISBN 0-07-018244-2
    1. Database management—Handbooks, manuals, etc. I. Title.
QA76.9.D3D852 1998
005.75'6—dc21   97-35362
                                                CIP

McGraw-Hill

A Division of The McGraw-Hill Companies

1 2 3 4 5 6 7 8 9 0 DOC/DOC 9 0 2 1 0 9 8 7

P/N 018245-0
PART OF ISBN 0-07-018244-2

The sponsoring editor for this book was Steve Chapman and the production supervisor was Sherri Souffrance. It was set in Century Schoolbook by Douglas & Gayle, Limited.

Printed and bound by R. R. Donnelley & Sons Company.

McGraw-Hill books are available at special quantity discounts to use as premiums and sales promotions, or for use in corporate training programs. For more information, please write to Director of Special Sales, McGraw-Hill, 11 West 19th Street, New York, NY 10011. Or contact your local bookstore.

*Because Jesus Christ, the son of God, was so gracious
to show me that He is real and save me from my sins, I would
like to dedicate this book and any honor derived from it, to Him.
Any dishonor, of course, belongs to the author.*

Contents

About the Book

This book is aimed at supporting the senior applications programmer, technical support specialist, or database administrator with a strong working knowledge of multiple databases and programming languages. Or any individual with a strong desire to become an expert in more than one database can benefit from the information. Even small businesses and home enthusiasts can benefit from the information provided.

The book has two goals. First and foremost is to present the collective tuning information available from several *Database Management Systems* (DBMS) and *Relational Database Managment Systems* (RDBMS), namely DB2, CA-IDMS, Microsoft® SQL Server™, Oracle, Sybase, and Xbased equivalents such as dBASE, CA-Clipper, BTRIEVE, and FoxPro. Second is to introduce several programs and techniques that have revolutionized tuning in the batch and online world. The examples can be ported from the mainframe to PC in Client/Server.

There won't be any lengthy discussions on probability and queueing theory, statistical analysis, usage of uniform, poisson, and exponential transaction distribution curves. Those are very nice principles, and there are plenty of books about them, but they hardly constitute the focus of this book. This book is dedicated to a streamlined practical tuning approach.

The most revolutionary tuning trick being used today is *smart caching*. Even if you use all the vendor-supplied buffering and caching technology available, your applications will still run faster with customized *smart caching* routines.

What is *Smart Caching*?

Regular caching technology uses buffer algorithms (ex. LIFO and/or FIFO, indexed) to save recently accessed fields, records, disk tracks, files, and so on. This technology is great. Don't get me wrong. With a 90 percent hit ratio, this method can regain half of the overhead associated with repetitive calls. But it misses a big piece of the pie. If these caching routines knew about the trends in your data, the nature of your processing, or the way you do business, they could double their effectiveness and make your applications scream.

That is *Smart Caching!*

This book helps you exploit this new technology. If chip manufacturers provided smart caching, encryption, compression, and even security at the hardware level, but controlled through software, you would have the perfect caching system. It doesn't exist today. Someday, the mass marketers of databases and operating sytems will take caching technology to that level. It shouldn't be far away. They estimate desktop computers will be 1000 times more powerful in the next decade, and they will be accessing many terabytes of information. Caching will be even more importeant then than it is now. Until then, it is up to you to blaze the trail. You will reap rewards galore by using smart caching, as will the software company which delivers on this idea.

"Why a multidatabase tuning book anyway?" The answer is pretty simple. Many of the older legacy database applications are now being converted or rewritten to utilize more advanced client/server based technology. The old idea of a corporate database of choice is dissolving away. Administrators are confronted with multiple database support as it relates to conversions, replication, and warehousing. The enterprise database is on many platforms and connectivity is in its heyday. This book makes it possible for you administrators, programmers, and techies to get all the tuning answers from one source guide.

One thing is certain. The enterprise investment is so large that it is estimated that a big Information Systems (hereinafter referred to as I/S) organization needs from two to seven years to convert from one DBMS to another. So while you build and convert those applications, remember to tune everything in sight. Today's savings are compounded tomorrow! I like to say that tuning can pay for new technology.

My choice of DBMS and RDBMS for inclusion in this guide represents the industry big boys. The same is true about third-party software products discussed herein. This book should provide an excellent source of information when cross training database professionals. I want you to read this book and become a highly paid *distributed database administrator*.

So, that's the ticket laddie! I hope this answers the question, "Why write a multiple-database tuning book?"

Top Players in the Database World

The Legacy:

ADABAS	DB2*	ORACLE*
BTRIEVE*	DB2/2*	PARADOX*
CA-Clipper*	IMS	PROGRESS
CA-DB	INFORMIX	Rdb
CA-DATACOM/DB	INTERBAS	RMS
CA-IDMS*	MICROSOFT® Access™[1]	SUPRA
CA-OpenIngres	MICROSOFT® FoxPro™ *	VISUAL dBASE*
CA-VAX/DB	MICROSOFT® SQL Server™ *	WATCOM/DB

*This book provides tuning information apaplicable to this database.

---

[1] Microsoft® Access™, Microsoft® FoxPro™, and Microsoft SQL Server™ are registered trademarks of Microsoft Corporation.

Introduction

The larger body of tuning knowledge can be inter-exchanged between computer platforms, operating systems, and database management systems. As you read this book, you will discover something. The types of tuning opportunities presented for DB2 databases also have corresponding applications with Oracle, Sybase, CA-IDMS, and the large repertoire of PC databases. Code examples will often be portable to other environments, with a few modifications.

The best way to get performance is to pay for tuning up-front. It is not a hidden cost if included in the initial design effort and is exponentially cheaper than performing tuning as an add-on feature. As an advocate of the "Performance Design Review," I always recommend that a tuning review is part of both the "Database Design Review" and "Application Design Review" processes.

Now, I would like to share with you some of my personal advice on tuning. These 10 principles were discovered through trial and error. I'm certain they will help you avoid heartaches.

10 Tuning Principles

1. Your biggest gain will not result from how well your tuned code performs. *Instead, your biggest gain will be derived from how your improvement is viewed by your peers.* Ask yourself these questions for each tuning objective. How can I be proactive with other members of the tuning team? How do I avoid setting management expectations too high? Have I touched all the bases and obtained all the approvals? What will guarantee accurate test results? How can I share my success with everyone involved? Will my proposed improvement sacrifice existing functionality, expansion, serviceability, or integrity of this application? Have I sought to make this tuning change a win-win scenario for everyone involved?

2. *Deliverables far outweigh projects in-progress!* Be sure to set attainable goals and then stay focused on each deliverable until it is in production. You will find that as you uncover layers of code in an application, many new opportunities will unfold. Each one will look like a pot of gold, but every new task will postpone the delivery of one already in progress.

3. *Avoid problems due to semantics.* There are so many terms floating around that it can be confusing. Clearly describe the ramifications of each tuning change and its benefits using concise terms and definitions.

4. *Concentrate on the big gainers.* Use the Pareto Principle: 80 percent of the results flow out of 20 percent of the activities. If your first tuning change involves making 100,000 lines of code changes, you've missed the point. Simple global tuning changes will yield larger returns, and sooner.

5. *Get help.* Tuning is not a one-man show. Sure, you can tackle some pretty big things. But in the end, the overall impact of a group of people can be quite astounding. This is the only way you will be able to defer a hardware acquisition and save your company millions of dollars. If you continually advertise your success to upper management and the I/S organization as a whole, you will gain supporters who want to achieve the same goals within their groups. You will gain visibility if you select a catchy name for your tuning group. The "Tuning Mission," "CPU Swat Team," or "Blitz Team" are good names for the people who have come together. It also helps to set up a status report to management on a weekly or monthly basis. Post this status in a public bulletin board on e-mail to gain further visibility. Visibility will help you to gain momentum for your tuning project.

6. *Measure your success accurately.* Don't promise 50 percent improvement, when in fact you only meant a 50 percent EXCP reduction. This suggestion will contribute greatly to your credibility and avoid embarrassing apologies later.

7. *Put simply, tuning involves three basic activities. The first is eliminating unnecessary processing. The second is eliminating redundant processing. The third activity is using more efficient processing in exchange for less efficient processing.* Stated differently, tuning merely changes the rate and amount of resource consumption, or exchanges an available resource for one that is exhausted. Keep this in mind while you are browsing line 33000 in a COBOL program for tuning opportunities. Let your brain find the solutions before your eyes become fatigued!

8. *Shared resources are affected by the principles of queueing theory.* You can often identify the bottlenecks for shared resources as being the code that runs the longest. In an online system, a correction to a program that ties up resources exclusively will often remove the peg holding up the whole table of cards. All the cards drop to the next level, where some other program now becomes the bottleneck. If you can remove enough of these pegs, the entire system will collapse down to very efficient processing. I like to think of this as the house-of-cards or cascading effect. I didn't invent it, but I have seen it happen. If you are instrumental in causing it to happen somewhere, it will bring you immense joy.

9. *Robust systems have special tuning needs.* You may identify a performance problem in a program nested 16 levels deep in an application thread, which is accessed concurrently. The design complexity alone may be responsible for any inherent performance problems. Recognizing

robust systems and their limitations is a labor intensive, but viable aspect of tuning. You may not recognize the true cause of poor performance until you have sifted through the many layers of the system architecture. But have faith. In time you will be able to tame the beast.

10. You must always remain cognizant of the fact that programs operate within a fixed arena. A processor has a fixed number of millions of instructions/sec (MIPs), DASD storage (3390s, Mass Storage Devices, etc.) and memory (200M real and virtual). Capacity planning is a process that works hand in hand with database, application, and system tuning. If an upgrade is inevitable, your tuning efforts were not in vain. *The resources you save today will postpone a hardware upgrade and carry forward to future processors.*

Well, that concludes my advice column. The remainder of this book is devoted to sound methods for deriving large savings in your applications, regions, and at your server. Keep in mind that you never really finish tuning. The demand for additional resources will always be present. Bottlenecks will always arise. And, as one application program is tuned and drops off your "TOP 10" list, another will take its place. In addition, there will be a constant influx of new programs. The tricks of the trade in this guide and the code examples will find their way into your new programs, database designs, and generation of regions.

1

Statistics Collection

1.1 Snapshots, Histograms, and Summaries

Flexibility in reporting gives you many options for identifying areas where systems and applications are suffering from problem performance. Prior to the war over relational *Data Base Management System* (DBMS) market dominance, both monitoring and reporting tools were limited. Competition has leveled the playing field and fueled the creation of many tools by primary and alternate software vendors.

This chapter introduces you to some of the most valuable reports and performance monitoring tools. In addition, most of the conventional sources of information for tuning DBMS systems, platforms, transactions, and batch processes are mentioned. In all, this information should provide you with a checklist of things to gather for your tuning effort. We will begin with reporting mechanisms.

The realm of reporting can be broken into three forms of statistic information. *Snapshots* are pictures of resource utilization at a given moment in time. *Histograms* extend your visibility by reporting resource utilization over minutes or hours, generally collected at a consistent time interval. A *summary,* on the other hand, captures the net or gross resource utilization for a job, program, task, or transaction. Not all reporting tools provide all three mechanisms. All can be useful to the serious tuner.

REPORT	DESCRIPTION
SNAPSHOTS	A picture of resource utilization at a moment in time
HISTOGRAM	Many individual pictures of resource utilization at different times plotted
SUMMARY	Net or Gross resource utilization for a job, program, task, or transaction

1.2   Making a Checklist

Call it planning or goal setting. You're going to have to do this essential step. Upper management is going to want to know what you are accomplishing. Whether you decide to tune only one program, several programs, or entire systems, you will be under the watchful eye. "Why," you ask? Because tuning is a last resort. Most shops won't attack performance improvements unless they have no other choice. If that's the case, the performance issue is already hot. Don't fret. Soon you will be able to identify the key elements for planning your attack.

I'm not going to waste your time explaining queuing theory or how CPU seconds are factored. Instead, this book is written with deliverables in mind. The first and foremost of these is the plan. A plan means research, goal setting, and tasks. The first step is research. You will need to go on an all-out scavenger hunt for tuning statistics. Figure 1-2 represents a checklist of what you will be hunting for in the *Computer Associates Integrated Database Management System* (CA-IDBMS) world.

You will find here a series of reports and job streams that will give you some idea of what kinds of tools and reports are available for this first all-important task.

1.3   Choosing Your Initial Tuning Targets

What's next? Given that you've gathered much of the information, the next step is to pick your first target. If you have a list of the top 10 CPU offenders, don't choose number 10. Instead, go after the worst offender, even if it is a vendor product. It is crucial that your visibility and credibility be established early in a tuning project. Don't push aside a vendor product that falls in the worst offender slot. Often these are the easiest to tune using vendor-supplied information.

Also, it is very important to stay focused. Once you start delving into code and designs, you are going to find lots of opportunities. Don't lose time catego-

Batch Window	Prime Time CPU	Decision Time for User
Paper Utilized (reports)	Disk Storage & I/Os	Memory

Figure 1-1   Start Thinking of Ways To Save These Resources

Online Programs and Dialogs	Batch
DREPORT 5	Longest batch application jobs
SREPORTS 3, 6, 7, 8, 9, 12, 13	Startup JCL and JESMSGS for each CV
JREPORTS 1-7	IDMSDUMP reports for all dictionaries and database files
IDMS Sysgen Listing	IDMSDBAN reports 4,5,6 on all databases
IDMS System Statistics	Global and Local DMCL listings
List of Transactions with Longest Elapsed Time	List of Batch CV and Local Mode Programs
List of Transactions Using the Most EXCP(s)	Schema Bachmans for Databases
List of Transactions Using the Most CPU	IDMS Archive Journal Reports
List of Transactions with Most Executions	List of File Blocksizes Used in Batch
List of Main and Subprogram Load Modules Executed Most	
List of Largest Subschema Load Modules	NetSpy VTAM Reports
Prime Time (6AM-6PM) Usage Chart	
I/O Network Diagram Showing Controllers, Channels, DASD	
MVS Paging Rates	
RMF Cache Reporter Reports	
CA-IDMS SQL Option Users (System Tables— refer to table in Appendix P)	
CA-IDMS SQL Option Users (EXPLAIN PLAN)	
CA-IDMS SQL Option Users (Create Key Definitions)	
CA-IDMS IDMSBCF Space Reports (see Appendix Q)	
Performance Monitor Reports 2, 4, 9, 10, 80, and 97	
Reports from DCMT displays	
Reports from dictionary displays	
IDMSRADM Export Table Counts	

Figure 1-2   CA-IDMS Resource Utilization Checklist

rizing and tackling too much. The sooner you produce a deliverable, the better. Management may appear patient for the short term. But, if you can't give them a quick deliverable, they will turn their attention to machine upgrades and probably cancel the tuning project.

1.4   Where To Focus Your Efforts

Suppose that, for example, program BILLING1 is using two hours of CPU per run and 2.5 hours elapsed time. It is safe to say that the program is CPU bound. If you view the *Job Entry Subsystem* (JES) run-time messages, and the program is doing 200,000 EXCPs (an EXCP equates to a physical I/O) to a file, then tuning the use of that file should address both CPU and elapsed time.

What if BILLING1 does very little file or database access? The CPU is being used in program instructions somewhere. With a tool like STROBE, you can see where every percent of CPU is utilized. Otherwise, it becomes a guessing game. What I consider the most valuable Strobe reports are those that provide wait time distribution, EXCP(s) by file, CPU usage by system component, CPU usage for dynamic calls, and CPU usage by instruction within the application program.

1.5 Making Your Programs Run Faster—The Big Picture

As you become more experienced with tuning application programs, you will inherently know what activities are associated with overhead. Later on, this book will introduce you to several programming techniques that can yield big returns on your tuning investment of time. If this is uncharted territory for you now, Figure 1-3 shows some ways to increase performance in your programs.

This list is not even close to all the possibilities for tuning that will unfold as we present topics in later chapters. Remember to generate a checklist, like the one shown here.

```
Regions:          IDMSPRD1-5      IDMSTST1-5      IDMSSYS1-5

Dictionaries:     PRDDICT1-5      TSTDICT1-5      SYSDICT1-5

Schemas:          PRDCHEM1-5      TSTCHEM1-5      SYSCHEM1-5

DMCLs:            PRDDMCL1-5      TSTDMCL1-5      SYSDMCL1-5

                  PBADMCL1-nn     TBADMCL1-nn     SBADMCL1-nn

Subschemas:       PRDSUBS1-nn     TSTSUBS1-nn     SYSSUBS1-nn
```

Following a checklist ensures that you've collected the required information for the entire CA-IDMS environment, before actual tuning begins.

1.6 Strobe Reports

Some of the most valuable reports will come from the STROBE product (by Programart Corporation). I've chosen to show those first. Let's look at some of them now.

The report in Figure 1-4 provides a histogram of CPU and file management usage during the course of execution. The larger the number, the more time spent during this portion of program execution. The bottom line shows the time line for execution from 0 to 100 percent.

In our example of the "Resource Demand Distribution" report (see Figure 1-5), 59 percent of the time was spent in the accessing of the BILLFILE on a 3390 pack.

Figure 1-6 shows that the greatest portion of wait time was spent doing VSAM file management. This correlates with the resource demand distribution shown in Figure 1-5.

REDUCING SEQUENTIAL FILE I/O ACTIVITY

- Consolidate files and processing.
- Maximize block sizes for BSAM, QSAM, and BDAM files.
- Reduce CISIZE for random processing in KSDS files.
- Increase CISIZE for sequential processing in KSDS and ESDS file.
- Increase buffering using the DCB=BUFNO and VSAM AMP parameters.
- Eliminate I/O by moving files into memory tables for repetitive processing.
- Use LSERV or other memory-resident buffering facilities to eliminate I/O.

WAYS OF REDUCING DATABASE I/O ACTIVITY

- Use LSERV for DB2.
- Use Release 12.0 of IDMS, FAST ACCESS, or DB-MEGABUFFS products.
- Tune buffering algorithms.
- Divide up files, area, table spaces, etc., for optimization.
- Eliminate redundant calls to the same record or groups of records.
- Use memory tables of frequently used record.

WAYS TO REDUCE CPU

- Avoid redundant processing.
- Use record save areas and total fields, etc., to avoid repetitive database accesses.
- Eliminate unnecessary calls to subroutines that may not be used in every iteration of a processing loop.
- Use optimizing compiler directives or vendor-supplied optimizers.
- Reroute processing to other platforms for strategic processing.
- Come forward to newer releases of vendor products that perform better.
- Use indexes in-lieu of subscripts for Cobol table processing.

Figure 1-3 Looking at Tuning Activities—The Big Picture

```
** TIME DISTRIBUTION OF ACTIVITY LEVEL
-TASK OR RESOURCE N X 10 PLUS OR MINUS 5 IS PERCENT OF FULL UTILIZATION * IS GREATER THAN 95% - IS LESS THAN 5%
  DDNAME    .-------------------------------------------------------------------------
 BILLING1  CPU .1 33222 124 1124 53122557 1 12241133754411363231132461222    175324314315 4241  33444 5522
73234813328.
 .FILEMGT  .9*76898*975 1   1 3     1    22   11    1 1
     0---0---1---1--2---2---3---3--4---4---5---5--6---6---7---7--8---8---9---9--*.
```

Figure 1-4 Strobe—Time Distribution of Activity Level

```
                  ** RESOURCE DEMAND DISTRIBUTION **
-       — PERCENT OF RUN TIME —      — PERCENT OF RUN TIME SPENT ——    CUMULATIVE PERCENTAGES
 TASK OR RESOURCE  SERVICED   SERVICED   SERVICED  SOLO     SOLO     SOLO        CAUSING    SOLO  CAUS-
ING
  DDNAME           BY CPU     BY I/O     BY EITHER IN CPU   IN I/O   IN EITHER   CPU WAIT   TIME  CPU
WAIT

BILLING1 CPU       26.25      .00        26.25     26.25    00       26.25   .     20       26.25  .20
  BILLFILE 3390    54.87      4.13       59.00     54.87    4.13     59.00       4.82       85.25 5.02
 .FILEMGT          13.37      .10        13.47     13.37    .10      13.47        .49       98.72 5.51
```

Figure 1-5 Strobe—Resource Demand Distribution

```
** WAIT TIME BY MODULE **
 MODULE   SECTION   FUNCTION              RUN TIME PERCENT    RUN TIME  HISTOGRAM   MARGIN OF ERROR: 3.07%
 NAME     NAME                            PAGE     TOTAL      .00   1.50  3.00   4.50  6.00

 .COBLIB  ILBOVOC   VSAM OPEN AND CLOSE    .10     .10       -
 .SVC     SVC 020   CLOSE                          .10     .10      20  -+
 .SVC     SVC 130   RACHECK                .10     .10       -
                                                            —     —
 .SVC     TOTALS    SUPERVISOR CONTROL     .20     .30
 .VSAM    IDA019L   VSAM RECORD MANAGEMENT .00     5.11     —++++++++++++++++++++++++++++++++++++++
                                                            —     —
PROGRAM BILLING1 TOTALS                             .30     5.51
```

Figure 1-6 Strobe—Wait Time by Module

With the "Data Set Characteristics" report we pinpoint the file activity, as well as buffer, RPL, and CI/CA splits. All are potential tuning opportunities (see Figure 1-7).

The I/O Facility Utilization Summary shows how much of the CPU run-time was attributed to individual files (based upon their DDNAME). In Figure 1-8, the BILLFILE used 3.93 percent of the CPU for the run.

The "Program Section Usage Summary" report isolates the run-time usage to the data portion of the BILLFILE cluster. See Figure 1-9.

You can see that the peak CPU usage is easily identified. In this case, it is the VSAM service routines chewing up CPU. Next, we will take a closer look at those routines.

Our suspicions are confirmed by the report shown in Figure 1-10. The small control interval length would be something to review further, based upon our findings.

In conclusion, the STROBE tool is unsurpassed in isolating a performance bottleneck. From our example reports we were able to make the following determinations quickly:

■ 59 percent of the run time was spent in accessing the BILLFILE.

■ This file is a VSAM cluster that may require additional buffering and RPLs.

- The data component of the cluster is where the bottleneck occurred.
- The interval control length is also a potential object of tuning.
- The CPU usage reports confirm that VSAM services consumes the most.

1.7 CA-IDMS Performance Monitor Reports

The CA-IDMS performance monitor comes with a series of CULPRIT-based (Parametric reporting language) reports that extend your tuning capabilities

DDNAME	ACCESS METHOD	-RECORD- FMT SIZE	BLK/CI SIZE	BUF NO	RPL STRINGS	-SPLITS- CI CA	EXCP COUNTS	DATA SET NAME
		** DATA SET CHARACTERISTICS **						
TIMEDATA								2
BILLFILE	VSAM KSDS 100	4096	2	1			3,223	PV.BILL.FILE
BILLFILE	VSAM INDEX	4089	4096	1	1		23	PV.BILL.FILE

Figure 1-7 Strobe—Data Set Characteristics

```
** I/O FACILITY UTILIZATION SUMMARY *
UNIT    DEVICE    VOLUME    DDNAME          RUN TIME PERCENT   RUN TIME HISTOGRAM  MARGIN OF ERROR: 3.07%
NO      TYPE      ID                        SOLO    TOTAL     .00      1.00    2.00    3.00    4.00
240     DA 3390   SMS142    BILLFILE        3.93    3.93      .*********************************
240     DA 3390   SMS142    BILLFILE INDEX  20      20        .**
                                            ---     ---
UNIT 240 TOTALS                             4.13    4.13

350     DA 3390   SMS135    .FILEMGT        .10     .10       .*
```

Figure 1-8 Strobe—I/O Facility Utilization Summary

```
                        ** PROGRAM SECTION USAGE SUMMARY
  MODULE    SECTION    SECTION  FUNCTION              CPU TIME PERCENT   CPU TIME HISTOGRAM  MARGIN OF ERROR: 3.16%
  NAME      NAME       SIZE                           SOLO    TOTAL     .00      18.00    36.00    54.00
72.00

.SYSTEM    .COBLIB             COBOL LIBRARY SUBROUTINE  20.40   20.40   .*********** **
.SYSTEM    .COMMON             COMMON AREA               .10     .10     .
.SYSTEM    .IOCS               DATA MANAGEMENT SERVICES  .10     .10     .
.SYSTEM    .SVC                SUPERVISOR CONTROL        1.35    1.35    .
.SYSTEM    .VSAM               VIRTUAL STORAGE ACC METH  71.18   71.18   .**************************************
                                                        -----   -----
.SYSTEM TOTALS                 SYSTEM SERVICES           93.13   93.13

CPXCEM             9416                                  .21     .21     .
CPXTERM            5400                                  .10     .10     .
BILLING1 BILLING1  4052                                  6.56    6.56    . ****
                                                        -----   -----
PROGRAM BILLING1 TOTALS                                  100.00  100.00
```

Figure 1-9 Strobe—Program Section Usage Summary

```
                          ** PROGRAM USAGE BY PROCEDURE
.SYSTEM    SYSTEM SERVICES   .VSAM VIRTUAL STORAGE ACC METH
MODULE     SECTION          FUNCTION     INTERVAL    CPU TIME PERCENT  CPU TIME HISTOGRAM  MARGIN OF ERROR: 3.16%
 NAME       NAME              LENGTH    SOLO  TOTAL   00   17.00    34.00    51.00   68.00

IDA019L1  VSAM RECORD MANAGEMENT  64    67.43  67.43 .****************************************
IDA019R0  VSAM                          3076         3.75   3.75    .***
                                                     ----   ----
          .VSAM                        TOTALS       71.18  71.18
```

Figure 1-10 Strobe—Program Usage by Procedure

dramatically for online CA-IDMS database transactions. JCL for running reports is shown in Figure 1-11.

In the JCL of Figure 1-11, the weekly CA-IDMS log file acts as input to the reporting facility, which extracts records for ADSO dialogs between 7 a.m. and 6 p.m. (prime time). The output reports generated by this job are shown in Figure 1-12.

You will find the average CPU, average wait, and average db-calls some of the most useful information reported. With this report you can quickly analyze the affects of tuning changes.

1.8   Generating the Right SREPORTS (Statistics Reports)

Some of you aren't going to have the luxury of the IDMS performance monitor tool. In that case, you will want to run the standard CA-IDMS SREPORTS to get equivalent information. As we did in the last section, we will now show you the JCL for generating statistics reports (see Figure 1-13) and the output for one of the key reports, namely SREPORT13 (see Figure 1-14).

```
//USERJOB1 JOB (ACCOUNT),'PERFORMANCE REPORTS',
//         TIME=30,CLASS=P,MSGCLASS=A
//CULP   EXEC CULPRIT
//CULPRIT.SYSCTL DD DSN=PROD.IDMS.SYSCTL,DISP=SHR
//SYS010   DD *
  REPORT FROM 07:00 ON 92/001 THRU 18:00 ON 92/001
  EXCLUDE INTERVALS FROM 10:30 THRU 14:00
//SYS011   DD DSN=IDMSPLOG.G0001V00,DISP=OLD,UNIT=TAPE   WEEKLY INPUT
//SYS020   DD DUMMY
//SYSIN    DD *
 PARAM=NOLIST
=COPY 'PMARPT00'
=COPY 'PMARPT01'               TASK DETAIL
=COPY 'PMARPT02'               TASK SUMMARY
=COPY 'PMARPT04'               ADS DIALOG AVERAGES
=COPY 'PMNAME'
=COPY 'PMARPT04'
 TYPE ADS/O
 TASK BILLONL1
//* TYPE BATCH
```

Figure 1-11   JCL for IDMS-PM (Performance Monitor Batch Reporter)

```
REPORT NO. 04                 CULLINET SOFTWARE              01/01/92  PAGE 1
IDMS/R-PM 10.2.1           ADS/O DIALOG SUMMARY REP
DC SYSTEM VERSION #:    1            AMALGAMATED             DATA FROM: 1/01/92
```

DIALOG NAME	VER NUM	NUM TIMES EXEC	NUM TIMES ABND	AVG STORAGE ACTIVE	AVG STORAGE KEPT	AVG CPU TIME (SECS)	AVG WAIT TIME (SECS)	AVG TP READ LNGTH	AVG TP WRITE LNGTH	AVG NUM OF I/O	AVG NUM OF DBCLS	AVG NUM OF LVLS	AVG NUM OF DBLVLS	AVG NUM OF BUFS
BILLONL1	1	12		64283	73000	.1586	. 8532	10	540	8	35	0	0	0
BILLONL2	1	94		51039	25833	.1914	1.6903	6	801	13	176	1	0	2
BILLONL3	1	6		56363	18933	.2745	1.2932	10	716	19	205	1	0	2
CUSTONL1	1	10		99296	18746	.2402	1.2811	19	679	29	335	1	0	2
CUSTONL2	1	18		141977	36804	.7210	4.6616	42	518	21	385	1	0	2
CUSTONL3	1	5		83699	43776	.1709	.8365	14	1210	190	1028	1	0	2

Figure 1-12 PM—Output from Figure 1-11 JCL

```
//USER1S JOB (ACCOUNT),'PLOGTEST CV1',CLASS=P,MSGCLASS=A,TIME=30
//*************************************************************
//*    DOC:  THIS JOB EXEC THE IDMS CULPRIT UTILITY
//*          SREPORT 8  - ERUS (BATCH) PROGRAM STATS
//*          SREPORT 13 - TASKS CALLED AND LOADED
//*          SREPORT 15 & 16 - TERMINAL RESPONSE TIMES
//*          SREPORT 21 - STATS BY DIALOG
//*************************************************************
//STEP010 EXEC CULPRIT,CV='CLOSE',CULLIB='IDMSPROD.SRCLIB'
//CULPRIT.STEPLIB DD  DSN=IDMSPROD.CV1.LOADLIB,DISP=SHR
//               DD  DSN=IDMSPROD.LOADLIB,DISP=SHR
//CULPRIT.SYS010  DD  DSN=IDMSPROD.CV1.IDMSLOGP(0),UNIT=TAPE,DISP=SHR
//DICTDB    DD  DSN=IDMSPROD.CV1.DICTDB,DISP=SHR
//DLODDB    DD  DSN=IDMSPROD.CV1.DLODDB,DISP=SHR
//DMSGDB    DD  DSN=IDMSPROD.CV1.DMSGDB,DISP=SHR
//SYSIN     DD *
DATABASE DICTNAME=DICTDB
PARAM=NOLIST
IN 6352 V
USE 'SREPORT 000' (92023 0001 92029 2359)
USE 'SREPORT 013'
```

Figure 1-13 Sample JCL for SREPORTS

```
REPORT NO. 13            IDMS-DC PROGRAM SUMMARY  C87     02/04/92 PAGE   15
SELECTED FROM:  92023  00:01    TO:  94029  23:59
ACTUAL:  92023  04:04    TO:  94029  22:01
```

PROGRAM NAME	VER	PGM DICTNAME	DICTNODE	CALLED	TIMES LOADED	TIMES CALLED/	RATIO OF LOADED	TIMES WAITED	TIMES CHECKED
BILLONL1	1		USERDICT		133	3	44.3333		
BILLONL2	1		USERDICT		29	1	29.0000		
BILLONL3	1		USERDICT		28	1	28.0000	✎	
CUSTONL1	1		USERDICT		36	1	36.0000		
CUSTONL2	1		USERDICT		12	1	12.0000		

Figure 1-14 Output from SREPORT 13

The real value of SREPORT 13 is the called/loaded ratio. The times called statistic shows up on other reports where it is more valuable to have that information. However, if your programs are being loaded more than once, you have an excellent tuning opportunity by enlarging your virtual storage pools. If they are being called many times, then the applications are great candidates for tuning. A small savings will be compounded over all the program executions. Not all of the SREPORTS are necessary for tuning. Neither are all the statistics fields. Figure 1-15 shows the basic ones needed to get the job done.

The SREPORTS are inadequate in effectively tuning individual programs and dialogs. You will need the performance monitor reports or your own statistics. Figure 1-16 presents you with the additional fields required from *the journal reports* (JREPORTS).

1.9   Generating the Right DREPORTS (Dictionary Reports)

The DREPORTS are reports that collect information from the CA-IDMS data dictionary. CA-IDMS utilize an active dictionary that is updated with valuable

---

SREPORTS 1, 5-11 & 21 (Database & Data Communications Statistics)

These are general numbers with some general actions.

SREPORT 3 (SYSTEM STATISTICS)		
PGMPOOL WAITS	☞	The pools should have no waits
XA PGMPOOL WAITS		
STORAGE POOL WAITS		
REENTPOOL WAITS		
TIMES AT MAX TASK	☞	Should be zero, raise MAX TASK in sysgen or processor at maximum
SHORT ON STORAGE	☞	Should be zero, increase pools or size
RUNAWAY TASKS ABRTD	☞	Should be zero in production

SREPORT 13 (PROGRAM SUMMARY)		
TIME LOADED	☞	Should be = 1 or 0, increase pools
TIMES WAITED	☞	Should be zero, increase loader run-units

SREPORT 15 (LINE SUMMARY)		
TOTAL READS + WRITES	☞	Activity shouldn't exceed line capacity

SREPORT 16 (PHYSICAL TERMINAL SUMMARY)		
CUMULATIVE RESPONSE TIME	☞	If high, VTAM tuning needed
AVERAGE RESPONSE	☞	Use to determine affects of tuning

SREPORT 21 (DIALOG TRANSACTION STATISTICS)		
RECORDS CURRENT	☞	If high, review code for improvements
RECORDS REQUESTED		
PROGRAMS CALLED	☞	If > 100, review calls to subprograms

Figure 1-15   List of Valuable SREPORT Fields

information when compiles for programs or *Application Development System/Online* (ADSO) for CA-IDMS dialogs are performed. Figure 1-17 shows JCL for creating these reports, and Figure 1-18 shows the output listing generated by the job.

JREPORT 2

NOT STORED ON TARGET	☜	Used to find areas for REORG
REQUESTED FROM DATABASE	☜	Used to find excess database calls
SHARED LOCKS HELD	☜	Used to locate excess locking

JREPORT 3 & 4

READ	☜	Used these to identify high # of I/O
WRITTEN		due to inefficient buffering
REQUESTED		
BUFFER UTILIZATION RATIO	☜	If low, increase buffers

Figure 1-16 List of Valuable JREPORT Fields

```
//STEP010    EXEC  CULPRIT,CULLIB='IDMSPROD.SRCLIB'
//STEPLIB    DD    DSN=IDMSPROD.CV1.LOADLIB,DISP=SHR
//           DD    DSN=IDMSPROD.LOADLIB,DISP=SHR
//SYSCTL     DD    DSN=IDMSPROD.CV1.SYSCTL,DISP=SHR,FREE=CLOSE
//DICTDB     DD    DSN=IDMSPROD.CV1.DICTDB,DISP=SHR
//DLODDB     DD    DSN=IDMSPROD.CV1.DLODDB,DISP=SHR
//DMSGDB     DD    DSN=IDMSPROD.CV1.DMSGDB,DISP=SHR
//USERDICT   DD    DSN=IDMSPROD.CV1.USERDICT,DISP=SHR
//SYSIN      DD    *
   DATABASE DBNAME=USERDICT
   DREPORT=005
   SEL       SSPROG-091  IN  PATH  EG  WHEN  SS-NAM-026  EQ  'USERSUB1'
   SEL       PROG-051  IN  PATH  EA  WHEN  BUILDER-051  NE  'A'
 *AND       BUILDER-051  NE  'C'
```

Figure 1-17 Sample JCL for DREPORT 05

```
REPORT NO. 05      DATA DICTIONARY REPORTER S1021  0204/92    PAGE 5
DREPORT 005               PROGRAM REPORT
***************************************************************************
               ESTIMATED     TIMES    ——DATE——
PROGRAM        LINES                  COMPILED COMPILE UPDATED CREATED
***************************************************************************
-BILLONL2  VER  1  6324        8       11/10/92  06/25/92
   PUBLIC ACCESS ALLOWED FOR ALL AUTHORITY
   MODE            BATCH-AUTOSTATUS
   LANGUAGE        COBOL
   SUBPROGRAM      DYNAMIC  VER  1
   RECORD COPIED   BILL-FILE-RECORD1 VER  1
   RECORD COPIED   CUST-FILE-RECORD1 VER  1
   CALLED BY       BILLONL1  VER  1
```

Figure 1-18 Output from DREPORT 05

The report pictured in Figure 1-18 is helpful in identifying several pieces of information for tuning. Everywhere a program is called and where the records are used are cross referenced here, which helps itemize the programs impacted by a tuning change. This particular run tied the USERSUB1 subschema back to programs that have been registered in the CA-IDMS dictionary at compile time.

The purpose of the JCL in Figure 1-19 is to generate the control cards that will be used to run a UCFBATCH job which displays all the programs in CV1. The output is edited to construct control cards of the form "DCMT DISPLAY PROGRAM PGMNAME."

1.10   Generating Reports Using DCMT and UCFBATCH Commands

From the next task code prompt in CA-IDMS DC (a.k.a. ENTC), you can issue commands for collecting system statistics. Using a list of programs taken from a DCMT display command as input to a dictionary display can provide a list of module sizes. Figure 1-20 shows the JCL necessary to start this process, using a batch job.

The output of the *Universal Communications Facility* (UCF) batch (CA-IDMS) job shown in Figure 1-20 contains the load module size. Your goal in using this procedure is to collect the size of all online load modules. Upon running the batch job, we have a file with all the programs defined to the online system and their attributes (see Figure 1-21).

It will be necessary for you to massage the output of these displays into a format suitable for a report. I usually edit the dataset and exclude all the lines

```
//************************************************************************
//*   IDMSDDL TO GET CTL CARDS FOR ALL PROGRAMS
//************************************************************************
//STEP010  EXEC  PGM=IDMSDDL,REGION=2M
//CDMSLIB  DD    DSN=IDMSPROD.CV1.LOADLIB,DISP=SHR
//         DD    DSN=IDMSPROD.LOADLIB,DISP=SHR
//STEPLIB  DD    DSN=IDMSPROD.CV1.LOADLIB,DISP=SHR
//         DD    DSN=IDMSPROD.LOADLIB,DISP=SHR
//SYSCTL   DD    DSN=IDMSPROD.CV1.SYSCTL,DISP=SHR
//SYSUDUMP DD    SYSOUT=*
//SYSLST   DD    DSN=IDMSPROD.PGMLIST,DISP=(,CATLG,DELETE),
//               UNIT=WORK,SPACE=(,TRK,  (5,5),RLSE),
//               DCB=(RECFM=FB,LRECL=133,BLKSIZE=27930)
//SYSPCH   DD    DUMMY
//SYSIPT   DD    *
         SIGNON  USER  USER1  PAS  USERPASS  DICT  USERDICT  USA  RET.
         DIS   ALL   PRO   .
         BYE
```

Figure 1-19 Sample JCL for Program Activity Displays

```
//UCFBTCH EXEC  PGM=UCFBTCH,REGION=4M
//STEPLIB  DD   DSN=IDMSPROD.CV1.LOADLIB,DISP=SHR
//         DD   DSN=IDMSPROD.LOADLIB,DISP=SHR
//SYSCTL   DD   DSN=IDMSPROD.CV1.SYSCTL,DISP=SHR
//SYSUDUMP DD   SYSOUT=*
//SYSLST   DD   SYSOUT=*
//SYSIPT   DD   *
SIGNON USERABLE
SOFTWARE
SOFTWARE
DCUF SET DICTNAME USERDICT
DCMT D PRO USERONL9
DCMT D PRO USERONL2
DCMT D PRO CUSTONL1
```

Figure 1-20   JCL To Generate Program Load Module Size Displays

```
DIS PRO USERONL9
PROGRAM NAME USERONL9
VERSION 00001
FROM DICTIONARY
DICTNAME USERDICT
DICTNODE
TYPE DIALOG
LANGUAGE ADSO
SECURITY 000
SIZE IN BYTES 00002444                    ☞   Size of Loag Modules
DATABASE KEY 01105115:007
ISA SIZE 00000
STORAGE PROT YES
STATUS ENABLED AND INSRV
RESIDENCE IN POOL AT 0F6AF000
DYNAMIC ALLOWED
TRHEADING MULTI THREADED
RELOAD NO
OVERLAYABLE NO
REENTRANT FULLY REENTRANT
NEW COPY ENABLED
TIMES CALLED 008150                       ☞   For tuning subprograms
TIMES LOADED 000001
```

Figure 1-21   Output from UCFBTCH Job in Figure 1-20

in which I'm not interested. The result is a list with the program name and load module size only. Sort the records descending on size, so you can see the biggest programs at the top of the file, something like this:

Program	Times Called
BILLONL9	192017
CUSTONL9	175000
CUSTONL8	111005

The "TIMES CALLED" is very valuable tuning information. In the Performance Monitor reports (sample 1), we were able to see that the times mainline programs were executed. One of the deficiencies in those reports is their inability to identify activity in subprograms. However, a simple DCMT DISPLAY program command will give you the "TIMES CALLED" figure. The number of times a program is called does not correlate exactly to the number of times executed. You can expect the number of calls to be much higher than execution counts that are tied to actual transactions. However, these numbers can be sorted to give you a detail report of the most actively called subprograms. But, the "TIMES CALLED" figures should not be used in formulas for estimating CPU and elapsed times. They will not give accurate results. After you have identified the most called subprograms, tuning these programs should yield great performance gains.

There is plenty of tuning information available from the various DCMT DISPLAY commands. For example, the DCMT DIS STATS SYSTEM command shown in Figure 1-22 displays many key fields, which are further explained with the aid of the cross reference Table 1-1.

1.11   Generating MXG Reports

The MXG reports provide a comprehensive set of statistics on all aspects of operating system and user program performance for MVS. These reports are an extension of the *System Management Facility* (SMF) in that they read the SMF file with its statistics records. Figure 1-23 shows two examples of running the MXG report generator. The first example extracts SMF records for program

TABLE 1-1   CA-IDMS System Statistics Table

Value Found	Conclusion
Large count in TIMES AT MAX TASK	The MAX TASK sysgen option is low or the CV system is running at peak utilization.
Large count in BUFFER WAITS	DMCL, AREAn, and INDEX tuning is needed, or a vendor XA/ESA buffering tool is justified.
Large count in CALC or VIA overflows	The database needs reorganization or a design change.
RLE, RCE, DPE, or ILE high water mark is reached or exceeded	The initial allocation numbers forthese resources should be increased in the sysgen.
Large number of abends or runaways	Quality control is missing something
Large number of SCAN2 and/or SCAN3 (release 10) searches for available storage in pool, or, short on storage count is incremented	Storage pools may be too small, or storage allocations too large
Large numbers seen in the QUEUE statistics	Some applications may be over using the QUEUE area. It is not intended to be a replacement for a well-designed user database.
CV has been running 61 hours and there have been 228,368 tasks	The task rate is 61 (3600) / 228,368 which works out to 1 task/second processed

```
                DIS STAT SYS
      18:57:28.21 97/105 Current Time      00:01:37.56 Tot Sys Time
      19:32:44.18 97/103 Startup Time      00:00:00.00 Tot User Time

TASKS:          194 Processed          9 Abended      39 Max Tasks
                132 System             0 Runaway       0 Times At Max
                  0 Deadlocks          0 Dead Victims

RUN/UNITS:       32 Processed         17 Norm Cmp     13 Max Conc
                  4 Ext Proc           1 Ext Norm      4 Ext Conc      5 Max Erus

DATABASE:      2467 Calls           4557 Pages Rqst     2181 Recs Rqst
                  0 Buff Wait       2821 Pages Read     1788 Recs Cur R/U
                 22 Page Writ          5 Calc Noflo        0 Via Noflo
               1330 Tot Locks          0 Calc Ovflo        0 Via Ovflo
                                       0 Frag Stord        0 Recs Reloc
    INDEX:        0 SR8 Splits         0 SR8 Stores        0 SR7 Stores
                  0 SR8 Spawns         0 SR8 Erases        0 SR7 Erases
                  0 Orph Adopt         0 Ix Searches       0 Min Level
                                       0 Lvls Srchd        0 Max Level
    SQL:          0 Commands           0 Tupls Fetched     0 Rows Inserted
                  0 AM Recomp          0 Rows Updated      0 Rows Deleted
                                       0 Sorts             0 Sort Min
                                       0 Tuples Sorted     0 Sort Max

JOURNAL:                   0 Buff Waits            4 User Putjrnl
    Page     11  0-10     0 11-20     0 21-30     7 31-40     2 41-50
    Dist      0 51-60     1 61-70     0 71-80     0 81-90    18 91-100

INTERNAL:      RLEs      RCEs     DPEs    Stack
                320       296      127     821 HWM
               1500      1500      600    1200 Sysgen Threshold
                  0         0        0         Times Exceeded

STORAGE:       4792 Gets           4562 Frees        0 SOS COUNT
                  0 PGFIXs            0 PGFREEs
                  0 Pages Fxd         0 Pages Freed
               3857 Scan 1            0 PGRLSEs
                935 Scan 2            0 Pages Relsd

PROGRAM:             Act Loads  Pages Load  Wait/Space
          Non-Reent      2          11          0
             Reent      27         921          0
     XA Non-Reent        3          20          0
         XA Reent      119        3196          0
SCRATCH:       81 Gets         105 Puts       103 Dels
   QUEUE:       13 Gets           5 Puts         5 Dels        0 Task AutoSt

TIME:        2503 Gets      171981 Post        0 Started Tasks
                0 Wait      171980 Canc
U12  ENTER NEXT TASK CODE:
```

Figure 1-22   IDMS Display Systems Statistics

USERBAT1 and provides a CPU time summary. The second example provides CPU time, EXCP(s), tape drive allocations, paging rate, number of swaps, and average working set (memory use), for all programs. These mainframe statistics are extremely beneficial in locating targets for tuning.

There are many different reports generated from the MXG SAS routines. For tuning purposes, the most useful are the batch history reports, batch job reports, and a report of the top CPU burners. The report in Figure 1-24 demonstrates how the caliber of information provided by these reports can propel your tuning effort. This single report could drive your entire tuning campaign.

At first glance, we see that this report is ideal for preparing your batch tuning game plan. Begin at the top and work your way down the list looking for ways to optimize the performance of each program. This report does not include CA-IDMS regions. DB2 foreground access from TSO may be included in the IK-JEFT01 time shown.

EXAMPLE 1:
```
//****************************************************************************
//* GENERATE ONE PROGRAM CPU TIME SUMMARY REPORT
//****************************************************************************
//S1 EXEC SAS6,SREG=3M,CONFIG='SYS1.MXG.SRCLIB(CONFIG)',
//                    SRCLIB='SYS1.MXG.SRCLIB2',
//                    SFDATA='SYS1.MXG.PRODDB1'
//SYSIN   DD *
DATA BNCHMARK;
 SET SF.STEPS;
DT = DATEPART(INITTIME);
DY = DAY(DT)
IF TYPETASK='JOB';
IF PROGRAM=: 'USERBAT1';
PROC SUMMARY;
  CLASS PROGRAM;
  VAR CPUTM SELAPSTM;
   OUTPUT OUT=SUM SUM=;
PROC PRINT;
VAR PROGRAM CPUTM SELAPSTM;
```

EXAMPLE 2:
```
//****************************************************************************
//* GENERATE ALL PROGRAMS CPU TIME SUMMARY REPORT
//****************************************************************************
//S1 EXEC SAS6,SREG=3M,CONFIG='SYS1.MXG.SRCLIB(CONFIG)',
//                    SRCLIB='SYS1.MXG.SRCLIB2',
//                    SFDATA='SYS1.MXG.PRODB1'
//SYSIN  DD *
PROC SORT;
  BY PROGRAM
PROC PRINT SPLIT='+';
  VAR JOB STEPNAME PROGRAM INITTIME CPUTM EXCPTOTL TAPEDRVS
     PAGETOTL SWAPS AVGWKSET;
    LABEL JOB      ='JOB+NAME'
          INITTIME ='STEP+BEGIN+TIME'
          CPUTM    ='CPU=TIME'
          EXCPTOTL ='TOTAL+EXCPS'
          TAPEDRVS ='TAPE+DRIVES+ALLOC'
          PAGETOTL ='TOTAL+PAGE+RATE'
          SWAPS    ='NO.+OF+SWAPS'
          AVGWKSET ='AVG+WORKING+SIZE (X1000)';
```

Figure 1-23 Sample JCL for MXG Reports

Because SMF saves statistics about all the resources in use within MVS, you also can use these reports to do your wait-time analysis or disk load balancing (see Figure 1-25).

Most remarkably, you will find that several of the vendor-supplied programs, as seen in Figure 1-24, are among the top 10 CPU burners in many shops. We will cover tuning methods that can be used with IEBGENER, SORT, IDCAMS, and user programs later on.

```
TOP 10 BATCH CPU USERS REPORT REPORT
JAN 29, 1995 THRU  FEB 6, 1995
```

					AVG CPU	AVG ELAPSED	
PROGRAM OBS	PROGRAM NAME	RUN	CPU TIME	ELAPSED TIME	TIME (MIN.)	TIME (MIN.)	CPU UTIL
1	GLBTCH1	238	13:00:30	119:09	3.28	30.0	2.7
2	EZTPA00	1336	6:08:10	100:34	0.28	4.5	1.5
3	IKJEFT01	1742	5:39:11	31:29:16	0.19	1.1	4.5
4	SASLPA	790	3:57:10	134:47	0.30	10.2	0.7
5	FDRABR	1646	3:49:07	251:59	0.14	9.2	0.4
6	IEBGENER	18972	3:45:06	10:59:18	3.13	9.2	8.5
7	BILLBAT9	101	3:11:54	11:01:37	1.90	6.6	7.3
8	ACTG0001	24	2:57:15	12:15:50	7.39	30.7	6.0
9	IDCAMS	2638	2:09:35	29:54:29	0.05	0.7	1.8
10	SORT	6887	1:40:52	87:45:59	0.01	0.8	0.5

Figure 1-24 Output from MXG Job in Figure 1-23

SHIFT	POOL	VOLSER	TOTAL I/O RATE	AVG RESPONSE TIME(MS)	AVG I/O QUEUE TIME(MS)	AVG PENDING TIME(MS)	AVG DISCONNECT TIME(MS)	AVG CONNECT TIME(MS)	AVG DSNS OPENED
N	TEST	T90001	0.566	25,4	1.5	0.3	10.4	13,7	9.5
N	TEST	T90002	0.492	26.2	1.3	0.3	11.0	13.8	13,3
N	TEST	T90003	0.466	23.2	0.8	0.3	12.1	10.0	49.0
N	WORK	W90001	0.418	23.3	0.9	0.3	10.8	11.2	22.0
N	WORK	W90002	10.505	35.5	10.2	0.6	20.4	4.2	125
P	IDMS	I90001	25.484	39.6	20.4	0.4	16.9	1.9	160
P	IDMS	I90007	10.270	21.0	3.7	0.3	13.2	3.7	141

Figure 1-25 Disk Device Activity Report

1.12   Prime Shift RMF Paging Statistics

Now, add to your measurements the gathering of a few key MVS paging statistics. This list of statistics is useful in determining the memory loads on a database system.

PAGING STATISTICS COLLECTION

```
PAGE RATE
DEMAND PAGE RATE
AVAILABLE FRAMES
AVERAGE FIXED FRAMES
AVERAGE FIXED FRAMES BELOW 16MEG LINE
AVERAGE TSO USERS
AVERAGE WORKING SET
```

Ideally, you want to see this information in columns on a report, with data broken out into different hours during prime shift.

That brings up the absorbing debate over PRIME SHIFT. Some data processing shops recognize the prime shift as the 8 a.m. to 5 p.m. window of time. Others feel this should be 7:30 a.m. to 5:30 p.m. Those of international persuasion consider it to be tied to international date lines and time zones. Logic dictates that the most meaningful time to adopt is the one that encompasses your mission-critical online applications.

AVG I/O times and TOTAL I/O rate are two other fields that can be used to identify already overworked DASD volumes. This, in turn, would drive data set placement, as a means to better throughput.

Strobe also provides some paging information. The first page of STROBE reports also gives you the PAGING RATE and EXCPS/SEC for programs or regions. For example, you could STROBE a TSO user using DB2 to find out these two values.

1.13   Generating PC Batch Program and Database Reports

On operating systems like Windows NT you can use built-in monitors to collect statistics about processes. But, on Windows 3.11 and older operating systems, batch processes are somewhat of a mystery. I have a routine that I use to capture elapsed time for batch programs on these systems. It involves using some DOS commands in a special batch routine. In Figure 1-26, I use the routine to capture elapsed time and cache performance on my own MSD.EXE program.

Wrapping the batch commands around the execution of program MSD makes it possible to collect start-and-stop times for PC programs, as well as SMRT-DRV buffer hit-and-miss counts. Use this information to identify and record PC run-times and buffer utilization. Figure 1-27 shows the results, which are piped into a file called MSDSTAT.JOB.

In this example, MSD.EXE ran for two hours and one minute (end time stamp minus begin time stamp). The buffer cache hits and misses come from SMARTDRV. This information shows that there were 357 cache hits and only

```
PROMPT TIME IS: $T$_DATE IS: $D
SMARTDRV /S > MSD.JOB
C:\DOS\FIND "cache hits"   MSD.JOB >> MSDSTAT.JOB
C:\DOS\FIND "cache misses" MSD.JOB >> MSDSTAT.JOB
DIR MSD.JOB /O:-D /-W >> MSDSTAT.JOB
MSD.EXE
SMARTDRV /S > MSD.JOB
C:\DOS\FIND "cache hits"   MSD.JOB >> MSDSTAT.JOB
C:\DOS\FIND "cache misses" MSD.JOB >> MSDSTAT.JOB
DIR MSD.JOB /O:-D /-W >> MSDSTAT.JOB
DEL MSD.JOB
PROMPT $P$G
```

Figure 1-26 PC Program Statistics Collection

```
------ MSD.JOB
There have been 37,942 cache hits

------ MSD.JOB
    and 2,137 cache misses

Volume in drive C is CDRIVE
Volume Serial Number is 123E-0FD0
Directory of C:\WINDOWS
MSD     JOB      600 02-07-94   3:02p
        1 file(s)         600 bytes
                    26904576 bytes free

------ MSD.JOB
There have been 38,299 cache hits
    and 2,138 cache misses

Volume in drive C is CDRIVE
Volume Serial Number is 123E-0FD0
Directory of C:\WINDOWS
MSD     JOB      600 02-07-94   5:03p
        1 file(s)         600 bytes
```

Figure 1-27 Output from MSDJOB.BAT Run

one cache miss. That means MSD.EXE exhibited superb caching. The MSD-JOB.BAT file is set up to continually add before and after job statistics. So, you could conceivably collect several months of data before doing any performance analysis.

Figure 1-28 contains a CA-Clipper program listing of source code. The program is designed to capture database file and index statistics. You need to wrap portions of the code around your own database program to use it on your application.

1.14 RISC Processors for UNIX

RISC stands for **R**educed **I**nstruction **S**et **C**omputing. Some of the machines incorporating RISC architectures are the Sun Microsystems SPARC workstation, MIPS Computers Rx000, HP 9000/700 and series9000/800, DEC, AT&T/NCR, Sequent, and IBMs RS/6000 or 9076 Scalable POWERparallel Systems. IBM has also delivered the *Parallel Transaction Server* (PTS), *Parallel Query Server* (PQS), and POWERparallel components necessary to access CICS and IMS/TM in parallel.

In some ways, the new Intel Pentiums use techniques similar to those found in RISC-based machines. The result is an open architecture with a smaller instruction set and phenomenal speeds. Because UNIX is the current operating system dominating RISC computers, I recommend that you consider RISC as the resting place for client/server applications requiring high performance. Microsoft is preparing NT for the RISC platform, and it may be ready by the time this book goes to print. That, too, will be a boon to developers of client/server systems on RISC computers. What are the key performance strategies used in RISC processors? Let's take a look.

```
                    SET HEADING OFF
                    SET SAFETY OFF
                    SET CONSOLE OFF
                    SET DEVICE TO SCREEN
                    SET STATUS OFF
                    SET STEP OFF
                    SET ECHO OFF
                    SET BELL OFF
                    SET SCOREBOARD OFF
                    SET DECIMALS TO 2
                    SET TYPEAHEAD TO 100
                    SET COLOR TO W+/B, GR+/RB, B
                    ************************************************************
                    * PROGRAM: NAMEFAST
                    * PURPOSE: TEST LARGE DATABASE SPEED AND INDEX SPEED
                    * RULES: TAKE TIME DELTAS ON SEQUENTIAL AND RANDOM INDEX PROCESSING
                    * DEBUG: DEBUGGING STATEMENTS TURNED ON WITH MDEBUG = .T.
                    ************************************************************
                    * FILE ALLOCATION AND VARIABLES
                    CLEAR SCREEN
                    STORE SPACE(9) TO MOPT
                    STORE 5 TO R, C
                    STORE 42 TO C2
                    STORE 1 TO MSUB2
                    STORE 0 TO SEC3, TOTAL, AVERAGE, ELAPSED
                    STORE SPACE(2) TO SEC1, SEC2
                    STORE SPACE(1) TO MOPT
                    USE NAMETBL
                    DO WHILE MSUB2 < 6
                       @ 0,0 TO 24,80 DOUBLE
                       @1,2   SAY '                  NAME DATABASE SEQ SPEED TEST'
                       @2,2   SAY 'SEQ START: '+TIME()
                       START = SECONDS()
                       DO WHILE R < 24
                          @ R,C SAY SUBSTR(MYXBASE,1,30)
                          @ R,C2 SAY SUBSTR(MYXBASE,1,30)
                          SKIP
                          R = R + 1
                       ENDDO
                       ELAPSED = SECONDS() - START
                       TOTAL   = TOTAL     + ELAPSED
                       AVERAGE = TOTAL     / MSUB2
                       @2,32  SAY 'SEQ END: '+TIME()
                       SKIP 100
                       @3,2   SAY 'DIFFERENCE/SEC(S): '+LTRIM(STR(ELAPSED))+' AVG:
                    '+LTRIM(STR(AVERAGE))
                       @1,2   SAY 'ENTER TO CONTINUE   NAME DATABASE SEQ SPEED TEST' GET MOPT
                       TONE(100,1)
                       READ
                       MSUB2 = MSUB2 + 1
                       STORE 'MAP'+LTRIM(STR(MSUB2)) TO MAPNAME
                       SAVE SCREEN TO MAPNAME
                       STORE 5 TO R
                    ENDDO
                    *
                    * RANDOM INDEX TEST
                    *
```

Figure 1-28 CA-Clipper Database Statistics Program

```
CLEAR SCREEN
STORE SPACE(9) TO MOPT
STORE 5 TO R, C
STORE 42 TO C2
STORE 1 TO MSUB2
STORE 0 TO SEC3, TOTAL, AVERAGE, ELAPSED
STORE SPACE(2) TO SEC1, SEC2
STORE SPACE(1) TO MOPT
USE NAMETBL INDEX NAMENDX1
DO WHILE MSUB2 < 6
   @ 0,0 TO 24,80 DOUBLE
   @1,2  SAY '                      NAME RANDOM INDEX SPEED TEST'
   @2,2  SAY 'SEQ START: '+TIME()
   START = SECONDS()
   DO WHILE R < 24
      IF R = 6
         SEEK 'A'
      ELSEIF R = 7
         SEEK 'B'
      ELSEIF R = 8
         SEEK 'C'
      ELSEIF R = 9
         SEEK 'D'
      ELSEIF R = 10
         SEEK 'E'
      ELSEIF R = 11
         SEEK 'F'
      ELSEIF R = 12
         SEEK 'G'
      ELSEIF R = 13
         SEEK 'H'
      ELSEIF R = 14
         SEEK 'I'
      ELSEIF R = 15
         SEEK 'J'
      ELSEIF R = 16
         SEEK 'K'
      ELSEIF R = 17
         SEEK 'L'
      ELSEIF R = 18
         SEEK 'M'
      ELSEIF R = 19
         SEEK 'N'
      ELSEIF R = 20
         SEEK 'O'
      ELSEIF R = 21
         SEEK 'P'
      ELSEIF R = 22
         SEEK 'Q'
      ELSEIF R = 23
         SEEK 'R'
      ELSEIF R = 5
         SEEK 'Z'
      ENDIF
      @ R,C SAY SUBSTR(MYXBASE,1,30)
      @ R,C2 SAY SUBSTR(MYXBASE,1,30)
      SKIP
```

Figure 1-28 CA-Clipper Database Statistics Program (Continued)

```
      R = R + 1
   ENDDO
   ELAPSED = SECONDS() - START
   TOTAL   = TOTAL     + ELAPSED
   AVERAGE = TOTAL     / MSUB2
   @2,32  SAY 'SEQ END: '+TIME()
   SKIP 100
   @3,2    SAY 'DIFFERENCE/SEC(S): '+LTRIM(STR(ELAPSED))+' AVG:
   '+LTRIM(STR(AVERAGE))
   @1,2  SAY 'ENTER TO CONTINUE   NAME RANDOM INDEX SPEED TEST' GET MOPT
   TONE(200,1)
   READ
   MSUB2 = MSUB2 + 1
   STORE 5 TO R
ENDDO
CLEAR SCREEN
STORE SPACE(9) TO MOPT
STORE 5 TO R, C
STORE 42 TO C2
STORE 1 TO MSUB2
STORE 0 TO SEC3, TOTAL, AVERAGE, ELAPSED
STORE SPACE(2) TO SEC1, SEC2
STORE SPACE(1) TO MOPT
DO WHILE MSUB2 < 5
   @ 0,0 TO 24,80 DOUBLE
   IF MSUB2 > 6
      SET COLOR TO B/B, B/B,,, W/N
   ELSEIF MSUB2 > 27
      SET COLOR TO G/B, RB,N+,,, B/G
   ELSEIF MSUB2 > 58
      SET COLOR TO R/R, R,B,,, W,N
   ELSEIF MSUB2 > 79
      SET COLOR TO RB,RB, R,R,,, U,I
   ELSEIF MSUB2 > 160
      SET COLOR TO N+,U,  GR+,R,,, N,W
   ELSEIF MSUB2 > 171
      SET COLOR TO GR+,R, R,R,,, R,R
   ELSEIF MSUB2 > 182
      SET COLOR TO I
   ENDIF
   @1,2  SAY '                    NAME SCREEN SPEED TEST'
   @2,2  SAY 'SEQ START: '+TIME()
   START = SECONDS()
   STORE 'MAP'+LTRIM(STR(MSUB2)) TO MAPNAME
   RESTORE SCREEN FROM MAPNAME
   ELAPSED = SECONDS() - START
   TOTAL   = TOTAL     + ELAPSED
   AVERAGE = TOTAL     / MSUB2
   @2,32  SAY 'SEQ END: '+TIME()
   @3,2    SAY 'DIFFERENCE/SEC(S): '+LTRIM(STR(ELAPSED))+' AVG:
   '+LTRIM(STR(AVERAGE))
   @1,2  SAY 'ENTER TO CONTINUE   NAME SCREEN SPEED TEST'
   TONE(50,0.01)
   MSUB2 = MSUB2 + 1
ENDDO
@ 10, 20 CLEAR TO 15, 60
@ 13, 30 SAY 'ALL TEST COMPLETE'
RETURN
```

Figure 1-28   CA-Clipper Database Statistics Program (Continued)

RISC PERFORMANCE STRATEGIES

■ 64-bit processing that implies very large memory pools are supported

■ Overlapping instruction execution (a.k.a. pipe-lining and scaling)

■ Simpler instruction set

■ Fast memory access

■ Multiple register sets eliminating register save and restore

■ More sophisticated caching than desktop computers

■ Multiprocessor arrays

1.15   UNIX Performance Tuning

UNIX is a contagious disease for many of us old mainframe folks. This operating system, which is becoming more widespread, entered on the scene in 1970 and has evolved to the prominent AIX, HP/UX, LINUX, SCO, and System V versions of today. Several standards committees have influenced UNIX, and *Portable Operating System Interface Cross Computers* (POSIX) is a term with which you will come to grips. I became interested in UNIX when it looked like I would need to know about its place in the downsizing/rightsizing world (a.k.a. scalar abilities). I didn't want to learn about it. In fact, I didn't want to learn things about any new platforms. But, the need gained momentum and eventually won. Many aesthetic downsizing and rightsizing solutions are UNIX centered strategies.

Well, there are a few reporting mechanisms of importance to the tuner. You must have SUPERUSER (yes, that's a real name) authority to gather this data on the UNIX system. The bare minimum is to produce a full complement of *System Activity Reporter* (SAR) reports. Additionally, there are individual displays that will have to be entered before, during, and after heavily used processes and programs to determine where their particular bottlenecks are. The *Process Status* (PS) commands are useful for this.

Two of the best tuning opportunities for UNIX systems (see Appendix R for SCO tuning options), are the kernel, buffer, page caches and blocksizes. You can recompile the kernel with only the devices that actually can be used. It's a good idea to do this, because UNIX usually comes with everything turned on. This will reduce the size of the kernel, as well as speeding up the bootup process. The second thing to do is increase the raw file blocksize from 1K to 8K. Larger blocks means fewer I/Os to get information.

Figure 1-29 shows the types of statistics you should collect for basic UNIX systems. If you use the commands in the following list of examples, you will capture most of the simple statistics rapidly.

Online and Batch

```
UNIX SAR Reports CPU, I/O and PAGING (Similar to RMF on Mainframe)
    SAR -A Command Will Give All Reports
UNIX TCP/IP Network Usage
UNIX PS (Process Status Displays)
IOSTAT, MPSTAT, VMSTAT, NETSTAT
```

Figure 1-29   fgc:UNIX Statistics Gathering Checklist

EXAMPLE 1:   SOME SAR COMMANDS

```
SAR                 - today's CPU activity so far
SAR  -d  -f  temp   - to later review disk and tape activity from that
                      period
SAR -A -            - all reports (both remote and local are printed
                      provided that a stats file exists)
```

EXAMPLE 2:   USING PS TO SEE PROCESS STATUS

```
ps -ef > temp       - The processing status command is useful for
                      looking at the elapsed time for individual users
                      or processes. The output from the temp file
                      would look like the following information.
                      Notice the STIME for user jeffboy. This is the
                      start time for the user. The TIME column shows
                      elapsed time. See Appendix C for complete
                      descriptions of the PS and SAR command syntax
                      and reported fields.
```

@	UID	PID	PPID	C	STIME	TTY	TIME	COMMAND
root	0	0	0	Feb 25	?	0:00	sched	
root	1	0	0	Feb 25	?	3:11	/etc/init	
root	2	0	0	Feb 25	?	0:00	vhand	
root	3	0	0	Feb 25	?	29:57	bdflush	
root	8532	1	0	Mar 15	console	0:00	/etc/getty console console	
root	113	1	0	Feb 28	vt01	0:00	/etc/getty /dev/vt01 vt01	
root	58	1	0	Feb 28	?	0:00	/usr/bin /strerr	
root	114	1	0	Feb 28	vt02	0:00	/etc/getty /dev/vt02 vt02	
root	63	1	0	Feb 28	?	0:00	/usr/bin /ipxd -start	
root	1	1	0	Feb 28	?	0:00	/usr/bin/dlixd started	

root	65	1	0	Feb 28	?	0:00	/usr/bin /loginixd -start
root	99	1	0	Feb 28	?	0:19	/etc/cron
root	103	1	0	Feb 28	?	3:37	/usr/lib /lpsched
root	11661	65	1	10:51:01	?	0:03	/usr/bin /loginixd -start
jeffboy	11662	11661	1	10:51:02	pts000	0:00	-sh
jeffboy	11689	11662	4	10:55:06	pts000	0:00	ps -ef

EXAMPLE 3:   COLLECTING SAR STATISTICS OVER 4 HOURS

sar -o temp 60 240   - This will capture SAR activity once each minute for 240 minutes and place the output into a file called temp. You will then be able to report from the temp file. Here are several examples of commands to capture reports from the temp file output.

EXAMPLE 4:   REPORTING DISK ACCESS STATISTICS

sar -a -f temp > saracces   - Will read the temp SAR history file and place the following information in report format in a file called SARACCES. You can use command "VI SARACCES" to view the file.

09:41:36	iget/s	namei/s	dirbk/s
09:42:36	1	0	1
...			
12:46:40	0	0	0
Average	1	0	1

EXAMPLE 5:   REPORTING BUFFER UTILIZATION STATISTICS

sar -b -f temp > sarbuff   - Will read the temp SAR history file and place the following information in report format in a file called SARBUFF. You can use command "VI SARBUFF" to view the file.

09:41:36	bread/s	lread/s	%rcache	bwrit/s	lwrit/s	%wcache	pread/s	pwrit/s
09:42:36	0	1	85	0	0	63	0	0
...								
12:46:40	0	1	100	0	0	67	0	0
Average	0	1	96	0	0	61	0	0

EXAMPLE 6:   REPORTING CPU UTILIZATION STATISTICS

```
sar -u -f temp > sarcpu          - Will read the temp SAR history file and
                                   place the following information in
                                   report format in a file called
                                   SARCPU. You can  use command
                                   "VI   SARCPU" to view the file.

09:41:36      %usr     %Sys     %wio    %idle
09:42:36       70       24        5      1
...
12:46:40       65       22       10      3
Average        68       23        7      2
```

A greater amount of user time compared to system time is preferred. If the
system time is the higher of the two, an I/O bottleneck may exist.

EXAMPLE 7:   REPORTING MEMORY UTILIZATION STATISTICS

```
sar -r -f temp > sarmem          - Will read the temp SAR history file and
                                   place the following information in
                                   report format in a file called
                                   SARMEM. You can  use command
                                   "VI   SARMEM" to view the file.
                                   These values are in 4K pages.

09:41:36 freemem freeswp
09:42:36     742    55296
...
12:46:40     738    55296
Average      741    55296
```

When the `freemem` value dips below 100 and `freeswp` begins dropping,
swapping has begun. This is an indication that more `freemem` is needed Increasing shared memory can result in less memory available to processes, resulting in undesirable swapping.

EXAMPLE 8:   REPORTING MESSAGE SERVICES UTILIZATION STATISTICS

```
sar -m -f temp > sarmsg         - Will read the temp SAR history file and
                                  place the following information in
                                  report format in a file called SARMSG.
                                  You can  use command "VI   SARMSG" to
                                  view the file.

09:41:36   msg/s   sema/s
09:42:36    0.00     0.00
...
12:46:40    0.00     0.00
Average     0.00     0.00
```

EXAMPLE 9: REPORTING PAGING STATISTICS

```
sar -p -f temp > sarpage       - Will read the temp SAR history file
                                 and place the following information
                                 in report format in a file called
                                 SARPAGE. You can  use command
                                 "VI  SARPAGE" to view the file.
```

09:41:36	vflt/s	pflt/s	pgfil/s	rclm/s
09:42:36	0.20	0.03	0.03	0.00
...				
12:46:40	0.00	0.00	0.00	0.00
Average	0.04	0.06	0.00	0.00

EXAMPLE 10: REPORTING QUEUE UTILIZATION STATISTICS

```
sar -q -f temp > sarbuff    - Will read the temp SAR history file and
                              place the following information in
                              report format in a file called SARBUFF.
                              You can use command "VI  SARBUFF" to
                              view the file.
```

09:41:36	runq-sz	%runocc	swpq-sz	%swpocc
09:42:36	1.0		12	
...				
12:46:40	1.0		12	
Average	1.0		12	

EXAMPLE 11: REPORTING SYSTEM CALL STATISTICS

```
sar -c -f temp > sarscall    - Will read the temp SAR history file and
                               place the following information in
                               report format in a file called
                               SARSCALL. You can use command
                               "VI  SARSCALL" to view the file.
```

09:41:36	scall/s	sread/s	swrit/s	fork/s	exec/s	rchar/s	wchar/s
09:42:36	1	0	0	0.00	0.00	1586	17
...							
12:46:40	5	1	0	0.00	0.00	1583	16
Average	1	0	0	0.01	0.01	1515	15

EXAMPLE 12: REPORTING PAGE SWAPPING STATISTICS

```
sar -w -f temp > sarswap       - Will read the temp SAR history file and
                                 place the following information in
                                 report format in a file called
                                 SARSWAP. You can  use command
                                 "VI  SARSWAP" to view the file.
                                 Blocks are 512 bytes in size.
```

09:41:36	swpin/s	bswin/s	swpot/s	bswot/s	pswch/s
09:42:36	0.00	0.0	0.00	0.0	1110
...					
12:46:40	0.00	0.0	0.00	0.0	1414
Average	0.00	0.0	0.00	0.0	1322

SWPIN/S and SWPOT/S are zero, which means that there is no swapping.

EXAMPLE 13:   REPORTING TTY TERMINAL STATISTICS

```
sar -y -f temp > sartty    - Will read the temp SAR history file and
                             place the following information in
                             report format in a file called SARTTY.
                             You can use command "VI  SARTTY" to view
                             the file.
09:41:36 rawch/s canch/s outch/s rcvin/s xmtin/s mdmin/s
09:42:36    0       0       0       0       0       0
```

EXAMPLE 14:   Disk Usage

```
sar -d 20 1  -  Provides I/O statistics on the system
09:41:36 device   %busy    avque      r+w/s      blks/s      avwait
avserv
09:41:48 sd1       33.15   200.12     149.99      333.11      248.81
7.50
         sd2      22.11    108.04     100.14      278.22      299.67
13.55
```

It is recommended that I/Os not exceed 50 per second for any physical volume. A device should not be busy more than 10 percent of the time, too. In example 14, both drives are overly busy. The implementation of additional drives can improve performance.

Another tool mentioned here, without examples, is the timex reporter. It will provide system-wide and per-process reports of activity during process execution.

One of the hurdles that non-UNIX individuals have to overcome is new commands. UNIX has commands to do the same things that other operating systems do, except that the syntax is different. There doesn't seem to be any standardization of operating system commands going on, nor ever will be, I presume. Table 1-2 shows some comparisons between UNIX and DOS commands. This may help you adapt gradually to UNIX.

1.16   VMSTAT, IOSTAT, and NETSTAT

The vmstat and iostat utilities produce comparable statistics to those provided by sar commands. They are very useful in tracking performance on Sybase and Oracle servers. vmstat needs to be run with a fairly large interval to capture

TABLE 1-2   DOS Versus UNIX Command Table

UNIX	DESCRIPTION	DOS EQUIVALENT
CD mydir	Change Directory	CD c:\path\mydir | CD mydir
CP myfile myfile2	Copy file	COPY myfile myfile2 XCOPY myfile myfile2
DATE	Display date and time	DATE and TIME
DU -a	Display files in tree	TREE
DU -scb	Display total space for all files in tree	DIR *. /S
LL *.*	Display files in current directory and whether they can cbe read, written or exected	DIR *.*
LS	Display all files in current directory	DIR *.* | DIR
MAN CD	Help text for commands	HELP CD
MKDIR mydir	Make Directory	MD mydir | MKDIR mydir
MORE myfile	Display file contents	TYPE myfile
MV myfile myfile2	Move or Rename File	REN myfile myfile2
PWD	Display which directory in	Dos prompt displayed C:\WIN95>
RM myfile	Remove File	DEL myfile
RMDIR mydir	Remove Directory	RD mydir | RMDIR mydir
./myprog	Execute a program or script	myprog

useful values for the number of runnable processes in the run queue, paging activity by the virtual memory driver and the percentage of CPU time allocated to system and user mode processing.

If the sr field in vmstat output is greater than zero, it is an indication that the system is attempting to allocate some physical memory in a shortage condition.

I/O disk statistics from the extended iostat command will wake you up to potential disk performance problems. Here is output from a sample extended iostat display.

SAMPLE IOSTAT–XC OUTPUT

disk	r/s	w/s	K r/s	K w/s	wait	actv
sd20	4.4	0.0	12.6	0.0	0.0	0.0
sd21	9.3	12.2	44.5	20.2	0.3	0.2

High wait times for any disk should sound the warning alarm. They will usually accompany high I/O service times. Service time is the number of milliseconds to complete a physical I/O and shouldn't exceed 100.

`Netstat` is effective in determining network collision rates. High collision rates for an ethernet network purport a bottleneck, while token ring will always have a zero collision rate from `netstat`. Calculate the collision rate by dividing the number of collisions by the sum of input and output packets.

1.17   Summarizing Reports and Selecting Tuning Targets

Based upon the reports generated so far, here is a list of target programs that would be chosen for our initial tuning effort.

MAINFRAME TUNING INITIAL TARGET LIST

Online Mainline Program	CUSTONL2 with the highest cpu usage 0.72 Avg cpu SECS / transaction
Online Subprogram	BILLONL9 with the highest number of executions 192,017 times called / week
Batch Program	GLBTCH1 with the highest cumulative cpu usage 13:00 hours cpu / week
Batch Program	FDRABR with the highest cumulative elapsed usage 251:59 hours elapsed / week

PC TUNING INITIAL TARGET LIST

PC Batch Program time	MSD.EXE with the longest single elapsed 2:01 hours elapsed

UNIX SYSTEM INITIAL TARGET LIST

Batch Program	COLLECT1 with the greatest CPU based upon SAR statistics

Assuming that CPU TIME and ELAPSED TIME were targets for our hypothetical tuning effort, the preceding list of programs is a fitting group to begin with. You would now be prepared to draft a memo to management spelling out the target programs and reasons for choosing them. It would be wise to work closely with the applications programming managers responsible for these applications. They will be able to identify a contact who can provide key information on the internal workings of the programs, a person who will make or coordinate code changes and someone to perform testing of the run-time improvements. Final implementation of changes is also a key issue to work out with the manager.

OMEGAMON for MVS from CANDLE Corporation is useful in identifying the overall bottleneck in a DBMS region. It will give a quick CPU and EXCP percentage used per type of figure. This information can be used by the systems programming staff in setting the dispatching priority. We won't be using OMEGAMON in this book.

1.18   DB2 Report Collection

DB2 is limited in the performance evaluation information it provides. For example, EXCP(s) are not directly available. If you perform a trace you can identify the requests for pages not found in buffers. However, this approach will report I/O(s) even if the page is found in the cache buffer (NO-IO should be reported). DB2 will tally reads and writes to the user address space. Sequential and list prefetch page requests are added to the statistics for the DB2 region. For this reason, I recommend you get hold of STROBE's DB2 interface and one of the many performance monitoring tools for DB2.

A comprehensive list of the reports necessary to perform complete DB2 tuning analysis can be seen in Figure 1-30.

Another recommendation is that you read the IBM *DB2 Data Administration Guide*, Volume 3, on performance monitoring and tuning. It contains more detail than could ever be included here. Be selective in your report gathering. Isolate your interest to the longest running transactions, queries, batch programs, and utilities.

After you have collected the correct reports, an analysis of symptoms will provide some insight into the causes of poor performance. Major related symptoms will be I/O waits, locking waits, high paging, high EXCP counts, large numbers of leaf levels in indexes, insufficient free space on pages, insufficient buffering, insufficient free pages in indexes, etc. A much more in-depth discussion of these topics is provided later in the book.

1.19   CICS/ESA Storage Statistics Utility (Release 3.3)

DFHOSTAT has been enhanced for release 3.3 of CICS. This utility provides a lot of useful information when sizing the five *Dynamic Storage Areas* (DSAs).

The thresholds presented in Figure 1-31 give you an indication of what minimums should signal your interest in tuning these values by changing the MXT (maximum tasks) and storage area sizes.

1.20   DB2 DASD Statistics Gathering Tools

I've saved a few more tools for the end of the DB2 reports discussion. I haven't had experience with these tools. For vendor contact information, refer to Appendix D. Obviously, based upon the tool names, they have to do with optimizing disk utilization and performance.

DASD Manager for DB2 from BMC Software.

!DB/DASD for DB2 from Candle Corporation.

Flex DASD from Succinct Software for DB2.

1.21   RMF Caching Reports

The **Cache RMF Reporter** from IBM consists of a user exit and reporting program. Tuning the operating system should be left up to the systems programming

Transactions and Queries	Batch
Transaction processors IMS, CICS	Longest batch appl jobs
VTAM line speeds	Longest batch utility jobs
Transaction/second rate	Allowable concurrent jobs
EXCPS/transaction	DB2 RUNSTATS facility (space usage indexes)
Resource limits & QMF Governor Limits	DB2 Catalog queries for reorg timing
Longest and most executed SQL queries	DB2 Runstats Utility
DB2 RUNSTATS Facility (space usage and indexes)	DB2 STOSPACE Utility
DB2 TRACE Facility (performance and monitor trace data)	DB2 EXPLAIN statement for path usage
	CICSPARS Performance Reports
DB2PM (Performance Monitor) Reports*	Crystal CICS & DB2 Performance Rpts
CMF (CICS Monitoring Facility)	NetSpy VTAM Reports
CICSPARS (CICS Performance Analysis Reporting Sys for response times and lock contentions)	
IMS DC Monitor for requests to DB2	
IMSPARS (IMS Performance Analysis Reporting Sys for response times and lock contentions)	
DB2 STOSPACE Utility for space allocated	
DB2 EXPLAIN Statement for path usage	
DB2 DISPLAY Command for transaction counts	
DB2 Catalog queries for reorg timing	
RMF for paging, channel usage and volume EXCP rates	
Diskview DEC VAX file reports	
AS/400 performance analyzer reports	
SMF/RMF Type 100 (Ifcid 1 2) DB2 System Services Information	
SMF/RMF Type 101 (Ifcid 3) DB2 Database Manager	
SMF/RMF Type 102 (ifcid 106) DB2 DSNZPARM Parameters	

* See Appendix D for a list of many other performance monitoring tools for DB2.

Figure 1-30   DB2 Resource Utilization Checklist

staff. The information shown here is to give you a flavor of the types of information that are useful when tuning cache routines. This is invaluable later on in the chapters where we show you how to build your own application-driven multilevel caching programs. The reason is not so obvious, though. As you expand the amount of XA or ESA memory buffering within your operating system, it will impact paging. The following statistics will help you to adjust paging after each expansion/reduction in the usage of caching mechanisms.

Field	Threshold	
Private Area Storage Available Below 16M	< 1 Meg	(threshold)
Other Modules Loaded in Region Below 16M	> 100K	"
Free Storage (including cushion)	< 500K	"
Cushion Size	< 20K	"
Times No Storage Returned	> 0	"
Times Request Suspended	> 0	"
Times Short on Storage	> 0	"
Program Load Totals by Type	> 0	"
Total and Average Fetch Time	> 1 sec	"

Figure 1-31 Key DFHOSTAT CICSPROD Region Report Thresholds

```
Read H/R = Demand Paging Read Hits / Demand Paging Reads

Read H/R (Sequential Paging) = Sequential Paging Read Hits / Sequential
Paging Reads

Read H/R (Swap-In) = Swap-In Read Hits / Swap-In Reads

Read H/R (Total Paging) = Total Paging Read Hits / Total Paging Reads *

Reads (Total Paging) = Demand Paging + Sequential Paging + Swap-In Reads

Read/Write (Read to Write) Block Ratio = Reads (Total Paging) / Block
Writes

* should be 0.7 or higher
```

1.22 FDRABR Reports

Most mainframe administrators are familiar with *Fast Dump Restore* (FDR). One of the things I found it extremely handy for was reporting on *Virtual Storage Access Method* (VSAM) cluster usage. It just makes sense to include this processing with your normal backup processing. Take a look at the parameters to collect this information along with the output from the job (see Figure 1-32). This report shows the DSN, SIZE, SIZEUSED, SIZEFREE, %FREE, and NOEXTENT fields. The fields are sorted on %FREE (ascending), SIZEFREE (descending), and DSN(ascending). A second example (see Figure 1-33) is provided. This example includes CISIZE and sorts primarily by CISIZE, which is useful in locating different CISIZEs for VSAM datasets.

1.23 DB2 Batch Display of Plans

Figure 1-34 shows how you would use a batch routine to display DB2 SYS-PLAN information that has been gathered.

1.24 Oracle Statistics Collection

There are abundant tools for tuning Oracle. Oracle comes with dynamic V$ views, utlbstat/utlestat.sql scripts (DBWR), dictionary reports, init.ora parameters, multithreaded server (MTS) parameters, and **x$** tables in

```
PARAMETERS
TITLE  LINE='SPACE REPORT01',SKIP=2
DEFAULT AUTOSTACK,DISPLAY=NO,ONLINE
XS   XDSN.EQ.PROD.BILLWORK.UNIT.PRD00001.*,DSORG=AM,UNITNAME=WORK
REPORT F=(DSN,SIZE,SIZEUSED,SIZEFREE,%FREE,NOEXTENT)
SORT F=(%FREE,SIZEFREE,DSN),SEQUENCE=(A,D,A)
PRINT FORMAT=PRT,RESETSEL=YES,SORT=COMBINE,SUM=YES,INFOMSG=NO,ONLINE

OUTPUT
                               SPACE REPORT01

DATA SET NAME              ALLOC      USED       FREE      %FR       EXT
-------------              -----      -----      -----     ----      ---
PROD.PRD00001.DATA    150   140        10                  7         1
PROD.PRD00001.INDEX    60    44        16                 27         1
FDR400   FDRABR REPORT STANDARD SUMMARIES - FDREPORT VER 5.2/06P  -
INNOVATION
                                    SPACE REPORTING

FINAL TOTALS --
DSN-------2  NOEXTENT------2  SIZE------210   SIZEFREE------26 SIZEUSED------188
```

Figure 1-32 FDRABR Report Parameters Example # 1

PARAMETERS

```
TITLE  LINE='SPACE REPORT02,SKIP=2
DEFAULT AUTOSTACK,DISPLAY=NO,ONLINE
XS   XDSN.EQ.PROD.BILL.*.DATA,DSORG=AM,UNITNAME=WORK
REPORT F=(DSN,SIZE,SIZEUSED,SIZEFREE,%FREE,NOEXTENT)
REPORT F=(DSN,%USED,SIZEUSED,SIZE,RECORDS,NOEXTENT,CISIZE)
SORT F=(CISIZE,%FREE,SIZEFREE,DSN),SEQUENCE=(D,A,D,A)
PRINT FORMAT=PRT,RESETSEL=YES,SORT=COMBINE,SUM=YES,INFOMSG=NO,ONLINE

OUTPUT
                                    SPACE REPORT02

%US      USED      ALLOC      RECORDS    EXT          CISIZ
---      ----      -----      ------------  ---        -------
DATA81       15079 18615        974494      23              12288

-1  NOEXTENT-----23  SIZE-----18615  SIZEFREE-----3536  SIZEUSED-----1507
```

Figure 1-33 FDRABR Report Parameters Example # 2

---

v$fixed_view. You can use the ANALYZE, TRACE, and EXPLAIN PLAN commands to capture statistics useful in tuning ORACLE queries. Then there are the sar, vmstat, iostat, and netstat commands for system and network statistics. Finally, don't forget the many performance monitors available, which we will discuss later in Chapter 1. Figure 1-35 provides a checklist of statistics and tools used to capture them.

INPUT

```
//BIG1 EXEC PGM=IKJEFT01,DYNAMNBR=20
//SYSTSPRT DD SYSOUT=*
//SYSPRINT DD SYSOUT=*
//SYSUDUMP DD SYSOUT=*
//SYSIN    DD *
//SYSTSIN  DD *
```

OUTPUT

```
DSN SYSTEM(DB2P)
DSN
RUN  PROGRAM(DSNWAIT) PLAN(DSNWAITX)        LIB('SYS1.DB2P.LOADLIB')
DSN
END
END
PAGE    1
***INPUT STATEMENT:  SET CURRENT SQLID = 'PRDDB2P' ;
RESULT OF SQL STATEMENT:
DSNT400I SQLCODE = 000,   SUCCESSFUL EXECUTION
SET      SUCCESSFUL
PAGE    1
***INPUT STATEMENT:  SELECT * FROM SYSIBM.SYSPLAN ;
```

	NAME	CREATOR	BINDDATE	VALIDATE	ISOLATION	VALID	OPERATIVE	BINDTIME	PLSIZE	IBMREQD
1_	DSNWAIT2	PRDDB2P	950414	R	S	Y	Y	10085007	1995	N
2_	DSN8SP22	PRDDB2P	950429	R	S	N	Y	13454236	2296	C
3_	BIL10000	BILPGM1	950406	B	S	Y	Y	16314096	2376	N

PAGE   2

	AVGSIZE	ACQUIRE	RELEASE	EXREFERENCE	EXSTRUCTURE	EXCOST	EXPLAN	EXPREDICATE	BOUNDBY	QUALIF
1_	0	U	C	N	N	N	N	N	PRDDB2P	PRDDB2
2_	1290	U	C	N	N	N	N	N	PRDDB2P	PRDDB2
3_	1176	U	C	N	N	N	N	B	BILLUS1	BILPGM

PAGE   3

	CACHESIZE	PLENTRIES	DEFERPREP	CURRENTSERVER	SYSENTRIES
1_	1024	0	N		0
2_	1024	0	N		0
3_	1024	0	N		0

SUCCESSFUL RETRIEVAL OF   3 ROW(S)

Figure 1-34 DB2 Batch Display of Plans

Command or Utility	Information of Interest
sar (UNIX system, disk and memory)	See Chapter 1 examples
vmstat (memory shortages)	"
iostat (I/O bottlenecks)	"
netstat (network bottlenecks)	"
init.ora (tuning parameters)	All available statistics
sqlnet.ora	"
v$session_wait (parallel sessions)	"
v$sgastat (system global area memory)	"
v$sga (system global area memory)	"
v$library_cache(library cache)	"
v$db_object_cache (object cache)	"
v$dispatcher (dispatcher)	"
v$latchname (latch names)	"
v$latch (latch contention)	"
v$shared_pool_reserved (flushes)	"
v$rollstat (rollback contention)	"
v$filestat (disk contention)	"
v$datafile (file activity)	"
utlbstat/utlestat.sql reports	All DBWR statistics
v$rowcache (gets/getmisses etc)	All available statistics
v$sqlarea	"
v$session	"
v$sessstat (full table scans)	"
v$sysstat (sorts buffers etc)	"
x$kcbrbh (alternative cache tuning)	cache_hits
x$kcbcbh (alternative cache tuning)	"
EXPLAIN PLAN (SQL tuning)	Access Paths/Optimization
ANALYZE	with LIST CHAINED ROWS option
TRACE	
RULES BASED EXPERT	Oracle Expert
RMF STATISTICS (Oracle MVS)	Resources
DBGENERAL SQLab	SQL activity by user
	SQL activity by object
	I/Os per table
	Automatic SQL statement tuning
SQL*DBA	MONITOR ROLLBACK SEGMENTS
SQL area reuse	open_cursors
Multi-Threaded Server (MTS) parameters	All available statistics
listener.ora (configuration file)	address_list
Dictionary Views	Generally useful information
dba_catalog	All database Tables, Views,
	Synonyms, Sequences
dba_clusters	Description of al clusters in the database
dba_constraints	Constraint definitions on all tables
dba_data_files	Information about database files
dba_extents	Extents comprising all segments in
	the databasedba_free_space Free
	extents in all tablespaces
dba_indexes	Description of all indexes in the database
dba_segments	Storage allocated for all database segments
dba_snapshots	All snapshots in the database
index_histogram	Statistics on keys with repeat count
index_stats	Statistics on b-trees

Figure 1-35 Oracle Statistics Collection Checklist

Command or Utility	Information of Interest
dba_triggers	All triggers in the database
DBAware, Precise/SQL, DB-Vision, Performance Monitor, Platinum Tools for Windows NT, DBGENERAL Monitor, ADHAWK Monitor, PerfoRMAx Monitor, ECOTools, PATROL	
	All available statistics
UnixWare Operating System Parms	aio_listio_max
	BUFHWM
	HVMMLIM
	MAXUP
	NBUF
	NPROC
	NUMAIO
	SHMMAX
	SHMSEG
	SVMMLIM
	TCPWINDOW
Pentium Kernal Parameters	pse_physmem

Figure 1-35   Oracle Statistics Collection Checklist (Continued)

1.25 Capturing Oracle V$ Statistics

There are more than a hundred V$ views that you could mull through on your own and then write SQL(s) to analyze your database. But, thanks to Menlo Software's Oracle Page (www.menlosoftware.com), you have a running start. Figures 1-36 through 1-61 show queries taken from that page.

The init.ora parameter, db_block_buffers, controls the amount of memory allocated for the data cache. When an application requests data, Oracle first attempts to find it in the data cache. The more often Oracle finds requested data in memory, a physical I/O is avoided, and thus overall performance is better. Under normal circumstances this ratio (see Figure 1-36) should be >=95%. Initially set db_block_buffers size to be 20 to 50 percent the size of the SGA.

The init.ora parameter shared_pool_size controls the amount of memory allocated for the shared buffer pool. The shared buffer pool contains SQL and PL/SQL statements (library cache), the data dictionary cache, and information on database sessions. This percentage (see Figure 1-37) will never equal 100 because the cache must perform an initial load when Oracle first starts up. The percentage, therefore, should continually get closer to 100 as the system stays "up." Ideally, the entire data dictionary would be cached in memory. Initially set the shared_pool_size to be 50 to 100 percent the size of the init.ora parameter: db_block_buffers; then fine tune the parameter.

The query in Figure 1-38 returns the first 1,000 bytes of the user SQL statement having the highest number of logical disk reads per statement execution. Each logical read means that Oracle accessed a buffer block instead of executing a physical I/O. The SQL statement with the most logical I/Os will consume the most blocks in the DB Block Buffer.

The query in Figure 1-39 returns the username associated with the user SQL statement having the highest number of logical disk reads per statement exe-

```
select round((1-(pr.value/(bg.value+cg.value)))*100,2)
from v$sysstat pr, v$sysstat bg, v$sysstat cg
where pr.name='physical reads'
and bg.name='db block gets'
and cg.name='consistent gets'
```

Figure 1-36   DB Block Efficiency

```
select round(sum(gets)/(sum(gets)+sum(getmisses))*100,2) from v$rowcache
```

Figure 1-37   Dictionary Cache Efficiency

```
select sql_text
from v$sqlarea, v$session
where address = sqlsql_address
and username is not null
and buffer_gets/executions =
(select max(buffer_gets/executions)
from v$sqlarea, v$session
where address = sql_address
and username is not null)
and username is not null)
```

Figure 1-38   Disk Reads Logical Max SQL

```
select username
from v$sqlarea, v$session
where address = sql_address
and username is not null
and buffer_gets/executions =
(select max(buffer_gets/executions)
from v$sqlarea, v$session
where address = sql_address
and username is not null)
```

Figure 1-39   Disk Reads Logical Max SQL

cution. Each logical read means that Oracle accessed a buffer block instead of executing a physical I/O. The SQL statement with the most logical I/Os will consume the most blocks in the DB Block buffer.

The query in Figure 1-40 returns the first 1,000 bytes of the user SQL statement having the highest number of physical disk reads per statement execution. It is designed to help determine the SQL causing the most physical disk reads per statement execution.

The query in Figure 1-41 returns the username associated with the user SQL statement having the highest number of physical disk reads per statement execution. It is designed to help determine the user causing the most disk reads per statement execution.

Every table requires at least one extent. Ideally, each table should reside in one extent, but this is sometimes not practical. However, each table should reside in the fewest extents possible. The query in Figure 1-42 returns the largest number of extents used by any database object (i.e. table or index). These objects do not include SYS- or SYSTEM-owned objects.

The query in Figure 1-43 returns the name of the object, table, or index, using the maximum number of extents in any tablespace. These objects do not include SYS- or SYSTEM-owned objects.

The select in Figure 1-44 returns the percentage that a request for data resulted in a wait for a free block. This value should be less than 1 percent. To reduce contention for a table's free list, the table must be recreated with a larger value in the FREELISTS storage parameter.

```
select sql_text
from v$sqlarea, v$session
where address = sql_address
and username is not null
and disk_reads/executions =
(select max(disk_reads/executions)
from v$sqlarea, v$session
where address = sql_address
and username is not null)
```

Figure 1-40   Disk Reads Physical Max SQL

```
select username
from v$sqlarea, v$session
where address = sql_address
and username is not null
and disk_reads/executions =
(select max(disk_reads/executions)
from v$sqlarea, v$session
where address = sql_address
and username is not null)
```

Figure 1-41   Disk Reads Physical Max User

```
select max(extent_id) + 1
from sys.dba_extents
where owner not in ('SYS','SYSTEM')
```

Figure 1-42   Extents Max Count

```
select segment_name
from sys.dba_extents
where owner not in ('SYS','SYSTEM')
and extent_id =
(select max(extent_id)
from sys.dba_extents
where owner not in ('SYS','SYSTEM')
```

Figure 1-43   Extents Max Object Name

The select in Figure 1-45 returns the largest percentage of latch contention from key latches. The value should be less than 3 percent. If the value is greater than 3 percent, try decreasing the value of the init.ora parameter `log_small_entry_max_size` to force more copies to use the copy latches. For multiple CPU systems, increase the number of "redo copy latched" by increasing the value of the init.ora parameter `log_simultaneous_copies`. It may be helpful to have up to twice as many copy latches as CPUs available to the database instance. Finally, try increasing the value of the init.ora parameter `log_entry_prebuild_threshold`.

The query in Figure 1-46 returns the percentage that a SQL statment did not need to be reloaded because it was already in the library cache. The init.ora parameter `shared_pool_size` controls the amount of memory allocated for the shared buffer pool. The shared buffer pool contains SQL and PL/SQL statements (library cache), the data dictionary cache, and information on database sessions. The percentage should be equal to 100. Maximum efficiency requires that no SQL statement be reloaded and reparsed. Initially set the `shared_pool_size` to be 50 to 100 percent the size of the init.ora parameter `db_block_buffers` and then fine tune the parameter.

Figure 1-47 exhibits a query to obtain the total number of recursive calls (Oracle-issued SQL statements). It may show dynamic extensions of tables or roll-

```
select round((sum(decode(w.class,'free list', count, 0))
/ (sum(decode(name,'db block gets', value, 0))
+ sum(decode(name,'consistent gets', value, 0))))
* 100,2)
from v$waitstat w, v$sysstat
```

Figure 1-44   Freelist Contention

```
select round(greatest(
sum(decode(ln.name,'cache buffers lru chain', misses, 0))
/ greatest(sum(decode(ln.name.'cache buffers lru chain', gets, 0)),1)),
(sum(decode(ln.name,'enqueues', misses, 0))
/ greatest(sum(decode(ln.name,'enqueues', gets, 0)), 1)),
(sum(decode(ln.name,'redo allocation', misses, 0))
/ greatest(sum(decode(ln.name,'redo allocation', gets, 0)), 1)),
(sum(decode(ln.name,'redo.copy', misses, 0))
/ greatest(sum(decode(ln.name,'redo copy', gets, 0)), 1)))
* 100,2)
from v$latch l, v$latchname ln
where l.latch# = ln.latch#
```

Figure 1-45   Latch Contention

```
select round(sum(pinhits)/sum(pins) * 100,2) from v$librarycache
```

Figure 1-46   Library Cache Efficiency

```
select value from v$sysstat where name = 'recursive calls'
```

Figure 1-47   Recursive Calls

back segments. Or, it may be caused by misses in the data dictionary cache, database triggers, stored procedures, functions, packages, anonymous PL/SQL blocks, DDL statements, and enforcement of referential integrity constraints.

The percentage (see Figure 1-48) of time that a process attempted to acquire a redo log latch held by another process should be less than 1 percent. This is rare on single CPU systems. If the value is greater than 1 percent, try decreasing the value of the init.ora parameter `log_small_entry_max_size` to reduce contention for the redo allocation latch. For multiple CPU systems, increase the number of "redo copy latched" by increasing the value of the init.ora parameter `log_simultaneous_copies`. It may be helpful to have up to twice as many copy latches as CPUs available to the database instance. Additionally, try increasing the value of the init.ora parameter `log_entry_prebuild_threshold`.

The query in Figure 1-49 returns the number of times a user process waited for redo log buffer space. This value should be near zero. If the value increments consistently, increase the size of the redo log buffer with the init.ora parameter `log_buffer` by 5 percent.

The percentage of times that a request for data resulted in a wait for a rollback segment is derived using the query in Figure 1-50. If this returns a value greater than 1 percent, then create more rollback segments.

The query in Figure 1-51 returns the size of the *System Global Area* (SGA). The SGA consists of the virtual memory dedicated to Oracle. Generally, the larger the SGA, the better. But, the SGA must stay within RAM (i.e., it must not get paged or swapped out of RAM by the operating system).

```
select round(greatest(
(sum(decode(ln.name,'redo copy', misses, 0))
/greatest(sum(decode(ln.name,'redo copy', gets, 0)), 1)),
(sum(decode(ln.name,'redo allocation', misses, 0))
/greatest(sum(decode(ln.name,'redo allocation', gets, 0)), 1)),
(sum(decode(ln.name,'redo copy',immediate_misses,0))
/greatest(sum(decode(ln.name,'redo copy',immediate_gets,0))
+ sum(decode(ln.name,'redo copy',immediate_misses, 0)), 1)),
(sum(decode(ln.name,'redo allocation',immediate_misses, 0))
/greatest(sum(decode(ln.name,'redo allocation',immediate_gets, 0))
+ sum(decode(ln.name,'redo allocation',immediate_misses, 0)), 1)))
* 100,2)
from v$latch l, v$latchname ln
where l.latch# = ln.latch#
```

Figure 1-48 Redo Log Allocation Latch Contention

```
select value from v$sysstat where name = 'redo log space waittime'
```

Figure 1-49 Redo Log Buffer Contention

```
select round(sum(waits)/sum(gets),2) from v$rollstat
```

Figure 1-50 Rollback Segment Contention

Figure 1-52 shows how to determine the percentage of free memory in the SGA shared pool area. This percentage should not drop below 5 percent.

A way to determine the number of items a SQL statement or procedure has been reparsed or reloaded because of a lack of memory is seen in Figure 1-53. If the number is too large, increase the init.ora parameter `shared_pool_size` or the init.ora parameter `open_cursors`.

The select in Figure 1-54 returns the percentage of SQL statement executions that result in a SQL statement reload. If the percentage is more than 1 percent, increase the init.ora parameter `shared_pool_size`. Although less likely, the init.ora parameter `open_cursors` may also need to be increased.

Sort performance can be ascertained using the query in Figure 1-55. The percentage of sorts performed in memory (preferred) as opposed to those in temporary segments on disk is calculated.

```
select sum(value)
from v$sga
```

Figure 1-51   SGA Size

```
select round((sum(decode(name,'free memory',bytes, 0))
/ sum(bytes))
* 100,2)
from v$sgastat
```

Figure 1-52   Shared Pool Free Memory

```
select sum(reloads)
from v$librarycache
where namespace in ('SQL AREA','TABLE/PROCEDURE','BODY','TRIGGER')
```

Figure 1-53   Shared Pool Reload Count

```
select round(sum(reloads)
/ sum(pins) * 100,2)
from v$librarycache
where namespace in ('SQL AREA','TABLE/PROCEDURE','BODY','TRIGGER')
```

Figure 1-54   Shared Pool Reload Ratio

```
select round((sum(decode(name,'sorts(memory)', value, 0))
/ (sum(decode(name,'sorts(memory)', value, 0))
+ sum(decode(name,'sorts(disk)', value, 0))))
* 100,2)
from v$sysstat
```

Figure 1-55   Sort Area Efficiency

The query in Figure 1-56 returns the largest percentage of used blocks by any tablespace. For example, if a database instance contains a tablespace with 10 percent free space, this query will return 90, assuming no other tablespace has a lower percentage of free space.

To determine the percentage of blocks used by a specific tablespace, edit and run the query shown in Figure 1-57. Supply your tablespace name as needed.

The query in Figure 1-58 generates a formatted SQL*Plus report with assorted buffer cache statistics.

The query in Figure 1-59 tells you how well your database blocks are used. It also gives you the current status of all database blocks. You must log as SYS to run this query.

```
select round(max((d.bytes - sum(nvl(f.bytes,0))))
/ d.bytes) * 100,2)
from sys.dba_data_files d, sys.dba_free_space f
where d.file_id=f.file_id(+)
group by d.bytes
```

Figure 1-56   Tablespace Max Used

```
select round(((d.bytes - sum(nvl(f.bytes, 0)))
/ d.bytes) * 100,2)
from sys.dba_data_files d, sys.dba_free_space f
where d.file_id = f.file_id(+)
and d.tablespace_name = '[INSERT YOUR TABLESPACE NAME]'
group by d.bytes
```

Figure 1-57   Tablespace Used

```
column phys_read heading "Physical?Reads" format 99999999990
column block_get heading "Block ?Gets" format 99999999990
column consi_get heading "Consistent ?Gets" format 99999999990
column bchr heading "BCHR" format 9999.90

select pr.value phys_read, bg.value block_get, cg.value consi_get,
(1 - (pr.value/(bg.value+cg.value))) * 100 bchr
from v$sysstat pr, v$sysstat bg, v$sysstat cg
where pr.name = 'physical reads'
and bg.name = 'db block gets'
and cg.name = 'consistent gets'
```

Figure 1-58   Buffer Cache Data

```
select decode(state, 0, 'Free', 1, 'Read and Modified', 2, 'Read and Not
Modified', 3, 'Currently Being Read', 'Other'), count(*) from x$bh group by
decode (state, 0, 'Free', 1, 'Read and Modified', 2, 'Read and Not Modi-
fied', 3, 'Currently Being Read', 'Other')
```

Figure 1-59   Database Block Usage

Figure 1-60's query will supply an ordered list by segment type, table, or index, and then by the size of the segment and again by segment name. Alternatively, you could order the numext field to see which segments have many extents.

To determine which user is connected to a dispatcher and server along with the current status of the user process, use the query in Figure 1-61.

The following additional queries against the V$ views have been collected from friends and associates around the world.

The query in Figure 1-62 will list important tuning fields from the v$sgastat.

The query in Figure 1-65 will identify objects that exceed a maximum size to be supplied by you. The resultant list of objects are candidates for pinning. All of this is done to reduce the number of misses during execution. Another means to eliminate misses is to place large PL/SQL objects in packages and mark them as kept.

```
select segment_name, segment_type, count(*) numext,
round(sum(bytes)/1024/1024,1) MB
from sys.dba_extents
where owner not in ('SYS', 'SYSTEM')
group by segment_name, segment_type
order by segment_type, round(sum(bytes)/1024/1024, 1) desc, segment_name
```

Figure 1-60 Extent List

```
select sess.username, sess.status, cir.queue "Query Location", dis.name
"Disp Name", dis.status "Disp Status", ss.name "Serv Name", ss.status
"Serv Status"
from v$circuit cir, v$session sess, v$dispatcher dis, v$shared_server ss
where sess.saddr = cir.saddr
and cir.dispatcher = dis.paddr
and cir.server = ss.paddr;
```

Figure 1-61 Multithreaded (MTS) Server Processes

```
select name, bytes
from v$sgastat
where name in (
'sql area',
'library cache',
'free memory',
'dictionary cache',
'log_buffer',
db_block_buffers,
```

Figure 1-62 List SGA Sizes

```
select namespace, gets, round(decode(gethits, 0, 1, gethits)
/ decode(gets, 0, 1, gets), 3)
"GET HIT RATIO" from v$librarycache
```

Figure 1-63 Get Hit Ratio

The queries in Figures 1-66 through 1-68 are useful in tracking table growth. This kind of information can help you predict when a data file needs to be added to the tablespace. Figures 1-69 through 1-77 are other queries.

```
select namespace, pins, round(decode(pinhits, 0, 1, pinhits)
/decode(pins, 0, 1, pins), 3)
"PIN HIT RATIO", reloads, invalidations from v$librarycache
```

Figure 1-64   PIN HIT Ratio

```
select *
from v$db_object_cache
where sharable_mem > "'[YOUR MAXIMUM]"
```

Figure 1-65   Objects for Pinning

```
select table_name, blocks*2048 from dba_tables;
```

Figure 1-66   Used Table Size Report

```
select index_name, leaf_blocks*2048 from dba_indexes;
```

Figure 1-67   Used Index Size Report

```
select tablespace_name,
round(sum(bytes)/1048576,2),
round(sum(bytes)1048675,2)
from sys.dba_free_space
group by tablespace_name
order by tablespace_name);
```

Figure 1-68   Tablespace Free Space

```
select trunc((1-(sum(decode(name,'physical reads',value,0))/
(sum(decode(name,'db block gets',value, 0))+
(sum(decode(name,'consistent gets',value,0))))))
* 100) "Buffer Hit Ratio"
from v$systat;
```

Figure 1-69   Buffer Hit Ratio

```
select
sum(gets) "Gets",
sum(getmisses) "Misses",
trunc((1-(sum(getmisses)/sum(gets)))*100) "Dictionary Cache Hit Ratio"
from v$rowcache
```

Figure 1-70   Data Dictionary Cache Hit Ratio

```
select
sum(pins) "Pins",
sum(reloads) "Misses",
((sum(reloads)/sum(pins))) "Library Cache Miss Ratio"
from v$librarycache
```

Figure 1-71   Library Cache Miss Ratio

```
select substr(name,1,30)
from v$sysstat
where name = 'redo log space requests';
```

Figure 1-72   Redo Log Buffer

```
select
sum(executions) "Total SQL Requests"
from v$sqlarea;
```

Figure 1-73   SQL Requests

```
select
sum(users_executing) "SQL Requests Running"
from v$sqlarea;
```

Figure 1-74   SQL Running

In Figure 1-75, the average number of waits per queue request is queried. If this number is greater than 1, it implies a server wait. Increasing the mts_max_servers parameter in init.ora is one option.

If the percent busy for a dispatcher derived from the query in Figure 1-76 is greater than 30 percent, bump up the maximum number of dispatchers (mts_max_dispatchers) in init.ora.

Most DBA(s) know how important file distribution is to overall database performance (see Figure 1-77). The greater the distribution across disks and the more even the distribution, the better. But, there is an added benefit quite often overlooked. Wide distribution of database files limits exposure for recovery in the event of a disk failure.

You will have to run many of the queries on your own. In Figure 1-78 you are shown a sample session with output for a query on hit ratios. Not every query in the book has an example. Instead, a few really good examples of output are provided to give you an idea of what to expect.

1.26   Capturing Oracle X$ Psuedotable Statistics

V$ view tables are derived from X$ base tables. There are some base tables for which no V$ view information is provided. In the event you have exhausted your search for information using V$ views, you may want to try these tables.

```
select decode(totalq,0, 'Total Queue Requests',
wait/totalq
from v$queue
where type = 'COMMON';
```

Figure 1-75 MTS Server Usage

```
select name,
(busy/(busy+idle))*100 "Percent Busy"
from v$dispatcher;
```

Figure 1-76 MTS Dispatcher Usage

```
select
substr(df.name,1,30) 'File Name",
df.bytes,
fs.phyrds,
fs.phywrts
from v$datafile df, v$filestat fs
where df.file# = fs.file#;
```

Figure 1-77 File I/O Distribution

For example, X$KCBRBH and X$KCBCBH tables are useful when evaluating changes to buffer cache; X$DB can provide the status of database blocks used; and X$KSPPI is useful in calculating the average number of buffers on the dirty buffer list using the following formula:

```
average number of buffers on dirty buffer list =
summed dirty queue length/write requests
```

1.27 Oracle ANALYZE

There seems to be a lot of confusion surrounding the ways to use ANALYZE (see Figure 1-79). I will try to clear it up here, so you won't fall prey to the rumors. This collection utility can be executed several ways as shown in the following examples.

In this example, table your_table is analyzed using a 20 percent sampling of rows. It is important to note that estimates are just that. The smaller the sampling, the less accurate the results. Some administrators won't even trust an estimate. But, if your table contains gigabytes of data, it makes sense to use only a sampling. The alternative is to use the COMPUTE STATISTICS option. With this option, ANALYZE will create a temporary tablespace up to four times the size of the one being analyzed. So, if you see message ORA-01547 saying that the system tablespace is out of room, you need to add segments/files or change

```
SQLDBA>
SQLDBA> set charwidth 18;
SQLDBA> set numwidth 11;
SQLDBA> Rem Sleeps should be low.  The hit_ratio should be high.
SQLDBA> select name latch_name, gets, misses,
    2>     round(decode(gets-misses,0,1,gets-misses)/decode(gets,0,1,gets),3)
    3>     hit_ratio, sleeps,
    4>     round(sleeps/decode(misses,0,1,misses),3) "SLEEPS/MISS"
    5>     from stats$latches
    6>     where gets != 0
    7>     order by name;
```

LATCH_NAME	GETS	MISSES	HIT_RATIO	SLEEPS	SLEEPS/MISS
archive control	28	0	1	0	0
cache buffer handl	753960	76	1	7	.092
cache buffers chai	-652465416	1114760	1.002	134506	.121
cache buffers lru	16865629	5046747	.701	649742	.129
dml lock allocatio	73610	0	1	0	0
enqueues	345684	85	1	16	.188
global transaction	81149	0	1	0	0
global transaction	254	0	1	0	0
latch wait list	68488	352	.995	51	.145
library cache	1092558	1901	.998	898	.472
library cache load	5602	0	1	0	0
library cache pin	33098496	650381	.98	35828	.055
messages	1110437	1164	.999	423	.363
multiblock read ob	1023865	299	1	13	.043
process allocation	788	0	1	0	0
redo allocation	6503169	16698	.997	1101	.066
redo copy	171	34	.801	12	.353
row cache objects	1532211	758	1	98	.129
sequence cache	19948	0	1	0	0
session allocation	114829	2	1	2	1
session idle bit	26532546	10164	1	386	.038
session switching	1801	0	1	0	0
shared pool	2196266	3103	.999	1965	.633
system commit numb	19416000	9289	1	1263	.136
transaction alloca	127112	6	1	0	0
undo global data	972206	718	.999	60	.084
user lock	4104	0	1	0	0
virtual circuit bu	107446724	21841	1	1532	.07
virtual circuit qu	105785907	281909	.997	17583	.062
virtual circuits	26492460	50861	.998	2200	.043

```
30 rows selected.
```

Figure 1-78   Hit Ratio Output

(login as table owner)

```
analyze table your_table estimate statistics sample 20 percent
```

(on PL/SQL)

```
execute dbms_utility.analyze_schema('owner','estimate')
```

Figure 1-79   ANALYZE with ESTIMATE STATISTICS

your strategy to ESTIMATE. The command for ANALYZE with COMPUTE STATISTICS is as follows:

```
analyze table your_table compute statistics
```

It is wise to collect statistics regularly, or for that matter, on some prescribed frequency. Otherwise, finding something as simple as the number of rows could mean an unnecessary table scan. For example, the two selects in Figure 1-80 achieve the same purpose.

The statistics collected by ANALYZE and referenced in our examples can be seen using the "dba" type system tables (i.e., dba_indexes, index_stats, and dba_clusters), as well as user type tables. This information is only as current as the last ANALYZE (use last_ddl_time in dba_objects), or in some cases the last IMPORT. If you have analyzed objects in the database before doing an EXPORT and if you don't specify STATISTICS=NONE or COMPUTE while doing the EXPORT, then the default EXPORT behavior is to generate SQL statements that will subsequently generate estimate statistics during an IMPORT. Of course, this adds to the time IMPORT takes to complete. On the other hand, if you EXPORT with STATISTICS=NONE, then you can IMPORT without statistics. Afterwards, if you decide you want the statistics, you can run ANALYZE as a separate job. You may also be able to create the tables first and then IMPORT the data, thus avoiding an ANALYZE.

The presence of the STATISTICS parameter in the EXPORT causes ANALYZE statements to be included in the EXPORT file. Subsequently, in IMPORT an ANALYZE will generate fresh statistics. However, you lose some functionality in the process. Specifically, you lose the ability to designate the desired "sample" population to use when generating statistics. The ANALYZE statement will let you specify an absolute number of rows or a fixed percentage of rows to use for the statistics. But, when using the STATISTICS=ESTIMATE parameter in the EXPORT, you are not given the opportunity to specify the number of rows or percentage to use. Therefore, the ANALYZE statement will use the default estimate value of 1064 rows. This population value is far too small to generate accurate statistics on all but the smallest tables.

```
select num_rows from sys.dba_tables where table_name = `your_table'
NUM_ROWS
_____

123412341234

select count(*) from dunham.your_table
NUM_ROWS
_____

123412341234
```

Figure 1-80 Number of Rows

If you decide to use STATISTICS=COMPUTE in the EXPORT, then the IMPORT may take a long time because it is now using 100 percent of the population to determine the statistics.

To view the results of ANALYZE just query a view of interest, like the ones shown in Figure 1-81. If you see statistics, then the table_name has been analyzed. It means that cost-based optimization is in effect. If not, then they were either deleted, or the table has never been analyzed. One of the most pretentious features of ANALYZE is its way of compelling you to use the cost-based optimizer. If statistics don't exist, then rule-based optimization is in effect, by default. If you want to delete statistics to force rule-based optimization just enter the query shown in Figure 1-82. You can set rule-based at the session level with the command: alter session set optimizer_mode = rule.

```
select owner, table_name, num_rows, blocks from sys.dba_tables;

select table_name, row_cnt, idx_cnt from user_tables
where table_name='your_table'
```

Layout of sys.dba_tables		Layout of sys.dba_extents	
Column Name	Data Type	Column Name	Data Type
owner	varchar2(30)	owner	varchar2(30)
table_owner	varchar2(30)	segment_name	varchar2(81)
tablespace_name	varchar2(30)	segment_type	varchar(17)
cluster_name	varchar2(30)	segment_type	varchar2(30)
pct_free	number	extent_id	number
pct_used	number	file_id	number
ini_trans	number	block_id	number
max_trans	number	bytes	number
initial_extent	number	blocks	number
next_extent	number		
min_extents	number		
max_extents	number		
pct_increase	number		
backed_up	varchar2(1)		
num_rows	number		
blocks	number		
empty_blocks	number		
avg_space	number		
chain_cnt	number		
avg_row_len	number		

Figure 1-81 Query sys.dba_tables

When one creates a primary key or a unique constraint, an index is automatically created by the Oracle engine as the constraint is enabled. Unless specified otherwise, when a constraint is created, the spawned index goes into your `default_tablespace`, which is displayed when you examine the user_users view. If you do not explicitly name the index, it has the same name as the constraint. If you do not name the constraint, it has a name of the form `sys_cnnnnnn`, where *nnnnnn* is an Oracle assigned sequence number. Index information goes into the `user_indexes` view. When you ANALYZE the owning table, all indices are also analyzed. The results of the analysis are visible in columns of the `user_tables`, `user_indexes`, and `user_tab_columns` views. Here is how you would query `avg_leaf_blocks_per_key` for `your_table` (see Figure 1-83).

You can run into some performance problems with or without cost-based optimization. For example, if you have ever analyzed `your_table`, and the optimizer mode is set for CHOOSE (default), then the cost-based optimizer may decide to perform a full table scan even if an existing index would be more efficient. Look at Figure 1-84. The cost-based optimizer may do a scan if more than 20 percent of the rows returned are like Dun%. Deleting the statistics will deactivate the cost-based optimizer. However, keep in mind that rule-based optimization is probably going away very soon. It is probably a good idea to understand cost-based processing completely.

Similar situations resulting in full scans can occur with many syntax combinations. An "order by" can also result in a table scan, if the optimizer is unable to choose the optimum path. See Figure 1-84 for an example of a select that will generate a table scan.

Oracle server uses the `optimizer_mode = {choosefirulefiall_rowsfifirst_row}` to determine the instance-wide query optimization mode to use. Or, this can be set using the `optimizer_goal` parameter in an ALTER SESSION command. If CHOOSE is in effect, then statements will not be optimized at compile time, but rather will be determined at execution time based on statistics gathered from ANALYZE. `All_rows` will use cost-based optimization with the path determined by all rows meeting selection criteria. `First_rows` is similar, except the path is determined by the first row retrieved.

```
analyze table your_table delete statistics;
```

Figure 1-82 Delete Statistics

```
select  avg_leaf_blocks_per_key from user_indexes
where table_name = 'your_table';
```

Figure 1-83 Query User_Indexes

```
select first_name, last_name from cust where last_name like 'Dun%';
```

Figure 1-84 Unexpected Table Scan

```
analyze index your_index validate structure
```

Layout of index_stats		Layout of dba_indexes	
Column Name	Data Type	Column Name	Data Type
height	number	owner	varchar2(30)
blocks	number	owner	varchar2(30)
name	varchar2(30)	table_owner	varchar2(30)
lf_rows	number	table_name	varchar2(30)
lf_blks	number	table_type	varchar2(11)
lf_rows_len	number	uniqueness	varchar2(9)
lf_blk_len	number	tablespace_name	varchar2(30)
br_rows	number	ini_trans	number
br_blks	number	max_trans	number
br_rows_len	number	initial_extent	number
br_blk_len	number	next_extent	number
del_lf_rows	number	min_extents	number
del_lf_rows_len	number	max_extents	number
distinct_keys	number	pct_increase	number
most_repeated_key	number	pct_free	number
btree_space	number	blevel	number
used_space	number	leaf_blocks	number
pct_used	number	distinct_keys	number
rows_per_key	number	avg_leaf_blocks_per_key	number
blks_gets_per_access	number	avg_data_blocks_per_key	number
		clustering_factor	number
		status	varchar2(11)

Figure 1-85   ANALYZE Index

Figure 1-85 shows how to ANALYZE an index. Afterwards, you can query the results from the index_stats table. Columns btree_space, used_space and blocks are helpful in determining the amount of space allocated by an index. It doesn't make sense to ANALYZE an index if you intend to ANALYZE its table. The ANALYZE of the table/cluster will automatically include all associated indexes. A separate index ANALYZE will just duplicate work.

One of the most versatile forms of the ANALYZE command is for identifying chained or migrated rows. When a row is too long for one block it is chained to additional blocks (poor hashing functions are instrumental in this). If the updates for a row won't fit in the free space (pctfree) of a block, then the entire row may need to be migrated to another block. If this is the case, a forward pointer is retained in the original block, pointing to the row's new location. Both these incidents will cause Oracle to incur additional I/O when the row is accessed for any reason. If the new block's location is displaced far enough from its original one, it can add head and rotational delay overhead to the processing. ANALYZE with LIST CHAINED ROWS will save entries for each of the chained rows in a table called `chained_rows` (you must build this using the utlchain.sql script). If more than 5 percent of the table constitutes chained rows, then tuning is a good idea. Adjusting the PCTFREE space, the database block size (`db_block_size` parameter) and even the table layout are some of the alternatives.

As you can see, ANALYZE populates many statistics in many tables. You will want to gather as much of this information as time permits during the planning stage of tuning. To get a better picture of how the cost-based optimizer may be affected performance, use the EXPLAIN PLAN and TKPROF commands. They are discussed in the next sections.

1.28   Oracle Trace

The standard Oracle procedure for monitoring programs is to perform a SQL trace on a process. First, you need create a trace file and then run the trace file through TKPROF. The TKPROF process will generate a printout that shows the SQL statements and the indexes used to obtain data. From the output, one can determine the inefficiencies of the program and take appropriate action. Oracle Server allows you to trace all the SQL statements sent to it and executed by the database engine. To activate trace choose one of the following setup procedures.

- Instance activation of TRACE (changes to init.ora)

```
user_dump_destination =  directory path location
max_dump_file_size = trace file size limit
timed_statistics = true   (this enables collection)
sql_trace = true
```

Follow with shut down and start up of system.

Instance seactivation of TRACE (changes to init.ora)

```
timed_statistics = false
```

- SQL*Plus sesson activation of TRACE

```
alter session set sql_trace = true;
```

SQL*Plus session deactivation of TRACE

```
alter session set sql_trace = false;
```

- PRO*C stored procedure trace activation

```
within a WHEN-NEW-FORM trigger;
begin
```

```
forms_ddl('alter session set sql_trace=true');
end;
```

or

```
EXEC SQL EXECUTE
begin
dbms_session.set_sql_trace(true);                 turn trace on
end;
END-EXEC;
```

■ **TRACE activation for other sessions**

```
dbms_system.set_sql_trace_in_session(SID,SERIAL#,TRUE)
```

Trace deactivation for other sessions

```
dbms_system.set_sql_trace_in_session(SID,SERIAL#,FALSE)
```

SID and SERIAL# can be found in v$session. This routine must be run by SYS user.

■ **Granting EXECUTE privileges in C programs**

```
CREATE PROCEDURE trace ... AS
BEGIN
...
END TRACE;
GRANT EXECUTE ON trace TO PUBLIC;
```

Not limited to PUBLIC, which is most general form of access.

Go to the `user_dump_destination` and get the name of the trace file. TKPROF can be used to look at the explained plan and statistics by performing the first command in Figure 1-86. The "explain=..." is optional. It will cause the execution plan for each SQL statement to be included in the report. This will show if statements are using indexes or performing table scans (access plan).

The report from TKPROF shows the text of each SQL, access plan used by the queries, number of rows passing through each phase of the query, cpu time used by each operation on the query (parse, execute, and fetch), and the elapsed

```
tkprof <tracefile> <outputfile> explain=<user>/<password> sort=<option>
tkprof <tracefile> <outputfile> explain=<username>/<password>
tkprof <tracefile> <outputfile>          (without the explain plan)
vi <outputfile>                          (view output file)
tkprof -help                             (get more information)
make -f oracle.mk tkprof                 (compile tkprof utility in install directory)
```

Figure 1-86   TKPROF Command Examples

time. The sort option can help you isolate the most resource intensive statements quickly. You must decide which of three major phases of SQL statement processing you are interested in (parse, execution, or fetch). A list of sort options is available in Figure 1-87.

The sample report in Figure 1-88 shows output of TKPROF.

Trace pinpoints the application areas that consume the most resources, thereby saving time and improving performance. It can also be used to identify error codes for processes that crashed while processing.

It can be more difficult using trace with programs executed by the Concurrent Manager. These programs require that trace be turned on for the entire RDBMS, resulting in substantial overhead and output. Concurrent Manager tracing should be reserved for the wee hours of the night when users are all nestled in their beds.

Sort Option	Description
EXECNT	EXECUTE CALL COUNT
EXECPU	EXECUTE CALL CPU TIME
EXECU	EXECUTE CALL BUFFERS FOR CURRENT READ
EXEDSK	EXECUTE CALL DISK READS
EXEELA	EXECUTE CALL ELAPSED TIME
EXEMIS	EXECUTE CALL LIBRARY CACHE MISSES
EXEQRY	EXECUTE CALL CONSISTENT DISK READS
EXEROW	EXECUTE CALL ROWS PROCESSED
FCHCNT	FETCH CALL COUNT
FCHCPU	FETCH CALL CPU TIME
FCHCU	FETCH CALL BUFFERS FOR CURRENT READ
FCHDSK	FETCH CALL DISK READS
FCHELA	FETCH CALL ELAPSED TIME
FCHQRY	FETCH CALL BUFFERS FOR CONSISTENT READ
FCHROW	FETCH CALL ROWS PROCESSED
PRSCNT	PARSE CALL COUNT
PRSCPU	PARSE CALL CPU TIME
PRSCU	PARSE CALL BUFFERS FOR CURRENT READ
PRSDSK	PARSE CALL DISK READS
PRSELA	PARSE CALL ELAPSED TIME
PRSMIS	PARSE CALL LIBRARY CACHE MISSES
PRSQRY	PARSE CALL CONSISTENT DISK READS
USERID	USER THAT PARSED THE CURSOR

Figure 1-87 TKPROF Sort Options

```
SELECT C.CUSTNO, C.FIRSTNAME || ' ' || C.LASTNAME, ROUND(SUM(A.ORDER * Q.PRICE),2)
TOTORDER FROM TST1.CUSTOMER C, TST1.ITEMS Q, TST1.ACCOUNT A WHERE A.CUSTNO = C.CUSTNO
AND A.ITEMNO = Q.ITEMNO AND Q.ORDERDATE = (SELECT MAX(T.ORDERDATE) FROM TST1.ITEMS T
WHERE T.ITEMNO = Q.ITEMNO) GROUP BY
C.CUSTNO, C.FIRSTNAME || ' ' || C.LASTNAME ORDER BY TOTORDER DESC
```

call	count	cpu	elapsed	disk	query	current	rows
Parse	1	0.05	0.07	0	0	0	0
Execute	5	0.18	0.24	15	169	39	0
Fetch	10	99.75	121.83	2792	969201	2519	20
total	15	99.98	122.14	2807	969370	2558	20

```
Misses in library cache during parse: 0
Optimizer goal: RULE
Parsing user id: 44  (DBA0001)              (recursive depth: 1)
```

Rows	Execution Plan
0	SELECT STATEMENT GOAL: RULE
30000	SORT (ORDER BY)
81000	SORT (GROUP BY)
159187	FILTER
159187	NESTED LOOPS
81000	NESTED LOOPS
81000	TABLE ACCESS GOAL: ANALYZED (FULL) OF 'ACCOUNT'
81000	TABLE ACCESS GOAL: ANALYZED (BY ROWID) OF 'CUSTOMER'
81000	INDEX GOAL: ANALYZED (UNIQUE SCAN) OF 'CUSTOMER_PK' (UNIQUE)
159187	TABLE ACCESS GOAL: ANALYZED (BY ROWID) OF 'QUOTES'
240187	INDEX GOAL: ANALYZED (RANGE SCAN) OF 'ITEMS_PK' (UNIQUE)
159187	SORT (AGGREGATE)
240187	INDEX GOAL: ANALYZED (RANGE SCAN) OF 'ITEMS_PK' (UNIQUE)

Figure 1-88 Viewing TKPROF Output

TKPROF is not a good choice of tools for measuring execution times inside PL/SQL packages. An article called "A Method for Measuring Execution Time for Packages That Have A Complex Hierarchy of Procedures and Functions" is published in *Select Magazine* (October, 1996 issue). You can obtain this article from the *International Oracle User Group* (IOUG) site at http://www.ioug.org/. Their procedure can even measure time intervals that intersect or overlap.

1.29 EXPLAIN PLAN

EXPLAIN PLAN is a means to a goal, namely optimizing SQL access paths. It is imperative that you optimize SQL access paths. With the rule-based optimizer a ranking is applied to each statement. The worst rank is 15 which equates to a table scan. The best ranking is 1. In contrast, the cost-based optimization prepares a cost estimate (cost=382). To choose the optimum cost-based access path prior to production implementation, you should test your SQL using hints.

Hints are implemented by concatenating syntax after select, update, or delete commands as follows:

```
select /*+  all_rows     */  Most efficient path for all rows
select /*+  first_rows   */  Most efficient path for first row
select /*+  rule         */  Uses rule-based optimization, ignore hints
select /*+  default      */  Uses the session mode established
```

Other potential hints are add_equal, cluster, full, hash, index, index_asc (index_name), index_desc (index_name), ordered, use_merge, and use_nl.

Oracle's hierarchy for selecting the optimization mode and hint to be used is not straightforward. If `optimizer_mode = {chooseﬁruleﬁall_rowsﬁﬁrst_rows}` is defined in init.ora, it will establish the default mode for query optimization instance-wide. `alter session set optimizer_goal = {chooseﬁruleﬁall_rowsﬁﬁrst_row}` will override the instance-wide default at the session level. SELECT, UPDATE, and DELETE commands with the `/*+hint*/` will either compliment or override an existing session or instance default. For example, an `optimizer_mode` of choose and a `/*+rule*/` will use the rule-based approach without any hints. See Figure 1-89 for mode settings.

The next step in using explain plan is to create a `plan_table`. The layout of the `plan_table` is shown in Figure 1-90.

Make sure to create the `plan_table` under the oracle user id that will run the SELECT statement. The CREATE TABLE syntax is located in `$oracle_home/rdbms/admin/utlxplan.sql` or your equivalent directory.

The syntax for EXPLAIN PLAN is shown in Figure 1-91. You will want to delete any existing `plan_table` entries for the statement you will be explaining by issuing the command `delete plan_table where statement_id = '&statement';` first.

The EXPLAIN PLAN statement is loaded into your `plan_table` using the `statement_id` supplied in `&statement`. Use a different `statement_id` for each SQL select that is run. After running the SQL statement, you can look at the EXPLAIN PLAN using the commands shown in Figure 1-92. The second command is in tabular format.

Mode	Goal
all_rows	Cost-based (best for all rows meeting selection)
first_row	Cost-based (best for first row meeting selection)
rule	Rule-based
choose	Cost-based (best decided at execution time)

Figure 1-89 Optimizer_mode / Optimizer_goal Options

Column Name	Data Type
statement_id	varchar2(30)
timestamp	date
remarks	varchar2(80)
operation	varchar2(30)
options	varchar2(30)
object_node	varchar2(30)
object_owner	varchar2(30)
object_name	varchar2(30)
object_instance	number(38)
object_type	varchar2(30)
search_columns	number(38)
id	number(38)
parent_id	number(38)
position	number(38)
other	long

Figure 1-90   Layout of the plan_table

```
explain plan set statement_id = '&statement'
for
select c.custno, c.firstname || ' ' || c.lastname,
round(sum(a.order * q.price),2) totorder     from tst1.customer c,
tst1.items q, tst1.account a
where a.custno = c.custno
and a.itemno = q.itemno
and q.orderdate = (select max(t.orderdate) from tst1.items t
where t.itemno = q.itemno)
group by c.custno, c.firstname || ' ' || c.lastname
order by totorder desc;
```

Figure 1-91   Explain Plan Syntax

```
select operation, options, object_name, id, parent_id, position from
plan_table
where statement_id = '&statement'
order by id;

select lpad(' ',2*(level-1))||operation||' '||options||'
'||object_name||'
'|| decode(id,0,'Cost = '||position)
from plan_table
start with id = 0 and statement_id = '&statement'
connect by prior id = parent_id and statement_id = '&statement';
```

Figure 1-92   Retrieving EXPLAIN PLAN Output

If you want to spool the information to a file, encapsulate the statements in the following statements:

```
set echo off term off feed off ver off
spool explan
select...
spool off
set term on
vi explan
```

The output from the EXPLAIN PLAN sample of Figure 1-91 is shown in Figure 1-93. The cost estimate of 382 on line one of the plan is relative. When compared with other plans using different hints, or incorporating more direct access paths using indexes, you can arrive at optimum access. For more information about EXPLAIN PLAN output, refer to the Oracle7 *Server Application Developer's Guide*. You must incorporate your findings into your SQL statements. Then, once ANALYZE has been run to generate statistics, Oracle's optimizer can examine the statistics built in the data dictionary.

1.30   Sybase Statistic Collection

Just as we've done in prior sections with other databases, we want to repeat the process here. Our goal will be to collect statistics on all the key tuning areas of Sybase (see Figure 1-94). The results will be the basis for tuning decisions made later when referencing Chapter 11.

 WARNING! A bug has been reported when issuing the following command. It may or may not be resolved by the time you read this warning message. Be cautious and research the bug before issuing the command.

```
select suid, cmd from sysprocesses group by suid
```

Here are various SQL statements designed to monitor Sybase SQL Servers, courtesy of Menlo Software Incorporated. DBAware from Menlo Software is profiled in Section 1.37, later in this chapter. It automatically collects and graphs statistics at user-defined intervals. It provides an aesthetic tuning solution for Oracle and Sybase.

One of the advantages of using DBAware is that it will account for the number of engines when averaging statistics.

```
SELECT STATEMENT   COST = 382
          2.0  SORT (ORDER BY)
                  3.1 SORT (GROUP BY)
                  4.1 NESTED LOOPS
                      ...
```

Figure 1-93 Viewing EXPLAIN PLAN Output

Command or Utility	Statistic
sar (UNIX system, disk and memory)	See book section 1.15
vmstat (memory shortages)	See book section 1.16
iostat (I/O bottlenecks)	"
netstat (network bottlenecks)	"
set showplan on	Query steps
set noexec on	Suppress SQL statements to isolate costs
	using the output from optimizer set statistics io on
	Reads and writes by query
set statistics subquerycache on	Cache hit ratio by subquery
set statistics time on	Parse, compile, and execution time for
	query steps
dbcc traceon (302)	See the calculations used by optimizer
sp_monitor	@@identity (last value inserted in
	identity column)
sp_sysmon	System Performance
sp_configure	List of current system parameter settings
sp_cacheconfig	Cache configuration
sp_helpcache	Cache bindings
sp_help	Table list
sp_estspace	Estimates size of index and table
sp_spaceused	Actual size of index and table, and unused space
sp_reportstats	CPU and I/O activity by user
sp_helpsegment	Segment list
sp_helpconstraints	Referential constraints
sp_helpjoins	Table joins
sp_helpthresholds	Thresholds
sp_helpuser	Users
sp_helplog	Log
sp_helplock	Locks
sp_helpindex	Index list
update statistics	Distribution and density of index keys
IQ DBCC CHECKDB	Interactive Query Accelerator
IQ SHOW INDEXSPACESTATS	"
CPERRLOG	
@@cpu_busy	Server Statistics
@@io_busy	
@@idle	
@@pack_received	
@@pack_sent	
@@packet_errors	
@@total_read	
@@total_write	
@@total_errors	
@@connections	
@@trancount	
Sybase Monitor Reports	All available statistics
DBAware Monitor Graphs	All available statistics
SQL Monitor	CPU and Trends
	Device I/O
	Hit Ratios
	Log Device
	Network Polling
	Memory Caching

Figure 1-94 Sybase Statistics Collection Checklist

At installation time, DBAware implements a few tables for archiving statistics and a couple procedures that grab statistics. The Windows-based monitor will capture the data at user-defined intervals. The following list of queries (see Table 1-3) gives you some idea of how extensive the product is in gathering information. Note that it is SQL-query based, which means that the product can be extended without the need to reinstall or upgrade software. Menlo Software provides new queries that can be imported into the product periodically.

TABLE 1-3   DBAware Sybase Queries

Query	Description
select @@connections	Number of logins since server was started
select @@cpu_busy	Returns the amount of time, in ticks, that the CPU has spent doing SQL Server work since the last time SQL Server was started.
select value from dba_monitors where field_name='cpu_busy_delta'	Server CPU Busy Delta
select value from dba_monitors where field_name='cpu_busy'	Server CPU Busy Total
select disk_errors_delta = value from dba_monitors where field_name = 'disk_errors_delta	Disk Errors Delta
select @@total_errors	Returns the number of errors that have occurred while the server was reading or writing.
select disk_read_delta = value rom dba_monitors where field_name='disk_read_delta'	Disk Reads Delta
select @@total_read	Returns the number of disk reads by the server since it was last started.
select disk_write_delta = value from dba_monitors where field_name = 'disk_write_delta'	Disk Writes Delta
select @@total_write	Returns the number of disk writes by the server since it was last started.
select blocking_locks = isnull(sum(n),0)from dba_monitor where type in (256+1, 256+2, 256+5, 256+6, 256+7)	Lock Blocking
select exclusive_locks = isnull(sum(n),0) from dba_monitors where type in (1, 5, 256+1, 256+5)	Lock Exclusive
select @@idle	Returns the amount of time, in ticks, that the server has been idle since it was last started.
select value from dba_monitors where field_name='idle_delta'	Server Idle Delta
select value from dba_monitors where field_name='idle'	Server Idle Total

TABLE 1-3   DBAware Sybase Queries (Continued)

Query	Description
select @@io_busy	Returns the amount of time, in ticks, that the server has spent doing input and output operations since it was last started.
select value from dba_monitors where field_name='io_busy_delta'	Server I/O Busy Delta
select value from dba_monitors where field_name='io_busy'	Server I/O Busy Total
select @@langid	Returns the local language id of the language currently in use.
select @@language	Returns the name of the language currently in use.
select @@packet_errors	Returns the number of errors that have occurred while the server was sending and receiving packets.
select pack_errors_delta=value from dba_monitors where field_name='pack_errors_delta'	Packet Errors Delta
select pack_received_delta=value from dba_monitors where field_name='pack_received_delta'	Packet Received Delta
select @@pack_received	Returns the number of input packets read by the server since it was last started.
select pack_sent_delta=value from dba_monitors where field_name='pack_sent_delta'	Packet Sent Delta
select @@pack_sent	Returns the number of output packets written by the server since it was last started.
select page_locks=isnull(sum(n),0) from dba_locks where type in (5, 6, 7, 256+5, 256+6, 256+7)	Lock Page
select @@servername	Returns the name of the local server.
select shared_locks=isnull(sum(n),0) from dba_locks where type in (2, 6, 256+2, 256+6_	Lock Shared
select @@spid	Monitor SPID
select table_locks=isnull(sum(n),0) from dba_locks where type in (1, 2, 256+1, 256+1)	Lock Table
select @@timeticks	Returns the number of microseconds per tick. The amount of time per tick is machine dependent.
select total_locks=isnull(sum(n),0) from dba_locks	Lock Total
select update_locks=isnull(sum(n),0) from dba_locks where type in (7, 256+7)	Lock Update

1.31   Sybase SQL Server 11 Monitor

In a coming section we will show you how to use DBAware from Menlo Software. Now we will mention some other means for collecting baseline measurements. Perhaps the two most popular tools are SQL Server Monitor and sp_sysmon.

sp_sysmon is a system procedure that monitors SQL Server performance. Its statistical output describes the behavior of your SQL Server system. See the next section for more about sp_sysmon. This section will focus on SQL Server Monitor.

SQL Server Monitor is a separate product from Sybase. A major advantage this monitor has over its competitors is that it is integrated into the Sybase system. As SQL Server runs, it saves performance data in shared memory. This makes the monitoring process run fast. The actual monitoring is accomplished with a Client application that avoids adding much overhead to the Sybase system. Also, recording is accomplished with another server, alleviating overhead. The architecture is composed of five pieces, namely:

- **SQL Server:** Gathers statistics and places them in a shared memory array.

- **Monitor Server:** A Sybase Open Server™ application that reads the shared memory array and passes information to Monitor Client.

- **Monitor Client:** A client application that connects to Monitor Server and accepts the statistics for GUI displays.

- **Monitor Historical Server:** An Open Server application that records statistics for future reference.

- **Monitor Client Library:** Routines for user-written programs accessing statistics.

Because there are several pieces of software involved, start up and shut down of the monitor must follow an orderly process. Start SQL Server first, SQL Monitor Server second, and SQL Monitor Client third. If for some reason SQL Server is rebooted, then both the Monitor Server and Monitor Client must also be rebooted. Here is how it is done.

There are some parameters to supply at start up which are good to know. Start SQL Server as user "sybase." Use the -M flag to specify the location of the server_name.krg file. For example:

```
setenv SYBASE /usr/local/system11
setenv DSLISTEN SYBASE11
$SYBASE/bin/dataserver -d/system11db/SYBASE11_master.dat
-e$SYBASE/install/errorlog_SYBASE11 -M$SYBASE &amp;
```

Start up the Monitor Server using the same "sybase" id on the same host machine (because they share memory). Use the -i flag (with no space) to point to an interface file that has both SQL Server and Monitor Server entries and the -m flag. For example:

```
$SYBASE/bin/monser -Usa -Ppassword -MMON_SYBASE11 -SSYBASE11 -n5 -0 \
-Lmonserver_config_file\
-l$SYBASE/install/MON11_SYBASE11.LOG\
-n -m$SYBASE -O &amp;
where monserver_config_file has the following line which will poll every
60 seconds for the presence of SQL Server
heartbeat_interval 60
```

Next start the Monitor Client application on any PC box that can be a client. The -i flag this time points to an interface file containing Monitor Server and SQL Server entries passed on the Monitor Server command line. The SQL Server name must match the one in the interface file (or .INI in the case of PCs). PC versions of this process involve executing SERVMON.EXE in a batch file or from the RUN dialog box. Before Monitor Client can start displaying information about a specific SQL Server, it is necessary to connect to the Monitor Server for the correct SQL Server. On UNIX, for example

```
/usr/directory/bin/sqlmon -M MON11_SYBASE11 -U sa -P password
-I\x11/usr/directory/interfaces &amp;
```

You must be endowed with `sa_role` when connecting Monitor Client. This privilege can be granted with the following command.

```
exec sp_role `grant', sa_role, `username'
```

PC users will actually use two TCP network connections for each open window in Monitor Client. So, if your default is six connections, you will be limited to three open windows, after which you will receive a SERVMON CANNOT ACCESS SERVER error message. Increase the `tcp-connection=` entry in the PCTCP.INI file and reboot the client machine.

 NOTE: There is a `ceventbuf` value in SQL Server that defaults to 100. If you are just setting up SQL Monitor for the first time, I recommend a setting of 10,000 to begin with. Monitor Client can slow SQL Server down by building a memory allocation chart. If this happens, new connections may hang up. You can avoid building the memory allocation chart by supplying the -nomem flag for UNIX clients or by using an associated checkbox on PC-based clients.

Sybase Monitor has some great features. First, it provides you with an overall picture of system usage, the ability to keep baselines, excellent pinpointing of bottlenecks, and alarms. I wouldn't advise anyone to attempt serious performance tuning without a monitor that lets them take a picture of performance before and after some tuning change.

In addition to graphic (two- and three-dimensional) and tabular displays of collected statistics, you can save multiple configurations and record statistics.

The Windows version of Monitor Client follows all of the usual Windows screen conventions. There is a main window with child windows for each of the different types of statistics being monitored. Helps, check boxes, and pull-down menus are familiar trademarks in all Windows-based products. They act and feel the same here.

When you first open a statistics window it will display all the possible processes, databases, database objects, or data caches in the system. Then you can limit what is viewed using filters. My favorite one is the SELECT TOP filter, which allows you to limit your viewing, for example, to the top 10 devices using logical or physical reads and writes, or the top 10 processes using the most CPU.

Each new child window can show statistics using a different sampling interval than some other window.

You can save your complete configuration in a *workspace* file. The next time you startup Client Monitor, just select the saved configuration. Different configurations provide a way to configure monitoring for different types of tuning, memory, I/O, processes, etc.

Once you arrive at the statistics window with a graph or table showing, you can print the window. I like to use screen capture tools. That way I can incorporate a window display in that all-important report to upper management.

There are check boxes for thresholds, which when exceeded can cause the display to change its color or pattern. I like to see things switch to the color red when something has happened that I would get in trouble for, if I overlooked it.

Client Monitor provides various statistics windows as itemized in Table 1-4.

MONITOR HISTORICAL SERVER

The Historical Server component allows you to record statistics. From the menu bar select RECORD, then DEFINE. Next, choose DATA to define what type of data collection recording you want. Any number of client windows can be recorded. Also, you can specify ALARMS for data windows or custom data windows. ALARMS will either send messages to the log or execute a file. Data sampling can be from 1 second to 1 day. Refer to the SQL Monitor Historical Server User's Guide for more information about recording statistics.

1.32 Sybase sp_sysmon Procedure

Naturally, you want to take the speediest approach to tuning you can. Tuning can be fun. Iterative tuning can become tedious. That's where the sp_sysmon procedure comes in handy. It's fast and easy to use. To invoke sp_sysmon, execute the following command using isql where the interval is an integer designating 1 to 10 minutes:

```
sp_sysmon interval
```

Picture your system as a house of cards. Each tuning improvement is like a small breeze that knocks down one level of cards. As each level drops, the remaining levels are left holding up the structure. This analogy is similar to the

TABLE 1-4 SQL Monitor Statistics Windows

WINDOW	ACTIVITY	STATISTIC	DISPLAY	DESCRIPTION
Cache Statistics	Page I/O	Logical Reads Physical Reads Physical Writes Data Cache Hit Rate Procedure Execution	GRAPHS	The request rates for data and stored procedure query plans indicates cache effectivenes
	Procedure I/O	Reads - from Disk Procedure Cache Hit Rate		
Data Cache	Data I/O	logical Reads by Cache Physical Reads by Cache	GRAPHS	Use statistics to configure data caches for best performance
Device I/O	Device I/O	Reads by Device Writes by Device	GRAPHS	Use I/O rates to perform device load balancing
Memory Allocation (not available Sybase release 11)	SQL Server Memory	% For Kerne % For Server % Data Cache % Procedure Cache	PIE CHART	Use to tune overall system memory settings
Network Activity	Traffic	Max Packet Size Avg Packet Size Bytes sent or received Network Reads by Server Network Writes by Server	GRAPHS	Use to tune packet sizes, need for additional network lines or adapters, maybe even servers
Object Lock Status	Locking	Database Name Object Name Page Number Lock Type Lock Status Process ID Login Name Time Waited Locks Blocked Count	DATA TABLE	Lock contention by lock type and table
Object Page I/O	Objects	Database Name Object Names Logical Reads Physical Reads Physical Writes	DATA TABLE	Page I/O on objects
Performance Trends	General	CPU Utilization Rate Data Cache Hit Rate Device I/O Lock Hit Rate Lock Request Rate Network Traffic Procedure Cache Hit Rate	METERS	As the Window is titled, this is useful for determining system trends
Performance Summary	Overall	CPU Utilization Rate * Process State Counts Server Hit Rates Network Traffic Device I/O Locks Requested Locks Granted by Type	GRAPHS	See throughput. Equate it to times when bottlenecks occur.

WINDOW	ACTIVITY	STATISTIC	DISPLAY	DESCRIPTION
Stored Procedure Activity	Stored Procedures	Database Name Stored Procedure Name Nbr of Executions Average Exec Time/Sample Average Exec Time/Session	DATA TABLE	How long are stored procedures running. Figure out which ones need some extra tuning effort
User Processes	Process Activity	CPU Utilization logical reads and writes physical reads and writes	GRAPHS	What are user processes up to. Identify those which cause bottlenecks. Data is available for single processes, selected groups or all processes
	Process Detail	Process Identification Status Page I/O Lock Details	DATA TABLE	
	Process Lock Activity	SPID Nbr Locks	DATA TABLE	
Transaction Activity	Transaction	Total by Type Transaction Processing Rates	DATA TABLE	See SQL Server transaction throughput. Useful in benchmark comparisons and growth studies

* SQL Monitor will show a different amount of CPU usage than OS monitors or commands. The reason is that OS is looking at SQL Server as a subtask and can't discern what is going on within it. Typically, OS will show SQL Server being busy, when in fact it is idling.

effects of tuning. When you take pressure off one area, it may transfer your focus to the next level. Until all levels have been optimized, you won't see the maximum benefit. Each level can equate to the layers of software making up the system or to different activities within the system. Both fit the analogy. With sp_sysmon you can quickly tune, and the process is robust enough to monitor several system activities, including:

- Disk I/O
- Data cache
- Indices
- Kernel utilization
- Locks
- Memory
- Network I/O
- Procedure cache
- Recovery
- Tasks
- Transactions

As an administrator, your biggest challenge may be locating a server that you can test your tuning changes on, without causing a ruckus. You need to have a standalone test environment to get accurate results. Also, you need some extra CPU. Machine time is always in demand. Sp_sysmon can account for an added 5 to 10 percent overhead. Once you find that machine, you can do some serious tuning.

First, start sp_sysmon. Next, run an application. Finally, fire up sp_sysmon again. That is the basic process. To test changes to sp_configure, run the basic process before and after making the changes. Your output should signify any benefit, or loss, from the tuning change. I've discovered that you really need to run your application several times during each test. This way, you can eliminate the possibility of unequal caching. Unequal caching will negate your results by favoring whichever test gets the best caching. If you can't repeat a test identically, then your before and after comparisons are like apples and oranges. They really don't have anything in common.

Depending on where you work, management may want to review your findings. This is easy. Gather your reports and sort them by run date and time. If you use tabs on the edge of the report indicating which test it belongs to, it helps other individuals to review your results. The reports represent an audit trail of your tuning efforts (see Figure 1-95). Statistics can be input to calculations that estimate overall system or application savings.

The example shown in Figure 1-95 shows performance information for SQL Server engines in an *Symmetric Multi-Processing* (SMP) environment. The last row of output shows the average utilization, which is of interest. Output tables are standardized and follow rules. These are some basic rules for samplings, as they apply to a sampling interval.

- Counts that are not printed may be zero

- Averages are per/second and per/xact (committed transaction) unless the designation is different

- Percent of total depends on the situation to which it applies

- Summary data is shown as total and average

```
========================================================================
Sybase SQL Server 11 System Performance Monitor
========================================================================

Run Date                      Jan 1, 1997
Statistics Cleared at         11:30:05
Statistics Sampled at         11:30:06
Sample Interval               1  min.

========================================================================
Engine Busy                   Utilization
========================================================================
Engine 0                      98.8 %
Engine 1                      98.8 %
-----------                   -------------        ---------------
Summary:                      Total: 197.6%        Average:  98.8 %
```

Figure 1-95 sp_sysmon Report

We will refer to sp_sysmon often in Chapter 11, where Sybase tuning is detailed.

 WARNING: The sp_sysmon procedure and SQL Server Monitor collect statistics into the same internal variables. You must run one or the other. They should not be run concurrently.

1.33   SHOWPLAN for Sybase

If poor query performance and a failure to understand their cause are the enemy, then SHOWPLAN is the ally. The only guarantee that a query will execute the way you want it to is to issue the following commands and review the resulting output.

```
isql > set showplan on
isql > set statistics io on
isql > set noexec on
isql > "run your query here"
isql > set noexec off
isql > set statistics io off
isql > set showplan off
```

SHOWPLAN will get the information you need. It is the primary instrument for seeing how the optimizer will execute queries. Figure 1-96 contains a sample query and its SHOWPLAN output. Notice that the invoice table is being scanned. This could be avoided by creating an index on inv_client.

```
select inv_nbr
from invoice
where inv_client = 'Dunham Software'

QUERY PLAN FOR STATEMENT 1 (at line 1).
    STEP 1
        The type of query is SELECT.
        FROM TABLE
            invoice
        Nested iteration.
        Table Scan.
        Ascending scan.
        Positioning at start of table.
        Using I/O Size 2 Kbytes.
        With LRU Buffer Replacement Strategy.
```

statistics io for the query shows a total of 90 physical reads and 101 logical reads:

```
Table: invoice  scan count 50,  logical reads: 101,  physical reads: 90
Total writes for this command: 0
```

Figure 1-96   Query and SHOWPLAN Output

The first thing you will notice is that the messages output by SHOWPLAN are cryptic. They need to have descriptions. Table 1-5 provides descriptions and identifies what level of tuning opportunity exists when you see the message in your SHOWPLAN output.

The output can often clue you in to obvious tuning opportunities, like a missing index or partial keys that will result in undesirable table scans. It can also be a reminder to run the *update statistics* command, which will provide the optimizer with better information at run-time. Sometimes, *forceplan* is being administered the wrong way. This will override any optimization in lieu of a user's own desired execution plan. The problem is that tables evolve. Forceplan can overlook new tuning opportunities.

1.34 Sybase DBCC Statistics

The database consistency checker is another utility that provides useful statistics. I will just mention one of them here, namely memory usage. If you issue the following command, you can watch what is going on with data caches.

```
dbcc memusage
```

When your hit ratio is dropping, it could be caused by insufficient cache memory or large table scans. Very large databases are susceptible to problems with data caching. You can use partitioning, segmenting, I/O sizing, and parallel processing with *Very Large Databases* (VLDB). You should also look into EMC disk arrays. Array controllers can often perform hardware caching that supplements the system's capabilities. Locating scans is relatively easy. The prior section showed how to use SHOWPLAN to locate queries that would result in table scans.

1.35 Microsoft® Windows 95™ Statistic Collection

Windows 95 is not really an operating system where you will be supporting large numbers of clients. In fact, you will probably only have one. Windows 95 is a good platform for use with monitors that are dedicated to monitoring other servers running on UNIX or NT. But, it is important to get the most out of Windows 95 that you can.

Dashboard 95 is a product from Starfish Software Incorporated. It is handy in finding out some of the information about your Windows 95 system. A resource gauge gives you the percent of swappable system memory. A meter shows CPU activity, threads for multitasking, and virtual machines (defined as WIN95 and DOS applications running). The drive watch meter shows the available free disk space by drive. There are alarms to warn you when disk space or available memory are low. I like the thread display. Threads are an indication of concurrent tasks running that can contend for resources. This display can clue you in to why resources are taxed. A sample Dashboard 95 panel is shown

TABLE 1-5 SHOWPLAN Tuning Opportunities

SHOWPLAN MESSAGE	DESCRIPTION	TUNING OPPORTUNITY
Table Scan.	A table scan is performed	HIGH
Using N Matching Index Scans.	The query is performing multiple index scans, one for each -OR- condition or -IN- list item.	HIGH
Position at start of table.	Scan positioning used	HIGH
WorktableN Created for REFORMATTING	Work table and index are being built automatically for join operation.	HIGH
Position at index start.	Scan position used	HIGH
Using I/O Size N Kbytes	I/O page size used	HIGH
Scanning only up to the first qualifying row.	Minimum optimization	MEDIUM
Positioning by Row ID (RID	Scan positioning used	MEDIUM
Keys are: key1, key2 ,,, keyn	Displayed in conjunction with the POSITIONING BY KEY message	MEDIUM
Using Dynamic Index	Queries with -OR- and -IN- clauses	MEDIUM
With MRU Buffer Replacement Strategy	Most recently used buffer cache replacement strategy used with this table	MEDIUM
Positioning by key	Scan position used	LOW
Log Scan.	Trigger has been activated which uses inserted or deleted tables from log.	LOW
With LRU Buffer Replacement Strategy.	Least recently used buffer cache replacement strategy used with table.	LOW
Using Clustered Index.	Query uses the clustered index on the table.	LOW
Scanning only the last page of the table.	Maximum optimization	NONE
Index contains all needed columns. Base table will not be read	Nonclustered index coverage	NONE
Ascending scan.	All scans are in ascending order, so this is superfluous.	NONE
Index: indexname.	Name of index used	NONE

in Figure 1-97. In the figure, CPU shows 47 percent utilization; there are 18 threads running and 51M of free disk space. Ouch! It's time for me to buy another drive.

Net Watcher can be used to monitor shared resource usage. With it you can see who is currently using resources on your computer. You can also add shared

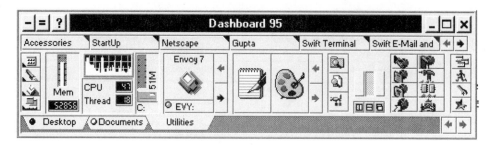

Figure 1-97 Dashboard 95

folders and disconnect users from your computer or from accessing specific files. To run Net Watcher, you must have Client for Microsoft Networks installed, and you must make sure that both printer and file sharing options in Windows 95 are enabled.

Print a copy of your CONFIG.SYS and AUTOEXEC.BAT files, so the information is handy when you get into the WINDOWS 95 tuning chapter.

1.36   Microsoft® Windows NT™ 4.0 Statistic Collection

With the aid of the Windows NT Performance Monitor, Task Manager, and Event Viewer, you can observe a number of statistics that will suffice for tuning Windows NT. There are other third-party tuning tools with additional monitoring facilities. A list of valuable statistics is shown in Figure 1-98. Chapter 8 provides additional information about these tools and shows how to fully tune the Windows NT system, using the Performance Monitor alone.

1.37   DBAware Monitor from Menlo Software

There are quite a few monitors to choose from, like Platinum's DB-Vision or EPM, Patrol from BMC Software, *Administrative and Performance Suite* (APS) toolkit, the *Performance Monitoring* (PM) toolkit2, and BRADMARK's DBGeneral Suite of performance monitoring products, ADHAWK Monitor from Eventus, PerfoRMAx Monitor from Aonix Software, Platinum Tools for Windows, as well as EcoTOOLS from Compuware. Here, we will take a look at DBAware from Menlo Software.

DBAware is the most versatile client-based RDBMS monitor available. It features customizable, graphical MS-Windows 3.1 and MS-Windows NT based RDBMS monitor (for Oracle and Sybase) with archiving and alarming capabilities. As I go to press, Paul Osborn of Menlo Software informs me of the imment release of DBAware 2.0. Enhancements include a Windows 95 version and an improved user interface. If I receive the new release in time, I will include it on the enclosed CD-ROM. Paul also informs me of extensive revisions to Menlo's web site, www.menlosoftware.com. The number of performance metrics

Tool	Statistic/Information of Interest
SMS Network Monitor	Preinst Process (SMS hierarchy manager)
	SiteIns Process (SMS site configuration manager)
	SMSExec Process (SMS multiple component executive)
	MSSQL Server Process (SQL server v.6.x)
PING	Network Latency for all terminals
Win32 Software Dev. Kit	Working Set Sizes
Event Viewer	System Resource Failures
Trace Logs	Application Calls
Windows NT Diagnostics	Devices
	Drivers
	Sector Sizes
Windows NT Task Manager	—Process Tab—
	Image Name (name of process)
	CPU Usage (percentage of processor usage)
	CPU Time (cumulative processor time)
	Memory Usage (working set in K)
	Page Faults (cumulative not found in memory/disk retrievals)
	Virtual Memory Size (paging file size in K)
	Base Priority (priority versus other scheduled threads)
	Handle Count (object handle count)
	Thread Count (current active threads in process)
	—Performance Tab—
	CPU Usage (current system-wide processor usage)
	MEM Usage (current system-wide memory usage in KB)
	Total Handles (current system-wide object handle usage)
	Total Threads (current system-wide thread count)
	Total Processes (current system-wide active process count)
	Physical Memory Total (installed memory in K)
	Physical Memory Available (current system-wide available memory in K)
	Physical Memory File Cache (current file cache memory in K)
	Commit Charge Total (current system-wide virtual memory usage in K)

Figure 1-98   Windows NT Statistics Gathering Checklist

Tool	Statistic/Information of Interest
	Commit Charge Limit (current system-wide free virtual memory in K)
	Commit Charge Peak (max. defined virtual memory in K)
	Kernel Memory Total (sum of paged and nonpaged kernel memory in KB)
	Kernel Memory Paged (paged pool size in KB)
	Kernel Memory Nonpaged (nonpaged pool size in KB)
Performance Monitor	CACHE: Data Map Hits %
	CACHE: Read Aheads/sec
	CACHE: Copy Read Hits %
	LOGICAL DISK: Average Disk Queue Length
	LOGICAL DISK: Average Disk Read Queue Length
	LOGICAL DISK: Average Disk Write Queue Length
	LOGICAL DISK: % Disk Time
	LOGICAL DISK: % Free Space
	PHYSICAL DISK: Average Disk Queue Length
	PHYSICAL DISK: Average Disk Read Queue Length
	PHYSICAL DISK: Average Disk Write Queue Length
	PHYSICAL DISK: % Disk Time
	PHYSICAL DISK: Current Disk Queue Length
	MEMORY: Pages/sec
	MEMORY: Pages Input/sec
	MEMORY: Pages Output/sec
	MEMORY: Page Faults/sec
	MEMORY: Available Bytes
	NETWORK INTERFACE: Bytes Total/sec for TCP/IP
	NETWORK INTERFACE: Bytes Total/sec for SNMP
	NETWORK INTERFACE: Bytes Total/sec for NetBEUI
	NETWORK INTERFACE: Datagrams/sec
	NETBIOS: Bytes Total/sec for NWLink
	OBJECTS: Processes
	PAGING FILE: % Usage
	PAGING FILE: % Usage Peak
	PROCESS: % Processor Time
	PROCESSOR: % Processor Time
	SERVER: Bytes Total
	SERVER: Context Blocks Queued/sec
	SYSTEM: % Processor Time

Figure 1-98 Windows NT Statistics Gathering Checklist (Continued)

Tool	Statistic/Information of Interest
	SYSTEM: Total Interrupts/sec
	SYSTEM: Processor Queue Length
	TAPI: Number of Devices
	TAPI: Active Lines
	TAPI: Incoming Calls
	TAPI: Outgoing Calls
	THREAD: % Processor Time 0/1
Operating System	MAXMEM
	PAGEFILE.SYS size
	Partitioning and File Architecture (NTFS vs. FAT)
Hardware	Modem Speeds
	Multi-Channel PPP Speeds and Aggregate Bandwidths
	Network Adapters and speeds
	Disk rated seek and track-to-track times
	Controller cards
	Stripe-sets
	Mother board bus speeds
	Write back shared memory options

Figure 1-98   Windows NT Statistics Gathering Checklist (Continued)

will double. Check the web site for the latest version of DBAware and additional metrics.

DBAware allows users to associate a SQL or OS alarm with a specific RDBMS error. For example, you can set DBAware to execute an OS batch file if an Oracle instance returns an `ORA-1034 Oracle not available` error. The monitor will automatically deal with formulas surrounding statistics, multithreading and multiple engines or instances. Additionally, DBAware will parse the SQL or OS command executed by the alarm, and it can pass the following parameters:

- RDBMS error number
- RDBMS error string
- Database name
- Alarm name
- Alarm timestamp
- User defined priority
- Whether the query was suspended
- Query name

- Query last execution time
- Query last execution result

DBAware's features are highlighted here. It is important to note that this tool is SQL statement driven, and as such, is very versatile and flexible.

Customizable: You can customize DBAware with your own SQL statements. Each SQL statement executes at its own rate over its own interval, or it may be grouped and administered simultaneously with other queries. You can further customize DBAware from an exhaustive list of preference options.

Graphical: DBAware includes a powerful selection of customizable graphing features. Graphs automatically update as new data are returned by the database. Graph types include: line, bar, layer, and step.

Archiving: Both alphanumeric and numeric data may be archived into a database, easing data retrieval, backup, and security. DBAware inserts archived data into a user-designated database. Archived data are directly accessible via SQL.

Alarming: DBAware's alarm features let you check returned data with your algebraic expression. If the data contain anomalies, the alarm can contain SQL statements and/or OS batch files or executables.

Reconnection: DBAware will automatically reset queries accessing a database that restarts after going down, minimizing the DBA's recovery involvement.

DB errors: If a query returns an error from the RDBMS, DBAware checks the error number against a user-modifiable list. If the error number matches a list entry, the query is suspended. DBAware will periodically attempt to reexecute the query until it executes without returning a listed error.

Clipboard: DBAware uses the system clipboard. Any SQL statements accessed via any editor may be cut and pasted into DBAware.

Import/Export: SQL statements may be imported and exported between instances of DBAware. This feature facilitates the sharing and backup of custom SQL statements.

Interface: DBAware's user interface can be set to emulate Apple Macintosh, OSF Motif, OS/2 CUA, or MS-Windows.

SQL STATEMENTS

Although DBAware comes complete with a continuously growing list of SQL statements designed to measure a spectrum of an RDBMSs internals, you can enter your own SQL statements. This lets you make site/application specific measurements.

You can group SQL statements and alter the parameters of the group simultaneously, relieving the administrative burden of performance monitoring. For example, all queries accessing a single database instance may be grouped and set to access the instance at the same rate, giving an accurate picture of what is occurring in that instance, at that time.

SQL statements execute at their own rate, over their own interval. This means that you can accumulate an individual statistic at an acceptable rate.

A SQL statement may be changed into a "benchmark" at any time. By running a benchmark statement at times of low and high activity, you can make more informed decisions for optimizing your database.

I installed DBAware on my Windows 3.1 system in under an hour and ran it against Personal Oracle7. The monitor was easy to use and truly flexible. It comes with SQL queries designed to capture statistics for all the tuning areas within Oracle. Take a look at the screen displayed in Figure 1-99. The shaded area is the SQL syntax. The lower box provides a description of the statistic and its importance. All the queries are available from pull-down menus. They are viewable and editable. Menlo Software provides updates in the form of new or revised queries on a disk that imports in minutes.

To use a predefined or custom query, you tell DBAware that you want to ADD a QUERY. Do this by clicking on the "Q" in the menu bar. In the example shown in Figure 1-100, I've selected the upper right two fields, which are pull-down menus. By default, my query will collect statistics from 8 a.m. to 5 p.m. daily, Monday through Friday. If you select the query box, then you can look at

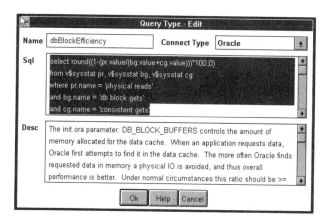

Figure 1-99 DBAware SQL Queries

statistics using graphs, while DBAware is running. If you also want to see the statistics later, then select ARCHIVE. You can use DBAware to view archived statistics, or you can extract the data from the `dba_archive_data` table built by DBAware. This is useful when you plan to input the data to a spreadsheet.

It isn't necessary to graph your statistics. That is done automatically for you, if you want. I selected three concurrent graphs to show statistics for three running queries (see Figure 1-101). My queries were created using the default 5-minute interval for statistics collection. As each query interval completed, the corresponding graph received a new entry.

Another neat feature are the alerts. If your database goes out-of-service, then the terminal beeps a couple of times. This beats trying to build your own watchdog routines.

You can tell DBAware to save as many entries as you like. This is a great tool. The price is exceptional for its power and versatility.

In the area of end-user SQL optimization there are quite a few tools to look at. There are Inspect/Analyze SQL by Precise Software, SQL Analyzer by Platinum, SQL*TRAX from Corner Stone Software, DBGENERAL SQLab by BRADMARK, ADHAWK SQL LAB by Eventus, ECOTools from Compuware, and Oracle's Enterprise Manager to name a few. Let's take a look at one now.

Just one final note on this product. I was able to fire up concurrent monitoring of multiple Oracle instances and Sybase systems from a single PC-based screen. Each separate instance/server was capable of being monitored from one location. This makes it possible to have an NT/WIN95 workstation set aside to do all your monitoring, a very favorable option.

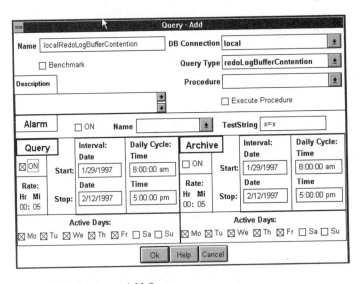

Figure 1-100   DBAware Add Query

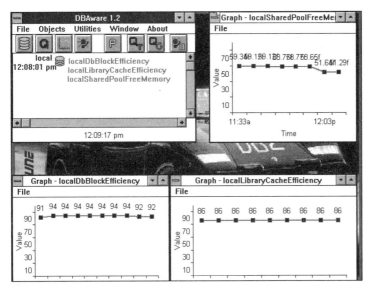

Figure 1-101   DBAware Queries and Graphs

1.38   Precise/SQL from Precise Software

While no one questions the value of SQL as the universal standard for RDBMS access, SQL applications often have a significant (and unanticipated) impact on RDBMS performance. What's more, most existing database tools focus on individual pieces of the RDBMS puzzle and reveal only the symptoms of performance problems, not their causes. Precise/SQL is a full life-cycle integrated set of performance monitoring tools for improving the performance of Oracle databases and applications. The Precise/SQL suite of products is first to deliver a full complement of performance tools that can be used throughout an application's life cycle from development through production. Precise/SQL looks at the whole puzzle.

According to the Oracle Performance Tuning Book, 60 percent of Oracle database performance problems (see Figure 1-102) are caused by applications, yet the performance tools today focus on monitoring and tuning the database. These tools address a small portion of the entire problem and reveal only the symptoms of poor performance—not the causes.

Let's take a look at how the Precise/SQL suite can help you identify, analyze, and correct SQL-oriented performance problems. The tool set includes the following:

- Inspect/SQL—Identifies problems within applications

- Analyze/SQL—Analyzes problems and models potential improvements

- Improve/SQL—Provides options for corrective action

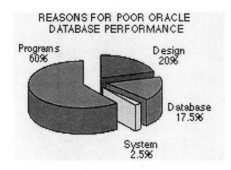

Figure 1-102   Reasons for Poor Oracle Database Performance

INSPECT/SQL

Inspect/SQL offers a host of innovative features that fully support all aspects of Oracle application and system tuning. Key features include Inspect/SQL's unique "drill down" capabilities that allow database administrators to identify problematic SQL statements in a matter of minutes or hours, as opposed to traditional methods that often take weeks or months. While standard performance monitors focus on statistical information that reveal only symptoms of the problems, such as CPU utilization, buffer hit ratios, and disk read rates, Inspect/SQL concentrates on the end-user's problem. It displays which programs and users consume the most resources, what percent of the database resource a program or user consumes, what percent of the end-user response time is due to CPU consumption, and what percent is due to CPU waits. Inspect/SQL also shows how the database, a single program, or even a single SQL statement is affected by database-related issues like checkpoint frequency, or system-related issues like system paging.

Computer resources are limited, and there is a limit to the number of processes that can simultaneously perform "productive" work. For example, there is an upper boundary to both the amount of CPU utilization and the number of I/O operations performed simultaneously. There are Oracle constraints caused by the locking mechanism that prevent more than one task from updating the same piece of data. The result of these constraints is that while there are productive processes performing user requests, there are also nonproductive victims waiting for resources used by the productive processes.

The Inspect/SQL display allows users to quickly identify processes that are in nonproductive states (i.e., waits for locks or waits for CPU). These victims are usually waiting because other "offender" processes are consuming excessive resources. Inspect/SQL pinpoints the offenders and the resources in use. Tuning these offenders will result in better response times for everyone.

Inspect/SQL contains its own scheduler and threshold mechanisms to allow sampling to be switched on and off at user-defined intervals. The feature supports remote unattended monitoring that can be analyzed at later stages and also helps diagnose hard to find problems that only occur under certain system workload conditions.

Information on currently active sessions is provided in real-time to show what is occurring on any Oracle database. This is very useful to the Help Desk and other staff members responsible for resolving real-time problems, so they can keep Oracle systems running efficiently.

Inspect/SQL displays Oracle sessions that are currently in Lock-Wait situations. It shows detailed information on the process waiting for the lock and on the object being locked. These displays help administrators quickly resolve the problem.

In addition to the intensive sampling, Inspect/SQL provides a background sampler option that runs at low-level sample rates. Background samplers can be set to run continuously without significant overhead. A sampler approach provides historical data that can be analyzed to diagnose any future problems that may occur. All historical data collected by the sampler is stored on any Oracle server and can be used to review system and application performance. Detailed information like which users were active, which SQL statements were running, and what resources were consumed are captured.

Client-Server Inspect/SQL is a true, cooperative client/server application that features a presentation-layer operating under MS-Windows and a server agent linked to the client via an efficient *Remote Procedure Call* (RPC) mechanism. This allows for real-time collection of information from Oracle and the UNIX host to provide a clear and accurate picture based not only on information available to Oracle, but also on operating system information (i.e., when Oracle applications are paged out or waiting for CPU). A single client can communicate with multiple Oracle database servers and display the sampled information in a single window.

STEPS TO INSPECT/SQL TUNING

1. Generate an overview of the type and amount of resources used as a percent of entire database resources available.

   The first step in using Inspect/SQL is to take a comprehensive look at the database resources consumed by the typical application. In this step, you will identify the areas of significant system and database resource utilization. The purpose of this high-level examination is to tag the areas in which the system is constrained, namely CPU, I/O, paging, internal waits due to latches, checkpointing, etc. The information at this stage will direct you to one of three tuning stages, all from the application perspective.

   ▪ System tuning

   ▪ Database parameter tuning

   ▪ Application tuning

   System Tuning is necessary if you reveal that the system is impacting application performance and end-user productivity. For example, if you identify that a typical application is spending 20 percent of its time paging, then you must resolve the paging problem before attempting application tuning. Solving the paging problem will immediately decrease the run time of all applications by 20 percent. However, if you see that a typical application is spending less than half of a percentage point of its time paging, then it is not necessary to tune system paging parameters.

Database parameter tuning is necessary if you identify that incorrect database parameters are impacting application performance and end-user productivity. For example, if a typical application is spending five percent of its time on Oracle checkpoint waits, you should not attempt to tune the application until you resolve the checkpoint wait problem. However, if the same application is not waiting due to checkpoints, it isn't necessary to change Oracle's checkpoint parameters, regardless of the number of checkpoints/hour occurring within the system.

Application tuning is necessary if you determine that CPU, I/O activity, or lock-waits are significantly affecting application performance.

Inspect/SQL's unique sampling mechanism will help you trap not only poorly performing applications but also those that seem efficient while frequently running and consuming large amounts of resources. For example, if you find that a typical application is spending 40 percent of its time consuming CPU, 30 percent waiting for I/O operations, and 30 percent in all other states, you should focus on application tuning. In order to perform application tuning, advance to steps 2 and 3.

2. Drill down to costly programs and users.

   From Inspect/SQL you can drill down to a detailed display showing resource consumption by program and/or user. You can easily identify areas of your Oracle workload that are consuming excessive UNIX or Oracle resources, requiring tuning.

3. Drill down to costly SQL statements.

   This detailed screen will pinpoint the problematic SQL statements within the costly programs and provide resource usage information at the statement level. This feature ensures that you are tuning the right statements for maximum performance gain, with a minimum investment of time, by focusing on the reduction of the disproportionate resource consumption category.

As mentioned earlier, Inspect/SQL is fully integrated with Analyze/SQL from Precise Software Solutions. Analyze/SQL determines the cause of problematic SQL statements by analyzing the access path and data dictionary information. Now let's shift our attention to this tool set member.

ANALYZE/SQL

The more you know about problematic SQL statements, the easier it is to tune them. In addition to offering EXPLAIN information, Analyze/SQL provides you with important Data Dictionary information. The ability to review this data provides the missing ingredient in identifying the root causes of high-consumption SQL statements.

In the traditional development model, tuning problem SQL statements require testing an alternate solution, evaluating its impact, undoing the solution if necessary, and starting over. Analyze/SQL reduces the time and risk associated with this process by modeling the impact of changes on overall database performance, such as changes in index definition or object statistics. Developers can also use Analyze/SQL to generate a list of alternate SQL statements that perform the same tasks, allowing them to choose the alternative that offers the best performance without altering functionality.

ANALYZE/SQL FEATURES

■ *Display information in convenient, intuitive formats*

Analyze/SQL's easy-to-use extract facilities allow users to retrieve SQL statements from many types of application code, trace file, or the V$ tables. With just a few mouse clicks, users can display access paths and present EXPLAIN information using intuitive tree structures. This information can be stored for future analysis. Analyze/SQL can also be used to compare the behavior of different statements using the Rule-Based or Cost-Based optimizers. This helps Oracle users make the transition from a Rule-Based to a Cost-Based orientation.

■ *View database objects and all their related SQL statements*

Analyze/SQL lets users query all aspects of tables, indexes, triggers, constraints, and PL/SQL statements. It will also show all statements directly related to a specific table, index, or column. Additionally, all statements performing a specific scan on one of these objects can be displayed.

■ *Generate logically equivalent alternative SQL statements*

Using knowledge-based engineering technology, it lets users automatically generate SQL statements and review explanations of their access path behavior. This reduces the time needed to manually look for alternate SQL statements and helps users learn how to write efficient SQL.

■ *Gauge the impact of changes to database objects on SQL statements*

Analyze/SQL allows you to simulate potential changes to database objects. For example, simulating the positive or negative implications that result from changes to table or index structures, or from defining new indexes without performing any physical changes to the database. These features reduce the time and risk involved in implementing changes.

1.39 SQLBench Simulation and Prototyping

SQLBench is a tool for testing database application systems. With SQLBench, the performance capabilities of database application systems based on the client/server model can already be determined in the system design phase—that is, even before the programming of the system starts. With SQLBench, the programmer is not bound to a special front-end development tool. That means the performance capabilities of database application systems for SQLBase® that are developed using C, C++, COBOL, SQLWindows®, or another front-end development tool can be tested before the system is implemented in the desired environment. The SQLBench name and the information shown in this section are being used with the permission of SQLBench International, Inc. These materials are their sole property.

The performance and, therewith, the quality of a database application system based on the client/server model depends on the performance of the database server used. Factors affecting the performance of a database application system are the database management system (like Oracle, Informix, Sybase, DB2, etc.) used, the hardware and software configuration to be used, the logical data model (the data structures) of the application system, as well as the transactions. Usually, proven claims regarding the performance of a database application system can be made only after bringing up the actual system. The reason for this is the strong dependence of performance on the workload (number of users, frequency of transactions, and data quantities). Testing the application system under actual load conditions arising during operation in the design and development phases of the system cannot be done using conventional methods because creating the load condition is impossible. If during actual operation bottlenecks are discovered that are a result of the data structure model or the access structure of the transactions to the database—that is, which point to weaknesses in the system design—adapting the system will prove to be very expensive in terms of time and costs.

To determine the performance of database application systems at an earlier stage, preferably before the development of the application software, the load conditions that can be expected during actual operation must be simulated. SQLBench supports the description, generation, and simulation of the workload up to the point in time when the database application system is designed. By permitting testing of the performance capabilities during the system design phase, SQLBench helps to detect and correct weaknesses early. Figure 1-103 shows the difference between the occurrence of the performance evaluation in the typical system life-cycle and that with SQLBench.

HOW DOES SQLBENCH WORK?

SQLBench uses simulation and prototyping concepts to test database application systems. The basic idea is to simulate the performance-critical components of a database application system using an application system prototype in order to be able to simulate the expected workload during actual operation.

WHAT IS A TRANSACTION?

The users of a system execute user transactions from their workstations. A user transaction is a sequence of database accesses intertwined with user interac-

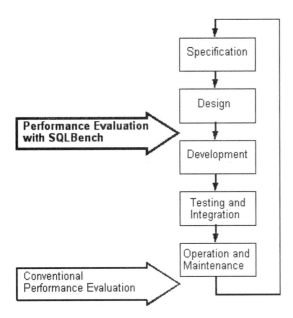

Figure 1-103 System Life-Cycle Model

tion and combined with control flow. A user transaction customarily consists of several database accesses and user interactions.

As opposed to a database transaction, which is defined as an atomic database operation ensuring the consistency of the database, a user transaction can consist of several database transactions and additionally contains the code for managing the user interface and the flow control. Examples of user transactions are the accounting procedures at a bank counter and the sales procedure at the cash register of a retail store. Figure 1-104 shows the relation between a user transaction and a database transaction. If we use the term "transaction" in this section, we will be referring to a user transaction.

In SQLBench, the user of the system is replaced with the simulation component of SQLBench, the transactions with transaction prototypes programmed in the SQLBench programming language, and the database of the application system with test data generated by SQLBench.

SQLBENCH SIMULATION COMPONENT

The simulation component starts a simulator for each user. Each simulator takes on the following functions.

1. Calling the transaction prototype for a user

2. Simulating control time resulting from the interaction of the user with a transaction (user time)

3. Managing the running of transaction prototypes; including the generation of the input values for a transaction prototype and the simulation of the flow control of a transaction prototype

The simulator uses random numbers to simulate the control time of the user, to generate the input values, and to simulate flow control of the transaction prototypes. The invocation of a transaction and the delay before the next invocation (= arrival interval) also occur randomly.

TRANSACTION PROTOTYPES IN SQLBENCH

A transaction prototype in SQLBench only simulates the database accesses and the flow control of the transaction associated with the access. Not specified is the user interface of the transaction; this does not contribute to the rating of the database application system based on a database server. Because the user interface is not specified, the cost of developing a transaction prototype is substantially lower than for developing the complete transaction. The database accesses are programmed in SQL. The SQL commands should already exhibit the form in which they will be used in the transaction of the application program (i.e., a SQLWindows or C application).

Figure 1-102 illustrates the structure of a cashier transaction in a retail store compared to the structure of the corresponding transaction prototype. Because the transaction prototype produces only the database accesses of the transaction, process steps not required for rating the performance are not considered (for example, calculating the sale total, printing article information on the receipt, and printing the sale total on the receipt). Instead of the user entering the article number, the simulator generates the article number in the transaction prototype. The simulator also generates the user time of the transaction

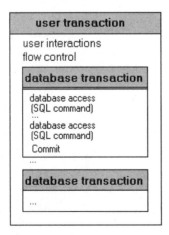

Figure 1-104   User Transaction and Database Transaction

(user time for entering the article number), and the flow control information, if more articles exist.

SQLBENCH TEST DATA GENERATOR

If no data regarding production mode operation is available at the time SQL-Bench is to be used, the requirements set related to the data system must be simulated as part of the workload to be generated using test data. To accomplish this, SQLBench offers numerous functions for generating random test data.

SQLBENCH TRANSACTION MONITOR

The response times of the transaction prototypes, as well as exception and error situations that occur during simulation, are measured and recorded by the SQLBench transaction monitor. Figure 1-105 illustrates a workload simulated with SQLBench as compared to an actual system (also see Figure 1-106).

BDL PROGRAMMING LANGUAGE

SQLBench has its own, easy-to-learn programming language (BDL: Benchmark Description Language). BDL can be used to specify test data, the frequency of transactions for a simulated user, transaction prototypes, and the SQL commands for those prototypes.

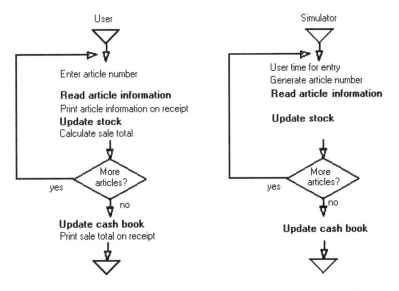

Figure 1-105 Transactions (left side) and Transaction Prototype (right side)

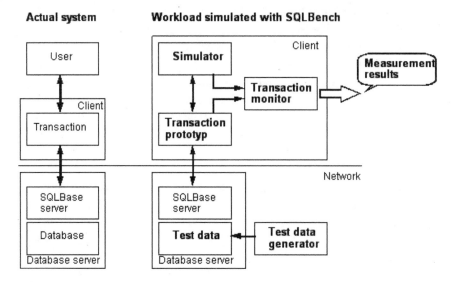

Figure 1-106   Actual System and SQLBench

SQLBENCH OPERATION

SQLBench consists of a compiler for programs, a run-time system, and a workbench. The workbench is where you edit your BDF (a SQLBench Program File) files, invoke the compiler and run-time system, audit the simulation and view the results. Figure 1-107 provides an overview of SQLBench's components.

USING A SQLBENCH PROGRAM

As mentioned earlier, *Benchmark Description Language* (BDL) is used for writing programs for database systems based on the client/server model. It is used to generate test data and simulate a workload.

GENERATING TEST DATA

Because no data regarding production mode operation of the application system to be developed is available at the time SQLBench is to be used, the requirements set related to the data system must be simulated as part of the workload to be generated using test data. Using SQLBench, random test data values can be generated. BDL offers numerous functions for generating test values. BDL also permits relationships (i.e., primary key, foreign key) to be simulated. The test data description limits itself essentially to the definition of the random functions for generating random values and the specification of SQL INSERT commands for inserting test data.

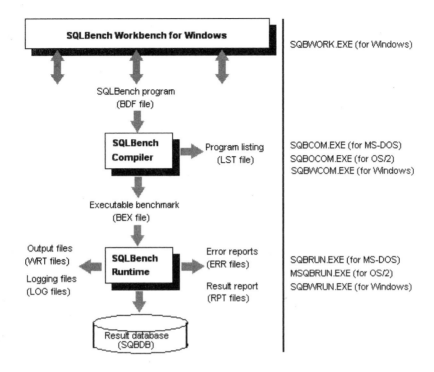

Figure 1-107   SQLBench Components

WORKLOAD SIMULATION

Using a SQLBench program, the workload for a client/server database system can be written. Accordingly, the users of the system, system transactions, and the SQL commands for the transactions are written in BDL.

SQLBENCH PROGRAM STRUCTURE

Each SQLBench program consists of four main sections:

- Random Variables Section
- Workload Section
- Transaction Section
- SQL Section

RANDOM VARIABLES SECTION

All random variables used in the SQLBench program are defined in the random variables section. Random variables are used for generating random input values and for specifying random repetition factors, the probability of running transaction sections, and random user times.

WORKLOAD SECTION

The system users to be simulated are defined in the workload section. A user is described by a simulation time slice and the transactions to be called along with their frequency.

TRANSACTION SECTION

The transaction prototypes used by the users specified in the workload section are defined in the transaction section. The transaction prototypes call SQL commands to access the database. A transaction prototype represents the basic structure of a transaction. It reproduces the access structure of the database transaction. The user interface of the transaction is not specified in the transaction prototype. In contrast to transactions called by the users of the system when a program goes live, transactions prototypes are called by SQLBench Runtime based on the information found in the workload section. Description of the transaction prototypes is handled with a Pascal-like syntax.

SQL SECTION

The SQL commands called by the transaction prototypes are defined in the SQL section. They are the reusable section of the SQLBench program. The SQL commands should already exhibit the form in which they will be used in the transaction of the application program.

The example in Figure 1-108 shows a portion of a SQLBench program for simulating a workload. Two random variables (randvar1 and randvar2) with two different random functions (RndUniN and RndStr) are defined in the *random variables section*. Three users (usr1, usr2, and usr3) are defined in the *workload section*. During its simulation time slice of 3,600 seconds, usr1 calls the transaction Selling 100 times and the transaction Order 10 times. usr2 and usr3 have the same workload profile. Both call the transaction StockQuery 20 times during a simulation time slice of 2,000 seconds.

The transaction prototypes of the transactions Selling, Order, and Stock-Query are defined in the transactions section of the SQLBench program. The transaction prototype Selling calls the SQL command SelArticle and InsSale to access the test database of the application system to be simulated (Figure 1-109).

The SQL commands used by the transaction prototypes SelArticle and InsSale are defined in the SQL section. SQL command parameters (ano, name, agr, and pr) and random variables can be used in SQL text as bind variables (with preceding ":"). See Figure 1-110.

SQLBench Compiler compiles the program SIMS.BDF and creates an executable file SIMS.BEX. A BEX file contains the complete description of the workload for all users.

```
BENCHMARK SIMS
...
DCLRAND
        randvar1:     RndUniN (1..1000);
        randvar2:     RndStr ("abcde1234"; 10..20);
...
DCLUSER
        USER usr1: 3600,300,200;
        TRANSACTIONS
            Selling: 100;
            Order: 10;
        USER usr2, usr3: 2000,300,200;
            StockQuery: 20;
```

Figure 1-108 SQLBench Program Example

```
DCLTRANS
    TRANSACTION Selling:
        VAR    i,artno: NUMBER;
               name,agr:   STRING;
            ...
    BEGIN
            ...
        FOR i:=1 TO 5 DO
        artno:=randvar1;
        c1: SelArticle(IN artno; OUT name,agr);
        c2: InsSale(...);
            ...
    END Selling;

    TRANSACTION Order:
    ...
    TRANSACTION StockQuery:
    ...
```

Figure 1-109 Transaction Prototype

```
dclsql
    selarticle(in ano: number);
            out name, agr: string; pr: number):
        select article_name, price, article_group
        into :name, :pr, :agr
        from article where artno = :ano;
        inssale(...):
        ..
        end sims
```

Figure 1-110 SQL Section

OPERATION OF SQLBENCH RUNTIME

SQLBench Runtime performs the simulation for one user defined in the workload section of the SQLBench program. It is responsible for the following tasks:

- Calling the transactions for a user randomly
- Fixing the delay of arrival between two transactions
- Managing the queue of waiting transactions
- Reporting the results of a simulation

CALLING THE TRANSACTIONS

FSQLBench Runtime selects the next transaction to be executed randomly. The probability of a transaction being called next depends on the frequency with which the user calls the transaction during the simulation time slice, in the workload section. According to the preceding example, the user usr1 calls the transaction Selling 100 times and transaction Order 10 times. Therewith the probabilities P(X) of the transactions to be called next are as follows:

$$P(X = Selling) = \frac{100}{110};$$

$$P(X = Order) = \frac{10}{110};$$

Every call of a transaction changes the probability of the transaction to be called next because the total number of transactions to be called changes, too. If the transaction Selling is called first, the probabilities P(X) of the transactions to be called change accordingly:

$$P(X = Selling) = \frac{99}{109};$$

$$P(X = Order) = \frac{10}{109};$$

DELAY OF ARRIVAL BETWEEN TWO TRANSACTIONS

The delay between the arrival of two transactions is also calculated randomly. The simulation time slice and the total number of transactions to be called determine the *mean arrival interval – **m*** of the transactions (equals simulation time divided by total number of transactions). The behavior of arrivals of transactions can be described by a Poisson Process. That is, the arrival interval of the transaction follows an exponential distribution with the mean vale *xxx*. For user usr1, the *mean arrival interval* between transactions will be calculated as shown:

$$m = \frac{3600}{(100 + 10)} = 32.7 \; seconds$$

Thus, the transactions for user usr1 arrive on an average of 32.7 seconds.

WAITING QUEUE OF TRANSACTIONS

A transaction is put into the waiting queue if there is another transaction being executed at the moment the transaction arrives or if there are already other transactions waiting in the queue for execution. The waiting queue discipline is *first in-first out* (FIFO).

REPORTING THE RESULTS OF A SIMULATION

SQLBench Runtime reports the response times and waiting times (minimum, maximum, and average times) of all transactions executed. Also the response times of all SQL commands, fetch statements, and user-defined timer statements are reported. The performance results are displayed on-screen during simulation. At the end of a simulation, SQLBench Runtime writes the performance results and database errors to result files (files with extensions RPT and ERR). These are optionally written to a result database called SQBDB. In the result database SQBDB, the results for several users can be related to simulation projects, which constitute the base for further reporting. Optionally a log file (file with extension LGO) is written during simulation, reporting all SQL C/API function calls. Figures 1-111 to 1-113 show some SQLBench Testdata Generator and Reporter screens.

To conclude, SQL/Bench is the CASE tool for performance testing of database applications during design, implementation, operation, and maintenance. This tool's ability to work in the design phase, to model unlimited virtual users, to produce salient data using a test data generator, and to simulate up to 300 users on one NT machine set it apart from any competitors.

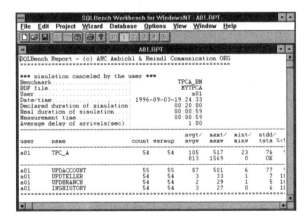

Figure 1-111   SQLBench Testdata Generator

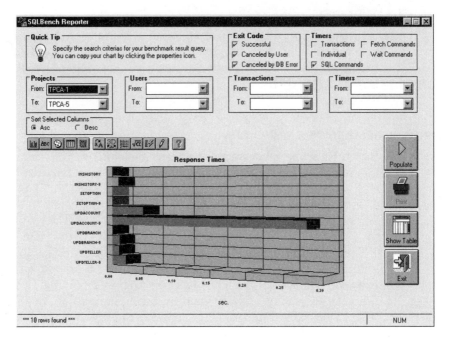

Figure 1-112 SQLBench Reporter Response Time Graphic

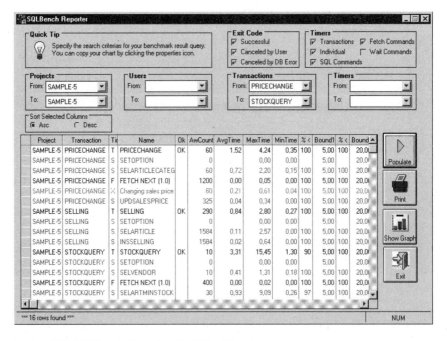

Figure 1-113 SQLBench Reporter (List View Mode)

1.40   Response Time Measurement Variances

Now, response time means to you something different than it means to me. How can that be? Just trust me. It can. More importantly, it may mean something entirely different than what we both think to your end user. For example, the percent of transactions within service level might be one person's definition of an acceptable response time. However, a tuning statistician recognizes that the percentage of time that the service level was attained is a more accurate display of what the user sees. The user, on the other hand, will sit down with you and repetitively run an individual transaction, over and over, to prove to you that it is above his service level agreement.

So, how do you satisfy your users if they don't accept your word that response time is acceptable. One way is to agree with them. One of the many faces of tuning is negotiation. Perhaps, if you fix the one transaction that your users are plagued with, those users may be more apt to approve a massive tuning requested by you later on.

1.41   Network Latency

Network delays can be confused with poor database or application performance. They add to the overall response time. One way to test network latency, or the communication time from the client to a server, and back, is with PING. Use ping to measure network latency. Figure 1-114 shows a ping display box with minimum, maximum, and average times in milliseconds. Latency periods greater than 10 ms signify a delay that needs to be researched.

Windows 95 & NT also have standard PING commands. From the DOS prompt you can enter PING yourid.domain to evaluate the time to communicate to your destination. The syntax for PING is available by using the command without any operands, as shown here.

```
C:\WIN95> PING
Usage: ping [-t] [-a] [-n count] [-l size] [-f] [-i TTL] [-v TOS]
       [-r count] [-s count] [[-j host-list] | [-k host-list]]
         [-w timeout] destination-list
Options:
     -t              Ping the specifed host until interrupted.
     -a              Resolve addresses to hostnames.
```

Figure 1-114   Ping Output from Swift by Net Manage

```
-n count      Number of echo requests to send.

-l size       Send buffer size.

-f            Set Don't Fragment flag in packet.

-i TTL        Time To Live.

-v TOS        Type Of Service.

-r count      Record route for count hops.

-s count      Timestamp for count hops.

-j host-list  Loose source route along host-list.

-k host-list  Strict source route along host-list.

-w timeout    Timeout in milliseconds to wait for each reply.
```

When you run PING with a host name, you will see output that contains the time in milliseconds for communications hops. A Windows 95 example is shown here.

```
C:\WIN95> PING jeffd.dsi.com

Pinging jeffd.dsi.com [198.111.111.210] with 32 bytes of data:

Reply from 198.111.111.210: bytes=32 time=1ms TTL=32

Reply from 198.111.111.210: bytes=32 time=1ms TTL=32

Reply from 198.111.111.210: bytes=32 time=1ms TTL=32

Reply from 198.111.111.210: bytes=32 time<10ms TTL=32
```

Another useful tool is TRACERT. In Windows 95, run `TRACERT host.name.net` where *host.name.net* is your remote host name, or the target location. TRACERT will determine the number of hops to get to your Internet/Intranet destination and the number of milliseconds for each hop (see Figure 1-115). Unfortunately, using a RUN command will cause the display to disappear before you can view all the output. So, you will want to execute TRACERT from the DOS prompt. The syntax for the command can be viewed by entering the command without any operands as shown here.

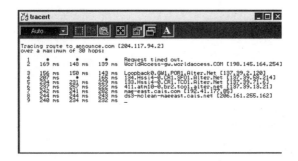

Figure 1-115 TRACERT Output

```
c:>WIN95\TRACERT

Usage: tracert [-d] [-h maximum_hops] [-j host-list] [-w timeout] tar-
get_name


Options:
    -d Do not resolve addresses to hostnames.
    -h maximum_hops Maximum number of hops to search for target.
    -j host-list Loose source route along host-list.
    -w timeout Wait timeout milliseconds for each reply.
```

1.42 Microsoft® SQL Server™ Statistics Collection

Just as we've done in prior sections on other databases, we want to repeat the process here. Our goal will be to collect statistics on all the key tuning areas of Microsoft SQL Server (see Figure 1-116). The results will be the basis for tuning decisions made later when referencing Chapter 6.

SQL Server and Windows NT Monitor are basically the same thing, with slight differences. The SQL Performance Monitor is accessed from the SQL Server for Windows NT Group, while the Windows NT Performance Monitor can be found in the Administrative Tools Group. When the SQL Performance Monitor is started, a file named C:\SQL\BINN\SQLCTRS.PMC is actually called instead of PERFMON.EXE. It in turn calls PERFMON.EXE (the conventional Windows NT Performance Monitor program) passing server-related parameters. Both monitors capture system statistics. But, the SQL monitor has an additional 70 plus counters with SQL Server information.

1.43 Your Best Tuning Opportunities

To recap, in Chapter 1, you have been taken along a straight and narrow path towards your first tuning accomplishment, the development of a plan with exact targets. You may be asking yourself, "What things, in general, should I be targeting for tuning in my shop, or for that matter, on my PC?" That's a good question. If you haven't found exactly what you need to address from previous sections in this chapter, then the next section will help you.

The following list of generalized tuning opportunities is in order from greatest impact on improving performance to least. However, this order does not necessarily coincide with the cost. Some big gainers are relatively inexpensive to implement (like more servers) versus reengineering a giant application system, which can run in the range of millions of dollars.

Greatest performance improvement

Hardware upgrades and right sizing

Server Clustering

(Massively Parallel Processing) MPP

SMP (Symmetric Multi-Processing)

Multiprocessors for Mainframes

Faster buses, adapters, and bandwidths

Increased numbers of servers

   Multitasking for Mainframes

   Optimize the operating system (MVS, VM, VSE, NT, UNIX)

   Optimize the RDBMS (Oracle, Sybase, CA-IDMS, DB2 ...)

   Optimize other regions (CICS, Monitors) and tune networks

      Third Party Tools (Sort, Reorg, etc)

      Restructures and reorganizations

      Re-engineering

      New Software Releases (with performance improvements)

         Parallel processes and bulk processing

         Local Mode Processing (CA-IDMS and DB2)

         SMART caching

         System caching

            Swap files

            Application caching

            Faster languages and code optimizers

            File striping and load balancing

            File buffering and blocking

               Bit-Mapped indexes

               Conventional indexes and sets

               Index rebuilds

               Data compression

                  Optimization of SQL or native calls

                  WorkFlow analysis and redesign

                  Application tuning

                  Multi-threading programs

                     Foreign keys

                     Eliminate deadlocks

                     Remove unneeded reports

                     Remove dead code

                        Programming workbenches

                        Least improvement

Command or Utility	Statistic/Information of Interest
set showplan on	Query steps (see Chapter 6 for directions)
set statistics io on	I/Os by queries
Windows NT Event Viewer	Logged events
Windows NT Performance Monitor	See Chapter 8 on using the monitor CPU, Disk I/O, Cache Utilization
	(Windows NT Administrative Group)
Disk Mirroring	List of disks using mirroring and which controller
Disk Sriping	List of disks using striping and which controller
RAID 0,1,5	List of RAID devices
DLL(s)	List of DLL(s) used and whether 16-bit or 32-bit
Network Settings	All settings
sp_configure	Complete listing of settings
Client Software	List of application programs and whether they are 16-bit or 32-bit
Peripheral devices	List of any other devices and their controllers
Backup schedule	When are backups done and how
Alerts	List of existing database alerts
Stored Procedures	List of existing stored procedures
Triggers	List of existing triggers
Memory	Physical memory and memory settings
SQL Programmer (workplace tool)	Parse, compile, and execution time for SLQ statements
SQLSTRES [1]	Stress multi-threaded SQL calls
i386 [1]	x86 Windows NT Disk Stress Utility
SQLHDTST [1]	Win32 utilitiy exercises Win32 overlapped asynchronous I/O
SQL Server Performance Monitor	All statistics
	(SQL Server for Windows NT Group)
MS Network Monitor (part of SMS) [2]	Monitor queries with network analyzer
4032 trace flag (see Transact-SQL Reference)	See SQL statements sent to the SQL errorlog
SQL Inspector from Blue Lagoon Software	Intercept SQL at the ODBC layer
Inspect/Analyze SQL by Precise Software	SQL tuning (product review in this chapter)

Figure 1-116 Microsoft SQL Server Statistics Collection Checklist

Command or Utility	Statistic/Information of Interest
SQL Analyzer by Platinum	SQL tuning [3]
SQL*TRAX from Corner Stone Software	SQL tuning [3]
DBGENERAL SQLab by Bradmark	SQL tuning [3]
ADHAWK SQL LAB by Eventus	SQL tuning [3]
ECOTOOLS from Compuware	SQL tuning [3]

[1] Download from Microsoft Internet site
[2] SMS is the System Management Server from Microsoft
[3] You need to verify that this tool works with Microsoft SQL Server

Figure 1-116 Microsoft SQL Server Statistics Collection Checklist (Continued)

2

Mainframe Blocking and Buffering

2.1 VSAM CISIZE, CASIZE, AMP, and BUFFERSIZE Parameters

IDCAMS is the backbone utility for VSAM files and clusters. You can define, delete, load, unload, redefine, and make modification to the VSAM-based files with one utility. In our first example, we will explore the management of these clusters for performance. Without getting into the internal design of *Control Intervals* (CIs) or *Control Areas* (CAs), many CIs make up a CA, and many CAs make up the entire data or index component of a cluster.

As updating takes place, CIs and CAs are inclined to split and spawn. These divisions into new CIs and CAs can degrade future performance. In fact, the larger the CA, the longer the wait for a split. To see the number of CI and CA splits in a VSAM file, you need to run only the IDCAMS utility with the LISTCAT command. This is done with the JCL shown in Figure 2-1.

The report in Figure 2-2 contains VSAM tuning information. First, notice that the CI SPLITS = 443 and the CA SPLITS = 96. These splits could be eliminated by running IDCAMS with the REPRO command. This would unload and reload the VSAM cluster. At that time you might consider increasing the size of

```
//IDCAMS01 EXEC PGM=IDCAMS,REGION=8M
//SYSPRINT DD SYSOUT=*
//SYSUDUMP DD SYSOUT=*
//SYSOUT   DD SYSOUT=*
//SYSIN    DD *
    LISTCAT LEVEL('PRODVS.BILLING') ALL
```

Figure 2-1 Sample JCL for IDCAMS Cluster Report

```
1IDCAMS  SYSTEM SERVICES                                     TIME: 19:00:01        02/07/94        PAGE    1
0
  LISTCAT LEVEL('PRODVS') ALL
0CLUSTER ----- PRODVS.BILLING
      IN-CAT --- CATALOG.USER001
      HISTORY
        DATASET-OWNER----(NULL)         CREATION--------1993.355
        RELEASE----------2             EXPIRATION------0000.000
        PROTECTION-PSWD---(NULL)       RACF-----------(YES)
      ASSOCIATIONS
        DATA-----PRODVS.BILLING.DATA
        INDEX----PRODVS.BILLING.INDEX
0DATA ------ PRODVS.BILLING.DATA
      IN-CAT --- CATALOG.USER001
      HISTORY
        DATASET-OWNER----(NULL)         CREATION--------1993.355
        RELEASE----------2             EXPIRATION------0000.000
        PROTECTION-PSWD---(NULL)       RACF-----------(YES)
      ASSOCIATIONS
        CLUSTER-PRODVS.BILLING
      ATTRIBUTES
        KEYLEN-----------64             AVGLRECL---------640         BUFSPACE---------18432       CISIZE-----------8192      ◄ Size
        RKP--------------8             MAXLRECL--------1017         EXCPEXIT--------(NULL)        CI/CA--------------84
        SHROPTNS(1,3)    SPEED          UNIQUE          NOERASE      INDEXED        NOWRITECHK     IMBED       NOREPLICAT
        UNORDERED        NOREUSE        NONSPANNED
      STATISTICS
        REC-TOTAL------230802           SPLITS-CI--------443         EXCPS-----------184438                                  ◄ CI Splits
        REC-DELETED----105610           SPLITS-CA---------96         EXTENTS------------4                                    ◄ CA Splits
        REC-INSERTED---76823            FREESPACE-%CI------30         SYSTEM-TIMESTAMP:
        REC-UPDATED----14500            FREESPACE-%CA------30           X'A8CC163C740E7B00'
        REC-RETRIEVED--640897           FREESPC-BYTES--48496064
      ALLOCATION
        SPACE-TYPE----CYLINDER          HI-ALLOC-RBA--619315200
        SPACE-PRI--------900            HI-USED-RBA---271810560
        SPACE-SEC---------90
      VOLUME
        VOLSER--------PRD195            PHYREC-SIZE------8192        HI-ALLOC-RBA----619315200    EXTENT-NUMBER--------4
        DEVTYPE----X'3010200F'          PHYRECS/TRK--------6         HI-USED-RBA-----271810560    EXTENT-TYPE------X'40'
        VOLFLAG--------PRIME            TRACKS/CA---------15
        EXTENTS:
        LOW-CCHH---X'02B00000'          LOW-RBA-----------0          TRACKS----------345
        HIGH-CCHH--X'02C6000E'          HIGH-RBA----15826943
        LOW-CCHH---X'04A60000'          LOW-RBA-----15826944         TRACKS---------1110
        HIGH-CCHH--X'04EF000E'          HIGH-RBA----66748415
        LOW-CCHH---X'09910000'          LOW-RBA-----66748416         TRACKS---------6945
        HIGH-CCHH--X'0B5F000E'          HIGH-RBA---385351679
        LOW-CCHH---X'0BB70000'          LOW-RBA----385351680         TRACKS---------5100
        HIGH-CCHH--X'0D0A000E'          HIGH-RBA---619315199
```

Figure 2-2   Output from STEP IDCAMS01 in Figure 2-1

102

the CIs and CAs. They are currently 8192 and 688,128 bytes, respectively. There are 84 CIs per CA. Since these sizes are already considered large, the splitting probably is not related to the size of these control blocks.

CI and CA splits occur in only KSDS files or alternate indexes when inserting records or updating variable length records. The splitting can also be avoided by increasing the FREESPACE (CI,CA), CI RESERVED AMOUNT, and CA RESERVED AMOUNT.

As a general rule, you want to allocate CAs in cylinders to get fewer CAs, and as a result, fewer sequence sets, index sets, and EXCP(s). Also, as a general rule, you want smaller CI sizes for records that will be accessed randomly.

Next, you should find the options IMBED and REPLICATE. These options are defined at cluster definition time. IMBED will store the sequence set records with the data records (for improved indexing performance). REPLICATE assigns each index set record to a dedicated track and duplicates the record as much as possible on that track. This requires a substantial increase in DASD space but makes it possible to find keys wthout hardware seek time or rotational delay. The only time spent is in positioning the head over the track to be read. In Figure 2-2, this option is turned off, so you see NOREPLICATE.

Another IDCAMS definition that can impact performance is the SPANNED option. You use this parameter when you want to allow very large or variable records to span control intervals. This parameter has some interesting problems, and I recommend you avoid it, except where an application design has no other choice. In our sample cluster, NONSPANNED indicates that it is turned off.

The remainder of the IDCAMS cluster report is in Figure 2-3. Displayed is data for the INDEX component of the cluster. The same kinds of tuning considerations apply. Keep in mind, that placing the DATA and INDEX component files on different volumes is a recommended approach to improving performance.

Another useful piece of information that is easily identifiable is the HI-USED-RBA. The HI-ALLOC-RBA indicates the allocated space, while the high used *Relative Byte Address* (RBA) is an indication of the highest address where records have been stored on the current extent. It is easy for VSAM to store records just beyond the high RBA. Each extent will have its own high RBA address. The addition of EXTENTS to a VSAM file can also degrade performance.

One way to control free space is with the FREESPACE parameter. At cluster definition time, you may assign a percentage of each CI and CA to be used for FREESPACE. Later, after the cluster is in use, you may modify this percentage upwards. However, it will apply only to new CIs and CAs built. To implement the new FREESPACE parameter globally requires a reload of the cluster. This again can be done with IDCAMS REPRO or with your own custom built COBOL programs.

Alternate indexes, although laid out internally in a different fashion than a primary index, have similar tuning concerns. Quite often, the best thing to do with these is to have regularly scheduled batch jobs run and rebuild them. This

```
1IDCAMS  SYSTEM SERVICES                                         TIME: 19:00:01    02/07/94    PAGE    2
0INDEX ------ PRODVS.BILLING.INDEX
0    IN-CAT -- CATALOG.USER001
     HISTORY
         DATASET-OWNER-----(NULL)        CREATION--------1993.355
         RELEASE-----------2             EXPIRATION------0000.000
         PROTECTION-PSWD---(NULL)        RACF-----------(YES)
     ASSOCIATIONS
         CLUSTER-PRODVS.BILLING
     ATTRIBUTES
         KEYLEN----------64     AVGLRECL----------0      BUFSPACE----------0      CISIZE-------------2048
         RKP--------------8     MAXLRECL-------2041      EXCPEXIT-------(NULL)     CI/CA----------------21
         SHROPTNS(1,3)  RECOVERY    UNIQUE    NOERASE    NOWRITECHK    IMBED       NOREPLICAT     UNORDERED
         NOREUSE                                                                  Tuning Hot Items
     STATISTICS
         REC-TOTAL-------408    SPLITS-CI--------96      EXCPS-----------23604     INDEX:
         REC-DELETED-------0    SPLITS-CA---------6      EXTENTS-------------5     LEVELS---------------3
number of levels in index
         REC-INSERTED------0    FREESPACE-%CI-----0      SYSTEM-TIMESTAMP:         ENTRIES/SECT---------9
         REC-UPDATED----8916    FREESPACE-%CA-----0         X'A8CC163C740E7B00'    SEQ-SET-RBA------43008
         REC-RETRIEVED-----0    FREESPC-BYTES-1050624                              HI-LEVEL-RBA------4096
highest level index record
     ALLOCATION
         SPACE-TYPE------TRACK  HI-ALLOC-RBA--1886208
         SPACE-PRI----------1   HI-USED-RBA----851968
         SPACE-SEC----------1
     VOLUME
         VOLSER--------PRD195   PHYREC-SIZE-----2048     HI-ALLOC-RBA-----43008    EXTENT-NUMBER--------1
         DEVTYPE--X'3010200F'   PHYRECS/TRK-------21     HI-USED-RBA------26624    EXTENT-TYPE------X'00'
         VOLFLAG------PRIME     TRACKS/CA----------1
         EXTENTS:
         LOW-CCHH--X'00290003'  LOW-RBA------------0     TRACKS--------------1
         HIGH-CCHH-X'00290003'  HIGH-RBA-------43007
     VOLUME
         VOLSER--------PRD195   PHYREC-SIZE-----2048     HI-ALLOC-RBA---1886208    EXTENT-NUMBER--------4
         DEVTYPE--X'3010200F'   PHYRECS/TRK-------21     HI-USED-RBA-----851968    EXTENT-TYPE------X'80'
         VOLFLAG------PRIME     TRACKS/CA---------15
         EXTENTS:
         LOW-CCHH--X'02B00000'  LOW-RBA--------43008     TRACKS------------345
         HIGH-CCHH-X'02C6000E'  HIGH-RBA-------90111
         LOW-CCHH--X'04A60000'  LOW-RBA--------90112     TRACKS-----------1110
         HIGH-CCHH-X'04EF000E'  HIGH-RBA------241663
         LOW-CCHH--X'09910000'  LOW-RBA-------241664     TRACKS-----------6945
         HIGH-CCHH-X'0B5F000E'  HIGH-RBA-----1189887
         LOW-CCHH--X'0BB70000'  LOW-RBA------1189888     TRACKS-----------5100
         HIGH-CCHH-X'0D0A000E'  HIGH-RBA-----1886207
1IDCAMS  SYSTEM SERVICES                                         TIME: 19:00:01    02/07/94    PAGE    3
0    THE NUMBER OF ENTRIES PROCESSED WAS:
                   AIX ------------------0
                   ALIAS ----------------0
                   CLUSTER --------------1
                   DATA -----------------1
                   GDG ------------------0
                   INDEX ----------------1
                   NONVSAM --------------0
                   PAGESPACE ------------0
                   PATH -----------------0
                   SPACE ----------------0
                   USERCATALOG ----------0
                   TOTAL ----------------3
0    THE NUMBER OF PROTECTED ENTRIES SUPPRESSED WAS 0
0IDC0001I FUNCTION COMPLETED, HIGHEST CONDITION CODE WAS 0
```

Figure 2-3 Continuation of Output from Figure 2-1

reestablishes the minimum number of index levels to the index structure and makes FREESPACE available for future updates.

Buffers can be assigned in BATCH JCL to optimize access to CLUSTERS on the whole or to their individual DATA and INDEX components. To code the BUFSP parameter so that 20K of buffer space is available, the AMP parameter would look like this:

```
//BILLFILE     DD     DSN=PRODVS.BILLING.CLUSTER,AMP=(BUFSP=20480)
```

In this example, three buffers are assigned to the index component, and 24 are given to the data component.

```
//BILLFILE     DD     DSN=PRODVS.BILLING.CLUSTER,
AMP=('BUFNI=3,BUFND=24')
```

When this is done, the buffers for the data and index components are the same size as the control intervals that reside within them.

2.2   VSAM Buffering Tools

VSAM Express by Software Diversified Services improves the performance of VSAM programs by selecting the best buffer allocations. The buffer allocations are made at run-time, thus adjusting to changes in processing.

2.3   QSAM, BDAM, BSAM BLOCKSIZE, and DCB=BUFNO

Non-VSAM datasets have just as much need to be tuned as any other file type. In Chapter 1, we showed you a list of the top 10 batch cpu offending programs. Within the list was a program called IEBGENER. This is one of the "IExxxxxx" utilities from IBM. Shops all over have opted to replace the original IBM program with SYNCGENR, which is a fully compatible replacement. It is more efficient. FASTGENR is another product from Software Engineering of America that also is a fully compatible replacement. In addition to speed, the basic facilities of IEBGENER have been enhanced. For example, you can copy many files in one step and copy fixed-to-variable block data sets.

With SYNCGENR and IEBGENER competing head-to-head on a 700 track file, SYNCGENR dropped the elapsed time by 8.5 seconds, the CPU time by 1.4 seconds, and the EXCP(s) by 2750. The product also cures a known bug with IEBGENER. Can't beat that.

But, here is something which may not be obvious to these shops, or yours. You can still see a significant savings from blocking and buffering, even if you are using SYNCGENR.

Step GEN01 in Figure 2-4 copies a file to a temporary pass file called &&TEMP. Step GEN02 repeats the same copy but utilizes 255 buffers. Figure 2-5 displays the JES job statistics for both steps.

Notice that the CPU time increased in step GEN02 while there was a nominal ELAPSED time savings. We ran the same job again changing the DCB=BUFNO=255 to DCB=BUFNO=50, and Figure 2-6 contains the results.

The ELAPSED time savings increased with fewer buffers. You may be asking why step GEN01 didn't yield the same results in both instances. This is because of the operating system loading and time-of-day. At different times of the day,

```
//GEN01      EXEC PGM=IEBGENER,REGION=2M
//SYSPRINT   DD SYSOUT=W
//SYSUDUMP   DD SYSOUT=W
//SYSOUT     DD SYSOUT=W
//SYSUT1     DD DSN=PROD.BILL.FILE1,DISP=SHR
//SYSUT2     DD SYSOUT=&&TEMP,
//           DISP=(NEW,PASS),UNIT=WORK,SPACE=(CYL,(1,1))
//SYSIN      DD DUMMY
//GEN02      EXEC PGM=IEBGENER,REGION=2M
//SYSPRINT   DD SYSOUT=W
//SYSUDUMP   DD SYSOUT=W
//SYSOUT     DD SYSOUT=W
//SYSUT1     DD DSN=PROD.BILL.FILE1,DISP=SHR
//SYSUT2     DD SYSOUT=&&TEMP,DCB=BUFNO=255,
//           DISP=(NEW,PASS),UNIT=WORK,SPACE=(CYL,(1,1))
//SYSIN      DD DUMMY
```

Figure 2-4   Sample JCL for Buffering IEBGENER

```
Step    GEN01       TCB=00.00.01.64         program CPU time
                    SRB=00.00.00.25         system CPU time
                    ELAPSED=00.00.27.84     wall clock elapsed time
                    DASD EXCPS=961          physical I/O

Step    GEN02       TCB=00.00.01.75         program CPU time        BUNO=255
                    SRB=00.00.00.28         system CPU time
                    ELAPSED=00.00.23.83     wall clock elapsed time
                    DASD EXCPS               physical I/O
```

Figure 2-5   Results of Running with BUFNO=255

```
Step    GEN01       TCB=00.00.01.58         program cpu time
                    SRB=00.00.00.23         system cpu time
                    ELAPSED=00.00.33.97     wall clock elapsed time
                    DASD EXCPS=961          physical I/O

Step    GEN02       TCB=00.00.01.65         program cpu time        BUFNO=50
                    SRB=00.00.00.22         system cpu time
                    ELAPSED=00.00.22.87     wall clock elapsed time
                    DASD EXCPS               physical I/O
```

Figure 2-6   Results of running with BUFNO=50

you will experience discrepancies in the time it takes to run a program versus another time of day. That is why it is important for you to follow the guidelines listed in section 2.4 when testing.

2.4   Rules for Getting Consistent Test Results

It can be very disconcerting to spend a great deal of time implementing a tuning change, just to find out that the performance degraded. You may say to yourself, "I tested it out, and it generates a great savings!" But, when that ill-fated day arrives, your users disagree with you. Why did the tuning change flop? It could be because you did not have a valid benchmark; or, you didn't run the exact same test against your benchmark; or, the implementation was somewhere entirely different than where testing was conducted. Here are some guidelines for getting consistent test results.

1. Always try to run before and after tuning tests under the same conditions. This can be the same day of the week, same day of the month, and same time of the day.
2. When testing relatively small batch runs or online transaction programs, run several tests and derive an average for cpu, elapsed, I/Os, and DB-Calls. These tests will show more reliable results.

The most helpful tools I have seen for getting good comparison times are STROBE and HIPERSTATION. HIPERSTATION enables you to run the same script 1-to-n times from 1-to-n terminals. HIPERSTATION executes without human error and stresses the applications in a tight window. It's a great tool for testing deadlock scenarios in database applications. Both tools are invaluable to the tuner.

The previous example is a good one for pointing out the tradeoffs of exchanging resources for performance. Buffers use memory and memory management routines in exchange for elapsed time savings. We ultimately discovered that DCB=BUFNO=40 was the ideal number for IEBGENERs. The main problem you will encounter is resistance to changing the buffer settings in the 10,000 JCL streams containing IEBGENER. Two things can aid you in this task. First, build a production supported PROCLIB member, which only requires programmers to supply the PROC name and input/output files. The PROCLIB member can supply the buffering automatically. Second, make the findings of IEBGENER tuning known in your shop with a bulletin publicizing the availability of the new PROCLIB.

Not every run of IEBGENER will benefit from buffering. The key on this change is to make an across-the-board savings. It can't be justified on one small step alone.

2.5   Reblocking Files

Reblocking all your production files to near track sizes will result in an ELAPSED and CPU time savings. ELAPSED times for files that were never optimized can be reduced as much as 80 percent, and CPU times can be reduced up to 40 percent.

These savings are not meager. This is particularly true if you implement the changes to all your production job streams at the same time. You probably will need to initiate an application team request-for-service, or, at least mount a major crusade for this, as JCL changes can take time away from other application requests. Management may just say, "Been there, done that."

You also will need to gather two key pieces of information. Charts (or a tool that computes the best block sizes) for files and a list of all existing file block sizes.

Here are two of the most common record sizes used. LRECL=80 is optimum at BLOCKSIZE=27920, and LRECL=133 is optimum at BLOCKSIZE=27930. I'll bet there are a lot of files using these record sizes in your shop. See Figure 2-7 for a cross reference to optimimum blocksizes.

The second key piece of information to identify when reblocking production files is a complete inventory of all data sets and their block sizes. This information can be found via several methods. Some CATALOG reporting facilities will give comprehensive information. If all your production JCL or *Procedure Library* (PROCLIB) JCL is in a single library, you can use a utility to do a find on the string "LRECL=". This find should get LRECL and BLOCKSIZE at the same time.

```
              BLOCKSIZE FROM BEST TO WORST TRACK UTILIZATION

80-byte records optimum blocksizes


                                       ——3390 Track Utilization——
BLKSIZE  Sample JCL                    %Used BLKs/TRK Bytes/TRK RECs/Tr
 27920   SPACE=(27920,(2,0),RLSE)       99%      2       55840      698
 18400   SPACE=(18400,(3,0),RLSE)       98%      3       55200      690
 13680   SPACE=(13680,(3,0),RLSE)......97%.....4.......54720....684
 10720   SPACE=(10720,(4,0),RLSE)       95%      5       53600      670
  8880   SPACE=(8880,(5,0),RLSE)        95%      6       53280      666
  7520   SPACE=(7520,(6,0),RLSE).......93%.....7.......52640....658
  6480   SPACE=(6480,(7,0),RLSE)        92%      8       51840      648
  5680   SPACE=(5680,(8,0),RLSE)        91%      9       51120      639
  5040   SPACE=(5040,(8,0),RLSE).......89%....10.......50400....630

133-byte records optimum blocksizes


                                       ——3390 Track Utilization——
BLKSIZE  Sample JCL                    %Used BLKs/TRK Bytes/TRK RECs/TRK
 27930   SPACE=(27930,(3,0),RLSE)       99%      2       55860      420 [wes]
best
 18354   SPACE=(18354,(4,0),RLSE)       98%      3       55062      414
 13566   SPACE=(13566,(5,0),RLSE)......96%.....4.......54264....408
 10773   SPACE=(10773,(7,0),RLSE)       96%      5       53865      405
  8778   SPACE=(8778,(8,0),RLSE)        93%      6       52668      396
  7448   SPACE=(7448,(9,0),RLSE).......93%.....7.......52136....392
  6517   SPACE=(6517,(11,0),RLSE)       93%      8       52136      392
  5719   SPACE=(5719,(12,0),RLSE)       91%      9       51471      387
  5054   SPACE=(5054,(14,0),RLSE)......90%....10.......50540....380
```

Figure 2-7 Optimum Blocking Charts

Here is what a string search for "PGM=IEBGENER" looks like using FILE AID from COMPUWARE (see Figure 2-8). This handy utility searches *entire Partitioned Data Set* (PDS) libraries looking for multiple search criteria. You may have this or other tools at your disposal.

As you can see, this information would be great for locating all the IEBGENER steps in production. It can be used to locate many global tuning opportunities in JCL or program source, and the output can be routed to a printer or a dataset for editing.

The same utility that was used to identify a string can be used to change a string. For example, if you wanted to FIND all LRECL=80 and BLOCKSIZE=6160 cards and then change them to LRECL=80 and BLOCKSIZE=27920, here are the File Aid control cards to do so.

```
FIND LRECL=80 ANDFIND BLOCKSIZE=6160

THEN CHANGE 'BLOCKSIZE=6160' 'BLOCKSIZE=27920'
```

Several sets of control cards can be input together. In this way, all the possible block sizes other than 27920 could be changed to 27920, where the record length is 80. Subsequently, all the block sizes are conveniently changed at one time.

Other products exist that specifically address the issue of maintaining shop standards throughout JCL, including block sizes. JOB/SCAN from Diversified Software Systems, Inc., is a good example. The product does JCL validation, enforces standards, makes changes, and reformats JCL for clarity and uniformity. All this can be done under the control of the data center and can be incorporated into migration products to automate the process. This product should be under serious consideration in your shop, if you need these controls.

2.6 DMCL Tuning

Device Media Control Language (DMCL) control block tuning has always presented challenges. Because the DMCL resides below the 16M barrier, shops have had to play a game of doubling up on buffer assignments and even starting additional IDMS/DC regions to work around this limitation. With CA-IDMS release 12.0, the DMCL will finally go 31-bit.

```
Library          :      PROD.PROCLIB
JCL MBR          :          BILLP010
     TEXT    :   //BILLS010    EXEC PGM=IEBGENER,
JCL MBR          :          BILLP020
     TEXT    :   //BILLS020    EXEC PGM=IEBGENER,
     TEXT    :   //BILLS021    EXECEXEC PGM=IEBGENER
JCL MBR          :          BILLP500
     TEXT    :   //BILLS550    EXEC PGM=IEBGENER,
......etc.
```

Figure 2-8 PDS Scan of JCL for IEBGENER

There should be room to properly tune the DMCL, eliminating or reducing buffer conflicts. The result will be fewer I/Os. Release 12.0, at the time this book was written, was gaining acceptance. Here are some basic rules for tuning the buffers.

Buffer pools are broken into page sizes that service database areas with the same page size. In Figure 2-9, you see a display of buffer pool utilization taken from the Buffer Pool Summary Display screen in the CA-IDMS Performance Monitor.

Under Release 10.0 of CA-IDMS, the P10796-BUFF in the diagram may have been the only one you could have defined. There may have been insufficient memory under the 16M line for an additional pool. However, in Releases 12.0 and above, you can break this up into several buffer pools, potentially reducing the number of forced writes. The *forced write count* is the number of times a READ of a database page forced another page in the same buffer pool to be written to disk. This count is an indication of buffer pool contention and can be reduced if more buffer pools are provided.

Another form of DMCL tuning is separating areas into independent files. When several CA-IDMS database areas reside in the same file, a disk head contention can exist. With separate files, the areas and their respective files can be distributed across several disk volumes based upon the load of activity on the volumes. This distribution can improve performance. To determine the activity on a volume, you should look at the file statistics in the JES2 job log for the IDMS/DC region and compare those statistics with the area statistics found in the detail section of the performance monitor buffer display. See Figure 2-10.

```
IDMS/R PM-R10.2        Cullinet Software, Inc. V1              17:03:12.81
CMD->
                                                              Window : 02
                                                              Refresh: 10
02 Buffer I/O Summary
                 Found    Read    Write   Forced  Bcr              Buffer
  Buffer_Name    In_Buf   Count   Count   Write   Waits  #Areas    Pages
_ DRUN-BUFF      166122   5152    6896    182     2      7
_ DMSG-BUFF      42870    1812    1               1      1         3
_ DSCR-BUFF      1        1               1       1      20
_ P6516-BUFF     411690   77992   6597    6497    8      3
_ P4564-BUFF     24841853 426396  191513  42144   623    500
_ P10796-BUFF    55516073 1504257 363721  157008  95     200
_ P27996-BUFF    2644858  68067   65              5      14
```

Figure 2-9 PM—Buffer Pool Summary Display

```
        03 Specific Buffer I/O Detail
                           Found        Read    Write
  File_Name    Area_Name   In_Buf       Count   Count   Buffer_Name

  BILLLOG      BILL-LOG-AREA    588876   39450   13105   P10796-BUFF
  CUSTITEM     CUST-ITEM-AREA  1204913   44140   12762
  CUSTLOG      CUST-LOG-AREA     24946    2341   15
```

Figure 2-10 PM—Buffer File Detail Display

As you can see from Figure 2-10, the BILLLOG and CUSTITEM areas are lumped into the same buffer pool. Because these areas occupy the same physical database file, it could be advantageous to use both of the tuning techniques described in this section of the book. The BILL-LOG-AREA and CUST-ITEM-AREA should get their own files. If we are in transition to release 12.0 of CA-IDMS, they can get their own buffer pools at the same time.

2.7   Fast Access from Allen Systems Group

ASG-Fast Access reduces the elapsed time of CA-IDMS *Central Versions* (CVs), local mode jobs, IDMSAJNL (archive journal), IDMSDUMP (dump facility), IDMSDBAN (database analyzer), IDMSRFWD (roll forward), IDMSRBCK (roll back), RHDCPRLG (print log), IDMSDBL2-3 (database loads), IDMSRSTR (restore), and application load programs, making only JCL modifications.

This utility enables you to define a large buffer pool that extends the capabilities of the DMCL. It also uses track read ahead and write ahead that make sequential database sweeps run much faster—about 75 to 80 percent faster.

The many intricacies of ASG-Fast Access occupy their own manual. The key parameters with their usual settings are shown in Table 2-1.

Four JCL changes must be made to accommodate ASG-Fast Access. The first is a STEPLIB or JOBLIB entry, identifying the fast access control programs. These must get precedence over the usual CA-IDMS facilities. Second is the FIOCNTL control cards defining the files to be buffered and any associated parameters. Third is the FIOSTAT output file for the statistics. Statistics can be turned off by using "DD DUMMY". The last change to the JCL is to increase the region parameter to accommodate the new memory used for buffering. Figure 2-11 is a working example of using ASG-Fast Access with a database sweep progam.

TABLE 2-1   ASG-Fast Access Control Parameters

PARAMETER	PURPOSE
MAXTRKS	Defines the number of buffers to be kept (by track). A Buffer = (Page +8) * Number of Pages/Track
READTRKS	Number of tracks that will read at one time.
ADAPT=ON/OFF/SEQ	ON (recommended setting) will buffer sequential and use database for random. OFF will update the buffers regardless of type of access. SEQ will assume that access is sequential.
WRITECPY=Y	Y causes buffers to be updated as the database is updated.
BUFTIMOT=0	Buffer timeout is off. Never release the allocated buffers. Do not use BUFTMOT on multiprocessor CPU(s).
DD=DDNAME(,parm1=...(,parm-n-)	DDNAME of database file and any parameters.
EXCLUDE	Disable for database files without DD control cards.

```
//STEP1     EXEC PGM=CUSTDUMP,REGION=20M                    ✎    Note #4
//STEPLIB   DD   DSN=IDMSPROD.FASTAC.LOADLIB,DISP=SHR       ✎    Note #1
            DD   DSN=IDMSPROD.CV1.LOADLIB,DISP=SHR
            DD   DSN=IDMSPROD.LOADLIB,DISP=SHR
            DD   DSN=IDMSPROD.SUBSCHEM.LOADLIB,DISP=SHR
            DD   DSN=ISPROD.LOADLIB,DISP=SHR
//CUSTFIL1  DD   DSN=IDMSPROD.CUSTFIL1,DISP=SHR
//CUSTFIL2  DD   DSN=IDMSPROD.CUSTFIL2,DISP=SHR
//FIOSTAT   DD   SYSOUT=*                                   ✎    Note #2
//FIOCNTL   DD   *                                          ✎    Note #3
 EXCLUDE
 ADAPT=OFF
 READTRKS=1
 DD=CUSTFIL1,MAXTRKS=50
 DD=CUSTFIL2,MAXTRKS=50

Changes to JCL:
Note #1: Fast Access Loadlib
Note #2: FIOSTAT DD card
Note #3: FIOCNTL DD card
```

Figure 2-11   ASG-Fast Access with a Database Sweep Program

The output statistics can be interrogated to determine whether the HIT RATIO (number of accesses satisfied from buffer) is 80 percent or higher. Adjusting the parameters can influence the *hit ratio*.

The display messages in Figure 2-12 were generated by ASG-Fast Access. These messages are designed to aid you in customizing MAXTRKS buffer parameters, thus capitalizing on the features of this product.

The block of messages in Figure 2-12 (FIOSTATS), which are taken from the FIOSTATS file, will be repeated for each file for which ASG-Fast Access was engaged. This information can be used to further tweek the parameters and achieve the maximum long-term savings. Often, processing changes based upon the cycle of the week or month. This change in processing can be accommodated by custom tailoring parameters for each cycle. Keep this nonstandard tuning in mind; it is a way to get that extra 10 percent achievable.

Would you put an entire database in memory, if it were feasible? The limitation, of course, is available virtual storage. Well, this tool enables you to do it. But, to be a viable candidate for using this facility, a database must be accessed heavily.

Take a look at the top ten batch database programs and determine whether ASG-Fast Access or another buffering tool will improve performance. Then continue to tweak the tool until maximum performance is obtained. Obviously, a database administrator needs to be involved in the process, and that administrator should already be using a tool like this to run day-to-day database utilities. Contact the vendor for more information on the Fast Load and Fast Sweep features. A list of vendors is in Appendix D.

```
JESLOG Messages....

03.32.33 JOB00655  IEF403I CUSTD0001 - STARTED - TIME=03.32.33
03.48.17 JOB00655+FASTSW 3.0 CUSTFIL1 TRACKING 1414 XA AD=OFF M=00050
R=00001
03.48.17 JOB00655+FASTSW 3.0 CUSTFIL2 TRACKING 1414 XA AD=OFF M=00050
R=00001
03.58.32 JOB00655+FASTSW 3.0 CUSTFIL1 R00: ENGAGED
03.58.33 JOB00655+FASTSW 3.0 CUSTFIL2 R00: ENGAGED
04.22.28 JOB00655+FASTSW 3.0 CUSTFIL1 C00: CLOSED
04.22.28 JOB00655+FASTSW 3.0 CUSTFIL2 C00: CLOSED
04.23.23 JOB00655  $HASP395 CUSTD0001 ENDED


FIOSTAT Messages...

FASTSW   3.0 1414   XA START( 93.040   3:35) END( 93.040    3:48)
JOB=CUSTD001(JOB00655) PROCSTEP=STEP1 STEP=STEP1   PGM=CUSTDUMP
 DD=CUSTFIL1           DSN=IDMSPROD.CUSTFIL1
  VOLSER=PRD108
  DEVICE=DASD
  ALLOCATED BY TRKS        NOT CYLINDER ALIGNED
  TRACKS PER CYL .......   15
  BLOCK SIZE ..........   10796
  BLOCKS PER TRACK .....   5
  BLOCKS ALLOCATED .....   4350
 FIOCNTL:
  ADAPTIVE TRACKING ....   OFF
  MESSAGE LEVEL .......   2
  WRITE COPY ..........   N
 READ  STATISTICS:
  MAX TRACKS ..........   615
  READ TRACKS .........   1
  READ  BUFFER GETMAINS   417
  READ  BUFFER SIZE ..   22526340
  READ  REQUESTS .......   3919     ➥   EXCPS without ASG-Fast Access
                         BDAM  FASTSW   TOTAL
  BLOCKS READ .........   0    2085    2085
  READ  EXCPS .........   0     417    417  ➥  EXCPS with ASG-
 Fast Access
  READ  HIT RATIO ......   89.4          ➥  EXCP efficiency
 WRITE STATISTICS:                      ➥ No Database Updates
  WRITE REQUESTS .......   0
  EXCPS SAVED ..........   3502          ➥ EXCPS reduced
```

Figure 2-12 ASG-Fast Access Output Messages

2.8 Compression Utilities

Some of the compression utilities on the market can help you achieve a space savings without compromising CPU performance.

CA-IDMS Presspack from Computer Associates can be used to achieve a higher level of performance for CA-IDMS database records. If there is a commonality of data, or a repetitive pattern to your data, greater compression can be realized. Give this some thought. If you can get 600 records into the database buffer with a single call, as opposed to 40, imagine the reduction in I/Os.

However, there is a CPU penalty. When the CPU overhead exceeds the savings in EXCP(s) and disk space, it isn't wise to compress your records.

Presspack will evaluate your records for repeating strings of data and save these patterns in a table called the *Data Characteristic Table* (DCT). This information is used to further compress records during real-time access. This is a great product, and you can get 10 percent more compression on records than with the standard DCT used by IDMSCOMP/DCOM programs. I recommend that you evaluate all the heavily used databases in your shop.

The DCT is an assembler translation table (see the sample provided in Figure 2-13) that contains common strings of information and a compact unique replacement string. This translation table maximizes compression while adding a level of encryption.

To better understand the concept, just imagine replacing the string "Customer Support Department" everywhere in a database with a hex value two bytes long like X'CF29'.

2.9   DB-Megabuf Plus from Cogito Limited

CA-IDMS buffering is best accomplished with third-party vendor tools. Here are some products from Cogito Limited that can save the day.

DB-Allocate allows dynamic allocation and deallocation of files from CA-IDMS. This product is particularly useful for maintenance of dictionaries and databases in which 24-hour availability of CV is critical.

DB-Buffer Plus enables you to dynamically manage the use of buffers in CA-IDMS. This product enables you to govern the size of buffers based upon the hit ratio for "finds in buffer," Very useful to tuning the online environment is the ability to change the number of buffers used for a given buffer pool at a given time of day. The reporting of buffer hits by file and area are necessary when using the DB-Megabuf Plus product, making this a partner product.

```
DCT        TITLE ' CUST DATA CHARACTERISTTCS TABLE '
CUSTTBL1 CSECT
DCTID1     DC    C'DCT '
           CRQID
           DC    AL2(LDCT) DCT LENGTH
           DC    X'CF'          DCT CHECK-BYTE
           DC    AL1(8)         NUM OF TABLES
           DC    A(ET1)         ADDR OF 1ST EXP. TABLE
* COMPRESSION TABLE 1
           DC    X'000102AB02AB70563157014001710A7201C300BC01760177'
           DC    X'002F019001850182018301880B89018A0061018C018A018C'
           DC    X'018E018F019401950064019601970198019901A019B019C'
           DC    X'019D01D000FF01A101A201C301B401A5001201A601A701AB'
           DC    X'00D401AC01AC01AE03AE04AF01B007C101D201E201B401A5'
           DC    X'001501C601D701E801A901BA01CC01DC01ED01BE03BF03C0'
...   * COMPRESSION TABLES 2 to 8 etc.
```

Figure 2-13 Presspack DCT Table Example

DB-Synchro makes XA DMCL buffers and dataspaces available to multiple CVs and batch jobs.

DB-EZReorg minimizes downtime during database reorganizations. You unload/reload affected areas while they remain available to users. First a quiesce point is established. An inflight or hot-backup is done, and the active journal is varied. Next, a BCF CLEANUP or IDMSLDEL removes logically deleted records. The DB-EZReorg jobs are run, which perform the reorganization. Finally, a catch-up phase rolls forward any updates using input from the journals and standard DMLs against the reorganized database. The new areas should be backed up and then placed in service. The only outage time is the time needed to take the backup, which is considerably smaller than the reorganization time.

DB-Megabuf Plus gives buffer constraint relief to users of CA-IDMS. With DB-Megabuf Plus, you can allow pools to grow to two gigabytes, and you can place particular database files into ESA dataspaces. The tradeoff is paging rates in MVS.

I'm going to provide you with some examples of using DB-Megabuf Plus, which is, in my mind one of your best tuning opportunities for CA-IDMS. DB-Megabuf Plus implementation involves preparing three tables that are linked with the IDMSDBIO module. First of these is the COXAMEG table, which is used to assign buffer pools to override the normal DMCL buffer pools. In Figure 2-14 BUFMAX is used to assign the number of pages in buffer pool. BUFRQST is the number at system startup.

Figure 2-15 shows you what JCL changes are necessary to implement this tool into your production CA-IDMS region. As you can see, it is simple to use. Now let's examine the results of using this enlarged buffer pool.

When using MODE=DUAL, DB-Megabuf provides shutdown statistics that show the effectiveness of simulated buffers alongside actual ones (see Figure 2-16). This is useful in determining the overall effectiveness of your COXACTL buffer assignments.

```
#COXAMEG TYPE=IDMS,ENTRY=DMCL,NAME=PRD5IDMS,POOL=DUAL,        X
        LOC=ANY,MODE=SYSTEM                        ➷ CV Region Buffers
#COXAMEG TYPE=IDMS,ENTRY=BUFFER,NAME=BUFF-4564,              X
        BUFMAX=300,BUFRQST=200
#COXAMEG TYPE=IDMS,ENTRY=BUFFER,NAME=BUFF-10796,            X
        BUFMAX=300,BUFRQST=200
#COXAMEG TYPE=IDMS,ENTRY=DMCL,NAME=BILLDMCL,POOL=OS,        X
        LOC=ANY,MODE=LOCAL,JRNLBUFF=NO             ➷ Local Mode Use
#COXAMEG TYPE=IDMS,ENTRY=BUFFER,NAME=BUFF-10796,            X
        BUFMAX=300,BUFRQST=30
#COXAMEG TYPE=DMCL,POOL=OS,                                 X
        BUFMAX=1000,BUFRQST=100                    ➷ Catch All Pool
#COXAGEG ENTRY=LAST,                                        X
        TYPE=IDMS                                  ➷ End of Table
```

Figure 2-14 DB-Megabuf Plus COXAMEG Table Example

```
//IDMS5      EXEC PGM=IDMS5,PARM='S=05', REGION=100M
//STEPLIB    DD  DSN=IDMSPROD.DBMEGBUF.LOADLIB,DISP=SHR
//           DD  DSN=IDMSPROD.LOADLIB,DISP=SHR
//CDMSLIB    DD  DSN=IDMSPROD.CV5.LOADLIB,DISP=SHR
//           DD  DSN=IDMSPROD.DBMEGBUF.LOADLIB,DISP=SHR
//           DD  DSN=IDMSPROD.LOADLIB,DISP=SHR
```

Figure 2-15   DB-Megabuf Production CV JCL Changes

```
Jes Log Messages

... at startup of CV
03.09.46 JOB00394  IDMS CO999221L COXADBIO - DB-MEGABUF LOADED

... at shutdown of CV
22.01.27 JOB00394  IDMS DC201003 V5 T1 IDMS CENTRAL VERSION 5 SHUTDOWN
22.01.27 JOB00394  CO999211 BUFFER SIMULATOR    (SIMULATED FOLLOWED BY ACTUAL)
22.01.27 JOB00394  CO999211 BUFFER NAME    # PAGE RE        # I/O    SIZE(K)
22.01.27 JOB00394  CO999212 BUFF-4564     1041049         235609    2229      ☜ Simulated I/O
22.01.27 JOB00394  CO999212                               440631    196       ☜ Actual I/O
22.01.27 JOB00394  CO999212 BUFF-10796    58504091        398822    5271
22.01.27 JOB00394  CO999212                              1701462    264
22.01.27 JOB00394  CO999212 BUFF-7548      288637          29039    3686
22.01.27 JOB00394  CO999212                                31143    184
22.01.27 JOB00394  CO999212 BUFF-27996     105748           1398    273
22.01.27 JOB00394  CO999212                                21533    273
22.01.27 JOB00394  CO999212 IXBUFF-10796   153412           2147    1054
22.01.27 JOB00394  CO999212                                 9842    158
22.01.27 JOB00394  CO999212 IXBUFF-27996   683285            827    2734
22.01.27 JOB00394  CO999212                               194569    164
22.01.28 JOB00394  CO999212 IXBUFF-4564    130974            688    446
22.01.28 JOB00394  CO999212                                 5984    98
22.01.28 JOB00394  CO999213 TOTAL         60907196        668530    15693
22.01.28 JOB00394  CO999213      .                       2405164   1337
22.03.12 JOB00394  IDMS DC200021 V5 T1 TOTAL-RUS:9287  NORML-COMP:9248
22.03.12 JOB00394  IDMS DC200021 V5 T1 TOT-EXT-RU:4765  NORML-COMP:4739
```

Figure 2-16   DB-Megabuf CV Message Output

The best way to achieve maximum effectiveness is to tune the buffers for the peak periods of online usage (see Figure 2-17). You can display similar statistics at different times of the day using the online command xast. If you do this hourly, you can assimilate the information for a table showing PAGE REQUESTS and I/O by hour (see Figure 2-18). This table becomes the basis for establishing buffer parameters to be used throughout the day.

Using the information gathered in the table in Figure 2-18, you may establish higher buffers during three periods. The daytime hours from 6:00 to 18:00 would have generally higher buffer assignments. The two periods from 07:00–09:00 and 14:00–16:00 would use higher buffer assignments for BUFF-4564. The result should be a reduction in the CA-IDMS I/O for these periods.

DB-Megabuf Plus (Release 3) has been improved to include a sequential *prefetch* option. This option enables you to optimize sequential processing, in much the same way that ASG-Fast Access operates. The advantages are pri-

```
DB-MEGABUF (R2.0)        ***  SIMULATOR STATISTICS  ***        V0005 10:00:01 94.04
------------------------------------------------------------------------------------
BUFFER-NAME     PAGE REQ      BSIM I/O      SIZE(K)      IDMS I/O      SIZE(K
------------------------------------------------------------------------------------
BUFF-4564       16,864,191    370,713       4,457        400,150       2,228
IXBUFF-4564     3,505,012     1,699         4,457        2,211         4,457
BUFF-10796      18,088,538    5,014         21,085       37,013        7,907
IXBUFF-10796    1,728,275     5,036         2,108        6,744         1,054
------------------------------------------------------------------------------------
GRAND TOTAL     401,860,016   382,462       32,107       446,118    15,646
------------------------------------------------------------------------------------
```

Figure 2-17 XAST Online Buffer Usage Display

```
      Buffer Name    T.O.D   IDMS I/O
      BUFF-4564      06:00     8,000
                     07:00    11,000        ⬲
                     08:00    13,000        ⬲    Peak Period 1
                     09:00    19,000        ⬲
                     10:00     7,000
                     11:00     4,000
                     12:00     3,000
                     13:00     9,000
                     14:00    21,000        ⬲
                     15:00    25,000        ⬲    Peak Period 2
                     16:00    11,000        ⬲
                     17:00     8,000
                     18:00     4,000
```

Figure 2-18   Prime Time Buffer Tuning Table

marily discernible in batch and utility processing of whole database areas and files. This is where the #COXASEQ table is used.

HOT SEQUENTIAL PREFETCH FEATURES

- Full track writes of records for local mode jobs
- Automatic release of buffers if not used for a specific time
- Buffers are not used until needed
- Places the whole database in memory or into a dataspace shared by multiple CV(s)

Remember back in Chapter 1, when we began our tuning mission. We determined that several programs could be targeted for tuning. One of those programs was BILLBAT9, which was experiencing high cpu and elapsed times, as well as lots of EXCPS. Further investigation has now shown that BILLBAT9 is an CA-IDMS database program issuing a large number of *random* calls for database records. Because it runs in LOCAL mode, we are going to try using DB-Megabuf Plus with the program. See Figures 2-19 and 2-20.

Figure 2-20 shows the results of program BILLPGM9 running with the aid of DB-Megabuf Plus. The pages requested from the buffer were 171,345, and

```
//JOBLIB    DD   DSN=IDMSPROD.DBMEGBUF.LOADLIB,DISP=SHR
//          DD   DSN=IDMSPROD.PROGRAM.LOADLIB,DISP=SHR
//          DD   DSN=IDMPROD.CV5.LOADLIB,DISP=SHR
//          DD   DSN=IDMSPROD.LOCALSS.LOADLIB,DISP=SHR
......
//BILLS010  EXEC PGM=BILLBAT9,REGION=90M    ☜ Extra Region
//STATOUT   DD   SYSOUT=*
//COXACTL   DD   *                          ☜ Megabufs Overrides
  COXATAB=COXLTAB9                          ☜ Customized Table for this program
  COXAMEG=COXLMEG9                          ☜ Customized buffer table
  COXASEQ=COXLSEQ9                          ☜ Customized seq pre-fetch table
```

Figure 2-19   DB-Megabuf Plus JCL Fragments for Local Mode Program

```
03.56.24 JOB00813  $HASP373 BILLJB09 STARTED - INIT 3 - CLASS P
03.49.27 JOB00813  +IDMS CO999221L COXADBIO  - DB-MEGABUF LOADED
03.49.27 JOB00813  +IDMS CO999201L COXAPOOL - BUFFER INITIALISATION COMPLETE
03.49.27 JOB00813  +IDMS CO999204L COXAPOOL - BUFFER POOL SIZE:    8396K
04.09.12 JOB00813  +CO999211 BUFFER SIMULATOR (SIMULATED FOLLOWED BY ACTUAL)
04.09.12 JOB00813  +CO999211 BUFFER NAME    # PAGE REQ    # I/O    SIZE(K)
04.09.12 JOB00813  +CO999212 BUFF-4564        36626        13       2229
04.09.12 JOB00813  +CO999212                               13       2229
04.09.12 JOB00813  +CO999212 BUFF-10796       41094        9685     3163
04.09.12 JOB00813  +CO999212                               9685     3163
04.09.12 JOB00813  +CO999212 IXBUFF-27996     93625        29332    2734
04.09.12 JOB00813  +CO999212                               29332    2734
04.09.12 JOB00813  +CO999213 TOTAL           171345        39030    8126
04.09.12 JOB00813  +CO999213                               39030    8126
```

Figure 2-20   Output from Local Mode DB-Megabuf Run

the actual I/Os were 39,030, which is roughly a 4:1 ratio. The actual number of I/Os before using DB-Megabuf Plus were 73,010, which is roughly a 2:1 ratio. The utility has cut the I/Os in half and the elapsed and CPU dramatically. In conclusion, this utility is worth having and implementing fully.

2.10   CA-IDMS Central Version Versus Local Mode and Mixed Mode Processing

A quick run down on these types of processing is in order. Most shops already use these, but they may not have fully implemented them. Remember that local mode is ideal for retrieval-only processing in batch. Mixed mode, which binds a run-unit for updates and then uses a separate run-unit for retrieval-only processing, is harder to implement and maintain. The savings shown in Figure 2-21 indicates that large savings are in order when running in local mode—approximately 40 percent.

Central version mode is detectable when: the "`//SYSCTL DD DSN=IDMSPROD.CV1.SYSCTL`" DD statement is present in the jobstep, or, if the IDMSOPTI module (CV=YES mode) has been linked with the application program. To run in local mode, the "`//SYSCTL DD DUMMY`" statement must be provided, or you must link

Jobname	Processing Mode	Records Processed	Elapsed Time
BILLJOB1	CV	27,090	1.20 min
BILLJOB1	LOCAL	30,520	0.72 min
BILLJOB2	CV	119,700	1.18 min
BILLJOB2	LOCAL	122,200	0.45 min
		Savings:	1.21 min

Figure 2-21   Sample Statistics for Central Version Versus Local Mode

the IDMSOPTI (CV=NO mode) into the application program. You also must supply the database, journal, and SYSJRNL DD statements in the JCL. The journals can be dummied out if you will not be using them for recovery. Use discretion, however. If you don't have backups before local mode updates are performed and the journals are dummied, then you do not have a valid path to perform recoveries.

CV mode processing sends requests for database records through the CA-IDMS SVC, where the CV region will service them. This is a single-threaded operation, and if lots of CV mode programs are executing concurrently, they can experience degradation. Also, the overhead of maintaining CONCURRENCY (record locking) adds to the cost. That is why running local mode does not have as long a run-time.

Mixed mode is more complicated than local mode processing. You need to build a driver program that binds multiple run-units. It is possible to have multiple run-units open concurrently or to have just one open at a time. Remember that the cost of binding a run-unit is high, so you will not want to perform the operation for every record in an input file.

2.11   VS Cobol II SYSPRINT Tuning

If you look at a pie chart of the distribution of processing in a data center, you may see that the percentage for development and testing outweighs production. The constant flow of requests for changes to existing applications drives this activity. Most of the overhead is associated with testing. There is a simple but effective change that can be made to VS Cobol II compiles to reduce EXCP(s). This change is the reblocking of the SYSPRINT file. The creation of the SYSPRINT file is usually responsible for a third of the EXCP(s) in a compile.

In the VS Cobol II compile step, you have the option of assigning your output in the various ways shown in Figure 2-22. The results will always look identical. However, the processing expended is very different, as Figure 2-23 portrays.

As this figure shows, you can specify SYSOUT or a data set to be the target of SYSPRINT output and still get the savings, as long as you remember to use

```
Option 1:  //SYSPRINT  DD  SYSOUT=*
Option 2:  //SYSPRINT  DD  SYSOUT=*,DCB=BUFNO=100
Option 3:  //SYSPRINT  DD  DSN=PROD.COMPILE.BILLPGM1,
           //              DISP=(NEW,CATLG,DELETE),
           //              UNIT=TEST,
           //              DCB=(RECFM=FBA,LRECL=133,BLKSIZE=27930),
           //                   SPACE=(27930,(500,50),RLSE)
Option 4:  //SYSPRINT  DD  SYSOUT=*,
           //              DCB=(RECFM=FBA,LRECL=133,BLKSIZE=27930,BUFNO=200)
```

Figure 2-22   Different VS Cobol II SYSPRINT Options

Option	TCB (CPU)	SRB(CPU)	ELAPSED	EXCP(s)	
1	10.01 sec	00.77 sec	07.46.06 min	4,389	
2	10.21 sec	00.91 sec	08.11.11 min	4,390	
3	09.07 sec	00.53 sec	03.08.38 min	4,653	☜ **optimum**
4	09.83 sec	00.72 sec	03.51.69 min	4,389	

Figure 2-23   VS Cobol II SYSPRINT Output from Job in Figure 2-22

blocking and buffering on the SYSPRINT file. This simple change, when multiplied across all the compiles in a shop, represents a significant savings.

2.12   Programmer Workbench

Your shop has probably implemented some ISPF Panels to expedite compiles. These panels are usually hit heavily. You can do a few things to speed compiles and at the same time reduce the overhead of general-purpose workbenches:

- Use DCB=BUFNO=nn to give buffers to all files in all steps of JCL that are using more than 100 EXCPS.

- Create user selection switches that will limit the number of steps which get added to JCL based upon the need. For example, you have three available preprocessors and two reporting steps. The default may be to just run the necessary preprocessors. The additional reporting steps would require the programmer to select them from the panel.

- Definitely use the SYSPRINT tuning option described in section 2.10 of this chapter.

- A panel option to "OPTIMIZE like production" is preferable. This option causes the VS Cobol II compile step to use the optimize option. Programmers may want to determine offsets like in production or get run-times like in production. Try to mimic production by default.

- A panel option to use the AMODE=31 option of VS Cobol II will cause the programmers to become familiar with 31-bit storage in their programs.

This is one way to enforce the use of 31-bit addressing while transitioning off the old OS/VS Cobol compiler.

2.13 PDSFAST

PDSFAST from Software Engineering of America is a product from which you can benefit. If you already use it in your shop for CICS, IMS, and DB2 library compression, you may consider implementing it into places where compile steps do similar work.

PDSFAST will give you an 80–90 percent improvement over IEBCOPY and TSO foreground issued COMPRESS/TSOCOPY commands.

2.14 Buffering and Compression Tools for DB2

Not long ago, we mentioned that there were some tools to do sequential prefetch (read ahead) into the buffer for CA-IDMS. Well, DB2 Release 2 has this as a built-in feature. For DB2 to use the feature, a table or index must require a scan and be at least 40 pages in size. DB2 will read from 32 to 40 pages and then begin using sequential prefetch. The performance will vary depending upon the number of available buffers in the pool.

DB2 Release 3 has an enhanced buffer manager allowing 60 buffer pools, hiperpools, and some new commands for managing buffers.

Extended Buffer Manager (XBM) is available from BMC Software. High-speed memory caching techniques eliminate I/Os.

Capacity Plus for DB2 from Softworks compresses DB2 databases up to 85 percent while improving system throughput.

Also available for DB2 are **Data Packer for DB2** from BMC Software, **DCC-Compact** from Tone Software Corporation, and **Infopak** from Infotel Corporation.

2.15 DB2 Rel 3 Hiperpools

In addition to the virtual pool that existed in Release 2, DB2 now supports a hiperpool (example in Figure 2-24). A one-to-one relationship exists between these two pools. Effectively, you cannot define a hiperpool without a corresponding virtual pool. Database pages are moved between the pools using a most recent used and least recent used algorithm. A page can only exist in one of the two types of pools at any time. Efficiency is greatly enhanced with the addition of hiperpools. This works a little like the multilevel caching we will show you later in this book.

A hiperpool is made up from 1-to-*n* *Expanded Storage Only* (ESO) MVS/ESA hiperspaces. Hiperspaces can be no larger than two gigabytes, and hiperpools can be a maximum of eight gigabytes. Just like traditional paging, these hiperpools move data in 4K pages.

Hiperpools should be defined with CASTOUT = YES. This means that MVS can steal pages from the pool when it needs them. Specifying NO could result in an extended storage shortage error.

Even though Release 3 allows for 50 4K buffer pools and 10 32K buffer pools, I still recommend that a single BP0 global buffer pool be used. This is the most efficient for the buffer manager. There may be an exception in which additional buffers for independent highvolume applications are justified.

With the addition of the DISPLAY BUFFERPOOL BP1 DETAIL command, you can obtain statistics on sequential prefetch, dynamic prefetch, list prefetch, and ADMF activity. Using the LIST and LSTATS keywords of the DISPLAY BUFFERPOOL command provides a cross-reference of tablespaces and index spaces to buffer pools.

With the extension of buffering within Release 3, DB2 now incorporates a state-of-the-art mechanism for providing faster table access than is used in other database management systems with their respective buffering products. I expect that this will add some lifetime to the DB2 mainframe engines that will propel data to end users. This adds credence to the concept of mainframe data servers for PC-based users in the future.

2.16   Strobe Rel 9.2 LSR Pool Statistics

The new release of Strobe provides another way to obtain hiperspace buffer usage and *Local Shared Resource* (LSR) pool statistics. In addition, reports show CI/CA ratios and the number of VSAM index levels.

2.17   MVS VIO (Virtual I/O)

Sometimes, *Virutal I/O* (VIO) is the best way to get throughput. The technique involves copying a database file or sequential file into memory where it can be accessed with the same file access methods used while on disk. The difference,

```
ALTER BUFFERPOOL BP1

VPSIZE 400              ┅     virtual pool buffers
VPSEQT 40               ┅     virtual pool sequential threshold
VPPSEQT 40              ┅     parallel sequential threshold
VDWQT 200               ┅     virtual deferred write threshold
HPSIZE 10000            ┅     hiperpool buffers
HPSEQT 1000             ┅     hiperpool sequential threshold
DWQT 200                ┅     deferred write threshold
CASTOUT YES
```

Figure 2-24   Creating a Hiperpool

Strobe Rel 9.2 Reports

REPORT	TUNING INFORMATION
VSAM LSR POOL STATISTICS	READS/WRITES/STR NO/HIPERSPACE
DATASET CHARACTERISTICS SUPPLEMENT	SMS DATA/CI-CA RATIO/INDEX LEVELS/FREESPACE
CPU USAGE BY DL/1 REQUEST	IMS CALL CPU

of course, is no disk access overhead. This technique works for relatively small files and should not be abused. Too many concurrent jobs using this facility will overload the operating system. Unlike other resources, there is no throttle to use when tuning VIO. If you overload it, online systems will suffer poor response.

In Figure 2-25 the CA-IDMS scratch database area is initialized using VIO. It then is passed to the CA-IDMS CV startup JCL. The scratch area can be used in this fashion because there is no need to perform database recovery during restart. Scratch area updates are considered transient. This same technique can be used to build temporary in-storage database files, which are used by subsequent job steps for loading, update, and retrieval. You must design around job failures, which will require reloading the database area. Again, VIO files are very useful in situations in which the number of EXCPS normally would be very high and in which recovery is not a major concern. For example, you could build a VIO file to hold stock exchange quotes. The data would be viewable online. Then after several minutes of viewing, you may read the VIO file and flush the information to a DASD based database. In the event of a system failure, you could refresh your tables to within minutes of the crash.

In Figure 2-26, VIO is used to hold a sequential data file with all the ZIP codes in the United States. Steps following ZIP1 can access the file and scan it quickly using randomized or binary-searching algorithms. There will be no EXCP(s) while retrieving from the loaded VIO file.

2.18 CA-IDMS Page Sizes for 3390

Figure 2-27 has a quick reference for 3390 page sizes. The correct page size will utilize the best possible paging under MVS.

```
//INITSCR   EXEC PGM=IDMSINIT,REGION=4M
//STEPLIB   DD DSN=IDMSPROD.CV5.LOADLIB,DISP=SHR
//DSCRDB    DD DSN=&&DSC5,
//            DISP=(NEW,PASS,DELETE),
//            UNIT=VIO,SPACE=(2676,(10000,0)),
//            DCB=(RECFM=FB,LRECL=2676,BLKSIZE=2676)
//SYSLST    DD SYSOUT=*
//SYSIPT    DD *
PROCESS=FILE,DMCL=PRODDM05
FILE=DSCRDB
```

Figure 2-25 VIO for CA-IDMS Scratch Area

```
//ZIP1      EXEC PGM=LOADZIP1,REGION=20M
//STEPLIB   DD DSN=PROD.ZIP.LOADLIB,DISP=SHR
//ZIPTBL    DD DSN=&&ZIP1,DISP=(NEW,PASS,DELETE),
//            UNIT=VIO,SPACE=(CYL,(100,0),RLSE),
//            DCB=(RECFM=FB,LRECL=69,BLKSIZE=27945)
//SYSOUT    DD SYSOUT=*,DCB=BUFNO=50
//SYSPRINT  DD SYSOUT=*,DCB=BUFNO=50
```

Figure 2-26 VIO for ZIP CODE/STATE/CITY Memory Table

```
33,390 tracks/3390 drive   2226 cylinders/3390 drive   56,700 bytes/track
```

Page_Size	Pages/Track	Bytes/Track	Track_Util	Pages/Gigabyte
27,996	2	55,992	98.75%	35,296
18,452	3	55,356	97.62%	52,944
13,680	4	54,720	96.50%	70,592
10,796	5	53,980	95.20%	88,240
8,906	6	53,436	94.24%	105,988
7,548	7	52,836	93.18%	123,536
6,516	8	52,128	91.93%	141,184
5,724	9	51,516	90.85%	158,832

Figure 2-27   Optimum CA-IDMS Page Sizes for 3390

2.19 ESCON Tape Drive

ESCON stands for *Enterprise System Connection*. It is the protocol for a fiber optic link between a mainframe and storage devices. You must have the right processor to use this protocol. For example, the IBM ES/9000 with MVS/ESA (Operating System) 3.1.0 is supported.

In the ESCON hardware world, the control unit is within the tape drive. A fiber optic cable goes from the drive to the channel. The drive costs little more than a standard drive, when compared with the batch execution window problems it can solve.

Customers report varying percentages of performance improvement; most are dramatic. It is not uncommon to see 30–40 percent improvement in tape activity, for example. And, when used specifically to improve full-volume backups, the savings can be 2:1 for elapsed time. CPU utilization seems to show minute improvements.

3

PC Files and Buffers

3.1 Obvious Tuning Opportunities

Before we examine the ways to improve I/O performance with file and buffer management, I think we should look at the most obvious methods. For example, hardware upgrades.

PROCESSORS

The processor is the most important facet of tuning PC file access. The engine speed and scalability determines the limit of your processing power. Did you know that a 200MHz Pentium nets only about a 5 percent boost over a 166MHz one? The rest is spent on other components. A P6 processor utilizes new features like processing stages, three instructions/clock cycle, and lots of L2/L3 cache memory and process decoders to avoid stalls. The Pentium Pro is better than a standard Pentium. The AMD-K6 233MHz is even faster than the Pentium Pro (using Winstone scale). What most people don't understand is that slower inputs and outputs degrade a high-end processor. Specifically, the 66MHz memory bus, the <33MHz PCI bus, and that old disk drive or graphics card. Consequently, the motherboard, supporting chip sets, and peripherals play a big role in performance. Also, choose the zero-wait state for better internal caching.

What is MMX? *MMX* is a class of new multimedia enabled processors. They use an extended instruction set with 57 more instructions. The instructions will manipulate video, audio, and graphical data more efficiently. Most noticeable is loop processing of this sort of data. A new process, called, *Single Instruction Multiple Data* (SIMD) will reduce compute-intensive loops. If it isn't already obvious, software manufacturers must recode their offerings using the new instructions in order to see any benefit from MMX technology. After they do this, you can expect faster multimedia and communications applications, provided you own an MMX CPU.

Symmetric Multi-Processors (SMP) come in boxes with 1, 2, 4, 8, 12, or more processors. *Massively Parallel* (MPP) machines can have thousands of processors. Clustering is another type of multiprocessor/server arrangement that we discuss in detail in other chapters. These can all increase raw processing power. Buying enough processor power never seems to be a limitation. High-end client/server machines today can handle in excess of 40,000 concurrent users.

DISK DRIVES

A 4 ms (millisecond) track-to-track disk access time is much better than 12 ms. You should evaluate the drive market and find the drives with the highest performance. More disk heads are better than less because each head can be positioned independently. Random and sequential access times are nice for initial comparisons. But, the real bottom line is the rate of data transfer on the PC bus. EISA is in high-end machines. Avoid VL-Bus/PCI combinations that can penalize performance.

There also is Ultra SCSI. Wow, I like Ultra SCSI. Companies like Source Computer GmbH, Iwill Corporation, and Giga-Byte Technology Co., Ltd., make motherboards with on-board Ultra-wide SCSI controllers and RAID port for incomparable performance.

Your next step after SCSI drives may be RAID controllers. Several storage systems on the market work with Windows NT, Sun, DEC Alpha, and RS/6000 machines. These controllers use Ultra SCSI and Fibre Channels to achieve data throughput up to 200M/sec.

GRAPHICS CARDS

How about a 128-bit graphics accelerator with 4M of VRAM or MDRAM to make monitor access scream? The Magic F/X 256 is a graphics accelerator that features embedded DRAM. Embedded memory does away with circuitry with inherent bottleneck problems.

LANS

In the world of LAN servers, often a memory upgrade is all that is needed to improve performance, but hardware and protocols make giant differences. We discuss lots of variations on this theme in the Chapters on Sybase, Oracle, and Microsoft SQL Server.

BUSES

There are several things to concern yourself with when evaluating bus speeds: The basic type of bus (eg. ISA, EISA, PCI); serial and parallel port speeds; and DMA data transfer.

When shopping for an EISA motherboard, keep your eyes peeled for 75MHz buses. They outperform the traditional 66MHz Pentium ones by 14 percent. Bus Mastered PCI slots are best. Here are some basic numbers to reference:

- ISA   10M/sec
- EISA   66M/sec
- IBM Micro Channel   160M/sec
- PCI   264M/sec

DMA bus speed is equally important. For example, the VIA VP2 chipset pushes hard disk transfers 50 percent faster—up to 33M/sec.

The new Microsoft PC97 specification is here to replace serial devices with the *Universal Serial Bus* (USB), which enables you to daisychain 127 devices, all 10 times faster than the fastest serial port ones. Some motherboards support this capability and a power management capability, also part of the PC97 specification.

TAPE BACKUP

Sony's *Advanced Intelligent Tape* (AIT) uses 8mm tape cartridges, each holding 23G of uncompressed data and a memory chip onboard. The chip stores the tape directory, negating the need to rewind to the beginning of the tape, where most units keep their directory. This dramatically speeds up access to files on the tape. AIT cartridges will work only with Sony SDX-300 drives boasting a 3-to-6 Mbps data transfer rate.

MEMORY

A lot of people think that the CPU is the biggest performance gain for a workstation or server. But, when it comes to raw power for investment dollar, memory beats everything. Recent drops in memory prices make it a very viable solution.

For conventional DOS-based PCs, overall performance equates to how much low DOS memory can be had. Through the use of MS DOS 6.2 and QUALITAS' 386MAX memory managers, up to 759K of available DOS memory can be obtained before loading network drivers. Judicious memory management and loading only the TSRs that are absolutely necessary will provide the best overall speed increase for all applications short of buying a high-end processor (the 64-bit P7 is on the drawing board). Of course, 40ns (nanoseconds) RAM is better than 70ns.

If you don't have, or can't afford, a memory manager, you can always try to do the best you can with the LOADHIGH= (AUTOEXEC.BAT) and DEVICEHIGH= (CONFIG.SYS) parameters of DOS. These have a lot of bearing on the available low DOS memory. Here are some obvious things that should be loaded HIGH. The order in which these are defined can greatly impact the full utilization of lower memory and the upper memory block.

AUTOEXEC.BAT	CONFIG.SYS
LOADHIGH=C:\DOS\DOSKEY.COM	DEVICEHIGH=C:\WINDOWS\MOUSE.SYS /Y on
	DEVICEHIGH=C:\corel drivers

RAM technology has evolved to the point where new changes are arriving faster than the market can cope with. Older types like *Random Access Memory* (RAM), *Dynamic* (DRAM), *Static RAM* (SRAM), SIMMS, and SIPPS have given way to the next couple generations of chips. Fast Page MODE (FPM) DRAM is faster in that it can search a page of memory quickly. *Extended Data Output* (EDO) is even faster than fast-page-mode DRAM. EDO can handle recursive calls more quickly. EDO memory enables the memory controller to save time by cutting out a 10ms wait period that is normally required before issuing the next address. This equates to a 10 percent processor speed up. Standard EDO memory comes in 60ns and 70ns speeds. *Burst EDO* (BEDO) is an extension of EDO that moves more data back to the CPU, in case it is the next requested memory chunk. Finally, there are the most recent synchronous memory series of chips, like *Synchronous DRAM* (SDRAM) and *Synchronous Graphics RAM* (SGRAM). These will synchronize with the system clock to optimize their speed. They are very fast in comparison to their predecessors.

Today's power-hungry workstations and servers need the punch that the new memory types offer. The best available memory types are DIMM and SDRAM, which both require that the motherboard sport DIMM memory slots. These slots are just now (vintage Summer, 1997) becoming standard. This is a major speed up, for almost no extra cost-per-M. DIMM memory transfers data at 64-bits (twice the rate of SIMMS). For example, the DIMM 3.3v Burst EDO (168 pin; 60ns) is available, as is the SDRAM 3.3v Unbuffered memory (168 pin) that runs at 10ns. The bottom line is that your motherboard and the memory are key factors to performance. A wise selection should include DIMM slots, SDRAM, and 512K or more of pipelined burst L2 cache (write-back and synchronized).

OPERATING SYSTEM SOFTWARE

You can't ignore your operating system when matching hardware and software. Your operating system determines your ultimate limitations for memory and paging. Windows 95, Windows NT, OS/2, and assorted UNIX operating systems can eliminate some of the traditional memory problems of good old DOS. Each has quirks that enable them to use, or not use, special features found within latest chip and board technology.

There are going to be specific areas of tuning that you will have to evaluate on your own. This book could never contain all of the possible tuning opportunities. For example, we won't spend time evaluating printer tuning. We make only these two suggestions. First, use a print spooler device. Don't let your system carry the burden of printing. Second, select a motherboard with a

EPP/ECP printer port. It is 10 times faster (doubles data transfer rates) than previously available parallel printer ports and can speed printing from supporting printers, like the HP LaserJet 5se (IEEE 1284 ECP compliance).

There is some wisdom in selecting hardware with a longer life-time. A good example is the wave of CD-ROM purchasing. For about the same price, you can get a rewritable optical drive that is as speedy as the fastest standalone CD-ROM unit (24x), has a 100 times longer media lifetime, and holds twice as much information. A rewritable optical is good for almost anything. Try using wisdom in leveraging your investments. But, don't write off CD-ROMS.

We usually assume that a CD-ROM is good only for taking delivery of some software, installing it, or putting a small library online. But, with the CD-ROM Network System from Procom Technology, you can hook-up 6–63 CD-ROMS with 10ms access. That is extremely fast. I can imagine a lawyers' library, or medical journals online, using that kind of technology.

Software setup modifications are a key method for making the best use of the hardware you have purchased. In the following sections, we take a look at standard DOS and Windows 3.x settings. In other chapters, we discuss settings for high-end computer systems, like servers.

3.2 FILES=, FCBS=, and File Management

The number of allowable open files that DOS can handle is 255. The number you select for your system can influence overall system performance, but only slightly. I would recommend that you select higher numbers for this parameter in the CONFIG.SYS file. If you are coding using CA-Clipper, you will need a few additional unseen file handles. If you are going to be using a maximum of 40 database and index files, then you may have a setting like FILES=60 (Note: the settings mentioned in this section are for DOS. See Chapter 9 for Windows 95).

Locating files on drives is more important than the number of FILE handles defined. The PATH command enables you to define the order of look up for files. The heaviest used files should be found first in the path search. Here's an example.

```
PATH=C:\WINDOWS;C:\DOS;C:\QEMM
```

If you have a series of database files that are opened and closed thousands of times in batch processing, you may want to have your path definition look like this:

```
PATH=D:\BILLING;C:\WINDOWS;C:\DOS;C:\QEMM
```

You should make every attempt to cluster your database files according to their usage. You can dedicate a physical drive to a given application or applications. To improve index performance, try this idea. Put the database on one drive and the index on another drive. If these are physical devices, then the heads will remain positioned based upon the last-or-prior access. This prevents repositioning or rotational delay times. See the following:

```
D:\BILLING\BILL.DBF
E:\BILLING\BILL.NTX or BILL.NDX or BILL.MDX
F:\BILLING\BILL2.NTX or BILL2.NDX or BILL2.MDX
```

3.3   BUFFERS=n,m (where n=number and m=number in secondary cache)

Set buffers equal to the FILES=parameter plus 4. I use BUFFERS=35 with no secondary because I have a special optical drive that won't support the second operand. However, you should keep FILES= and BUFFERS= large enough for database applications.

3.4   STACKS=n,s (where n=number and s=size in bytes)

Set stacks arbitrarily high, which will prevent any stack errors. These do not utilize enough memory on today's systems to cause problems. I prefer to use a setting of STACKS 8,256 for my CA-Clipper applications.

3.5   SMARTDRV Tuning

DOS 5 comes with SMARTDrive version 3.1. Windows 3.1 comes with SMART-Drive version 4.0 that supports more hard drives. SMARTDrive's caching routines are superior to RAM Disks when tested. Figure 3-1 shows the SMART-Drive command parameters, and Figure 3-2 has the best tips for using SMARTDrive version 4.0.

```
SMARTDRIVE aaaa bbbb /E:cccc /B:dddd  drive-/+ /R /C
```

aaaa	Size of primary cache buffer in kilobytes. Make as large as possible for batch processing and try 512 for Windows work.
bbbb	Size that Windows can reduce the cache to get memory. Make this 256K less than the cache size or equal to the cache size.
/E:	Size in bytes that cache moves at a time. Use 8192 default all thetime.
/B:	Buffer size should be a multiple of /E: parameter. Use 16384 all the time.
/R	Clear the cache and restart SMARTDrive. This doesn't act like you would expect it to. You will not be able to reset the size of the cache and other parameters without a reboot.
/C	Flush the cache buffers. This is recommended as the last statement in your batch files to force the remaining buffer contents of disk files to be written when you have specified the write caching feature.
d-/+	Drive name alone turns on read-only caching. Adding the plus sign will cause write caching. The minus sign is used to drop the drive from SMARTDrive caching.

Figure 3-1   SMARTDrive Parameters

- Use DOS batch files to control the drives and size of caching buffers for use with long-running programs.

- The SMARTDRV /C command should be added to the end of batch files that execute long-running programs. It will force the write cache to be flushed, thus protecting your files.

- It is recommended that you turn on write caching for long-running batch programs. It will cut considerable run-time off the processing. This is done with the command SMARTDRV C+ (the plus sign turns on write caching). Repeat the command for each drive with files used during the long-running program.

- Turn off caching for drives that will get very little activity during the long program run. This is done with the command SMARTDRV E[ms] (the minus sign turns off caching.

- SMARTDrive 4.0 may have installed double buffering. Look in your CONFIG.SYS file for a `DEVICE=C:\WIN31\SMARTDRV.EXE/DOUBLE_BUFFER` statement. If your hardware doesn't require double buffering (try taking it out), then you should remove this statement. It will cause additional overhead. Enter `SMARTDRV /S` for status on the need for double buffering. If the column titled `BUFFERING` says `NO` that drive does not require double buffering. If it says `YES`, it does need double buffering; if it has a dash, then SMARTDRV doesn't know whether this drive needs double buffering.

- There is a necessary statement in your AUTOEXEC.BAT that invokes SMARTDRV at system boot time. This statement enables you to tune the SMARTDrive software. Enter `SMARTDRV ?` on your terminal to view the syntax for setting SMARTDRV driver parameters.

Figure 3-2 SMARTDRV Recommendations

The performance tests in Figures 3-3 and 3-4 were run on an IBM PS2 Model 70 (386) machine with 8064K of RAM memory. They will provide you with valuable information for tuning your SMARTDrive caching.

In the next test we decided to take the best performing initial cache size and test for the optimum buffer size to use in conjunction with the cache size. Because buffer size must be a multiple of the data movement size (/E:8192 parameter), we began at 8192 and progressed upward to 64K buffers (see Figure 3-4 for the results).

Having determined ideal cache and buffer read ahead sizes for sequential read and write of files, the next test was to see what impact turning off the write caching would have. To accomplish this, two commands were issued: SMARTDRV C and SMARTDRV D. These commands effectively leave, the read-only caching on. See Figure 3-5 for results of the testing. As you see, turning off the write caching resulted in a tremendous degradation in performance. For this reason, it is recommended that write caching be turned on for long-running batch programs and that the SMARTDRV /C command be issued at the conclusion of processing.

Test # 1:   XCOPY 1.4M from Drive C: to D:

Test	Size of Cache	Elapsed Time	Cache Hits	Cache Misses
Baseline	SMARTDRV Off	52.56(secs)	N/A	N/A
16x8192	128KB	37.61	1209	1161
32x8192	256KB	35.24	1209	1086
64x8192	512KB	33.37	1317	1058
128x8192	1024KB	32.26	1376	1024
256x8192	2048KB	30.24	1384	1012
512x8192	4096KB	25.61	1401	999 ⬅ **Best**

Figure 3-3   SMARTDrive Statistics for Determining Best Initial Cache Size

Test # 2:   XCOPY 1.4 Megabytes from Drive C: to D:

Cache Size K	Buffer Size Bytes	Elapsed Time Secs	Cache Hits	Cache Misses
4,096	8,192	24.83	1394	985
4,096	16,384	24.66	1401	999 ⬅ **Best**
4,096	32,768	25.05	1410	1030
4,096	65,536	24.72	1394	985

Figure 3-4   SMARTDrive Statistics for Determining Best Buffer Size

Test # 3:   XCOPY 1.4 Megabytes from Drive C: to D:

Cache Size K	Buffer Size Bytes	Elapsed Time Secs	Cache Hits	Cache Misses
4,096	16,384	24.66	1401	999
4,096	16,384	43.95	975	1455 ⬅ **Ouch!!**

Figure 3-5   SMARTDRV Statistics for Determining Absence of WRITE Caching

There are three remaining tests to present, which will help you fully understand the impact of different variables when using the SMARTDrive caching routines. First is the difference between high-speed and slow-speed drives. In the previous examples, the C: drive was a faster physical device than the D: drive. Figure 3-6 will show how the times varied when the copies were performed to the same drive. You will see a small performance gain going from drive C: back to drive C:. This is because of the difference in read/write speed for the drive and the physical organization (fragmentation) of the data.

The final test with SMARTDrive was conducted to determine what impact, if any, using the FASTOPEN tuning option has. FASTOPEN is an option you specify in your AUTOEXEC.BAT that will keep a table of files last opened. The time for subsequent reopens is greatly reduced. However, the cost of FASTOPEN is not free. The command we added to the AUTOEXEC for FASTOPEN was as follows:

```
LOADHIGH C:\DOS\FASTOPEN.EXE C:=30 D:=30
```

This parameter loads the FASTOPEN routine in upper memory and tells it to keep track of 30 files on drives C and D. See Figure 3-7 for the test results. FASTOPEN resulted in about a 10 percent degradation in performance. However, in normal usage day-to-day, where you open and close the same files repeatedly, fast open can yield a performance gain. When you are running long batch programs that will open and close files only once, you may want to turn off fast open.

Our testing indicated that we should define the most initial cache memory possible, use a 16K read ahead buffer, use 8K data movement chunks, and turn on write caching for all drives involved in long batch processes. To accomplish all of these things, you need the following statement added to your AUTOEXEC.BAT file (replacing any other SMARTDRV statements).

BATCH OPTIMUM

```
SMARTDRV 4096  2048 /E:8192 /B:16384 C+ D+
```

If you have a lot of memory available, you can improve performance further by increasing the size of the initial cache more.

As of DOS 6.22, SMARTDRV will cache CD-ROMS.

Test #4: XCOPY 1.4 Megabytes from Drive to Itself

From Drive	To Drive	Cache Size K	Buffer Size Bytes	Elapsed Time Secs	Cache Hits	Cache Hits	
C:	C:	4,096	16,384	23.50	1516	972	☜ **Best**
D:	D:	4,096	16,384	36.20	782	1350	

Figure 3-6 SMARTDRV Statistics for Determining Drive Speed Importance

Test #5: XCOPY 1.4MB from Drive C: to C:

FASTOPEN Utility	Elapsed Time Secs	Cache Hits	Cache Misses	
Off	23.50	1516	972	
On	25.93	1420	986	☜ **Ouch!!**

Figure 3-7 FASTOPEN & SMARTDRV Together

3.6   Ram Disks

A RAM disk can speed up an application that does a lot of disk accesses if the files being accessed are relatively small. If the file is large, for example 1M or larger and is lightly accessed, a RAM disk would actually degrade the speed of the PC.

A *Random Access Memory* (RAM) disk consists of setting aside some of the PCs volatile RAM and utilizing it like a small disk drive. For this to work, you must first have the RAM available in the PC. Whether running DOS or Windows, you probably wouldn't want a RAM drive of less than 1M in size. To really be worthwhile, it should be from 2M to 5M in size. If running just DOS this would mean that your PC should have a minimum of 4M to 8M. If running Windows, your PC should have 10M to 16M. Files kept in RAM drives will be lost if the PC is powered off.

In a LAN environment, you would use a swap file in lieu of a RAM disk. You would put the PC's swap file on the server. Placing a swap file on the network is not a good idea as it tends to take slightly longer to access a network drive than it does a local hard drive. Many users concurrently accessing swap files would cause a bottleneck on the network resulting in longer access times for everyone.

I think that you will be astonished with the information in Chapter 10 on using smart caching and SMARTDRV. A comparison showed that SMARTDRV outperformed a RAM DISK and that smart caching outperformed everything. There may still be places where a RAM DISK is the easiest way to tune an application. However, it is far from the fastest solution available.

3.7   Windows 3.11/95/NT 32-Bit Disk Access

If you have a few bucks, upgrade to Windows 3.11 for WorkGroups and DOS 6.22 or jump straight to Windows 95/NT. Word is that the 32-bit disk read/write is twice as fast. This can be a serious performance boost in database applications that churn a lot of disk I/Os. Of course a boost in Windows performance alone isn't a bad thing.

The *installable file system* (IFS), including MS-DOS 6.2 compressed drives, *virtual file allocation table* (VFAT) access, and disk caching (VCACHE) are handled by five additional virtual device drivers (VxDs):

DEVICE=IFSMGR.386	VFAT
Real-Mode Device Driver Interface	
DEVICE=IFSHLP.SYS	VFAT and NETWORKING
Real-Mode Device Driver	
DEVICE=VFAT.386	21h Requests Intercepted
DEVICE=IOS.386	I/O Services Supervisor
DEVICE=*VCACHE.386	32-bit Disk Caching

The IFSHLP.SYS manager services both VFAT and network access. If it is not loaded, then VFAT is automatically disabled along with 32-bit disk and file access.

From the 386 Enhanced Control Panel in Windows, you can configure the paging file, 32-bit disk access, file access, and disk caching. These settings will equate to their stored counterparts in the SYSTEM.INI file.

3.8   Windows Permanent Swapfile

Defining a swapfile will cause Windows to substitute disk space for RAM. The size of this swap file will determine its effectiveness. If defined too small, online performance drops. If made too large, disk space is wasted. To define a permanent swapfile, choose the 386 ENHANCED ICON from the Windows control panel and then choose the virtual memory button. I would recommend starting with a 4M swap file and adjust it up or down until disk access is minimized. Use your drive light as a means for determining the amount of access.

4

DB2 System Tuning

Chapters 2, 5, and 6 contain a great deal of information that could be considered system tuning. Refer to those chapters, along with the information contained in this chapter.

4.1 Release 4.x Tuning Using Performance Monitor

Perhaps the best way to tune DB2 is with the DB Performance Monitor Online Monitor. The performance monitor can be viewed by selecting option 3, `View online DB2 activity`, from the IBM Database 2 Performance Monitor primary options menu in TSO.

PM displays subsystem-wide performance information including CPU times, buffer pool usage, locking, log, and I/O activity. For an individual thread, the Online Monitor displays information such as the elapsed time, the time spent in DB2, the time it was suspended, the read and write activity involved, the locks obtained, and the SQL statements executed.

The PM main menu (DGOMMENU) requests selection of one of the following options:

1. `Display Thread Activity` (Thread and locking detail)

2. `Display Statistics` (View all statistics)

3. `Display System Parameters` (See DSNZPARM System Parms)

4. `Options` (Change PM options)

5. `Control Exception Processing` (Identify threshold exceptions)

6. `Collect Report Data` (Start and stop tracing)

7. `IRF–Create and execute DB2 PM commands` (Create/Execute PM commands)

8. IRF-Display and print graphs (Output reports and graphs)

9. IRF-Maintain parameter data sets (Set thresholds)

10. Explain (Examine PLAN_TABLE access)

Exception processing (menu option 5) can be used to monitor the following:

- Deadlocks
- Timeouts
- EDM pool full
- Authorization failure
- Thread commit indoubt
- *Coupling Facility* (CF) rebuild/alter start
- CF rebuild/alter end

Figure 4-1 contains a sample output screen showing output statistics detail from the monitor.

In the remainder of this chapter, we will take a look at some of the important areas of DB2 performance tuning. Then, in Table 4-1 you will see an easy way to cross reference your tuning symptom to a possible solution. If you have gathered PM statistics and useful information, as documented in Chapter 1, your tuning effort should progress smoothly.

4.2 Datasets

The following data set options affect the size of the EDMPOOL, and therefore, performance in DB2. More threads and connections allow more concurrent processing. The tradeoff is I/O bottlenecks and memory usage.

```
MAXIMUM OPEN DATASETS
MAXIMUM THREADS
MAXIMUM CONNECTIONS
```

4.3 Environmental Descriptor Manager (EDM) Pool

This is where *Data Base Descriptors* (DBDs), skeleton cursor tables (or plans), and program cursor tables (threads) are located. The number of loads per request should be almost nonexistent in the EDM pool. Figure 4-2 contains the values to monitor. The pool should never exceed 80 percent utilization.

4.4 Buffer Pools

The buffer pool usage is tricky to understand but easy to tune. When the DEFERRED WRITE threshold exceeds 50 percent, the Data Manager will begin writing updated pages to disk. When the PREFETCH DISABLED threshold exceeds 90 percent, DB2 will cease using read ahead, which affects batch

```
DGOMSPSM 12:48            DB2 Statistics Detail DUNHAM          APC5 V4
                            GROUP003 MEMBER03
                                             INTERVAL 12:59:59
For details, type any character next to heading, then press Enter.
                                                    More:    - +
_ EDM Pool
   EDM Pool full . . . . . . . . . . . . . . . . . . . . . . :       0
   EDM Pool pages in use (%) . . . . . . . . . . . . . . . . :    81.6
   CT requests/CT not in EDM pool  . . . . . . . . . . . . . :     7.1
   PT requests/PT not in EDM pool  . . . . . . . . . . . . . :    11.8
   DBD requests/DBD not in EDM pool  . . . . . . . . . . . . :    21.9
  Buffer Manager
   Synchronous Reads . . . . . . . . . . . . . . . . . . . . :    88.3
   Deferred write threshold reached  . . . . . . . . . . . . :       0
   Data manager critical threshold reached . . . . . . . . . :       0
_Locking Activity
   Suspensions - all . . . . . . . . . . . . . . . . . . . . :    1501
   Deadlocks . . . . . . . . . . . . . . . . . . . . . . . . :       2
   Timeouts  . . . . . . . . . . . . . . . . . . . . . . . . :       1
   Lock escalations - all  . . . . . . . . . . . . . . . . . :      44
Open/Close Management
   Open data sets - High Water Mark  . . . . . . . . . . . . :     114
_ Bind Processing
_ Plan/Package Allocation, Authorization Management
_ Log Manager
   Reads satisfied - output buffer . . . . . . . . . . . . . :    2275
   Reads satisfied - Active Log  . . . . . . . . . . . . . . :     204
   Reads satisfied - Archive Log . . . . . . . . . . . . . . :       0
   Write-no-wait . . . . . . . . . . . . . . . . . . . . . . :    1115
   Unavailable output log buffers  . . . . . . . . . . . . . :       0
_ Subsystem Service
   Queued at create thread . . . . . . . . . . . . . . . . . :       0
   System event checkpoints  . . . . . . . . . . . . . . . . :       2
_ SQL Activity
_ Query Parallelism Data
_ RID List Processing
  Distributed Data
_ CPU Times and Other Data
_ Data Sharing Locking Activity
_ Group Buffer Pool Activity
_ Global Group Buffer Pool Statistics
_ Stored Procedures
Command ===> _____
 F1=Help      F2=Split     F3=Exit     F5=Auto     F6=History   F7=Up
 F8=Down      F9=Swap      F10=Delta   F11=Interval F12=Cancel  F16=Look
 F17=Collect
+---------------------------------------------------------------------------
```

Figure 4-1 DB2 Performance Monitor Statistics

EDM Pool	Skeleton Cursor Table Sections	Database Descriptor	Cursor Table
# Pages	# Pages	# pages	pages
# Pages Used	# Pages Used	# Pages Used	# Pages Used
	# Loads/Request	# Loads/Request	

Figure 4-2 EDM Pool Statistics

programs. At 97 percent, IMMEDIATE WRITE takes over, and DB2 is in serious trouble. For this reason, you need to be aware of the fullness of buffer pools. Eighty percent is the magic number again. Figure 4-3 contains some of the buffer statistics to monitor.

Multiple index paths reduce EXCPS by avoiding costly table scans. If the buffer pools are insufficient to satisfy the needs for index paths, a scan is forced. DB2 will monitor the query. If the query attempts to use more than 50 percent of the buffer space or 25 percent of the table data in satisfying the query (and DB2 estimates that this will exceed the maximum buffer usage), then a scan ensues.

By defining separate buffer pools for data, indexes, and exception processing, you can manage the use of the pools for better performance.

A third-party solution for tuning buffer pools is the **Buffer Pool Tool** from Responsive Systems. This tool has the Ability to simulate different pool sizes, thresholds, and the effect of moving objects to other pools, without impacting your production system.

4.5   DB2 Catalog Locking

Excessive *Data Definition Language* (DDL) and BIND statements without commits can lock the DB2 catalog. You should reduce PLAN binding to less than a dozen DBRMs at one time, because catalog tables are in a single table-space. A single user can effectively lock the entire system this way.

4.6   IRLM

Most individuals will agree that a single IRLM per DB2 host is best. The settings for the IRLM are adjustable. Here is a basic set from which to work. Adjust timeouts up or down as needed. For example, the query timeout of 5 seconds may be too low.

IRLM Parameter	Setting
AUTOSTART	Yes
Cross Memory	PC=NO
Deadlock Timeout	5 seconds
Query Timeout	5 seconds
Transaction Timeout	5 seconds
Bind Timeout	10 seconds
IMS BMP Timeout	20 seconds
Fast Path Timeout	30 seconds
Stop Database Timeout	60 seconds

Here is a list of accepted standards to consider when setting up your DB2 locking environment.

Reads Versus Logical Reads

Writes Versus Logical Writes

Updated Pages Not Written SWS/PWS

\# Times Multiple Index Path Accessed (reduces scans)

\# Times Multiple Index Path Not Used (due to insufficient buffers)

Figure 4-3 Buffer Statistics

- Use one IRLM per DB2 subsystem.
- Use a separate IRLM for IMS.
- Run IRLM nonswappable, with high dispatching priority.
- Define ECSA storage and use PC=N, if OK to do so.

  Cross memory services are not needed for lock requests.
- NUMLKTS is the maximum page locks for a program on a table(space).

  Define with LOCKSIZE ANY and set high enough to avoid lock escalations.
- NUMLKUS is the maximum page locks for user on all table(spaces).

  Define as LOCKSIZE ANY or PAGE and set high enough to avoid lock escalations.

4.7 Logging

Everyone agrees that dual active logging is the best way to go. Adjust the number of buffers, buffer size, and number of active logs upwards to the point where there are not thresholds exceeded or measurable waits in DB2. If a user performs an unqualified update that floods the log, deal with that issue separately.

4.8 Checkpoints

Checkpointing needs to be based upon latent read-only versus update activity. This is done via the LOGLOAD parameter in DSNZPARM. Set this value to 10 minutes from 10 a.m. to 2 p.m. and to 30 minutes in the off hours. These are experimental settings. You can adjust them up or down gradually in your shop.

4.9 MVS Dispatching Priority

DB2 subsystems should be assigned dispatching priorities greater than IMS message processing regions, TSO, and CICS, but less than VTAM and the IMS control region. Other DBMSs like CA-IDMS should be dispatched equal to the DB2 regions. The order for DBMSs is determined by how they tax the overall system and where the bulk of supported users are logged on. It is recommended that the IRLM receive a very high dispatching priority so that the other DB2 regions do not need to wait upon it.

4.10 Snapshot Copy from BMC Software

BMC provides a high-speed image copy for DB2 tablespaces that don't require anything else to run and can happen concurrent with table updating. Images are registered in SYSIBM.SYSCOPY with SHRLEVEL REFERENCE and can be used for recovery. Snapcopy works in conjunction with BMC Software's **COPY PLUS** and **Extended Buffer Manager (XBM)** products. Outages to the data can be minimized with these products.

IBM, on the other hand, provides the **DFSMS/MVS 1.1** component that requires 3990-3 or 3990-6 Cache Controllers along with the supporting macro code to replicate this kind of processing. I don't know which way is faster or cheaper. You'll have to find out for yourself.

4.11 Number of Users

The number of users is an easy one to tune. Determine the true number of users for each DB2 region and set the system parameter equal to this number plus 10 percent, thus allowing for expected growth.

4.12 Sorting

This is another easy one. More temporary tablespaces will improve sort performance.

Try to fit all the sorted table rows into the temporary tablespace primary allocation. It is better to guess high and avoid unnecessary overhead. If you want to avoid sorts, consider building indexes that will eliminate the need to sort rows. Also, consider loading rows into tables in sorted order, to reduce the overhead within the sort routine.

Here are a couple things to keep in mind when sorting DB2 on the 6000.

- Avoid sort overflows and obtain as many piped sorts as memory will allow.
- The `bufferpool`, `sortheap`, and `sortheap` threshold settings provide big performance gains.

4.13 Distributed Databases

The next important decision for DB2 relational databases is whether to distribute data to target tables on target nodes.

With distributed databases, data can be available for update, retrieval, or both. The shared tables are available to users in other data centers with direct telecommunications links. Large corporations will distribute their data in myriads of ways. Figure 4-4 shows how data tables might be distributed and accessible from multiple data centers.

In this example, Subsidiaries A and B maintain local general ledger tables with journal entries for their own respective businesses. The data from these tables is available for retrieval from the Holding Corporation, so that quarterly and annual consolidated accounting can be performed.

There are tuning benefits to distributed data. It is easier for smaller data centers to make hardware and software upgrades. If one center goes down, the others will continue working. It may be possible to use the Holding Corporation's data center as a disaster site.

There are no hard and fast rules for breaking up data for distributed processing. Almost any scenario you dream up can be built. So, use a design that has accounted for all the ways in which data must be accessed. With distributed database technology, data from several locations can be incorporated into a single query. Telecommunications times can play a big role in the overall response time in these types of queries. *Virtual Telecommunications Access Method* (VTAM) and the hardware in use can be configured to optimize distributed performance down heavily used paths. We will touch lightly on some opportunities for this in Chapter 17.

Most of the data that has been normalized will exist in only one table. The data from several tables will comprise a query or view. The bottom line is that overall processing speeds will hinge on several aspects: data normalization, VSAM cluster performance, the indexing and placement of data in tables,

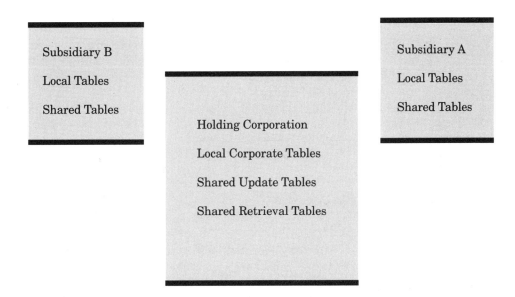

Figure 4-4 Corporate Distributed Database

placement of tables in storage groups, the placement of storage groups on physical drives, the location of physical drives on channels, distributed database software, distributed definitions, regular performance maintenance of tables, regular performance maintenance of indexes, query optimization, SQL predicate usage, etc. Let's take a look at each of these items.

4.14 DB2 and VSAM

Because we have already covered design policies and VSAM in great detail in Chapter 2, the only points left to make are these: indexes should be rebuilt often to reduce the numbers of levels. Also, tables should be resized to incorporate all the rows in the primary allocation. Both of these tasks should occur regularly depending on how often updates occur. Both activities also should be automated to free the DBA for other tasks.

4.15 DB2 Storage Groups

Storage groups are used to allocate VSAM datasets, tablespaces, and indexes. You may want to divide up the available volumes for storage groups into three categories—fast devices, medium, and slow. As you find heavily used DB2 objects, especially indexes, you should place them on the high-speed volumes.

It is possible to create your own tablespaces, partitioned tablespaces, indexes, and partitioned indexes using VSAM cluster definitions in *Access Methods Services* (AMS). This procedure avoids storage groups; however the same placement concerns exist that would have existed with storage groups. Notice the volume parameter in Figure 4-5. With storage groups you can group like resources, but you can't necessarily load balance an individual file. By the way, DB2 ignores any SPANNED and BUFFERSPACE parameters at run-time. If you'll remember, these are the parameters used for tuning VSAM files, which were discussed in Chapter 2.

```
CREATE STOGROUP FASTG001                       ☜    Busy Tables
    VOLUMES (PRD00001)
    VCAT PRODVS
    PASSWORD SYSBOOT;

CREATE STOGROUP MEDMG001
    VOLUMES ('PRD00070','PRD00076')
    VCAT PRODVS
    PASSWORD SYSBOOT;

CREATE STOGROUP SLOWG001                        ☜    Low Use Tables
    VOLUMES ('PRD00041','PROD00043')
    VCAT PRODVS
    PASSWORD SYSBOOT;
```

Figure 4-5 Building DB2 Storage Groups

NOTE: If DB2 and *Storage Management System* (SMS) storage groups are not identical, then the DB2 volume inventories may not reflect where tables actually reside. See the IBM publication titled "SMS Migration Planning Guide" for more information.

4.16 DB2 Databases

Central to tuning, when creating databases, is to assign the appropriate buffer pool. Figure 4-6 shows how the database object is created and assigned a buffer pool.

4.17 DB2 Simple and Segmented Tablespaces

There is much ado about tuning when we talk tablespaces. The two types discussed here are *Simple* and *Segmented*.

A *Simple* tablespace can be used implicitly, or explicitly, to hold rows for a table. When you want to combine multiple tables in a *Simple* tablespace, you merely use the IN clause during table creation. The rows from more than one table will be interspersed in the tablespace (see Figure 4-7). This can have positive or negative performance ramifications, depending on what you were trying to achieve. For example, one table's operations on interspersed rows can lock an entire tablespace, preventing others from getting at their tables. Also, the *Query Management Facility* (QMF) allows creation and dropping of entire tables. This can impact concurrency. Finally, you will need to run the MODIFY utility to delete records of obsolete copies from SYSIBM.SYSCOPY. However, if the clustering of rows in a simple tablespace more closely matches the order of their usage, you could reap a significant performance advantage.

```
CREATE      DATABASE    CUSTD001
            STOGROUP    FASTG001
            BUFFERPOOL  BP1;
```

Figure 4-6 DB2 Database Creation

```
CREATE      TABLESPACE CUSTS001
       IN CUSTD001
       USING STOGROUP FASTG001
            PRIQTY    10
            SECQTY    10
            ERASE     NO
       LOCKSIZE      ANY            HINTS:
       BUFFERPOOL BP1                     4K pages speedy
       CLOSE NO                           Prevent repeat open/close
       PCTFREE 30;                        Leave room
```

Figure 4-7 DB2 Simple Tablespace Creation

Scanning a table in a simple tablespace can result in the entire table's space being scanned. More than one table can be locked when only one table was being acted upon. For these reasons, *Segmented* tablespaces are recommended. Scanning tables, single table locking, space reusability, faster deleting, reduced logging, and fewer open files are the many performance benefits of segmented tablespaces.

Figure 4-8 shows the DB2 definitions for a segmented tablespace. In the example, the first three segments are in use, while segments four and five are not.

If all of the tables in the CUSTS001 segmented tablespace are large, then you may want to specify 32 pages per segment. This is done with a subcommand like the one shown in Figure 4-9.

4.18 DB2 Partitioned Tablespaces

Although you may have thought we were through talking about tablespaces, there is one more type of tablespace, as you can see from the section title. If you have the mother of all tables, this is the way to define it. The single table

```
STORGROUP
     DATABASE
               SEGMENTED TABLESPACE
                    SPACE MAP
                         SEGMENTS 1-3 IN USE
                              SEGMENT 1
                                      PAGES 1-4        TABLE CUSTT001
                                                             ROWS
                              SEGMENT 2
                                      PAGES 5-8        TABLE CUSTT002
                                                             ROWS
                              SEGMENT 3
                                      PAGES 9-12       TABLE BILLT001
                                                             ROWS
                              SEGMENT 4
                                      PAGES 13-16      UNUSED
                              SEGMENT 5
                                      PAGES 17-20      UNUSED
```

Figure 4-8 Segmented Tablespace Creation

```
CREATE TABLESPACE        CUSTS001
        IN CUSTD001
        USING STOGROUP FASTG001
              PRIQTY        64
              SECQTY        32
              ERASE         NO        HINTS:
        SEGSIZE      32               ☜ 32 pages per segment
        LOCKSIZE     TABLE            ☜ Only lock one table at a time
        BUFFERPOOL   BP1              ☜ 4K pages for speedy
        CLOSE        NO               ☜ Prevent repeat open/close
        FREEPAGE     10;              ☜ Free pages per segment
```

Figure 4-9 DB2 Segmented Tablespaces

occupying a partitioned tablespace (creation syntax is shown in Figure 4-10) can span many storage groups and volumes.

Individual rows are divided among partitions based upon their cluster index keys. You can assign partitions to specific storage groups, which in turn have the fastest performance. In this way, certain cluster keys will run faster than others. View Figure 4-10 for an example of how you would do this at index creation time.

DB2 will allow locking of tablespaces, tables, or pages. Depending on the type of processing anticipated, it can be to the application's benefit to have one or another of these types of locking.

Customer numbers are assigned to the customer base as they begin doing business. High-volume clients are automatically assigned a customer number in partition 1. This makes the process of tuning a key-oriented one. It also makes the application programs bear some of the responsibility for accomplishing this feat.

DB2 indexes use root and leaf pages. There can be many leaf page levels. Leaf pages can be broken into subpages, which determine how much is locked in a run-unit. As the number becomes smaller, processing costs rise. Use smaller

```
                                        HINTS:
CREATE TABLESPACE      CUSTS001          ▼ 64 Gigabytes max
        IN CUSTD001
        USING STOGROUP    MEDMG001
              PRIQTY      40
              SECQTY      20
              ERASE       NO
        NUMPARTS     16                   ▼ 4 Gigabytes max/each
             (PART 1 USING STOGROUP FASTG001
              PRIQTY      40
              SECQTY      20)
        LOCKSIZE       PAGE               ▼ Lock one page at a time
        BUFFERPOOL BP1                    ▼ 4 KB pages for speedy
        CLOSE          YES;               ▼ Open/close one table
```

Figure 4-10   DB2 Partitioned Tablespace Creation

```
CREATE UNIQUE INDEX CUSTI001.INDEX
        ON CUSTC001.MAIN
             (CUSTNO   ASC)
        SUBPAGES 2
        CLUSTER
             (PART 1 VALUES ('00599')        HINTS:
              USING STORGROUP FASTG001,      ▼    Fast Storage Group
             (PART 2 VALUES ('00999')
              USING STORGROUP MEDMG001,
              .... etc
             (PART 16 VALUES ('99999'))
        BUFFERPOOL BP1                       ▼    Fast Buffer Pool
        CLOSE YES;
```

Figure 4-11   Creating High Performance Partitions

subpages for heavier transaction flow. Allowable values are 1, 2, 4, 8, and 16. In the example in Figure 4-11, middle ground was chosen.

PCTFREE reserves space within leaf pages to reduce splitting. FREEPAGE tells DB2 how often to leave a page of free space to prevent spawning. See Figure 12-29 for free space formulas to use.

BUFFERPOOL, LOCKSIZE, FREEPAGE, PCTFREE, and USING STOGROUP can all be changed with an ALTER TABLESPACE statement. If the STOGROUP is changed, it will not take effect until the tablespace is LOAD REPLACE'd or REORG'd.

4.19   Changing Performance by Environment

DB2 datasets can be moved from volume to volume. Also, DB2 databases (and their objects) can be moved from one DB2 subsystem to another. These are ways of segregating the TEST and PROD environments. Under a different subsystem, like PROD, performance would be better than TEST, in theory. Confirm that optimum buffer pools and devices are picked up during such migrations.

The DSN1COPY utility is fastest for database moves but requires knowledge of internal DB2 object identifiers. Migration can also be a way to segregate SLOW PROD databases from FAST PROD databases in different subsystems.

Finally, entire DB2 subsystems can be moved to other processors. This is one way to move distributed data en-masse. DFDSS is the fastest and easiest way to accomplish these copies. For more information on optimizing data and object movement, see Chapter 2, "Mainframe Blocking and Buffering."

4.20   DB2 Tables

Rather than give you a class in defining DB2 tables, this small section will just point out some of the obvious tuning opportunities that you should keep in mind when creating and altering tables.

Primary keys that cannot be updated will prevent overhead. A primary key that uses the minimum number of columns to enforce uniqueness will also reduce overhead. Choosing ASCENDING or DESCENDING, so that rows requested are always stored or retrieved first, can save processing time. For example, if TIMESTAMP is in the key, and you will be accessing the latest records most frequently, make the index DESCENDING.

If you are using ON DELETE CASCADE, many rows can be deleted with a single request. This could create a bottleneck in processing. Also, there may be many dependent records impacted in other tables. You can solve this by creating indexes on foreign keys. This will eliminate scans of dependent tables. Placing this kind of table in its own tablespace, or segmenting it, will also reduce the scope of a scan.

Dropping a table is a serious prospect, but it can be better from a performance standpoint than deleting all the rows in a table. There are distinct differences in the results of both methods. Dropping a table will cause the foreign keys not to be checked in related tables. That could spell disaster, if you expected them to be wiped out.

4.21 DB2 Security Checking

This one is simple. A less rigorous security check will result in improved performance. Therefore, don't over-enforce and don't under-enforce. Use of concise generic profiles will help reduce the time spent in security checking.

4.22 DB2 Symptoms and Solutions

We will spend very little time describing the use of the resource limit facility and audit trace in managing performance. The resource limit facility can time-out long running queries. The amount of CPU and number of commits are available with audit trace.

A long evaluation of the DB2 environment has made it apparent that DB2 is relatively efficient in its I/O handling. The cost of SQL and queries is therefore relegated to ways of building and using tables. First and foremost of these is the decision of how much normalization is really necessary. Second is the selection of the clustering index that drives the physical clustering of rows. Third is the provision for other indexes as needed. Fourth is the careful monitoring and selection of SQL predicates and use of pre-fetch. Fifth is re-engineering for throughput and response improvement. Sixth entails proper tweaking of clusters, tablespaces, free space, buffer pools, and the many other system parameters governing the system as a whole.

Table 4-1 is a tuning decision table. Begin by searching the left column for a poor performance symptom in your database. Upon finding your symptom, refer to the right column for a solution. Multiple symptoms and solutions may apply.

TABLE 4-1 DB2 Tuning Decision Table

SYMPTOM	SOLUTION
Too many I/Os resulting from SQL commands against a large table.	Use multiple indexes to satisfy requests. Reorganize tablespace and check that data fits in first extent. DB2 will allocate the next extent when half of the current extent is used. Check all of the design information in Chapter 5 for hints on improvement of database design.
Too many OPEN/CLOSE operations for a tablespace.	Use CLOSE NO in the CREATE for tablespace or in the CREATE for INDEX.
Access times are increasing on indexed tables, reorganizations are frequent, index splits are high, locking is high, or clustering is poor.	PCTFREE and FREEPAGE need to be increased.
There is I/O contention on clusters and poor buffer performance.	Use a large single buffer pool, or multiple pools, whichever is best.

(Continued)

TABLE 4-1   DB2 Tuning Decision Table (Continued)

SYMPTOM	SOLUTION
Sort is slow. I/Os per second is high.	Create additional temporary tablespaces. Fit all the rows in the primary allocations.
IMS CPU/transaction is high on high volume transactions.	Specify PROCLIM > 1, reduce WFI (wait for input).
CICS CPU/transaction is high.	Check for AUTH(SIGNID)= on RCT. Use a name that will not change. Grant execute AUTH to public on all plans.
Response time is slow.	First determine how much time is in transmission versus different DB2 SQL calls. Then isolate what resources were used most in SQL calls. Use indexing, buffering, table reorganizations, etc. to improve SQL calls. Use VTAM modifications, hardware, and routing changes to improve transmission time. Look at I/O locking, switching from serialization of SQL to parallelism.
Some DB2 jobs need higher performance than others. times.	Use dispatching priorities, job classes, high speed DASD devices, and buffering tools to reduce run
How do I identify where table scans are occurring?	Use DB2's instrumentation facility to retrieve information similar to EXPLAIN. Use the EXPLAIN statement to collect path information and save it in the PLAN_TABLE or in a QMF form. Then query PLAN_TABLE or the form output. Use the EXPLAIN statement of BIND or REBIND to get similar information for embedded queries in application programs.
How do I prevent table scans?	Modify table views to add indexes and use the QMF governor to limit available query resources. The DB2 governor will perform the same limits for dynamic SQL.
High I/O on DSNDB01.SCT02 and DBD01 is present. Long response times loading SKCTs and DBDs is experienced.	Increase the size of the EDM pool.

DB2PM statistics show one of the following conditions:
  Buffer pool expansions > 0
  Current active buffers > 0
  DM critical threshold > 0
  Prefetch disabled
  No-buffer or No-read-engine >0
  Getpages requests vs. total reads < 2 : 1
  Pages-written vs. Write-IO-
    operations < 5 : 1
  Write engine not available > 0
	Increase the minimum size of buffer pool.

DB2PM datasets opened = DSMAX or DSN6SPRM.	Increase the DSMAX.
DB2PM buffer pool manager activity report shows Unavailable-Output-Log-Buffers > 0.	Increase the OUTPUT BUFFER size or WRITE THRESHOLD number.
Reads-Delayed-Due-to-ARC-Limit > 0	Increase DSNTIPL logs number.

TABLE 4-1   DB2 Tuning Decision Table (Continued)

SYMPTOM	SOLUTION
Reads-Satisfied-From-Archive-Log > 0	Increase number or size of log files. Move the logs to better volumes and channels.
Any of the following files showing high I/O contention: DB2 trace reports DSNDB01.DBD01, DSNDB01.SCT02 and index DSNDB06.SYSPLAN, DSNDB06.SYSDBASE DSNDB06.SYSVIEWS tablespace and index on SYSVTREE DSNDB07.DSN4K01 and any other temporary tablespaces QMF system data sets User tablespaces and indexes	Separate these files and place them on faster volumes and channels. DSNB07 performance is affected by tuning the size of its virtual pool, number of data sets, placement of data sets, number of buffers and avoidance of synchronous I/O. See the work file statistics on the statistics report to view sort efficiency which is an indicator.
GROUP BY, ORDER BY, JOIN, DISTINCT, UNION (except UNION ALL), IN subquery, ANY or ALL with logical operators like <, >=, <= on large tables takes too long.	SORT is invoked with these types of calls and can be avoided by building indexes.
All the referential constraints are slowing processing.	Some of these may be extraneous. There are cases where systems are designed overly protective in the case of data integrity. An agreement on the real source of valid data can allow you to turn off some of these checks. And, then using the LOAD and CHECK utilities in conjunction with the ENFORCE option will allow you to identify records which have fallen out of synchronization.
DB2 catalog and directory performance is poor.	Check to see if the catalog and directory have many extents. If so, move them to a volume with enough room to contain everything in one extent. Leave some room for growth.
Too many I/Os. Too much CPU. Too long response time. Too many buffer pools in use.	Consolidate and use one large buffer pool.
High volume transactions running slow.	Identify the most heavily executed transactions with the largest number of SQL statements and enforce reuse of threads. Consider putting tablespaces in memory or smart caching them (see Chapter 10). Look into database reengineering for performance. Place system code like ISPF, QMF and GDDM in the LPA/ELPA to reduce swapping. Avoid using group AUTHIDs which reduce concurrency. Verify that locking is using LOCKSIZE ANY on the TABLE CREATE. Reduce the number of pages locked by any one application using the LOCKS PER USER parameter on the IRLM Panel 2 (DSNTIPJ and DSNTIPK). It may help to adjust page sizes to change page management CPU, or locking. Restrict batch and DB2 utilities to the

(Continued)

TABLE 4-1   DB2 Tuning Decision Table (Continued)

SYMPTOM	SOLUTION
	night batch window. Try to use multiple index access paths. Avoid stage 2 predicates (nonsargable) where possible. Structure queries with column functions like TRY MERGE JOIN SCAN - DB2 release 2.
COLUMN_FN_EVAL = blank in PLAN_TABLE	Queries using MAX, MIN, AVG, SUM and COUNT will perform better if operating on single columns, using 1 function at a time, as stage 1 predicates and if columns operated on are in the innermost table (provided that a JOIN was taking place). A composite index with the predicate column as its primary columns and the MIN/MAX column immediately following is best for functions without GROUP BY clauses. GROUP BY with SORT is better than without.
IMS SQL users and requests are queuing. DB2PM Queued-at-create thread > 0	Use IDMS Fast Path, use an empty SSM (subsystem member) for regions that don't connect to DB2 and maximize the number of IMS regions connected to DB2. Give DB2 transactions a higher scheduling class.
TSO SQL users and requests are queuing. DB2PM Queued-at-create-thread > 0	Increase the MAX USERS, MAX REMOTE, MAX TSO CONNECT and MAX BATCH CONNECT parameters in install panel DSNTIPE.
CICS SQL users and requests are queuing. DB2PM Queued-at-create-thread > 0	Increase the MAX USERS and MAX REMOTE parameters. Increase THRDM in CICS and set the RCT DPMODE=EQUAL for high priority DB2 threads. Caution: More threads implies more overall resources. If your system is relatively well tuned and this is not a sporadic event, you have to consider an all out tuning project, or a processor upgrade.
DB2 Load utility runs too long.	Use UNLOAD CONTINUE instead of UNLOAD ONLY and UNLOAD PAUSE. Use SYNCSORT instead of DFSORT. Use 6+ sortworks with large primary cylinder allocations which are defined as CONTIG.
DB2 Copy utility runs too long.	Evaluate the use of incremental image copies, or merged full and incremental copies.
DB2 Recover utility runs too long.	Evaluate rebuilding indexes for individual partitions instead of the whole tablespace.
DB2 RUNSTATS utility runs too long.	Use indexes. For non-indexed column statistics, only specify the columns you really need to see.
Batch processing won't go fast enough.	Use LOCK TABLE to make IRLM lock at the table instead of the page. Use LOCKSIZE TABLESPACE to eliminate page locks. This is not a good idea, though, if you have users querying the tables. Increase buffering. TRY MERGE SCAN JOIN - DB2 Release 2.
Deadlocks are prevalent.	Use ACQUIRE(ALLOCATE) to reduce the number of deadlocks on the network.
	Beware, all tablespaces and tables in plan are then locked.

TABLE 4-1   DB2 Tuning Decision Table (Continued)

SYMPTOM	SOLUTION
	Use RELEASE(DEALLOCATE) to release the locks as soon as possible.
	Reduce the time frame locks are held.
	Use cursor ISOLATION whenever possible.
	Use the FOR UPDATE clause to avoid lost updates when this can lead to deadlocks in SELECTs.
	Use frequent commit points with RR (Repeatable Read) ISOLATION.
	Cluster tables relevant to the same application.
	Use the fewest databases possible in an application.
	Enforce standard entry sequences for table access. Reduce the window in which table locks are held by rearranging code. Issue rollback after a failure to release locks.
QMF is creating and dropping table spaces resulting in a lot of overhead.	Add the SPACE parameter to Q.PROFILES in order to use SPACE database for SAVE DATA commands.
Accounting elapsed times for QMF are long.	Set ISPSTART F parameter lower for general queries.
Remote access queries are slow.	Use BLOCK FETCH by specifying FOR FETCH ONLY in the DECLARE CURSOR statement. Try DEFER(PREPARE) instead of NODEFER(PREPARE) to package all the SQL requests before transmission.
IEAVXSTK is consuming a large amount of CPU.	Tune the cross memory services. Try the PC=NO option in panel DSNTIPJ of the IRLM install.
JOINS are running longer.	The more tables that are joined, the higher the cost becomes. As the number of rows increases, there is a geometric increase in time to complete a JOIN. Indexes will improve JOIN performance.
Subquery is running long.	A JOIN is faster than using a subquery in a multi-table retrieval.
A RANDOM index SQL request is not performing well.	There are many differences in performance depending on the number of rows and different predicates employed. Try exchanging an EQUALITY predicate for an OR predicate. You may find performance improves.
Denormalized table runs faster than normalized. Why?	It is typical to experience 40-50 percent CPU reductions and 25-30 percent faster response times with denormalized tables. There is a tradeoff for the performance, which is the amount of redundancy introduced. You must decide what middle ground is acceptable to your design.
How can we get more throughput in a mixed IMS & DB2 environment?	Increase the amount of IMS transactions and reduce the number of SQL transactions. A 2:1 balance will achieve higher processor throughput.

(Continued)

TABLE 4-1   DB2 Tuning Decision Table (Continued)

SYMPTOM	SOLUTION
Is a dual or quadratic processor upgrade better?	Tests have shown that increasing processors speed is preferred to the number of processors in a complex. An increase in the number of processors can cause a direct increase in the number of lock suspensions per transaction. Also, multiprocessor task managers add a level of overhead in exchange for throughput.
Too much CPU on one DBRM is experienced.	Identify the problem SQL and fix it. Try joining tables and using "FOR FETCH ONLY" or "OPTIMIZE FOR" clauses.
Index access is slow.	Consider index-only access.
CPU for commits high or low.	Issue checkpoints every 10 seconds online and every five minutes in batch without concurrency, or every minute in batch with concurrency. Adjust frequency up or down accordingly.
Batch commits need to be variable.	Set parameters internally based upon the time-of-day or other factor driving this need.
Package lock duration high.	Consider NO ACQUIRE option. Use same RELEASE() option as plans.
Batch jobs run long or high volume CICS transactions need to reuse thread.	Use ALLOCATE/DEALLOCATE in BIND.
Don't need thread reuse and batch needs concurrency.	Use ACQUIRE(USE) RELEASE(COMMIT) on BIND.
Read only and no concurrency in batch needed.	Use LOCKSIZE TABLESPACE.
Updated by multiple online, or batch concurrent users.	Use LOCKSIZE ANY or PAGE.
Updated by multiple online only.	Use LOCKSIZE ANY or PAGE or LOCK TABLE in EXCLUSIVE/SHARE mode in program.
Control tables with high concurrency.	Add dummy columns to make row > 1/2 page and force 1 row/page.
Control indexes with high concurrency.	Use PCTFREE = 99 and define SUBPAGE for 1/page.
High contention on DBD.	Embedded dynamic SQL which releases locks sooner than static SQL is best.
Temporary tables are contending with main tables.	If tables are created in program, this can happen. Consider isolating these to temporary database partitions.
SUBPAGE locking is high.	Use SUBPAGE=1.
Lock escalation is high.	Reduce subpages so the number of index entries per SUBPAGE is equal to the number of rows/page.
There are too many secondary extents.	Use IDCAMS REPRO or DFDSS on user-managed VSAM DB2 data sets, or tablespaces using STOGROUPS to release unwanted extents.

TABLE 4-1   DB2 Tuning Decision Table (Continued)

SYMPTOM	SOLUTION
Sequential prefetch is disabled.	Check to see if tables with cluster indexes are out of order. If so, run reorganize, image copy and RUN-STATS in that order, then rebind the programs.
Rows are located more than 64 pages from where the main index indicates they should be (FARINDREF has been incremented).	Reorganize the table.
LEAF DISTANCE is incremented.	Index is out of sequence. Reorganize.
Checkpointing is causing synchronous I/O to queue up.	Reduce the checkpointing in 50 percent increments during peak periods until the optimum level is realized.
EDM pool is heavily fragmented.	Increase pages in the pool in 50 percent increments until an optimum size is obtained. CICS storage may need to be increased concurrently, to accommodate an increase in DB2 threads and throughput. Otherwise, short on storage conditions can arise in CICS.
Deadlocks are occurring in adjacent subpages.	Set the SUBPAGE value for indexes to 1.
Program is performing a scan.	Modify the index column sequence or content to eliminate. Collect column statistics so the DB2 optimizer will choose a better path.
Strobe is showing a large amount of overhead associated with INTERTEST routines.	Turn off INTERTEST for production applications.
The buffer hit ration is decreasing.	Increase buffer pool pages and specify pools for more active tables and indexes.
A large amount of DB2 service time is categorized as class 2 time.	This is probably OPEN and CLOSE of data set related. Try using CLOSE=NO on the DB2 table parameter.
Contention on rows stored sequentially with common keyfields is being experienced.	Switch the access mode to random.
Increased transactions are causing an increase in new row insertion.	Increase FREESPACE and reorganize indexes. Check for deadlocks and timeouts, with activity related primarily to unclustered data and the need for more indexes.
Tuning indicates a need for scalability.	Consider using V4 and V5 of DB2. They capitalize on parallel processing, and processor coupling. 32 9672-RX3 10-engine machines can be coupled together, with 5000 users on each machine. A 57 TB database is possible, partitioned across 254 disk controllers.
Need faster queries.	Consider using the new V5 temporary tables which do not require logging, and reside in memory.
Suspect long running units of recovery.	Use the UR CHECK FREQ entry on the DSNTIPN install panel, which detects long running units of recovery.

(Continued)

TABLE 4-1   DB2 Tuning Decision Table (Continued)

SYMPTOM	SOLUTION
LOAD or REORG is slow.	Try the new SORTKEYS parameter in V5. It forces sorts into memory, eliminating bin files and their I/O.
REORG, LOAD and COPY run a long time.	Try the new V5 utilities which have been enhanced. Check out the new V5 On-line REORG Utility.
DB2 is picking inefficient access paths	The new V5 REOPT(VARS) statement can cause a reoptimization and force a new access path.
Applications are beating the same tables to death with SELECTs.	Consider rewriting applications to use the new V5 CASE statement, which can eliminate redundant table access.
Need more density for rows.	Consider V5 of DB2, which allows 255 rows per page. Increased density can make it possible to use 32 KB pages more effectively.
Backup to disaster sites over T3 lines takes too long.	Consider using the 45-Mbps circuit compression from Computer Network Technology Corp. It cuts the amount of networking enormously. You might even shut down some T3 lines.
Locking is preventing access.	Consider using Selective Partition Locking (SPL) in V5 of DB2. Individual partitions can be locked reducing user impact.
I/O throughput is poor.	Consider partitioning. V5 allows 254 partitions which can be accessed in parallel, which reduces the Mean Time to Access Data (MTAD).
Network traffic is high.	Consider using more stored procedures. In V5 they have the added benefit of returning an entire result set.
Transactions are seeing large wait times in the CICS terminal owning (TOR).	Increase the CICS MAX TASKS and ATASKS in 50 percent increments until an optimum region level is attained. Increase the number of threads and buffer pool pages in DSNZPARMS and the number of send and receive sessions in the same manner.

The single best way to analyze the way your query is performing is with EX-PLAIN. There are three ways to invoke this facility. One is to put EXPLAIN(YES) on programs bound. Alternatively, you can use QMF or SPUFI to test queries.

A query's performance can be analyzed closely by looking at the PLAN table fields collected with EXPLAIN. Some of the key fields to review in an attempt to eliminate expensive processing are shown here.

EXPLAIN PLAN Tuning Fields

■ ACCESSNAME is the index name.

■ ACCESSTYPE has codes for scans or multiple index access.

■ COLUMN_FN_EVAL indicates whether SUM used and at what time.

■ MATCHCOLS gives counts of columns in index which matched.

■ METHOD is used to check for joins and sorts

EXPLAIN PLAN Tuning Fields

- MIXOPSEQ shows how indexes were utilized.
- PREFETCH indicates whether sequential or list prefetch were used or not.
- PLANNO shows the order of table usage.
- SORTC and SORTN shows reasons why sorts were performed.

4.23 DB2 Predicates

DB2 predicates play an important role in performance. The right choice, when multiple methods are available, can greatly reduce the cost of queries. Figure 4-12 shows predicates in increasingly complex order. The greater the complexity, the greater the cost.

4.24 DB2 New Releases

In addition to the things listed so far, there are several performance enhancements in DB2 Release 2, DB2 Versions 3, 4, and 5. Key areas impacting performance are listed in Figures 4-13 through 4-16. Note that versions 4 and 5 have an incredible amount of changes impacting DB2 performance in every area.

4.25 CA-FASTDASD

One of the more esoteric types of tuning, which is routinely overlooked, is data set placement for DB2 data sets. It seems like such a big trial. Mainly, because we just don't know enough about the operating system types of things.

Well, CA-FASTDASD from Computer Associates generates a single report that will make your job easier with information like that shown in Figure 4-17.

PREDICATE	SAMPLE USAGE
*	SELECT * (unqualified)
CALC	
LIKE	SELECT WHERE LIKE '%THIS'
OR	SELECT WHERE condition OR condition
IN	SELECT WHERE IN (A B C)
NOT	SELECT WHERE NOT condition
AND	SELECT WHERE condition AND condition
BETWEEN	SELECT WHERE BETWEEN A and Z
EQUALITY	SELECT WHERE col >= val
COUNT	SELECT COUNT(*)
AVG	SELECT AVG(col)
MIN	SELECT MIN(col)
MAX	SELECT MAX(col)
SUM	SELECT SUM(col)
NULL	SELECT WHERE col is NULL
=	SELECT WHERE col = val

Figure 4-12 DB2 Order of Predicate Complexity Affecting Performance

■ Multiple Index Access

■ Ordering of Candidate List into a Clustering Sequence

■ Column Functions

■ Statistics on Data Distribution

■ Subquery Processing

■ Merge Scan Join

■ Index Field Retrieval

■ Transaction Performance

■ RUNSTATS Performance

Figure 4-13   Some DB2 Release 2 Enhancements

■ Parallel I/O reduces response time

■ Hiperpools improve buffering and response time

■ Data compression reduces DASD costs and potentially response time

■ Parallel utility job execution on partitioned tables reduces unit of work time (accomplished with partition independence)

■ Multiple recover jobs can share the archive log

■ I/O scheduling reduces response time

■ SMF accounting provides additional tuning data

■ Data propagation (using DFPROP exits) allows data to propagate from IMS to DB2 or DB2 to DB2.

■ Improved independence of index pageset access from table access

■ Read-only (RO) switching mechanism reduces logging

■ Improved SYSLGRNG recording for CLOSE YES and NO pagesets

■ Adding and deleting pagesets from the deferred close drain queue

■ Reduced pageset logging

■ Improved dataset open failure processing

■ Improved dataset open for update timestamp recording

■ Detection of down-level pagesets (things backed up with HSM or other data manipulators

■ Pagesets will be closed on a local DB2 whenever applications no longer are using them for read or write. DSNZPARM determines how long they sit inactive before closing.

Figure 4-14   Some DB2 Version 3 Highlights

- Client/Server enhancements
  - Stored procedures for locals and remotes
  - Larger network support (more threads)
  - Improved DRDA
- Data sharing on S/390 Parallel Sysplex
- Performance enhancements and availability
  - Parallel query processing
  - Tunable DB2 catalog
  - Faster COPY, LOAD, REORG utilities
  - RUNSTATS
  - New Type 2 indexes
  - Uncommitted Read (UR) isolation
  - Read Stability (RS) isolation
  - Partition independence
  - CONCURRENT Option on COPY Utility
- User Productivity
  - Table check constraints
  - Nested table expressions
  - Additional SQL standards
  - OOPS
  - Managing threads
  - DB2 Online Help
  - New CICS and DB2 adapters
  - Performance monitoring
  - SQL syntax changes
- Standards
  - DRDA, Open Blueprint, ISO, ANS, IBM SQL Standard

Figure 4-15 Major DB2 Version 4 Highlights

There is a data set report that gives you similar information for data sets. With these two reports you should be able to locate optimum drives for placement of DB2 files.

- Client/Server enhancements
  - Native TCP/IP for DRDA
  - Two-phased commit for TCP/IP Connections
- Distributed Computing Environment (DCE)
  - Single login
- Stored Procedures
  - Return Entire Result Set
  - Access to Global Temporary Tables
  - Workload Manager Transaction Prioritization
  - Multiple Stored Procedure Address Space (SPAS) are Allowed
- ASCII Server Support
- CLI/ODBC Support (sharing client code on mainframe)
- New Resource Recovery Services (RRS) Attach Facility (two-phased commit)
- New DB2 World Wide Web Connection Version 1 (multi-platform connectivity)
- Partitions
  - Large Partitioned Table Spaces (254 partitions)
  - RIDs were increased to 5-bytes to accommodate large partitions
  - The DB2 Catalog was also changed to accommodate large partitions
  - Selective Partition Locking (SPL)
- Rows per page increased from 127 to 255
- New sample program for new On-line REORG Utility
  - Allows on-line updates while reorganization (uses shadow files)
- New SORTKEYS statement for REORG and LOAD Utilities (faster sorts)
- New CHANGELIMIT and REPORTONLY keywords on COPY Utility
- New DSNJLOGF Log Preformat Utility
- Comments allowed for SYSIN input streams
- New Extended Sequential Datasets (ESDs) for striping
  - Stripes can be written to in parallel
  - Striped datasets can have up to 123 extents
- Language Support
  - Support for IBM Cobol for MVS and IBM C/C++ for MVS/ESA
- Detection of long running units-of-recovery (UR)

Figure 4-16 Major DB2 Version 5 Highlights

- DB2 Estimator for Windows
- DB2 Installer
- SQL-92 Entry FIPS 127-2/ISO 9075:1992/ANSI X3.135-1991 Supported
- SQL Temporary Tables which only exist for duration of task and do not incur logging overhead are supported (part of SQL-92 standard)
- CASE Expressions allow the result to be processed, without incurring overhead (part of SQL-92 standard)
- Visual EXPLAIN (GUI workstation tool for working with the PLAN_TABLE)
- Data Sharing Enhancements
  - Automatic recovery of group buffer pools (GBP)
  - Dynamic rebuild of group buffer pools (SETXCF command)
- Performance Enhancements
  - Reoptimization for static and dynamic SQL variables - REOPT(VARS)
  - Prepared statement caching for dynamic SQL minimizes binds
  - KEEPDYNAMIC(YES) option to retain dynamic SQL across commit
  - Selective partition locking for Sysplex Query Parallelism
  - Scans of non-contiguous partition ranges for Sysplex Query Parallelism
  - Improved index-only scans
  - Key column correlation statistics
- New RUNSTATS SAMPLE keyword does column sampling (reduces CPU)
- Some year 2000 support changes

Figure 4-16   Major DB2 Version 5 Highlights (Continued)

```
Controller ID       CU-ID          CNTRL101
Device              VENDOR NAME    IBM
Device              MODEL          3880-23
Device              ADDRESS        102
Device              VOLSER         VSAM01
Performance         I/O PER SEC    1.50
Performance         READ RATIO     70.0
Performance         RD HIT RATIO   95.0
Performance         CACHE SIZE     64M
```

Figure 4-17   CA-FASTDASD Device Report

4.26   The Platinum Collection

It wouldn't be appropriate to bypass Platinum Technology. They are a software leader with the right tools. Here are the hot buttons on the list of DB2 utilities that every shop needs.

DATA COMPRESSOR

- A library of different types of compression with quick online analysis of which is best
- Transparent compression to ease table management
- Reduced CPU and I/O on DB2 logging
- Sometimes increased and sometimes decreased CPU on table processing
- Less I/O on compressed tables
- Big space savings over all other compression utilities

The next series of highly flexible tools reduce CPU, elapsed time, and EXCPS. They can all improve the downtime maintenance window

RAPID REORG

- Faster reorganization times for tablespaces and indexspaces
- Supports multiple requests in one run
- Integrated image copy creation
- Multitasking concurrent processing of partitioned tablespaces

QUICK COPY

- Quickly makes copies of DB2 table data, similar to the Rapid Reorg utility
- Multitasking concurrent processing of partitioned tablespaces

FAST LOAD

- Much faster than IBM LOAD
- Multitasking of BUILD and ALL load formats
- Data reclustering

FAST UNLOAD

- Much faster than DSNTIAUL
- Multiple requests in a single job
- Data manipulation during unload

FAST INDEX

- Much faster than CREATE INDEX
- Multiple requests in a single job

■ Incorporates a hook to SYNCSORT product

■ Eliminates space lockouts

FAST RECOVER

■ Moderately faster than DB2 RECOVER

■ Extensibility features

■ Utility Submission Facility

■ Ties product line together to add productivity

4.27   Expressway 103

This indexing tool uses bitmapped indexes requiring one half the space of conventional B-TREE indexes. The tool is targeted at DB2 tough SQL queries that are resource intensive. Speed is touted at 10 to 100 times faster than a conventional lookup. Sybase has acquired Expressway Technologies, and it is my understanding that this great technology was incorporated into Sybase IQ. The fate of Expressway 103 is undetermined, as yet.

4.28   Other Vendors with DB2 Performance Utilities

This section is devoted to a list of other great performance tools.

■ **!DB/DASD for DB2** from Candle Corporation will optimize DB2 tablespaces without having to use compression or run utilities.

■ **CDB/Batch, CDB/Superload, CDB/SuperReorder,** and **CDB/SuperReorg** products from CDB Software allow for things like DB2 commands in a batch job, faster table loads, customized optimization of clustering, and table accessible reorganizations.

■ **Copy Plus for DB2, Load Plus for DB2** and **Recover Plus for DB2, Opertune for DB2 and Reorg Plus for DB2** are high speed image copy, loading, reorganization, and recovery utilities from BMC Software. Optertune for DB2 is unique in that it allows you to dynamically tune the DB2 subsystem, including buffer pool size, checkpoint frequency, maximum threads, and prefetch quantity.

■ **Smart/Restart** from Relational Architects Int'l allows batch programs to perform automatic restarts without code changes.

■ **Omegamon for DB2** from Candle Corporation is a real-time DB2 performance and exception monitor.

■ **Scalpel for DB2** from Responsive Systems is a buffer pool analyzer that generates the desired pool sizes, which will achieve the best hit ratio.

■ **SMF/Xpress** and **SQL/Xpress** from RDS include a DB2 performance monitor and prototyping tool for SQL queries that can evaluate response time during the development cycle. **Vista Performance Workbench (VPW)** provides lock, plan, SQL, DB2 object analysis and other tuning information.

Refer to Appendix D's list of Vendors and Tools or to Appendix N's list of World Wide Web tool sites for a much larger list of DB2 specific tools.

4.29   Strobe Rel 9.2 SQL Analysis

APMPower from Programart Corporation identifies SQL statements using excessive amounts of resources. In addition, an analysis facility will provide coding tips for SQLs. Figure 4-18 has a list of the best Strobe SQL analysis fields and report where they come from.

4.30   JOIN Performance

SELECT, PROJECT, and JOIN are features of relational database management systems that extend their power. Beginning users have a tendency to abuse the power they have. One form of abuse is the 3-way, 4-way, 5-way join through n-way JOIN. The more databases participating in a JOIN, the greater the cost. Resolving this issue often requires an analysis of what the user intended to achieve with the query and utilizing indexes or smaller join sets. Sometimes, JOIN is avoided altogether by extracting data from tables and manipulating it outside of the database environment.
Check out Figure 4-19 to see how a 5-way join is accomplished.

4.31   Very Large Decision Support Systems (DSS)

When used with DSS systems in the past, DB2 has had a bad report card. However, the new features in the past two versions (4 and 5), along with the right hardware, can provide a solution to large data warehouses and DSS use. Here are five points that can make a DSS DB2 solution really work for you.

Report	Tuning Fields
EXPLAIN Data Report	Table Name/Table Number/Access Type/Indexed
Translation Report	Synonyms/Aliases/Views/Referential Constraints
Opportunities Report	Coding Hints
Catalog Statistics Report	DB2 Catalog Statistics

Figure 4-18   Strobe SQL Analysis Reports

```
create view all_states (year, volume, state, region)
as select to_char (l.shipdate, 'YY'),  l.price*(1-1.discount/100.0),
c.state, c.region
from part p, supplier s, item l, order o, customer c
where p.part_num = l.part_num
and s.supp_num = l.supp_num
andl.order_num = o.order_num
and o.cust_num = c.cust_num
and c.state = s.state
and o.orderdate between trunc
(to_date('1995-01-01', 'YYY-MM-DD'))
and trunc (to_date(1999-12-31','YYYY-MM-DD'))
and p.part_num >=1
and p.part_num <=9999;
```

Figure 4-19 5-Way Join Example

1. It is important to have a plaform that will yield the high-performance results needed.

   A standard S/390 9672 machine may not do the job. Instead, you want to have a 10-engine 9672-RX3. Why? Because you want to be able to exploit the partitioning and parallelism in V4 and V5 of DB2. DB2 V4 supported 64 partitions. But V5 will now support 254 partitions.

2. You want to partition your database across at least as many storage controllers as there are engines on the CPU. So, if you get a 20-engine machine (even better), then you can spread the partitions across 20 disk controllers.

3. You want to use the fastest disk devices available (Fibre would be ideal). But, 10 3390 storage controllers, each with 16 drawers of RAMAC2 storage have a total capacity of 1.8 TB, and an aggregate data path capacity of around 132 M/sec. Since the 9672 is a scalable machine, you can couple 32 of them, which extends disk capacity to 57 TB.

4. You want a lightning networking solution. A high-speed packet protocol or Fast Ethernet may work, if the network load is balanced correctly. Using clustered 9672 processors, you could put 5,000 users on each system.

5. You want to take advantage of as many of the new V5 performance features as possible. Temporary tables that work entirely in memory are one example. Another would be the CASE expressions that can reduce overall database access.

Chapter

5

Logical Database Design

The processes we undergo to design applications and databases have matured rapidly in the last decade. It wasn't that long ago when we plucked an idea from our minds and scribbled the design onto a piece of paper. Not long afterward, the database definitions were in place, and application coding began. Today, we must follow a regimented design methodology. No two individuals seem to follow them identically, though.

Also, not so long ago, the first step in building a new application system was to gather requirements. This task has been replaced by a new assessment routine. The techno-babel name for this new method is *workflow*. A workflow will yield the real way we should be doing business. It is then possible to determine where computers and automation can garner savings.

Eventually, we get to the logical database design stage. In this stage, the data used in a computer-based system is massaged into records or rows with primary and foreign keys. This step must occur before any physical implementation of a design is attempted. Otherwise, the fields of data can lose the properties that relate them to each other properly. The relationship of the fields is the basis for *relational* databases.

In this chapter, we lightly touch on logical database design. Physical database design is the next step following logical database design. However, the actual implementation can vary by RDBMS. So, physical constraints have been relegated to chapters about individual database products.

5.1 Normalization

Before identifying the key performance concerns for DB2, some conventions for relational tables must be defined.

First normal form tables have been designed so that one value exists in each row-and-column point in a table. Second normal form extends the design by enforcing that all nonkey columns provide information about their respective whole key. Third normal form is violated when nonkey columns become information about other nonkey columns. Finally, fourth normal form is attained when all multivalued relationships with entities have been decomposed into their own unique tables. For the newcomer to relational database design concepts, these laws may appear cryptic. So, I've given you an easy example to reference in Figure 5-1. As you view the figure, reread the four rules for normalization.

A rule of thumb is to get all your tables in fourth normal form and then sacrifice normalization for performance, as necessary. As you can see from Figure 5-1, the foreign keys begin to eat up more and more space. This is the cost of keeping all other elements in fourth normal form. You also will need to weigh the tradeoff of maintaining referential integrity across all tables. Referential integrity means that all references to a field in disjunct tables are kept in synchronization. Sometimes this integrity is handled automatically and sometimes by your application. But, in all cases, it costs something extra. One of your design steps should be to determine where it is not critical and can be disregarded.

Here is a list of very good reasons to normalize your data.

■ Accelerate searching, sorting, joins, and index creation due to narrower tables.

■ Build more and more compact, clustered indexes because there are more tables.

Unnormalized Table	1st Normal Form	2nd Normal Form	3rd Normal Form	4th Normal Form
Cust_Name_Addr*	Cust_Name*	Cust_Name*	Cust_Name*	Cust_Name*
Invoice_#*	Cust_Addr	Cust_Addr	Cust_Addr	Cust_Addr
Invoice_Amt	Invoice_#*			
Sales_Regn	Invoice_Amt	Cust_Name*	Cust_Name*	Cust_Addr*
Sales_Rep	Sales_Regn	Invoice_#*	Invoice_#*	Invoice_#*
Sales_Dept	Sales_Rep	Invoice_Amt	Invoice_Amt	Invoice_Amt
	Sales_Dept	Sales_Regn	Sales_Rep	Sales_Rep
		Sales_Rep		
		Sales_Dept	Sales_Rep*	Sales_Rep*
			Sales_Dept	Sales_Dept
			Sales_Regn	
				Sales_Rep*
* key column				Sales_Regn

Figure 5-1 Normalization of Relational Tables

- The need for fewer nonclustered indexes reduces maintenance and update activity.
- More tables allows for more and better segmentation and partitioning of data.
- Reduced storage requirements and NULL processing.
- Fewer referential integrity constraints to define and process.
- Better data cache utilization.

5.2   Xbase Design Tools

Many of the things that were pointed out in DB2 database design can be applied to Xbase databases. Because databases on the PC are represented as records that look like tables, not much is different. Records on the PC are linked by primary and foreign keys, just like the mainframe relational tables. In fact, we are beginning to see many design and migration tools that enable you to choose between the mainframe or PC relational databases. The logical design effort is usually the same, but the physical implementation will vary dramatically.

DDL to Xbase Converter Tool from CASEware Technology is an example of one of the new tools. This product will take DDL for DB2 and create Xbase databases and indexes.

5.3   perfoRMAx from Aonix

perfoRMAx is a unique, easy-to-use graphical tool suite that applies the mathematical principles of Rate Monotonic Analysis and other scheduling techniques to your real-time system. Used during proposal, specification, design, implementation, and maintenance phases, perfoRMAx can save months of wasted effort, millions of wasted dollars, and can even save lives and assets (see Figure 5-2).

Utilizing an engineering approach to real-time development sets perfoRMAx apart from other tools. Through its unique analysis process, perfoRMAx provides a framework for analyzing system timing behavior.

FEATURES

- Mathematically guarantees system performance
- Analyzes real-time performance before, during, and after system implementation
- Ensures the ability to schedule under worst-case scenarios
- Isolates individual subsystems and operational nodes
- Pinpoints bottlenecks and recommends redesign strategies

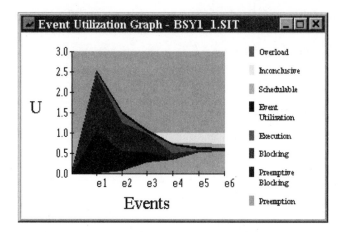

Figure 5-2 PerfoRMAx Utilization Chart

- Is completely language and target independent
- Supports analysis of all major scheduling policies

SYSTEM REQUIREMENTS

- Windows 3.1, Windows 95, Windows NT
- 2M RAM
- 4M hard disk space

STATIC PERFORMANCE ANALYSIS

Developers and engineers can use perfoRMAx to analyze the runtime performance of real-time systems before, during, and after implementation. perfoRMAx gathers system characteristics, performs a static analysis, and measures the Ability of the system to meet performance requirements. The analysis considers worst-case and combinations of system load, phasing, and resource consumption.

Worst-case analysis ensures real-time performance and stability under heavily loaded conditions. perfoRMAx also provides an average-case analysis for normal operation.

ANALYZING EXISTING SYSTEMS

In addition to engineering new real-time systems, perfoRMAx measures the capacity and limitations of existing designs and implementations. With perfoRMAx, real-time developers and engineers are able to quantify the potential for increasing load and adding capabilities to any system.

If a real-time system does not meet its performance specifications, perfoRMAx presents the timing anomalies along with suggestions for a corrective action. perfoRMAx presents synchronization, resource allocation, and processor throughout metrics (refer to Figure 5-3), taking the guesswork out of determining the real performance issues. perfoRMAx helps you develop an overall solution strategy before buying new hardware or modifying any part of the real-time system.

How does perfoRMAx work? perfoRMAx is designed to provide you with the benefits of real-time analysis technology, without getting you caught up in the details. perfoRMAx has several components for analyzing your real-time system.

- Collects system characteristics
- Checks for completeness and consistency
- Determines the real-time performance capabilities of the system with a static schedule-ability analysis
- Presents the analysis results in an intuitive, comprehensive manner
- Provides suggestions for corrective actions when necessary

RATE MONOTONIC ANALYSIS

perfoRMAx is an engineering tool based on proven analytical techniques defined by fixed-priority scheduling theory and *Rate Monotonic Analysis* (RMA).

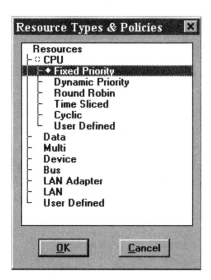

Figure 5-3 PerfoRMAx Resource Types and Policies

RMA is practical, theoretically sound, and provides quantitative methods for understanding, analyzing, and predicting timing behavior. RMA was developed by the *Software Engineering Institute* (SEI) to address real-time analysis (see Figure 5-4).

perfoRMAx provides an analytical approach to understanding and measuring the timing behavior of real-time systems. perfoRMAx consists of a scheduleability engine, transformation and analysis dialogs, comprehensive diagnostics, and customized reports.

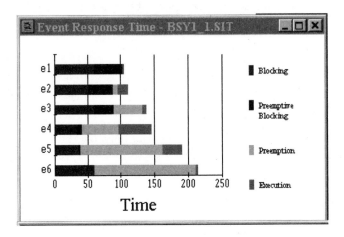

Figure 5-4 PerfoRMAx Event Response Time

6

Microsoft® SQL Server™ 6.5 Tuning

Unlike chapters on other RDBMS in this book, a discussion of new terms for Microsoft SQL Server[1] will not be presented here. The reason is that there are so many correlations between Sybase and Microsoft SQL. So many, in fact, that they appear to be the rule, not the exception. If you read the beginning of Chapter 11, you will become familiar with many terms that have the same meanings in Microsoft SQL.

Microsoft SQL Server is not just another RDBMS. SQL Server, as it will be called from now on, is a top contender for the midrange database market, which is rapidly becoming the high-end market. A single server can support 5,000 users, executing several million transactions per day on a database in the hundreds of gigabytes. With clustering, it is possible to configure 16 servers (each on an SMP box) today, many more in a couple years. In fact, just prior to print, I read an article explaining how IBM ran a system with 1 billion transactions per day. That is almost beyond belief. But, this is no ordinary database, and Microsoft is no ordinary vendor. Much of the technical information for their products is available over the Internet. If you sign up to become a member of the *Microsoft Developers Network* (MSDN), you can get access to even more technical information.

SQL Server is tightly integrated with the Windows NT operating system. This is good in two respects. First, the product runs better because it talks with the operating system. Second, you don't have to decide which operating system to go with. Windows NT is all there is. We discuss the tuning of Windows NT in Chapter 8, including how to use the Windows NT Performance Monitor.

---

[1] Microsoft® SQL Server™ is a registered trademark of Microsoft Corporation.

As with most RDBMS, the greatest benefit in SQL Server performance can be gained in the areas of logical database design, index design, query design, and application design. However, these areas can be personnel intensive. Sometimes you will identify a query that is run frequently and can be optimized. Often you will spend inordinate amounts of time trudging through queries that will not return anything for your investment. But, when they do pay off, they pay off big. We will discuss these types of tuning opportunities first in this chapter. Then we will look at system tuning areas like memory, disk arrays, cache buffers, and so forth.

6.1   SQL Server 6.5 Performance Enhancements

Back in release 6.0, we were surprised to get *symmetric multi-processing* (SMP), parallel data scan, disk striping, a faster server, and some optimizer enhancements. Release 6.5 adds an impressive list of new additions. Here are a few of the important ones.

RELEASE 6.5 ENHANCEMENTS (PARTIAL LIST)

- Built-in support for Internet applications
- Improved support for distributed transactions
- Heterogeneous replication
- New dynamic-locking architecture
- Compaq Proliant failover support
- SMP CPU affinity masks
- Remote Connection Timeout

6.2   Normalized Databases

If you read the database design chapter, you already know the slant I have on database design. You need to normalize your tables to third or fourth normal form and then back off for the sake of performance. More tables of a narrow nature characterize a normalized database, while wider tables tend to proximate denormalized ones. Normalized databases do possess the following qualities:

- Sorting is faster because there are fewer columns
- Index creation is faster because there are fewer columns
- There are typically fewer indexes per table
- Less redundant data
- Fewer NULLs
- Less referential integrity processing

- Reduced table locking
- Increased clustered indexes, due to more tables

Normalized databases are routinely associated with complex joins, an area of poor performance. There are several techniques for handling joins. One way is to denormalize the table. Another is to create a coverage index that satisfies the request. This won't always work, and faster devices are a last resort, as is 64-bit processing.

6.3 Indexes

The presence or absence of an index can make or break performance. A poorly designed index is just as devastating. The optimizer depends on effective path alternatives to access tables. An inadequate number of these alternative paths, or inefficient paths, will degrade response times. It's impossible to examine all the WHERE clauses in your queries to identify your index needs. Instead, you need to isolate poorly performing queries and review their SQL code. In Chapter 1, we provided the names of several third-party vendors with tools for tuning SQL code. A low-budget alternative is to use SHOWPLAN to locate queries that would result in scans. These particular queries could benefit from a faster access mode, like indexes. In order for the optimizer to have the information it needs to best use indexes, distribution pages must be built.

DISTRIBUTION PAGES

When you issue the UPDATE STATISTICS statement, a database page is built which logs the distribution of the index key. A sampling of data values is used to produce the statistic. If you use DBCC SHOW_STATISTICS to see the statistics, a value indicating selectivity of an index is presented (the lower the density returned, the higher the selectivity). Selectivity is the basis for determining whether or not an index would be useful to the optimizer. Here is an example of using the UPDATE STATISTICS command on the invoice table. If the table has any indexes, the distribution page is built.

```
update statistics invoice
```

Indexing is a science. It isn't enough to just build a truckload of indexes and hope for the best. You need to understand how the optimizer will choose paths and provide the best indexes for the bulk of your processes.

INDEX SUGGESTIONS

- Narrow indexes have more rows per page and fewer index levels. Therefore, they are processed faster and satisfy more general queries and join requirements.
- Too few indexes result in additional scanning.

- Too many indexes result in additional update overhead.
- A clustered index will improve access to a frequently accessed range of values.
- Run UPDATE STATISTICS regularly to provide the optimizer with distribution pages needed to make accurate access choices.

CLUSTERED AND NONCLUSTERED INDEXES

A table can have only one clustered index. Clustered indexes will group like information. For example, a query to find all the bolts of a particular type in a parts database would benefit by having a clustered index on bolt category. Here is an example of this query.

```
select * from part
where category = 'bolt'
```

But, how do you know which columns in a table are good candidates for a clustered index? Here is a query that will count the number of unique data values for the category column.

```
select count (distinct category)
from parts
```

If the parts table contains three million rows, and the count returns two million categories, it is best to use a nonclustered index on category. But, if there are only 5,000 unique categories, a clustered index would be a good choice. As the number of unique values drops near to zero, it becomes futile to build an index, because it would almost require an entire table scan to get all rows for any one value. Likewise, a join on a column with only a few unique values could equate to a scan.

6.4 Application Design

Client connections submit queries that drive SQL Server locking, I/Os, CPU utilization, and multithreading services. For this reason, it's important to make the correct decisions during the application design phase. A well-designed application is capable of supporting thousands of concurrent users. A poorly designed application will bog down, even with the most powerful server platform. Here are some application design suggestions to avoid the quagmire:

- Use small query result sets (enough for one display screen).
- Avoid applications designed to browse the database endlessly (wildcards).
- Capacity plan to take advantage of parallel processing, multiple servers, SMP, MPP, or server clustering.
- Request fully qualified unique key searches (no ad-hoc queries).

- Reduce the path from request to result (forms, instructions, calls, sorts, predicates, math functions, etc.).
- Use 32-bit and 64-bit programming languages for speed.
- Reduce the number of tables involved in join operations.
- Allow `dbcancel()` or ODBC `sqlcancel()` so applications can cancel a query in progress without rebooting the machine.
- Use `dbsettimer()` or ODBC `SQLSetStmtOption()` query timeouts to avoid runaway queries.
- Use query row limits to catch runaway queries.
- Design out extra locking.
- Design out deadlocks.
- Design out extra I/Os.
- Use table partitioning and striping from the ground up.
- Separate *Decision Support* (DSS) and *OnLine Transaction Processing* (OLTP) transactions on different platforms and servers.
- Design clustered and nonclustered indexes to handle the bulk of queries.
- Use workflow design to achieve optimum business requirements before building a computer-based solution.
- Use Kai-zhen, Paradigms, and Total Quality Management to refine the application and the processes used to create and maintain it. These business philosophies can have as significant a result on design, development, and maintenance as any technically based issue.

6.5 Query Design

Any query can run inefficiently. Experience teaches that certain types of query syntax and SQL predicates will result in poor performance. Everything you can do to curb your use of the following items, will improve queries:

- Large result sets and table scans
- IN, NOT IN, and OR predicates
- Highly nonunique WHERE clauses
- Expressions, data conversions, nonunique values, and local variables in WHERE clauses
- Complex GROUP BY views
- Complex ORDER BY views
- != (not equal) comparison operators

■ SUM function

■ UNION with SELECT INTO will create an intermediate worktable if the `select into bulkcopy` option is not set

The real work is modifying a query to make it less resource intensive. For example, adding a WHERE clause can force the optimizer to use an index and avoid a scan. See the following example, where the user wants to determine the gross sales of lawnmowers in the town of Yacolt, Washington. The first query performs a table scan because the SALES table does not have a city index. The second query is a little better, because there is a ZIPCODE index. The optimizer is able to utilize the index. However, the result set contains PARTS that are not needed by the user.

LARGEST RESULT SET

```
SELECT SUM(GROSS)
FROM SALES
WHERE CITY='YACOLT'
```

MEDIUM RESULT SET

```
SELECT SUM(GROSS)
FROM SALES
WHERE ZIPCODE='98675'
GROUP BY PART
```

SMALLEST RESULT SET

```
SELECT SUM(GROSS)
FROM SALES
WHERE ZIPCODE='98675'
AND PART='LAWN MOWER'
```

The final query qualifies its search on ZIPCODE and PART type. This search returns the smallest result set. Large result sets are costly on most RDBMS. They use more locks and transmit more data over the networks. The more you are able to restrict the result set, the more efficient the query. There is a point of diminishing returns. More restrictive access generally means more indexes. Indexes save on retrievals but cost more on update.

6.6 Query Tuning

Tuning the server is important, but it can be an exercise in futility, if the queries are the cause of adverse performance. You may be tuning the effect of congestion, not the cause. Query tuning, on the other hand, addresses the reason performance is unfavorable. Queries drive resource utilization. Therefore, their initial design is crucial. Even if you design a query for good performance, however, you may have to revisit it from time to time because the application will evolve. Users ask for more functionality, which leads to more complex queries, and so on. As this evolution pursues, performance can degrade further and further, until you are forced to do something about it. That is the nature of tuning. We do it when we have no other choice.

The first task is to locate the top 10 queries that run the longest, use the most CPU, and are executed the most. Use one of the many tools described in this book to find these queries; there is the NT Performance Monitor (see Chapter 8), SHOWPLAN (see Chapter 6), the Microsoft SQLSTRES program (see Chapter 6), or Inspect SQL from Precise SQL (see Chapter 1). ODBC applications can use the ODBC administrator to trace calls.

The next step is to determine why the query is performing the way it does. The following suggestions will help:

- Use ISQL to run the query in isolation and local pipes. Redirect the output to a file, so you can be certain that network and screen I/O do not play a part in the performance. Sometimes, this also can identify a software layer that is causing additional overhead.

- Determine whether the query is I/O bound or CPU bound:

  - If Windows NT Performance Monitor shows 80 percent or higher CPU usage consistently, while % Disk Time is consistently low, then the query is CPU bound. Take a look at where CPU is being consumed in query. SHOWPLAN may help isolate the cause.

  - If Windows NT Performance Monitor shows consistently low CPU usage (under 60 percent) and consistently high I/O, then the query is I/O bound. Use the information in the next bullet to further isolate the cause of I/O.

- Use SET STATISTICS IO ON to examine the I/O consumed by the query. See the sections in this chapter on I/O devices and I/O tuning. Also see the Windows NT Performance Monitoring information in Chapter 8. If a query is I/O bound, these are some of the things you can do to improve performance:

  - Table partitioning and disk striping

  - Table space management

  - Index creation (to satisfy WHERE clauses and joins)

  - Index rebuilding (to collapse levels)

  - Cache buffer tuning

  - Load balancing

  - Faster devices and controllers

- Use SET SHOWPLAN ON to see the plan steps. See the section on SHOW-PLAN to understand how to interpret SHOWPLAN output.
- Use server-based stored procedures for better performance.
- Run the query outside of a view or stored procedure. This will identify if the problem is in stored procedures or views and how they are optimized.
- Triggers can transparently perform I/O. Remove triggers to determine whether they are the source of overhead.
- Be aware of possible triggers on the involved tables that can transparently generate I/O as the trigger runs.
- Determine whether more rows are returned to the client than needed.
- Run UPDATE STATISTICS regularly.
- Optimize queries that build temporary worktables.

After identifying the causes of poor query performance, make your changes and retest the query in isolation. If there is an improvement, move your changes to production. Be certain that you are not introducing a different resource bottleneck. You can use the SQLSTRES program to try the change out with multiple concurrent clients. If you have made a change that will improve memory usage, you should compute the required increase for the number of users. You may need to increase available memory on the machine to support your change.

6.7   Uses for SQL-Programmer

SQL-Programmer provides its users with an abundance of functionality. The same functionality designed to make development flexible provides the means to gather information used in tuning applications. For example, SQL-Programmer can be used to identify the following:

- Stored procedures
- Triggers
- Batch objects
- Views
- Rules
- Document tables and indexes
- Assemble execution plans
- Assemble I/O and time statistics

EXECUTION TIME STATISTICS

SQL-Programmer displays the time it took to parse and compile each command and the time it took to execute each step of the command. Times are given in time ticks, the exact value of which is machine dependent. The Execution Time statistics of a procedure may be obtained from either the Access Manager or SQL-Programmer Workplace Main Tool Bar.

6.8   Deciphering SHOWPLAN

Microsoft's cost-based query optimizer can quickly determine the best access method for retrieving data, including the order in which to join tables and whether or not to use indexes that may be on those tables. The query optimizer relieves the System Administrator from having to determine the most efficient way of structuring the query to get optimal performance. It is cost-based because it picks the access method that costs the least, in terms of page I/Os.

To get detailed information about the access method that the optimizer will choose, you can execute the SET SHOWPLAN ON command. SHOWPLAN will list step-by-step processing the way the optimizer processes a query. In this section, we want to illustrate the different SHOWPLAN messages and how they can be used to tune queries. In this section we will look at the following SHOWPLAN messages and their relevance to tuning queries.

SHOWPLAN Message

```
Step n
The type of query is SELECT (into a worktable) and GROUP BY
The type of query is <query type>
The update mode is deferred | direct
Scalar | Vector Aggregate
FROM TABLE | TO TABLE


Nested iteration | EXISTS TABLE: nested iteration
Table Scan
Using Clustered Index
Index : <index name>
Using Dynamic Index
```

STEP *n*

Figure 6-1 contains SHOWPLAN output for a single step query. Steps represent a way for SQL Server to break up processing, which cannot be completed in one unit of work. A good example of this is a query with a GROUP BY clause. SQL Server will select the qualifying rows in the first step of processing and group them in a second step. This requires an internal sort, which is the reason for the second step. As the number of steps increases, so does the potential for tuning. Multiple steps imply added processing, which can sometimes be circumvented.

THE TYPE OF QUERY IS *SELECT* (INTO A WORKTABLE) AND GROUP BY

If the optimizer needs to create an intermediate worktable for selected rows, this is the message displayed. In the example in Figure 6-2, a GROUP BY statement on in_zipcode forces SQL Server to build an intermediate worktable. Consequently, you see two steps in the plan output, both of which reference a worktable. Queries that contain a GROUP BY clause will always be at least two-step queries: Worktables are an indication of additional processing. They may be a signal that some variation on the query could avert the added processing.

THE TYPE OF QUERY IS *<QUERY TYPE>*

Queries will be SELECT, INSERT, UPDATE, or DELETE types. In Figure 6-2, the type was SELECT. Each type of query has its own tuning properties. By

```
SELECT in_company, in_number, in_total
      FROM invoice
      WHERE in_company = "Dunham Software"

SHOWPLAN:   STEP 1
      The type of query is SELECT
      FROM TABLE
      invoice
      Nested iteration
      Table Scan
```

Figure 6-1 SHOWPLAN Output with Single Step

```
SELECT in_zipcode, total_zipcodes = count(*)
      FROM invoice
      GROUP BY in_zipcode

SHOWPLAN:   STEP 1
      The type of query is SELECT (into a worktable)
      GROUP BY
      Vector Aggregate
      FROM TABLE
      invoice
      Nested iteration
      Table Scan
      TO TABLE
      Worktable

      STEP 2
      The type of query is SELECT
      FROM TABLE
      Worktable
      Nested iteration
      Table Scan
```

Figure 6-2 SHOWPLAN Output with Worktable

and large, most queries are SELECTS and, therefore, these generally get the greatest attention when tuning.

THE UPDATE MODE IS DEFERRED | DIRECT

SQL Server can make updates directly to the database pages, or it can store them in the transaction log and apply them at the end of the transaction. The latter method is known as *deferred update* and incurs dual costs. There are special types of processing that require deferred updates. Cascade table updates are an example. They must be logged first to avoid key conflicts before actually updating the pages.

You should review queries whose SHOWPLAN indicates deferred update mode is being used. Watch for operations like reading from a table that is being updated or populating a table from a SELECT. Also check that unique indexes exist for WHERE clauses. Otherwise, more than one row could qualify for update, requiring update to be deferred. Most of these queries can be converted to direct mode, by breaking up the operations into two or more queries, which build an interim table or separate update from retrieval. If you eliminate work, that is fine. In some instances, however, you may transfer only the deferred processing overhead to another table.

Direct updates are faster and require fewer log records than the deferred method. Because this is the desired mode, you do not need to do anything with queries whose SHOWPLAN indicates this mode. In Figure 6-3, the invoice row is deleted using direct mode, because there is a clustered index on the in_number column.

SCALAR | VECTOR AGGREGATE

Scalar aggregate is just a fancy term to describe a query function that returns a value which is the product of averaging, counting, summing, or comparing values in some field within the query. These are the aggregate query functions:

```
Query 1:        DELETE
       FROM invoice
       WHERE in_number = "1997-05-22-001"

SHOWPLAN 1:     STEP 1
       The type of query is DELETE
       The update mode is direct
       FROM TABLE
       invoice
       Nested iteration
       Using Clustered Index
       TO TABLE
       invoice
```

Figure 6-3 SHOWPLAN Output with Mode is Direct

Aggregate Function	Description
AVG()	Return average of all rows selected
COUNT()	Return count of all rows selected
COUNT(*)	Return count of all rows selected for all columns
MAX()	Return value in row with highest value
MIN()	Return value in row with lowest value
SUM()	Return sum of all rows

Figure 6-4 shows a query that produces a scalar aggregate. When the result of aggregation is one value, a scalar aggregate is used. When the result is multiple values, as in a GROUP BY clause, the result is considered a vector aggregate. SHOWPLAN shows two steps, one to process rows for the WHERE clause and a second to return the COUNT.

Now let's take a look at a similar query that will return a vector aggregate (see Figure 6-5). The GROUP BY in_zipcode requires that SQL return a COUNT for each unique ZIPCODE in the database. Consequently, it must build a table of values (vector table) to hold the variables, until the second step when they are returned as output. From a tuning aspect, it should now be easy to understand that a vector aggregate must store more interim results and do more work.

FROM TABLE | TO TABLE

SHOWPLAN indicates the table being read in the FROM TABLE output and the table written to in the TO TABLE output. If the query optimizer is joining tables it will list multiple tables in the FROM TABLE output. The order they are listed is also the order in which they are joined, even if this disagrees with the order the tables were used in the SQL syntax (see Figure 6-6). In the example, the invoice table in_part rows are first retrieved and joined with the part table pa_number rows. As the number of join operations increases, so does the cost of the query. There are 3-way, 4-way, and 5-way joins. You can optimize

```
Query:      SELECT COUNT(in_number)
            FROM invoice
            WHERE in_zipcode = "98675"

SHOWPLAN:   STEP 1
            The type of query is SELECT
            Scalar Aggregate
            FROM TABLE
            invoice
            Nested iteration
            Table Scan

            STEP 2
            The type of query is SELECT
            Table Scan
```

Figure 6-4 SHOWPLAN Output with Scalar Aggregate

joins sometimes by breaking up the join operations using multiple queries. This can cut some of the overhead out. TO TABLE table names can sometimes be the same table as was in the FROM TABLE output. The TO TABLE also may indicate a worktable. A worktable implies interim processing, which may represent an opportunity to tune the query. For example, what if the worktable is being used to sort output? This may be an indication that a new index is required.

NESTED ITERATION | EXISTS TABLE: NESTED ITERATION

Nested iteration is a way for SHOWPLAN to tell you that it is using a program loop to accomplish the step. It sounds like it may be an easy way to find a tuning opportunity, but it isn't. A nested iteration may be indicating that the query

---

```
Query:       SELECT COUNT(in_number)
             FROM invoice
             WHERE in_partnum = "lawn mower"
             GROUP BY in_zipcode

SHOWPLAN:    STEP 1
             GROUP BY
             Vector Aggregate
             FROM TABLE
             invoice
             Nested iteration
             Table Scan
             TO TABLE
             Worktable

             STEP 2
             The type of query is SELECT
             FROM TABLE
             Worktable
             Nested iteration
             Table Scan
```

Figure 6-5 SHOWPLAN Output with Vector Aggregate

```
Query:       SELECT part.pa_number, pa_stock, in_qty
             FROM part, invoice
             WHERE part.pa_number = invoice.in_part

SHOWPLAN:    STEP 1
             The type of query is SELECT
             FROM TABLE
             invoice
             Nested iteration
             Table Scan
             FROM TABLE
             part
             Nested iteration
             Table Scan
```

Figure 6-6 SHOWPLAN Output from Table

---

has to walk an index, which is not necessarily a bad thing to do. Just treat this output as information. When you specify EXISTS, IN, or =ANY in the query qualifiers, SHOWPLAN displays the `EXISTS TABLE: nested iteration` output. EXISTS requests may represent a tuning opportunity if they are being issued frequently and if they are causing the tables to be accessed using scans.

TABLE SCAN

The most optimistic tuning opportunity lies with the SHOWPLAN statement `Table Scan`. If a table has one or more indexes on it, the query optimizer may still choose to do a table scan instead of using one of the available indexes if the optimizer determines that the indexes are too costly. A table scan reads every row in a table, no matter how large the table is. The WHERE clause criterion or other query and subquery predicates determine the path taken. Because a scan was chosen, the other paths are not considered optimum. One of the challenges of administration is determining which queries to optimize. If you created an index, or in some cases another index, to satisfy every query, you would have a real problem on your hands. Additional indexes require additional maintenance. Even though indexes provide faster retrievals, they also require additional overhead to update. So, you must be selective in your tuning efforts. Table scans represent an opportunity for normalization, denormalization, or adding indexes. Figure 6-1 shows a prime example of where an index may be warranted, but you want to count the costs versus the benefits of tuning these queries, too. It just may be that the query is not qualified properly. The query in Figure 6-1 may have used an existing index, if the where clause had been written differently.

Existing WHERE clause (no index)

```
where in_company = "Dunham Software"
```

New WHERE clause (uses existing index)

```
where in_number = "1997-05-22-001"
```

USING CLUSTERED INDEX

The `Using Clustered Index` SHOWPLAN output identifies the unique index for the table that is being used. Figure 6-2 shows a clustered index being used. The clustered index is commonly called the primary index, because you can have only one of these types of indexes per table.

INDEX : <INDEX NAME>

This output statement (in Figure 6-7) will accompany a nonclustered index for a table. Tables can have up to 249 nonclustered indexes, which do not have to contain unique keys. The more unique they are, though, the fewer that need to be returned in the query selection process. Often, it can be advantageous to revisit these indexes and determine whether the columns used in their keys are optimum.

USING DYNAMIC INDEX

The Using Dynamic Index SHOWPLAN output signifies that SQL Server has decided to build its own index during the query execution. Figure 6-8 shows a query with an OR clause. Each OR clause results in a pass at the table. The results for each pass are row IDs (RIDs) stored in a worktable for the next step of processing, where they are sorted and where duplicates are removed. The RIDs equate to a dynamic index, because the table rows can be accessed directly using the RID. A final scan will use the RIDs to obtain rows directly. This entire process is very inefficient. This is only one example of the types of queries that result in this kind of processing.

```
SELECT in_company, in_number, in_part
      FROM invoice
      WHERE in_part = "lawn mover"

SHOWPLAN:   STEP 1
      The type of query is SELECT
      FROM TABLE
      invoice
      Nested iteration
      Index: pninvoice
```

Figure 6-7 SHOWPLAN Output with Single Step

```
Query 1:    SELECT *
            FROM invoice
            WHERE in_part = "lawn mower"
            OR in_month = "12"

SHOWPLAN 1: STEP 1
            The type of query is SELECT
            FROM TABLE
            invoice
            Nested iteration
            Index : part_idx
            FROM TABLE
            invoice
             Nested iteration
             Index : month_idx
             FROM TABLE
             invoice
             Nested iteration
             Using Dynamic Index
```

Figure 6-8 SHOWPLAN Output Using Dynamic Index

You may want to consider building your own permanent nonclustered indexes for the columns expressed in the OR clause, if the queries are going to represent a significant load on the server.

In this example, the SQL Server optimizer will evaluate if a table scan is more cost effective than using a dynamic index. It will choose the least costly method. If any of the OR clauses require a table scan, scan will be used for the entire query, instead of the dynamic index.

6.9   Tuning Transactions

Data consistency is a term that means the database is both logically and physically correct. This can be considered a state, because it is time dependent. At any given moment, the database can be in flux. Internally, the SQL Server is maintaining integrity using locking, logging, and other enqueuing. Each query running is allowed to update a row only after its predecessor has committed its changes. In many instances, the predecessor query must commit its changes to many rows and tables before another process can proceed. The work that occurs between these commits is known as a *unit-of-work* (UOW). A transaction is the processing responsible for one or more units-of-work. The larger a unit-of-work is, the greater the wait period for subsequent processes. Therefore, transactions should hold onto resources for the shortest possible time. In other words, they should use small units-of-work. Otherwise, shared resources can be held longer than necessary and result in bottlenecks. Transactions are characterized by properties having the acronym ACID (wherein lies the term acid test for transactions), which stands for **A**tomic, **C**onsistent, **I**solated, and **D**urable.

Acronym Character	Description	RDBMS Implementation
Atomic	The transaction is a complete set of instructions representing a business function (process)	Process or Batch
Consistent	A transaction will transform the database to a new consistent state if successful, or return it to a prior consistent state, if it fails.	Units-of-work (UOW)
Isolated	A transaction stands on its own and is not visible to other transactions. Thus, we consider transactions as single-threaded entities.	Row Locking Page Locking
Durable	A transaction survives system failures. Unlike a batch file update which might lose its entire file if the system is lost, the changes for an individual transaction are kept.	Transaction logs

The following batch file shows how a transaction works. The statements would be considered a single transaction as seen in the SQL Server Performance Monitor, where I/O Transactions/sec is the number of batches (or remote procedure calls, RPCs) per second. The elapsed time between commits represents a critical factor in tuning. It could be the time that page and row locks are held. That is why it is a good idea to commit work as soon as you are ready to release locks. So, you could use a batch routine with time displays to determine where performance slows in a batch process.

```
begin tran
-display beginning of tran time here-
insert invoice values ("159","Dunham Software","lawn mower","289.95")
commit tran
-display done with invoice insert time here-
begin tran
delete order where or_comany = "Dunham Software"
commit tran
-display done with order delete time here
begin tran
select sum(in_qty) from invoice where in_part = "lawn mower"
commit tran
-display done with sum parts invoiced time here
go
```

On an SMP processor, you can provide for *Distributed Transaction Coordinator* (DTC) transactions that protect the ACID properties of your transactions. On clustered systems, DTC automatically manages the work of transactions that span multiple servers on different nodes. To configure the system to use DTC, make the following system configuration change. Sessions begun after this option is set inherit the revised configuration setting.

```
sp_configure ' remote proc trans', 1
reconfigure go
```

To summarize about transaction tuning, here are some things that you can do when designing transactions, reengineering transactions, or scheduling them:

- Make transactions simple, not complex.
- Decrease the number of rows or pages accessed in a transaction. The maximum number of rows accessed in a transaction should be equal to the number that could fit on a single page in the table, or on a single screen when returned.
- Reduce the time for a unit-of-work (from commit-to-commit).

- Design systems to match business work flows.
- Design business functions to match business needs.
- Design the physical database to optimize transaction processing.
- Design transactions to use faster resources.
- Prioritize high-volume transactions.
- Reserve high-speed devices like fiber optics, memory, and fast networks for priority transactions.
- Load balance transaction processing over a 24-hour day, not just an 8-hour day. You also can load balance transaction processing over multiple CPUs, servers, clusters, and distributed database regions, using replication or networking.
- Separate *Decision Support* (DSS) and *OnLine Transaction Processing* (OLTP) transactions onto different platforms that are highly tuned for those kinds of transactions.
- Perform long-running batch transactions off-shift.
- Fine tune the transaction log, which affects the speed at which transactions process.
- Eliminate deadlocks through tuning and redesign.
- Write batch routines that are restartable, ignoring already processed rows.
- Don't leave a transaction open that depends on user input.

6.10   Transaction Logs

There are two key factors to logging performance. One is the size of the transaction log and the other is where it is located. The transaction log is made up of records, which have 16-byte headers and a variable portion. The variable portion is filled with update, delete, insert, and commit information about rows. It is used to roll out aborted transactions. If the log fills up an error like this is displayed:

```
error 1105: Can't allocate space for object syslogs in database dbname
because the log segment is full.
```

When this happens, you need to dump the transactions log. Researching the dumped log data, you may be able to locate the cause of the full syslog: an uncommitted transaction, bulk processing, or truncation threshold exceeded. Next, you will want to address whether or not the log should be increased in size or dumped more frequently.

The next option for log performance is placement. The log should be placed alone on the fastest device available (Ultra SCSI Fast-n-Wide, for example), using its own high-speed controller. Never place the log on the same drive with databases. This opens an integrity exposure, in the event of a drive failure.

6.11   Tuning Delphi Applications

Delphi is an extremely powerful development tool. With power, comes a need to make decisions. Some of those decisions are performance oriented. That is our focus here, not using the Delphi product. When using Delphi, you need to consider the following performance issues.

INTERCEPTING EXCEPTIONS

Intercepting exceptions in Delphi is costly. If you have to intercept them for large numbers of records, then online performance can be impacted. Off hours processing is preferred.

DATABASE COMPONENTS VERSUS ALIASES

How you access databases in your application can greatly influence performance. The easiest way for programmers to access databases is to place the full path information to a table in the table name property. You can also set up an alias in the DatabaseName property dataset component. A third method is to use a database component. Here are some of the benefits of using a database component:

- A database component is global to the application.
- The connection to SQL Server can be kept open independent of datasets and open or close datasets through a single connection. The number of connections is reduced.
- You can specify the transaction isolation level, so you can choose the optimum one.
- You can connect to the database using the fastest ODBC drivers available. To do this you need an alias that uses the ODBC driver. Using aliases makes the application harder to deploy, but enables you to choose the fastest driver.
- Avoid record-at-a-time access.
- You can use TList objects for high-performance tables-in-memory.

When creating an alias, there are several important parameters to specify. Look at the following example.

```
DATABASE NAME=invoice
SERVER NAME=server1
USER NAME=jad
OPEN MODE=
SCHEMA CACHE SIZE=8                    <==size affects performance
BLOB EDIT LOGGING=
LANGDRIVER=                            <==driver speed
SQLQRYMODE=
```

```
SQLPASSTHRU MODE=SHARED AUTOCOMMIT
DATE MODE=0
SCHEMA CACHE TIME=-1
MAX QUERY TIME=                              <==limits
MAX ROWS=-1                                  <==limits
BATCH COUNT=200
ENABLE SCHEMA CACHE=FALSE                    <==use cache?
SCHEMA CACHE DIR=
PASSWORD=
```

WHICH ISOLATION LEVEL SHOULD I USE?

Isolation, by its name, implies some kind of separation. That is the nature of transaction isolation, to prevent one transaction from affecting another. Per the SQL-92 standard, there are four basic isolation levels available to you: Read uncommitted, Read Committed, Read Repeatable, and serializable. However, SQL Server and Delphi do not support the same levels. Each level is designed to deal with different kinds of processing anomalies. Table 6-1 is a cross reference of supported levels and their respective anomalies.

So why bother with isolation? It is an integral part of your locking strategy, and locking affects performance. Also, isolation is going to be part of an ODBC solution. So, you must decide how important the integrity of your application data is. For OLTP applications, a higher isolation level is probably a good idea. Serializable may be the only acceptable mode for OLTP. But, in a *Decision Support* (DSS) one, you can let your guard down, because updates may be nonexistent. In these applications, Read Uncommitted may be adequate and preferred, for the reduced locking.

Using the database component described in the previous section, you can set isolation levels to control how transactions behave in a multiuser/multithreaded setting. The major factors affecting your decision, after performance, are going to be with regard to the anomalies: dirty reads, nonrepeatable reads, and phantom reads.

A dirty read is where uncommitted updates from transactions can be viewed by other transactions. If the transaction that made the updates is rolled out, those updates never occurred. But to some transactions, they appeared to. The data is dirty. After you select an isolation level that allows this to occur, it could happen frequently. You have no control over how often a user might see garbage.

A nonrepeatable read is similar to a dirty read, in that uncommitted updates are available to other transactions. This anomaly occurs when a transaction sees an update from another transaction before it has been updated and again after it has been updated. Repeated reads do not return the same information for a row.

The third anomaly is called a phantom read. The only difference between this and the other types of anomalies is that the transaction performing uncommitted updates has inserted a new record. In other words, this is not an update scenario. So, other affected transactions may issue multiple queries, where the

TABLE 6-1   SQL Server and Delphi Supported Isolation Levels

Isolation Level	SQL	Delphi	Delphi	Shared	Exclusive	Dirty	Nonrepeatable	Phantom Reads
Read Uncommitted	Y	Y	tiDirtyRead	N	N	Y	Y	Y
Read Committed	Y	Y	tiReadCommitted	Y	Y	N	Y	Y
Read Repeatable	N	Y	tiRepeatableRead			N	N	Y
Serializable	Y	N			N	N	N	

results do not include the row in one query but do in another query. The row appears to have appeared out of nowhere (a phantom).

Your decisions regarding isolation should be based upon your need for transaction consistency and performance. Don't take consistency for granted.

In conclusion, here are some useful hints at tuning Delphi SQL Server applications:

- Avoid intercepting exceptions whenever possible.

- Use database components.

- Use ReadUncommitted isolation for DSS systems to reduce locking overhead.

- Inserting data into a temporary table with TTable or TQuery and then moving it to the base table is faster than moving individual records to a base table with a clustered index.

- Use TTable with a WHERE filter to reduce the rows returned in a query.

- Avoid using TDataSource and a grid control to browse the entire table with SQL Server.

- Avoid auto-creating data-entry forms, because the BDE queries system tables adds overhead.

- Only open and close datasets once. These are expensive operations.

- Use TStoredProc stored procedures that are faster than views. SQL Server will cache the query tree for views, it will not cache the access plan for views. However, this is one of the problems with a stored procedure. You should create stored procedures that tell SQL Server to generate a new access plan upon each execution, to get around this problem.

- Use `CachedUpdates` to queue updates on your PC and then use `ApplyUpdates` to move these changes to SQL Server databases.

- Place read-only tables in memory by creating a TList object or array and loading it with rows of data. Good examples of tables for memory are tax codes and rates, ZIPCODE, and other static information. One approach might be to load heavily used tables into memory on the Server and use a stored procedure to access them.

6.12 SQLSTRES Program

SQLSTRES.C is a sample Windows NT-based C-language program downloadable from Microsoft. It can simulate a large number of client connections running Transact-SQL queries. This enables you to prototype production environments or to tune a system in preparation for scaling up and out. You can use this technique to scale systems, load balance servers, tune disk I/O, or debug deadlocking. Queries are read from standard text files.

SQLSTRES enables you to specify the number of clients and iterations to perform. Windows NT threads simulate client connections, and query output is displayed in MDI windows.

6.13 Database Alerts

The Windows NT Performance Monitor has the capability to monitor SQL Server and Alert selected clients/workstations of database conditions. This is particularly useful for things such as the following:

- CPU overload
- Runaway processes
- Log space used
- Cache overload
- Database space getting low

Using the SQL Performance Monitor workspace configuration file (.PMW extension), you can define a SQL Server Database Alert. These are the steps necessary to do this:

SETTING UP DATABASE ALERTS

1. Start SQL Performance Monitor from SQL for Windows NT Group.
2. Select Alert from the View menu.
3. Select Add to alert from the Edit menu.
4. Enter Server id.
5. Select an object to alert on (e.g., SQLServer-log) from the drop-down Object list box.
6. Select a counter to alert on (e.g., Logspace Used (%), Processor Used (%)) from the Counter list box.

7. Click on `Alert If` and put 80 in the `Over` box or some threshold value. See Chapter 8 for many potential thresholds.

8. In the `Run Program` place the .BAT or .CMD file to execute when the alert is triggered.

9. Select the database from the `Instance` list box.

10. Click on the Add button, then the Done button.

11. Return to the `View` menu.

12. Select `Chart` from the `View` menu.

13. Enter the workspace file name `c:\sql\my.pmw` and click OK to save.

14. Enter `Exit` to leave SQL Performance Monitor.

15. Select the `Startup Group`.

16. Select `New` from the `File` menu.

17. Select `Program` from the `New Frame` box.

18. Click on OK.

19. Enter the name for an ICON to be used with the alert.

20. Enter `perfmon.exe c:\sql\my.pmw` in the `Command Line` box.

21. Click OK to save.

22. Now relogon to Windows NT.

If the setup was successful, the new alert will show up in the new instance of SQL Performance Monitor, when you double-click on the icon to start it up.

 NOTE: System Administrator or Administrators group authority is required to perform this procedure.

6.14 Stored Procedures

Stored procedures are faster than views. They execute on the server and return the results to the client workstation. Administration is easier, because you only need to make a change to a procedure to have all applications see the change. They reduce the use of ad-hoc queries that deteriorate performance. So, they are useful in enforcing database access standards. When you create a stored procedure, the text part of the stored procedure is kept in the syscomments system table. A normalized version of the procedure with a query tree is kept in the sysprocedures system table. It is read into memory the first time the procedure is invoked, at which time the procedure is compiled and the optimizer creates the access plan. Subsequent executions of the procedure are very fast. If the database has changed, an embedded command can cause a fresh copy to be built. However, if a table has new columns and the procedure uses SELECT*, the procedure must be deleted and readded to force a new compile.

Stored procedures are written in Transact-SQL (SQL Server's native language). The language is robust, having the ability to perform any kind of logic needed. It can also be used to pass parameters to the TStoredProc function, making procedures dynamic (Delphi works, too). To create a dynamic stored procedure that will enforce access to the invoice table by an index, use a procedure like the following:

```
create proc invoices_for_company
@company char(30)
as select *
from invoice
where in_company = @company
```

In this stored procedure, @company is a 30-byte character variable passed to the invoices_for_company procedure. At execution time the variable you pass is substituted. Because you, as an administrator, know of the existence of a nonclustered index on company name, you are aware that the query will optimize to use the index. Execution of our sample procedure is easy. Just enter a command like the following:

```
execute invoices_for_company "Dunham Software"
```

Microsoft's SQL Server supports three types of stored procedures: system stored procedures, user-defined stored procedures, and extended stored procedures. System stored procedures are used to administer and maintain the database server. User-defined stored procedures are created by the application developer to perform data manipulation and retrieval functions. Extended stored procedures give the administrator access to the server's operating system functions.

To derive the most benefit from stored procedures, you need to follow these steps:

1. Obtain a list of all queries being executed and how often they are executed.

2. Take the highest volume queries and find those which use the most CPU or I/O.

3. Further reduce the list to those queries that are part of mission-critical applications.

4. Build stored procedures for those remaining on the list.

5. Make sure there is adequate memory to hold all the stored procedures.

6. Have the application program teams switch to executing the stored procedures.

6.15 Server Performance

A process, batch, or transaction can have one or more threads executing concurrently. In multiuser systems, the number of active threads can be in the hundreds or thousands. For example, an NT system that is just idling with Performance Monitor running uses a hundred threads. Threads are assigned priorities by Windows NT. There are 32 levels, one being lowest and 31 the highest. Zero is reserved for the operating system, which makes sense. The operating system must have precedence over other tasks, or it wouldn't be able to terminate ones that run away, etc.

Windows NT manages threads using two distinctly different types of priorities. First are *Variable Priorities* that include thread priorities 1 to 15. The others are *Real-Time Priorities* that include the remaining 16 to 31 thread priorities. Variable priorities mean just that. They are automatically adjusted by the Windows NT scheduler. The real-time priorities are not adjusted by the scheduler. Because they do not change, they are termed real-time.

Optimizing SQL Server means giving it priority over other less important threads. To do this, the SQL Server Setup program enables you to select an option to boost its performance (from Set Server Options). By default, SQL Server runs at thread priority 7. On a uniprocessor, with the option turned on, it will run at thread priority 13. On supported symmetric multiprocessors, it goes up to thread priority 24. It is recommended that the option be turned on only for servers dedicated to running SQL Server. However, because it is also recommended that a server be dedicated to running SQL Server, it is kind of a nit.

Administrators can easily monitor multiserver environments, if they have the right tools. Here are four tools which can make the job a snap:

SE-6M6M15V-4-A from Network Technologies Incorporated is a device for controlling 32 Windows NT Servers with one monitor and keyboard (www.networktechinc.com).

Sentry Shutdown Remote Power Module from Server Technologies Incorporated allows administrators to initiate an orderly shutdown and restart of a remote NT server.

SiteScope 2.0 from Freshwater Software Incorporated can reboot servers, allocate additional space, and notify an administrator via e-mail or pager.

SpaceGuard for NT from Simac Software Products will let administrators limit the disk space for individual users or groups. When the limit is exceeded, the administrator is notified via e-mail.

6.16 Processor Tuning

Processor Tuning for Microsoft SQL Server should be broken into three categories. Category one is capacity planning—what kind of hardware to buy. By hardware, we mean more than the processor alone. The second category is server tuning. Category three is application tuning. All three categories have CPU tuning tasks that affect overall throughput. We will take a look at each category independently.

CAPACITY PLANNING

There is an old Chinese parable, "He that mounteth the panther, must not dismount." The responsibility for purchasing the correct amount of processing horsepower on a large project is like this parable. After you have the job, you can't back out. If you make the wrong decision, you may be updating your resume. A high estimate could result in a $75K clustered processor purchase. An estimate too low might leave your company with an unneeded $2K mail-order mistake. Here are some questions to answer before you pick up the phone to place an order:

- Will the system be dedicated to Microsoft SQL Server? The answer should be yes.
- How many users or processes will access SQL Server?
- What will the level of transaction throughput be?
- Is the SQL Server a departmental system or an enterprise system? You really need to find out up front whether distributed database replication is going to be a major factor in your planning.
- Must the server be scalable? If you will have 100 users at the end of the first year and 5000 at the end of the third year, the answer is yes. You want to be able to scale up and out. Aggregation or clustering is a wise choice.
- How many processors will be needed?
- How much memory will be needed?
- How many disk drives, RAID arrays, and controllers will be needed?
- Which networking software and protocol(s) will be used?
- How many network controllers will be needed and which type?
- How much disk mirroring will be done?

After you get your workload estimates, you need to feel out the marketplace. Any tuning book that claims to have all the answers is lying. Technology and price/MIP are changing so rapidly that today's answer is out-of-date in a month. A wise decision should include council from multiple sources. Ask vendors how many users and transactions are rated on their machines. Then, send out USENET messages on the Internet to ask fellow database veterans about their experiences. Finally, dig into the current trade journals for benchmarks. When done, you will be able to draft an intelligent proposal including your estimates and recommended choices for hardware. The bottom line on capacity planning is that it is better to error in favor of buying a little more CPU power than coming up short. By the way, capacity planning never ends. Systems always seem to grow and change. It's their nature.

After you have the right processor and the first application is running, CPU monitoring will begin. The following pointers will aid you in determining where CPU problems originate, as will the information on CPU tuning in Chapter 8.

ARE YOU FEEDING CPU HOGS?

Given the Windows NT Performance Monitor, or SQL Server Performance Monitor, CPU monitoring is a cinch. The monitors will identify whether the processor(s) are overloaded or whether individual processes are responsible for bottlenecks.

If `Processor: % Processor` Time consistently registers more than 85 percent, the processor(s) may be the bottleneck. (Use `System: % Total Processor Time` for multiprocessor systems.) However, if a process is consuming all the CPU, then use the `SQLServer-Users: CPU time` statistic. Other than a rarely occurring CPU loop, most process problems originate with poorly designed queries or inefficient database access. Follow the guidelines for tuning transactions and queries in this chapter, as well as the tuning guidelines in Chapter 8.

If `Processor: % Privileged Time` is consistently over 20 percent and `Processor: % User Time` is consistently below 80 percent, then SQL Server is likely generating excessive I/O requests to the system.

See the sections on I/O tuning in this chapter and in Chapter 8 for ways to resolve I/O bottlenecks.

If the CPU bottleneck is not associated with a few processes, system tuning is in order. After that, it is time to address an upgrade in hardware or memory. Here is a list of general tuning suggestions:

- Improve query performance.

- Improve I/O performance.

- Improve Server Performance.

- Consider denormalizing tables.

- Consider additional indexes or index maintenance.

- Schedule CPU-intensive queries during off-peak hours.

- Boost the MS SQL Server priority.

- Increase memory for caching.

- Increase the number of servers.

- Increase the number or speed of processors (SMP and Clustering).

- Move unnecessary processes to another server or platform.

- Set Windows NT Tasking to `Foreground and Background Applications Equally Responsive`.

- Use bus mastering.

- Use faster network hardware and protocols.

- Place tempdb in RAM.

6.17 SCALABILITY

SQL Server achieves its scalability by supporting *symmetric multiprocessing* (SMP). Beyond that, a clustering approach is used to scale out. Clustering requires partitioning a large database so that each server in the cluster performs the work for a given partition. As far as I know, SQL Server will not work with *Massively Parallel Processors* (MPP), although I could be wrong. In this section we will look at tuning SMP and Clusters.

SYMMETRIC MULTIPROCESSING

Scale-up or *up-sizing* are terms applied to growing a server system by adding multiple processors. It can involve increases in the number of processors, shared memory, disks, and network cards. SMP servers can provide 2-way through 12-way processing throughput of a processor depending on the hardware chosen. SMP tuning is accomplished through scaling up a system and tuning it. Use Table 6-2 as a scalability reference to get some idea of what type of system you might use, if you knew your resource requirements. You really need to query the marketplace and vendors to derive a more realistic table. This one is supplied as a sample and is speculative.

The downside of SMP is that memory is shared and access to it must be serialized. This serialization limits the practical scalability for individual applications.

SETTING SMP PROCESSOR AFFINITY

Under heavy system loads, thread management overhead increases as threads jump from processor to processor. Setting processor affinity in SMP machines can reduce the reloading of processor cache responsible for this overhead. This is accomplished by assigning specific threads to a processor. A bit mask is used to define all of the processors. Setting specific bits to 1 means that they are available for thread assignment. In the following example, bits 1 through 6 are available for assignment. The resulting binary value is 01111110, or decimal 126. When determining bit locations count from right-to-left, not left-to-right.

Bit Position	Bit Setting	Usage
0	0	All system I/O handling
1	1	Thread affinity assignment in SQL Server
2	1	Thread affinity assignment in SQL Server
3	1	Thread affinity assignment in SQL Server
4	1	Thread affinity assignment in SQL Server
5	1	Thread affinity assignment in SQL Server
6	1	Thread affinity assignment in SQL Server
7	0	Delayed Process Call (DPC) activity for Network Interface Card 1 (NIC)

There are some quid-pro-quos when messing with processor assignments. Some of the processors in an SMP have operating system activities defaulted to them. In our example, the first processor is used by the system for all I/O

TABLE 6-2 **Scalability Table (based on speculation, not real data)**

Scale	tpmC [1]	Memory	Users	Disk
1 processor	1400	128 M	500	100 G
2-processor SMP	2800	256 M	1000	250 G
4-processor SMP	3600	512 M	2500	500 G
8-processor SMP	5676	1 G	5000	1 TB
12-processor SMP	9,000	2 G	7500	1 TB
2 node (4-way)	10,000	512 M/node	10,000	2 Cluster
4 node (4-way)	10,000	512 M/node	20,000	2.5 Cluster
8 node (4-way)	18,000	512 M/node	30,000	5 TB Cluster
16 node (4-way)	24,000	512 M/node	40,000	10 TB Cluster

[1]The *Transaction Processing Performance Council* (TPC) is the authority for determining industry standards used in comparisons. They also provide audited benchmarks for database systems and are a good source of all kinds of information (Internet address: www.tpc.org). A series of benchmarks are used, but the most widely accepted one is the tpc-C one for performance and scalability of OLTP systems. Our sample table variable called tpmC stands for transactions per minute, using the tpc-C standard.

activity. The highest processor is assigned by the system for delayed process calls (DPCs). By assigning SQL Server processing with thread affinity, we help to reduce contention between this kind of processing and operating system activities. Without affinity, they could compete for the same processors. In our example, the system has eight processors.

To change the sp_configure options and implement the affinity mask shown in our example, you would execute the following command procedure. Notice that the mask is entered as a decimal value:

```
sp_configure 'affinity mask', 126
reconfigure go
```

Another reason to have a processor available for assigning threads is to handle those special user requests. For example, on Friday afternoon a user requests to run a join of two billion record tables. The output must be available by close of business. You as an administrator don't want to work on Saturday, and you know that the join will cause response problems for other users. The solution is to assign the join to its own processor.

Here is a short list of vendor machines well suited to SMP:

SMP Platforms
Intel Pentium Pro 4xP6
DEC Alpha AXP
IBM PowerPC
SGI MIPS

SMP Platforms
Compaq Proliant
Intergraph's high-end ISMP6x server
Advanced Modular Solutions Modular Fault Tolerant Server (MFTS) comes with Windows NT Server Enterprise Edition, with Wolfpack (clustering)
NCR S26 and S46 Servers
Sequent

CLUSTERING

To grow beyond SMP boundaries, Microsoft has provided a clustering solution, in which the workload and database are partitioned among an array of networks, processors, memories, and database systems. Clustering is not new. The Teradata DBC 1024 and IBM MVS Sysplex are examples of clustering machines used with other non-SQL Server databases. For Windows NT and MS SQL Server, the Data General AviiON AV6600 and AV2100 (with clustering) is a good choice.

A cluster is two or more loosely coupled processors or SMP systems. These are commonly referred to as nodes. Currently, clusters can have up to 16 nodes. But, in the years to come, that number will grow. Communication between individual nodes is handled by a commodity network. In fact, individual components of a cluster are called *commodity components*. Clustering is really powerful. Here are some the benefits derived from clustering:

- The Microsoft SQL Enterprise Manager enables an operator to monitor and manage multiple SQL Servers from a single console.

  - Monitor clients and servers
  - Use job scheduler to automate performance tuning tasks
  - Use exception handling to isolate performance problems
  - Use third-party API to hook into performance products
  - Use replication interface to automate replication performance tasks

- Cluster technology leverages distributed system technologies like replication, remote procedure call, distributed systems management, distributed security, and distributed transactions.
- Scalability can combine SMP and Cluster architectures.
- 4-way SMP is supported. 8-, 16-, and 32-way are a future goal, which would make a Microsoft solution the deepest and widest available.
- Supports high-availability databases via fail-over from one node to another.
- Provides modular growth, in small increments, one node at a time.

- A 10-terabyte partitioned database (in theory).
- Partitioning of databases is mandatory for clustering.
- Transparent partitioning (future goal).
- Very high tpmC throughput of 10,000 to 18,000 (future goal).
- Partition parallelism, where tasks are spread across processors and database partitions.
- Pipeline parallelism, where parts of a thread are spread across parallel tasks.
- Parallel processing capabilities for utilities (future goal).
- 64-bit programming architecture (future goal).
- More cost effective than high-end SMP solutions.
- Shared disk or Shared Nothing clustering.
- *Remote Procedure Calls* (RPCs) allow node related processing.
- Large client population management using simple domain controllers.
- *System Management Server* (SMS) centralized client software administration.
- DHCP Protocol automatic dynamic TPC/IP address assignment.

Clustering and SQL Server must come together. Here is the basic architecture. Each node in the commodity network runs Windows NT Server along with a single SQL Server address space. The SQL Server address space has two pools of threads, one for system tasks (like logging) and the other for user processes (like SQL requests). Your mongo database is partitioned across the different SQL Servers, as are your users. The cluster appears to clients as a single server, because their messages (Remote Procedure Calls or Transact-SQL) get routed to other nodes. Ideally, you may want to situate your users on the server with that portion of the database they frequent most. That will help cut down on messaging traffic. In fact, tuning becomes a networking and proximity game. Is tuning therefore easy? Not really.

Tuning a clustered system is a giant undertaking. For example, suppose that you want to back up a 6 TB database, using high-speed tape systems in parallel, averaging 20 G/hr. This would run non-stop for about 12 days, if nothing went wrong and if you had enough tapes. Regular maintenance is only one area where clustering becomes challenging. Picking and choosing between setup options is another. Nowhere else is this more true than with shared disk and shared nothing clusters.

In a shared disk cluster, disks and a global cache area are shared, much like they are in Oracle's Parallel Query Option. This is a disk caching area, so a distributed cache manager and lock manager are needed to handle concurrency. The advantage of shared disk is that less memory is needed by using a global cache. Each system has to maintain its own local cache, also. The disadvantage is that it can become a bottleneck, as shared memory is in SMP systems. This isn't the case with shared nothing clusters.

With shared nothing clusters, each node owns its own disks and memory (like IBM Sysplex). Nodes communicate with each other using messages. The problems associated with sharing resources go away. However, message traffic increases. One alternative is to capture result sets returned by remote procedure calls directly in node-local tables.

Fail over is handled by assigning disk devices to more than one node. In the event one node fails, another takes over. Both shared and nonshared configurations require quite an amount of setup, and there are significant performance differences.

Microsoft claims that SQL Server and Windows NT Server clusters will bring scalability and fault tolerance to the commodity marketplace. To this end Microsoft is building clustering technology directly into the Windows NT Server operating system. The goal is to take advantage of the existing best-of-breed hardware and software technology. I give Microsoft two thumbs up on its processing solution, because it promises to give the most power to the user.

6.18   Memory and Cache Tuning

In Table 6-2 we speculated on how a system may be scaled based upon transaction volumes database size and number of users. It was only a guess because real market figures aren't available. In this section we need to build upon the idea of scaling, with respect to memory requirements, as required by the Windows System components. Thus, Table 6-3 can be considered an extension of the table from the prior section. It shows how we might select our memory based upon factors already discussed. Because Windows NT has a physical memory limit of 4G, and SQL Server has a 2G limit, we can use these values for fixing high-water marks on machine memory, even though we don't foresee an individual system or node using that amount of real memory in practice.

DISPLAYING SP_CONFIGURE MEMORY VARIABLE

To see the sp_configure current setting for SQL Server memory, type the following:

```
sp_configure 'memory'
name        minimum     maximum     config_value     run_value
-------     --------    --------    ------------     ---------
memory      1000        1048576     16384            16384
```

Notice that the maximum allowable amount of server memory is 1048576 (2K pages) or 2G. The run_value is the amount actually being used, which in this case is 16384 (2K pages) or 32M, which is an entry-level server size.

The *Virtual Memory Manager* (VMM) maps things into physical memory. When requirements exceed what is available, paging and page faults result.

TABLE 6-3   Memory Table (based on speculation, not real data)

Processor Scale	Number of Users	Machine Memory	Windows NT and SMS Memory	SQL Server Memory
1 processor	500	128 M	32 M	96 M
2-processor SMP	1,000	256 M	48 M	208 M
4-processor SMP	2,500	512 M	64 M	448 M
8-processor SMP	5,000	1 G	128 M	896 M
12-processor SMP	7,500	2 G	256 M	1792 M
2 node (4-way)	10,000	512 M/node	10,000	448 M/node Cluster
4 node (4-way)	20,000	512 M/node	20,000	448 M/node Cluster
8 node (4-way)	30,000	512 M/node	30,000	448 M/node Cluster
16 node (4-way)	40,000	512 M/node	40,000	448 M/node Cluster

Paging will utilize PAGEFIL.SYS, which should be large enough. It should also be placed where contention will not be an issue. Now let's look at conventional memory tuning for SQL Server.

SHOULD I GIVE MEMORY TO WINDOWS NT OR SQL SERVER?

Using the SQL Server monitor cache hit ratio, you can identify whether a server is bottlenecked, when this value drops below 80 percent. You have several options. First, allocate less memory to Windows NT and SMS and more to SQL Server. If Windows needs the memory, allocate more physical memory. Another option is to move some users or processing to another server. You can also restrict the amount of concurrent processing or force less important processing into off shift hours. The hit ratio is the single most important tuning counter of interest.

If `page faults/sec` is consistently high, give Windows NT additional memory and SQL Server less. Obviously, if SQL Server then runs into a problem, you need more physical memory to divide among the hungry servers.

 NOTE: If the number of SQL connections currently in use is close to the maximum defined, you should increase it immediately. If the system runs out of connections, SMS may stall. Also, if the current number of commands queued is larger than the number of network cards installed in the SQL Server computer, a network bottleneck is occurring. Resolving these two performance issues could impact the need for additional memory.

PROCEDURE CACHE

SQL Server uses memory for its procedure cache, data, and index page caching, static server overhead, and configurable overhead. SQL Server reserves 30 percent (by default) of available memory for procedure cache. Procedure cache holds stored procedures, triggers, and rules. If you make extensive use of extended stored procedures, you should release memory after their use by unloading the DLLs. This can be done like as follows:

```
dbcc dllname(FREE) command
```

The amount of memory specified must be sufficient for the SQL Server static memory needs (kernel overhead, user stack space, and so on), as well as for the procedure cache and the data cache (also called buffer cache). Procedures are stored in this cache area, as the name implies. It is also used when a procedure is being created and when a query is being compiled. If SQL Server can find a routine in the cache area, it doesn't need to compile it or read it from disk. Therein lies the savings.

You can use DBCC MEMUSAGE and statistics from the Windows NT Performance Monitor to help you adjust this value. Change this value only when you add or remove memory or when you change how you use your system. The amount of procedure cache should drop in respect to the amount of data cache, as the server system becomes larger and physical memory is greater. The reason is that the amount of data caching will need to increase, while the number of procedures will not.

DATA CACHE

Data cache is used for caching data and index pages. There are a few monitor counters that can aid you in determining when more data cache is needed.

If SQLServer: Cache-Ave. Free Page Scan or SQLServer: Cache-Max. Free Page Scan are more than 10, a memory bottleneck may be indicated due to excessive buffer scanning while searching for a free page. Two things can help resolve this. First, increase the data cache size. Second, checkpoints can be increased via the recovery interval value.

If SQLServer: I/O-Page Reads/sec remains high during peak shift hours, it is probably another indication that you are seeing excessive page faults. The data cache is inadequate. Decreasing the procedure cache or increasing SQL Server memory will cause the data cache to increase. Query tuning can also reduce the work that drives data cache usage.

Another monitor value is lazy writes/sec. This counter should remain at zero. When it starts incrementing, it is an indication that there is insufficient memory for data page caching. SQL Server needs additional memory.

Here is how you would calculate the amount of SQL Server cache memory for the first row in Table 6-3. First estimate the overhead for 500 users on the server as shown.

Calculate Overhead for 500 User Server

$$500 \; users \; \times \; \frac{40,000 \; bytes}{connection} = 19 \; MB$$

$$5000 \; database \; objects \; \times \; \frac{72 \; bytes}{object} = 360 \; KB$$

$$100,000 \; locks \; \times \; \frac{32 \; bytes}{lock} = 3.2 \; MB$$

$$other \; system \; overhead = 2.2 \; MB$$

$$Tempdb \; in \; RAM \; = \; 14 \; MB$$

$$Total \; = \; 40 \; MB$$

Next you need to use the following formula and compute the memory cache needed. In row 1 of Table 6-3, 96M are set aside for SQL Server. Therefore, using the formula, we arrive at a memory cache size of 96M – 40M = 56M.

SQL Server Memory Cache = Physical Memory – Overhead

Since the procedure cache is 20 percent of the computed amount, it is 11.2M. The remaining 80 percent of the memory cache or 44.8M is used by the data cache.

6.19 Tuning DBCC

The *Database Consistency Checker* (DBCC) utilities are a collection of programs used to verify integrity of a SQL Server Database. Running DBCC on a large table is like running a table scan because it hits every page in the table or index. That is why it is important to tune this access. Here are several actions you can take to maximize the performance of DBCC:

- Parallel index checking and read-ahead is used, so optimize their use.
- Run DBCC off shift to avoid spurious errors caused by concurrent update activity.
- Use hardware with plenty of I/O capacity (RAID disk arrays with as many physical drives as possible). Running DBCC at the same time as dumps helps avoid these errors. Errors mean you have to run in single-user mode (very slow and restrictive).
- More SQL Server data cache memory is better.
- Run CHECKDB less frequently than NEWALLOC.

- Use the NOINDEX option to avoid index checks.

- Run DBCC on a *hot backup* server. Backup sites or mirror sites are ideal for backups and consistency checks, because they offload the primary server from doing this processing.

- Run CHECKTABLE in production, by preloading the page cache with the table and index contents using a nonblocking SELECT with the NOLOCK optimizer hint. By checking one index at a time, you can minimize the elapsed time that the table is share locked. Here is how you would preload the table into memory and run dbcc on it:

```
select * from invoice (nolock index=0) where in_number < 0
dbcc checktable (invoice, 0)
```

If table blocking is hanging out spids, then issue a kill command on the dbcc checktable to free up the table. Issue the following query to track the blocking:

```
select status, blocked, hostname, spid, cmd, program_name
from master..sysprocesses
where blocked > 0
```

6.20 Locking

When queries request a large number of rows from a particular table or tables, SQL Server generates page-level locks. If a query requests a large percentage of the rows from the table (the LE threshold percent option of sp_configure), then lock escalation will occur. This makes table scans and operations against a large results set more efficient. The lock escalation options apply per state-ment and not per transaction. The lock escalation options are detailed in the last section of this chapter.

With release 6.5, Microsoft is delivering row-level locking (part of its Dy-namic Locking Initiative). (I guess that means they now have the initiative to put it in their software.) All laughing aside, release 6.5 has these features:

- Customizable locking at SELECT time with Isolation.

- ODBC Isolation support (discussed earlier).

- Optimistic concurrency reduces locking while a cursor is populated.

- Page-level locking.

- Insert row-level locking: IRL (update and delete in future).

- Dynamic Locking Initiative, whereby the locking manager uses the intelli-gence of the database engine to determine whether a row, page, multipage or table lock should be used. Another aspect of the initiative is mixed-pages, whereby rows from different tables are grouped together on a page to improve performance. This is row clustering.

ROW VERSUS PAGE LOCKING

Locking is a process of escalation. It begins with the least intrusive level of locking and becomes more severe. The more severe the locking, the more costly. For example, a SELECT implies retrieval, and therefore no locking, or at worst a shared lock. Updates will be satisfied with page locks first. Once 200 page locks per SDES are held, locking is escalated to a shared or exclusive table lock instead. This is done to lower locking overhead. Indexing has a dramatic affect on locking.

If updates can be accomplished using a clustered index, then only exclusive page locks are necessary. Otherwise, the optimizer will detect a table scan, and locking will once again escalate to a table lock. To see which types of locks are being held, you can review the SHOWPLAN output or issue the sp_lock command as follows:

```
sp_lock
spid    locktype          table_id    page    dbname
-----   --------          ---------   ----    -------
2       Ex_table          15002012    0       invoice
```

In this example, the invoice table has an exclusive table lock, probably the result of escalation. The reason is not apparent, but it could be because of a table scan. This would represent an opportunity to determine whether an index is needed. It may even be something simple like a query change.

Page-level locking is used for deletes and updates and is also used for inserts by default, unless insert row-level locking has been specified. When a transaction needs to update or delete a row on the locked page, the lock is escalated to an exclusive page-level lock.

To understand where the new row-level insert (IRL) locking benefits, it is best to describe how insert contention arises. Contention is particularly evident on insert, because new rows are added to the last page in a table page chain. For this reason insert row locking was implemented first. Prior to IRL, page locking would result in elongated waits for the last page. The problem was compounded by the need to chain in a new page for rows and was also evident during leaf-page creation of indexes.

Figure 6-9 is a summary of locking behavior for assorted SQL statements, lock types, concurrent locking, and promotions.

6.21   Tempdb

Temporary databases are a necessary evil associated with RDBMS. Most RDBMS have a tempdb, or its equivalent. All RDBMS have the same kinds of performance concerns for these system work databases and often depend on the same tuning initiatives.

I call the tempdb a necessary evil. My reason for labeling it so is because many users concurrently building temporary tables have the tendency to use a

SQL Statement	Table Lock	Page Lock	Row Lock
Insert	IX	X	X
Using Select	IS	S	none
Index Select w/Holdlock	IS	S	none
Update	IX	U, X	none
Delete	IX	X	none
Without Select	IS	S	none
Using Select w/Holdlock	S	none	none
Index Update	X	none	none
Delete	X	none	none
Create cluster Index	X	none	none
Create nonclustered Index	S	none	none

where lock types are:

```
IS = Intent Shared; Intent locks flag at table level type of page locks
     held
IX = Intent Exclusive
S  = Shared
X  = Exclusive
U  = Update; Used for read/modify/write operations
```

Table Lock Compatibility

	IS	IX	S	X
IS	YES	YES	YES	NO
IX	YES	YES	NO	NO
S	YES	NO	YES	NO
X	NO	NO	NO	NO

Page Lock Compatibility

	S	U	X	X
S	YES	YES	NO	NO
U	YES	NO	NO	NO

Figure 6-9   SQL Lock Types Allowed

whole heck of a lot of disk space. Database administrators have different ways of dealing with the issues surrounding temporary table proliferation. Some just resign from their jobs. Others request the purchase of terabyte RAID arrays for each end user. Then there is the administrator who sparingly gives each user 1 track with which to play. Honestly, the issue deserves a more serious exposition.

So, we will take a serious look at the kinds of queries that inflict this misery and some tuning alternatives for the tempdb database.

Certain types of queries will trigger the need to build a temporary table in the tempdb database. The SQL Server optimizer may determine that a temporary worktable is needed to hold intermediate results during execution of certain steps in a query, typically those with GROUP BY or ORDER BY clauses, where sorting became mandatory for whatever reason. Figure 6-5 has an example of a GROUP BY query where a worktable is built. Here is a list of other query operations that can result in the creation of temporary worktables. We will expand on each of these operations, providing examples.

Queries Generating Worktables	SHOWPLAN Output
ORDER BY	Worktable
GROUP BY	Worktable
SELECT INTO	Worktable Created for SELECT_INTO
SELECT DISTINCT	Worktable Created for DISTINCT
WHERE T1.COL = T2.COL (join)	Worktable Created for REFORMATTING
DISTINCT or ORDER BY	This step involves sorting
DISTINCT or ORDER BY	Using GETSORTED

WORKTABLE CREATED FOR SELECT_INTO

The SELECT INTO (see Figure 6-10) operation creates a table with the exact same structure as the table being selected from, and then it inserts all selected rows into the newly created table. Even though the TO TABLE indicates a temporary worktable, it really isn't temporary. The newly created table will survive the query. The new table will go to the users directory, unless tempdb is

```
Query:      SELECT *
            INTO big_companies
            FROM invoice
            WHERE amount > 500

SHOWPLAN:   STEP 1
            The type of query is TABCREATE

            STEP 2
            The type of query is INSERT
            The update mode is direct
            Worktable created for SELECT_INTO
            FROM TABLE
            directory
            Nested iteration
            Table Scan
            TO TABLE
            Worktable
```

Figure 6-10 SHOWPLAN Output for SELECT INTO

specified. Actually, the new table could be a temporary table, in the sense that the user has control over its location and lifetime.

WORKTABLE CREATED FOR DISTINCT

Step 1 of execution of a query with the DISTINCT keyword causes rows to be read into a worktable sort. The rows are sorted on the column used in the DISTINCT query. Company is the column in the example shown in Figure 6-11. Rows with duplicate company names are excluded from the final result set as the sorted file is passed in step 2 of query execution.

WORKTABLE CREATED FOR REFORMATTING

A *reformatting strategy* is used to join large tables without useful indexes. The smallest table in the query is inserted into a worktable and indexed. It is then used to join with the other table involved in the query. This is how SQL Server avoids as much I/O as possible. Figure 6-12 provides an example of this query strategy.

THIS STEP INVOLVES SORTING AND USING GETSORTED

Two other SHOWPLAN output statements that further indicate the use of a worktable are the `this step involves sorting` and `Using GETSORTED` displays. Queries with DISTINCT keywords or the ORDER BY clause cause the optimizer to build a temporary worktable, if the access plan doesn't have a suitable

```
Query:      SELECT DISTINCT company
            FROM invoice

SHOWPLAN:   STEP 1
            The type of query is INSERT
            The update mode is direct
            Worktable created for DISTINCT
            FROM TABLE
            invoice
            FROM TABLE
            invoice
            Nested iteration
            Table Scan
            TO TABLE
            Worktable

            STEP 2
            The type of query is SELECT
            This step involves sorting
            FROM TABLE
            Worktable
            Using GETSORTED
            Table Scan
```

Figure 6-11 SHOWPLAN Output for DISTINCT Query

```
Query:       SELECT invoice.part, part.qty
             FROM invoice, part
             WHERE invoice.part = part.part

SHOWPLAN:    STEP 1
             The type of query is INSERT
             The update mode is direct
             Worktable created for REFORMATTING
             FROM TABLE
             part
             Nested iteration
             Table Scan
             TO TABLE
             Worktable

             STEP 2
             The type of query is SELECT
             FROM TABLE
             invoice
             Nested iteration
             Table Scan
             FROM TABLE
             Worktable
             Nested iteration
             Using Clustered Index
```

Figure 6-12 SHOWPLAN Output for REFORMATTING

index. In these cases, a sort ensues, and these messages become part of the execution plan.

Let's summarize what has been learned by studying the SHOWPLAN output for queries involved in the building of temporary worktables. In all cases, the optimizer was unable to find a more efficient access method, even if one existed. In every case, the absence of an index could be the cause for using tempdb. Thus, one solution to problematic usage of tempdb is to provide more satisfactory index access. Now let's take a look at tuning tempdb.

TUNING TEMPDB

Tempdb (temporary database) tuning is divided into three tasks. The simplest task is to place tempdb on its own dedicated storage device, with its own controller. Because temporary tables are dropped at the conclusion of queries, a non-RAID device can be used. In fact, integrity is not an issue. Raw speed is the issue, so high-speed I/O devices with a lot of cache memory fit the picture. A device solution works, but if you use this technique with every I/O bottleneck encountered, soon you will be the proud owner of a mountain of disk drives and controllers.

The second task is to review the queries driving the use of temporary tables and to make changes that would eliminate temporary table building. This requires more labor than the first solution. Management, however, doesn't have to sign a purchase order for new hardware, unless you build too many new indexes.

The third and last option is to speed tempdb access by making it resident in memory. Allocating memory to tempdb effectively reduces the amount of memory available to allocate to the SQL Server data cache. Accordingly, you need enough physical memory to store the entire tempdb in RAM without impacting the memory required for Windows NT Server, SQL Server, and applications. Thus, you should consider using tempdb in RAM only when you have large amounts of memory available.

If most OLTP transactions use worktables, placing tempdb into RAM could provide a performance gain. If most of the work currently centers around hits in the data cache, however, you could destroy performance by stealing memory that would increase the cache hit ratio. If the latter is true, your system is probably suffering from a need for more data cache, not tempdb tuning. Of course, you could always do both, increasing the system's physical memory for the sake of a larger data cache and for forcing tempdb into memory.

The process of trying out tempdb in RAM is a trial-and-error routine. Here are the steps:

1. Query tempdb space consumption over a couple days using this query:

```
SELECT SUM(DPAGES) FROM TEMPDB..SYSINDEXES
```

   Note that because the query optimizer creates worktables internally, their names cannot be found in the tempdb.sysobjects table.

   Concurrently, monitor the cache hit ratio for the data cache during the same period (SQL Performance Monitor Cache Hit Ratio counter for the SQLServer object).

2. Determine the average tempdb space usage during the period it was monitored in step 1.

3. Determine whether the system has adequate free memory to match the average tempdb space usage.

4. If not, buy more memory or reduce your expectations. If yes, then use the following commands to establish the `avgsize`:

```
sp_configure 'tempdb in ram',avgsize go
reconfigure go
shutdown go
```

5. Monitor the cache hit ratio for adverse performance. Turn tempdb in RAM off, or adjust it for the best performance.

WARNING! If the SQL Server tempdb in RAM value is configured to a value higher than the available RAM remaining on the computer, SQL Server fails on the next startup attempt. Several error messages are logged, one of which says that the system is unable to move tempdb into RAM, the RAM device does not exist, or it cannot be created. You will need to startup a minimum configuration server using the commands in step 4 of the preceding.

6.22   Disk Subsystems

Achieving optimal disk I/O is your goal. The way you arrive at your goal is entirely up to you. But, keep this in mind. It is hard to tune a system built upon presumptions about throughput. It can be a very painful lesson to learn. You must build upon a knowledge of the applications and resource consumption that will exercise the system. The number of servers and distribution of data are equally important. I suggest that you prepare a document stating your objectives. It should include a chart with devices, controllers, bandwidths, and random and sequential loading estimates (based on transaction analysis). After these things are done, you can have fun shopping for hardware.

A proper hardware foundation is the basis for achieving the optimal disk I/O goal we began discussing. Therefore, we will use the rest of this section to discuss available hardware and software used in successful high-performance subsystems. *Integrated Drive Electronic* (IDE) and *Enhanced-IDE* (EIDE) controllers and devices can be used but aren't recommended. The following chart shows some basic differences in speed.

Controller	Speed
IDE	2.5 Mbps
ESDI	3 M/sec
SCSI-2	5 M/sec
Fast SCSI-2	10 M/sec
Fast-n-Wide SCSI	20 M/sec
Ultra SCSI	40 M/sec

Your choice for hardware controllers boils down to these: SCSI-2, Fast SCSI-2, and Ultra SCSI (the best). On a daisy-chained SCSI system, the SCSI controller has more of an impact on your total performance than your disk drive. Some of the manufacturers of high-end controllers include Adaptec, BusLogic, Digital, Future Domain, Mylex, Qlogic, Trantor, and UltrStor. You aren't limited to individual controllers, either. A system could have several in it. Disk drives probably play the next biggest role.

Look for the fastest seek times and average latency[2]. Seek time is the time required to move the disk head over the track requested, and is generally used to determine random access performance. The ratio of time spent seeking to the

---

[2] Average latency is the time it takes the drive to make half a revolution. You can simply calculate average latency from rotational speed; the two are inversely proportional. For example, a 10,000 rpm driver makes 10,000/60 revolutions per second, or about 166.66. The reciprocal of this is 0.006 seconds to make one full revolution. Therefore, half a revolution takes 0.003, or 3 ms.

time spent transferring data is usually 10:1, or higher. You are after a low ratio. Your search will quickly educate you in the benefits of higher rpm (revolutions per minute) drives.

Here is a list of premium features to watch for.

SCSI Features To Die for

Intelligent SCSI-2 (Fast-n-Wide), Ultra SCSI Wide (best)

Controller cache memory (this can vary from 1M to 256M and above)

Bus Mastering cards with on-board processors are best

Asynchronous read and write support

32-bit EISA or MCA

Hardware-level RAID 0, 1, and 5 support

Faster rotation drives (7,500 and 10,000 rpm, and above)

Read Ahead Drive caching (the more there is, the better)

Built-in Failover (hot swap of power supplies and drives)

Smallest track seek times

Smallest average latency times

Personally, I wouldn't want to own a RAID 0 device. I like the security that comes with RAID 1 and 5. But, this isn't the only reason for owning RAID. Automatic load balancing and striping are tremendous features. Average read and write performance can be better with the right RAID configuration; overall performance can be substantially better.

WHAT RAID LEVEL SHOULD I USE?

Redundant Array of Inexpensive Disks (RAID) offers logical partitioning, easy striping, load balancing, redundant disk mirroring, error-free recovery, and parallel I/O. However, you must choose the correct RAID level depending on which of these features you must have. RAID levels 0 through 7, 10, and 53 exist. Windows NT 4.0 support RAID levels 0, 1, and 5. So, we will limit our discussion to these. To see any performance improvement with RAID arrays in Windows, you need to have three or more physical drives. The best performance is achieved when data is striped across multiple controllers with only one drive per controller.

RAID level 0 implements a striped disk array, the data is broken down into blocks, and each block is written to a separate disk drive. I/O performance is greatly improved by spreading the I/O load across many channels and drives. This results in better *Mean Time to Data Availability* (MTDA) over conventional drive setups. Differently sized drives can be mixed.

RAID level 1 supports disk mirroring. Updates for each hard drive are mirrored to another drive. In the event of a drive failure, the backup drive can take over instantly. Quality RAID 1 systems allow the primary and backup drive to be read concurrently, to satisfy read requests. This is a big performance improvement. Writes on the other hand, take twice as long (dual controllers reduce the hit taken here). In OLTP systems, writes account for 20 percent or less of the activity. In *Decision Support Systems* (DSS) write activity depends on how much ad-hoc querying is done. Generally write activity is less on DSS systems than on OLTP ones. RAID 1 has two disadvantages. First, it takes twice the number of disk drives. Second, if drives are different sizes, then RAID 1 will partition them according to the smaller of two drives. The extra space is lost or with quality controllers used for nonmirrored partitions. For the highest performance, the controller must be able to perform two concurrent separate reads per mirrored pair or two duplicate writes per mirrored pair.

RAID level 5 combines striping and parity error correction codes. Each entire data block is written on a data disk. Parity for blocks in the same rank is generated on write requests, recorded in a distributed location, and then checked on reads. In a recovery, this data is used to reconstruct lost data. Some major drive failures can't be recovered from, though. So, RAID 1 is still best for serious fail-over requirements. RAID 5 is the fastest available, because it allows for parallel read-and-write operations. On small arrays with a few drives, you won't necessarily see the savings, but with a lot of drives, parallel access improvement is dramatic.

Table 6-4 has been constructed to quickly compare tradeoffs of using SQL Server supported RAID levels.

Most of the RAID subsystem vendors provide excellent data sheets on their products, via Internet web sites. I reviewed a few and saw things like high-end Fibre systems with 5 SCSI buses, 100 M/sec data transfer, 256M internal cache, ECC memory correction, triple redundant power supplies, on-the-fly array reconfiguration, hot-swap (instantaneous disk recovery), hot-spare standby, various battery backup options, and 7800 I/O/second ratings. This gives you a sample of some high-end features. Some subsystems even offer failover protection on all components making up the subsystem. The following list will speed your

TABLE 6-4   Windows NT and SQL Server Supported RAID

Feature	RAID Level 0	RAID Level 1	RAID Level 5
Disk Striping	YES	NO	YES
Disk Mirroring	NO	YES	NO
Parity CPU Overhead	NO	NO	YES (varies by device)
Fault Tolerant	NO	YES	YES
Disk Overhead	NONE	2:1 (mirroring)	LOW (ECC)
Mixed Drives	YES	NO	YES
Read Performance	GOOD	FAIR	BEST
WritePerformance	GOOD	POOR	BEST

research and shopping for RAID devices. The RAID Advisory Board has also been added to the list of great web sites. This is where to go, to find out which products have been tested, the ratings, and standards.

RAID Vendors	Web Site	Special Notes
Adaptec	www.adaptec.com	SCSI, RAID, Fibre
Adjile Systems	www.adjile.com	
Amdahl	www.amdahl.com	RAID
Andataco	www.andataco.com	RAID
ArteconIncorporated	www.artecon.com	RAID
BoxHill Systems Corporation	www.boxhill.com	Fibre Box
CMS Enhancements	www.cmsenh.com	RAID
Ciprico Incorporated	www.ciprico.com	UltraSCSI & Fibre
CLARiiON Advanced Storage Solutions (Data General)	www.clariion.com	Fibre
Compaq	www.compaq.com	RAID
Conley	www.conley.com	SCSI-3 Fast-n-Wide
CyberStorage Systems	www.cyberstorage.com	
Conner Storage Systems (now Seagate Inc)	www.conner.com	Every type of drive alive
DataStor Incorporated	www.datastor.com	
Digital Equipment Corp	www.storage.digital.com	RAID
Distributed Processing Technology	www.dpt.com	SCSI-2,3, and Ultra
ECCS Inc	www.eccs.com	RAID
EMC	www.emc.com	RAID
Eurologic Systems Limited	www.eurologic.com	
Hitachi	www.hitachi.com	RAID
IBM	www.storage.ibm.com	RAID
MicroNet Technology	www.micronet.com	RAID
Micropolis Pte Ltd	www.micropolis.com	SCSI-2,3, and Ultra drives
MTI	www.mti.com	RAID
nStor	www.nstor.com	SCSI-2
Open Storage Solutions	www.openstore.com	Fibre & Desktop RAID
Raidtec Corporation	www.raidtec.com	Fibre Channel
RAID Advisory Board (RAB)	www.raid-advisory.com	Standards and Ratings
Storage Dimensions Incoporated	www.storagedimensions.com	
StreamLogic	www.streamlogic.com	RAID
Symbios Logic	www.symbios.com	RAID

I have to admit that I was blown away by Adaptec. They have quite a series of controllers. I would consider the AHA-1542 CPK (ISA Bus Mastering Fast SCSI-2) and AHA-2940 K (PCI Bus Mastering Fast SCSI-2) boards as the entry-level cards for database aficionados. The AHA-2940K sports 133 M/sec data transfer across a PCI bus, supports seven 8G drives and uses a 32-bit bus width. It is also Windows NT compatible. However, then we begin working on the bigger server requirements. The Adaptec ARO-1130 card will plug into an existing SCSI motherboard slot, converting it to a RAID controller port. The next step would be the AAA-130 Ultra SCSI Array Adapter. It supports RAID levels 0,1, and 5, as all the Adaptec cards appear to. This card can also handle 133 M/sec data transfer across bus. But, Adaptec ships a CI/O Array Management Software that enables you to handle configuring the array, making quick drive changes, alerts for devices that fail, verifying parity information, and monitoring the array. Finally, there is the AEC4312A SCSI-to-SCSI External RAID Controller, for the big boys. With Ultra SCSI wide, you can have 15 devices per channel (30 total). It comes with a 133 Mhz on-board processor, and you can swap daughter cards when you want to upgrade from a SCSI host to a 100 M/sec Fibre channel interface.

Beware of magazine benchmarks. Even though two controller cards may show the same throughput, one may consume a lot of CPU. A good example is comparing a PCI bus mastering controller versus a PIO (programmed I/O) SCSI card. The PCI card will not use any of the motherboard CPU, because it handles I/O without taxing the motherboard. But the standard SCSI card, which shows the same amount of throughput, taxes the CPU by 30 percent.

6.23   I/O Tuning

The cardinal rule to tuning I/O is that adding CPUs to an I/O-bound system will not make it go faster. Instead, I/O tuning involves other hardware and software alternatives. In the last section, we went over the many hardware options open to you. Now we want to discuss the software ones.

APPLICATION I/O TUNING

The SQL Server `Statistics I/O` option available from the main toolbar is one method to get statistics on I/O. As procedures are executed, you will be able to select these statistics for the procedure:

- Number of scans
- Number of logical page reads
- Number of physical page reads and writes

These statistics afford you the ability to tune individual applications that may have resource utilization problems. After locating these procedures, you would identify individual queries needing special attention. This can be done with the query monitoring tools shown in this chapter and Chapter 1. The last step in the process would be to tune those queries using the sections on query tuning.

Asynchronous I/O is a feature built into the hardware controllers and subsystem. Developers can take advantage of asynchronous I/O in their own programs. The Win32 API calls ReadFile(), ReadFileEx(), WriteFile(), and WriteFileEx() all perform asynchronous or overlapped I/O. The added advantage of being a 32-bit driver can result in some real performance boosts for homegrown business applications.

SYSTEM I/O TUNING

Asynchronous I/O tuning is an option at the system level. The benefit from concurrent writes using asynchronous I/O is realized most with striped data sets.

Tuning this feature only involves adjusting the `max asynch io` option of sp_configure. The installation default is 8, which is adequate for most I/O subsystem hardware and software. But, increasing the value can improve performance sometimes. The rule-of-thumb for tuning is just try it. Increase `max asynch io` while monitoring `SQLServer: I/O-Batch Writes/sec`. Ideally, the number of concurrent writes will increase, indicating more throughput and effectively shortening the period that the system is checkpointing or doing lazy-writes. You should also monitor `SQLServer:I/O-Batch reads/sec` during this change, because I/O queuing could overload the subsystem and adversely affect read performance. Therefore, if write performance is improved without a penalty to read performance, the change should be accepted.

 NOTE: To counteract any impact asynchronous I/O has on read performance, you can increase the data cache memory size.

DISK PARTITIONING

Windows NT Server allows logical volumes to be partitioned across multiple conventional disks, or RAID disks. A disk array organizes multiple independent disks into one large, high-performance disk. RAID offers parallel read and write capabilities, as described in the prior section. The speeds vary depending on CPU, RAID level (0,1, or 5), and hardware features. The length of time taken to execute a read or write on a disk is determined by the time taken for the data area on the disk surface to pass under the read/write heads of the drive. Reading or writing an 8K block on a conventional disk takes eight times as long as a 1K block. However, in a RAID array, if the 8K block is written to a disk array with eight disks, the data is split into eight stripes of 1K, which are written to individual disks in parallel. In this way, disk arrays achieve a higher data transfer rate than nonparallel drives.

RAID is the recommended choice for your system, because it provides load balancing, incredible speeds (mostly because of the caching and bus mastering features in the hardware), and because RAID 1 and 5 offer great mirroring and fault tolerance, respectively. If you don't use the partitioning features of SQL Server, you can take a look at third-party tools. Here are a few:

Third-Party Striping Software

Anubis Formatting and Partitioning Software from Charismac

ExpresStripe Striping software from ATTO technologies

Silicon Graphics XLV Striping Disk Driver

6.24 Networks

A server box has four major areas that can become bottlenecks. They are the processor, the disk subsystem, network subsystem, and memory. In this section we will discuss some network controller recommendations, how the technology surrounding those recommendations works, and then talk about network tuning.

NETWORK CONTROLLER RECOMMENDATIONS

Not all *Network Interface Controllers* (NICs) are equal. Even though many devices show the same features in their data sheets, they may not perform the same. Subtleties can exist between devices that make them deliver varying degrees of performance. Here are some things to look for in a good NIC:

- The NIC should transfer data over the system bus at the maximum rate allowed.
- Minimum host processor loading. A fast on-board processor with a lot of L1 cache. Use only bus-mastering cards, which offload your main CPU.
- A high *Mean Time Between Failure* (MTBF).
- The NIC should be easily scalable.
- Modular: because most of today's high speed LANs operate over a user selectable variety of physical media (e.g., twisted pair cable, coax cable, fiber optic cable, etc.), modularity is desired to permit a common base design to support all the different media options.
- Portable across different computers and operating systems.
- Match the network interface card (NIC) to the system bus. If you have a 16-bit bus, use a 16-bit network adapter; if you have a 32-bit bus, use a 32-bit network adapter.
- The NIC should provide the fastest network data transfer rate, with zero latency. Compare manufacturer data sheets on cards and their features. This can be done quickly by visiting their web sites. Here are some examples of devices:

- 3COM 100 Mbps/sec NIC
- CISCO 2514 Router (load balances line at 3.0 Mbps)

- There are a wide variety of products covering a wide range of technologies:

  - Ethernet *Wide Area Network* (WAN) Routers
  - *Integrated Services Digital Network* (ISDN)
  - X.25
  - *Fiber Distributed Data Interface* (FDDI) LAN
  - Know which technology will fit your current and future needs

- Choose a high-speed 32-bit bus architecture. Choose from these:

  - EISA = 32 M/sec (OK, but not the best)
  - PCI = 132 M/sec (best choice)
  - MCA (also 32-bit, speed unknown)

- Avoid ISA which is slow (5 M/sec) and limited to 16M memory addressing.

WHAT IS BUS MASTERING?

Bus mastering is a term for a bus design that allows add-in boards to process independently of the CPU and to be able to access the computer's memory and peripherals on their own. Peripheral devices such as disk, tape, or communications cards, must move large amounts of data to or from the computer's RAM. The different methods used to move this data achieve different levels of performance.

Programmed Input/Output (PIO)   is a data transfer method that depends on your motherboard's CPU to move blocks of data using string moves. A string move will move a 512-byte sector in 256 separate 16-bit operations. The processor receives one interrupt for each sector. This method is limited to 2.5 M/sec, as witnessed in conventional IDE disk drives.

Direct Memory Access (DMA)   uses other hardware to move data between a peripheral and memory buffers. There are two types of DMA controllers. One is the type built into your motherboard. The second is known as Bus Mastering DMA. This type will move data without the need to use the motherboard CPU, or a motherboard DMA chip. It is autonomous. Bus mastering controllers have on-board processors of varying power. They move larger amounts of data using fewer bus cycles, resulting in much faster transfers. On top of this, system memory can be accessed using high-speed page mode. ISA controllers typically move data at 5 to 10 M/sec, EISA at 33 M/sec, and PCI/FDDI ones at 100 M/sec.

NIC Software Drivers for Windows NT Not all software drivers perform the same either. NIC card manufacturers often supply their own proprietary drivers to use with their cards. This can be good, and it can be bad. If the programmers know what they are doing, the driver may run great. What if they didn't do a very good job programming the driver? There are DMA considerations, buffers, Windows NT API calls, and other things that could have an impact on how many instructions are executed in the in NIC driver path. Unfortunately, I don't know of any benchmark studies on actual drivers. You will just have to survive on the occasional benchmarks offered in trade journals.

TUNING SQL SERVER NETWORKS

You can use any of the following monitors to capture information about network throughput, which is the basic indicator of performance:

- SQL Server Performance Monitor
- Network Monitor (provided with Systems Management Server)
- Windows NT Performance Monitor

For our tuning in this section, we will use the SQL Server Monitor. The following three scenarios will identify network bottlenecks:

1. If `SQLServer: Network Reads/sec` is substantially lower than `Server: Bytes Received/sec`, this can be an indication of excessive network activity.

2. If `SQLServer: Network Writes/sec` is substantially lower than `Server: Bytes Transmitted/sec`, this can be an indication of excessive network activity.

3. If `SQLServer: Network Reads/sec` or `SQLServer: Network Writes/sec` is high, this indicates a great deal of network traffic.

The first two scenarios could also be a red flag that Windows NT Server administrative processes are eating up resources. If so, determine which processes or protocols are responsible for the overhead and move them off the server. You have a second alternative if this is true.

The database server should be the only major application running on NT Server. An NT Server can be used for print and file sharing, application sharing, and domain controller functions. In a database climate, it is recommended that you avoid conflicts between the database and other services like *Backup Domain Controllers* (BDCs) or *Primary Domain Controllers* (PDCs). Try to dedicate the server to the database.

There is no doubt when you encounter the third scenario. Review the number of `SQLServer: User Connections` and the `SQLServer: Network Command Queue`

Length. If these values are high, you can increase the number of threads, to allow more work through or to restrict the number of user connections (sp_configure), which reduces the load. Reducing user connections means some users can't get on the system. If this is unacceptable, consider upgrades to the machine. More and faster memory, followed by more and faster NICS, followed by more servers, and then more and faster processors, would represent stepping stones to better network throughput.

TDS packets (tabular data stream) are 512 bytes, by default. Try increasing packet sizes if network traffic consists mainly of large query result sets. For example, if the average query returns more than two screens of data, 2 to 8K packet sizes will perform better. If the system is strictly for DSS, the largest sizes available may be warranted. Individual applications can also change packet size, thus customizing TDS packet usage. Change the packet size by using the DB-Library DBSETLOACKET() call. The packet size may also be changed while using the BCP and ISQL utilities using the [/a packetsize] parameter. Increasing the packet size will only work for naming pipes clients to SQL Server on Windows NT. Larger packets will result in fewer network reads/sec and writes/sec, as witnessed in the performance monitor.

Increasing Netlogon service updates notice periods on the SQL Server if your SQL Server is a Primary Domain Controller. I recommend that they be as high as possible, to reduce the load to the database and to equalize traffic. The following parameters are key ones:

Netlogon Value	Default	Minimum	Maximum	Recommended
Pulse	300 sec	60 sec	3600 sec	3600 sec
PulseConcurrency	20 pulses	1 pulse	500 pulses	1 pulse
Randomize	1 sec	0 sec	120 sec	120 sec

Pulse defines the typical pulse frequency (in seconds). All User/Security database account changes are queued up for this period. Then a pulse is sent to just the Backup Domain Controllers (BDCs) needing the changes. By setting this interval as high as is allowed, the PDS will not wake up as often and spend time researching which BDCs need changes.

PulseConcurrency defines the maximum number of simultaneous pulses the PDC will send to BDCs. Increasing this value increases the load on the PDC. Decreasing this parameter increases the time it takes for a domain with a large number of BDCs to get a database change to all of the BDCs. It is best to spread the network traffic as thin as possible, by limiting pulses to one-at-a-time.

Randomize is used to calculate the timing for pulses. Set this value as high as allowed to help spread the changes out over the longest time period.

6.25 SNA Performance

The *Systems Network Architecture* (SNA) was introduced by IBM in 1974 as a networking architecture allowing applications to run ignorant of the underlying communications devices. It is not a communications standard. Instead it is a framework that corresponds to the *Open Systems Interconnect* model (OSI) layers 2 through 6. See Chapter 17 for a description of OSI. SNA supports IBM compatible devices only, for the most part. Support for non-SNA devices is limited.

WHAT IS SDLC?

Synchronous Data Link Control (SDLC) is the piece of SNA that resides at the data-link layer of the OSI model. In an SNA network each 3270 terminal connects to a cluster controller using coaxial cable and communicates using SDLC at approximately 2.4 Mbps. SDLC uses asynchronous communications and terminals only transmit when polled. A controller can handle from 1 to 32 terminals (depending on the model).

WHAT IS X.25?

X.25 (CCITT standard) is a communications standard that defines the interconnection of *Data Terminal Equipment* (DTE) and *Data Circuit Termination Equipment* (DCE). X.25 is much like SDLC but uses the High-Level Data Link Control protocol. Without getting into a lot of detail about the underlying framework, it is sufficient to state that X.25 NPSI V3R3 supports line speeds up to 256 Kbps.

WHAT IS DLC 802?

The next type of communications worth mentioning is DLC 802.2 (IEEE standard). The 802 standard is really a family of standards.

- 802.2 Logical Link Control
- 802.3 CSMA/CD for Baseband
- 802.4 Token Bus

These are token access protocols where the OK to transmit, known as the token, is systematically passed from node to node on the network. When a node receives the token, it can transmit. This is where we get token ring from, and our traditional LAN networks. Depending on which method is employed, different speeds can be achieved. CSMA/CD provides 10 M/sec using 50Ω (ohm) coax cable, and 2 or 10 M/sec using 75Ω coax cable. On a token bus expect 1 M/sec using 75Ω coax with Phase Continuous FSK, 5 or 10 M/sec with Phase Coherent FSK, or Multilevel Duobinary AM/PSK. Typical Token Ring gets 1 or 10 M/sec with 150Ω twisted pair, and 4, 20, and 40 M/sec with 75Ω baseband coax. So you can see that the last one mentioned is the fastest.

LOCAL SNA DEVICES

In addition to protocol and standard selection, which are probably already in place at your site, you have several parameters in members within the MVS

SYS1.VTAMLST dataset with which to work. The following VBUILD parameters are examples of definitions used to define a local 3278/9 model 4 terminal:

```
* 3270 Model 4 *
MYNODE1 VBUILD TYPE=LOCAL
*
MYNODE1      PU      CUADDR=100,           CU ADDRESS                      X
                     DELAY=0,              MAXIMUM SPEED (COATTAILING)      X
                     ISTATUS=ACTIVE,       INITIAL STATUS ACTIVE           X
                     MODETAB=MT32704,      MODE TABLE FOR 3270 MOD 4       X
                     DLOGMOD=MD32704,                                      X
                     USSTAB=USSTAB,                                        X
                     SSCPFM=SSCPFM,                                        X
                     DISCNT=NO,            VTAM DISCONNECT                 X
                     MAXBFRU=15,           MAXIMUM NUMBER OF BUFFERS       X
                     PUTYPE=2,             PU TYPE                         X
                     PACING=4,             PACING                          X
                     VPACING=4             PACING                          X
             TITLE='MD32704'
MD32704              MODEENT  LOGMODE=MD32704,
                     FMPROT=X'03',
                     TSPROF=X'03',
                     PRIPROT='B1',
                     SECPROT='90',
                     COMPROT='3080',
                     RUSIZES='87C7'
                     PSERVIC='02800000000018502B507F00'
```

Now we want to look at the three major areas of tuning SNA *Virtual Telecommunications Access Method* (VTAM) and tie these back to the parameters just showed to you.

VTAM tuning is accomplished by monitoring *Common Storage Area* (CSA) usage by the network, analyzing slowdowns, using the VTAM Performance Monitor to gather and analyze statistics, and making changes to the system.

VTAM uses CSA storage for major and minor node control blocks, buffer pools, session and routing tables, and temporary work spaces. CSA is a type of storage within the MVS operating system. The first step is to monitor VTAM buffers and CSA usage. This can be done by issuing the command:

```
d net,bfruse
IST924I ——————————————
IST920I APOO    BUFF SIZE  56          EXP INCREMENT    56
IST921I         TIMES EXP  7           EXP/CONT THRESH 10  / *NA*
IST922I         CURR TOTAL 56          CURR AVAILABLE   56
```

```
IST923I          MAX TOTAL   56          MAX USED          0
...
IST449I CSALIMIT = NOLIMIT, CURRENT = 1891K, MAXIMUM = 1908K
IST790I MAXIMUM CSA USED = 1911K
IST449I CSA24 LIMIT = NOLIMIT, CURRENT = 33K, MAXIMUM = 33K
IST790I MAXIMUM CSA24 USED = 33K
IST595I IRNLIMIT = NOLIMIT, CURRENT = 0K, MAXIMUM = 0K
IST981I VTAM PRIVATE: CURRENT = 3741K, MAXIMUM USED = 3787K
IST314I END
```

The general formula for determining unused CSA is:

$$AP00 \; Buffer \; Pool \; unused \; CSA = (maxtotal - maxused)° \; buffsize$$
$$3136 = (56 - 0) ° 56$$

Applying the formula to the buffer pool displayed, we come up with 3136 bytes of unused CSA in buffer pool AP00. If this number is high, then the buffer pool has too much CSA allocated. If it is low, then it may be short on CSA. CSA shortages are one of the causes of slow performance. Notice that in the totals at the bottom of the output display it shows the total CSA usage for all pools and systems.

The second area of VTAM tuning is isolating slowdowns. Insufficient buffers are the cause of slowdowns, which can be detected using SLODN statistics from SNA. Whether slowdown occurs in a channel-attached SNA controller or in a multipath channel connection, it is always a shortage of buffers. Increase buffers accordingly.

The third step in tuning is gathering general tuning statistics by buffer pool and acting upon them. If you are using the TNSTAT start option or have issued the MODIFY TNSTAT command, you can collect statistics to SMF. Then using the following online tuning statistics report for a SNA controller, you can evaluate performance for devices on a controller:

```
IST440I    TIME = 12310500      DATE = 99193          ID = 0D0-L
IST441I    DLRMAX = 1           CHWR = 178          CHRD = 135
IST442I     ATTN = 31           RDATN = 0           IPIU = 155
IST443I     OPIU = 180          RDBUF = 155         SLODN = 4
IST314I END
```

Here is how to evaluate the statistics shown and how to adjust your VBUILD parameters accordingly:

▪ Notice that the SLODN output shows a count of 4. This is the number of times the controller went into a slowdown because buffer threshold was reached.

▪ CHWR is the total number of write channel programs issued.

- CHRD is the total number of read channel programs issued.

- IPIU is the total number of inbound (to VTAM) PIUs received from the controller. If RDBUF is much larger than IPIU, the value specified for the I/O buffer size might be too small.

- To analyze inbound data transfer, multiply MAXBFRU by the number of channel READs (CHRD). MAXBFRU is shown in our VBUILD example earlier. The product should be close to the value of RDBUF (the number of read buffers used). Otherwise, data is not being transferred for all the channel command words (CCWs) in the read channel program. Reducing the value of MAXBFRU should solve this problem. MAXBFRU is the number of 4K page buffers used.

- The value of MAXBFRU times UNITSZ must be at least as large as the largest PIU received.

- RDATN is the number of times that VTAM, after reading data, is requested by an attention to read more data. This occurs if the CCW string is not long enough to hold the data or if more data comes into controller during read. If this occurs, you should increase MAXBFRU which will allow for a larger CCW string. MAXBFRU is the number of 4 KB page buffers used.

- To determine the average number of PIUs for each write operation, divide the outbound PIU (OPIU) count by the number of channel WRITEs (CHWR). This average number of PIUs indicates the effectiveness of the VTAM blocking algorithm (or coattailing). *Coattailing* is efficient. It is where more than one message gets routed to or from the host, because more than one transaction comes in before the scheduled polling. If the DELAY value is too low, then you don't get enough coattailing. If it is too high, and there aren't enough transactions, it could be a while before anything happens. Use the DELAY to help achieve a good level of coattailing. MAXBFRU is also influential, because a full buffer will cause an interrupt, just like DELAY.

- ATTN is the number of attention requests sent to the controller. These requests are CPU intensive. It could be an indication of too high a polling rate.

OTHER DEVICE TYPES AND NODE CONNECTION TYPES

Now that you have seen how general tuning is performed for VTAM, it is time to explain that the beast is bigger than we've chosen to show you so far. There are many other node and device types that can be defined in the network on MVS. Some are SNA, and some are non-SNA types. There are peculiarities for each type of line, device, and connection defined to VTAM. Here are some keywords associated with performance for other types not discussed so far.

Definition	Type Used By	Description
MAXTSL=	NCP Major Node	Maximum Data Transfer
RCVBUFC=	NCP Major Node	Maximum Receive Data
MAXDATA=	Switched Major Node	Maximum Data Transfer
SPEED=	Switched Subarea Link	Link Speed (BAUD, like modems)
MAXTSL=	Token Ring NTRI	Maximum Data Transfer
RCVBUFC=	Token Ring NTRI	Maximum Receive Data
DUPLEX=	BSC Connection	Full or Half Duplexing
PAUSE=	BSC Connection	Wait
SPEED=	Routing Node	Link Speed (BAUD, like modems)
DUPLEX=	Routing Node	Full or Half Duplexing
PAUSE=	Routing Node	Primary and Secondary Pause
SPEED=	Subarea Link	Link Speed (BAUD, like modems)
MAXDATA=	Dynamic Defined Switched Maximum Bytes PU Receives in on PIU	
MAXBFRU=	Dynamic Defined Switched Maximum Buffers (4 KB pages)	
MAXOUT=	SDLC	Link Level Response
PASSLIM=	SDLC	Maximum PIU Send Count

X.25 TUNING

The final area of tuning we want to explore in the SNA world is X.25. Tuning X.25 connections is a little different than those discussed before. The primary reason for this is that packet technology is more current, and it represented a different framework than SNA was familiar with, prior to its introduction. Consequently, the data required some new programs and tools to provide tuning data. You begin capturing statistics about performance by including parameters on the NPACOLL keyword of the X25.MCH statement. The X25.MCH statement is the main statement used to define X.25 connections. Here is the syntax used:

```
NPACOLL =      (MCHLINE, MCHPU, VCPU)
(NO, NO, NO)
where:

MCHLINE     Collects performance data at the frame level.
MCHPU       Collects global performance data at the packet level.
```

```
VCPU        Collects individual VC performance data at the packet level.
NO          Data is not kept at the level.  NO is the default.
```

Refer to the *X.25 Tuning Guide* from IBM for a description of tuning using the output statistics gathered. The amount of packet traffic information is pretty significant, and I think it exceeds what we have time to show you here. But, here are some of the major tuning hints useful with X.25 connections:

- If the PLPIGGB option on the X25.MCH statement has been used to turn off piggybacking, performance may be poor. *Piggybacking* means that received frames or packets are acknowledged in the next outgoing packet. To tune piggybacking, use the SPEED and T1TIMER parameters.

- X25 buffering is different than NCP. Use MAXDATA and BFRS to set buffers large enough to reduce excess packet processing (124 or greater depending on type).

- Turn pacing off to eliminate delays.

In conclusion, tuning the SNA network should be a prerequisite to attempting to provide better performance for SNA devices on SQL Server. Some other things you can do that haven't been mentioned yet are to achieve line load balancing on MVS, use faster modems (which equates to the SPEED= parameter mentioned in previous tables), and use higher speed dedicated lines (up to 256K or fiber).

MICROSOFT SNA SERVER TUNING

For SQL Server to connect to the SNA world, as with anybody that wants to talk SNA, it is necessary to write a communications program. Lucky for you, it already exists and is called the Microsoft SNA Server. There are two sides to SNA communications tuning for SQL Server. One side is SNA itself. The other is MS SNA Server.

On the MS SNA Server side (see four basic services of SNA Sever listed), there are some things you can do to improve performance.

SNA Component	Description
SnaBase Service	SNA servers coordination domain services support
SnaServer Service	Physical Unit (PU) Node Support
Link Services	DLC 802.2, SDLC, X.25 support
Net View	The NetView commands can be used to query the network

SNA Server acts as a Windows NT process and competes for operating system resources, as opposed to Microsoft BackOffice applications. This server uses Windows NT multithreading and asynchronous facilities. The only concerns when tuning SNA Server are that there is adequate CPU and memory. Because its memory requirements are small (the SNA protocol was designed to fit in 32K cluster controllers) the task is even lighter. See the following table for memory guesstimates.

Users	SNA Server Memory
500	32 M
1,000	48 M
2,500	64 M
5,000	72 M
7,500	90 M
10,000	128 M
20,000	150 M
30,000	192 M
40,000	256 M

Here are some additional tuning hints for SNA Server:

■ Tune SNA Server so there is no paging due to SNA process faulting (`Process: Page/Faults/sec` in Performance Monitor). More memory will reduce faults.

■ If SNA Server is using more than 90 percent CPU (`Processor: % Privileged Time`), CPU or interrupts could be a problem. The following solutions may apply:

   ■ Use a faster processor or more processors

   ■ Use a faster protocol (like X.25)

   ■ Use multiple NIC cards

   ■ Use 32-bit bus mastering

   ■ Use some of the other alternatives listed under network tuning in Chapters 8 or 17.

■ If `SNA Connections: Throughput Bytes/sec` is high (see Chapter 8), you can load balance user connections over several SNA Servers by creating a LU pool that contains LUs from more than one SNA Server. The load will be shared according to the number of users per SNA Server.

 NOTE: Common TP monitors such as CICS, Encina, Tuxeda, and Top End all work with Windows NT Server and interface with Microsoft SQL Server. They may provide additional information used in tuning networks.

IBM's **Communication Server for NT** features Web-to-host connectivity, an SNA gateway, TN3270E server support, high-performance routing, common client services, and emulation, to name a few. See their website at www.ibm.com.

6.26 SMS Tuning

Automated hardware and software inventory packages have become a popular past-time in most shops. The newer second generation tools now distribute system changes and install software remotely. The days of walking around and reading the labels on machines, then jotting them down on a clip-board are passing away forever. Microsoft *Systems Management Server* (SMS) is a computer management system that enables you to inventory and support computers on LANs and WANs. Believe it or not, this product must be tuned. Why? The primary reasons for tuning this product are its extensive use of disk and network resources.

Tuning SMS, as it will be referred to, requires identifying the different components, their resource usage, what they are responsible for accomplishing, and listing available tuning options. The following list of services gives you some idea of the impact this product can have on your system.

SMS Services	Network Activity	Disk Activity
Site Hierarchy Manager	Low	Low
Site Configuration Manager	High	High
Executive	High	High
Package Command Manager	Medium	Medium
Inventory Agent	High	High
Bootstrap	High	High
SNA Receiver	None	None

Following is a brief summarization of the different components and their purpose. The component named Executive is actually a bunch of separate facilities, which we won't describe in detail.

Executive: This service is the master controller for several other components including: Maintenance Manager, Inventory Processor, Site Reporter, Scheduler, Despooler, Inventory Data Loader, Senders (LAN, RAS, and SNA), Applications Manager, and Alerter.

Site Hierarchy Manager: This service monitors the site database for changes to the configuration of that site or its direct secondary sites. Configuration changes are stored in a control file that is sent to the site they affect. Changes are recorded in the primary and secondary site SQL Server database.

Site Configuration Manager: This service takes the control file built by the Site Hierarchy manager and implements the changes. An interval value drives monitoring, which can be adjusted.

Package Command Manager: The PCM service runs on all Windows NT Servers and provides unattended package installation.

Bootstrap: The Bootstrap service is used to set up the site server for a secondary site.

Inventory Agent: This service performs inventory on all the servers. This service is also interval controlled.

SNA Receiver: The SNA Receiver processes SNA Sender information.
   Here is a list of tuning hints for SMS:

- Move the Scheduler component of SMS Executive to a SMS Helper server to balance work across multiple hardware platforms.
- Move the Despooler component of SMS Executive to a SMS Helper server to balance work across multiple hardware platforms.
- Move the Inventory Data Loader component of SMS Executive to a SMS Helper server to balance work across multiple hardware platforms.
- Move the Inventory Processor component of SMS Executive to a SMS Helper server to balance work across multiple hardware platforms.
- Move the Sender(s) component of SMS Executive to a SMS Helper server to balance work across multiple hardware platforms.
- Change the Package Command Manager (PCM) posting interval (default 1 minute) to 60 minutes or even higher to cut down polling overhead.
- Adjust the Inventory Agent scan and service intervals so activity happens less frequently. Increase the number of minutes between scans in value:

```
<SMS Root>\Components\SMS_MAINTENANCE_MANAGER\Inventory Agent Service
Interval
```

- Very large networks with many servers should setup SMS and its primary database on a dedicated box, potentially with a dedicated RAID subsystem.
- Delete unneeded packages to save disk space.
- Adjust the Windows NT Server compression value downwards, to save on CPU due to compression. The value can be from 1 to 7, 7 being the most CPU intensive. The registry key value is:

```
HKEY_LOCAL_MACHINE\SOFTWARE\Microsoft\Systems Management Server\Compression
```

Disable the SMS_Site_Config_manager service from overwriting manual modifications to the registry, to avoid overlaying this change with future changes.

```
<SMS Root>\Sites\<Site code>\Properties\Service Responcs\data = FFFFFFFF.
```

■ Increase the amount of time in minutes that the Executive waits before sending changes in files to child servers. A good choice might be daily or weekly.

```
<SMS  Root>\COmponents\SMS_Applications Manager\Processing Delay
```

■ Increase the Sender wait times, causing it to become active less frequently.

```
<SMS Root>\Components\<Sender name>
```

■ Increase the number of concurrent threads used by the LAN Sender to complete sendings faster.

6.27   DBArtisan for SQL Server

If you are working with both Sybase and Microsoft SQL Servers, DBArtisan from Embarcadero Technologies Incorporated consolidates your tool set into a single workbench. Newcomers to SQL Server appreciate how DBArtisan's intuitive interface accelerates their understanding of SQL Server.

MIGRATE AND SYNCHRONIZE DATABASES

The proliferation of databases in many organizations has elevated the need to manage the process of copying and synchronizing distributed databases. Copy management is often the most time-consuming and problematic aspect of a DBA's job. To help you address this critical task, DBArtisan offers powerful copy management facilities to migrate and synchronize all or part of a database. The Copy Manager logically orders database schema to eliminate dependency errors when building database objects and chooses the fastest available method for migrating data.

VISUAL SCHEMA MANAGEMENT

Every administrator and developer knows how important it is to synchronize source and object code so that a database can be reconstructed from scratch if necessary. However, maintaining source code becomes cumbersome, especially in comparison to visual programming against a database. DBArtisan helps you bridge the gap that often exists between source and object code. Its visual editors, which are the most intuitive visual editors available for SQL Server, enable you to create and modify database objects efficiently. Its schema extraction facilities, which capture complete and accurate DDL, enable you to secure the underlying definition of your database objects with ease. By using DBArtisan, you can enjoy the speed of visual programming without sacrificing the security of maintaining source code.

CHANGE MANAGEMENT

Altering database objects is difficult because of the intricate dependencies that can exist between objects. Administrators and developers often don't have the luxury of simply dropping and recreating objects because of the residual effects of losing object permissions, accurate object dependencies, and in the case of tables, their data, indexes, and triggers.

DBArtisan constructs intelligent object alteration strategies for you to ensure reliable change management. Moreover, it extends the functionality available for altering tables so that you can now add, delete, and modify table columns as needed.

SPACE AND STORAGE MANAGEMENT

Managing space is vital to ensuring the availability and performance of your databases. If you have ever run out of room on a database segment, suffered table or index corruption, or experienced a hard drive failure, you know that these events can shut down your databases. DBArtisan incorporates a number of major feature sets that help you steer clear of such problems, including utilities to:

- Monitor free space by analyzing device, database, and segment space utilization
- Estimate table and index sizes so that you can manage the growth of databases and segments
- Perform database consistency checks to diagnose and correct corruption
- Update index statistics to maintain performance
- Dump and load databases and transaction logs for disaster recovery
- Mirror devices to guard against hardware failures

SECURITY MANAGEMENT

DBArtisan can help you establish and maintain security on your SQL Servers. It provides full support for managing logins, roles, users, groups, and aliases so that you can control access to your database servers and individual databases. In addition, it offers permissions management utilities so that you can set the system and object-level permissions for any role, user, or group.

SERVER CONFIGURATION AND OPTIMIZATION

As your databases and number of users grow, it becomes vitally important to optimize the configuration of your SQL Servers. Because of their sophistication and high performance, both Sybase and Microsoft SQL Server offer a dizzying array of configuration options.

To guide you through the process of optimizing your SQL Servers, DBArtisan features dedicated facilities that organize and explain each configuration parameter, from basic ones, such as available memory, to advanced ones for tuning SMP servers. Figure 6-13 is a sample Data Cache Summary screen. It shows how concise and comprehensive information in DBArtisan is.

SCALABLE AND INTEROPERABLE

DBArtisan is specifically designed to facilitate the effective management and control of many distributed, heterogeneous SQL Servers. From the same tool, you can achieve secure and consistent control of your distributed databases. You will find that DBArtisan can meet your needs as you add and distribute databases throughout your organization. Moreover, Embarcadero's no-nonsense licensing policy, which excludes any server-based fee, makes cost-effective administration of many SQL Servers a reality.

6.28 Microsoft DMO

With Microsoft's Distributed Management Framework comes SQL Enterprise Manager (a GUI interface), SQL Server, and SQL *Distributed Management Objects* (DMO) with a set of objects for OLE automation. Theoretically, you can use the DMO to build your own applications to perform many of the Database Administrator tasks in unattended mode. These include the following:

- Automate backups of all tables
- Automate consistency checks of all tables

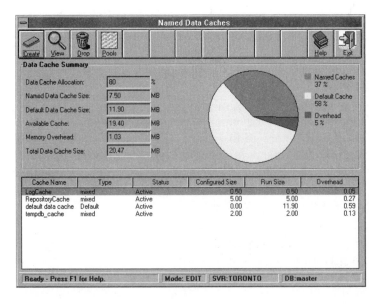

Figure 6-13 DBArtisan Data Cache Summary Screen

▪ Automate index rebuilds for performance

▪ Automate performance reporting

6.29 Choosing sp_configure Settings

The sp_configure options can be set with `isql` or using the SQL Enterprise Manager, accessed off the SQL Server program group (see Figure 6-14).

CONFIGURATION OPTIONS AND VALUES

Table 6-5 lists each configuration option, its minimum and maximum acceptable value, the default value, and runtime settings for 100, 1,000, or 10,000 users. Memory and other resources were calculated based on systems with heavy transaction loads. So, some of these may be high on systems with less throughput.

Dynamic options are noted with an asterisk (*). A new setting for a dynamic option takes effect immediately. A new setting for a nondynamic option takes effect after the server is restarted. You can also change or display settings using line commands like this:

Command	Description
sp_configure	display all configuration options
sp_configure "locks", 10000 go	change locks to 10000

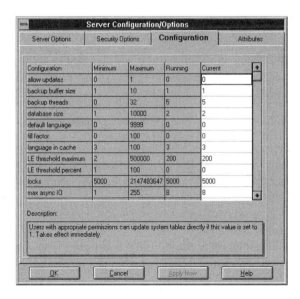

Figure 6-14 Changing sp_configure

Anyone can issue the first command shown. However, only a system administrator can make changes, as in the second command. After making a change, remember to issue the reconfigure command, like this:

```
RECONFIGURE go
```

Dynamic changes will take effect immediately; nondynamic ones at server restart time.

TABLE 6-5   Configuration Options Table

config_name	Min	Max	100 users	1,000 users	10,000 users
allow updates*	0	1	0	0	0
backup buffer size*	1	10	2	4	8
backup threads	0	32	4	8	16
cursor threshold*	-1	2147483647	512	512	512
database size	1	10000	2	2	2
default language	0	9999	0	0	0
default sortorder id	0	255	52	52	52
fill factor	0	100	0	0	0
free buffers*	20	524288	3276	6553	13107
hash buckets	4999	265003	8191	16381	32749
language in cache	3	100	3	3	3
LE threshold maximum*	2	500000	400	200	100
LE threshold minimum*	2	500000	20	20	20
LE threshold percent*	1	100	0	0	0
locks	5000	2147483647	4000	200000	1000000
logwrite sleep (ms)*	-1	500	4	0	-1
max async IO		1	255		
non-RAID conventional	8	8	8		
RAID SCSI 1 channel	8	8	8		
RAID SCSI 2 channel	16	16	16		
RAID SCSI 3 channel	24	24	24		
max lazywrite IO*	1	255			
non-RAID conventional	8	8	8		
RAID SCSI 1 channel	8	8	8		
RAID SCSI 2 channel	16	16	16		
RAID SCSI 3 channel	24	24	24		
max worker threads*	10	1024	255	512	1024
media retention	0	366	32	32	32
memory	1000	1048576	65536	131072	262144

TABLE 6-5   Configuration Options Table (Continued)

config_name	Min	Max	100 users	1,000 users	10,000 users
nested triggers*	0	1	1	1	1
network packet size*	512	32767			
Ethernet NICS/EISA buses	4096	4096	4096		
Fast Ethernet NICS	8192	8192	8192		
Decision Support Servers	8192	8192	8192		
FDDI NICS/PCI buses with mastering	16384	16384	16384		
open databases	5	32767	100	1000	10000
open objects	100	2147483647	1000	10000	100000
priority boost	0	1			
not SQL Server dedicated	0	0	0		
SQL Server dedicated	1	1	1		
procedure cache	1	99	15	10	5
RA cache hit limit*	1	255	4	4	4
RA cache miss limit*	1	255	3	3	3
RA delay*	0	500	15	15	15
RA pre-fetches*	1	1000			
RA slots per thread	1	255			
RAID 0, 1, 5 SCSI-2	5	5	5		
RAID 0, 1, 5 FAST SCSI	10	10	10		
RAID 0, 1, 5 ULTRA SCSI	20	20	20		
RAID FDDI	30	30	30		
RA worker threads	0	255	100	1000	1000
recovery flags	0	1	0	0	0
recovery interval*	1	32767	5	10	15
remote access	0	1	1	1	1
remote login timeout*	0	2147483647	5	30	60
remote query timeout*	0	2147483647	30	60	120
resource timeout*	-1	2147483647	120	120	120
set working set size	0	1	0	0	0
show advanced option*	0	1	1	1	1
SMP concurrency	-1	64			
uni-processor	1	1	1		
SQL Server dedicated SMP	-1	-1	-1		

(Continued)

TABLE 6-5   Configuration Options Table (Continued)

config_name	Min	Max	100 users	1,000 users	10,000 users
non-dedicated SMP	0	0	0		
sort pages*	64	511	128	256	511
spin counter*	1	2147483647			
uni-processor	10	10	10		
SMP	10000	10000	10000		
tempdb in ram (MB)	0	2044	8	16	32
user connections	5	32767	100	1000	10000
----------------------------new release 6.5 options----------------------------					
affinity mask	0	2147483647			
uni-processor	0	0	0		
2, 4, 8, 12 way SMP	(read manual on assigning affinity)				
max text repl size	0	2147483647	65536	65536	65536
remote conn timeout	-1	32767	10	10	10
remote proc trans	0	1			
with consistency (slower)	1	1	1		
without consistency	0	0	0		
user options	0	4095	0	0	0
NOCOUNT (if not an issue)	512	512	512		

To see advanced options, you must change the show advanced option to 1, before displaying all options. This is the command:

```
sp_configure 'show advanced option', 1 go
```

The following detail describes the purpose of, and some safe settings for, the sp_configure options. Most of the tuning options end up using more memory if you increase them. However, if you do, the overall system memory must be increased to make up for the added memory requirement, or some other option must be reduced.

■ affinity mask—specifies a bit mask in which each bit represents the processors on which the thread is run. Use decimal values to specify affinity mask settings.

Affinity mask specifies which processor(s) the SMP SQL Server will use and allows the system administrator to associate a thread with a processor.

■ allow updates*—option (1) allows direct system table updates, via ad hoc user procedures. When off (default option 0), they can only be updated by the system. It is recommended that this option be set to off (0).

▪ `backup buffer size*`—specifies the size of the dump and load buffer, in 32-page increments. Increased buffering will speed up backup processing.

▪ `backup threads`—specifies the number of threads to be reserved for striped dump and load operations. A setting of (0) turns off striped dumps.

▪ `cursor threshold*`—specifies the optimizer estimated threshold number in rows, after which an asynchronous cursor is generated. Small results are faster to build synchronously. When set to (0), all keysets will be built asynchronously. When set to (-1), all keysets are built synchronously.

▪ `database size`—is the number of megabytes allocated to a new database. This is the system default used when the size is not specified in the CREATE DATABASE statement.

▪ `default language`—specifies the ID of the language that is used by the server to display system messages, unless a user has chosen another language from those available on the server. English is always ID (0). Other languages are assigned unique ID numbers when they are added.

▪ `default sortorder id`—specifies the number of the sort order currently installed as the default on the server. Do not use the sp_configure system stored procedure to change sort orders.

▪ `fill factor`—specifies the page free space in percent, which SQL Server will reserve as a new index is created. It is recommended that free space be assigned using the CREATE INDEX statement, because not all indexes need to have additional space. Filling of pages depends on database update activity.

The default for this option is (0). A fill factor of (0) does not mean that pages are 0 percent full. It is treated similarly to a fill factor of 100 in that SQL Server creates clustered indexes with full data pages and nonclustered indexes with full leaf pages. It is different from 100 in that SQL Server leaves a space within the index B-tree.

▪ `free buffers*`—is a threshold value used to guarantee that the number of buffers in the option is the minimum number available at all times. The lazy writer process ensures that the number of free buffers available to the system does not fall below this threshold. If the `memory` option is changed then this value will automatically be reset to 5% of the new memory option. It must then be adjusted readjusted manually.

▪ `hash buckets`—are buckets used for hashing pages to buffers in memory. If the value specified is not a prime number, the closest prime number is used. For example, specifying 8000 creates 7993 hash buckets (the default). Here are some numbers you may want to try:

System Memory	Prime Number Hash Value
128 M	8191
256 M	16381

System Memory	Prime Number Hash Value
512 M	32749
1 G	65521
2 G	131071

 NOTE: I have not had a chance to test my theory. But, if my calculations are right, using smaller or larger prime numbers with different memory settings may increase SQL Server memory performance, by reducing hashed target collisions. If different requests randomize to the same page more frequently, then memory walk or scan routines must ensue. The right *prime* will reduce this activity. Perhaps you the reader can test this out. There are complete lists of prime numbers on the Internet. They can be found using *prime* and *numbers* in major search engines.

- `language in cache`—is the maximum number of languages that can be simultaneously held in the language cache. The default is 3.

- `LE threshold maximum*`—is the maximum number of page locks to hold before escalating to a table lock. Escalation will occur, whether or not the `LE threshold percent` value has been reached.

- `LE threshold minimum*`—is the minimum number of page locks required before escalating to a table lock. A table lock will occur only if this minimum is reached when the `LE threshold percent` is exceeded. LE threshold minimum prevents the server from escalating to a table lock for small tables where the `LE threshold percentage` is reached quickly.

- `LE threshold percent*`—specifies the percentage of page locks needed on a table before a table lock is requested. The default (0) causes a table lock to occur only when the `LE threshold maximum` has been reached.

- `locks*`—sets the total number of available locks. To determine the amount of memory designated for locking, multiply this number by 32 bytes. On very large systems with thousands of users, this number may need to be pretty big. Larger systems almost inherently have more ad-hoc queries which drive locking requirements up also.

- `logwrite sleep (ms)*`—sets the number of milliseconds that a write to the log will be delayed if the buffer is not full. This increases the chance that more data will be added to the log buffer by other users, so that fewer physical log writes will be needed. Acceptable values for this option are –1 through 500. The default (0) will cause the server to write unless users are ready to execute. A value of (-1) writes immediately. The many options available create a dilemma. Here are key issues at play:

  - You really don't want to slow down logging. Logging is usually a hog in most RDBMS. If you select a number, then a wait can ensue.

- If you select (0), then the server must walk the current processes, or check some kind of flag before continuing.

- The I/O associated with logging is reduced if you wait the right amount of time, which can save time ultimately.

- An immediate write (-1) is fast, but incurs extra I/O.

- Most RDBMS will wait for a log write to complete before doing the next one. This is a way of maintaining data consistency. However, writes can become a bottleneck for the whole system. Multiple commits can queue up.

The best way to deal with the dilemma is to analyze the system first. Very small systems have fewer users performing less transactions. The frequency of commit and update is less. Therefore, it is possible to set a sleep value, thus allowing blocks to fill up more.

A medium sized system with 500-2000 users has enough throughput to justify setting the option to (0). Waits are not desirable and it is still worthwhile to attempt to fill the blocks being written.

Very large systems shouldn't incur any waits or added processing. A value of (0) or (-1) will provide the best performance. Because the I/O to the log is going to be tremendous, the real bottleneck will lie in the speed with which I/Os complete. The device, controller, computer bus speed and technology (FDDI Fibre is recommended) will make a big difference to overall system performance. The log will probably work better on a non-RAID controller, or a RAID controller with asynchronous I/O features (see max async IO).

- `max async IO`—sets the number of asynchronous I/Os that can be issued. Asynchronous I/O will be used for bulk copies and checkpoints. This value should be changed only on systems with databases defined on multiple physical database devices that reside on separate physical disks, or on systems taking advantage of disk striping. The hardware must support asynchronous I/O. The number of channels available on RAID devices can impact this setting.

- `max lazywrite IO*`—sets the priority of asynchronous I/Os for use by the lazy writer. It must be less than or equal to the value in `max async IO`. Tunes the priority of batched asynchronous I/Os performed by the lazy writer. Do not change this option unless your primary support provider instructs you to do so.

- `max text repl size`—sets the number of bytes that can be added to a replicated column, or the maximum size in bytes of text and image data that can be added to a replicated column in a single INSERT, UPDATE, WRITETEXT or UPDATETEXT statement.

- `max worker threads*`—is the number of worker threads that are in the user pool. If the number of connections exceeds this value, thread queuing occurs. Make this number equal to the number of user connections, plus 1.

- `media retention`—sets the number of days to retain a database or transaction log dump. This is a shop specific setting. If you attempt to reuse the space before the retention has expired, then a warning is issued.

- `memory`—is the total memory allocation for SQL Server, in 2 KB pages. The maximum value is 2G. The memory option does not include memory needs for tempdb if you have placed tempdb in RAM using the `tempdb in ram` (M) option. Refer to the previous sections in this chapter for details on computing memory settings for SQL Server.

- `nested triggers*`—will allow (1) nested (or cascading triggers), while (0) does not.

- `network packet size*`—sets network packet size. Use a packet size that will optimize the greatest amount of network traffic. Larger packets work better. The default is 4096. See the section on network tuning for ways to tune this value.

- `open databases`—sets the maximum number of concurrently open databases. Start with a high number and adjust it downward based upon actual usage. This option affects access and memory usage.

- `open objects`—sets the maximum number of concurrently open database objects. An error message is issued if this number is exceeded. Set the value high enough above the error threshold to prevent any errors. This option affects memory usage and access.

- `priority boost`—is set to (1) on Windows systems dedicated to SQL Server. Otherwise, (0) the default is used.

- `procedure cache`—specifies the percentage of memory allocated to the procedure cache after all other SQL Server memory requirements are met, including system blocks, code and data cache. The procedure cache defaults to 30 percent. But, you need to adjust this number downward as the systems and amount of memory on the systems become very large.

READ AHEAD OPTIONS

The next six options are used to tune asynchronous read-ahead processing. Asynchronous I/O occurs in parallel. Read ahead is an industry-wide feature used to scan ahead and prefetch pages into memory before they are needed. With read ahead (RA), DBCC queries and bulk copy functions will run much faster.

- `RA cache hit limit*`— defines the number of cache hits that a read-ahead request can have before it is canceled. If every page is being found in memory already, then read ahead isn't needed. This is the threshold before aborting read ahead. The default value of (4) is adequate in small and medium systems. Very large systems may need a higher value. Check with your primary support provider before changing this value.

- RA cache miss limit*— sets the threshold for horizontal cache misses before triggering read ahead. Any setting lower than (3) can result in thrashing. My recommendation is to go with your primary support providers instructions.

- RA delay*— Specifies the delay of read ahead, in milliseconds. A delay is necessary to allow the read-ahead manager to fire up before I/Os begin. Use the default value of (15).

- RA pre-fetches*— defines how many pages are pre-fetched at a time. In many RDBMS, performance can increase as this amount is increased. But, the CPU processing and I/O subsystem must be able to keep up with each other. If both processor and subsystem are fast, try increasing this value in increments, until the maximum throughput is achieved. Monitor the effects on other I/O activity.

- RA slots per thread— is instrumental in designating how many concurrent RA scans can occur. The number of RA threads multiplied by RA slots is equal to the maximum number of concurrent RA scans. Fast I/O subsystems with available unused bandwidth can have this option increased over the installed default.

- RA worker threads— sets the number of threads used to service read-ahead requests. This option should be set to the maximum number of concurrent users on the system.

- recovery flags— affects the amount of error logging. Use (0) for reduced logging. Use (1) when more information is needed for debugging. Afterwards, set it back to (0) again.

- recovery interval*— sets the warmstart recovery period in minutes. This value affects the frequency of system checkpointing. During a checkpoint, the logging and buffering are all impacted. It can appear as a glitch in the system. The vendor recommendation is to raise this value as the amount of system activity increases. Personally, I disagree with that recommendation. For small server systems, it is OK to set this value small, like (5). As systems get larger, you can improve performance by raising the number to (30). The tradeoff is in the time required to recover, when necessary.

- remote access— will prevent remote access (0) to the server, or allow it (1).

- remote conn timeout— sets the number of minutes of inactivity before a server-to-server connection is disconnected. Timer based routines are both good and bad. They provide a means to terminate a bad connection, without shutting down everything. But, they also require the server system to service wait routines. They have to wake up frequently and walk around control blocks. My twist on this is to set it as high as tolerable. If you have a lot of server-to-server problems and need to act on them quickly, then maybe (5) minutes is good. If you don't, then maybe (60) minutes is acceptable. This option will not work for MS DTC coordinated distributed transactions.

- `remote login timeout`*— sets the timeout (in seconds) for remote login attempts. An infinite wait (0) is not acceptable. A typical timeout might be between 5 and 30 seconds. On a really large system, the network could be tied up for a while and a larger number might be warranted.

- `remote proc trans`— will use MS DTC coordinated distributed transactions (1), or not (0, the default). DTC transactions maintain consistency of data in server-to-server environments. This is recommended.

- `remote query timeout`*— sets the wait in seconds for remote queries. An infinite wait (0) is unacceptable. This value should be high enough to prevent premature timeouts.

- `resource timeout`*— sets the number of seconds to wait for a resource to be released. The default is 10. Increase this value if the SQL Server error log shows a lot of `logwrite` or `bufwait` timeout warnings.

- `set working set size`— will tell Windows NT to reserve memory the working set size memory for SQL Server and tempdb in RAM, if it is specified.

- `show advanced option`*— is used to display advanced sp_configure options (1), or not (0, default).

- `SMP concurrency`— should be set to (1) on uni-processors. On a symmetric multiprocessor (SMP) computer, it sets the multi-threading limit. For a dedicated SQL Server machine, use (-1), meaning there is no limit. On non-dedicated machines, it can be adjusted to provide balance between Windows NT processes and SQL Server processes.

- `sort pages`*— sets the maximum number of memory pages/per user for sorting. Memory sorts are far superior to those conducted using bins on disk. The added memory can be computed by determining the number of users with concurrent queries requiring sorts, and multiplying it times the memory page setting here. The larger this value can be, the better performance will be.

- `spin counter`*— sets the amount of spins performed in attempting to obtain a resource The default is 10 on uni-processors and 10000 on SMP machines. Read the information in the chapters on Oracle and Sybase for a better understanding of spin counters used in RDBMS.

- `tempdb in ram (MB)`— is the amount or RAM in megabytes set aside for tempdb processing. The tempdb will reside on disk (default option 0) if tempdb cannot hold the worktable. If memory is available, this facility can optimize work operations. Remember that the same pages may reside in the data cache, which means they are already in memory. If data cache is already constrained, this option will not help.

This option can be altered 10 times before the server must be restarted to make a modification. Altering tempdb while it is in RAM causes each alteration of the database to allocate a new chunk of contiguous memory to tempdb. Prior tempdb RAM allocations are not necessarily useful. It is best to restart the server if the tempdb in RAM value is altered.

 NOTE: If tempdb is in RAM at the time of an upgrade, it will subsequently be moved out of RAM. The default disk device(s) must have the minimum amount free (2M) to create tempdb. If not, SQL Server startup will fail. To temporarily force a 2M tempdb in RAM, use the -f flag on the command line with SQLSERVR.EXE. This will allow the server to start. Once it has started, you must perform one of the following options immediately: increase the size of a default device, free space on a default device, or add a default device.

- `time slice`— sets the threshold number of times that a user process is allowed to pass through a yield point without voluntarily yielding. If the time slice is set too low, SQL Server can spend too much time switching processes. If it is set too high, users can experience long response time.

  The default is 100. This value can act as a governor on very large systems. You may need to increase this value in those types of systems.

- `user connections`— sets the maximum number of simultaneous connections to SQL Server allowed. The number of connections actually used will determine how many concurrent processes, and how much concurrent memory usage exists in the system. This value can be reduced to improve performance, at the expense of some users not gaining access. If set too high, the system can come to a halt because both hardware and software resources may not support the load.

  Use this statement to get a report on the maximum number of user connections:

```
select @@max_connections
```

  Users of DB-Library need to increase this value by one for each process started with a call to dbopen().

- `user options`— sets the global session defaults for all users. These can be overridden individually with the SET statement.

Here are the settings, which correspond to bit positions in the @@OPTIONS variable of SQL Server. Several options that are mutually exclusive, like ANSI_NULL_DFLT_ON, cannot be enabled when ANSI_NULL_DFLT_OFF is enabled. The only one that appears to have a positive tuning impact might be NOCOUNT, which if used, would reduce some network traffic and tallying.

User Option	Description
1	DISABLE_DEF_CNST_CHK. Controls interim constraint checking.
2	IMPLICIT_TRANSACTIONS. Controls whether a transaction is started implicitly when a statement is executed.
4	CURSOR_CLOSE_ON_COMMIT. Controls behavior of cursors once a commit has been performed.
8	ANSI_WARNINGS. Controls truncation and NULL in aggregate warnings.
16	ANSI_PADDING. Controls padding of variables.
32	ANSI_NULLS. Controls NULL handling by using equality operators.
64	ARITHABORT. Terminates a query when an overflow or divide-by-zero error occurs during query execution.
128	ARITHIGNORE. Returns NULL when an overflow or divide-by-zero error occurs during a query.
256	QUOTED_IDENTIFIER. Differentiates between single and double quotation marks when evaluating an expression.
512	NOCOUNT. Turns off the message returned at the end of each statement that states how many rows were affected by the statement.
1024	ANSI_NULL_DFLT_ON. Alters the session's behavior to use ANSI compatibility for nullability. New columns defined without explicit nullability will be defined to allow NULLs.
2048	ANSI_NULL_DFLT_OFF. Alters the session's behavior to not use ANSI compatibility for nullability. New columns defined without explicit nullability will be defined not to allow NULLS.

All of the definitions of sp_configure parameters were extracted from information found in the following documents:

sp_configure System Stored Procedure

sp_configure (version 6.5)

© 1997 Microsoft Corporation. All rights reserved.

Portions reprinted with permission from Microsoft Corporation.

You may want to refer to the originating documents for additional information about sp_configure. The most current version of these documents are located at the following Internet sites:

```
http://www.microsoft.com/msdn/sdk/platforms/doc/backoff/sqldrop/tsql-
ref/src/tsql19.htm
```

```
http://www.microsoft.com/msdn/sdk/platforms/doc/backoff/sqldrop/hydra/ts
ql/src/addsproc_37.htm
```

7

Oracle 7.3 Tuning

7.1 Introduction

Before scrutinizing the many facets of Oracle 7.3 tuning, I need to clarify the use of some terms for those administrators coming from other RDBMSs. In DB2, Informix and CA-IDMS, a *database* is defined as the schema defined table/network relationship constituting the user's data. Multiple databases are accessible from a DBMS region. However, in Oracle database means the *instance* or region where the RDBMS resides. Oracle's equivalent for a DB2 database is called the schema (owner).

The next term which may throw the non-Oraclite for a loop is *segment*. This is the name given to the space allocated to a table or other object in a tablespace, consisting of a number of extents. This, of course is nothing like an IMS segment, which is a database record (similar to a record in CA-IDMS). In RDBMSs, a record is a row.

A *sequence* (feature to get next sequence number) allows you to get and use a unique sequential number. These are cached across users (the number cached defined when you create a sequence), and you have to get the NEXTVAL (next value) before you can use the CURRVAL (current value).

When you create or alter them, you can specify minimum and maximum numbers, standard gap width (good for text: remember in BASIC how line numbers were usually 10 apart), and whether the sequence recycles or not. The sequence can even go backwards (good for demos with related columns checked so they cannot be negative). You might be tempted to have a cache=1, thus helping to avoid gaps, but this can often screw up the use of CURRVAL. And anyway, the sequence is meant to be arbitrary and distinguish rows, not to have any meaning (sometimes date and time are substituted for this).

A *set* is a group of operations (UNION, INTERSECT, MINUS) for "vertical joins." This might be confused with a CA-IDMS set, which defines the relationship between schema records and their connecting pointers. In Oracle, set operators can be used to get stuff from two (or more) select statements at a time, often from different tables, as in this example:

```
'emp_id, phone_num from emp

union

select 's', store_name, store_id, phone_num from store

union

select 'd', dept_name, dept_id, reception from dept

order by 2;
```

The next all-important term (parameter) is *SID* (Oracle System ID). It is held in the `$oracle_sid` environment variable in UNIX and `ora_sid` in VMS. Under UNIX, your SID must match the `oracle_home` `${oracle_home}` directory in the directory specified in the /etc/oratab file. Throughout this book we will refer to init.ora. In fact, this should be initSID.ora, as each database or instance of Oracle will have a unique SID.

SYS is the owner of Oracle database objects. Some of the standard userids in Oracle are SYS, ORACLE, and SYSTEM. SYSTEM is used by DBAs.

SYSTEM is also the name of a tablespace used for internal tables. It is good practice to move all the non-Oracle internal tables out of this tablespace. New users get the SYSTEM tablespace by default unless you explicitly point them elsewhere.

INIT.ORA or initSID.ora is a file containing initialization parameters. A majority of the aspects of tuning revolve around changes to parameters within this file. In the DB2 and CA-IDMS worlds, this file would be the equivalent of the system generation (SYSGEN).

Latches are an internal locking mechanism used by Oracle to control access to buffers, system tables and the dictionary. They do not work the same as regular locks on tables and rows. Instead, they are very fast.

Some of the more frequently used acronyms include those associated with background processes running in Oracle, namely *DBWR* (Database Writer), *LGWR* (Log Writer), *PMON* (Process Monitor), *SMON* (System Monitor), *RECO* (Recovery Process), *ARCH* (Archival Process), and *CKPT* (Checkpoint Process).

Tuning Oracle 7.3 consists of taking measurements, modifying initSID.ora (just init.ora from here on) initialization parameters, file placement, server management, and a few other fun things. Parallel processing is one of the hottest pay-backs for your efforts. The single biggest thing you can do with a basic Oracle system is tune the SGA (System Global Area). We will discuss all these things and more.

7.2 Benefits of Right Sizing to Oracle

You can get a major savings by converting your MVS, CICS, or VSAM based application to an ORACLE HP-UX/AIX/RS6000 based one. In doing so, you will reduce future maintenance costs, while reaping the benefits of relational-database technology along with the large repertoire of third-party relational tools. Also there may be some serious hardware and software licensing and maintenance cost incentives.

If you undertake this scenario, you would most likely use a tool set that would include Oracle and Developer/2000. Communications could very well be Novell LAN based. Quite a few other well known communications packages are also available to choose from.

Just why are so many shops making this transition? Increased productivity is being realized in systems with dial-up to database access, along with the newer wireless access. Legacy systems without these features may be suffering from people bottlenecks, where employees or customers wait until the next day to do business; while those with these features have both employees and customers continuing to get answers the night before information is needed or out in the field, where crucial decisions can be made immediately.

One of the hottest topics in the information marketplace is *warehousing*. We should all be familiar with the benefits of warehousing. DSS (Decision Support Systems) allow corporations to respond quickly in the market and win. To be successful at warehousing, you need a recipe for success. So, I've prepared a culinary fare for "Warehouse Pie." The recipe includes the following ingredients:

Recipe for Successful Warehouse Pie	
1 Cup	RDBMS (the more relational, the better)
1 Tsp	Read-only tables are ideal (but not required)
3 Cups	Fast processing (parallel architectures are best)
1 Cup	Cluster processor (Up to 32 cpus)
5 Tsp	Fast Networking (NICs utilizing Fibre FDDI)
2 Cups	Replication agents (asynchronous update and full copy)
1 Tbls	Extremely fast data loaders (a must)
2 Tbls	Extremely fast index builds and rebuilds
1 Cup	The best complex query optimizer that money can buy
5 Tsp	Many third-party DSS/MSS tools
9 Cups	Gigabyte-to-terabyte database support

Based on the contents of this recipe, you would think that Oracle had been doing nothing but cooking up culinary masterpiece. And you'd be right. They have been concentrating on this pastry for some time. In fact, the RDBMS winners in the big database shootout are going to be the ones who can provide this sorely needed solution. It isn't easy to juggle *Online Transaction Processing* (OLTP), *Symmetric Multi-Processing* (SMP), *Massively Parallel Processors* (MPP), OOPS technology advances, an ever growing list of hardware and operating system platforms on the mainframe, server, and desktop, coupled with the new media open initiative, Internet/Intranet offerings, artificial life/intelligence in tools and the ho-hum day-to-day upgrades of a large product line. While you're at it, add to this replication and warehousing the big new areas of industry competition. I know of no other company that has risen to the challenge like Oracle. Oracle 7.3 appears to have all the necessary ingredients, too. Now, it is up to us to eat the pie. Oracle's unparalleled support of warehousing requirements may make them an ideal choice for those companies contemplating a move from mainframe to client/server.

If this weren't enough to convince a big-blue addict that they had never eaten a really great apple pie, maybe a look at the bottom line of the budget report would. I keep turning up magazine articles about companies in transition to client/server based warehouses at a fraction of the cost of their mainframe counterparts. These stories can't all be bogus. Sure, I'm aware that the cost of retooling to new software and technology is high (some say 2-to-1), but the benefits are so appetizing. Besides, it never seems to be the information systems professional that decides what new technology will be used. It always seems to be some drooling wack-o end-user that sees a pretty picture in a magazine, or hears some hyped-up marketing demonstration. Can you blame them? They waited 35 years for the delivery of the last system which was approved. And it didn't do what they asked.

There are some companies helping make the transition from older legacy databases to Oracle. One such company is SMART Corporation. They make SMART DB, a point-n-click tool for data conversion.

So, if you're the unlucky decision maker in your organization, consider switching to Oracle. And, while you're at it, plan a mainframe garage sale. Those babies are much too big for boat anchors. Along these lines, take a look at the enhancements for Oracle Release 7.3 in the next section. Also, there is a dandy chart listing reasons to go client/server in Section 12.52 (Chapter 12).

7.3   Oracle Release 7.3 Performance Enhancements

In Release 7.1, we saw a milestone for performance enhancement. We got things like a flexible data loader that can load large amounts of data from a database into a warehouse, quicker index builds, complex query optimization, parallelized utilities (recovery, import/export, bulk loading), and read only tablespaces. Release 7.2's data warehousing improvements were notable. And in Release 7.2.2 the trend continued with a reduction of the load on DBWR (the database writer). This was accomplished when table scans and sorts began bypassing the buffer cache (set `sort_direct_write` = `true` in init.ora). But, Oracle

Release 7.3 is a landmark release for performance enhancements and new productivity. Check out the list in Figure 7-1.

- System enhancements to memory management
- Hash joins eliminate the need to perform sorts by providing in-memory hash tables constructed at runtime. The optimizer chooses the best method for joins, incorporating this significant improvement.
- Bit-mapped indexes improve ad-hoc queries on low-cardinality column data. Oracle utilizes a patented data-compression technology with bit-mapped indexes.
- Most aspects of parallel processing
  - Execution of UNION and UNION ALL
  - Execution of NOT IN
  - Execution of GROUP BY
  - Cost-base optimizer
  - Improved EXPLAIN PLAN
  - Locking mechanism to enables the specification of parallel-cache management locks that minimize the need for inter-instance communication.
- Internet usability
- Asynchronous read ahead for table scans delivers performance improvements for queries involving large tables. Additional data is asynchronously retrieved from disk while the current set is being processed.
- Improved space management for sort operations is accomplished by using TEMPORARY tablespaces designated exclusively for sorts. This scheme eliminates serialization of space-management operations involved in the allocation and deallocation of sort space.
- Using the knowledge of data locality (disk affinity), the system optimally allocates work to query slaves located on nodes where the data resides and minimizes inter-node data movement.
- Cost-based optimizer
  - Cost-based optimizer can automatically select the most efficient execution plan for the complex, data-intensive queries typical of warehouse environments.
  - Histograms provide the optimizer with the finer granularity information needed to select the fastest execution plan.

Figure 7-1 Oracle Release 7.3 Performance Enhancements

> Histograms and support for multidimensional queries, more transformations and execution strategies allow enhanced DSS (Decision Support Systems) optimization.

> The optimizer chooses defaults for parallelism based on the number of available processors and disk devices for storing table data.

■ Space-management improvements facilitate superior support for very large objects (VLOs) and better utilization of available space. Limitations on the number of extents per object has been removed. On demand release and coalescence of contiguous space is available.

■ An option for online analytical processing (OLAP) provides tools and facilities for complex drill-down and multi-dimensional data analysis.

■ Scalability enhancements eliminate potential serialization points and provide major improvements (including XA-compliant TP monitors) in scalability and performance under heavy loads.

■ Serializable transactions allow a high degree of isolation between concurrently running transactions (using the command SET TRANSACTION ISOLATION LEVEL SERIALIZABLE).

■ Disaster Recovery

> Faster instance startup via deferred transaction-recovery

> Standby Database

■ PL/SQL 2.3 Enhancements

> Updateable JOIN Views

> Multithreaded Client Applications

> OCI Enhancements

■ New Oracle TRACE performance data collection tool

■ New Rules Based Expert (ORACLE EXPERT)

Figure 7-1   Oracle Release 7.3 Performance Enhancements (Continued)

7.4 Freelist Contention

Every Table has a value for FREELISTS. This specifies the number of linked-lists maintained for the free blocks within available extents for the table. INSERT statements require reference to a FREELIST to identify an available block.

Concurrent table inserts can result in waits for FREELIST blocks. If the number of FREELISTS is less than the number of concurrent table inserts, a wait can ensue. In some instances, additional I/O is incurred. As the number of update transactions increases, there is a tendency for increased I/O and contention for resources.

You can specify the FREELIST value for a table at creation time. In Figure 7-2 this is set to 20 FREELIST blocks (free list of blocks used for segment extents) and 5 FREELIST groups (freelists for different database instances).

The select in Figure 7-3 returns the percentage that a request for data resulted in a wait for a free block. This value should be less than 1 percent. To reduce contention for a table's free list, the table must be recreated with a larger value in the FREELISTS storage parameter.

Oracle 7.4 added new *Oracle Parallel Server* (OPS) performance features, including freelist groups on indexes and elimination of the need to preallocate extents to freelist groups.

7.5 SMARTSTART Oracle

With SmartStart Oracle, users can take a new, un-configured server and turn it into a fully tuned and optimized Oracle7 database system. We're talking about a tool designed to optimize applications running on a Compaq ProLiant server (with TriFlex Architecture and SMP capabilities). Contingent upon answering a series of questions pertaining to the user's application, the tool produces recommendations for disk configuration, operating-system tuning, and database tuning. The user then accepts or modifies these recommendations. SmartStart automatically installs the software and has unlimited scalability. How can I hope to sell tuning books if Oracle makes the whole process turnkey?

7.6 Commonly Supported Platforms

This section is provided to list some of the more common platforms (see Figure 7-4) on which Oracle is running. I don't think anyone could compare all the tradeoffs for these because there are so many operating systems and third party software complexities which go along with the hardware. Just reference this list if you are interested in whether Oracle will run on a platform you may

---

```
create table tune_freelist
(tune_fl_cnt number,
tune_fl_gets number)
freelists 20
freelist groups 5;
```

Figure 7-2 Freelist Allocation

```
select round((sum(decode(w.class,'free list', count, 0))
/ (sum(decode(name,'db block gets', value, 0))
+ sum(decode(name,'consistent gets', value, 0)))))
* 100,2)
from v$waitstat w, v$sysstat
```

Figure 7-3 Freelist Waits

have. The software industry undergoes major changes every six months and hardware platform support can double every two years. Keep this in mind.

Platforms/Operating Systems	Disks
SunOS 4.1.3, 4.1.4	Common
Sun Solaris 2.3, 2.4, 2.5, 2.5.1	RAID
Sun Ulta Enterprise 6000 with Sun Solaris 2.6	CDROM
(with 16 CPUs capable of 23,143 tpmC[1])	ECC Cache
Sequent DYNIX/ptx	
IBM/AIX and RS/6000	
IBM RS/6000 + PowerPC Server R40	
(with 32 clustered CPUs capable of 14,283 tpmC)	
HP9000/715, HP9000/8887 &HP-UX (i.e. 9.05)	
HP-UX 10.20 on a HP9000 EPS30 (with 48 clustered CPUs capable of 17,826.5 tpmC)	
SGI IRIX	
DEC Alpha/Digital Unix	
DEC Alpha (i.e. 2100) Open VMS (i.e. 6.1)	
DEC VAX/VMS	
Digital UNIX V4.0A on AlphaServer 8400 (with 32 clustered CPUs capable of 30,390 tpmC*)	
Compaq ProLiant (e.g. Models 4000 and 5000) Servers (i.e. with Novell UnixWare 2.0)	
IBM S/390 Parallel Sysplex Mainframes with MVS/ESA, VTAM & CICS/ESA (IBM 9674 Coupling Facility)	
AS/400	
BULL ESCALA Power Cluster P4404-HE (with 32 clustered CPUs capable of 14,285 tpmC)	
SCO UNIX	
NetWare	
Pyramid Nile	
Fujitsu UXP/DS, DS/90 (UXP/DS)	
Hitachi 3050RX HI-UX/WE2, 3500 HI-UX/WE2, 3050 HI-UX/WE2	
NEC UX/4800	
Oracle Rdb on Alpha AXP and VAX	

  * tpmC values pulled off a web-site. Check with the Transaction Processing Council for documented benchmarks (www.tpc.org).

Heterogeneous Database Access from Oracle
ODBC Compliance
Sybase
DB2
Informix
CICS
IMS

  [1] Benchmark tpmC values mentioned were found at the Transaction Processing Councils website at www.tpc.org.

Figure 7-4 Commonly Supported Oracle Platforms (partial list)

7.7   Sizing the System Global Area (SGA)

The *System Global Area* (SGA) is one of the major tuning points for Oracle. The SGA is a memory area which contains work areas for several major components of Oracle. The database block buffer cache, redo log file cache, archive buffer cache, shared pool, and several other structures reside in the SGA.

- Database Buffers contain recently accessed records and updated ones not yet flushed to permanent storage data files.

- The redo log file buffer cache holds records used in database recovery before they are flushed to a sequential file. Transaction rollback and warm-start use the redo log files.

- The shared pool is comprised of the library cache and the data dictionary cache.

  - SQL and PL/SQL areas reside in library cache.

  - Dictionary and session information for multi-threaded processes occupy the data dictionary cache.

You can list summary information on the size of the main components of the SGA using the query in Figure 7-5, or you can get a complete component list and total byte usage report using the queries in Figure 7-6.

Figure 7-7 shows some SQLDBA and operating system displays for a very large SGA.

Since the SGA usually comprises the largest chunk of memory on your system, you can also use the UNIX "ipcs -b" command (see Figure 7-8) to get an approximate memory system for the operating system, plus the SGA. This command is helpful in determining rough estimates of memory usage. For example, you would never want to allocate an SGA so large that it occupied more than 90 percent of the entire system. UNIX would have trouble if there weren't enough memory for semaphores and background processes.

 NOTE: In Figure 7-8, only one memory segment is shown. No semaphores have been allocated indicating that post-wait is in operation. Utilizing a single shared memory segment is more efficient than several smaller segments.

```
select name, bytes
from v$sgastat where name in
('db_block_buffers,
 'log_buffer',
 'dictionary cache',
 'sql area',
 'library cache',
 'free memory');
```

Figure 7-5 Main SGA Components

```
compute sum of value on report
break on report
column value format 999,999,999
select * from v$sga;

column bytes format 999,999,999
compute sum of bytes on report
select *
from v$sgastat;
```

Figure 7-6 SGA Usage by Component

```
SQLDBA> connect internal
Connected.
SQLDBA> show sga
Total System Global Area        503568120 bytes
            Fixed Size              47936 bytes
         Variable Size          191896504 bytes
      Database Buffers          311296000 bytes
         Redo Buffers             327680 bytes
SQLDBA>
SQLDBA> show parameters

cpu_count                            =  2
db_block_buffers                     =  38000
db_block_size                        =  8192
db_domain                            =  WORLD
db_files                             =  100
db_name                              =  swow
db_writers                           =  1
gc_db_locks                          =  38000
ifile              file /users/home/dba/oracle/admin/swow/pfile/configswow.ora
instance_number                      =  0
log_archive_buffer_size              =  32
log_archive_buffers                  =  4
log_buffer                           =  327680
log_checkpoint_interval              =  999999999
log_checkpoints_to_alert             =  FALSE
log_files                            =  255
open_cursors                         =  255
parallel_default_max_instances       =  0
parallel_default_max_scans           =  0
parallel_default_scansize            =  100
parallel_max_servers                 =  5
parallel_min_servers                 =  0
parallel_server_idle_time            =  5
pre_page_sga                         =  FALSE
processes                            =  100
recovery_parallelism                 =  0
rollback_segments                    =  r01,r02,r03,r04,r05,r06,r07,r08
shared_pool_reserved_min_alloc       =  5000
shared_pool_reserved_size            =  0
shared_pool_size                     =  180000000
single_process                       =  FALSE
sort_area_retained_size              =  1310720    ☜ Sort
sort_area_size                       =  5242800    ☜ Tuning
sort_write_buffer_size               =  32763
sort_write_buffers                   =  2
spin_count                           =  20
temporary_table_locks                =  150
transactions                         =  126
transactions_per_rollback_segment    =  71

SQLDBA>

The OS parameters:

# ipcs -a
IPC status from /xyz/zyz as of Tue Oct  18 18:11:10 1996
T     ID     KEY        MODE        OWNER     GROUP   CREATOR   CGROUP CBYTES
```

Figure 7-7 SQLDBA and OS Displays

```
QNUM QBYTES LSPID LRPID   STIME    RTIME    CTIME
Message Queues:
  q       0 0x3c0421a5 -Rrw--w—w-     root     root     root     root     0
0   32768    0      0 no-entry no-entry 19:12:41
  q       1 0x3e0421a5 --rw-r—r--     root     root     root     root     0
0     264    0      0 no-entry no-entry 19:12:41
  q       2 0x04917dff --rw-rw-rw—    root     root     root     root     0
0    2400  416    204 4:05:57  4:05:58 19:12:43
  q       3 0x0045dcf8 --rw-rw-rw—    root     root     root     root     0
0    5520    0      0 no-entry no-entry 19:13:11
  q       4 0x0d5dcf71 --rw-rw-rw—    root     root     root     root     0
0    5520 24620    415 4:02:53  4:02:54 19:13:11


  T     ID    KEY       MODE      OWNER    GROUP   CREATOR   CGROUP NATTCH
SEGS Z  CPID  LPID  ATIME    DTIME    CTIME
 Shared Memory:
  m       0 0x410421ad --rw-rw-rw—    root     root     root     root     0
51 2    94     94 19:12:32 no-entry 19:12:32
  m       1 0x410421af --rw-rw-rw—    root     root     root     root     1
1462 0    94     98 19:12:36 19:12:36 19:12:32
  m       2 0x4110002b --rw-rw-rw—    root     root     root     root     1
819 2    94     98 19:12:36 19:12:33 19:12:33
  m       3 0xff0c0146 --rw-rw-rw—    root     root     root     root     2
8 4   189 24623  4:03:08 no-entry 19:12:43
  m       4 0xfe0c0146 --rw-rw-rw—    root     root     root     root     2
2465 2   204 24623  4:03:08 no-entry 19:12:49
  m       5 0xfd0c0146 --rw—rw-rw—    root     root     root     root     2
260 8   204 24623  4:03:08 no-entry 19:12:49
  m       6 0xfc0c0146 --rw-rw-rw—    root     root     root     root     2
2081 2   204 24623  4:03:08 no-entry 19:12:49
  m     107 0x764b6d6f --rw-r----- oracle71      dba oracle71      dba    35
50356 8392   456 26454 16:10:37 16:10:37 19:15:44


  T     ID    KEY       MODE      OWNER    GROUP   CREATOR   CGROUP NSEMS
OTIM E   CTIME
 Semaphores:
  s       0 0x410421af --ra-ra-ra—    root     root     root     root     2
19:12: 36 19:12:32
  s       1 0x4110002d --ra-ra-ra—    root     root     root     root     2
no-ent ry 19:12:33
  s       2 0x01090522 --ra-r—r--     root     root     root     root     1
no-ent ry 19:12:38
  s       3 0xff0c0146 --ra-ra-ra—    root     root     root     root     1
4:05: 56 19:12:43
  s       4 0x00000000 --ra-r----- oracle71      dba oracle71      dba   100
16:10: 46 19:15:44
  #
```

```
ipcs -b
```

```
T     ID    KEY       MODE      OWNER    GROUP      NSEMS
m     900 0x10043232  -re-r—   oracle    dba      41923455
```

Figure 7-8 IPCS -b Display

The maximum size of the SGA is related to two parameters on UNIX systems, SHMMAX (Maximum shared memory segment size) and SHMSEG (Maximum number of shared memory segments per process). If you specify an SHMMAX of 20M (see Figure 7-9) and an SHMSEG of 10, then the total segmented memory available is 200 M. However, the variable portion of the SGA (mainly the SHARED POOL) must reside within a single shared memory segment or you will see the error message ORA-7331. So, in our example, it would have to reside in 20M. In addition to these OS tunable parameters, the SVMM-LIM and HVMMLIM are used to define the maximum amount of shared memory available to a user. They must be large enough to accommodate the complete SGA.

When you start an Oracle instance it allocates the SGA in virtual memory. Database use causes paging into real memory. An init.ora parameter called pre_page_sga will cause everything to get paged into real memory during startup. But, it is not aware of the database rows which will be used during processing. Those must be loaded by allocating them in processes.

Everyone's SGA size will be different. I've heard of Novell server based systems with 170M SGAs and ones on Solaris systems with 250M SGAs. The real physical limit is up in the gigabyte memory range. But, you can always have more databases and more servers.

Typically, you want to tune all of the components of the SGA so that they are getting more than 90 percent hit ratios. Then, you don't need an SGA that is any larger. Try to make the SGA fit in real memory (paging can cost I/O). And insure there is sufficient memory to handle peak-load user processes. If your system provides support for it, you can optimize the use of real memory by installing the Oracle supplied software allowing several users to share a single executable image.

The free memory statistic (refer to Figure 7-5) should be low, not high. If the free memory value is too high, it could indicate that Oracle has aged objects out of the shared pool, which has become fragmented. Finally, the maximum memory available minus free memory gives an indication of memory used.

Another object found in the SGA are SEQUENCES. Oracle defaults 10 and will allow up to 32000. If a SEQUENCE were not found in memory cache an existing one would need be flushed out before it could be used. Each entry is 110 bytes (parallel server). Specifying NOCACHE is not advised, as Oracle would have to read these each time they are requested.

```
set shmsys:shminfo_shmmax=2000000
set shmsys:shminfo_shmmin=1
set shmsys:shminfo_shmmni=100
set shmsys:shminfo_shmseg=10

shmmax * shmseg = max segment memory        (which governs SGA)
```

Figure 7-9 Unix Kernel Parameters

The `small_table_threshold` parameter in init.ora determines the number of buffers that are available for full table scans. Tables smaller than this size are read into buffers entirely and added to the most recently used end of the LRU (least recently used) list. Tables larger than this buffer size get aged out as they are put at the head of the LRU list. This value is to be increased only if you want full table scan blocks to be retained in the SGA.

OPENVMS AND THE SGA

SGA varies by platform and on VMS Oracle creates a paging file for it. This is required by VMS that uses virtual memory and paging. This file is the basis of the SGA pad.

The SGA pad is a chunk of VMS address space that is allocated for the SGA so that each process that wants access to the SGA must reserve that address space within their own process address space. When run, the processes simply map to the real shared SGA area instead of to their own memory.

Having a larger than necessary SGA pad merely uses up more page space and doesn't waste real memory. If the process never accesses the portion of the SGA that is not part of the current database instance's SGA area, then it never gets paged into real memory.

If you want each instance to have its own SGA pad, then you need to link separate copies of Oracle with different pad sizes.

7.8   Sizing the Shared Pool

The shared pool consists of the library cache, the dictionary cache and MTS (Multi-threaded session information.). We will discuss tuning the library cache first and then the dictionary cache, which is the way you should proceed with tuning.

7.9   Library Cache

The queries in Figures 7-10 return the percentage that a SQL statement did not need to be reloaded because it was already in the library cache. The init.ora parameter `shared_pool_size` controls the amount of memory allocated for the shared buffer pool. The shared buffer pool contains SQL and PL/SQL statements (library cache), the data dictionary cache, and information on database sessions. The percentage should be equal to 100. Maximum efficiency requires that no SQL statement be reloaded and reparsed. Initially set the `shared_pool_size` to be 50-100 percent the size of the init.ora parameter `db_block_buffers * db_block_size` and then fine tune the parameter.

If the data dictionary hit ratio as determined using the query in Figure 7-10 is less than 80 percent, increase the `shared_pool_size` parameter in init.ora. Memory limitations may limit you from attaining the highest hit ratio possible. The inverse method shown in Figure 7-11 (Library Cache Miss Ratio) is another way to achieve the same goal. In this case, the resulting miss ratio should remain below 1 percent; otherwise, adjust the `shared_pool_size` parameter.

Using the output from the query in Figure 7-12, it is easy to discern from the pinhit ratio PHRATIO that the library caching is effective.

7.10 Dictionary Cache

The init.ora parameter shared_pool_size controls the amount of memory allocated for the shared buffer pool. The shared buffer pool contains SQL and PL/SQL statements (library cache), the data dictionary cache, and information on database sessions. More specifically, the data dictionary cache stores information relating to database objects. This percentage (query in Figure 7.10.1) will never equal 100 because the cache must perform an initial load when Oracle first starts up. The percentage, therefore, should continually get closer to 100 as the system stays "up". Ideally, the entire data dictionary would be cached in memory. Initially set the shared_pool_size to be 50-100 percent the size of the init.ora parameter: db_block_buffers, then fine tune the parameter.

Ideally, the entire data dictionary is cached in memory. If the data dictionary hit ratio as determined using the query in Figure 7-13 is less than 90 percent,

```
select
round(sum(pinhits)
/sum(pins) * 100,2)
from v$librarycache
```

Figure 7-10 Library Cache Hit Ratio

```
select
sum(pins) "Pins",
sum(reloads) "Misses",
((sum(reloads)/sum(pins)))
"Library Cache Miss Ratio"
from v$librarycache
```

Figure 7-11 Library Cache Miss Ratio

```
SQLDBA> set charwidth 12
SQLDBA> set numwidth 10
SQLDBA> Rem Select Library cache statistics.   The pin hit rate shoule be high.
SQLDBA> select namespace library,
   2>        gets,
   3>        round(decode(gethits,0,1,gethits)/decode(gets,0,1,gets),3)
   4>          ghration,
   5>        pins,
   6>        round(decode(pinhits,0,1,pinhits)/decode(pins,0,1,pins),3)
   7>          phratio,
   8>        reloads, invalidations
   9>  from stats$lib;
```

LIBRARY	GETS	GHRATIO	PINS	PHRATIO	RELOADS	INVALIDATI
BODY	3679	1	3679	1	0	0
CLUSTER	0	1	0	1	0	0
INDEX	23	.043	23	.043	0	0
OBJECT	0	1	0	1	0	0
PIPE	0	1	0	1	0	0
SQL AREA	107737	.911	16192572	.999	781	266
TABLE/PROCED	88792	.949	186375	.984	1490	0
TRIGGER	1060	1	1060	.994	6	0

8 rows selected.

Figure 7-12 Pin Hit Ratio

increase the `shared_pool_size` parameter in init.ora. The same is true if the percentage of misses increases while your application is running.

Memory limitations may limit you from attaining the highest hit ratio possible. It is common to see shops increase from 30M to 200M just to avoid dictionary cache misses.

Dictionary cache information is stored in the v$rowcache table, and like the v$librarycache table, it begins accumulating statistics from scratch every time the database is restarted. Only attempt to tune this cache after your application has been running long enough to build meaningful statistics in the v$rowcache table.

DBArtisan for Oracle is a comprehensive tuning tool for Sybase, Oracle and Microsoft SQL Server. One of its features is tuning cache.

7.11 DB_BLOCK_BUFFERS

Database block buffers reside in a cache area within the *System Global Area* (SGA). As with any conventional buffer mechanism requests for data first search the buffer. In the event the requested data is not found in the cache, it signals a physical read to place the data in the cache buffer. In some instances where the cache is full, the DBWR (Database Writer) is signaled to flush buffers to make room. Update and checkpoint activity also influence buffer utilization. The bottom line is the buffer hit ratio. It is derived from the formula:

$$1 - \frac{(physical\ reads)}{(physical\ gets\ and\ consistent\ gets)}$$

If the buffer hit ratio derived from the query in Figure 7-14 is less than 90 percent, you should increase the `db_block_buffers` parameter in init.ora. The maximum value allowed is 65536. Keep in mind that a change to this setting can cause an affect orders of magnitude in very large applications and tables.

Most operating systems will page-out the SGA if it does not fit entirely into real memory. If the cache is large enough, operating-system degradation can

```
column "Gets" format 999,999,999
column "Misses" format 999,999,999
select
sum(gets) "Gets",
sum(getmisses) "Misses",
trunc((1-(sum(getmisses)/sum(gets)))*100) "Dictionary Cache Hit Ratio"
from v$rowcache;

or

select round(sum(gets)/sum(gets)+sum(getmisses))
* 100,2)
from v$rowcache
```

Figure 7-13 Data Dictionary Cache Hit Ratio

make tuning the SGA counterproductive. It is a good idea to try to always have enough real memory to hold the SGA and other operating system requirements.

The `db_block_size` parameter defines the size of each block and is instrumental in controlling row migration and chaining (discussed in Section 1.27). Interestingly enough, the default `db_buffer_size` is 2048 bytes. It is related directly to the size of database blocks. In DSS (Decision Support Systems) where it is common to have queries return large amounts of data on average, a larger block and buffer size of 8K or 16K has been found to result in large savings.

Another init.ora parameter to look at is `db_file_multiblock_read_count` which determines the number of blocks read into the buffers in a single I/O (operating systems dependent). This is particularly relevant when cost-based optimization is selected. The optimizer capitalizes on the row statistics generated by ANALYZE (see Section 1.27 for more on ANALYZE), using the value in `db_file_multiblock_read_count` when computing the cost of full table scans. A larger parameter value equates to fewer I/Os necessary for full table scans.

7.12 Table and Tablespace Tuning

By paying attention to the needs of your tablespaces regularly, you will not be surprised with huge tuning projects. If you implement regular schedules for table and index reorganization, space management, backup, and disaster recovery, you will achieve the delicate balance needed for a supreme operational environment. It is also important to remember that changes to the database structure and other irregular changes need to be part of your maintenance plan.

For example, there are two ways to handle tablespace backup using scripts. First, you could alter tablespaces all at once or one at a time, placing them into backup mode. Altering them all at once is easier to do, but leaves tablespaces out of service longer. Timing is also important. Automated scheduling can reduce down time.

The same issues apply to index rebuilds, replication and any maintenance based procedure. There are lots of third party tools to help minimize the impact of maintenance windows.

The following tips will enhance tablespace performance:

■ Use separate tablespace for system, user tables and indexes, rollback segments, temporary areas (SQL statements, sorts etc.), and Oracle tools data.

```
select trunc((1-(sum(decode(name,'physical reads',value,0)))/
(sum(decode(name,'db block gets',value, 0))+
(sum(decode(name,'consistent gets',value,0)))))))
* 100) "Buffer Hit Ratio"
from v$sysstat;
```

Figure 7-14 Buffer Hit Ratio

- All objects in a tablespace should be a multiple of the db_block_size and they should all be a factor of the overall tablespace size, to avoid fragmentation.

- Set the size of the TEMPORARY tablespace to a little bit more than the space needed to perform your largest sort. Most likely, this is what you will use when creating your largest index.

- Place redo log files and the duplexed copies on different volumes to reduce contention and provide additional safety in the event that a controller or drive fails.

- Set MAXEXTENTS to 80 percent of the software maximum your table resides on. This will allow you to get an error message and still be able to increase extents before you hit a hardware or software limit.

- Have database triggers call stored procedures. Database triggers are interpreted each time they are executed. Stored procedures, on the other hand, are already parsed, so Oracle 7 handles them more efficiently.

- Optimize tablespace, freespace, and extents. Oracle returns error message ORA-1547 when there is insufficient free space to dynamically allocate an extent for a table or index.

To determine the percentage of blocks used by a specific tablespace, edit and run the query shown in Figure 7-15. Supply your tablespace name as needed.

Fragmentation of tablespaces, especially the SYSTEM tablespace, increases I/O. Tablespaces become fragmented as new extents are built all over the place because contiguous space is not available. You can recreate a tablespace during a reorganization to eliminate fragmentation. But, there are better ways to deal with it. DFRAG is a product available from Aris Corporation (http://www.ariscorp.com/).

DFRAG is the original Oracle database defragmentation and space management utility. DFRAG improves database performance and disk usage by rebuilding tables and indexes into single contiguous extents, eliminating row chaining and compressing row data in Oracle blocks. DFRAG works with both versions 6 and 7 of Oracle.

```
select round((((d.bytes - sum(nvl(f.bytes, 0)))
/ d.bytes) * 100,2)
from sys.dba_data_files d, sys.dba_free_space f
where d.file_id = f.file_id(+)
and d.tablespace_name = 'your_tablespace'
group by d.bytes
```

Figure 7-15 Tablespace Used

DFRAG FEATURES

- On-line defragmentation while database is in use
- Off-line defragmentation for jet fast reorganizations of entire tablespaces
- Parallel data load/unload
- GUI client-based front end, Virtual DBA
- Utilization based thresholds for defragmentation
- Defragment indexes independently of tables
- Graphical and statistical reports
- Calculates and recommends optimal storage parameters
- Ability to move objects to different tablespaces

Figures 7-16 through 7-18 depict ways that DFRAG will reduce fragmentation and physical I/Os.

Adhawk Spacer Version 2.0 is a competitive tool from Eventus Software. It provides detailed information about tablespaces and database objects.

7.13 Checkpointing

At checkpoint time, the DBWR (Database Writer) performs updates to all data and control files of the database. LGWR assume this duty if DBWR is not present.

Checkpoints occur at pre-defined intervals when modified blocks are written back to data files by the DBWR (Database Writer). Checkpoints facilitate instance restarts, since only the data since the last checkpoint needs to be rolled out or reapplied. Checkpoints occur when transactions are committed, redo log files switch, tablespaces are taken offline, online tablespace backups are started, and at shutdown (NORMAL | IMMEDIATE).

Checkpoint frequency is determined by the `log_checkpoint_interval` paramater in init.ora. The `log_checkpoint_timeout` parameter (default is 0 seconds) permits time-based checkpointing. Other init.ora parameters influencing checkpointing include:

```
checkpoint_process = true        (enables a process other than LGWR to
                                  handle checkpoints)

ckpt                             (name of other process)
```

It has been my experience that too few, or too many checkpoints can both cause serious performance impediments. Too few can increase the time for instance recovery and eat up more memory. Too many can overload the DBWR and the system as a whole.

An advisable initial setting is to make `log_checkpoint_interval` larger than the size of the redo log files setting (numbers in the tens of millions work best). Then if LGWR is too busy, tune the parameter based on application needs. For example, if a typical application is spending 5 percent of its time on Oracle

COMBINED EFFECT

NO PHYSICAL I/O

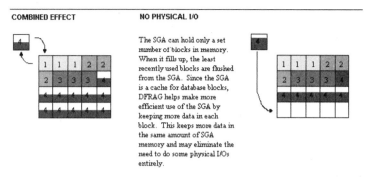

The SGA can hold only a set number of blocks in memory. When it fills up, the least recently used blocks are flushed from the SGA. Since the SGA is a cache for database blocks, DFRAG helps make more efficient use of the SGA by keeping more data in each block. This keeps more data in the same amount of SGA memory and may eliminate the need to do some physical I/Os entirely.

Figure 7-16   DFRAG and SGA Usage

ABLE FRAGMENTATION

FASTER I/O

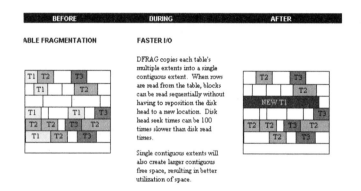

DFRAG copies each table's multiple extents into a single contiguous extent. When rows are read from the table, blocks can be read sequentially without having to reposition the disk head to a new location. Disk head seek times can be 100 times slower than disk read times.

Single contiguous extents will also create larger contiguous free space, resulting in better utilization of space.

Figure 7-17   DFRAG and Fragmentation

DATA DISPERSION

REDUCED I/O

DFRAG analyzes the existing data blocks for poor utilization. It then compresses the rows into fewer blocks. Now, rather than reading five blocks that are partially full, only three blocks are read, reducing I/O by 40%.

ROW CHAINING

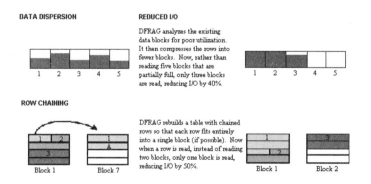

DFRAG rebuilds a table with chained rows so that each row fits entirely into a single block (if possible). Now when a row is read, instead of reading two blocks, only one block is read, reducing I/O by 50%.

Figure 7-18   DFRAG Block Utilization and Row Chaining

checkpoint waits, you should not attempt to tune the application until you resolve the checkpoint wait problem. However, if the same application is not waiting due to checkpoints, it isn't necessary to change Oracle's checkpoint parameters, regardless of the number of checkpoints/hour occurring within the system (query in Figure 7-19 issued hourly).

```
select name, value from v$sysstat where name = 'dbwr checkpoints'
```

Figure 7-19 Checkpoint Query

Too small a value in db_block_write_batch can cause checkpoints to take longer. This value is the maximum number of blocks that DBWR will write in one batch for a checkpoint. The bigger the batch, the faster it flies. The value db_block_checkpoint_batch can be computed as db_block_write_batch * 4.

A subject which goes hand-in-hand with checkpointing is the DBWR, discussed next.

7.14 DBWR (Database Writer)

In section 7.13 we talked about checkpointing and its tuning implications. In conjunction with this, the DBWR (Database Writer) is the focus of our next discussion.

After making a rudimentary study of the information available surrounding the DBWR, I have come to the conclusion that there is a need by gurus to identify new ways to tune this facility. Generally speaking, tuning today involves interrogating a handful of values queried from statistics and tweaking a handful of init.ora parameters. This is pretty straightforward. But I noticed while doing my research that the potential exists to expand tuning options, based upon other existing values, perhaps using new formulas. For now, this book will present the traditional information available.

Most the information you need to make determinations in tuning DBWR can be found using the utlbstat/utlestat.sql reports. A sample run is shown in Figure 7-20. In addition, Table 7-1 lists useful values and Figure 7-21 provides formulas for calculating your own statistics.

TABLE 7-1 Useful DBWR Report Values

STATISTIC	DESCRIPTION
Make free requests	LRU requests for free buffers
Free (clean) buffers found	Number of already clean buffers found
Dirty buffers inspected	Number of times a foreground process looking for a buffer to reuse encountered a dirty buffer that had aged out through the LRU queue to make clean
Summed Dirty Queue Length	Dirty queue length after writer requests complete
Summed scan depth	Accumulated scan depth at LRU scan time
Scans	LRU queue scans for buffers to write
Scanned buffers	The number of buffers looked at during LRU scans
Timeouts	Incremented if no DBWR activity

```
SQLDBA>
SQLDBA> set charwidth 27;
SQLDBA> set numwidth 12;
SQLDBA> Rem The total is the total value of the statistic between the time
SQLDBA> Rem bstat was run and the time estat was run.  Note that the estat
SQLDBA> Rem script logs on as "internal" so the per_logon statistics will
SQLDBA> Rem always be based on at least one logon.
SQLDBA> select n1.name "Statistic",
    2>        n1.change "Total",
    3>        round(n1.change/trans.change,2) "Per Transaction",
    4>        round(n1.change/logs.change,2)  "Per Logon"
    5>    from stats$stats n1, stats$stats trans, stats$stats logs
    6>    where trans.name='user commits'
    7>    and   logs.name='logons cumulative'
    8>    and   n1.change != 0
    9>    order by n1.name;
```

Statistic	Total	Per Transact	Per Logon
CPU used by this session	21409299	940.49	11121.41
CPU used when call started	21788526	979.58	11110.92
CR blocks created	166872	4.77	86.64
Current blocks converted fo	24028	1.19	14.04
DBWR buffers scanned	74749846	1640.44	19402.52
DBWR checkpoints	297	.01	.15
DBWR free buffers found	75479966	1556.84	18410.74
DBWR lru scans	284762	12.49	144.42
DBWR make free requests	248171	12.22	144.48
DBWR summed scan depth	74898746	1664.84	19684.45
DBWR timeouts	17470	.59	6.98
background checkpoints comp	24	0	.01
background checkpoints star	28	0	.01
background timeouts	84874	7.47	44.04
calls to kcmgas	61241	2.69	71.81
calls to kcmgcs	140429	4.49	88.57
calls to kcmgrs	18856606	828.75	9495.64
change write time	57484	2.75	24.49
cleanouts and rollbacks - c	24760	1.2	14.21
cleanouts only - consistent	716644	17.91	164.49
cluster key scan block gets	155464	6.87	80.46
cluster key scans	55282	2.47	28.42
consistent changes	1206248	52.99	626.62
consistent gets	859852295	48058.88	844845.75
cursor authentications	62467	2.46	72.6
data blocks consistent read	1164925	51.71	606.41
db block changes	12440857	546.51	6462.48
db block gets	17100201	545.48	6805.7
deferred (CURRENT) block cl	45789	1.99	27.58
dirty buffers inspected	214646	9.47	111.52
enqueue conversions	25461	1.17	17.78
enqueue releases	114024	5.14	60.49
enqueue requests	114041	5.14	60.8
enqueue timeouts	24	0	.01
enqueue waits	26	0	.01
exchange deadlocks	2	0	0
execute count	15841944	694.24	8245.14
free buffer inspected	744044	15.25	180.7
free buffer requested	16457477	422.48	8544.24
immediate (CR) block cleano	744259	15.12	148.84
immediate (CURRENT) block c	158714	6.95	82.24
logons cumulative	1925	.08	1
logons current	81	0	.04
messages received	709464	17.61	160.92

Figure 7-20 UTLBSTAT/UTLESTAT Script Output

```
messages sent                      709468       17.61      160.92
no work - consistent read g     1690424577    44241.86    848298.46
opened cursors cumulative          172955        5.84       69.04
opened cursors current               1828         .08         .95
parse count                        204564        9.12      104.87
parse time cpu                      54512        2.79       28.72
parse time elapsed                  88876         7.9       46.15
physical reads                   15460644      692.75     8184.75
physical writes                    901667       79.61      468.4
process last non-idle time      944887716    40529.05    815487.54
recursive calls                  12884281      566.17     6694.69
recursive cpu usage               8748789      768.05     4752.41
redo blocks written               2900840      124.47     1506.97
redo buffer allocation retr            44           0         .04
redo entries                      6245542      245.68     7260.02
redo log space requests               264         .01         .14
redo log space wait time            19689         .86       10.27
redo size                      1472879974    62947.24    444772.47
redo small copies                  687415       70.02      755.02
redo synch time                     41622        7.15       74.21
redo synch writes                    6484          .7        7.52
redo wastage                      4852844      217.18     2520.96
redo write time                    459515       20.19      278.41
redo writer latching time             449         .02         .27
redo writes                         79564        1.44       20.55
rollback changes - undo rec         40406        1.44       20.99
rollbacks only - consistent        165542        4.24       86.01
session connect time            9744887716    60529.05    415487.54
session cursor cache count           2444         .12        1.44
session cursor cache hits           99870        4.79       51.86
session logical reads          9448900899   104544.49   1242156.71
session pga memory             9780764916   104564.21   1276554.46
session pga memory max         9051698456    90129.08   1065814.78
session uga memory               11561016      504.86     6005.42
session uga memory max          168442292     4412.68    84658.77
sorts (disk)                           77           0         .02
sorts (memory)                    1225945       57.85      676.85
sorts (rows)                      4241022       186.7     2207.17
summed dirty queue length          159092        6.99       82.65
table fetch by rowid            814454099    75491.74    427248.88
table fetch continued row         5564070      244.42     2890.41
table scan blocks gotten         78744025     1684.42    19918.94
table scan rows gotten           49442084     7489.81    41268.62
table scans (long tables)            1472         .08          .9
table scans (short tables)         110054        4.87       54.14
transaction rollbacks                 904         .04         .44
transaction tables consiste           847         .04         .44
transaction tables consiste         76485        1.62       19.11
user calls                       17240051      581.62     6844.95
user commits                        22464           1       11.83
user rollbacks                       7193         .32        3.74
write requests                     118068        5.19       61.33
96 rows selected.

SQLDBA>
SQLDBA> set charwidth 20
SQLDBA> Rem The times that bstat and estat were run.
SQLDBA> select * from stats$dates;
STATS_GATHER_TIMES
------------------
22-jan-97 11:13:07
23-jan-97 18:41:03
2 rows selected.
```

Figure 7-20 UTLBSTAT/UTLESTAT Script Output (Continued)

The first init.ora parameter disclosed here is `db_block_write_batch`. It defines the number of dirty buffers DBWR will write back to disk in the following situations:

- When a user process moves a buffer it has modified to the dirty buffer list and finds that the list has reached a threshold which is half the value of `block_write_batch`
- When a user process scans the LRU list for a free buffer and the number of entries scanned exceeds `db_block_max_scan_cnt`
- When a DBWR time-out occurs (every 3 seconds)
- When a checkpoint occurs

Another query is provided in Figure 7-22 which will capture the average length of the dirty buffer write queue. If this is larger than the value of the `db_block_write_batch` parameter in init.ora, then consider increasing the value of `db_block_write_batch` and check the distribution of I/Os on disks.

As we saw in section 7.11, too small a value for `db_block_write_batch` can slow down checkpointing. Increase this parameter to allow DBWR to clean out the buffer cache faster. Dirty buffers are also discussed in section 1.26.

The next init.ora parameter to look at is the `db_file_simultaneous_writes`. This is the number of simultaneous writes for each database file written by DBWR. The value should be set to 1 on platforms not supporting multiple writes to a single device (default is 4 and maximum is 24). Obviously, there may

---

scans = scans + current scan depth

average scan depth = LRU scans / scans

average buffers scanned = buffers scanned / LRU scans

average reusable buffers in LRU queue = free buffers found / make free requests

average number of dirty buffers = summed dirty queue length / write requests

Figure 7-21   Useful DBWR Formulas

```
SQLDBA> select queue.change/writes.change "Average Write Queue Length"
    2>    from stats$stats queue, stats$stats writes
    3>    where queue.name  = 'summed dirty queue length'
    4>    and  writes.name = 'write requests';

Average Write Queue Length
-------------------------
1.34746078531016024663758309
1 row selected.
```

Figure 7-22   Average Write Queue Length

be some benefit in increasing this value where it is supported. Please check your Oracle installation and user guide for OS, to see if you can benefit by this.

The last init.ora parameter examined is db_writers. This is the number of DBWR processes to be forked. On platforms using asynchronous I/O, it should be 1 (default). On others it can be increased up to the number of disks in use by the database. Again, check your support for this.

7.15   REDO Log

When a redo log file is filled, the ARCH process archives it out to a UNIX file. LGWR continues writing to the next redo log file. If LGWR uses all available files and wraps around to the current file being archived, then LGWR and all database processing is suspended. A message is written into the alert_log file.

Several things can be done to improve logging and archival performance. Let's look at the most advantageous options. Avoiding a media failure is the easiest action you can take. To setup mirrored logging, you only need to add a member to each redo log group. You can create as many mirrored members as you wish, up to the maxlog_members value.

Place these mirrored images on different devices to avoid outages.

In parallel mode, each redo has a different thread number. This is one of the great advantages of parallel processing.

Broadly speaking, the performance of ARCH is not an issue. The log archive and redo log files should be on separate dedicated disk drives, to avoid contention. Provide enough redo log files to avoid wrapping during archival and to handle the longest transactions. Be sure that redo logs are on the fastest disks, where there are no competitive files stored.

Adjusting log_archive_buffers to 1 and log_archive_buffer_size to the maximum (as defined in the Oracle Installation and User Guide for OS) will make ARCH work slowly. Setting log_archive_buffers to 2, 3, or 4 and log_archive_buffer_size to a lower value will increase the speed of ARCH. This is a catch-22 situation. If ARCH runs too quickly, it can saturate the CPU time. And if it runs too slow, it can wrap and all database processes will enter a wait.

Other areas of tuning the redo log include latch contention, latch allocation contention, spin count, and redo log buffer waits.

The select in Figure 7-23 returns the largest percentage of latch contention from key latches. The value should be less than 3 percent. If the value is greater than 3 percent, try decreasing the value of the init.ora parameter log_small_entry_max_size to force more copies to use the copy latches. For multiple CPU systems, increase the number of "redo copy latched" by increasing the value of the init.ora parameter Log_simultaneous_copies. It may be helpful to have up to twice as many copy latches as CPUs available to the database instance. Finally, try increasing the value of the init.ora parameter log_entry_prebuild_threshold.

Equivalent latch output derived using the UTLBSTAT/ESTAT scripts is shown in Figure 7-24.

The percentage of time that a process attempted to acquire a redo log latch held by another process should be less than 1 percent (see Figure 7-25). This is rare on single CPU systems. If the value is greater than 1 percent, try decreasing the value of the init.ora parameter `log_small_entry_max_size` to reduce contention for the redo allocation latch.

For multiple CPU systems, increase the number of "redo copy latched" by increasing the value of the init.ora parameter `log_simultaneous_copies`. It may be helpful to have up to twice as many copy latches as CPU(s) available to the database instance. The number of redo copy latches is defined by `log_simultaneous_copies`, which by default, is equal to `cpu_count`. Oracle should automatically set `cpu_count` to the number of processors in a multi-processor

```
select round(greatest(
sum(decode(ln.name,'cache buffers lru chain', misses, 0))
/ greatest(sum(decode(ln.name.'cache buffers lru chain', gets, 0)),1)),
(sum(decode(ln.name,'enqueues', misses, 0))
/ greatest(sum(decode(ln.name,'enqueues', gets, 0)), 1)),
(sum(decode(ln.name,'redo allocation', misses, 0))
/ greatest(sum(decode(ln.name,'redo allocation', gets, 0)), 1)),
(sum(decode(ln.name,'redo.copy', misses, 0))
/ greatest(sum(decode(ln.name,'redo copy', gets, 0)), 1)))
* 100,2)
from v$latch l, v$latchname ln
where l.latch# = ln.latch#
```

Figure 7-23 Latch Contention

```
SQLDBA>
SQLDBA> set numwidth 18
SQLDBA> Rem Statistics on no_wait gets of latches.  A no_wait get does not
waite
SQLDBA> Rem latch to become free, it immediately times out.
SQLDBA> select name latch_name,
    2>      immed_gets nowait_gets,
    3>      immed_miss nowait_misses,
    4>      round(decode(immed_gets-immed_miss,0,1,immed_gets-immed_miss)/
    5>          decode(immed_gets,0,1,immed_gets),
    6>          3)
    7>        nowait_hit_ratio
    8>      from stats$latches
    9>      where immed_gets != 0
   10>      order by name;
```

LATCH_NAME	NOWAIT_GETS	NOWAIT_MISSES	NOWAIT_HIT_RATIO
cache buffers chai	25766284	7209	1
cache buffers lru	1470900853	339105013	.769
library cache	68464	92	.999
library cache pin	7603	183	.976
redo copy	6223523	468	1
row cache objects	1058	3	.997

6 rows selected.

Figure 7-24 Sample Latch Statistics

machine. Therefore, the cpu_count value must not be set in the init.ora. If the miss ratio is high, increase log_simultaneous_copies to a maximum of twice the number of processors on the machine. Log_entry_prebuild (default 0) can be increased to permit user processes to prebuild entries before attempting to copy into the log buffer.

The redo-buffer cache holds the redo records used in database recovery before Oracle 7 flushes these records to the online redo log. This cache area is yet another one of the many caches kept in the SGA.

The queries in Figure 7-26 return the number of times a user process waited for redo log buffer space. This value should be near zero. If the value increments consistently, increase the size of the redo log buffer with the init.ora parameter log_buffer by 5 percent. This parameter is defined in bytes and does not support the K (kilobytes) or M (megabytes) suffix notation.

With Oracle Release 7.2, an optional checksum computation and verification became available for redo log blocks, facilitating earlier detection and improved diagnosis of corrupted media. Using this new facility and making sure to backup redo logs are just common sense items.

Users can optionally disable the generation and logging of redo information for bulk data loads, CREATE TABLE AS SELECT and CREATE INDEX operations. If you are running in NOARCHIVELOG mode and use DIRECT = TRUE, you will bypass redo log generation.

The last thing covered in this section is spin count. The spin_count parameter is the number of times an Oracle process will attempt to get a latch before going to sleep. Oracle will try to acquire a latch; if it is busy, the process will

```
select round(greatest(
(sum(decode(ln.name,'redo copy', misses, 0))
/greatest(sum(decode(ln.name,'redo copy', gets, 0)), 1)),
(sum(decode(ln.name,'redo allocation', misses, 0))
/greatest(sum(decode(ln.name,'redo allocation', gets, 0)), 1)),
(sum(decode(ln.name,'redo copy',immediate_misses,0))
/greatest(sum(decode(ln.name,'redo copy',immediate_gets,0))
+ sum(decode(ln.name,'redo copy',immediate_misses, 0)), 1)),
(sum(decode(ln.name,'redo allocation',immediate_misses, 0))
/greatest(sum(decode(ln.name,'redo allocation',immediate_gets, 0))
+ sum(decode(ln.name,'redo allocation',immediate_misses, 0)), 1)))
* 100,2)
from v$latch l, v$latchname ln
where l.latch# = ln.latch#
```

Figure 7-25 Redo Log Allocation Latch Contention

```
select value from v$sysstat where name = 'redo log space waittime'
or
select value from v$sysstat where name = 'redo log space requests'
```

Figure 7-26 Redo Log Buffer Contention

spin and then attempt to acquire the latch again. It will do this until it either acquires the latch or it reaches `spin_count`. Then it goes to sleep for a set amount of time, wakes up, and tries again. The higher the spin_count, the longer Oracle will try to get the latch without sleeping. Spinning requires CPU cycles. Obviously, you don't want to use too much CPU and you don't want to go into excessive waits. So, have plenty of latches and set the spin count high enough to avoid sleeping. I'd recommend 4000 on small machines and 8000 on big ones.

7.16 Rollback Segments

Like other segments, rollback segments are allocated in groups of contiguous blocks known as extents. Each rollback segment contains at least two extents.

There is a SYSTEM rollback segment created automatically in the SYSTEM tablespace when a database is created. This segment is devoted to SYSTEM tablespace activity. In addition, other rollback segments are created to accommodate the expected number of concurrent transactions, and their size. All rollback segments should be the same size, with the exception of a limited number of large or small ones to handle unusual transactions.

Rollback segments are also used for read consistency. A volatile transaction can have an impact on performance if the rollback segments are not sized to deal with the effects of read consistency.

The system will register a transaction to a rollback segment, putting information in the rollback segment header. The number of transactions which can be registered in the header limits the number which can use a rollback segment concurrently. Increasing the block size will increase the number of transactions handled. For example, a 4K block can handle approximately 60 transactions. The syntax for creating a rollback segment follows:

```
create rollback segment your_rs
storage (
initial 100K
next 100K
minextents 20
maxextents 100
optimal 500K);
```

The system will allow you to create rollback segments on the fly, but it is important to add them to the init.ora, or they will not be recognized at the next startup.

The OPTIMAL parameter in our example is the size a rollback segment will shrink back to after a lengthy transaction. OPTIMAL should match the average size for most of your transactions to get the best performance. This is because every added extent slows the system. A higher OPTIMAL value will keep rollback segments in memory.

One method of obtaining information about rollback segment performance is MONITOR ROLLBACK SEGMENTS in SQL*DBA. Also, the v$rollstat system table (see Figure 7-27) contains statistics which aid in identifying the major tuning needs for rollback segments. Rollback segment contention and extent usage are the primary areas to focus on. Of lesser importance are extends, shrinks, and wraps, which incur recursive SQL. Let's look at contention first.

The percentage of times that a request for data resulted in a wait for a rollback segment is derived using the query in Figure 7-28. If this returns a value greater than 1 percent, then create additional rollback segments. A rule of thumb is to compute the number of rollback segments as `transactions/4`. This is one way to deal with contention.

The queries in Figure 7-29 provide counts for waits related to headers and blocks respectively using the v$waitstat table. The higher these counts, the greater the impetus to increase the number of rollback segments.

Column Name	Data Type
usn	number
extents	number
rssize	number
writes	number
xacts	number
gets	number
waits	number
optsize	number
hwmsize	number
shrinks	number
wraps	number
extends	number
aveshrink	number
aveactive	number
status	varchar2(15)

Figure 7-27 V$ROLLSTAT Table Layout

```
select round(rum(waits)/sum(gets),2) from v$rollstat
```

Figure 7-28 Rollback Segment Contention

```
select class, count
from v$waitstat
where class in ('system undo header','undo header')

select class, count
from v$waitstat
where class in ('system undo block','undo block')
```

Figure 7-29 Rollback Segment Waits

Another aspect of contention is managing rollback segment caching. This is primarily accomplished with the buffer size defined in the `db_block_buffers` parameter.

Contention is also reduced by ensuring that rollback segments have their own tablespace. This is just common sense because segregation using tablespaces and files is a common method for avoiding excessive extents and table fragmentation.

Extents, shrinks, and wraps statistics can be obtained using the query in Figure 7-30. These activities can be controlled using the OPTIMAL parameter online. If the number of `shrinks` is low and `aveshrink` is high then OPTIMAL is tuned properly. Otherwise, adjust OPTIMAL upward to reduce the number of `shrinks` and downward to increase `shrinks`.

The number of rollback segments as defined in the `rollback_segments` parameter can be modified online. You might find cause to create a few new segments on the fly and bring them online. After deciding that they are making a positive difference, you would make the changes permanent by adding them to init.ora. Long running batch processes have special needs including much larger rollback segments. It is best to assign one using the following command as the first line in transaction execution or a .SQL file.

```
set transaction use rollback segment <segment name>
```

A sample report with output provided by the UTLBSTAT/ESTAT scripts is shown in Figure 7-31. If the trans_tbl_waits field is high (as it is with undo segment 20) it implies that you should add rollback segments.

In summary, here is a list of key parameters affecting rollback segment performance and their specific use.

- `processes`—The number of concurrent processes allowed

- `transactions`—This number is computed as *1.1 * processes* (default 30)

- `rollback_segments`— This is the number of private rollback segments and should remain less than the number of transactions divided by transactions_per_rollback_segment

- `max_roll_back_segments`—Is the maximum number of rollback segments that can be kept online (default 30)

```
select n.name, s.xacts, s.waits, s.gets, s.shrinks, s.wraps, s.extends,
s.rssize, aveactive, aveshrink
from v$rollname n, v$rollstat s
where n.usn = s.usn
and n.status = 'ONLINE'
order by n.name
```

Figure 7-30 Rollback Segment Usage

```
SQLDBA> select * from stats$roll;
UNDO_SEGMENT          TRANS_TBL_GETS      TRANS_TBL_WAITS      UNDO_BYTES_WRITTEN
------------------    ------------------  -------------------  ------------------
               0                   324                    0                    00
               1                 36155                    5             611277323
               2                 79765                    0             142364923
               3                 40850                   30             713743665
               4                 11441                   42             119697003
               5                  8869                   50             118263553
               6                 13500                    1             130265683
               7                 17279                    0             260479256
               8                 14533                    1             203414875
               9                  7081                    5              60371882
              10                  7937                    1              71897551
              11                  4102                    0              43510611
              12                 12003                    1             177683964
              13                  6423                    2              78628822
              14                  8013                    3              92542452
              15                  4865                    0              48795861
              16                  2668                    1              19415991
              17                  5223                    0              59321621
              18                  7468                    0              72927431
              19                  7340                    0              90308402
              20                  7716                  710              70232031
20 rows selected.
```

Figure 7-31   Transaction Table Waits

- gc_rollback_segments—Parallel server rollback segments shared across multiple database instances. This number must be identical in the different instances.

- db_block_buffers—Rollback segments are cached and therefore impacted by the size of the buffer area.

- cleanup_rollback_entries—This is the number of row entries that PMON will clean up in case of an aborted transaction. Long running transactions can require more than the default value of 20.

- set transaction use rollback segment —Batch process rollback segment defined in the first line in transaction execution or a .SQL file.

- Sample Parameter Settings:

```
db_block_buffers                        = 38000
processes                               = 100
rollback_segments                       = r01,r02,r03,r04,r05,r06,r07,r08
transactions                            = 126
transactions_per_rollback_segment       = 71
cleanup_rollback_entries                = 30
```

7.17 Table Loading

Some might say it's a waste of time to use your own procedures and programs to perform unloads and loads, when there are so many tools to choose from. They may be right. But that's no excuse for not knowing the basic issues associated with load performance. Consider this section a short education into issues surrounding the LOAD.

The good news is that everyone taking this table loading course will get a passing grade on the final exam. The bad news is that you may fail in real life, where it really counts. There are quite a few factors governing efficient loading and unloading of tables. For example, the size of the table, the number of indexes, referential integrity constraints, stored procedures and triggers, the time frame in which the load must occur, and the frequency of table loading. Obviously, a mission critical application which gets reloaded frequently has special needs.

What is the best way to load a table? Even a well written C program that is loading many tables with rows of data as they are read from a sequential input file is not the fastest method available. It may be much better to pre-process an input file into separate files for each of your tables, and let SQL*Loader perform the load. Look at Table 7-2 for a long list of ways to facilitate faster loading of tables.

Figure 7-32 provides a rudimentary SQL*Loader example. Some of the things mentioned in our tuning suggestions table (Table 7-2) are shown in small type.

When using PRO*C, especially in a networked environment, it is important to use array inserts for performance. For example, the code in Figure 7-33 will incorporate 100 rows, or whatever fits, in a single network message.

```
load data                          (parallel=yes direct=yes)
infile file1.dat                   (can be sorted for faster index creates)
replace
into your_table
(t1f1 position(1:10) char)         (multiple files, tablespaces, striping)

or

load
infile 'my.txt'
terminated by ','                  (delimited field separator)
enclosed by '"'                    (delimited field enclosure)
into table your_table
(zip_code,
zip_plus_4)
```

Figure 7-32 SQL Loader Syntax Examples

TABLE 7-2   **Table Loading Techniques**

TECHNIQUE	BENEFIT
PARALLEL=YES in SQL*Loader	Bulk load in parallel when SMP processors are available
DIRECT=YES in SQL*Loader	Bypass DBWR and LGWR eliminating logging I/O and Database Writer overhead. Can save 75 percent. QUID PRO QUOS: ▓ won't work with clustered tables ▓ snapshot log won't show inserts ▓ no active SELECT(s) if table is indexed
Parallel index build	Saves elapsed time
Remove indexes before loading	Reduces elapsed time and CPU
CREATE INDEX | TABLE AS SELECT with UNRECOVERABLE option	Eliminates LGWR writing to log saving CPU and elapsed time
Use multiple FREELISTS	Avoid contention between multiple loader programs
Provide sufficient extents for load	Eliminates need to create extents during load
Avoid delimited records in input files	Reduces speed by half
Must have delimited data in input files	IMPORT should run faster than the loader.
Use IMPORT over SQL*Loader	Reduces elapsed time. But, make sure that you don't have indexes on tables during an import, or you won't save any time. Also set DB_BLOCK_BUFFER very large for IMPORT and use a giant BUFFER clause on IMPORT.
Sort input data file for indexing	Reduces elapsed time and CPU by being able to specify SORTED INDEXES clause.
Sort input data file for heaviest queries	Pick the index servicing the greatest query volume and sort input file to accommodate row locations after load.
Disable triggers	Reduces overhead, but invalidates snapshot logs that won't register inserts
Disable declarative constraints	Reduces CPU
Disable FKEY as opposed to dropping a constraint	Reduces amount of typing and scripting involved in removing and adding constraints
Eliminate "interested transaction entries"	Subsequent SELECTS incur overhead while Oracle cleans them up
Increase db_block_buffers	Reduces I/Os and CPU
Increase size of shared pool	Improves caching
Spread heavily accessed files. Stripe using ALTER TABLE ALLOCATE	Better transaction performance. Less disk contention with multiple loaders running.
EXTENT or FILE = clause of parallel loader	Boosts transaction performance after the load and helps parallelize queries.

TABLE 7-2   Table Loading Techniques (Continued)

TECHNIQUE	BENEFIT
Partition the data in tablespaces	Takes advantage of parallel loading and reduces impact of recovery
Place small reference tables in memory	Avoids repetitive I/O
Denormalize some tables	Reduces JOIN time in queries and helps to ease the transition to partitioned and parallelized processing
Spread the loading across multiple servers and/or multiple instances	Really big loads have special needs.
Avoid RAID 5 controllers	RAID 5 arrays are slower due to writeback verification of data resulting in extra I/O. Some newer drives don't have this problem. They have increased memory caching to eliminate overhead. They are superior for integrity checking and cost. These are tradeoffs.
Use more powerful hardware	This works, but isn't always the most cost effective method.
Commit regularly	Avoids Rollback Segment blowout by taking commits every so many DMLs
Commit less frequently	Reduces elapsed time and CPU
Run multiple user load programs concurrently	Reduces elapsed time
Avoid using your own program, if possible	SQL*Loader is very efficient
Use batch inserts in your own programs	Faster than single inserts
Use OCI in C++ to insert rows	Fastest native C++ method
Use multiple clients for loading	Shorter time frame for loading
Use hot backups with ARCHIVELOG	Prior to loads, these can accomplish a useful backup before load starts and satisfy the old copy requirement. Be sure to turn it off before running a big load from SQL*Loader.
Run load program on server	Client loading adds network time
Use array inserts in PRO*C	Very fast

7.18   Mass Delete

Now that we've talked about table loading, let's address the flip-side of the same subject, table deletes. We worked so hard in the last section to find ways to insert rows efficiently during loading. And what do we have to show for our efforts? A new desire to remove the same rows. Mass delete is the rule, not the exception, in the database world. A simple example of the need for mass delete is general ledger information. It is data with a useful history. After it is no

```
exec sql begin declare section;
    int   zipcode[100];
    char  city[30][100];
exec sql end declare section;

for ( i = 0 ; i < n ; i++ )
    {
    zipcode[i] = zipin. ;
    strcpy( city[i], "cityin" ) ;
}
exec sql for :n insert into your_table values (:zipcode, :city);
exec sql commit work;
... repeat
```

Figure 7-33   PRO*C Array Inserts Example

longer useful, it instead becomes a liability to performance. Some shops keep accounting information online for 3 months, some for 6 months, some for a year. But, not too many shops want to see it online anymore after 18 months. So, the mass delete exists for this purpose.

Pruning tables can be efficient. This is more likely if delete and archival were addressed during the design stages of the application. Even then, delete performance is usually sacrificed in favor of insert and update for the same rows. This is because insert and update generally happen in online transactions, more than delete. Delete is not entirely reserved for batch processes. However, mass delete is almost always directed at batch processing.

Approaches to mass delete vary. You might write a program to pass through the tables and delete rows. If you do this, be sure to commit properly, maybe only once every 1000 rows. You want to avoid commit overhead and avoid filling the rollback segments completely.

Another way to deal with logging overhead is to convert a mass delete into a selective load. This is done by unloading tables with user programs and massaging the data, removing unwanted rows. The resultant file is input to a standard load. And, SQL*Loader or a third party product would be the program to use. One of the key advantages to this approach is that the indexes can be rebuilt in the process. This is generally required to optimize index performance after a giant purge of records anyway. The steps listed below provide another very similar process to accomplish the same thing. The key difference is the use of an online SELECT instead of an unload program.

MASS DELETE VIA TABLE REBUILD

1. Rename your_table to your_table_copy

2. Create your_table as select * from your_table_copy where your_table_fields = ones to keep

3. Create indexes

4. Drop table your_table_copy

5. Reestablish ownership, roles, constraints, and triggers

7.19   Sorts in Oracle

In Release 7.2.2 sorts began bypassing the buffer cache (parameter `sort_direct_write = true`). This positive change reduced the load on DBWR. Release 7.3 eliminated the need to perform sorts for hash joins by providing in-memory hash tables constructed at runtime.

A temporary tablespace designated exclusively for sorts also reduced serialization of space management operations. Enhancements aside, you will still need to improve sort performance, especially if you build DSS (Decision Support Systems).

The `sort_area_size` parameter in init.ora determines the space allocated for sorts. If this is not ample in size, Oracle will allocate disk segments from the temporary tablespace for sort shadow processes to perform bin operations. Therefore, increasing `sort_area_size` can reduce the total number of runs, eliminating I/O. At sort conclusion, Oracle shrinks the `sort_area_size` to that in parameter `sort_area_retained_size`. Memory over and above this size is freed for use elsewhere, unless Oracle determines that the same data will be accessed again within the transaction. Ideally, the `sort_area_retained_size` would be set a small amount larger than the average bytes used by all sorts. And `sort_area_size` would be equal to the size of the largest sort. Any overage will go into the temporary tablespace.

ORDER BY, GROUP BY and CREATE INDEX invoke sort processing. The largest sort typically equates to the sort requirements of the largest index created. For this reason, it is best to pre-sort files used in index creation, thus eliminating sort overhead at index creation time. If these files are sorted, then the NOSORT option of CREATE INDEX can be used.

Several init.ora parameters affect sort sizing. They are shown in Figure 7-34. These are not the only parameters affecting sort performance. Performance is a balancing act. Too many processes concurrently sorting can influence paging. Parallel processing is a key factor in sort performance, as is temporary tablespace size.

Matching `db_file_multiblock_read_count` to `sort_read_fac` increases merge width and diminishes the number of sort shadow processes.

Sort performance can be ascertained using the query in Figure 7-35. The percentage of sorts performed in memory (preferred) as opposed to those in temporary segments on disk is calculated.

SyncSort UNIX can help cut Oracle sort and aggregation time (externally) by 60-80 percent, depending on the data and type of operation. Syncsort Incorporated is a company with incredible sort products. You can find company contact information in Appendix D.

7.20   Extents and Free Space

The initial, next, minextents, maxextents, pctfree, pctincrease, freelist, inittrans, and maxtrans parameters are the key ingredients to tuning extents and free space. These are all parameters on the CREATE TABLE and CREATE INDEX commands. Examples are provided in Figure 7-36.

In our example, the db_block_size is 8K. All objects in a tablespace should be a multiple of the db_block_size and they should all be a factor of the overall tablespace size, to avoid fragmentation.

Example: Setting initial and next extents

```
create table dept (
deptno integer,
depname varchar2(14),
loc varchar2(13))
tablespace temp
storage (initial 100K next 100K maxextents 3);
```

The pctincrease parameter helps you to tweak the size of extents by allowing you to adjust the size upward for each extent allocated after the first. So,

```
sort_area_retained_size        = 1310720   (defaults to sort_area_size)
sort_area_size = 52428800 (divisible by memory page size)
sort_write_buffer_size = 32763      Settings
sort_write_buffers      = 2
sort_read_fac  = 5000000
db_file_multiblock_read_count = 5000000
```

Figure 7-34 Oracle Sort Parameters

```
select round((sum(decode(name,'sorts(memory)', value, 0))
/ (sum(decode(name,'sorts(memory)', value, 0))
+ sum(decode(name,'sorts(disk)', value, 0))))
* 100,2)
from v$sysstat
```

Figure 7-35 Oracle Sort Area Efficiency

```
create table dept (              create index dept_index
deptno integer,                  on dept (
depname varchar2(14),            seq,deptno)
loc varchar2(13))                storage (
tablespace temp                  initrans 1
storage (                        maxtrans 3);
initial 800K
next 160K
pctincrease 0
maxextents 5)
pctfree 10
pctused 70
freelist 20;
```

Figure 7-36 Extents and Free Space Parameters

specifying 10 percent would make the second extent 10 percent larger than the size of the first, the third extent 10 percent larger than the second, and so on. However, it can also negatively affect fragmentation, creating many different size extents across the tablespace.

The `initial` parameter defines the amount of space allocated at table creation time. You should endeavor to make this size as close to the real needs of the table. For every rule there is an exception. In the case of disk striping, it is advantageous to fit individual extents on files spread out across disk devices.

The `next` parameter is the size of an extent which will be allocated when free space is needed. This size is determined by the nature of your application. I use 20 percent of the initial size in my tables unless update and insert activity justify something else.

The `maxextents` parameter specifies how many extents can be allocated overall. In our example, we set this to 5, which means that our table could grow from its original 800K size an additional 800K (5 times 160K) before it would run out of space and need to be recreated.

The `minextents` parameter reflects the minimum number of extents to be allocated. This defaults to 1 for tables, 1 for indexes and 2 for rollback segments. Since it is intentional to keep the number of extents to a minimum, this value was excluded from our example.

The `freelist` parameter of 20 establishes a list of free blocks in memory for inserts by concurrently running processes. Read more about `freelist` contention in section 7.4.

As inserts add rows to blocks, they increase the `pctused` (percent used) value. In our example, Oracle will continue to add rows while the block is less than 90 percent full. At that time the `pctfree` (percent free) value will prevent additional inserts. When enough rows have been deleted from the block to return it to its 70 percent used state, Oracle will resume inserts. The nature of processing should determine the optimum values for these two parameters. Table 7-3 suggests values based on different processing regimes. Please note that `pctfree` plus `pctused` must be less than or equal to 100.

TABLE 7-3 Table and Index Creation Versus Processing

PARM/UPDATE	LIGHT	MEDIUM	HEAVY
db_block_size	8192	4096	2048
initial	100% rows loaded	120% rows loaded	140% rows loaded
next	5% rows loaded	10% rows loaded	20% rows loaded
maxextents	10	50	100
pctused	90%	80%	70%
pctfree	5%	10%	20%
initrans	1	2	3
maxtrans	2	4	9

All of the CREATE TABLE and INDEX parameters (except INITIAL) can be modified after creation using the ALTER command. However, new values will only be effective for extents obtained after alteration.

There are yet two more parameter to discuss. The `inittrans` parameter defines the initial number of transaction entries allowed within a database block. For tables this defaults to 1; for indexes and clusters it is 2. Each transaction will create an entry specifying the types of locks it is acquiring for a row in the database block. The `maxtrans` parameter specifies the maximum number of entries for this purpose. When exceeded, new transactions must wait. Since database and application design can have a lot of bearing on this number, it should be adjusted based on application usage. As a general rule, many concurrent transactions hitting the same blocks should not be high.

NOTE: We set our block size smaller for heavy update applications in Table 7-3. Fewer rows per block would justify a smaller `maxtrans` value.

7.21   Regular and Bit-Mapped Indexes

Indexes have many of the same performance issues that tables do. In fact, the methods employed for tuning indexes are similar to those for tables. For example, take a look at the information about the DFRAG utility in Section 7.12. This utility, like many others, provides a complete solution for tuning tables, tablespaces, and, yes, indexes.

The following tips will enhance index performance:

- Indexes should reside within one extent, unless this becomes impractical.

- Bit-mapped indexes improve ad-hoc queries on low-cardinality column data. Oracle utilizes a patented data-compression technology with bit-mapped indexes.

- Use a tool like DFRAG or Export/Import to compress table data back into a single extent. Indexes may be dropped and recreated with the appropriate size. DFRAG can defragment indexes independent of tables and while they are online.

- Release 7.1 and above have faster index building utilities.

- Oracle 7.4 added freelist groups on indexes and eliminated the need to pre-allocate extents to freelist groups.

- If you implement regular schedules for table and index reorganization and space management, you will achieve the delicate balance needed for a supreme operational environment.

- Use a separate tablespace for all indexes. Use separate disks to avoid head contention between accesses to table and index.

- Set the size of the TEMPORARY tablespace to a little bit more than the space needed to perform your largest sort. Most likely this is what you will use when creating your largest index.

- Optionally disable the generation and logging of redo information for CRE-ATE INDEX operations. If you are running in NOARCHIVELOG mode and use DIRECT = TRUE, you will bypass redo log generation.

- Use parallel index building.

- Sort input data files used to rebuild indexes so that the SORTED IN-DEXES clause may be specified. This will reduce elapsed time and save CPU.

- Set extent and free space parameters to optimize updates to the index. See Section 7.20 for more information on doing this. Also, Figure 7-37 shows a query which returns the largest number of extents used by a table or index.

- Reserve hash and indexed clusters for queries which must have the absolute fastest response time. There are down sides to clustering, like overflows to neighboring blocks. However, they are very effective in reducing the overhead associated with JOIN operations.

- Build indexes on all the columns needed to fully qualify searches.

- Do not build indexes using columns that are predominantly used in searches with a function (i.e. SUBSTR).

- Use ANALYZE TABLE or ANALYZE INDEX commands to generate statistics used in determining the effectiveness of an index (see Section 1.27 and Figure 7-39). Those indexes with a high ratio of `distinct_keys` to `num_rows` are good candidates for indexes.

- SQL statements WHERE and AND contain candidate columns for indexing.

- Run the utloidxs and utldidxs scripts to obtain a report on a columns capacity for inclusion in an index. The report will percentage or rows with keys matching, a good indicator for indexing.

```
select max(extent_id) + 1
from sys.dba_extents
where owner not in ('SYS','SYSTEM')
```

Figure 7-37 Extents Max Count

```
select index_name, leaf_blocks*2048 from sys.dba_indexes;
```

Figure 7-38 Used Index Size Report

```
select i.distinct_keys, t.num_rows
from user_indexes i, user_tables t
where i.table_name = t.table_name
order by t.table_name
```

Figure 7-39 Oracle Index Effectiveness

BIT-MAPPED INDEXES

I don't know who gets credit for building the first bit-mapped index. Model 204 had them a couple decades ago, Burrough's DMSII has had them just as long and I've heard tell that they really existed in the punched card era. Nevertheless, they have become very popular in this decade. So many PC databases employ them that they are quite common.

What is the fixation with bit-mapped indexes? Well, they can hold hundreds of thousands of bits of data in tens of bytes of real storage space. This is due to the compression. Remarkably, search routines can access the data without decompressing it. This provides for lightning fast searches.

Another major advantage is their ability to divide data logically into sections, overcoming the problems associated with cardinality of data. These sections are associated with repeating bit patterns, tied to—you guessed it—index keys. When bit-mapped files are updated, only the section impacted needs to be updated. This means that only one section needs to be locked by a transaction in order to resolve concurrency issues. Not all bit-mapping routines can claim they are using these kinds of features.

There are many BMI (Bit-Mapped Index) compression and search algorithms in the marketplace. Some are better than others. The tradeoffs alone would make for a book on the subject. Oracle has their own patented compression algorithm, as does Sybase, Redbrick and many other vendors.

If your tables have indexed columns with only a few possible values and the update activity is minimal, as with many DSS systems, then bit-mapped indexes may fit. You must be on release 7.3.2 to use them. Specify `compatible = 7.3.2` in init.ora. At creation time, substitute CREATE BITMAP INDEX for the conventional CREATE INDEX clause.

In summary, bit-mapped indexes do not fit all database requirements. They tend to work best in nominal update, high cardinality, heavy ad-hoc query applications. Sure sounds like DSS to me.

7.22 Locking

Oracle supports table and row level locking. Row level locking is with the transaction processing option in version 6 and the procedural option in version 7. Oracle 7's lock manager is defined as a set of stored procedures, the lock package provides locking primitives (get, release, convert) for a set of locks independent of data locks and transaction events. A variety of lock modes, lock conversion, deadlock detection and multinode operation on clustered platforms (parallel server) are available. There are `row share`, `row exclusive`, `share`, `share row exclusive`, `exclusive`, and `none/null` lock types.

To enable row level locking specify `serializable = false` and `row_locking = always` in the init.ora file.

Unlimited locking at the row level, for both data and indexes, has become a trademark of Oracle. Users and applications may execute SQL statements that update local or remote data without knowledge of the data location. Stored procedures and triggers can access local and remote data equally easily, for retrieval or update. These are powerhouse locking facilities.

Select transactions acquire share locks while update ones acquire exclusive locks. Reader and writer transactions don't block one another. And, readers take no locks, unless requested. If two transactions enter a deadlock, information about the SQL is written to a trace file. In the absence of tracing, users receive an error message. Readers and writers don't block one another, yet readers always automatically see a consistent view of data.

A variety of methods and products are available to help you identify locking performance problems. To begin with, two scripts are provided by Oracle to analyze lock performance. CATBLOCK.SQL creates the dba_locks view and UTLLOCKT.SQL identifies processes waiting to acquire locks and processes waiting on.

MANAGING LOCKING WITH INSPECT/SQL FROM PRECISE SOFTWARE

In Oracle there are constraints caused by the locking mechanism that prevent more than one task from updating the same piece of data. The result of these constraints is that while there are "productive" processes performing user requests, there are also "nonproductive victims," waiting for resources used by the "productive" processes.

Inspect/SQL from Precise software allows users to quickly identify processes that are in nonproductive situations, such as waits for lock or waits for CPU. These "victims" are usually waiting because other "offender" processes are consuming excessive resources. Inspect/SQL pinpoints the offenders and identifies the resources they are consuming. Tuning these offenders will result in better response times for everyone since the offenders will consume fewer resources and more resources will be freed up for the victims.

Inspect/SQL shows detailed information on the process waiting for the lock and on the object being locked. These displays help administrators quickly identify and resolve the problem.

MANAGING LOCKING WITH DB-VISION

DB-Vision helps in the tracking down and monitoring of record locks. The tool monitors the database and reports the amount of time that a lock has been held and the time that another process has been waiting on the lock. This helps to identify programs that are improperly locking records and are causing performance problems.

I think you get the point. This is not something you have to tackle alone. There are many products to complement your tuning efforts. However, some of us like to do it ourselves. Here are some queries and tuning tips for the do-it-yourself enthusiast.

ENQUEUE TIMEOUTS

If you are encountering enqueue timeouts (using select in Figure 7-40) you should increase the `enqueue_resources` parameter in init.ora. Set `enqueue_resources` (number of resources locked) equal to `er1`, where:

$$er = ((((processes\ -\ 10) \times 2 + 55) \times 1.1)$$

Figures 7-41 to 7-43 provide some queries for obtaining DDL, DML, and USER locks. DDL (Data Definition Language) consists of statements like CREATE TABLE, DROP TABLE, ALTER TABLE, CREATE INDEX, DROP INDEX, CREATE VIEW, and DROP VIEW. So, the lock information reported in the query from Figure 7.22 will identify locks on these kinds of statements against the catalog. Conceivably, these could happen in user programs issuing dynamic SQL requests.

DML (Data Manipulation Language) consists of statements like outer JOINS, positioned UPDATE, positioned DELETE, SELECT FOR UPDATE, and UNIONS, SELECT, INSERT, UPDATE, SEARCHED, and DELETE SEARCHED. The locks reported on in Figure 7-42 are for DML locks. Figure 7-43 is a general purpose catchall query for locks. The `dml_locks` parameter of init.ora is the target of tuning activities surrounding DML. Begin by setting it to 100 for small, 200 for medium, and 500 for large systems. Then adjust it to eliminate locking contention.

```
select name, value
from v$sysstat
where name = 'enqueue timeouts'
```

Figure 7-40   Oracle Enqueue Timeouts

```
select
substr(username,1,12) "User name",
substr(owner,1,8) "Owner",
substr(name,1,15) "Name",
substr(fid.type,1,20) "Lock Type",
substr(mode_held,1,11) "Lock Mode"
from sys.dba_ddl_locks fid, v$session tid
where ddl.session_id = tid.sid;
```

Figure 7-41   DDL Locks

```
select
substr(username,1,12) "User name",
substr(owner,1,8) "Owner",
substr(name,1,20) "Name",
substr(mode_held,1,11) "Lock Mode"
from sys.dba_dml_locks fid, v$session tid
where fid.session_id = tid.sid;
```

Figure 7-42   DML Locks

```
select
substr(username, 1, 12) "User Name",
substr(lock_type,1,18) "Lock Type",
substr(mode_held,1,28) "Lock Mode"
from sys.dba_lock fid, v$session tid
where lock_type not in (
'Media Recovery',
'Redo Thread',)
and fid.session_id = tid.sid;
```

Figure 7-43   Locks and Latches

SEQUENCE GENERATORS

Oracle uses sequence generators to provide unique numbers without the transaction locking or I/O inherent to table based schemes. This reduces contention and locking overhead. These facilities should be implemented in your applications to improve performance.

PARALLEL SERVER LOCKING

A series of enhancements in Oracle release 7.2 have improved performance in the area of locking. First, blocks of data exchanged between instances are now released earlier. Second, multiple block changes can be applied by either instance before switching control. Third, block allocation is faster. And finally, lock recovery after an instance crash divides the workload across multiple lock processes that operate in parallel.

In summarization, row level locking, sequence generators, and selected init.ora parameter tuning can eliminate data contention as a transaction processing bottleneck. Traditional tuning includes identifying where locks are held for long periods of time and in great numbers and issuing commits in applications, or restructuring application logic to hold locks for a shorter duration.

7.23   Resource Limits

Oracle allows you to limit the resources used by individuals and sessions. This can be advantageous in preventing runaway SQL which brings the system to its knees. A typical application of resource limits might be SQL*NET where users run random ad-hoc SELECT statements. Several limits are enforceable as seen in Figure 7-44.

By default, any new profile has unlimited resource usage. Specific overrides are required to limit resource consumption. Resource limits can be enabled and disabled globally using the `resource_limit = true` parameter.

7.24   Number of Processes

The number of processes defined to Oracle affords a simple means to put a governor on the system. When the CPU or memory are exhausted, you can limit the number of user processes allowed to connect to Oracle. This may be necessary to achieve acceptable response for those processes that do connect. To do this, adjust the `processes` (default 50) parameter in init.ora.

7.25 SQL and PL/SQL

One of the most obvious means for improving SQL performance is tuning the shared pool. This pool is used to save parsed copies of SQL statements so that the parsing phase is avoided and execution is speeded up. The shared pool contains the library cache, dictionary cache, and MTS session information components. The separate tuning of each component was covered earlier in this chapter. To summarize here, the primary causes of shared pool performance problems include fragmentation, contentions for the library cache latch, reloads and reparsing of objects. We will discuss each of these here.

Figure 7-45 lists some common statistics and their meaning. Statistics in the V$LIBRARYCACHE begin each time the data base is restarted. The next query (Figure 7-46) selects these basic statistics.

The dual queries from Figure 7-46 return the percentage that a SQL statement did not need to be reloaded because it was already in the library cache. The percentage should be equal to 100. Initially set the `shared_pool_size` to be 50-100 percent the size of the init.ora parameter `db_block_buffers` and then fine tune the parameter. Increasing the `shared_pool_size` in init.ora is the primary method for combating reloads.

Fragmentation is a normally occurring process. A consequence of fragmentation is flushing. Large objects which will not fit into available fragments cause Oracle to flush other objects from the pool, thus making room for them. A LRU

```
create profile              lowly_user
sessions_per_user           =  1
cpu_per_session             =  2400    (hundredths of seconds)
cpu_per_call                =  1200    (hundredths of seconds)
connect_time                =  30      (minutes)
idle_time                   =  10      (minutes)
logical_reads_per_session   =  24000
logical_reads_per_call      =  2400;

alter user fredl profile lowly_user;
```

Figure 7-44 Limit Oracle Resources with Profiles

PINS	(show the number of times objects were executed)
RELOADS	(show the number library cache misses on execution, where an object must be reparsed and allocated to a new SQL area)
RELOADS-to-PINS	(indicates the proportion of reparsing)

Figure 7-45 Understanding V$LIBRARYCACHE Statistics

(least recently used) algorithm provides the rationale for flushing objects. One way to deal with fragmentation is by pinning large objects, usually PL/SQL ones, in the shared pool. To accomplish this goal you need to identify large objects (query in Figure 7-47) and how often they are accessed (script in Figure 7-48). It doesn't make sense to pin objects which are seldom used.

After generating your list of candidates, you can have Oracle keep the objects in the shared pool by using dbms_shared_pool.keep() which is created by running dbmspool.sql. You need to place all large PL/SQL objects into packages and mark the packages as "kept". Packages relate procedures and functions together and allow their storage as a single unit in the database, with SQL text and compiled code located in the data dictionary, while executables reside in the shared pool.

Setting parameter cursor_space_for_time = true in init.ora will cause implicit pinning of SQL statements for all open cursors. The problem with this method is that Oracle has nowhere to go if the shared pool is exhausted. So, use this method cautiously.

Another mechanism is available which reserves large chunks of memory in the shared pool. The shared_pool_reserved_size parameter in init.ora will

```
select namespace, pins,      —or—    select(round(sum(pinhits)
round(decode(pinhits, 0, 1, pinhits)    /sum(pins)
/decode(pins, 0, 1, pins), 3)           * 100,2)
"PIN HIT RATIO",                        v$librarycache
reloads, invalidations
from v$librarycache
```

Figure 7-46   PIN HIT Ratio Queries

```
select v$db_object_cache where sharable_mem > threshold
```

Figure 7-47   Oracle Object Sizes

```
col owner format a12
col name format a25 trunc
col tablespace_name format a10 hea 'TBS' trunc
col type format a10 trunc
col load format 9999 hea 'Loads'
col exec format 99,999 hea 'Exec'
spool object_usage
select o.owner, o.name, o.type, nvl(loads,0) load, nvl(executions,0) exec
from v$db_object_cache o
where o.executions > 100
order by executions desc
/
spool off
```

Figure 7-48   Oracle Object Frequency of Access Script

reserve memory for this cause. But, what is to keep this extension from also fragmenting? The answer is the `shared_pool_reserved_min_alloc` parameter. Set the minimum allocation parameter to the size of your largest object initially. Then adjust it based on statistics available in the v$shared_pool_reserved table.

After an object is flushed, it must be reparsed if requested again. This is considered a miss, because the parsed representation was not found in the library cache. Oracle has to allocate a shared SQL area in this case. Reparsing along with initial parsing of objects is expensive business. There are some things you can do while writing SQL statements which will reduce misses.

- Use bind variables rather than explicitly specified constants and ensure the same names are used on equivalent statements
- Standardize text case and spacing conventions for SQL statements and PL/SQL blocks. Any difference between functionally equivalent statements results in reparsing.
- Use packages and stored procedures to promote reuse of the same SQL area
- Use fully qualified table names including the schema name
- Set `hold_cursors` = `true` in pre-compiled applications
- Set `session_cached_cursors` = `true` in init.ora to allow caching of closed cursors

Figure 7-49 exhibits a query to obtain the total number of recursive calls (Oracle issued SQL statements). It may show dynamic extensions of tables or rollback segments. Or, it may be caused by misses in the data dictionary cache, database triggers, stored procedures, functions, packages, anonymous PL/SQL blocks, DDL statements, and enforcement of referential integrity constraints.

NUMBER OF CURSORS

The private SQL areas are used for parsing. As applications reuse SQL areas there is a memory savings. But, these applications will have to make more parse calls to reuse the SQL areas. Your goal is now to control the frequency of parse calls by increasing the initialization parameter `open_cursors` in init.ora. This will increase the number of cursors permitted for a session. Along with this parameter go the `hold_cursor`, `release_cursor`, and `maxopencursors` specified at pre-compile time. The Trace utility will provide you with the number of open cursors, reparses, and reexecutes that the application encountered.

```
select value from v$sysstat where name = 'recursive calls'
```

Figure 7-49 Oracle Recursive Calls

As a last note on the subject of object tuning, don't forget the many third party vendor tools that do this job for you. I should say that they do varying amounts of the job for you. Some tools only identify the SQLs and PL/SQLs needing attention. Others help you package and standardize your statements.

In the area of SQL optimization there are quite a few tools to look at. There are Inspect/Analyze SQL by Precise Software, SQL Analyzer by Platinum, SQL*TRAX from Corner Stone Software, DBGENERAL SQLab by BRADMARK, ADHAWK SQL LAB by Eventus, ECOTools from Compuware, and Oracle's Enterprise Manager, to name a few. Chapter 1 takes a closer look at Precise/SQL.

7.26   Physical Disk I/O

To get a grip on disk contention, you first need to identify those files with long wait queues. The `sar -a`, `sar -b`, and `sar -d 25 1` UNIX operating system commands will identify disk service times, waits, queue lengths, and buffer utilization. Sample SAR command output is shown in Chapter 1 and here in Figure 7-50. Notice that the r+w/s for sd032 is relatively high, as is its average wait time. This makes it a candidate for tuning.

Next map the disk activity to database files using the v$filestat table (as shown in Figure 7-51), with emphasis on a per-tablespace and per-file basis.

Most database administrators know how important file distribution is to overall database performance. The greater the distribution across disks and the more even the distribution, the better. There is an added benefit quite often overlooked. Wide distribution of database files limits exposure for recovery in the event of a disk failure. The query in Figure 7-52 will show tablespace I/O distribution across files.

In addition, objects that are accessed concurrently, such as a table and its indexes, should be in separate data files on separate disks. Another technique to

```
sar -d 25 1

14:01:05 device    %busy  avque   r+w/s  blks/s  avwait   avserv
14:02:11 sd031      37.09  111.14  47.04  101.41  332.75   1.40
         sd032     100.00   44.08  232.32  222.57 1024.33  13.54
...
```

Figure 7-50   SAR -d Output

```
select
substr(df.name,1,30) 'File Name",
df.bytes,
fs.phyrds,
fs.phywrts
from v$datafile df, v$filestat fs
```

Figure 7-51   File I/O Distribution

deal with contention due to concurrent access is striping. Stripe large tables that are subject to a high degree of concurrent activity across disks using the `alter table allocate extent`, or using the parallel loader and the `file = clause`. Finally, try operating-system striping, with the choice of interleave determined by the nature of the application.

Another way to gather the same information we just did is with the UTLBSTAT and UTLESTAT scripts.

Having gathered the information in the queries, or using the scripts, now find out the manufacturer's recommended device loading for disk drives. Spread files across disks evenly, making sure to keep tables and indexes on different devices. Ensure that individual disks are not loaded beyond their recommended capacity (consider 50 I/Os per second per drive as a good goal) and be certain that online transaction related files/tablespaces are given precedence. The REDO logs must be placed on disks with very little usage.

Are there tools which will help database I/O perform better? Well, Data Optimizer from DATATOOLS allows the compression of tables. Their advertisements claim savings in the 75 percent range. My experience with compression routines is that it costs something to compress and decompress the data in CPU, but usually you can get so much more data in blocks returned to buffers, that sweeps of data use fewer I/Os. The I/O savings reduces CPU and the end result is a compromise. Generally speaking, compression is a good idea.

7.27   Asynchronous I/O

Available with the UnixWare 2.0 operating system, AIO (Asynchronous I/O) will push RAW devices to maximum performance. To take advantage of this, enable this mode with the init.ora and OS parameter changes shown in Figure 7-53.

```
select ts.name, df.name, fs.phyrds, fs.phywrts, fs.readtim, fs.writetim,
fs.phyblkrd, fs.phyblkwrt
from v$filestat fs, ts$ ts, v$datafile df, file$ fi
where df.file# = fi.file#
and ts.ts# = fi.ts#
and fs.file# = fi.file#;
```

Figure 7-52   Tablespace I/O Distribution

`use_async_io = true`	(init.ora for DBWR)
`lgwr_use_async_io = true`	(init.ora for LGWR)
`numaio`	(OS AIO control blocks)
`aio_listio_max`	(OS AIO request list)
`ls -alst /dev/async`	(OS aysnc file updateable)

Figure 7-53   Oracle Asynchronous I/O and Post-Wait

Post-Wait is available on the UnixWare 2.0 operating system and eliminates much of the use of semaphores. This can be done in the init.ora parameters using these parameters:

```
use_post_wait_driver = true
post_wait_device = /dev/pw
```

7.28 Multi-Threaded Server (MTS)

Without any changes to your application programs, you can benefit from one of many Oracle 7 features. The (MTS) Multi-threaded Server architecture in Oracle helps capitalize on the scaling qualities of SMP (Symmetric Multiprocessing). Dispatching processes route requests to response queues (one per dispatcher) where one of multiple servers picks them up and processes them. The results go back into the queues where the dispatcher returns it to client. The server automatically loads balance connections among dispatchers and dynamically adjusts the number of server processes to the workload. The end result is the ability to support many concurrent clients. However, this puppy requires some real tuning to make it pump them through.

This select (Figure 7-54) shows which user is connected to which dispatcher/server and the current status of the user process. The SERVER output column will indicate "SHARED" if the user is connected via MTS. Here are some sample initialization parameters, if you are setting up MTS for the first time.

Sample Initial MTS Parameters	
init.ora parameters	
mts_dispatchers = "tcp, 5"	(initial number and type of dispatchers)
mts_max_dispatchers = 5	(maximum number of dispatchers)
mts_listener_address = "(address=(protocol=tcp)(host=)(port=1521))"	
mts_max_servers = 20	(the maximum servers that can be started)
mts_servers = 20	(initial number of servers started)
mts_service = "prod1"	(service id matches oracle_SID)
sqlnet.ora parameters	
use_dedicated_server = off	(force client to use MTS)

The mts_listener_address is the address of a TNS (Transparent Network Substrate) listener process to use with an MTS configuration. You can configure an Oracle server with several mts_listener_address parameters, one for each address to listen to. These addresses match those found in the address_list of the listener.ora file. After bumping the system with the new parameters in place, use the Shared Server/Dispatch monitors of Server Manager to verify the existence of new dispatchers and servers.

In Figure 7-55, the average number of waits per queue request is returned by the first query. If this number is greater than 1, it implies a server wait. Increasing the `mts_max_servers` parameter in init.ora is one option. If you suspect that the number of dispatchers is too low, you can issue an ALTER SYSTEM command to increase them (query in Figure 7-56 can be used to determine dispatcher usage).

There are alternatives to MTS. I read an article called "The Oracle Churchill Benchmark" about Vortex-Software from Trifox. In the article, it claimed that Vortex-Software outperformed MTS by 30 to 50 percent and used 50 percent less memory. Please don't quote me on this. Contact the vendors about the article and any updates to the figures. Furthermore, Vortex-Software had two operational modes. ST means that the vtxhost-program has been linked in single-task and TT means it has been linked in two-task mode. Apparently, MTS uses a single-task architecture. Things were benchmarked both ways. TT mode definitely showed more improvement than ST mode. But, both were outstanding.

```
select
sess.username,
sess.status,
circ.queue "Query Location",
disp.name "Dispatcher Name",
disp.status "Dispatcher Status",
        serv.name "Server Name",
serv.status "Server Status"
from v$circuit circ, v$session sess,
 v$dispatcher disp, v$shared_server serv
where sess.saddr = circ.saddr
and circ.dispatcher = disp.paddr
and circ.server = serv.paddr;
```

Figure 7-54 Multi-threaded Server Processes Display

```
select decode(totalq,0, 'Total Queue Requests',
wait/totalq
from v$queue
where type = 'COMMON';
```

and

```
select count(*) servers
from v$shared_server
```

Figure 7-55 MTS Server Usage

```
select name, network, busy, idle
from v$dispatcher
```

Figure 7-56 MTS Dispatcher Usage

7.29   Tuning Oracle 7.3 with NetWare 3.11

Pretty much everything we've discussed about tuning Oracle also applies in the NetWare world. It seems that each operating system has its own peculiarities. NetWare also fits this scenario. NetWare has its own tuning parameters to allocate hefty chunks of RAM for caching. Oracle also depends heavily on its ability to cache data. The trick is where to draw the line.

You don't want to over allocate the SGA, or paging performance becomes a problem. You don't want to under allocate the SGA, or caching performance in Oracle becomes a problem. In NetWare, the `cache_buffer` parameter is the one which generally contends with SGA usage. As the SGA value approaches the value of `cach_buffer`, less memory is available by the operating system.

NetWare also has its own full volume mirroring scheme. You don't want to use it and Oracle's mirroring together, or you are doing a lot of redundant processing. Since Oracle's mirroring is geared around transaction based recovery, it is probably the way to go for all database tablespaces. Let NetWare handle the rest of the devices.

7.30   64-bit Processing

Many of us are satisfied with 32-bit technology. It seemed like such a large leap to go 32-bit when it first hit the streets. And golly, 32-bit isn't all that bad. You can have an SGA memory pool of 4 G; 30 G of UNIX buffer cache. And your database can be as large as 400 G using 32-bit technology. Besides, it is hard to pick the best processing environment when you have so many choices. You can have 16-bit, 32-bit, SMP, MPP, and now 64-bit machines. I haven't seen a reliable set of benchmarks matching all these possibilities. Perhaps someone will read this paragraph and create a useful benchmark.

Is it worth it to you to go 64-bit? The computer industry doesn't sit still for a moment. Bigger and faster is better. The jump to 64-bit, or 2*2*2*2*2*2, means faster hardware processing speeds (should help those notorious 5-way joins), larger memory pools, terabyte tables, new tools, and larger block sizes. Yes, you read correctly. With 64-bit you can go from the current 8K maximum to block-sizes of 16K and 32K. These larger blocks (`db_block_size`) might reduce I/O significantly on DSS applications. "What's it going to cost me?" you may be saying to yourself.

You always pay a price for this jump. First there is the necessary burden of new hardware. Those Digital Alpha processors running at 300 megahertz sure look sweet. The next likely expense will be memory. Keep in mind that a more powerful processor can run more processes, which in turn will need more memory for caching. More users and processes mean more temporary tablespace DASD, user tables, etc. And during a transition to new technology you will probably keep the older technology around for a short time, as a safety net. Finally, 64-bit means better tools that take advantage of faster processing; database management tools, application development tools, and the like. All these things cost moolah—cash. When should you invest?

Before the next millennium we will be dealing with speeds in the Ghz (Giga-hertz) range. It's all happening so quickly. What did take 10 years, now takes 2 and soon only 1. The market is having trouble buying the technology because it declines in value so rapidly. Your investment today is worth 50 percent in a year and nothing in 5 years. But if you don't buy now, your business becomes obso-lete in the same time frame. Can you afford to fall very far behind your com-petitors? Timing is everything nowadays. If you buy into new technology on day one, it could cost a lot more than waiting a year. And if you wait too long, you have more work to do, in order to come forward to the current industry stan-dard. Sounds like the only winners are the guys selling the new technology. Maybe, but you're damned if you don't buy in and in debt if you do.

Assuming that we all must go 64-bit within a year of two, what will the tran-sition be like? Well, disk device speeds are lagging behind processing capabili-ties. Consequently, they will continue to be a bottleneck. Memory caching of disk I/O will be the workaround. That means you will need lots of memory. Fortu-nately, some gurus will have found ways to further improve caching, even to the point where the system will read your disk before you ask for the information.

Today, Digital's 64-bit Alpha supports configurations of 14 G (gigabytes) of RAM; soon this will be 50 G. Oracle Corporation announced their VLM (Very Large Memory) technology to facilitate new sizes for database entities. SGAs larger than 2 G, known as LSGA (Large System Global Areas) mean more caching. BOBS (Big Oracle Blocks) will take advantage of block sizes as large as 32K. It stands to reason that blocks this size will compress better, too. We should start seeing some blocks containing tens of thousands of rows, quite a lot for a single I/O, or memory buffer. Early benchmarks tell of query improve-ments in excess of 10,000 percent.

It stands to reason that these larger sizes mean that many of our traditional formulas for tuning will change soon.

On a side note, Oracle is getting an early start on supporting Intel's 64-bit microprocessor, by agreeing to optimize future versions of Oracle 8 for it. Intel and Oracle will also be cooperating on advanced clustering scalability.

Attention all 32-bit bigots, it's time to step aside. You can't stop technology. If you try to stand in front of it, you just get run over.

7.31   SMP Versus MPP

All *Online Transaction Processing* (OLTP) users have one thing in common: heavy data sharing. For example, all users of transactions for an order entry application may hit on the same parts, inventory and pricing tables and related indexes. Sharing of data within an SMP (Symmetric Multi-Processing) system is quick and efficient and requires no data transfer. To this end, you can use Or-acle Parallel Server to cluster multiple SMP systems with dozens of processors. *Massively Parallel Processing* (MPP) systems can also benefit OLTP applica-tions that have highly partitioned data. However, since the resources (like disk and cache memory) are not tightly coupled, MPP is better suited for DSS (Decision Support Systems) and data warehousing where partitioning. Processing in these climates requires much higher bandwidth(s) for movement of megabytes of data. This is needed to satisfy enormous queries and fast loading of partitioned data. MPP offers greater scalability, on the order of hundreds of processors. Remember though, that these processors intercommunicate with each other. There is an operational limit where communications saturate the system.

HARDWARE

Buying into the SMP and MPP world is not as expensive as one might think. If you try it on an IBM mainframe you might run out of money quickly. But, the same architecture is available with a Compaq Proliant using Pentium processors, or a Micron SMP 2x90 Mhz machine. So, think seriously about this avenue for performance.

OPERATING SYSTEMS

This list is by no means complete. SCO UNIX, Novell UnixWare, Microsoft Windows NT, and IBM's OS/2 support SMP architectures. I personally prefer Window's NT, just because it is so easy to use.

Remember that the parallel query option takes full advantage of multiprocessors.

7.32 Parallel Query Processing

What is a parallel query? A parallel query involves two or more processors completing a single SQL request. For example, one processor may be assigned to read one table and another processor will read a second table. Each of the first two processors may be shipping results to another processor that sorts the results. CPU usage is expended to reduce the elapsed time of the query.

The parallel query option can increase performance dramatically in DSS applications with large tables. If your queries are performing table scans, JOINS, UNIONS, DISTINCT, INTERSECTS, GROUP BY, and ORDER BY operations, then execution time is reduced. Tuning this option involves monitoring, changing init.ora settings, and reviewing SQL hints.

Parallel direct database reads benefit the types of queries we just mentioned, while parallel direct writes improve SORT-MERGE, JOINS, ANALYZE, GROUP BY, ORDER BY, CREATE TABLE AS SELECT, and CREATE INDEX. Direct read and write avoid concurrency overhead and bypass the normal buffer caching. This streamlines I/O activity in parallel processing. Additional information is available in the section on sorting. Where supported, asynchronous I/O can be used. Additional information is available on asynchronous I/O later in this chapter.

Another feature of immense value is the user-defined functions embedded in SQL. Because the user function is executed in conjunction with the SQL, it will automatically be parallelized.

There are a few basic approaches to using parallel query. First, you can specify the amount of parallelism at the table level, using an ALTER command like shown here.

```
alter table your_table parallel (degree x instances y);
```

The next method is to specify this information from within your program using a hint. Here is an example, where 20 instances are specified for parallelism.

```
select /*+ FULL(your_table) parallel(your_table, 20)*/
count(*) from your_table;
```

The two init.ora parameters `parallel_default_max_scans` and `parallel_default_scansize` are for the servers to use when you don't specify the degree in a hint clause in your program. So by failing to specify these, it should allow the init.ora settings as overrides.

Alternatively, you can specify the amount of parallelism using the init.ora parameters shown below. The `parallel_server_idle_time` is useful in specifying an amount of time before an idle server will shut itself down. While idle, they attach themselves to process 1.

```
parallel_min_servers = 20                (minimum servers running)
parallel_max_servers = 20                (maximum servers running)
parallel_default_max_scans = 20          (scan before parallel)
parallel_default_scansize = 500          (scan before parallel)
parallel_default_max_instances = 5       (max instances each)
parallel_server_idle_time                (time before closing)
gc_db_locks                              (shared distributed locks)
gc_files_to_locks                        (files to locks)
gc_rollback_segments                     (rollback segments shared
                                          between multiple instances)
```

You can temporarily turn off parallel query using the following command, which lowers the instances to 1.

```
alter table your_table parallel (degree 1 instances 1);
alter index your_index parallel (degree 1 instances 1);
```

Specifying `noparallel` will turn it off entirely.

```
alter table your_table noparallel;
```

Finally, you might want to set up a method to dynamically set the parallel option. This could be done in this fashion: with a PRO*C program., issue a sysconf() system call using the sc_nprocessors_conf argument. It will return the number of processors available on the system. Next, query the dba_segments table to get the size of the table (unless the program already knows this). If it is large, then the program could alter the table setting the degree and number of processors to use for parallelism. At the conclusion of processing, it could use the alter to shut off parallelism. Add to this mechanism a table entry somewhere which says how many processors are being used by programs and how many are available, and you have a fully automated system for utilizing as many processors as possible.

PARALLEL SERVER

Oracle Parallel Server maximizes processing on SMP and MPP computers. It balances the query execution across processing nodes and disk devices, eliminating the need to manually perform this as a tuning task. In case a node fails, it will recover transactions through surviving nodes. Multiple instances (usually running on different nodes of a cluster) can access the same database. Queries split across multiple instances are utilizing multiple CPU(s).

SERVER MANAGER

This tool provides monitoring for system performance and administration of Oracle, including parallel queries and symmetric replication. It is possible to monitor several distributed servers for performance, backups, and space management from one location. Manager is a GUI tool which will work with Windows or Motif. Many mundane tasks like adding users, files, and testing SQL and PL/SQL commands are automated for the database administrator.

From the UNIX command line you can display the number of parallel processes being used with the command:

```
ps -ef |grep ora
```

This will list all of the Oracle processes. If a process name repeats 5 times, then there are five parallel processes for that name.

7.33   Stored Procedures

I just love stored procedures. If anything was ever designed to take advantage of client/server computing, they were. They can reduce redundant code while enforcing database access standards for security, conformity, and performance. Stored procedures are distributed at remote servers, increasing efficiency in several important ways. They allow query results to be queued up for transmission, reducing network traffic. They allow optimum use of buffer caches by accruing information while blocks are still in the buffers.

You can combine your stored procedure (example in Figure 7-57) with your program code in the form of a package which is loaded as a single executable.

Make sure there is room in the SGA to load the package; you can do this right after startup, or you can clear the SGA by logging into SQLPLUS as SYS and typing:

```
alter system flush shared_pool;
```

```
procedure compute_comission (emp_name in varchar2, emp_comm_pct in number)
is
begin
      update emp
      set emp_comm = emp_sales * emp_comm_pct
end;
```

Figure 7-57 Stored Procedure Sample

Don't do this on a mission critical system, as the performance will drop off for a while. Now have Oracle keep it in the shared pool with the following command:

```
execute dbms_shared_pool.keep('compute_commission');
```

 NOTE: Are you having a security problem with your procedure? When you execute a stored or packaged procedure, Oracle simply switches to the procedure owner's security domain. Don't confuse this with login security. Switching to the procedure owner's security domain does not enable the procedure owner's default roles. Therefore, the procedure has security to only see and do what is directly granted to its owner.

There are some tools out there to help you with the all important job of building stored procedures. SQL Navigator from Techno Solutions lets you code, execute, test, and tune stored procedures within an integrated development editor. ADHAWK SQL STUDIO from Eventus lets you edit and compile stored procedures and triggers.

7.34 Disaster Recovery

Since disk I/O is the bottleneck during recovery, multiple process threads can be an advantage. With Oracle Version 7.1 comes parallel recovery which allows multiple processes to perform recovery, thus decreasing the time it takes to recover the database. On multiprocessor machines this is significant.

Also available with Version 7.1 is symmetric replication. Multiple copies of tables located remotely facilitate major recoveries.

With Oracle 7.3, instance startup is faster thanks to deferred recovery. Standby databases are a reality, too. But Oracle has had a large complement of disaster recovery capabilities building over the last few releases. With the advent of replication agents it has been possible to accomplish recovery with remote servers and databases. Most people don't realize that there can be a productivity boost by insuring 7x24 (7-day by 24-hour) availability of systems.

SmartSync recovery accelerator by Veritas Software can speed the recovery of mirrored databases after a system failure.

7.35 Wait Time

In the battle to run faster, you can get a quick idea of where your problems lie using the output from UTLBSTAT. This query (see Figure 7-58) shows the average wait time for events in the system. If you capture this information once each hour, on the hour, for the entire prime shift, you can get an idea of how much more wait time is being incurred at traditionally slower periods (say 10 AM and 2 PM). For example, the free buffer waits shown in our report are 33.38. If this number is much higher at the busiest times of the processing day, then it implies that there are insufficient free buffers at those times.

```
SQLDBA>
SQLDBA> set charwidth 27;
SQLDBA> set numwidth 12;
SQLDBA> Rem System wide wait events.
SQLDBA> select  n1.event "Event Name",
     2>          n1.event_count "Count",
     3>          n1.time_waited "Total Wait",
     4>          (n1.time_waited/n1.event_count) "Average Wait"
     5>     from stats$event n1
     6>     where n1.event_count > 0
     7>     order by n1.time_waited desc;
Event Name                     Count     Total Wait  Average Wait
------------------------       --------  ---------   ------------
client message                 13252195  173751332   13.11113608
virtual circuit status         13126224  163580005   12.462076299
dispatcher timer               25291006   69078918   2.7313629992
rdbms ipc message                271510   40923397   150.72519244
db file sequential read        10215066   24541196   2.4024510463
smon timer                          324    8987110   27737.993827
pmon timer                        30235    8883525   293.81594179
free buffer waits                 83775    2796622   33.382536556
db file parallel write           118060    2694164   22.820294765
buffer busy waits                808316    1978187   2.4472941275
db file scattered read           392636    1403270   3.5739718212
latch free                       847657     904391   1.066930374
log file parallel write           39556     459209   11.609085853
enqueue                             924     271911   294.27597403
log file sync                      9406     100569   10.692005103
library cache pin                   223      66469   298.06726457
write complete waits                942      45084   47.859872611
rdbms ipc reply                     307      28657   93.345276873
log file space/switch               264      19688   74.575757576
control file parallel write        1876      12983   6.920575693
control file sequential read       2770      10624   3.8353790614
db file single write               1090       5946   5.4550458716
log file single write                56        329   5.875
log file sequential read             28        135   4.8214285714
buffer deadlock                       2          2   1
25 rows selected.
```

Figure 7-58 System Wide Wait Time

TABLE 7-4   INIT.ORA Tuning Parameters

PARAMETER	DESCRIPTION
cache_size_threshold	unknown
checkpoint_process=true	Enables a process other than LGWR to handle checkpointing
chpt	Name of other process for checkpointing
cleanup_rollback_entries	Number of row entries PMON will clean up in case of an aborted transaction
cpu_count	Maintained by Oracle. Shows count
cursor_space_for_time=true	Causes implicit pinning of SQL statements for all open cursors
db_block_buffers	Number of database block buffers
db_block_max_scan_cnt	Number will affect writes back to disk
db_block_size	Size of database blocks
db_block_write_batch	Number of dirty buffers
db_file_multiblock_read_count	Number of blocks read into the buffers in a single I/O (operating system dependent)
db_file_simultaneous_writes	Number of simultaneous writes for each database file written by DBWR
db_files	Number of database files
db_writers	Number of database writer processes to be forked
dml_locks	Number of Data Manipulation Language locks
enqueue_resources	Affects enqueue timeouts and number of resources locked
gc_db_locks	Distributed lock manager locks
gc_files_to_locks	Number of locks per file
gc_rollback_segments	Rollback segments shared across multiple database instances
lgwr_use_async_io=true	Use asynchronous I/O (RAW) for LGWR
log_archive_buffer_size	Size of archive buffer; affects speed of archive which can saturate CPU
log_archive_buffers	Number of archive buffers; affects speed of archive which can saturate CPU
log_buffer	Bytes for log buffer. Used to tune waits on REDO log buffer, reducing contention
log_checkpoint_interval	Checkpoint frequency
log_checkpoint_timeout	Time used for time based checkpointing
log_entry_prebuild	Permits user processes to prebuild entries before attempting to copy to the log buffer
log_entry_prebuild_threshold	Can reduce latch contention
log_simultaneous_copies	Can increase the redo copy latches in multiprocessing systems
log_small_entry_max_size	Forces more copies to use copy latches
max_dump_file_size	Limits the size of dump and TRACE files

TABLE 7-4   INIT.ORA Tuning Parameters (Continued)

PARAMETER	DESCRIPTION
max_rollback_segments	Maximum rollback segments that can be kept online
mts_dispatchers	Initial number of dispatchers
mts_listener_address	TNS processor address
mts_max_dispatchers	Maximum number of concurrent dispatchers
mts_max_servers	Maximum number of concurrent servers
mts_servers	Initial number of servers
mts_service	Matches the SID and DBNAME
open_cursors	Control frequency of parse calls
optimizer_mode	Use to set default mode for query optimization
parallel_default_max_instances	Maximum instances for each request
parallel_default_max_scans	Used in determining degree of parallelism when you don't provide a hint
parallel_default_max_scansize	Used in determining degree of parallelism when you don't provide a hint
parallel_max_servers	Maximum concurrent parallel servers
parallel_min_servers	Minimum concurrent parallel servers
parallel_server_idle_time	An amount of time before an ideal server will shut down
post_wait_device=/dev/pw	Directory for post wait device. Helps eliminate semaphores
pre_page_sga=true	Will cause everything to get paged into real memory during startup
processes	Number of concurrent processes. Used to set a governor on the system
recovery_parallelism	Use parallel processing during recovery
resource_limit=true	Enables resource limits for users and profiles
rollback_segments	Tune to reduce rollback segment contention
row_locking=always	Enable row-level locking
serializable=false	Enable row-level locking
session_cached_cursors	Number of cached closed cursors in a session
session_cached_cursors=true	Allows Oracle to cache closed cursors in a session
sessions	Number of concurrent sessions
shared_pool_reserved_min_alloc	Controls fragmentation in the shared pool reserve
shared_pool_reserved_size	Reserve memory for large objects
shared_pool_size	Assigns the size of the shared buffer pool
small_table_threshold	Determines the number of buffers that are available for full table scans
sort_area-retained_size	Amount of space retained after sort is done (Continued)

TABLE 7-4   INIT.ORA Tuning Parameters (Continued)

PARAMETER	DESCRIPTION
sort_area_size	Space allocated for sorts
sort_direct_write=true	Use to reduce load on DBWR. Will bypass buffer caching on sorts and table scans
sort_read_fac	Affects the merge width and can diminish the number of sort shadow processes
sort_write_buffer_size	Size of sort buffer
sort_write_buffers	Number of sort buffers
spin_count	How many times the system will spin while attaining a latch before waiting
sql_trace = true	Enable SQL trace
temporary_table_locks	Number of temporary table locks
timed_statistics=true	Enables statistics collection
transactions	Number of transactions (1.1 * processes)
transactions_per_rollback_ segment	Number of transactions per rollback segment
use_async_io=true	Enable asynchronous I/O (RAW)—operating system dependent
use_dedicated_server=off	Force client to use MTS
use_post_wait_driver=true	Helps eliminate use of semaphores
use_readv = true	Turn on multiblock reads
user_dump_destination	Directory where you can look to find trace file name

7.36   Setting INIT.ORA Parameters

It's time to recap. Here we will reiterate the names of init.ora tuning parameter and their general use. The intention here is not to repeat the ways to go about tuning these parameters. You can see minutiae about them, locating them with the index at the tail end of the book. Refer to Table 7-4 as a checklist of parameters you should have tuned. If it isn't in this list, it probably is not a high priority for tuning.

7.37   New Rules Based Expert

Many aspects of the RDBMS world exist only to boost performance; indexes, cache, buffer pools, striping, partitioning, device configuration, capacity planning, parallel processing, table extents, table freespace, and optimizers, not to mention all the server load management parameters. It is safe to say that tuning is an activity which has not been fully automated until all these categories have likewise been automated. Oracle Expert is one of six tools included in the Performance Pack, available with Oracle Enterprise Manager (Release 7.3). I rate it as a first cut at automation. But its target isn't every category mentioned. And it is best suited for novice database administrators, or experienced administrators that are burdened with managing too many instances.

PERFORMANCE PACK

- Oracle Expert
- Oracle Locks Manager
- Oracle Performance Manager
- Oracle Tablespace Manager
- Oracle Trace

The Oracle Expert GUI application is built using standard windowing techniques and well suited folders. The flow of control within the application matches the tuning methodology employed. More specifically, the steps are COLLECT, VIEW/EDIT, ANALYZE, REVIEW RECOMMENDATIONS, and IMPLEMENT, in that order. Each step of the tuning methodology is handled with an individual windows folder. You are usually only required to click on check-boxes or pull down menu items. It's very simple to use.

Oracle Expert is a rules based expert system. The rules can be viewed or edited, as can their attributes. For example, one of these rules is the statistical sampling. You choose the sampling rate, as well as start and stop times. All of the samples collected are input to the tuning recommendations phase. So, if you know that the peak periods of OLTP processing are 10:30 AM and 2:30 PM, for example, you could limit your sampling to those periods and the recommendations generated would handle your heaviest processing load. Another sampling for night time batch processing would in turn yield tuning recommendations specifically for batch.

After collecting statistics and analyzing them, you arrive at the much awaited recommendations. In this folder, you are supplied a list of recommendations. Each recommendation can be viewed in detail by clicking on it. You can accept or reject a recommendation by double-clicking it. Be careful what you do, though. Let's say that you reject a change to db_block_buffers. This can have a ripple affect on the shared_pool_size or some other parameter.

If you decide to implement the recommendations, you will click on "generate" in the recommendations folder. A file is created which contains revised

```
#             Recommended Instance Parameters
#
#      Tune Session:   OR1
#      Database name: ORACLE
#      Instance name: oracle
#----------------------------------------
compatible = 7.3.2.2.0                    #previous value: 7.3.0.0.0
sort_area_retained_size = 131072          #previous value: 65536
sort_area_size = 131072                   #previous value: 65536
```

Figure 7-59 Oracle Expert Recommendations

parameters for your `init.ora` control file. Some of the values (see Figure 7-59) will be new and some will replace existing values. I recommend that you add a time/date stamp to all old values in case you decide to fall back to some back level of tuning. Tuning is of course an iterative process. You will probably repeat the process a few times to get it right. And what is good for today may be bad for tomorrow.

At first inspection, Oracle Expert looks comprehensive. With closer surveillance, you discover that there are business tuning answers which Oracle Expert won't provide for you. Some of the things I envision for fully automated tuning might include:

FOR A BRIGHT FUTURE, "THESE ARE A FEW OF MY FAVORITE THINGS!"

1. An answer to the question "Do I need additional engines or should I divide up applications on different computers?"

2. An answer to the question "What is the most effective implementation of partitioning and striping?"

3. Easy exportation of archived statistics to spreadsheets for use in tracking, graphing, reporting, and capacity planning.

4. Dynamic memory and buffer expansion and reduction, and dynamic increases and decreases in servers (even engines), while an instance is running, depending on the system load and introduction of new applications.

5. Automatic unattended modification of the operating system settings to correspond to changes in the database.

Don't blame me if I expect a lot. Users always want more. I'm just another user. For now, Oracle Expert will have to do. In time, this tool may grow to encompass my imaginations and yours too. For now, it is a welcome addition to the supreme tools provided by Oracle. Besides, who else provides this much automation now!

7.38   Oracle 8's Arrival

The arrival of Oracle 8 is slated for summer '97. This is going to be another big performance release. Here is a list of some things to expect:

■ *Advance Queuing Facility:* Database resident queues allow applications to shift logic to a background process, thus improving transaction response times. A foreground task can continue to work while the background process performs a task.

■ *Improved Checkpointing:* New algorithms make use of larger buffer caches.

■ *Better Memory Sharing:* Data structures are shared to improve per-user memory utilization.

- *Parallel DML Option:* New releases of Oracle always seem to have some parallel enhancement. In Release 8, insert, update, and delete operations for bulk data processing, along with more parallel processing of bit-mapped indexes, is new.

- *Integrated Lock Manager:* The Distributed Lock Manager is faster and tuneable. New views allow DBAs to see parallel server statistics.

- *Parallel Server:* Automatic load balancing via a fail-over feature which routes users to an available server, if one fails. Oracle 8 can be deployed on Windows NT clustered servers.

- *Partitioning:* This is a big enhancement in Release 8. Both tables and indexes are partitionable, with parallel processing of partitions an obvious addition. And, applications can actual, reference partitions to speed execution.

- *Very Large Data Bases:* VLDBs can now be hundreds of terabytes in size.

- *Pooling and Connection Multiplexing:* Support for tens of thousands of concurrent online users. Multiplexing allows users to share connections and pooling drops idle connections.

- *Parallel Replication:* Multiple replication tasks handle subsets of data which results in faster replication.

- *Object / Relational:* Oracle 8 is positioned for network computing which reduces the cost of hardware and software for many end-users. The Network Computing Architecture (NCA) is another wave of technology including major vendors like Sun Microsystems, with their Java and hardware solutions. Object technology in Oracle 8 positions the database for network computing.

PARTITIONED TABLES AND INDEXES

Perhaps the most compelling reason to come forward on Release 8 is the partitioning. Large databases for warehousing and enterprise schemes are the candidates for better manageability and performance. With partitioned tables, individual rows in different partitions have the same attributes. But, the rows are automatically routed to their owning partition by a range key. This key is provided when the table is first defined. See Figure 7-60 for the syntax to create a partitioned table.

In Figure 7-60, the partition key determines which partition a row will reside in. A partition key can consist of up to 16 columns. In our example, the key is siteid. Siteid is assigned to a customer when they are added to the database. It is determined by their respective country which places them in the correct region of the world. This makes it possible to separate the regions into different tablespaces. By doing so, maintenance to different regions can occur during off-peak hours without affecting other regions.

```
create table sites
(
siteid number(5) primary key,
company varchar(60) not null,
address1 varchar(60) not null,
address2 varchar(60) not null,
address3 varchar(60) not null,
city varchar(40) not null,
state varchar(40) not null,
country varchar(40) not null,
postcode varchar(9) not null
)
partition by range (siteid)
(
partition p0 values less than (09999)
tablespace usa,
partition p1 values less than (19999)
tablespace canada,
partition p2 values less than (29999)
tablespace britain,
partition p3 values less than (39999)
tablespace ireland,
partition p4 values less than (49999)
tablespace scotland,
partition p5 values less than (59999)
tablespace spacific,
partition p6 values less than (69999)
tablespace africa,
partition p7 values less than (79999)
tablespace asia,
partition p8 values less than (89999)
tablespace europe,
partition p9 values less than (99999)
tablespace samerica,
)
```

Figure 7-60   Oracle Partitioned Table Creation

To create a partitioned index which can also take advantage of this table design, we issue index creation syntax like that shown in Figure 7-61.

The following select clause will take advantage of the partitioned index. It will use the company name prefix to reduce the search via the index. Oracle 8 may not be able to readily identify the partition which the company row resides in. But, an alternative approach is available:

```
select * from sites
where company = "Dunham Software"
```

If you already know which partition a row resides in, you can direct your query with a new declarative. In the following select, the partition is supplied. Via an extension to ANSI SQL, Oracle 8 makes it possible to direct queries to the partition. In our table example, if a user or programmer knows the country for a query, they can supply the partition as part of the query.

```
create index sites_company
on sites (company, siteid)
partition by range (siteid)
(
partition p0 values less than (09999)
tablespace usa,
partition p1 values less than (19999)
tablespace canada,
partition p2 values less than (29999)
tablespace britain,
partition p3 values less than (39999)
tablespace ireland,
partition p4 values less than (49999)
tablespace scotland,
partition p5 values less than (59999)
tablespace spacific,
partition p6 values less than (69999)
tablespace africa,
partition p7 values less than (79999)
tablespace asia,
partition p8 values less than (89999)
tablespace europe,
partition p9 values less than (99999)
tablespace samerica,
)
```

Figure 7-61   Create a Partitioned Index

```
select * from sites
where company = "Dunham Software"
partition (p1)
```

All said and done, partitioned tables and indexes provide an easy way to maintain ranges of data while enhancing performance. With the size of databases now available in the new release, it just makes sense to automate the setup and control of partitions. Oracle gets a big "atta-boy" for this one.

8

Microsoft® Windows NT™ 4.0 Tuning

For the newcomer, Windows NT has been available for general consumption since October, 1996, in two versions, one for desktop (Windows NT Workstation) and one for server (Windows NT Server). NT is scalable, supporting 4G of physical RAM and multiple CPU(s). Windows NT works on the following platforms:

NT Platforms (Uniprocessors, SMP, and Clustered)

Mips Microsystems R4x00

Data General AviiON AV6600 and AV2100 (with clustering)

Digital Alpha AXP 21x64

Motorola Power PC 6xx

Pentium, Pentium Pro, Pentium Pro 4xP6

Compaq Proliant Series

Intergaph's high-end ISMP6x server

IBM PowerPC

SGI MIPS®

NCR

Sequent

Intel 386/486 machines (high end)

There are many new features with Release 4.0. We will limit our discussion in this chapter to those surrounding performance. We also will take an in-depth look at tuning the NT Workstation and Server. Besides the Task Manager and

Performance Monitor within Windows 4.0 NT, many other tools can aid with your tuning efforts. It would be remiss not to mention them because they can be used to drill down into more complex tuning problems. Here is a list of some prominent third-party tools, along with ones with NT.

HELPFUL TUNING TOOLS

Microsoft NT Resource Kit Book and CD-ROM: Contains everything you would ever need to tune NT and a bunch of utilities on CD-ROM, ISBN 1-57238-343-9 (purchased separate from NT).

Microsoft Test: Lets users record or script keystrokes for replay. This is useful for running tuning scripts, system control scripts, and application scripts. You could connect multiple users and replay scripts to measure tuning changes against a base line (purchased separate from NT).

Win32 Software Development Kit: Several items in this kit deal with performance tuning. The working set tuner will recommend changes to your application code that will reduce its maximum memory usage (purchased separately from NT).

Event Viewer: A handy tool for reviewing the Event Log, where entries can be selected based upon event source, category, user, computer, event ID, date, and time. The log will contain information about system resource failures that can help to identify major problems requiring your immediate attention (included with NT).

Trace Logs: SMS and individual applications have their own trace logs. The information in these logs is helpful when trying to identify specific calls that are contributing to a performance problem. Interpreting the ASCII information in these files can be time consuming (included with NT).

SMS Network Monitor: This tool is useful in monitoring the network load, monitoring clients, deploying software, and performing remote PC inventories. The following Systems Management Server processes should be monitored.

Processes	Description
Preinst	SMS hierarchy manager
SiteIns	SMS site configuration manager
SMSExec	SMS multiple component executive
MSSQLServer	SQL server v.6.x

Exchange Administrator: The Exchange Administrator within Exchange comes with a Server Monitor, which is helpful in controlling restarts of servers. The more automated and quickly this function can be performed, the less downtime experienced by users.

Windows NT Diagnostics: Useful in determining the hardware devices and drivers, as well as disk sector sizes, which are key to tuning I/O performance (included with NT).

Windows NT Task Manager: Shows instantaneous and histogram displays of major resources. Very useful in spot checking the system's status (included with NT and a subject of this chapter). This is also known as the diagnostic wizard in Windows NT 4.0 Server.

Windows NT Performance Monitor: Allows capture and archival of statistics for all resources. Allows reporting, charting, and export for use in spreadsheets (included with NT and a subject of this chapter).

8.1   Windows NT 4.0 Enhancements

Windows NT 4.0 with its redesigned and rewritten kernel is faster than NT 3.5.1. Other performance enhancements include better task management, reduced system crashes with bulletproof dedicated address spaces, an improved caching algorithm, scalable multiprocessor support to 64 CPU(s), faster networking, faster graphics, and faster print and file sharing. *Point to Point Tunneling Protocol* (PPTP) and *Remote Access Server* (RAS) now allow full PPP multichannel aggregation, which allows users to combine multiple lines to aggregate throughput. NT 4.0 supports Fast Ethernet and 100VG AnyLAN highspeed networking for up to 100 Mbps. When using these more advanced network protocols, frames transmitted are smaller and fewer, while transfer rates are double that available on NT 3.5.1. New APIs, including a fiber API, position NT for fast peripherals. The *High Performance File System* (HPFS) is no longer supported.

Release 4.0 changes to the Performance Monitor include new instances for objects, along with new and revised counters for cache, disk, and *telephony* (TAPI) objects. A new difference counter type enables you to create a counter and to monitor the change between the last two measurements of that counter.

Some of the nonperformance related enhancements include *Peer Web Server* (PWS), Network OLE (now called Distributed COM or DCOM), *Internet Information Server* (IIS), cryptography APIs, Win95-style GUI, Win95-compatible System Policy Editor, DirectDraw, DirectSound multimedia support, and the Internet Explorer 2.0 browser.

The question many Database Administrators and I.S. Managers are asking is, "Will an NT-based database application system deliver the performance and scalability I need?" The answer is most certainly yes. Systems with 100 to 300 users are commonplace, not an exception. Multiprocessing boxes utilizing *Symmetric Multi-Processing* (SMP) and *Massively Parallel Processing* (MPP) in conjunction with NT are also becoming commonplace. The result is enough processing power to meet your needs most of the time. Some experts agree though, that a switch to a high-powered UNIX-based operating system is a better choice as the system gets larger. I heartily agree, even though I don't know where the cut-over to UNIX becomes necessary.

If you are a Windows 95 user and want to test drive NT before committing yourself to this operating system, you can install both Windows 95 and NT on the same system. They must be installed separately. You also have to repeat the installation of your application under NT. The file system differences will give you headaches. Keep the aspirin bottle handy. *NT File System* (NTFS) files are not viewable from Windows 95. Likewise, Windows 95 FAT32 and DriveSpace drives cannot be seen from Windows NT. NT is administration-heavy in comparison to Windows 95. So, be forewarned, it will take more of your already valuable time.

The following two softwares are being added to Windows NT 4.0, which will strengthen distributed applications.

■ *Microsoft Transaction Server* (MTS, code named Viper) was added to Windows NT Server in the summer of 1997. MTS is tightly integrated with the *MS Message Queue Server* (MSMQ), in order to provide transaction-level support and unit-of-work integrity.

■ *Microsoft Message Queue Server* (MSMQ, code named Falcon) also was added to Windows NT Serrver in the summer of 1997. This product allows applications to send and receive messages. Messages are queued and are not lost if the application fails. MSMQ supports the new ActiveX ccomponents and calls.

8.2   Windows NT 4.0 System Requirements

My own slant on minimum suggested memory is 32M for an NT 4.0 Workstation and 64M for an NT Server. A Pentium or Pentium Pro processor allows larger memory pages (for reduced paging) and the power to run NT optimally. Alternative machines once included RISC-based processors, such as the Mips Microsystems R4x00, Digital Alpha AXP 21x64, and Motorola Power PC 6xx, but some systems have had a falling out. IBM halted Warp for PowerPC in 1996, and Novell killed NetWare for PowerPC in 1995. Also, Microsoft killed NT for PowerPC in early 1997. Prior to this, MIPS/NT development was halted. It seems that only Intel and DEC Alpha remain as contenders for NT sales, with Intel capturing 95 percent.

What about disk and memory? Allow yourself a couple hundred megabytes of disk space for software. Also, it would be a good idea to use a fast and wide

Ultra SCSI boot drive to speed up your swap file. Memory varies from 12M for a stripped-down workstation up to 90 or more megabytes for full-blown servers.

The exact numbers you choose for memory and processors are the ongoing discussion for the rest of this chapter.

8.3   Windows NT 4.0 Workstation Performance

Windows NT Workstation performance issues pretty much align with those of the Server version. Tuning is accomplished in the same way and usually for the same reasons. The big difference with Workstation is scope. It is usually re-signed to performing standalone tasks. A very noble use for a Workstation is as a centralized performance monitoring platform for many other boxes. Some folks don't realize that it makes a capable server on its own. You can have 10 simultaneous connections to a Workstation system, which means that you could be monitoring Sybase, Oracle, and Microsoft SQL databases remotely. Another prospect for Workstation is as a test bench for applications before they are placed on an NT Server system.

8.4   Windows NT 4.0 Server Performance

The database server should be the only major application running on NT Server. An NT Server can be used for print and file sharing, application sharing, and domain controller functions. In a database climate, it is recommended that you avoid conflicts between the database and other services like *Backup Domain Controllers* (BDCs) or *Primary Domain Controllers* (PDCs). Try to dedicate the server to the database.

MULTIPLE SERVERS

A significant boost in performance can be obtained using multiprocessing. Even though print and file servers don't realize much gain, most databases will get 80 percent gains with a second processor and some percentage with each additional processor. To take full advantage of more processors, it is best to define more servers, too. Databases such as Oracle and Sybase relegate different services to different servers, which in turn will utilize available processors.

REMOTE ACCESS SERVER (RAS)

Remote Access Server (RAS) capacity planning is simple. First determine the anticipated number of simultaneous users and their channel bandwidth. Windows NT 4.0 RAS supports up to 256 serial devices. Standard serial ports have a maximum speed of 115,200 bits per second (bps).

If you install enough modems to ensure no busy signals during peak usage, the number will be close to the number of simultaneous users. Some users will connect for only a short time to pick up email, while others will remain connected all day. You must evaluate user trends to come up with safety margins.

The channel bandwidth is usually equal to the modem speed, but multichannel PPP will aggregate modems and speed.

DHCP/WINS SERVER TUNING

NT Server 4.0 supports on-the-fly *Internet Protocol* (IP) address allocation using DHCP. The downside of DHCP is that lease periods can give rise to a performance issue.

As records become obsolete in the WINS database \SYSTEM32\WINS\WINS.MDB or the DHCP database \SYSTEM32\DHCP\DHCP.MDB, they introduce table fragmentation, which translates to a slowdown in server performance. Microsoft provides a utility called JETPACK.EXE, which will remove fragmentation in these database files. To execute the utility, type JETPACK database_name temp_name.

8.5   Importance of the Operating System

You could purchase multiple tools to tune Windows NT, but that alone would not guarantee that your system would run optimized. Likewise, you could also buy several manuals and books dealing with tuning Windows NT and not be assured of a speedy system. It doesn't matter how much power you have if you don't know it's there or how to use it. There is no substitute for reading the manual and no substitute for experience. To get from a poorly running NT system to an optimized one requires some determination and sweat. The information in the next three sections can help you develop a high-performance NT system. You must also perform the tuning steps necessary for databases found in other chapters. NT is an operating system, or layer of software, on which RDBMS rest. Your applications are another layer that sit on top of your RDBMS. Each layer must be tuned, but the lowest layer, the operating system, can slow all the other layers above it.

8.6   Task Manager

Windows NT Task Manager provides graphic and digital displays of CPU, Memory, Threads, Processes, Cache, and Paging. Navigation is pretty simple. There are two applets. The first is selected by clicking the Processes Tab (see Figure 8-1). It offers an easy-to-view table of all processes running and provides information on CPU time and memory use.

VALUABLE PROCESS TAB FUNCTIONS

- If you suspect a program has a memory leak, you can compare memory use against its normal operational level.

- A runaway process can be identified by viewing CPU consumption.

- If the process is out of control, this is from where you will terminate it.

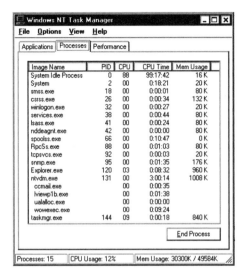

Figure 8-1   Task Manager Processes Tab

- If a process needs to be expedited, you can change the base priority to Real-time, High, Normal, or Low (good for current run of process). WARNING! Realtime can lockout other threads.

- On multiprocessors, you can expedite a process by reserving a processor for it and setting its affinity to the reserved processor.

VALUABLE PROCESS TAB STATISTICS

- Image Name (name of process)
- CPU Usage (percentage of processor usage)
- CPU Time (cumulative processor time)
- Memory Usage (working set in kilobytes)
- Page Faults (cumulative not found in memory/disk retrievals)
- Virtual Memory Size (paging file size in kilobytes)
- Base Priority (priority versus other scheduled threads)
- Handle Count (object handle count)
- Thread Count (current active threads in process)

The Task Manager Performance Tab (see Figure 8-2) shows histograms of CPU and memory usage graphically. This applet provides a way to determine when resources are low and to identify peak periods. The Performance Tab is executable from the NT 4.0 interface as a small bar graph, so system resources can be monitored while other tasks are being performed.

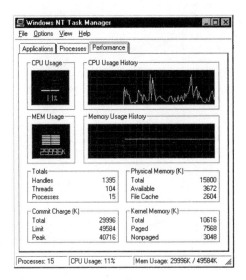

Figure 8-2   Task Manager Performance Tab

VALUABLE PERFORMANCE TAB FUNCTIONS

▪ The CPU History option can be used to view multiprocessor nonidle time.

VALUABLE PERFORMANCE TAB STATISTICS

▪ CPU Usage (current system-wide processor usage)

▪ MEM Usage (current system-wide memory usage in kilobytes)

▪ Total Handles (current system-wide object handle usage)

▪ Total Threads (current system-wide thread count)

▪ Total Processes (current system-wide active process count)

▪ Physical Memory Total (installed memory in kilobytes)

▪ Physical Memory Available (current system-wide available memory in kilobytes)

▪ Physical Memory File Cache (current file cache memory in kilobytes)

▪ Commit Charge Total (current system-wide virtual memory usage in kilobytes)

▪ Commit Charge Limit (current system-wide free virtual memory in kilobytes)

▪ Commit Charge Peak (maximum defined virtual memory in kilobytes)

▪ Kernel Memory Total (sum of paged and nonpaged kernel memory in kilobytes)

- Kernel Memory Paged (paged pool size in kilobytes)
- Kernel Memory Nonpaged (nonpaged pool size in kilobytes)

Some of the terms used in the statistics display are fuzzy, including kernel memory, paged memory, and nonpaged memory. Kernel memory is memory reserved for operating system programs. Paged memory is memory that can get paged out to disk when a process needs memory. Nonpaged memory is real memory that cannot get paged out. The nonpaged pool contains objects such as system routines and internal data structures.

8.7   Tuning Using Only the Performance Monitor

The Performance Monitor in NT uses class objects with corresponding counters within the object types. Each Windows NT Server node has more than 500 performance counters for its internal behavior. Microsoft SQL Server, Exchange, and many other products ported to Windows NT Server integrate with NT's performance monitor, providing important statistics. For example, Microsoft SQL Server Performance monitor adds more than 70 additional counters. The counters supplied by Windows NT Performance Monitor and SQL Server Performance Monitor are sufficient for tuning, but your application can create its own entries in the database. Statistic collection includes instantaneous readings, average readings, and a new *Difference* type that shows the delta between the latest two readings. Data is displayed graphically. An Alert feature of Performance Monitor enables administrators extensibility where normal counters do not provide a threshold option. With alerts, you can generate a message when a counter reaches some predetermined panic level. Table 8-1 lists the objects and counters that provide a basis for general tuning.

LOGGING

To view performance information already logged without interrupting the logging process, you need to start a second copy of Performance Monitor. Otherwise, logging is stopped. It is a good idea not to set intervals too small. The amount of information and overhead added by the Performance Monitor should be minimized. You need only enough information to tune the running system and occasionally resolve individual bottlenecks. Performance Monitor runs at a higher base priority than other tasks to ensure it can capture statistics at the update interval selected. If it is being preempted by other processes, try using a longer interval.

Logging is flexible. You can collect data from multiple systems in a single log file or chart or report on a single log file with multiple running copies of Performance Monitor.

I recommend that you begin by logging statistics for all the objects shown in Table 8-1. Set your update interval anywhere between 1 and 30 minutes. Start one copy of Performance Monitor for each computer. Direct each Performance

Monitor to separate log files. After you have logged for a full week, chart the results. This is the baseline for your tuning effort. The charted information will help you locate bottlenecks and shortages of resources. It will also show your peak hours and peak days.

TABLE 8-1   Windows NT Performance Monitor Objects and Related Counters

Object Name	Object Description	Counter	Counter Description
Cache	File system cache	Data Map Hits %	Percentage of data requests found in cache. This number should not drop below 85% or memory is needed.
		Read Aheads/sec	Sequential read aheads per second. These are more efficient, but may be an indication of unnecessary sequential processing
		Copy Read Hits %	Values less than 80% indicate data not found enough in cache
Logical Disk	Logical disk partitions	Average Disk Queue Length	Read/write queued request. If this number minus the number of spindles is greater than 2, then disk is a bottleneck.
		Average Disk Read Queue Length	Average read queue length.
		Average Disk Write Queue Length	Average write queue length.
		% Disk Time	Read/Write elapsed time.
		% Free Space	Amount free. If drops below 25%, it is time to address shortage.
Memory	Real memory	Pages/sec	Disk-to-memory page requests/second. Paging greater than 5 means there is a bottleneck. Greater than 10 is an indication of thrashing.
		Pages Input/sec	Disk reads per second to satisfy page faults (hard faults). If greater than 5/sec, there is a memory shortage
		Pages Output/sec	Disk writes per second to free memory to satisfy page faults.
		Page Faults/sec	Hard page faults require disk I/Os, while soft page faults are satisfied out of memory.

TABLE 8-1   Windows NT Performance Monitor Objects and Related Counters (Continued)

Object Name	Object Description	Counter	Counter Description
		Available Bytes	If drops below 10% of total memory or 2M, it is time to address shortage.
Network Interface	Network Interface	Bytes Total/sec for TCPIP/SNMP	Network throughput
		Bytes Total/sec for NetBEUI	Network throughput
		Datagrams/sec for NetBEUI	Network Activity
		SNA Connections Bytes/sec	Network Throughput (whether more SNA Servers are needed
NetBIOS	Network BIOS	Bytes Total/sec for NWLink	Network throughput
Objects	System software objects	Processes	Number of processes executing
Paging File	Virtual memory (swap) file	% Usage % Usage Peak	Use of virtual memory. If this number is greater than 15%, increase real memory.
Physical Disk	Physical disk device (spindle or RAID)	Average Disk Queue Length	Average of all logical disk partition queue lengths. (hardware RAID)
		Average Disk Read Queue Length	Average read queue length. (hardware RAID)
		Average Disk Write Queue Length	Average write queue length. (hardware RAID)
		% Disk Time	Percentage of time disk is busy. If greater than 90%, bottlenecks may be present.
		Current Disk Queue Length	Disk requests queued. If >= 3, then a bottleneck is present.
Processor	Object for a processor	Interrupts/sec	If greater than 1000, then the efficiency of network cards and I/O devices should be addressed
Process	Object for an executing program	% Processor Time	Process CPU usage. If greater than 85%, the processor is experiencing sporadic bottlenecks.
Server	Server Activity	Bytes Total/sec	Server network activity
		Context Blocks Queued/sec	

(Continued)

TABLE 8-1 Windows NT Performance Monitor Objects and Related Counters (Continued)

Object Name	Object Description	Counter	Counter Description
Processor	CPU	% Processor Time	Overall CPU usage
System	Assorted system counters	% Total Processor Time	Overall CPU usage in for multi-processors. If 85% or above, it's time to address.
		Total Interrupts /sec	Server load
		Processor Queue Length	Backlogged threads awaiting a processor. If => 3, then system is backed up.
Telephony	Telephone API device counters	Number of Devices	
		Active Lines	
		Incoming Calls	
		Outgoing Calls	
Thread	Portion of a process executing on one CPU	% Processor Time 0 % Processor Time 1	CPU time by thread

In addition to the counters shown in Table 8-1, there is a new _Total instance. For Process, Thread, Paging File, Physical Disk, and Logical Disk objects, the _Total value is equal to the sum of the values collected for an object counter. I find these values very helpful when trying to graph or chart interval statistics, such as values for each hour of the day, day of the week, or week of the month.

An example of _Total time can be seen in the B-line in Figure 8-4.

DATA POINTS

After 100 data points are collected, Performance Monitor will compress data to fit in the 100 available display slots. Windows of data will lose precision the longer that this compression continues. For this reason, you may want to narrow the Time Window by using the left- or right-arrow keys in the Input Log Timeframe dialog. Narrowing is one way to regain visibility to all the data points in a time window. A data export will retrieve all the data points, so your spreadsheets will have access to all data points.

SPIKES ON CHARTS

Another anomaly of Performance Monitor are invalid data spikes, which usually occur at the inception of a process or thread. These data points should be dropped from your statistics charting and reporting by setting the Time Window to exclude them.

Whether you are using the Windows NT Performance Monitor or the SQL Performance Monitor (for Microsoft SQL Server), there are two configuration files that you can setup, the `Alerts` file and the `Workspace` file. The Workspace file, which contains PERFMON chart settings and alerts, is saved with a default extension of `PMW`. The other file has an extension of `PMA` and contains user-configured alerts.

ALERTS

One way to monitor the system is with alerts. Alerts are tied to thresholds. Only one alert can exist for each object counter. When you set up an alert (from the Options menu), you specify the interval and a method. There are three methods of being alerted. The system will display the alert view, log the event, or send a network alert. You also can append a program to be executed. However, this isn't recommended because the resource shortage that triggered the alert may make it impossible to run the program.

PHYSICAL MEMORY

On an Intel platform, the MAXMEM parameter of the `BOOT.INI` file is used to set the maximum physical memory for use by NT. This is done by appending the parameter to the multi line under the [operating systems] section as follows:

```
Multi(0)disk(0)rdisk(0)partition(1)\
WINNT40="Windows NT Version 4.00" /MAXMEM=16
```

The MAXMEM parameter has several uses. It can be used to locate failing memory chips by limiting memory used by NT, using a process of elimination. For capacity planning, it can be used with a stress program to determine how many users are supported on a server, with varying bootable memory settings. Unfortunately, MAXMEM isn't the best method to determine whether more memory is needed. To determine that, you need to know the cause of memory shortages.

To establish the correct memory level for server memory usage, use the Network applet. It will display a dialog box like that shown in Figure 8-3.

Figure 8-3 Server Memory Setting

There are four settings from which to choose. Use the Minimum Memory Used setting for 1 to 10 users and the Balance setting for 11 to 64 users. The other two settings will handle more than 64 users. However, only use the Maximize Throughput for File Sharing option if Windows NT is the file server. This option gives file cache priority to memory over applications. Otherwise, the bottom option should be chosen. This is what you would select for Microsoft SQL Server, SNA Server, and Microsoft System Management Server.

There are several culprits that could be responsible for physical memory shortages. First is virtual memory paging, which we look at in the next section. Second is improper load balancing of processes in a multiprocessing environment. Third is over allocation of memory to subsystems and caches. And fourth is leaky processes, which eat up all available memory. Let's look at these various culprits and determine ways to tune memory.

VIRTUAL MEMORY

The paging file is used to hold information when memory is exhausted. The good part is that you don't just stop processing when memory runs out. The bad part is that the paging file incurs I/Os and slows the system down in two ways. First is paging results in I/Os that otherwise would have been memory operations. Second, Windows has to go through some serious instructions just to put information on the file and retrieve it later.

Performance Monitor will show your virtual memory usage, which is an indication of paging.

The following formula, using Performance Monitor statistics, is an indication of high I/O activity for paging. When the result is greater than one, paging is excessive, and more memory is in order.

$$\frac{Pages\ per\ read}{sec} = \frac{Pages\ Input}{sec} \div \frac{Page\ Reads}{sec}$$

You have a bunch of options available to avoid excessive swapping. First, you can migrate unnecessary processing off the current NT box to another one. Second, you can increase available physical memory. See Page Reads/second (D line) in Figure 8-4. Next, spreading paging files across multiple disk drives and controllers will improve performance as multiple disks can process I/O requests concurrently (up to 16 separate page files). Windows NT has several system files that are frequently accessed. Definitely locate page files on different disks than these files, or any heavily used files. Use drivers and devices that support asynchronous I/O (avoid the ATDISK driver that single threads I/O). Go to the Control Panel Virtual Memory tab and set the page file size such that extension of it will rarely occur. Finally, you should uninstall unnecessary drivers, which eat up memory.

Oh, by the way, you should make the boot disk your fastest disk on NT. Why? Because the boot drive also contains the paging file. Because paging can be a major area of contention and overhead, it should be the fastest device.

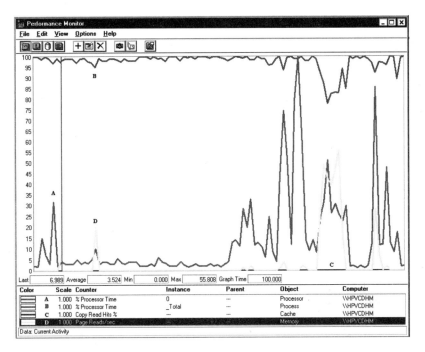

Figure 8-4 Performance Monitor Screen

LEAKY APPLICATIONS

Leaky applications are ones that over time gobble up all available memory. It doesn't require any fancy utility to locate these offenders. The system has lots of bells and whistles that clue you in to a problem. First, the PAGEFILE.SYS paging file will grow as physical memory is exhausted because paging must accommodate the memory shortage. Also, the Page File Bytes _Total statistic will show the current size of the paging file In Performance Monitor; the Available Bytes indicator will bottom out. The paging rate will climb as Pages Output/sec increases. The offending process also is at the top of the memory usage by process list.

CACHING

The file system in Windows NT uses memory for caching. As records are read, they are placed in the memory cache, where they can be found again and again. That is, until another page takes precedence or until memory is trimmed by the operating system. The demand for memory can result in a cache bottleneck. The conventional method for detecting a problem is to view the Copy Read Hit % statistic (see the C-line in Figure 8-4 for an example). If this value drops below 80 percent, caching is losing effectiveness—either the demands for memory are too high, or physical memory is too low. In our example, the value is bottomed out is because there is so little activity-required caching, a common cause for seeing an exceptionally low value.

In a multiprocessor system, shared memory must maintain cache coherency; that is, each processor's cache must be synchronized. You can realize a performance boost in heavily laden systems by choosing a hardware architecture that supports a write-through caching strategy. This strategy will outperform others when the shared cache must be updated, for the sake of synchronization.

Page faults are another indication of cache overloads. They are discussed in the virtual memory section.

Apparently, custom tuning is not necessarily the best way to optimize caching. Here are some tools that can exceed your own efforts. The marketing literature states that they do great. You should research them further to verify that you see equivalent results.

SUPERCACHE-NT AND SUPERDISK-NT FROM EEC SYSTEMS, INC.

SuperCache-NT is a multithreaded device driver that reduces disk I/O by saving areas of disk and programs that are reread in memory. It works on NT V3.51 and NT V4.0 (Workstation and Server) and supports Intel and Alpha AXP platforms and NTFS and FAT partitions. Marketing literature boasts 25 times the savings for users or batch jobs, depending on the power and number of CPU(s) in the system and the amount of free memory available for caching.

SuperDisk-NT creates RAM disks on NT systems. These RAM disks can be accessed from anywhere on the NT network. Updates are applied to a mirrored physical disk partition transparently. After a power failure, SuperDisk will reestablish the RAM disk to its state before the failure. Both FAT and NTFS partitions are supported. Marketing literature boasts a 30 times improvement (100 percent cache-hit levels).

PROCESSORS

The `%Total Processor Time` is an indication of processor usage (A-line on Performance Monitor Graph in Figure 8-4). On uniprocessors it indicates a shortage of processing power as the number is sustained above 85 percent. You need to have a grace period, in which to perform tuning, shift workloads, or to buy more processing power, so you don't want to wait until this statistic is sitting at 98 to 100 percent. For multiprocessors, this statistic is the total of all processors divided by the number of processors. So, a number like 80 percent is probably a safe limit before addressing processor throughput overall. But, it does not indicate whether an individual processor is exhausted. To accomplish the latter, you need to start up Performance Monitor sessions for each processor. Then you need to capture the `%Processor Time by Thread`. This will show the amount of saturation on each processor, by thread, of course.

Remember that a problematic process could cause a sustained processor usage above 85 percent. You must determine whether the problem is in a program before buying additional processing power. This can be done by looking at two indicators. First is the Processor Queue Length. It is an indication of back-logged threads that are awaiting an available processor. If Performance Monitor charts show sustained queue lengths greater than three, then a problem backlog is present. The second indicator is the %Processor Time for Thread objects. If an individual thread is hogging the processor, this is the first place to look. The solution could involve changes to the application, a database, or capacity management. You will need to take a closer look at the program associated with the thread.

Cyrix 6x86 Configuration v2.01 (by Olivier Gilloire) is a utility that can get a 75 percent performance increase for Windows NT 4.0.

THREADS

As the number of threads increase, so does CPU consumption. If the number of threads exceeds some magic number, you need more CPU. If the third tab on Task Manager (Memory and CPU usage) shows that you are consistently above 85 percent, then performance is already degraded. You can move unnecessary services or applications to less-used servers or boxes, or you can increase the number of processors on the current box. This means that you should buy scalable boxes and design distributed environments.

When using Performance Monitor to track threads, include the thread ID in graphs. If the thread ID changes, an unrelated event is now being charted. Thread IDs remain with a thread until it stops (unlike thread numbers).

I/O THROUGHPUT

Tuning I/O is the greatest test of your NT skills. There are several steps required to optimize I/O performance. First, you need to determine whether any of the disks are being exercised beyond their rated maximum. This is done by reviewing the Disk Reads/sec statistic in Performance Monitor. Anything more than 80 percent of the rated maximum can cause bottlenecks. For example, if Disk Reads/sec shows 43, and the device is rated at 50, then it is already causing delays.

The second step is to load balance disk activity. We discuss striping several times in the chapters on Oracle, Sybase, and other RDBMS. This is a viable way to handle I/O bottlenecks. You can also improve I/O performance by load balancing other I/O activities like paging files, log files, dump files, and monitoring files. The number and speed of disk controllers also directly impacts I/O performance. My personal favorites are Ultra SCSI Fast-n-Wide, RAID 5, and Fiber (also known as Fibre). These three alternatives have tradeoffs, first of which is their respective price tag. SCSI is cheap but requires that you manage the many controllers and devices. RAID manages the load balancing for you and can give your system the expansion necessary to define mirrored databases and logs. However, some people have reported problems with RAID.

FILE ARCHITECTURES

Use FAT instead of *NT File System* (NTFS) to get a little more performance on small folders, although some techies are denying that there is any gain. It may not be possible to use FAT, depending on the requirements of the RDBMS you are using. FAT's inherent problems with lost clusters and cross-linked files should also be considered. Another consideration is that NTFS added a security tab to every file and folder's properties sheet. Security is something most of us try to avoid. Somebody might actually need it. NTFS also allows compression on a file-by-file basis. Again, this isn't something that would sway me one way or the other. However, a FAT file system can have a maximum of 4G (2^{23} bytes), whereas an NTFS file system supports 16 Exabytes, or 18,446,744,073,709,616 bytes (2^{64} bytes). Even a single NTFS volume can contain 2 TB (2^{41} bytes), which is more than FAT can hold. This may affect any decisions you make about choice of file systems.

BootPart 2.0: Partition for NT is a utility that adds partitions (by Gilles Vollant).

DETECTING I/O BOTTLENECKS

Waiting on I/O is perhaps the biggest culprit of database systems running on Windows NT. With the aid of the Windows NT Performance Monitor, you can observe several statistics that can aid in determining whether bottlenecks exist. For disk performance you need to activate `diskperf` (the Disk Performance Statistics Driver). Diskperf will collect data for the Performance Monitor. Here are the commands used to start up diskperf.

STARTING DISKPERF (METHOD 1)

1. Choose the Command Prompt icon in the Main group.

2. Type:

```
diskperf -y or
diskperf -y \\mycomputer          (View disk subsystem statistics)
```

STARTING DISKPERF (METHOD 2)

1. Start control panel.

2. Choose devices and change the startup value of diskperf to boot.

3. Reboot computer.

Using either method, the disk performance monitoring will be enabled after rebooting the computer. Because this service represents significant overhead, you should turn it off again after the statistics collection is completed. To do this and to ensure the best performance, issue the following command from the command prompt.

HALTING DISKPERF

1. From the command prompt type:

```
diskperf -n
```

The key statistics for viewing are `%Disk Time and Current Disk Queue Length`. If `%Disk Time` is approaching 100 percent, then the disk is bottlenecked. If the Current Disk Queue Length shows sustained values greater than or equal to three, then there is a bottleneck. Solutions vary depending on the device speeds, number of adapters, buffers, caching, fragmentation, sector sizes, and type and implementation of disk striping being used. See the following paragraphs on these subjects.

FRAGMENTATION

Two obvious things to do when tuning NT 4.0 disk performance are to make the boot disk the fastest device available and to take care of disk fragmentation. Why bother with fragmentation? Because it is responsible for additional unnecessary I/O. Here are some vendor tools to help you manage fragmentation.

DISKEEPER FROM EXECUTIVE SOFTWARE

Windows NT 4.0 does not include a disk defragmenter. Diskeeper from Executive Software is a defragmenter for Windows NT. It will consolidate fragmented files and free space. Using only idle resources, this utility will defragment multiple disks and back off when the system kicks in to do something.

NORTON UTILITIES FOR WIN NT 4.0 BY SYMANTEC

Good old reliable Norton comes through again. **Norton Utilities Speed Disk** will defragment your disk and allow you to monitor the process. The same utilities package comes with a virus scanner, recovery for deleted files, and a resource monitor.

SECTOR SIZES

NT supports sector sizes from 512 to 64K. Even though larger sizes show substantial improvements in performance, they may not be supported by the device in use, or an application may not make proper use of the larger sector size. For example, OLTP transactions may be better adapted to smaller and mid-sized sectors, while warehousing (Read Only) environments work best with the largest sector sizes available. Also, database buffers have to accommodate the sizes being used. The bottom line is that larger is better where supported and warranted.

When determining the best sector size to use, look at the Disk Read Bytes/sec and Average Disk Bytes/Read statistics. Average Disk Bytes/Read will be close to the sector size for the device. Disk Read Bytes/sec will show more throughput for larger sector sizes, provided that a fair comparison test is being conducted.

REDUNDANT ARRAY OF INEXPENSIVE DISKS (RAID) AND STRIPE SETS

The %Disk Time counter in Performance Monitor treats hardware RAID sets as a single device. It cannot show individual statistics for devices making up the RAID set. For this reason, you need to use the Avg. Disk Queue Length, Avg. Disk Read Queue Length, and Avg. Write Queue Length statistics for these configurations. These statistics will show values in excess of 100 percent, which is typical for RAID.

SCSI technology outperforms IDE and EIDE. The gains are in the tens or hundreds of percent, depending on the combination of devices, controllers, and drivers. Also, striping is a benefit of using SCSI. It is easy to daisy chain several small disk drives to one SCSI controller and much more effective than owning one big EIDE drive. The more physical devices, platters, and read/write heads, the greater the potential to improve performance. With SCSI, you can add controllers to improve performance, too.

I/O CONTROLLER CARDS

32-bit controllers that use bus-mastering *direct memory access* (DMA) are best because they allow the DMA controller to perform I/O, freeing the processor for other things. It makes sense to choose a system with the fastest bus rate to match the controller (100M or better). Then there is the disk itself. It should be the fastest device or at least fast enough to take advantage of the bus and controller speeds.

NETWORKS

Response time is a product of the operating system overhead, client and server program overhead, network programs overhead, and network latency. In Chapter 1, we showed how you can use PING to determine the network latency. If you determine that network transmission time is poor, or unacceptable, you can choose between a number of advanced protocols and hardware options. For example, 32-bit network cards outperform their 16-bit predecessors, or you could put in Fast Ethernet between your servers and an Ethernet Switch. Finally, you could run fiber. Within NT itself, you can check the `Maximize for Network Applications` box in the NT Network Applet.

Make sure to use Network Monitor to determine whether slow network response is due to system performance, collisions, hub speeds, or other causes. One common mistake is to run an accelerated video card with a standard VGA driver. You must first isolate the cause of bottlenecks to the hardware or software in order to avoid spending time and money in areas that will not benefit performance.

If there are a high number of collisions, your LAN needs to be segmented. You can replace your LAN hubs with smart switching hubs, like **SuperStack** from **3Com**, which lets you mix 10 Mbps and 100 Mbps segments. A smart switching hub will learn the network addresses and perform fast routing of packets.

SERVICES

One area often overlooked is cutting out unnecessary services. Several services can be suspended when Windows NT is used as a database server. These include Computer Browser, DHCP, WINS, Clipbook Server, Alerter, Schedule, Messengers, and Network DDE. These can be turned off from the Services Applet. Likewise, unnecessary drivers and protocols also can be disabled.

CAPACITY MANAGEMENT

Capacity management can best be performed using Systems Management Server, Network Monitor, Server Manager, or the Performance Monitor. There are several third-party tools trying to do a better job of performance monitoring and capacity planning. One is **Dynameasure** from **Bluecurve Incorporated**. It is a capacity and performance measurement tool for NT-based networks. It supports file service, decision support system, and transaction processing workloads, in addition to client-server system performance testing and stress measurement. Others include **Performance Works** from **Landmark Systems Corporation** and **PerfMan** from **The Information Systems Manager Incorporated**.

8.8   Windows NT 5.0 Preview

On the horizon for 1998 is NT 5.0. This release isn't aimed at performance. It will introduce architectural changes and protocols that make NT more manageable. The old *Cairo* code name is still tied to NT 5.0. Microsoft is apparently trying to secure the distributed networking environment, which is tied to so much new business these days. Using *Distributed COM* (DCOM) to integrate components on a network and ActiveX controls to communicate DCOM requests, an Active Platform is provided. Distributed security (Kerberos and X.509 Public Key Certificates) and file directories (Active Directory) are intended to provide the kind of administrative capabilities and fire wall security needed in the Internet/Intranet and Client/Server networks spreading though the business world.

All the big RDBMS software vendors are taking advantage of *Symmetric Multi-Processing* (SMP) and *Massively Parallel Processing* (MPP) now. We discuss these in detail in Chapters 7 and 11. SMP's marked disadvantage is shared memory, which results in contention as more processors are added to a configuration. MPP does not have this contention problem. Now Microsoft is getting on the bandwagon with clustering. A cluster is a group of autonomous NT servers integrated into a single system. They work more like MPP, avoiding SMP's deficiencies. Clustered systems are scalable, increasing available transaction volumes. The new NT clustered system software is termed WolfPack. Even though it is not directly tied to Windows NT 5.0, expect to see it as a stable product in the same time frame. It will ship in phases. The first will support up to 16 server machines. Other vendors are jumping on the clustering bandwagon. Data General, with its *Cluster-in-a-box* solution has agreed to support Wolfpack.

Data General makes a high-end server, the AViiON AV 6600, and a new low-cost departmental server, the AV 2100. The AV 6600 has six 200MHz Intel Pentium Pro processors, each with 512K cache and up to 4G of memory. Both systems can access up to five terabytes of fault-tolerant CLARiiON storage (RAID). To ensure high availability, the AV 6600 has fully redundant power and cooling, as well as automated recovery from CPU, memory, and disk or I/O channel failures. The clustering technology is included, so scalability would allow two AV6600 machines, for a total of 12 Pentium processors. Sweet! Data General provides these machines for NT and UNIX. They also provide SMP servers that utilize cache-coherent memory.

9

Microsoft Windows 95 Tuning

9.1 Windows 95 Enhancements

Windows 95[1] enhancements include support for thread-based multitasking, independent message queues, better user interface development, a 32-bit operating system, the plug-n-play initiative, 8.4G drive IDE support, fewer reboots due to individual program crashes, and a GUI user interface. By the way, DOS is no longer needed, but keep it around if you're given a choice. You will find that some of your applications will still need to run native in DOS, or they will just run faster that way. That's why we will provide you with some more information on tuning your Windows 95 system.

Thread-based multitasking is a big winner. Programs can execute concurrently, and you will immediately notice an improvement in your performance. Windows 95 uses process and thread-based multitasking. A *process* is a program that is executing; Windows 95 supports multiple concurrent programs executing. A *thread* is a dispatchable unit of executable code. All processes have at least one thread but can have several more. For example, an application can start up several threads that run in parallel. This greatly reduces the elapsed time for a process.

9.2 CONFIG.SYS File Changes

I didn't discover a lot of the Windows 95 Enhancements and the potential for better performance until many months after converting from Windows 3.1.

---

[1] Microsoft® Windows 95™ is a registered trademark of Microsoft Corporation.

Then I discovered that some simple things such as the CONFIG.SYS and AU-TOEXEC.BAT parameters could be changed. For example, you can move control blocks into the *upper memory block* (UMB), the block of memory between the 640K line and the 1M line on all DOS/Windows computers. The more you can put in the upper memory block, the better. You won't have a problem with this because Windows 95 really needs an upper memory area of about 16M. Of course, Windows 95 also needs a low memory area of about 16M, too.

NOTE: Use the MEMMAKER program to optimize system memory by moving as many bytes as possible into the upper memory block, including resident programs and drivers. This process frees conventional memory for application use.

The BUFFERS/BUFFERSHIGH commands of the CONFIG.SYS file allocate memory for disk buffers. Using the BUFFERSHIGH command attempts to allocate memory from the upper memory block, if it is available. Otherwise, it uses below the 640K line memory. Set buffers equal to your FILES setting, divided by two.

EXAMPLE

```
BUFFERS=p[,s]
BUFFERSHIGH=p[,s]
```

where *p*=primary allocation   (min=0, max=99, default=30)

and *s*=secondary allocation   (min=0, max=8)

DEVICE/DEVICEHIGH commands of the CONFIG.SYS file load device drivers into memory. The DEVICEHIGH command attempts to allocate memory from the upper memory block, if it is available. Otherwise, it uses below the 640K line memory. The minsize parameter is particularly useful because a driver may use more memory while running than when initially loaded. This is used to guarantee that enough memory is reserved for the full size utilized by the driver.

EXAMPLE

```
DEVICE=[drive:][path]filename [parameters]
DEVICEHIGH [drive:][path]filename [parameters]
```

or

```
DEVICEHIGH [[/L:region1[,minsize1][;region2[,minsize2] [/S]]=
[drive:][path]filename [dd-parameters]
```

where the last command is used to load the device driver into 1 or more regions of memory

The next command is DOS. This command determines whether a portion of MS-DOS will be loaded into the *high memory area* (HMA); *upper memory block* (UMB), or both. In your CONFIG.SYS, specify one of the following:

```
DOS=HIGH|LOW[,UMB|,NOUMB][,AUTO|,NOAUTO]
DOS=[HIGH,|LOW,]UMB|NOUMB[,AUTO|,NOAUTO]
DOS=[HIGH,|LOW,][UMB,|NOUMB,]AUTO|NOAUTO
```

where *UMB* indicates that MS-DOS should manage the upper memory block; *NOUMB* indicates that MS-DOS should not manage the upper memory block; *HIGH* indicates that MS-DOS should load part of itself into the high memory area; *LOW* indicates that MS-DOS should remain in the low memory area (640K); *AUTO* indicates that MS-DOS should automatically load stuff into the UMB; *NOAUTO* indicates that MS-DOS should not automatically load stuff into the UMB.

It is to your advantage to use UMB. Whether or not you go all out using the HIGH and AUTO commands depends on whether you are getting the best utilization of the high memory by doing so. If you choose AUTO, MS-DOS will automatically use the -HIGH versions of all the commands described here, whether they were specified or not.

The FCBS/FCBSHIGH commands define *file control blocks* (FCBs). If you set FCBS=10, then you can only have 10 open files at one time. The eleventh will get an error. I recommend that you start with 100 because you need at least that much to run personal versions of database managers. Once again, the HIGH version of the command takes advantage of upper memory.

EXAMPLE

```
FCBS=n              (min=1, max=255, default=4)
FCBSHIGH=n          same
```

The FILES/FILESHIGH commands go hand-in-hand with their FCBS/FCBSHIGH counterparts. You should set them equal to each other, unless a specific software requires you to do otherwise.

The INSTALL/INSTALLHIGH commands are used to load memory-resident programs into low or high memory. Many of the supplied MS-DOS routines are available to load high using the INSTALLHIGH command.

EXAMPLE

```
INSTALL=[drive:][path]filename [parameters]
INSTALLHIGH=[drive:][path]filename [parameters]
```

MS-DOS keeps track of the last drive available. It uses this when searching available drives. The variable that keeps track of the last drive can also be loaded into low or high memory by using the LASTDRIVE/LASTDRIVEHIGH commands.

EXAMPLE

```
LASTDRIVE=d
LASTDRIVEHIGH=d
```

where *d* is a value from A to Z

STACKS and STACKSHIGH are used to handle interrupts and nested program calls that must save registers on the stack. These, too, can be allocated out of high or low memory. Always set stacks to the maximum allowable to eliminate the chance of a stack error.

EXAMPLE

```
STACKS=n,s
STACKSHIGH=n,s
```

where *p*=number of stacks   (min=0, range=8-64)
and *s*=size in bytes   (min=0, range=32-512)

9.3   PERFORMANCE SETTINGS

From the Performance Panel in Windows 95, you can optionally make some basic performance changes. Access is via the Control Panel. Select the SYSTEM icon and then the PERFORMANCE tab (see Figure 9-1).

 WARNING! Before making any changes to your system that could potentially expose you to a recovery situation, it is a good idea to have backups. You can back up your entire system with Windows 95 backup, but software that comes with a tape backup system is generally your best choice. You want to use a backup system that will find hidden files. Here is a BAT file that you can create that will let you capture the Windows 95 Registry. This is an important step to take before experimenting with changes to your Windows 95 system.

```
REM Backup Windows 95 Registry
CD ..
CD ..
CD WINDOWS
ATTRIB SYSTEM.DAT -h -r -s
ATTRIB USER.DAT -h -r -s
COPY SYSTEM.DAT mydrive:
COPY USER.DAT mydrive:
REM Backup of SYSTEM and USER files complete
```

In the event that Windows 95 is affected by a tuning change, you can copy these registry files back to the WINDOWS directory and reboot. Now back to the tuning features available.

The Performance Panel has three options in the advanced settings box: FILE SYSTEM, GRAPHICS, and VIRTUAL MEMORY. If the FILE SYSTEM button is selected, another window is displayed, this time with HARD DISK, CD-ROM, and TROUBLE SHOOTING tabs. Let's select HARD DISK. Figure 9-2 shows the displayed HARD DISK window.

Figure 9-1   Windows 95 Performance Panel

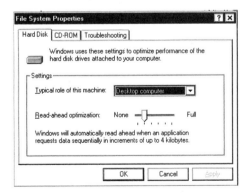

Figure 9-2   Windows 95 Hard Disk Performance

The read-ahead optimization slide control enables you to set the point where read-ahead will kick in. It is not set to full in the figure. But, you can set it to none or increments stepping up to 64K. When read-ahead kicks in, Windows 95 will read ahead from sequential files, placing the blocks into cache memory. These blocks will be accessed faster from memory as they are needed by the application. The optimum setting depends on the nature of files being read. If many of your files are small, then the lowest setting above NONE is best.

The other tabs on the performance panel lead to screens that also enable you to tune them by using slide controls. The CD-ROM window has a slide allowing you to set it from 214K to 1238K of physical memory used for optimizing CD-ROM access. The Graphics window has a NONE to ALL slide control for functions supported in graphics acceleration. The last tab is VIRTUAL MEMORY. The window displayed enables you to decide between having Windows 95 control virtual memory or controlling virtual memory yourself. Your only option is to define a virtual memory swap file. I'd recommend letting Windows 95 control virtual memory, unless the amount of RAM in your PC is very limited (12M or less).

9.4   CD-ROMS

The Performance Panel isn't the only avenue for tuning. (Note that CD-ROMs run better on Windows 95). Your choice of hardware has the greatest influence on CD-ROM performance. But, it is almost a joke to suggest which hardware to use. While writing this book, CD-ROMs evolved from two times faster (2x) to twenty-four times (24x) faster. For example, there is the Panasonic 24x ATAPI CD-ROM drive. I can't even speculate where this will go. By the time you read this line, the speeds will probably have changed, as will the features. There were some rumors of rewritable CDs being researched. You get what you pay for when performance is your primary concern. Modems are the perfect example.

If you need a large-capacity CD-ROM library system, take a look at the new jukeboxes from JVC. The MC-1200 loads up to 200 CDs. The MC-1600 loads 600. Both come standard with four eight-speed drives, expandable to six. They are excellent price/performance jukeboxes and work fine in network environments.

9.5   MODEMS AND ISDN

Modem performance is a product of several variables. The 16550 UART is prevalent and fast. This computer chip makes modems transfer data on the PC computer bus much faster than predecessor UARTs. So, don't use older UARTs. If you buy almost any internal modem today, it will have the faster UART.

The conventional dial-up network modems available today run at 33.6 Kbps. Many ISP providers have modems of various speeds. Your chances of getting a 33.6 Kbps connection depend on the modem available at the other end and on the line quality. Most connections end up between 14.4 Kbps and 28.8 Kbps, but there are alternatives worth looking into.

Telephone systems have undergone a gradual change from analog to digital communications in recent years. Along the way, *Integrated Services Digital Network* (ISDN) was developed. Today, the *National ISDN 2* (NI-2) standard is used industry wide, thus freeing users from needing to know the underlying support facilities. Unfortunately, the *Regional Bell Operating Companies* (RBOCs) have been slow to implement ISDN.

ISDN speeds are typically around 128 Kbps but can be as high as 1536 Kbps in the United States and 1984 kbps in Europe. Your basic ISDN service is known as *Basic Rate Interface* (BRI), which provides you with two 64 Kbps "B" channels for voice and data, as well as a 16kbps "D" channel for signaling (two channel aggregation is handled via bonding or multilink PP, with uncompressed data). *Primary Rate Interface* (PRI) service aggregates more "B" channels to achieve greater capacities. The channels are 23 Kbps, and you can have 24 in the United States and 30 in Europe. To handle the increased signaling requirements, a 64 Kbps "D" channel is paired with PRI "B" channels.

ISDN offers speed, faster line connects, single-line multiple device support (for ISDN types of devices), and fewer line quality interruptions. If you're interested in finding out more about ISDN hardware and services, check out these Internet sites:

```
www.ascend.com
www.bellcore.com/NIC
www.alumni.caltech.edu/~dank/isdn/index.html
www.ziplink.net/~ralphb/ISDN/
www.niuf.nist.gov/misc/niuf.html
```

Another alternative is cable modems, which run 80 times faster than ISDN and 5 times faster than dedicated T1 lines. They can even address multiple IP addresses at one time. Wouldn't that make surfing the Net more entertaining?

Corporations buy dedicated lines to bypass the nonsense surrounding hops., but the cost is high. A dedicated line can run $600/month. Several companies are switching to TCP/IP Internet and Intranet connections. Sophisticated firewall mechanisms are employed to reduce the chance of piracy and network sabotage.

Protocols make a big difference. Packet communications (TCP/IP) are much faster than conventional synchronous and asynchronous transmissions because there is less header and trailer information to send and receive and less handshaking.

9.6 DriveSpace 3 Disk Compression

When you compress a drive, the contents are contained in a single file known as a *compressed volume file* (CVF). Windows 95 creates this file on an uncompressed drive known as a host drive. DriveSpace and DoubleSpace, its predecessor from DOS 6.x, are compatible, so you can come forward to drivespace with your backups from another world. Figures 9-3 and 9-4 show the properties of a drive.

Windows is able to estimate the amount of free space available on a Drive-Space drive by using an estimate of the compression ratio. Compression is not exclusive. You can mix uncompressed and compressed drives. Compression is ideal for large static data sets or directories. Noncompressed drives are best suited for database and OLTP type applications.

9.7 Incremental Backups

Windows 95's system backup utility will backup my 1.2G drive to a rewritable optical one in about four hours. That's a long time, but the compression option saves both time and space on the target drive. It actually runs about 20 percent

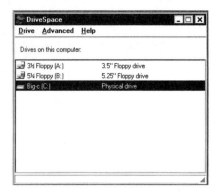

Figure 9-3 DriveSpace Drive List

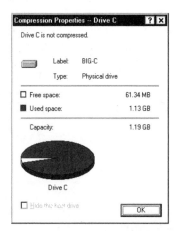

Figure 9-4 DriveSpace Disk Properties

faster and uses only half the space for the backup. The time isn't really an issue because incremental backups will catch regular updates in less than a half hour. Using incremental backups can reduce system down time because they only back up files that have changed since the last full backup. Plus, Windows 95 allows a hot backup, one that is occurring while updates are still happening to disk drives, although I'm not certain how you would recover your files with one. Maybe the database vendors can take advantage of this feature.

Figure 9-5 shows the system backup options for backups, where you can select incremental backups.

9.8 DISK DEFRAGMENTER

Another system utility available in Windows 95 is the Defragmenter. Fragmentation occurs as files are deleted, and new ones use their space. If a file is saved to an area that can no longer hold it, it will be saved in fragments across the disk drive. This fragmentation accounts for additional I/Os and head seek time. Defragmentation reassembles the files into single allocations. It clusters the files together and clusters the free space. It is like starting with a new drive until fragmentation takes its course again.

Before you can defragment a drive, you need to run Scandisk. Scandisk will check the FAT table and clusters for problems. If Scandisk gives the drive a clean bill of health, then you can run defrag. When you begin the defragmentation process, it will tell you whether the disk needs to be defragmented. If you have only a few percent of fragmentation, you don't need to defragment the disk. If this number is greater than 5 percent, it can be advantageous to defragment the drive. Figure 9-6 shows what the Defragmenter looks like before running. It will indicate 0 percent fragmentation after running.

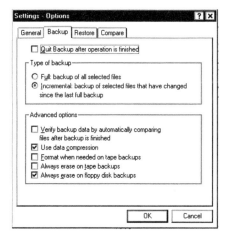

Figure 9-5 Windows 95 Incremental Backups

Figure 9-6 Windows 95 Disk Defragmenter

9.9 CPU USAGE

In Chapter 1, we showed you how to display the active CPU used with Dash-board 95. If you are experiencing a maxed-out CPU condition, you have some choices. Your first choice is to tune your applications. Another choice is to up-grade your hardware, but when the average CPU used finally exceeds 80 perc-net, you are losing productivity by not taking action.

9.10 CREATING THREADS

In Chapter 1, we showed you how to display the active threads running in Win-dows 95. Now, we want to discuss the benefits of using more threads. Multiple threads allow an application to parallelize activities. For example, one thread may be reading data into the application, a second one sorting the information, and a third formatting the output. More processing power is being used, and the payback is in elapsed time.

When an application runs, it has a main thread (mainline) and as many sub-threads as are created and given control. To create a subthread in an applica-tion program, you use an API function like the following:

```
HANDLE      CreateThread(LPSECURITY_ATTRIBUTES lpAttr,
            DWORD dwstack
            LPTHREAD_START_ROUTINE lpfunc,
            LPVOID lpParam,
            .DWORD dwFlags,
            LPDWORD lpdwID);
```

where

lpAttr   Is a pointer to a set of security attributes
              pertaining to the thread.

              If it is NULL, then no security is used.

dwStack   Is the size of the stack in bytes. If it is set to 0,
              then the size is set to match the size used in the
              main thread.

lpfunc   Is the address or entry point to the thread and must
              have this program.

for run prototype: DWORD thread func(LPVOID param);

`lpParam`	Is used to pass the new thread an argument, a 32-bit value.
`dwFlags`	If set to 0, the thread will begin execution immediately. If set to CREATE_SUSPEND, it will be suspended. It can be restarted by a call to ResumeThread().
`lpdwID`	The thread identifier is returned into this variable.
`beginthread( )`	Is a Microsoft C++ equivalent function.

9.11   Deleting Threads

There are three ways to terminate a thread. The first is when its entry thread returns. The second is the `TerminateThread()` function, and the third is the `Exit-Thread()` function, whose prototypes are shown here. `ExitThread()` can be used to terminate only the thread that calls it. And `TerminateThread()` kills a thread immediately, without cleanup.

```
BOOL TerminateThread(HANDLE hThread, DWORD dwStatus);
VOID ExitThread(DWORD dwStatus);
```

where

`hThread`	Is the handle to be terminated
`endthread( )`	Is a Microsoft C++ equivalent function

10

PC and Client/Server Program Coding

10.1 Sybase Set Processing (Client/Server RDBMS)

Sybase SQL Server is based on handling sets—not row-at-a-time processing. This fact makes for a great tuning opportunity when using Sybase. So, whenever you begin to code a new program, keep this fact in mind. RDBMSs are geared more toward set processing, anyway.

If your bulk processing of data has caused you to code row-at-a-time SQL processes, you need to identify these and consider conversion to set coding. Figure 10-1 shows how a master table merge is handled via group-row processing. Although both methods shown are functionally equivalent, the bulk-row processing on the right is much faster than the fetch-row processing on the left. Array fetches can yield I/O reductions of 10 percent to 15 percent.

10.2 ODBC Solutions

Now users can access data in more than one type of *database management system* (DBMS) by using the standard *application programming interface* (API) *Open Database Connectivity* (ODBC). ODBC enables users to access data in heterogeneous environments of relational and nonrelational DBMSs. As a result, developers no longer need to learn multiple database APIs. Instead, they can access, view, and modify data from multiple diverse databases, as well as easily port new and existing applications to new data sources.

The average company has from one to three major *relational database management systems* (RDBMSs) in-house. This is a result of purchasing end-user applications on different data sources. A major reason to use ODBC is to leverage connectivity of these data sources from new software. Technically, this goal

Row Processing (slower)	Set Processing (faster)
| ```
EXEC SQL DECLARE change_cursor FOR
     SELECT new_part_no,
             new_part_name,
             new_cost
     FROM part_updates;
EXEC SQL OPEN change_cursor;
WHILE change_cursor_rows_returned
part_cost)
BEGIN
   EXEC SQL FETCH change_cursor INTO
     new_part_no, new_part_name, new_cost;
   EXEC SQL SELECT part_no, part_name, part_cost
     FROM parts
     WHERE part_no = new_part_no;
   IF not_found THEN
         EXEC SQL INSERT
              INTO parts (part_no, part_name, part_cost)
              VALUES (new_part_no,
                   new_part,
                   new_cost);

   ELSE
         EXEC SQL UPDATE parts
              SET name = new_part,
                 cost = new_cost,
              WHERE part_no = new_part_no;
``` | ```
EXEC SQL UPDATE parts
SET part_name = new_part_name,
    part_cost = new_part_cost,
FROM part_updates;
WHERE new_part_name = parts.part_o;
EXEC SQL INSERT INTO
  part  (part_no, part_name,

SELECT new_part_no, new_part_name,
        new_part_cost
FROM   part_updates
WHERE new_part_no NOT IN
        (SELECT part_no FROM parts);
``` |

Figure 10-1 Row Versus Set Processing

is not easily accomplished. Each relational DBMS may supply proprietary programming interfaces and sophisticated procedures to set up connectivity. ODBC standards are not strictly enforced, either. Standard compliance levels will help you determine whether your solution will fit.

THE ODBC STANDARD

An ODBC-based application can help your organization shift away from database dependence and toward capability dependence. ODBC is a data-access specification that guarantees that data on different platforms can be accessed concurrently (known as *enterprise access*) by using a standard language; SQL is the industry-accepted language (ANSI standards). The specification includes three levels of API conformance: core, level 1 and level 2. ODBC also defines three levels of SQL grammar conformance: minimum, core, and extended. The best you can buy is API level 2 and extended SQL; these yield the most ODBC support.

ODBC PERFORMANCE

ODBC adds a software layer between multiple applications and multiple data sources, which by design adds some degradation. Choosing the right vendor ODBC driver can provide excellent performance, but because there are so many

ODBC vendor products to choose from, I can't offer you any help in choosing one. Here are a couple vendors worth researching, though.

Visigenic Software, Inc. provides components for developers whose applications need to operate with more than one database. Founded by Roger Sippl in February 1993, the company is a leading provider of database connectivity software for the enterprise, including **ODBC** *Software Development Kits* **(SDKs), ODBC DriverSet,** and **ODBC Test Suites**.

Neon Systems Incorporated makes **Enterprise Direct** (LAN-based DBMS access) and **Shadow Direct** for high-speed mainframe ODBC connectivity. The Shadow Direct product offers tuning controls such as these:

- Per-session CPU limit
- Per-SQL-query CPU limit
- Inactivity time-out
- CPU time slicing
- Maximum rows limit
- Static SQL control facility
- Maximum concurrent users
- Query cost governor
- Datastream compression
- Sysplex parallel processing (for CICS)

XBASE USERS

Client/server processing is in high demand by Xbase users looking for better throughput. One of the biggest concerns for Xbase users is providing a fully operational ODBC or client/server solution. Xbase languages let you roll your own LAN code, but they don't work well at all for client/server. Equally valuable to Xbase users are ODBC solutions allowing connectivity to high-end RDBMSs.

A perfect fit for accomplishing a migration from a single-user CA-Clipper database application to a network environment is the **Advantage Xbase Server**, from Extended Systems. This server product improves multiuser performance and seamlessly puts CA-Clipper applications in the client/server realm.

Bridgit, from Unelko Corporation, is another product that provides a multiuser solution for dBASE/Clipper applications.

Q+E Database Library ODBC Pack, from Q+E software, is another multiuser development package that supports 20 different PC and SQL databases.

CA-Ramis/Server is an interesting product. Ramis databases are not the mainstream. However, this product accepts data from multiple sources in Windows and has gateways to DB2, IMS, SQL/DS, VSAM, Terradata and CA-IDMS. The output can be converted to Xbase format. Wow—now that's a lot of connectivity.

GUPTA SQL Network is good for DB2, Oracle and much more.

DB2 NetWare SQL and **SQL Server Bonds** are two products from Revelation Technology. They provide *rapid application development* (RAD) for client/server applications.

XDB-Link, from XDB Systems, provides two components for interfacing the PC to host DB2 data. One component resides on the PC, and the other component resides on the host that ties CICS to the PC through an LU 6.2 protocol interface.

ShowCase Gateway, from Rochester Software Connection, enables Microsoft SQL Server client applications to access DB2/400 (AS/400) data on the host. A companion tool called **WindowLink** links Windows DDE applications to DB2/400 databases, thereby enabling state-of-the-art Windows applications to work with mission-critical data.

The **FoxPro Connectivity Kit**, from Microsoft Corporation, gives developers FoxPro, DB2 and Oracle data access from Windows and DOS applications that will run on client/servers.

Finally, there is the **Enterprise Data Access** (EDA)/SQL product line from Information Builders. This provides access to DB2, DB2/2, DB2/6000 and others with myriad connections and gateways, including UNIX.

These products are just some examples of the ever-growing commitment to client/server as the next platform frontier. Even IBM, with its CICS/6000, APPC, TCP/IP, X/Open DTP, X/Open XA, X/Open SQL, CICS OS/2, CICS/400, AS/400 and RISC System/6000 product lines is looking forward to providing a wide variety of scaleable solutions.

10.3   Software Portability and Database Compatibility

It is important to you, as a developer, to stay abreast of which coding languages provide the best runtime performance. There are several languages to code in that provide varying degrees of performance for Xbased database applications. You will want to pick the best language and maintain your code in a format that is portable to other languages as the times and speeds of competing products change. Figure 10-2 provides a list of some languages. The products listed are quite diverse and vary in their level of compatibility and portability to use the code you already have built.

10.4   Combining Searches in CA-Clipper

I want to share a great technique for reducing searches in a database—assuming, of course, that the user of an application is going to perform several searches, one after another. First, design and build your search key screen to allow the entry of multiple key occurrences. Allow the user to save as many search keys as desired. The application program can place the keys into a memory array or a work database file. Second, sort the keys according to the way they will perform best in index searches against the database. Third, make one pass at the database to satisfy all the search criteria. This technique eliminates redundant scanning or positioning in the database. Although the user can ask

FoxBase

FoxPro

dBase IV

CA-Clipper

Paradox for Windows (mix and match Paradox and Xbase databases)

SuperBase V 2.0 (Super Basic Language with read/write to Xbase databases)

MultiLink/VE (Visual Basic for an Xbase database)

Microsoft Access

Btrieve

Visual Basic

CA-Visual Objects

GUPTA SQL Windows

PowerBuilder

Figure 10-2   Xbase Compatible/Portable/Usable Products

for more at one time, he or she will use less overall because the application will not have to do I/O for the same database blocks multiple times.

10.5   Global Versus Local Variables

Global (or public) variables and arrays are addressable in all procedures in the current application program. Globals generally are defined in the highest-level program so that they are available early in the processing. Globals provide a means to pass information between programs. Because they are available for long periods of time, you should use them discreetly. Here is a sample definition of a public variable called HOTCACHE:

```
PUBLIC HOTCACHE[1000]
```

Local (or private) variables are available for the current procedure and those invoked below the current procedure. Here are three variables defined as private. The first, ZIPARRAY, is a table that can contain 1000 entries:

```
PRIVATE ZIPARRAY[1000], ZIPLAST, ZIPCURR
```

One way to keep storage use under control is not to define globals until the second level of the application. The first level might be a menu. When a person selects a menu option, the second level is invoked. The second level defines the globals. On return to the menu, you have two choices. You can let the global variables remain. In this way, only paths from the main menu that actually were used would have global variables in memory. The other alternative is to issue the CLEAR MEMORY command, which releases all public and private variables —as opposed to the RELEASE ALL command, which releases only private variables. The idea is to free up valuable memory.

10.6   Memory Managers for CA-Clipper

SmartMem, from Integrated Development Corporation, reduces CA-Clipper's memory use and fragmentation in the database's free pool. **ExoSpace** is another tool that permits programs to break the 640KB barrier. By breaking the barrier, you are freed from linking your applications with complex ritualistic overlays. The application will run faster because it is depending on the paging routines of the operating system, which are faster.

10.7   Fast Compilers, Linkers and Runtime Programs

ExtendBase, from Extended Systems, is a tool to provide client/server performance for dBASE and CA-Clipper databases. With ExtendBase, indexing and retrieval functions run faster.

Object linking and embedding (OLE), *dynamic data exchange* (DDE), and the many aspects of *object-oriented programming* (OOP) can enhance development with a degradation in runtime performance. There is hope, though. Vendors are working to provide compilers that translate these high-level interpretive object languages directly into native machine code that will run hundreds of times faster than today.

An example of this kind of development is **CA-Visual Objects**, from Computer Associates. The vendor's literature talks about faster runtimes, giant strides in GUI, object technology and an open database architecture—using *replaceable database drivers* (RDD)—to many of today's leading mainframe and PC databases.

Windows 95, from Microsoft, is a 32-bit preemptive multitasking software with features such as plug-and-play devices. A major benefit of coming forward to Windows 95, Windows NT, or UNIX operating systems is 32-bit and 64-bit architectures and processing speeds. Literally hundreds of drivers have been rewritten to take advantage of 32-bit processing in recent Windows releases.

I can't even keep up with the list of PC software performance enhancements; they happen so fast that if you blink, you miss one. That is the primary reason to have books like this on your shelf. They provide quick reference power for serious administrators.

10.8   Commits for CA-Clipper

The CA-Clipper commit flushes all buffers to DOS and then writes data to the disk drive. Use a counter to determine how often to commit. You even may want to write a checkpoint message. If you do, put the current time in it to enable you to tune your commit logic. Ideally, commits should happen frequently enough to prevent concurrent locking by online users, but not so frequent that they pre-occupy the processor. The rule of thumb is *one for two* and *two for one*, which means that one checkpoint every two seconds and two checkpoints every one second represent the range for online processing. Strictly speaking, a batch doesn't even need to issue a commit unless it is part of some restart logic.

10.9 Avoiding Database Scans with CA-Clipper

Scans of a database can be avoided by using indexes, query optimizers, pre-sorting of records and GOTO commands in programs. A simple GOTO can bypass repetitive processing. To see whether you are incurring duplicate database lookups, put displays of record names and keys after each call. The output will show when the same key is being accessed repetitively.

10.10 Printer Performance

This section addresses printer performance by adjusting the Window's printer options and CA-Clipper alternatives and building your own print-buffer routines.

The most obvious thing you can do to reduce wait time for print queuing is to purchase print-buffering hardware or memory upgrades for printers, such as the Hewlett Packard LaserJet.

Programmatically, you can opt to send printed output to a dataset, which is saved for later printing. With a little ingenuity, you can view a print dataset with an application program, perhaps negating the need to ever actually print it on paper.

Within Windows 3.1, you can change the printing speed from within Print Manager. By selecting Low Priority, printer processing gets fewer ticks, which frees CPU time for other applications. By selecting High Priority, printing gets more ticks.

10.11 Soundex for CA-Clipper

The soundex (or sounds like) key method has been grossly underused. It is a means to access data in a fashion other than alphabetically. Most indexes are alphabetical, and data is accessed by reading a tree with key fields in ascending or descending order. A soundex key is a derivation of the way something sounds. It is ideal for tasks such as spell checkers or name and address directory lookups. For example, *Jeff* also might be spelled *Geoff*. A soundex lookup would bring up both entries on your screen. To create an index on last name and street name is as simple as doing the following:

```
INDEX ON Soundex(LASTNAME) TO LASTNAME
INDEX ON Soundex(STREET)   TO STREET
```

When you need to look up a record, you access the index, as in this example:

```
MOVE soundex("JEF")                    TO LASTNAME
SEEK LASTNAME
```

The SEEK statement returns names that sound like JEF, including JEFF, GEOFF, JEFFF or even GEFF. Now add this interesting code to a database lookup program and allow users to query by using it. Even if the key entered at the terminal is spelled wrong, all possible variant spellings that sound like the search key will be found. Pretty incredible, isn't it? This is why soundex is the basis for spell checkers: It can take variant spellings and match them with a correct spelling.

For items such as Yellow Pages listings (telephony), mass mailing lists, street and address indexes, or customer order screens, a soundex index provides a means to do cleanup of misspelled names, cities, states and streets. One of the main benefits of soundex is that its keys are smaller than their alphabetic counterparts.

Soundex functions are available in SQL Server, FoxPro, Oracle, dBASE and CA-Clipper. Appendix L provides a reasonable COBOL routine that will meet your needs in online batch and database programs for which soundex functions are not provided.

10.12   Metric Analysis of Xbase Databases

One of the current trends is to use quality assurance metrics to improve the quality of data, software, systems, and processes in data processing. There's a lot of this buzzing around in the mainframe world. Well, one specifically for the Xbase folks, **QDB/Analyzer**, from QDB solutions, will measure and analyze Xbase datametrics.

10.13   The SCSI Advantage

Small Computer System Interface (SCSI) controllers have marked advantages over rival *Integrated Development Environment* (IDE) disk controllers. Most of the clonemakers ship machines with IDE or *Enhanced IDE* (EIDE) controllers, which are good for one to four disk drives. But, when you want to build big database systems on the PC, there are several other concerns that IDE won't deal with appropriately. Here are some of the blessings of SCSI:

■ SCSI quadruples the speed of CD-ROM applications.

■ SCSI handles seven drives per SCSI board, each consisting of several gigabytes. You can opt to plug in additional SCSI boards and repeat the process. The result is hundreds of gigabytes of disk storage. This would be a nightmare using IDE, where there are even limitations on the size of a drive that can be used.

■ Because of the incredible flexibility of SCSI and drivers such as COREL, you can mix and match different devices, such as scanners, sound boards,

CD-ROMs, assorted rewriteable optical drives, magnetic drives or *digital signal processors* (DSPs) for voice recognition. With IDE, you often are confronted with discarding devices that are not compatible with other devices.

■ Backup using high-speed SCSI tape drives or rewriteable optical drives is much faster and cost effective than IDE solutions.

■ The most recent SCSI controllers sport higher DMA speeds (greater than 6 Mbps) and expand your capability to optimize performance using SYNC NEGOTIATION and Fast SCSI features. Review these carefully for each device added to the SCSI chain:

SCSI-1	5 Mpbs transfer speed
SCSI-2 (Fast SCSI)	10 Mbps transfer speed
SCSI-2 (Fast-and-Wide)	20 Mbps transfer speed
SCSI-3 (UltraSCSI)	40 Mbps transfer speed

■ Ultra-SCSI controllers are backward compatible with both SCSI-2 and SCSI-1 peripherals. Of course, you won't see a performance boost without an upgrade to the peripherals.

10.14 Performing Rollback and Program Restarts

This is a controversial subject. PC products are just beginning to address the need to roll forward or backward database updates associated with transactions or batch processing. This kind of processing generally is out of the reach of home-grown utilities; it is better to buy a product. Here are some of the vendor-supplied tools:

Restart-Related Products

Product	Description
RDDKit	Produces journal
DB-LOG	Rolls forward and backward

10.15 FoxPro 2.6 Rushmore Query

With FoxPro 2.6, you can rebuild (automigrate) your dBASE indexes to FoxPro format, which will enable you to use Rushmore Query optimization. This query optimizer is one of the fastest for small databases. So, if your applications have many untuned queries, you might want to choose the best optimizer.

10.16 Tuning CA-Clipper Overlay Files

If you create .EXE files that use dynamic overlays, you will want to be sure to assign sufficient filehandles at runtime to increase the speed of loading the overlays, as needed. You can do this by using the dynf parameter:

```
SET CLIPPER=//dynf:6
```

Your changes become a DOS environment variable in the AUTOEXEC.BAT file, or you can implement your changes at execution time by using a command such as this:

```
MYPROG //dynf:6
```

Another way to speed up applications that are linked with overlays is to put the most active functions into the root memory area and tell the Overlay Manager to bypass pageouts of these functions. You can accomplish this with the RESIDENT statement:

```
RESIDENT HOTKEY
RESIDENT CALC
RESIDENT SEARCH
```

Consult your *CA-Clipper Reference Manual* for more information.

10.17   CA-Realia II Workbench
from Computer Associates

CA-Realia is a PC COBOL workbench from Computer Associates that enables you to compile, run, and debug your mainframe programs on the PC. It comes with a mainframe link that retrieves programs from PANVALET, LIBRARIAN ,or a PDS. Also, you can use CICS, CA-IDMS, IMS, and DATACOM DB databases with CA-Realia COBOL. Some other products may be necessary. Tables 10-1 and 10-2 detail the many tuning opportunities with this product.
COBOL programs are the legacy of the 1980s and 1990s. Some of your code can be migrated to the PC. To test the validity of running COBOL batch programs

Platform	Elapsed Time (mm:ss.hh)
IBM 2091 130 MIPS (unoptimized program)	00:07.35
IBM 2091 130 MIPS (optimized program)	00:06.42
386 DX20 (unoptimized program)	07:21.00
386 DX20 (optimized program)	07:19.00
386 DX25 (optimized w/coprocessor)	07:08:00
486 SX33 (optimized program)	03:28.00

Figure 10-3 PC Versus Mainframe COBOL Runtimes

TABLE 10-1   CA-Realia II Workbench Compile and Link Optimization

Method	Benefit
Code optimization	The default is optimized code which runs faster
Optimized performs	CALL and RET instructions will be used which are more efficient
COMP-5	Variables are in INTEL format and are processed faster
Allow LINKAGE/USING mismatch	Saves on LINKAGE moves
Auto segmentation size	Allows code segmentation into pieces smaller than the 64K maximum
Maximum displacement	Avoidance of code segment boundary overlays
/EXEPACK:nnn link parameter	Reduces EXE size
/FARCALLTRANSLATION link parameter	Improves code performance and reduces EXE size
/PACKCODE link parameter	Improves code performance for /FARCALLTRANSLATION parameter
/REORDERSEGMENTS link parameter	Maximizes use of /PACKCODE parameter
/PMTYPE link parameter	For creating segmented EXE or DLL modules
RAM disks	REALCOB.EXE and all files associated with the program (source, object, etc) can be placed on a RAM disk to speed compiles
Alternate link modules	Will reduce EXE file size
Memory management	Link all OS/2 subroutines with the main routine
	OS/2 swapping will manage storage efficiently

TABLE 10-2   CA-Realia II Workbench Runtime Optimization

Method	Benefit
Make calls dynamic	Data name calls default to dynamic
	Literal label calls default to static
	Overrides change the rules
EPDCALL directive	This is faster than dynamic calls for programs compiled with NOEPDCALL
	Using the NOEPDCALL directive will leave the subroutine in memory until the CANCEL verb is issued in the calling routine
Validate numeric sign & decimal digits	Default is to do these checks. Turning off eliminates checking
Abend if DIVIDE by ZERO	Default is not to abend
	Therefore, default is not to do checking
STRING & UNSTRING overflow condition testing	Default is to do checking. Turning off eliminates checking

(Continued)

TABLE 10-2   CA-Realia II Workbench Runtime Optimization (Continued)

Method	Benefit
File status abort	Affects compiler
Validate SUBSCRIPTS and VALUE RANGES	Default is to do checking Turning off eliminates checking
Minimum stack space requirement	Set at compile time and used at run-time
	This only impacts potential abends due to insufficient stack
COMPUTE expression	Replace computes with simple math (ADD SUBTRACT MULTIPLY DIVIDE) where possible to save on unnecessary code generated
Dead code	CA-Realia II will identify unreferenced code and storage variables which can be removed from the program for simplicity
File blocking & buffering	The Bnn, Dnn, Inn and Knn file descriptors allow you to define the block size, number of data blocks, number of index blocks and size of key table respectively.
Alternate READ & WRITE	Identical buffer sizes increase the likelihood of I/O occurring at the same time for input and output files
	Mismatched buffer sizes reduces the coincidence for this
Large BLOCK sizes	More of these improve sequential access
Small INDEX blocks	More of these improve keyed access
Large INDEX & DATA blocks	More of these improve random access
I-O processing	Should be tuned like random access
Memory management	Actions that allocate memory should deallocate them in reverse order to reduce or eliminate fragmentation
	Calling subroutines, opening files, calling DOS_ALLOC and sorts cause memory allocations (true for DOS)

on the PC, I built a program and tested it on the mainframe and the PC. The code is available in Appendix K. Figure 10-3 provides statistics for comparison. The program performed 1.8 million moves and computations.

10.18   32-Bit Compilers for the PC

Microway Inc. out of Kingston, MA, has two cherry products: the **NDP CIC++ C compiler** and **NDP FORTRAN compiler**. Both tools create 32-bit supported programs that will work with Windows NT, MS-DOS, UNIX, and OS/2. And, both knock down the program-size barrier. Programs can be up to 4GB and can run on the Pentium using the architecture for they were designed.

MetaWare Inc. out of Santa Cruz, CA, has the **High C++ 32-bit compiler**, which works with Windows, UNIX, and OS/2. This is another compiler that takes advantage of Pentium power.

10.19 Searching for Slow Motion in Your Programs

Another useful way to find places in your program where performance tuning would benefit is by using a completion gauge. In Visual Basic, for example, you can define a gauge that will display a color bar or meter that indicates processing from 0 to 100 percent. You can watch the processing and determine where the processing is excessively slow. In Figure 10-4, this is at 35 percent. You then would return to your program code and match the slow processing to lines of code where the gauge was incremented.

10.20 Super-Fast File Opens for CA-Clipper

I found this great tuning feature by accident while trying to improve the installation properties of a program written for a customer. If you test for the existence of a file in each of the PC drives C through J, it is possible to set default and path directories in your Clipper program. In this way, you don't search additional paths and subdirectories looking for database files that will be written to or read from. This saved me 50 percent elapsed time: I mean, the program really screamed. I never realized that so much time had been wasted before. The benefit was derived in the USE and SELECT statements.

10.21 Parallelization of User Programs

Parallelization is not a reality in your applications today—that is, unless you have a guru in your midst. Wouldn't it be nice to be able to update your tables using code similar to that in the following statement, which theoretically fires up four parallel processes to do table updates automatically?

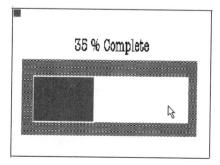

Figure 10-4 Completion Gauge

```
BEGIN PARALLEL
        LOOP
        UNTIL END_OF_INPUT
                BEGIN_PROCESS
                                IF GL_MONTH < 12 INSERT INTO GL_QTR_4
                END_PROCESS
                BEGIN_PROCESS
                                IF GL_MONTH < 9 INSERT INTO GL_QTR_3
                END_PROCESS
                BEGIN_PROCESS
                                IF GL_MONTH < 6 INSERT INTO GL_QTR_2
                END_PROCESS
                BEGIN_PROCESS
                                IF GL_MONTH < 3 INSERT INTO GL_QTR_1
                END_PROCESS
        ENDLOOP
    END PARALLEL;
```

Well, as I was saying, parallelization of user programs isn't much of a reality today. Don't get the wrong idea. You can write parallel applications, but it sure isn't easy. It wouldn't take much for the software giants to provide this capability in their development tools. Why should this be limited to utilities such as load, unload, backup, and restore? This architecture should be available for everything.

The squeaky wheel gets the grease, so don't be afraid to ask for something.

10.22   Xbase PC Database and System Tuning

I already covered file buffers and handles in earlier chapters. At this time, I will just mention a few products that will provide faster than normal *replaceable database drivers* (RDDs) specifically designed for CA-Clipper and FoxPro 2 databases.

First is **Six Driver**. It shrinks indexes, which saves valuable disk space, and increases index build and access speed. This product enables you to selectively build indexes on specific index keys, which further reduces access times.

The second product is **COMIX**, which speeds index building by 10 times. Support for .cmx multikey format, scoped indexes, smaller indexes, and Exo-Space are some of the finer sales points.

Flex File II is really neat. You can have compressed database files or strings. Files can contain a mixture of compressed and uncompressed fields. Variable length fields also are supported.

ExoSpace is a DOS extender for CA-Clipper programs that allows .exes of up to 16MB. You even may find that some of those pesky swap files and *virtual memory* (VM) errors will just disappear. The tool is implemented by linking with your application programs.

11

Sybase 11 Tuning

As with all *relational database management systems* (RDBMSs), high performance in Sybase is a product of proper database design, query design, system hardware and software implementation. There are many decisions to make during an application's life cycle. When dealing with the operating system, the network, servers, and hardware issues, the decisions are compounded. An awareness of every available option during application and server design can prevent costly errors in judgment. Performance is not an add-on; it must be designed into your servers and applications. The following subsections list the major tuning subjects covered in this chapter. Refer to Chapter 1, "Statistics Collection," for additional information about collecting Sybase statistics. When tuning a RDBMS as robust as Sybase, you need to decide where to begin. There are so many different areas to address, as this list suggests.

APPLICATIONS AND API

Client processing	Client library facilities
Bulk processing	Queries
Stored procedures	Triggers
Deadlock prevention	Replication
Cursors	Optimizer

DATABASES

Table structures	Clustered and nonclustered indexes
Page size	Partitioning/Striping/Segments

Mirroring   Read-only cursors and tables

Space thresholds   tempdb

Bitmapped indexes (IQ)

NETWORKS

NetWare   Protocols

Packets   NLMs

SQL SERVER

RDBMS release level   Spinlocks and thresholds

Parallel processing options   Configuration of server(s)

SMP, MPP, and clustering   Housekeeper tasks

Data and named caches   Hot backups

Procedure caches   *Private log cache* (PLC)

Checkpointing   Workload management

Total locks   Recovery intervals

Task and transaction throughput   Local and remote users/servers

SysAudit security   Sleeping processes

OPERATING SYSTEM

OS (UNIX versus NT)   Shared memory or engines

HARDWARE

Number and speed of engines   Disks/RAID/Controllers

Amount and speed of memory   Bus speeds

Number and speed of NICs   Fast Ethernet/Fibre

Fail over   Workstations

Because several RDBMSs are covered in detail in this book, many facets of tuning could be presented redundantly. I've chosen to uniquely address specific subjects in one RDBMS or another, and let the reader use the index to find these. Most of the common network-administration knowledge is in Chapter 17, "Communications and Networking," for example. You can find a good essay on *Systems Network Architecture* (SNA) and VTAM tuning in Chapter 6, "Microsoft SQL Server 6.5 Tuning," however, as well as a discussion of *redundant array of inexpensive disks* (RAID) technology. You can find additional terms common to client/server databases at the beginning of Chapter 7, "Oracle 7.3 Tuning." This approach avoids two problems that every writer faces: too many chapters and too much redundancy.

Sybase terminology will be unfamiliar to the newcomer. I will try to introduce a handful of commonplace terms peculiar to Sybase (many also are peculiar to Microsoft SQL Server). It is important to understand these terms before stumbling over them later in the text. Also, repetition of terms will solidify your understanding. Advanced readers may now skip ahead to section 11.1, "Sybase SQL Server 11 Performance Enhancements."

Many manuscripts try to familiarize the reader with complex terms by supplying an exhaustive glossary instead of offering points of reference based on the reader's experience. Because so many *distributed database administrators* (DBAs) and programmers are faced with a transition between database worlds, a point of reference probably would be welcome. In response to this need, correlations between DBMSs are presented along with definitions of the terms.

We live in the information age. One of the benefits of being here is that a great deal of information is available, as well as plenty of software to deal with it. One of the detriments is that there is too much information to accumulate and too much software to learn. Today's DBA must learn multiple databases, development tools, network protocols, and more. A commonplace problem that comes with the turf is semantics. A good example is the term *SQL Server*. Both Sybase and Microsoft have SQL Servers. When you refer to *SQL Server*, which one do you mean? For the rest of this chapter, SQL Server refers to the *Sybase SQL Server*. Now take a look at some Sybase terms that could be confused with other databases or that have unique meanings.

One widely used term that can mean different things to different people is *scalability*. For some, *scalability* means that software can be ported to a platform with greater or less processing power. For others, *scalability* means that the underlying hardware platform can be upgraded. Either of these definitions works with Sybase. Scalability can be a product of moving applications across hardware platforms or using *symmetric multiprocessing* (SMP) to increase the number of processors available on the current platform. Therefore, both software and hardware are scaleable.

Another term is *engineering bug fix* (EBF). For mainframers, an EBF is the same as a *program temporary fix* (PTF), a patch or APAR (IBM's official name). EBFs in the Sybase world arrive on disks and are applied differently than in the mainframe world. Mainframe PTFs can arrive on disk, via e-mail, or on tape (9-, 18-, and 36-track).

Hopefully, you are familiar with the term *client/server*; this is when some of the work is done on the client machine and some on the server. Well, prepare for a real focus on client/server. Sybase is the mother of client/server database systems.

If you are used to Oracle, here are some subtle differences. Type `go` on a line by itself to indicate the end of the command line (instead of a semicolon (;), as in Oracle). Forget *decode, spool* and *column*—these are Oracle-specific extensions that have no Sybase equivalent. You can change databases (on one server) without logging out; just issue the command `use <database_name>`. Wow. That's the same way it's done on dBASE and CA-Clipper.

Sybase provides a collection of system procedures that are quite helpful. If you want to get a list of objects in a database, for example, execute the procedure `sp_help`. If you want a list of databases on the server, execute `sp_helpdb`. If you want help on a particular database or object, use `sp_helpdb <database_name>` or `sp_help <object_name>`.

A *temporary tablespace* is a database that is shared by all databases on a server and is called tempdb. Yes, it has the same purpose as tempdb on Microsoft SQL Server. All RDBMSs have to do this kind of work somewhere. Even DB2 uses a temporary worktable.

Sybase has its share of caching mechanisms. A *procedure cache* is used for query plans, stored procedures, and triggers, whereas a *data cache* is for data, index and log pages. Specific databases or database objects can be bound to named data caches for the sake of performance. Data caches can come in different page sizes.

Perhaps the most enduring term you will learn is `sp_configure`. This term is like the sysgen in mainframe databases or the `init.ora` file in Oracle. Yes, again, it has the same purpose as `sp_configure` in Microsoft SQL Server. What a coincidence. It is at the crux of system tuning.

Two vehicles actually exist to implement system parameters for Sybase: the `sp_configure` procedure and the `buildmaster -y` mechanism. Many of the system parameters can be found in both tools. However, the `sp_configure` procedure should take precedence because it actually causes some buildmaster parameters to be recomputed and changed. If you attempt to make changes after that, you could lose valuable tuning changes when `sp_configure` is modified. For this reason, it is recommended that you also keep a copy of the parameters used in `sp_configure` and the output from `buildmaster -yall`.

Network communications in Sybase uses *tabular datastream* (TDS) packets, as does Microsoft SQL Server. DBAs can address many items when tuning TDS packet communications; an obvious item is the packet size.

The *Database Consistency Checker* (DBCC) is a utility that validates the integrity of a database. Several DBCC commands are useful when tuning a database.

A *heap table* is a table without a clustered index (a table can have one clustered index and up to 249 nonclustered indexes). The rows on this type of table are in insert order. Essentially, all inserts to a heap table are made to the last page of the page chain.

The *Private Log cache* (PLC) is a release-11 enhancement. This feature maintains log records in memory instead of writing them to the log file. This feature also is referred to as the *User Log cache* (ULC).

The area at the end of the buffer cache is called the *wash area*. If it is too small, I/Os might have to wait. Generally, the wash area is OK, but it might need adjustment.

I find the *row ID* (RID) intriguing. It is effectively identical to the RID in a CA-IDMS network database. In fact, the RID table is built the same way. Row IDs are managed by an offset table on each data page. The offset table is filled beginning with the last byte on the page. A 2-byte entry with the offset to a row on the page is stored. As the offset table grows, it backfills the page.

The similarities between RDBMSs are quite logical. It is easier to use something that exists and works than to invent something new. Most database systems are a collage of existing features brought together from other products. Sybase has *leaf pages*, for example; these are the lowest-level pages in an index, which contain the keys. Leaf pages work almost identically to those in DB2. *Page splits* and *overflows* in Sybase are pretty much identical to those in CA-IDMS. So, as you can see, much of the knowledge attributed to database management can be used with any RDBMS.

One of the fastest ways to process on the mainframe is to do an *index sweep*, during which you look only at the index pages. With Sybase, this is known as *index coverage*. Only the leaf pages actually are read. So, you can build multicolumn indexes with lots of valuable information and sweep them in a standalone fashion.

Global allocation map (GAM) pages are used to locate free extents in the database where objects can be stored. If all the bits are turned on in the GAM page, no free extents are available in the database.

An *extent* is a block of eight pages. It is the smallest amount of space that can be allocated to a table or index. Normally, an extent is owned by whatever object/index combination first uses it.

Space allocations vary from the eight-page minimum up to a 256-page maximum, each with an *allocation page* as the first page. Extent use by objects and individual page use within the 256 pages is recorded in the allocation page. It also stores the page ID for the *object allocation map* (OAM) page of any object stored on an extent.

Object allocation map (OAM) pages are control pages embedded in each table and index. They store index, table, and text object pointer chains to allocation pages. You quickly can find space by using these chains. One OAM page can map 250 allocation units (2000 to 63,750 data or index pages). Multiple OAM pages may be needed to store the mappings for an entire database.

A database can be broken up into 32 *segments*, with each segment residing on one or more logical devices. The system creates three additional segments— system, log, and default—in addition to the user-defined segments.

When a task alters a cache, a mechanism called a *spinlock* single threads access to the cache while changes are made. The duration of the spinlock is very brief. Because these locks are single threaded, they must be tuned.

Query variables derived by using the COUNT, SUM OR AVERAGE, MINIMUM, or MAXIMUM functions are *aggregates*. When combined with the GROUP BY clause, they are called *grouped* or *vector aggregates*. If the function produces a single value, it is a *scalar aggregate* or *ungrouped aggregate*.

Numerous Web sites provide more information on these topics. You can find the Sybase FAQ at

```
http://reality.sgi.com/pablo/Sybase_FAQ/
```

Also, a large list of Sybase sites is provided at

```
http://announce.com/~jdunham/power.htm
```

11.1   Sybase SQL Server 11 Performance Enhancements

I don't know how to describe release 11. It's big—really big. This was Sybase Corporation's attempt to get back on top. They tackled every major area of complaint with release 10, gambling on the high-stakes race for market share.

ENHANCEMENTS

- Showplan enhanced to show

  Line numbers to help locate statements in query text

  Subquery numbers and nesting levels for each subquery's plan

  Type of subquery

  Where each subquery is nested

  Types of scans

  Index coverage

  Index keys used to limit scan

  Worktable numbers

  Clustered index name

- Queries and subqueries

  Short circuiting

  Better flattening

  Materialization

  Caching

  Elimination of sort for DISTINCT expression subqueries

  No more GROUP BY ALL for quantified predicates

  Most recently used (MRU) or fetch-and-discard strategy

  Set dup no longer supported (rewrite query as join)

  Subqueries no longer allowed in updatable cursors

Maximum 16 subqueries on one side of a UNION restriction

Inside-out and unnest subqueries changed to nested loop

Group By All no longer used by quantified predicates

NOT IN, NOT EXISTS and ALL subqueries run faster

Subqueries in OR clauses run faster

- Deadlock checking period added
- Page use percent parameter
- New user log cache
- New sybsystemprocs stored procedures
- New system messages added to table sysmessages
- Two new ANSI keywords
- New stored procedure output
- Backup server tape support changes
- Threshold changes
- New *Private Log cache* (PLC)

It is really important that you test your queries under release 11 before cutting over to production. Think about this: Stored procedures, triggers, or views that contain subqueries won't automatically take advantage of the new subquery changes until you drop and re-create the compiled objects. There is no way to know what to expect until the new query behavior is monitored. Subqueries with large outer tables and small inner tables may not perform well. You may be forced to modify these queries to emulate release-10 processing. You can use the procedure sp_procqmode to determine which compiled objects contain subqueries.

More memory is required for the 11 kernel, new user log cache, locks, and larger compiled objects (stored procedures, triggers and rules). Consequently, the procedure cache also must be increased for these objects.

It's a good idea to run sp_checkreswords on each database from a sybinit session (installation and upgrade utility) to discover any conflicts between your names and the new ANSI-reserved keywords in Sybase 11.

11.2 Commonly Supported Platforms

This section lists some of the more familiar platforms on which Sybase is running (see Table 11-1). I don't think anyone could compare all the trade-offs for these platforms because there are so many operating systems and third-party software complexities that go along with the hardware. Just reference this list if you are interested in whether some release of Sybase will run on a platform you have. Keep in mind that the software industry undergoes major changes every six months, and hardware platform support can double every two years.

Just for the record, my favorite platform is DEC Alpha OSF/1 3.0. I've heard of benchmarks with 14,176+ tpmC on the Digital Alpha Server 8400 (10 CPUs),[1] 14,739+ tpmC on the HP9000 Model K460 Enterprise Server (RISC 4 CPUs), and 18,438+ tpmC on the Sun Ultra Enterprise 6000 (20 CPU cluster). These are whoppers indeed. I haven't seen big numbers like these for Windows NT-based systems, but that doesn't mean they don't exist. However, this lack of information could imply that Sybase on Windows NT isn't going to yield the same throughput as some of the 64-bit operating systems. Time changes everything, though. We will just have to wait to see what happens when Windows NT goes 64-bit, and Microsoft's clustering technology extends beyond 16 clusters.

TABLE 11-1   Commonly Supported Sybase Platforms/Software (partial list)

Supported Platforms and Software
AT&T (NCR) SRV4 2.03.01
AT&T (NCR) System 3000 UNIX SVR4 MPRAS
AT&T System 3000 UNIX SVR4 MPRAS
AT&T UNIX 2.02
Chinese character sets
Data General DGUX 5.4, 5.4.2, 5.4.2.01, 5.4R2, 5.4R2.1, 5.4R3.10
DB-Library for DOS, OS/2, Windows
DEC 2100 sable machines
DEC Alpha AXP OpenVMS 1.5, 6.1, OpenVMS 1.5+UCX, OpenVMS+UCX 3.1
DEC Alpha OSF/1 1.3, 1.2.1, 2.0, 2.0b, 3.0
DEC RISC Ultrix 4.3, 4.3a, 4.4
DEC VAX OpenVMS 5.4+UCX 3.1, OpenVMS 5.4+Wollongon
DEC VAX OpenVMS 5.5-2, 6.0, 6.1
DECnet Phase IV, UCX 3.2 and Multinet 3.2 or Multinet 3.3
Digital OpenVMS Alpha 1.0, 1.5
Digital OSF/1
Digital VAX OpenVMS
EISA bus
Embedded SQL/C Precompiler for Windows
Embedded SQL/COBOL Precompiler for Windows
HP 9000 Series 800 HP-UX
HP300 HP-UX 8.0, 8.01, 8.02, 8.05, 8.07, 9.0, 9.0.1, 9.03, 9.05
HP800 HP-UX 8.06, 8.08, 9.0, 9.0+LVM, 9.04, 9.04+LVM, 8mm tape device
HP9000/800 (Network Gateway)
IBM RISC System/6000 AIX

---

[1] The tpmC benchmarks shown were found at the Transaction Processing Councils Web site at www.tpc.org.

TABLE 11-1 Commonly Supported Sybase Platforms/Software (partial list) (Continued)

Supported Platforms and Software

IBM RS6000 4mm tape device

IBM RS6000 3.2.*X* SP/1, 3.2.*X* SP/2, 4.1.1 (UP)

IBM RS6000 AIX 3.2, 3.2.1, 3.2.2, 3.2.3e, 3.2.4, 3.2.5, 3.2.5+PowerPC Chi, 3.2.5+SPX/IPX

ICL DRS 6000 DRS/NX V7L2

Manager Server for Windows NT

Motorola SVR4 R$V4.1

NEC SVR4 R6.1

Net-Library FTP PC/TCP for DOS, Windows

Net-Library IBM TCP for OS/2

Net-Library Microsoft TCP for DOS

Net-Library Named Pipes for DOS, OS/2, Windows

Net-Library Novell IPX/SPX for DOS, OS/2

Net-Library Novell LAN Workplace for DOS, OS/2, Windows

Net-Library WinSock for Windows

NetWare 386 3.11, 3.12, 4.0.1, 4.0.2

NetWare 4.02

Novell NetWare

ODBC for Windows

Open Client/C Developers Kit for DOS, OS/2, Windows NT

Open Client/CICS/LU6.2 (mainframe access)

Open Server for OS/2, Windows NT

Open Server/CICS/TCP_IP (mainframe access)

Open Server/IMS/LU6.2 (mainframe access)

OS/2

OS/2 1.2.1, 1.3*x.x*, 2.0, 2.1

OS 2.00.01

OS/2 Net-G (Network Gateway)

OSAM/DB2/CICS/LU6.2 (mainframe access)

OSAM/DB2/CICS/TCP_IP (mainframe access)

OSAM/DB2/IMS/LU6.2 (mainframe access)

Pentium

Pyramid N 1.1 93d067, Nile D067

Pyramid S 1.1 93c062, SVR4 C034, SVR4 C044, SVR4 C062

Pyramid T 5.1a 93a060, OSx 5.1A

Replication Server for Windows NT

RS6000 (Network Gateway)

SCO 3.2.4, 3.2.4.2, R3.2 V4.2

TABLE 11-1   Commonly Supported Sybase Platforms/Software (partial list) (Continued)

Supported Platforms and Software
SCO Open Desktop Release 3.0.
SCO Open Server Enterprise System Release 3.0
Sequent DYNIX 1.2, 1.4, 2.0.1, 2.1.0, 4.0
Silicon Graphic IRIX 3.2, IRIX 5.1, IRIX 5.1.1.1, IRIX 5.2, not IRIX 6.2
Solaris (Network Gateway)
Sony NEWS R6.0.1
Sparccenter 1000
SPARCserver 1000E
SPX/IPX
SQL Monitor Client for Windows
SQL Server Manager for Windows
SQR Execute for DOS
SQR for OS/2
SQR Workbench for DOS
SQR Workbench for Windows
Stratus FTX 2.2.2(y), VOS 10.5, VOS 11.6, FTX 2.2.2, FTX 2.2.2.3
Sun OS Release 4.*x* (BSD)
Sun Solaris 2.*x*
SUN *Japanese Feature Package* (JFP)
SUN *Japanese Language Environment* (JLE)
SUN *Korean Feature Package* (KFP)
SUN *Korean Language Environment* (KLE)
Sun4 Solaris 2.2, 2.3, 2.3+SPARCstor, 2.3+SPX/IPX
Sun4 SunOS 4.1.1, 4.1.1+DBE 1.1, 4.1.2, 4.1.2+DBE 1.2, 4.1.3, 4.1.3+DBE 1.3
Sun4 SunOS 4.1.3, 4.1.3c, 4.1.3.u1, 4.1.3.u1b, 4.1.3/sparc10
SunOS (Network Gateway)
SunOS Release 4.*x* (BSD)
Unisys 65 SVR4 1.2
Unisys 75 Dynix 1.3.1
Unisys U6000 75 SVR4 1.3, 65 SRV4 1.2
WIN-TPC: (i386) 02.00.04.02
WIN-TCP/IP 2.00.04, 2.00.05, 2.01.00.12, 2.01.01.08, 2.02.00.07
Windows DB-Library (4.2)
Windows Net-Library
Windows NT, NT 3.5

While operating systems are fresh in your mind, realize that there are limits to hardware performance. CPUs, disk subsystems, and networks have physical limits. Faster processors often help, as do additional controllers and memory. At some point, however, hardware will no longer deliver any benefit. Even though it is wise to regularly tune an RDBMS and its applications, it isn't always a necessity. When your application is confronted by the boundaries of the hardware, however, tuning is no longer a luxury: It now becomes a necessity. The next section takes a look at the logical starting point for tuning Sybase SQL Server: the memory pool.

11.3 Memory Tuning

Memory tuning in Sybase SQL Server, as in Microsoft SQL Server, is tricky because many of the parameters are interrelated. A change to one area of memory can adversely affect another area. During SQL Server startup, internal structures are allocated based on `sp_configure` parameters. The memory that remains after internal data structures are allocated is divided between the procedure and data caches. Your goal is to assign the proper amount of memory for these two cache areas and the internal structures of SQL Server. Here is a list of items constituting memory use and the corresponding setting you use to control them.

Memory Use (peak shift use desired)	Configuration Parameter
Number of users connected	Number of users connected
	Number of remote connections
Number of locks used	Number of locks
Number of devices used	Total memory*
Static server overhead (fixed)	Total memory*
Number of databases open at peak hours of use	Number of open databases
Cache requirements for query plans in use during peak shift	`sp_cacheconfig` default or named caches
Cache requirements for tempdb	`sp_cacheconfig` named cache
Cache requirements and I/O size for log	`sp_cacheconfig` named cache
Cache requirements for user tables and indexes	`sp_cacheconfig` named caches
Number of initial stack entries	Stack size
Procedure cache size	Procedure cache percent
Memory size	Total memory*
Data cache size	Total memory*

*These items come out of the total memory allocation.

HINTS FOR BETTER MEMORY USE

- The percentage of cache buffers to memory should never drop below 50 percent for nondedicated servers.

- The percentage of cache buffers to memory should never drop below 30 percent for dedicated servers.

- If SQL Server is issuing errors, make sure `Minimum Number of Cache Buffers` is not set too high.

- Configure memory pools and bind objects to caches during off-peak hours.

- Binding and unbinding objects can slow performance because they may need to be flushed to disk (if dirty) or read from disk again when needed.

- SQL Server acquires an exclusive lock on the table or index while the cache is being cleared, so binding can slow other users of the object.

- Solaris 2.*x* users can configure *intimate shared memory* (ISM), which improves paging for heavily loaded systems. You must set the server to a size at which the Solaris kernel can lock into physical memory.

- Using `dbcc memusage`, if the sum of the pages represented by the top 20 objects in the buffer cache is greater than or equal to the number of page buffers, increase the size of the buffer cache. Decrease the size of the `Procedure Cache Percent` parameter or increase the `Total Memory` parameter in `sp_configure`.

- If the CPERRLOG shows 701 or 702 errors, increase the size of the `Procedure Cache Percent` parameter using `sp_configure`.

- If `% of Total` on `Procedures Read From Disk` or `Procedure Removals` is greater than 2 percent of `Procedure Requests` (`sp_sysmon` report), increase the size of the `Procedure Cache Percent` parameter.

- If negative timeslice errors on the log occur frequently, increase the `Time Slice` and `CPU Grace Time` `sp_configure` values.

- Make stored procedures out of frequently executed views and queries.

- One of the biggest problems for SQL Server is operating system page faults. When a page fault occurs, the entire server goes into a wait state. Multithreading ceases to exist for the duration of the fault. Therefore, it is of utmost importance to provide adequate memory for the operating system. It is better to configure SQL Server with less memory and to suffer an increase in physical I/O than to incur page faults.

- Bind syslogs to a separate data cache and configure a 4KB memory pool in its named cache to benefit from a larger I/O size, as defined by the `sp_logiosize` parameter. If you do not have a 4KB memory pool, logging may default to 2KB.

- Provide 4-, 8- and 16KB pools as `sp_sysmon` tuning indicates. Begin with a 16KB pool and transfer space to a different pool using `sp_poolconfig`.

- Bind tempdb to a separate data cache using 16KB I/O.

- Bind sysindexes, sysojbects, syscolumns, and sysprotects to a separate data cache.

- Use multiple data caches when spinlock contention exceeds 10 percent.

- If the `sp_sysmon` data cache management value `Cache Hits` is less than 98 percent, or the value `Cache Misses` is greater than 2 percent, the default or named cache performance may improve if enlarged.

- If the `sp_sysmon` data cache management value `Buffers Grabbed` is high, the default or named cache performance may improve if enlarged.

- If the `sp_sysmon` data cache management value `Pages by Lrg I/O Used` percent is low, the memory pool size or caching strategy should be changed.

- If the `sp_sysmon` data cache management value `Dirty Reads` or `Dirty Read Re-starts` is not zero, the buffer cache should be larger or the wash size should be smaller.

- If the `sp_sysmon` data cache management value `Spinlock` is high, using named caches may improve performance for SMP systems.

- If the `sp_sysmon` data cache management value `Utilization` is low, you need to reevaluate the named cache size or caching strategy.

- If the `sp_sysmon` data cache management value `LRU Buffer Grab` is greater than 2 percent, the pools are too small. If the `Grabbed Dirty` value is greater than 2 percent, the wash area is too small.

- If the `sp_sysmon` data cache management value `Wash Hits` is high, the wash area size may be too large. If decreasing the wash-area size reduces the cache hit percentage, increase the cache size.

- If the `sp_sysmon` data cache management value `Large I/Os Denied` exceeds 50 percent, try using a smaller pool size.

- If the `sp_sysmon` data cache management value `Large I/O Pages Used` divided by the `Large I/O Pages Cached` value is less than 50 percent, try using a smaller pool size.

- If heavily accessed table pages are being written to disk too frequently, try increasing the `cbufwashsize` parameter.

- If heavily accessed index pages are being written to disk too frequently, try increasing the `Number of Index Trips` parameter.

- If heavily accessed OAM pages are being written to disk too frequently, try increasing the `Number of OAM Trips` parameter.

- If any memory pool is underused, eliminate it. If it is experiencing a poor cache hit ratio, tune it.

dbcc memusage

dbcc memusage takes a snapshot of your procedure and buffer cache memory use. Figure 11-1 shows a sample DBCC execution.

I won't discuss everything you could possibly learn about dbcc memusage output. You should refer to the Sybooks manuals for complete instruction. I will provide you with the information I think is important for quickly tuning, though. To begin with, you need to understand what each of the output lines

```
1> dbcc traceon(3604)
2> go
1> dbcc memusage                                                    (A)
2> go

Memory Usage:

                              Meg.        2K Blks          Bytes

       Configured Memory:256.0000         131072       268435456     (B)
             Code size:    2.8144           1441         2951168     (C)
      Kernel Structures: 78.3691           40125        82176000     (D)
      Server Structures: 58.5907           29999        61436832     (E)
             Page Cache: 92.9785           47605        97495040     (F)
           Proc Buffers:  1.0722             549         1124352     (G)
           Proc Headers: 22.1738           11353        23250944     (H)

Number of page buffers:    44221                                     (I)
Number of proc buffers:    15286                                     (J)

Buffer Cache, Top 20:

           DB Id       Object Id     Index Id      2K Buffers

              7         505980312          0           10433         (K)
              7         594416976          0            9320         (L)
              7         886359889          0            5288         (M)
              7         116331948          5            4378         (N)
              7        1082800587          2            1997         (O)
...

Procedure Cache, Top 20:

Database Id: 6
Object Id: 2024357111
Object Name: daves_stuff
Version: 1
Uid: 1
Type: stored procedure
Number of trees: 0
Size of trees: 0.000000 Mb, 0.000000 bytes, 0 pages
Number of plans: 14
Size of plans: 0.630859 Mb, 661504.000000 bytes, 323 pages     (P)
...
1> dbcc traceoff(3604)
2> go
```

Figure 11-1 A dbcc memusage Example

means; they are labeled A through P in the figure and the following text. All items are in 2KB pages; so you can multiply pages by 2KB to arrive at bytes and then divide by 1024 twice to arrive at the megabytes column.

(A) The command is easy enough. If you precede the command with `dbcc traceon(3604)`, the output is directed to the screen instead of CPERRLOG.

(B) `Configured Memory` is the total of the other items listed in C through H. It does not have to match exactly.

(C-D) Not important

(E) This is affected directly by changes to `sp_configure` items affecting the number and size of internal data structures.

(F-H) These three items represent the caches. **(G)** is the maximum number of compiled procedural objects that can reside in the procedure cache at one time. Each object requires at least one page. **(H)** is the number of 2KB pages that make up the procedural cache area.

(I) `Page Buffers` equates to the number of 2KB pages in the allocated data cache. In Figure 11-1, 44,221 pages or 86.4MB of data is cached.

(J) `Proc Buffers` equates to the number of 2KB pages in the allocated procedure cache. In Figure 11-1, there are 15,286 pages or 29.86MB of procedure cache.

(K-O) The 20 largest objects are listed, of which you see five. The information is cryptic, but these notes will help you decipher its meaning. Working from left to right on item **(O)**, the DBID is 7 (entry repeated here):

```
    DB Id          Object Id      Index Id       2K Buffers
    7           1082800587            2             1997      (O)
```

You can see a less cryptic database name with the following command:

```
select db_name(7)
```

```
accounts
```

The OBJECT ID is `1082800587`. You can determine the name of this object by entering the following:

```
select object_name(1082800587)
```

```
invoice_indx
```

The INDEX ID is `2`. Some of the values for INDEX follow:

0	Table data
1	Clustered index
2-250	Nonclustered index
255	Text pages

The total 2KB buffers is 1997, which equals 3.9MB. Notice that the five entries shown in (K-O) total 31,408 pages or 61.34MB of storage. This represents 71 percent of the total 86.4MB of storage allocated to the buffer cache.

(P) The final elements displayed are the top 20 procedure cache objects. In Figure 11-1, you see the first in the list: a stored procedure called daves_stuff. The plans for this object use .63MB of storage. It just so happens that this is the largest plan in your system, too.

In addition to the dbcc memusage output, you need to display the Number of Locks, Number of User Connections and Number of Open Objects from sp_configure, as in the following:

```
1> sp_configure "number of locks"
2> go


Locks
100000


1> sp_configure "number of user connections"
2> go


User Connections
500


1> sp_configure "number of open objects"
2> go


Open Objects
5000
```

CACHE USE FROM CPERRLOG

A third source of valuable memory-tuning information is CPERRLOG. If you search from the end of the log backward and locate the most recent occurrences of the following three messages, you will be able to determine the actual cache use:

```
Server: Number of buffers in buffer cache: 28000
Server: Number of proc buffers allocated: 10500
Server: Number of blocks left for proc headers: 5500
```

The first message shown is an indication of the size of the data cache. The second message shows the number of proc buffers, not pages. Because 21 objects fit on a standard page, this number represents 500 pages of memory.
Data cache pages = 10,500/21 = 500 pages
The third number is the size of the procedure cache. Summed, these three items make up 34,000 memory pages. This total represents the cache in use (or

the sum of items F, G, and H) in the dbcc memusage display. So, of the 59,507 pages in both caches, only 34,000 pages are in use.

There is yet another way to determine the memory use of currently running procedures, which is effectively the size of the procedure cache:

```
1>      select sum(memusage) from sysprocesses
2>      go
```

COMPUTING sp_configure MEMORY-RELATED SETTINGS

The method used to determine each of the sp_configure settings is based on formulas. When you first install Sybase, you must make some assumptions about numbers for different parameters. After you install Sybase, you will monitor with dbcc memusage and adjust the system memory based on the following formulas. You will substitute the values from your findings so far.

User-Connections Storage
User_connection_MB = (number of user connections * 40,960) / 1,048,576
   19.53MB = (500 * 40,960) / 1,048,576

Open Databases and Objects Storage
Open_databases_MB = (number of open objects * 644) / 1,048,576
   3.07MB = (5000 * 644) / 1,048,576

Devices
Devices_MB = number of devices * 45,056
   4.29MB = 100 * 45,056

Locks Storage
Locks_MB = (number of locks * 32) / 1,048,576
   3.05MB = (100000 * 32) / 1,048,576

Server Static Overhead Storage
1.2MB = Static_overhead_MB

Stack Storage
Stack_storage_MB = (stack size * 100)
   9.7MB = (102,400 * 100)

#1 Top Plan Size
Top_plan_MB = (#1 plan from dbcc memusage / # of plans)
   0.045MB = (0.63MB / 14)

Procedure Cache Storage
Procedure_cache_MB = (number of user connections * Top_plan_MB) * 1.25
   28.1MB = (500 * 0.045MB) * 1.25
   Procedure_cache_pages = (Procedure_cache_MB * 1,048,576) / 2,048

14,387 = (28.1 * 1,048,576)/2,048

Procedure_cache_pct = Procedure_cache_pages/(number of proc buffers + number of page buffers)

24 percent = 14,387/(15,286 + 44,221)

Revised_memory_pages = Procedure_cache_pages/(number of proc buffers/total memory)

123,364 = 14,387/(15,286/131,072)

Based on the example that showed 15,286 proc buffers, you could set the size of the `Procedure Cache Percent` parameter to 24 percent. This would release the extra memory for use by the buffer cache. Alternatively, you could reduce the configured memory to 123,364, releasing 7,708 pages to the operating system kernel. These two alternatives were computed in the formulas for

```
Procedure_cache_pct and Revised_memory_pages
```

As useful as these formulas are in calculating memory use and `sp_configure` parameters, they do not determine the effectiveness of the cache areas. You need to take a closer look at tuning the procedure and data cache based on the performance statistics reported using `sp_sysmon`.

11.4 Procedure Cache

At execution time, SQL Server looks in its own MRU-to-LRU (*most recently used to least recently used*) chain to find out whether an object is already in memory. If it is found to be in memory, execution is immediate. The procedure is moved to the head of the MRU chain, which helps keep the most frequently used procedures in memory. If the procedure is not found, the query tree for the procedure is read from the sysprocedures table. After it is optimized, the procedure is added to the MRU chain. This processing may result in physical reads. Also, if necessary, another object may be aged off the LRU end of the chain. A subsequent request for that object would require its loading from sysprocedures. So, the idea is to minimize physical reads.

The procedure cache holds as many optimized triggers, views, queries, or stored procedures for which there is room. A query tree also is loaded into the cache sometimes. Furthermore, identical copies of objects can coexist in the procedure cache for different processes executing concurrently. Earlier in this chapter, you learned about using `dbcc memusage` to display system and cache memory allocations and uses. You also looked at useful formulas for making rudimentary determinations of system memory settings. This exercise is to determine whether the cache is performing efficiently and how to adjust it. The size of the procedure cache defaults to 20 percent of `Total Memory` at install time. Your intention, though, is to establish a size that conforms with the best possible performance.

With your goal of high-performance in mind, take a look at the procedure cache management information for `sp_sysmon`:

Procedure Cache Management	per sec	per xact	count	% of total	
Procedure Requests	109.4	1.0	39121	n/a	**(A)**
Procedure Reads from Disk	0.3	2.0	1555	3.9 %	**(B)**
Procedure Writes to Disk	0.0	0.0	0	0.0 %	**(C)**
Procedure Removals	0.1	0.1	117	n/a	**(D)**

(A) `Procedure Requests` shows that stored procedures are being executed at the rate of 109.4/sec and that 39,121 have been executed. Based on the numbers, many query plans already must be found in memory when needed.

(B) `Procedure Reads from Disk` indicates that 555 stored procedures were read from disk. Also, `% of Total` indicates the (`Procedure Reads from Disk` count/`Procedure Requests` count). If this number exceeds 2 percent, you should increase the size of the `Procedure Cache Percent` parameter using `sp_configure`.

(C) `Procedure Writes to Disk` indicates procedures built during the reporting interval. Typically, this number is very low. If applications are generating stored procedures, you need to review the application.

(D) `Procedure Removals` shows that 117 procedures have been aged out of the procedure cache. This is not a very high number in relation to the number of procedure requests. If this number exceeds 2 percent of the procedure requests, the `Procedure Cache Percent` parameter should be increased.

In addition to the `sp_sysmon` report, tuning with Sybase SQL Server Monitor is easy by using the following statistics. See Chapter 1 for a complete description of using Sybase SQL Server Monitor.

Activity	Statistic	Description
Procedure I/O	`Procedure Cache Hit Rate`	Cache effectiveness
SQL server memory	`% Procedure Cache`	Pie chart for use

11.5 Stored Procedures

All stored procedures are located in the sybsystemprocs database. Stored procedures improve performance in a couple of ways. First, the information for a query is collected and batched back to the client; this reduces network traffic. Second, locks can be held for a shorter duration. Because many users and applications can share a stored procedure, it is easy to maintain or upgrade with a tuning enhancement. Sharing data access via stored procedures results in fewer cached objects and better memory use. Also, stored procedures are faster than views, probably because they do not require caching of a query tree.

To get the most benefit from stored procedures, you need to follow these steps:

1. Obtain a list of all queries being executed and how often they are executed.

2. Take the highest volume queries and find those that use the most CPU or I/O.

3. Further reduce the list to those queries that are part of mission-critical applications.

4. Build stored procedures for those remaining on the list.

5. Make sure there is adequate memory to hold all the stored procedures.

6. Have the application program teams switch to executing the stored procedures.

TIMESLICE IMPROVEMENTS

Stored procedures that take a long time to complete are susceptible to timeslice errors like the one shown here:

```
00:97/06/19 07:58:48.02 kernel  timeslice -nnnn, current process infected
```

A procedure is allotted a maximum amount of time determined by adding the values defined in the `Time slice` and `CPU grace time` parameters of `sp_configure`. Initially, a procedure uses the amount of time in milliseconds permitted with the `Time slice` parameter; it yields to the system. A grace period then extends the allowed CPU execution. When the grace time expires, the process is infected and dies. Ideally, you would never see a timeslice error on the log because it could be an indication of a wrong parameter setting. These settings also are valuable in catching runaway procedures, however; you should set them as high as is practical. Here are some good initial settings:

```
sp_configure "time slice", 3000        <3 seconds
sp_configure "cpu grace time", 30000   <30 seconds
```

11.6   Default and Named Data Caches

The buffer cache (data cache) holds data pages in memory, reducing physical I/O. Sybase uses the data cache to store pages from system tables, system indexes (sysindexes), system objects (sysobjects), user tables, user indexes and the log. Just as you did with the procedure cache, you want to evaluate `sp_sysmon` reports for the default buffer cache and any other named caches.

Figure 11-2 shows sample `sp_sysmon` output for the `Data Cache Management` category. Information for each cache is provided, as well as a summary that includes information applicable to all caches.

The output in **(A)** through **(L)** is summary information for all caches. There is one named cache called `gl_super_cache` that has itemized information in items **(M)** through **(CC)**.

(A) `Cache Hits` provides a quick way to determine overall cache effectiveness. If this value is less than 98 percent, the default or named caches are not sized properly. Sizing issues could be the result of the way cache memory is distributed or insufficient cache memory.

```
begin_sample
sp_sysmon "01:00:00", dcache
end_sample
```

Data Cache Management

  Cache Statistics Summary (All Caches)

    Cache Search Summary
      Total Cache Hits   7211.5   2213.2   145442   69.9 % **(A)**
      Total Cache Misses   121.4   55.5   66633   30.1 % **(B)**
    ------------------------   ------   ------   ------
    Total Cache Searches   8932.9   2268.7   212075
    Cache Turnover
      Buffers Grabbed   771.4   330.5   14532   96.6 % **(C)**
      Buffers Grabbed Dirty   7.4   15.0   528   3.4 % **(D)**
    ------------------------   ------   ------   ------
    Total Turnover Requests   778.8   345.5   15060
    Cache Strategy Summary
      Cached (LRU) Buffers   4489.1   112.8   79769   100.0 % **(E)**
      Discarded (MRU) Buffers   0.0   0.0   0   0.0 % **(F)**
    Large I/O Usage
      Large I/Os Performed   542.4   11.0   7682   93.4 % **(G)**
      Large I/Os Denied   43.2   13.7   522   6.6 % **(H)**
    ------------------------   ------   ------   ------
    Total Large I/O Requests   585.6   24.7   8204
    Large I/O Effectiveness
      Pages by Lrg I/O Cached   5.0   3.0   10   100.0 % **(I)**
Pages by Lrg I/O Used   0.0   0.0   0   0.0 % **(J)**
    Dirty Read Behavior
      Page Requests   1.0   1.0   0   100.0 % **(K)**
      Re-Starts   0.0   0.0   0   0.0 % **(L)**
----
gl_super_cache

                                 per sec   per xact   count   % of total
   ---------------------------- -------   --------   ------   ----------
   Spinlock Contention   n/a   n/a   n/a   2.2 %   **(M)**
   Utilization   n/a   n/a   n/a   54.9 %   **(N)**
   Cache Searches
     Cache Hits   4366.5   3302.0   115099   98.7 %   **(O)**
       Found in Wash   0.0   0.0   0   0.0 %   **(P)**
     Cache Misses   155.7   80.3   1405   1.3 %   **(Q)**
   ------------------------   ------   ------   ------
   Total Cache Searches   4522.2   3382.3   116504

   Pool Turnover
     2 Kb Pool
        LRU Buffer Grab   15.5   7.2   768   87.3 %   **(R)**
           Grabbed Dirty   0.0   0.0   0   0.0 %   **(S)**
     8 Kb Pool
        LRU Buffer Grab   13.5   8.2   89   12.2 %   **(T)**
           Grabbed Dirty   0.0   0.0   0   0.0 %   **(U)**
   ------------------------   ------   ------   ------
   Total Cache Turnover   29.0   15.4   463
   Buffer Wash Behavior   **(V)**
Statistics Not Available - No Buffers Entered Wash Section Yet
   Cache Strategy
```

**Figure 11-2**  Data Cache Output for sp_sysmon
```

Cached (LRU) Buffers	4211.1	3382.3	99711	100.0 % **(W)**
Discarded (MRU) Buffers	0.0	0.0	0	0.0 % **(X)**
Large I/O Usage				
Large I/Os Performed	4.0	0.0	0	100.0 % **(Y)**
Large I/Os Denied	0.0	0.0	0	0.0 % **(Z)**
--------------------	------	------	------	
Total Large I/O Requests	4.0	0.0	0	
Large I/O Detail				
8 Kb Pool				
Pages by Lrg I/O Cached	32.0	0.0	0	100.0 % **(AA)**
Pages by Lrg I/O Used	4.0	0.0	0	100.0 % **(BB)**
...				
Dirty Read Behavior				
Page Requests	0.0	0.0	0	n/a **(CC)**

Figure 11-2 Data Cache Output for sp_sysmon (Continued)

(B) Cache Misses shows the inverse side of the cache-effectiveness equation. If this value is greater than 2 percent, the default or named caches are not sized properly. This value is an indirect indicator of disk reads.

(C) Buffers Grabbed is a count of buffers grabbed from the LRU end of the buffer chain. If this number is high, it also is an indication of insufficient buffer cache.

(D) Buffers Grabbed Dirty is a count of LRU buffers that had to be written to disk (dirty). This results in waits.

(E) Cached LRU Buffers is a count of buffers placed at the MRU end of the chain.

(F) Discarded MRU Buffers is a count of buffers placed at the wash marker.

(G) Large I/Os Performed is a count of large I/Os.

(H) Large I/Os Denied is a count of large I/Os that were not performed and should be researched.

(I) Pages by Lrg I/O Used % can be used to determine whether large I/O is buying anything. A low value means that the pool size or caching strategy is ineffective.

(J) Pages by Lrg I/O Used shows use after being cached.

(K) Page Requests is an average for isolation level 0 requests.

(L) Dirty Read Re-starts is displayed only for server, not named, caches. Both dirty reads and dirty read restarts are expensive.

Here is a breakdown of the information for the active gl_super_cache data cache:.

(M-Z) Many of the reported values in this section mean the same thing as their counterparts in the overall cache statistics. So, this explanation concentrates on those that are different.

(M) Spinlock Contention is useful in determining whether a wait for the cache occurred in an SMP environment. If the value is high, creation of a new named cache may reduce the contention. Each cache is controlled by its own spinlock.

(N) Utilization Percentage refers to searches for the gl_super_cache, as opposed to all active caches. The sample value of 54.9 percent is arrived at by dividing the Total Cache Searches value for all caches (for example, 212,075) into the Total Cache Searches value for the gl_super_cache (for example, 116,504).

(R) Pool Turnover reports the number of times a buffer is replaced from each pool in a cache. Each cache can have up to four pools, with I/O sizes of 2KB, 4KB, 8KB, and 16KB. If there is any pool turnover, LRU Buffer Grab **(R, T)** and Grabbed Dirty **(S, U)** information is shown for each pool that is configured, as well as a total turnover figure for the entire cache. LRU Buffer Grab (> 2%) is an indication of pools that are too small. Grabbed Dirty (> 2%) is an indication that the wash area of the pool is too small.

(V) If wash hits are high in comparison to all cache hits, the wash may be too large. A large wash is not good. SQL Server issues a write for dirty pages in the wash area, which increases the I/O. Reducing the wash to a size too small is not good either; it can result in more dirty buffer activity. If you see counts for Dirty or Already in I/O, the page was dirtied while in cache, and a write is necessary. There will be a wait until the I/O completes, which could be an indication of too small a wash area. There were no accumulated counts in this example.

(W) Cached LRU Buffers is cached buffers using the normal caching strategy.

(X) Discarded MRU Buffers is the number of buffers using the fetch-and-discard strategy.

(Y) Large I/O Performed is a count by page size.

(Z) More important is Large I/O Denied, which is an indication of poor large I/O performance. If this number exceeds 50 percent, try using a smaller pool size.

(AA-BB) Large I/O Usage summarizes activity for page sizes larger than 2KB. Pages Cached divided into Pages Used gives the hit ratio for large I/O. In this example, this is 4/32 = 12.5 percent.

(CC) Pages requested at isolation level 0.

WASH AREA SIZE AND RECYCLING

A wash area can be configured for each pool. The size should be tuned by using the caching statistics returned in sp_sysmon. If the wash area is too large, Sybase may push a lot of pages beyond the marker, which requires that they be written if they are dirty (item **P** in the example). This can result in unnecessary I/O. If the wash area is too small, Sybase may wait a process until a buffer is available. Buffer activity is controlled by using two different buffer strategies and a chain called LRU/MRU.

Objects that have aged toward the LRU end of the chain and are ready for deletion are identified quickly with a wash marker. Objects on one side of the marker are ready for deletion, whereas objects on the other side are not. The fetch-and-discard strategy lets Sybase place pages just before the wash marker when initially read in. This is advantageous for heavy sequential processing. A table scan that processes many pages, for example, would be more likely to flush pages quickly. The LRU caching strategy, on the other hand, takes objects and places them at the head of the MRU chain when they are used. Over time, they age off the chain. MRU objects have a shorter lifetime on the chain than LRU objects, mainly because they already are way down on the chain just before the wash marker when they begin life.

When a page is requested that already exists on the chain, it is moved to the head of the chain. This phenomenon is known as *recycling* and cannot be repeated indefinitely. The RDBMS must have a way to guarantee that pages are written from time to time to disk. When checkpoints are issued, they are written automatically. At checkpoint time, all dirty pages are written to disk and flushed from the MRU/LRU chain. The housekeeper task helps to flush pages that are dirty during server idle times. But what about pages that don't get flushed by these means? You can use parameters to control the pages' cache life expectancy:

- `cbufwashsize` is the number of recycles before a page is flushed to disk.
- `Number of OAM Trips` is the number of recycles for an OAM page before it is flushed to disk.
- `Number of Index Trips` is the number of recycles for an index page before it is flushed to disk.

NAMED DATA CACHES

The installation default is a single data cache. However, individual caches (named caches) can improve performance. If the cache is filling frequently with modified pages, for example, it has a tendency to flush retrieval-only pages, which will be needed again. When they are subsequently requested, additional I/O results. Sequential table scans cause the cache to flush frequently used pages also. As the cache hit percentage drops, the efficiency could indicate that the cache is too small or that named caches would be of benefit.

How do you determine when it's OK use a named cache? Do not use a named cache when indexing, query optimization, large I/O, or increased default cache size would resolve any performance problems with caching. A named cache is ideal for resolving cache conflicts due to multiple forms of database activity (for example, table scans and logging), multiple application systems contending for cache (tempdb use, for example), high-volume transaction spinlock waits (SMP processing, for example), and mission-critical applications. A mission-critical table can be bound to its own cache, for example.

How do you determine where a named cache should be used? The answer is to use Showplan and `set statistics io` to on for your queries. If you can identify where the largest amount of activity is occurring, you can try building a named cache for that application system or subsystem. Activity by file also is useful.

When building and monitoring named caches, you can use the following commands:

Command	Function
sp_bindcache	Binds database or database entities to a cache
sp_cacheconfig	Creates, drops, reports on size or defines size of named caches

Command	Function
sp_helpcache	Produces a cache report
sp_sysmon	Produces a cache and pool-use report
sp_unbindcache	Unbinds database or database entities from a cache
sp_unbindcache_all	Unbinds all entities from a cache at once

In addition to the sp_sysmon report, tuning with Sybase SQL Server Monitor is easy by using the following statistics. See Chapter 1 for a complete description of using Sybase SQL Server Monitor.

Activity	Statistic	Function
Page I/O	Data Cache Hit Rate	Reports on cache effectiveness
SQL Server Memory	% for Kernel	Generates a pie chart for use
	% for Server	
	% Data Cache	

LARGE I/O POOLS

Sybase 11 enables you to configure pools within the default or named caches; this is commonly called *large I/O*. Heavy sequential processing benefits from large I/O. You can configure the default cache and any named cache for 4-, 8- or 16KB reads and writes. A 16KB read, for example, reads eight pages at once. Ad-hoc table scans, bulk copies, joins and index queries, which walk the native index (Boolean calls to clustered indexes, for example), accomplish I/O processing faster. However, you may be able to get better performance by eliminating a table scan with proper query analysis and indexing.

If any large I/O pool is underused (less than 20 percent), eliminate it. If any large I/O pool is producing a poor cache hit ratio, tune it.

When building and monitoring pools, you can use the following commands:

Command	Function
sp_poolconfig	Creates, drops or defines I/O pools
sp_sysmon	Produces a cache and pool-use report

To force the optimizer to use a large I/O pool of your choice, you can specify the prefetch specification on queries (the index clause of select, delete or update statements). Here are some examples that set the size to 16KB I/O, which causes Sybase to process eight pages at a time (if a 16KB memory pool is available and the optimizer doesn't override your request because the object is already in another pool):

```
set prefetch on
select *
from invoice
(index inv_indx prefetch 16)
[, invoice ...]
where inv_nbr > 100
delete from invoice (index inv_indx
prefetch 16) ...
update invoice set inv_company = 'Dunham Software'
from invoice (index inv_indx
prefetch 16) ...
```

11.7 I/O Subsystem Analysis and Tuning

You will now take a look at tuning the I/O subsystem. The goal of I/O tuning should be to provide sufficient hardware that can meet the I/O rates required while load balancing I/O across that hardware in the most effective manner. Another goal is to provide adequate free space for future growth of applications.

You have quite a few tools at your disposal to achieve these goals. In Chapter 1, you looked at SQL Server Monitor and the device I/O statistics it provides. You also examined DBAware, a monitor from Menlo Software (a complimentary trial copy of DBAware is included with this book). This section also references output statistics from the sp_sysmon procedure and native UNIX commands. By touching on several tools, you will gain familiarity with the many options available for tuning the I/O subsystem in Sybase. You'll begin by looking at available space.

TOTAL DISK STORAGE

Total disk storage consumption is gauged with regular monitoring. The best way to do this is to create a small script that displays the size of all tables and indexes. The sp_spaceused procedure returns the information needed. Here is an example:

```
sp_spaceused invoice
```

name	rowtotal	reserved	data	index_size	unused
invoice	100000	27840 KB	25000 KB	1880 KB	960 KB

You also can issue the following query to see all the objects on a segment and the amount of space they use:

```
select object=o.name, 'index'= i.indid, segment=s.name,
size=reserved_pgs(i.id, i.doampg) + reserved_pgs(i.id, i.ioampg)
from sysobjects o, syssegments s, sysindexes i
```

```
where o.id = i.id<br>
and s.segment = i.segment<br>
order by s.name, o.name, i.indid<br>
compute sum(reserved_pgs(i.id, i.doampg) + reserved_pgs(i.id, i.ioampg))
by s.name
```

If you collect the pertinent data into a worktable, you can feed it into a spreadsheet and track table and index growth. The trickiest thing about controlling growth is timing. You need to allocate enough disk space to handle growth until the next window of opportunity opens during which maintenance can be performed. Regular rebuilding of indexes for performance and rebuilding of tables that are segmented or partitioned are the driving forces behind meticulous planning and timing. Because tables don't expand or contract at the same rate, you need to track them and compute the speed at which they change.

NUMBER OF DISK CONTROLLERS

Section 1.16 includes a sample of using the `iostat` command to display read/write-per-second rates on physical devices. You can use this information to determine the need for additional disk controllers. The I/O rate is compared with the maximum rate allowed for a device in its manufacturer's specifications.

 NOTE: You also can use the following UNIX command to see I/O rates:

```
sar -d -rptm
```

Section 1.31 provides a complete write-up on using Sybase SQL Server Monitor. The monitor collects Reads by Device and Writes by Device statistics, which are adequate for disk controller load balancing and I/O rate analysis.

Another tool that can simplify the job of managing disk devices and controllers is DBAware from Menlo Software. The disk reads and writes can be accumulated and reported in intervals. You can see the use of devices during prime shift periods of heavy use. You can archive statistics for historical analysis. This is very valuable in measuring changes over time. You want to be able to project the date when additional controllers or devices will be needed. Here are the important statistics to examine:

Query	Description
select @@io_busy	Amount of time in ticks the server has spent performing input and output operations since it was started
select @@total_errors	Number of read/write errors since server was started
select @@total_read	Number of disk reads since server was started
select @@total_write	Number of disk writes since server was started

If you began with a server using non-RAID technology that has grown substantially, you will want to investigate the latest advances in RAID. The cost has become more acceptable to smaller shops, and RAID systems are scaleable. Chapter 6 provides a complete discussion of RAID. RAID has the advantage of automatic load balancing of I/O. If RAID is out of your reach, consider using more controllers with small- to medium-size devices; this also will balance the I/O load better.

An I/O subsystem diagram is a prerequisite for any server with more than three devices. Show all the logical and physical drives, their controllers, and speeds. Also include the maximum I/O speed the disks will support and the bandwidth of the controllers and motherboard. Superimpose the I/O rates for devices found using a monitor or iostat. Now you have the information to see where I/O bottlenecks exist or will exist as system use increases.

The `sysdevices` table contains a Status column with information about the type of device and its mirroring status. Include this information when creating an I/O subsystem diagram. The column is bitmapped. Here is a cross-reference of bitmapped values:

Decimal	Hexadecimal	Status
1	0x01	Default disk
2	0x02	Physical disk
4	0x04	Logical disk
8	0x08	Skip header
16	0x10	Dump device
32	0x20	Serial writes
64	0x40	Device mirrored
128	0x80	Reads mirrored
256	0x100	Secondary mirror side only
512	0x200	Mirror enabled
1024	0x400	Device information in configuration area
2048	0x800	Mirror disabled

I/O ANALYSIS WITH sp_sysmon

Figure 11-3 shows the output from `sp_sysmon`'s disk I/O management report on a four-engine SMP.

(A) `I/Os Delayed By` may be an indication that the kernel asynchronous I/O limit needs to be increased.

(B) If `Disk I/O Structures` is non-zero, try increasing the `sp_configure Disk I/O Structures` parameter.

```
Disk I/O Management
-------------------
  Max Outstanding I/Os         per sec   per xact   count  % of total
  ------------------------     -------   --------   -----  ----------
    Server                       n/a       n/a        66      n/a
    Engine 0                     n/a       n/a        22      n/a
    Engine 1                     n/a       n/a        24      n/a
    Engine 2                     n/a       n/a        10      n/a
    Engine 3                     n/a       n/a        17      n/a
  I/Os Delayed by                                                       (A)
    Disk I/O Structures          n/a       n/a         0      n/a     (B)
    Server Config Limit          n/a       n/a         0      n/a     (C)
    Engine Config Limit          n/a       n/a         0      n/a     (D)
    Operating System Limit       n/a       n/a         0      n/a     (E)
  Total Requested Disk I/Os     73.7       0.8      3761      n/a     (F)
Completed Disk I/O's
    Engine 0                    22.0       0.2       850    23.9 %
    Engine 1                    24.3       0.2       914    25.9 %
    Engine 2                    11.2       0.2       779    21.9 %
    Engine 3                    15.0       0.2      1001    28.3 %
  ------------------------     -------   --------   -----  ----------
  Total Completed I/Os          72.5       0.8      3544              (G)
Device Activity Detail
----------------------
/dev/jad/work01
jad                            per sec   per xact   count   % of total
------------------------       -------   --------   -----   ----------
    Reads                       18.1       0.6       750    57.5 %  (H)
    Writes                      12.6       0.2       555    42.5 %  (I)
  ------------------------     -------   --------   -----   ----------
  Total I/Os                    30.7       0.8      1305    36.8 %  (J)
  Device Semaphore Granted      30.7       0.8      1305   100.0 %  (K)
  Device Semaphore Waited        0.0       0.0         0     0.0 %  (L)
  --------------------------------------------------------------------
c_sybmstr
master                         per sec   per xact   count  % of total
------------------------       -------   --------   -----  ----------
    Reads                       34.4       0.2      1249    56.0 %  (M)
    Writes                      31.0       0.2       982    44.0 %  (N)
  ------------------------     -------   --------   -----  ----------
  Total I/Os                    65.4       0.4      2231    63.2 %  (O)
  Device Semaphore Granted      39.9       0.3      1775    79.6 %  (P)
  Device Semaphore Waited       25.5       0.1       456    20.4 %  (Q)
```

Figure 11-3 Disk Management I/O Output for sp_sysmon

(C-E) If Server Configuration Limit, Engine Configuration Limit, or Operating System Limit is non-zero, try increasing the sp_configure Max async I/Os per Server parameter. Sybase automatically uses asynchronous I/O (AIO) if the operating system and hardware have been enabled for its use. You do not need to set parameters in SQL Server. In UNIXWare 2.0, you can use asynchronous I/O with raw devices by setting the async flag as the following:

```
chmod 666 /dev/async              (Give system admin auth)
Edit file /etc/conf/node.d/async  (Change mode number to 666 in file)
```

(F) If `Total Requested Disk I/Os` is a lot higher than `Total Completed I/Os`, the server is saturated and more I/O bandwidth is required.

(G, J, O) `Device Activity Detail` is shown for the master and each logical device. `Total I/Os` for each device adds up to `Total Requested Disk I/Os` and is used to see the percentage of activity on each device. This is how you can see whether device activity is balanced. If many devices are used and the load balance is poor, consider switching to high-speed RAID devices.

(H, I, M, N) The `Reads` and `Writes` counts can give you an idea of how different types of activity are balanced. Some devices read faster than they write. This may tell you how to assign devices to the type of activity they will service.

(K, L, P, Q) The `Device Semaphore Granted` and `Waited` show counts of requests for device semaphores. If the number of semaphore waits is high, the requests are not well balanced or the bandwidth for the device is being exceeded. Alternatives include RAID arrays, more controllers, segmentation and partitioning of data.

HINTS FOR TUNING THE I/O SUBSYSTEM

- Specify LRU or MRU in a `select`, `update`, or `delete` statement if it will improve the caching.

- If `Semaphores Waited` in the `sp_sysmon` output is high, balance I/O better and consider more or faster disk controllers.

- If the `Disk I/O Structures` count in the `sp_sysmon` output is non-zero, increase the `sp_configure Disk I/O Structures` parameter.

- If the `Device Activity` in `sp_sysmon` output is approaching the physical device rating for a disk device, balance I/O better or provide additional bandwidth.

- If `Total Disk I/Os Requested` is a lot higher than `Total Disk I/Os Completed` in `sp_sysmon` output, load balance the I/O better or provide additional bandwidth.

- Separate objects with heavy write activity onto devices rated for higher write performance.

- If the `Server Config Limit`, `Engine Config Limit`, or `Operating System Limit` count in the `sp_sysmon` output is non-zero, increase the `sp_configure Max Async I/Os per Server` parameter. Also, verify that the operating system doesn't have a maximum asynchronous I/O parameter that needs to be turned on or increased.

- Use `sp_cachestrategy` to disable or reenable the MRU strategy if it will improve caching. In this example, the "table only" option is added because there is no clustered index on the `invoice` table:

```
sp_cachestrategy invoice, "table only", mru "off"
```

Now the `invoice` table will use the LRU strategy, which is better for heavy concurrent access.

- Spread data across disks to avoid I/O contention.

- Add the INDEX clause to select statements to force the use of LRU caching.

- Isolate server-wide I/O from database I/O.

- Keep random disk I/O away from sequential disk I/O.

- Implement RAID arrays to balance the I/O and provide additional bandwidth.

- Increase the number and speed of I/O controllers.

- Mirror devices on separate physical disks.

- Place log data on a separate device with its own controller.

- Place specific tables or nonclustered indexes on specific devices. You might place a table on one device and its nonclustered indexes on a separate device.

- Place the text and image page chain for a table on a separate device from the table. The table stores a pointer to the actual data value in the separate database structure, so each access to a text or image column requires at least two I/Os.

- Increase the number of logical devices to reduce contention on internal I/O queues. There is a 128 device limit per database. Segmentation is the best method to use.

- Create databases that can perform parallel I/O on up to six devices at a time, giving a significant performance leap to the process of creating multigigabyte databases.

- Avoid mirroring when it is not needed.

- Configure the Number of Extent I/O Buffers parameter to 60 for index maintenance to occur off-peak. When index maintenance is complete, deallocate the extra I/O extents and resume normal memory allocations.

- Build an I/O subsystem diagram and collect statistics for tuning monthly.

- Systems requiring increased log throughput today must partition database into separate databases. Breaking up one logical database into multiple smaller databases increases the number of transaction logs working in parallel.

- If indexes are responsible for most of the database access, allocate small memory pools for large I/O.

- Set the Utilization parameter to 100 to continue using release 10 OAM space management. Set Utilization to a percentage to use faster release 11 space location.

- Verify that the default and named data caches are adequate.

- If the I/O Device Contention (number of times a task was put to sleep while waiting for a semaphore for a particular device) in the sp_sysmon task management report is high, tables need to be striped or segmented across devices more. Also, separate tables and indexes on different devices.

11.8   Tuning tempdb

Tempdb is a utilitarian database that is shared by many users and is quite active. Individual use is not shared, but system tables kept in tempdb can cause contention. Also, a significant amount of locking and buffer contention can occur. Use the following options for tuning the tempdb database:

- On some UNIX systems, tempdb can be altered onto a system file instead of a raw device.
- Place tempdb on a separate device with a separate or lightly used controller.
- Assign tempdb its own data cache and make sure that it is using a 16KB memory pool:

```
sp_bindcache "tempdb_16k_cache", tempdb
```

Because tempdb is not as important from the standpoint of recovery, it does not have to be mirrored or placed on a recoverable RAID array.

- Make sure that tempdb is large enough to handle all current and future requests. Set it quickly with this little formula using statistics I/O output:

Est_ tempdb_size_in_MB

((Temporary Table Bytes +

Worktable Bytes +

Temporary Index Bytes +

Sort Bytes +

*Maintenance Activity Bytes) * 1.2)/1,048,576*

- You can use the `sp_helpdb` command to see the current size and status of tempdb. Here is an example:

```
1> sp_helpdb tempdb
name        db_size  owner  dbid  created        status
----        -------  -----  ----  -------        ------
tempdb      1.0 GB   sa     5     July 13, 1997  select into/bulkcopy
device_frag  size    usage          free kbytes
-----------  ----    -----          -----------
temp01      1.0 GB   data and log   1048000
```

- Do not segment or partition the tempdb database.
- Perform the tasks for optimizing sorts shown in this chapter.

■ Consider making some worktables permanent, instead of temporary, depending on their reuse, segmentation, and partitioning properties.

■ Drop the master device from the default and logsegment segments after altering tempdb to its own device. Then verify that the default master segmap does not indicate 1 for the tempdb segment:

```
alter database tempdb on temp01 = 20
sp_dropsegment "default", tempdb, master
sp_dropsegment logsegment, tempdb, master
select dbid, name, segmap
from sysusages, sysdevices
where sysdevices.low <= sysusages.size + vstart
and sysdevices.high >= sysusages.size + vstart -1
and dbid = 5
and (status = 2 or status = 3)
dbid    name            segmap
----    ----            ------
5       master          1
5       temp01          7
```

■ Reduce logging activity in tempdb with SELECT INTO operations, selecting fewer columns.

■ Use temporary table indexes to improve query performance.

■ Break up queries that scan tables multiple times into separate passes. This way, the optimizer knows the size of tables used in subsequent passes.

■ Place tempdb on a low-numbered device because SQL Server looks up the device number chain beginning at zero for a device. Because tempdb is used so much, devices should be ordered for quick lookup, with the most active being the lowest device number.

■ Both tempdb and the log should be relatively low in number.

■ Avoid locking contention on tempdb's syscolumns table by creating tables before they are used in stored procedures and queries. Create the tables dynamically to improve performance even more. Never create the tables in the procedures that will use them; this is very inefficient.

11.9 Sort Performance

Here are some suggestions for optimizing sort operations. Sort performance works hand in hand with tempdb tuning and index-performance tuning. Refer to the sections in this chapter on those subjects for more ideas.

- Increase the `Number of Extent I/O Buffers` parameter to speed index creation. This value configures the number of extents (eight data pages) used for buffering intermediate results. Sybase 11 uses 16KB I/O buffers to save with this option.

- Increase the `Number of Sort Buffers` parameter. This value configures how many buffers can be used in cache to hold pages from the input tables. This is the number of cache buffers used to hold pages read from input tables. SQL Server does not allow processes to reserve more than half this number.

- Set the `Sort Page Count sp_configure` parameter. It specifies the maximum amount of memory a sort operation can use. These pages store rows in memory during the sort. Sorts require about 50 bytes per row while processing the input table. The `Sort Page Count` borrows pages from the default data cache for each sort operation. This value, and the other two mentioned just prior to this one, must all be computed using the formulas provided in the *Sybase SQL Server System Admin Guide*.

- Normalize your table data to optimize sorting and indexing.

- Build clustered indexes where sorting is frequent, thus avoiding the need to sort. If your data already has been sorted and is in the desired clustered index order, use the with `pre_sorted_data_file` clause of the `index create` command to speed index building. This saves the time normally spent on the sorting phase:

```
create clustered index index_name on table (column) with
pre_sorted_data_file
```

- Evaluate queries that use `OR`, `ORDER BY`, and `GROUP BY` strategies to find ways to avoid sorting. Prior to release 11, the `DISTINCT` expression also resulted in a sort to eliminate duplicates. Now a system aggregate tests for uniqueness, which avoids the need for a sort.

- For Sybase IQ, increase the value of the `mbsort` parameter. This value determines the amount of memory used for IQ session sorts (default 5MB).

- Size the tempdb for sorts based on the `set statistics io` writes for queries that perform sorts. Tune the tempdb area. Proper sizing, placement, and caching of the tempdb can reduce sort times.

- Read-only cursors using `UNION` create a worktable when the cursor is declared and sort it to remove duplicates. Fetches are performed on the worktable. Cursors using `UNION ALL` can return duplicates and do not require a worktable.

- If you are creating very large indexes at a time when other SQL Server activity is at a minimum, setting `Number of Sort Buffers` and `Sort Page Count` can greatly speed the index build because sorts are used for index building. `Sort Buffer` and `Page Count` parameters use memory from the default data cache; they both can be set dynamically, as needed.

11.10   Denormalizing Tables

This isn't the first time in this book this technique is mentioned. In fact, it is repeated for every RDBMS. Denormalizing tables is a way to sacrifice your design principles and referential integrity in exchange for happy users. If you are beginning with a third or fourth normal form database, you can denormalize it to optimize queries that need frequent access to joined data or entire joined sets. Or you can eliminate the need for worktables that are of a size and scope to prohibit building them. Avoid denormalization at all costs; it can increase costs in other areas of processing, such as referential integrity constraints, increased storage, indexing, and so on.

Denormalization implies that you already are normalized. If not, you may be building on a weak foundation. The first way to achieve better performance is to normalize the data. Only then does denormalization make sense.

11.11   Splitting and Collapsing Tables

Normalization and denormalization represent ways in which tables may be split or collapsed. They aren't the only ways, though; segmentation and partitioning are two other ways. Each method accomplishes different goals. Segments enable you to map data across physical volumes. Segments work well with large tables that suffer from maintenance and concurrency strains. Segmentation also is a good technique to use when scaling multiprocessors. Another use is separation of data and indexes.

Segments become a problem when they run out of space, so you must plan for their growth and allow a window of opportunity to maintenance them when they approach full utilization.

Partitioning and unpartitioning are other ways to split and collapse tables. These methods differ from segmentation in a few ways. First, partitions can be built only for heap tables—tables without a clustered index. Partitions are built for a single segment. If one partition runs out of space, Sybase steals a page from one of the other partitions to meet the need for space. When inserts are performed on a heap table, they occur on the last page. Heavy insert activity can result in contention. Partitions are a logical choice in these cases; they balance inserts across the different partitions.

The next few sections take a closer look at segmentation, striping, and partitioning.

11.12   Segments

A *segment* is a subset of database devices (logical and physical) available to a database. Placement of objects on segments is one way to control physical data placement and influence performance. Of the 32 allowed segments that make up a database, three are designated for the default, system, and log segments. You are allowed a total of 256 segments for a server.

Tables and indexes are stored on segments. If no segment is named in the `create table` or `create index` statement, the objects are stored on the default segment for the database. This should be avoided. Instead, tables and indexes should be assigned segments at creation time. You can use the `sp_placeobject` system procedure to designate the segment to be used for subsequent disk writes. In this way, tables can span multiple segments.

HINTS FOR SEGMENTATION

- Place the tempdb on its own segment and device to reduce contention.

- Place the log on its own segment and device to reduce contention.

- Place tables on one set of disks using a segment, and place indexes on another set of disks with a segment. This will isolate I/Os that would cause contention. Here is an example of the `create` syntax to use:

```
create table invoice (...) on seg1
create nonclustered index inv_indx on invoice (...) on seg2
```

- Split a large table across devices using a segment that can span multiple devices. A large number of equally sized devices is best because you can give them their own controllers for added performance. Make sure that the segment size is large enough to handle the table's growth until a large enough maintenance window is available. (Section 11.13 contains a striping example.)

- Tables with text or image datatypes perform one access for the text or image chain and another access for the actual text or image data. These will benefit by placing the text or image chain on a separate segment from the data. By default, they are placed on the same segment as the table. Use the `sp_placeobject` procedure to move all future allocations to a separate segment.

11.13   Striping

The easiest way to implement disk striping is to purchase an LVM or RAID array. Most of these are striped automatically, and I/O is load balanced across the physical drives and channels. Chapter 6 includes a complete write-up on RAID arrays.

A simple analogy for striping is to picture a table as a piece of paper with lots of information written on the page. Now cut the page into strips and place the information from each strip on adjacent disk drives. You can better understand striping by looking at a working example. The INVOICE database is very large. It needs to be striped onto three devices. Each drive is 2GB. The process of striping involves adding the devices to the system, initializing them, and then creating a database with segments that are striped. Suppose that the three devices (5-7) already have been added. Lower device numbers should be reserved for logs and tempdb. Also, a separate segment should be used for logging. The next step is to initialize the devices as the following:

```
ISQL

....
1>     disk init name = "inv01",
2>     physname = "volume1:inv01dat",
3>     vdevno=5,
4>     size=1048576,
5>     go
1>     disk init name = "inv02",
2>     physname = "volume2:inv02.dat",
3>     vdevno = 6,
4>     size = 1048576,
5>     go
1>     disk init name = "inv03",
2>     physname = "volume3:inv03.dat",
3>     vdevno = 7,
4>     size = 1048576,
5>     go
```

Each of the devices has 2048 usable megabytes, which equates to 1 million 2KB pages per drive. You need to partition the database as the following to avoid filling a single drive at a time:

```
1>     create database inv_db on
2>     inv01=256, inv02=256, inv03=256
3>     inv01=256, inv02=256, inv03=256
4>     inv01=256, inv02=256, inv03=256
5>     inv01=256, inv02=256, inv03=256
6>     inv01=256, inv02=256, inv03=256
7>     inv01=256, inv02=256, inv03=256
8>     inv01=256, inv02=256, inv03=256
9>     inv01=256, inv02=256, inv03=256
...
>      go
```

This example shows how to define the segments so that they flip-flop between volumes inv01, inv02 and inv03. This design uses 24 stripes of 256MB each. The interleave balances I/O across the database. Now create one segment that spans the three volumes to use for the invoice table:

```
1>      exec sp_addsegment invseg, inv01
2>      go
1>      exec sp_extendsegment invseg, inv02
2>      go
1>      exec sp_extendsegment invseg, inv03
2>      go
```

 NOTE: On SUN Solaris boxes with disk arrays, avoid using cylinder 0 on the disks. Place a metadb there to avoid striping problems.

11.14   Partitioning

A new feature in release 11 is the partitioning of heap tables. Heap tables have an inherent contention problem with inserts because they always occur on the last page of the page chain. With partitions, the table appears to have many last pages, which reduces the contention on inserts.

To facilitate this new feature, Sybase allowed for multiple page chains for a table, some new syntax, and a new type of page called the *control page*. When you partition a table, the root value for that table becomes obsolete. SQL Server now inserts a row into the syspartitions table for each partition and allocates a control page and first page for each partition.

Partitioning reduces page contention, which has little impact on I/O speed. You still need to use segments and multiple drives/controllers to get the best possible performance. Your goal is not just to improve insert performance on a heap table. You need to consider read, update, and delete performance as well.

In this example, you have chosen the invoice table, which is noted for its very high concurrent insert activity. There is no clustered index on this table. To create a partitioned table, you must allocate the segment, create the table and then add the partitions. Here is the syntax to add the invseg segment on three drives, initialized as inv01, inv02 and inv03:

```
1>      exec sp_addsegment invseg, inv01
2>      go
1>      exec sp_extendsegment invseg, inv02
2>      go
1>      exec sp_extendsegment invseg, inv03
2>      go
```

Next, you create the table:

```
create table invoice on invseg
(company char(30) not null,
 date datetime not null,
 ...
 nbr int(8) not null)
on invseg
```

Finally, you partition your table into 12 partitions by using the `alter table` command:

```
alter table invoice partition 12
```

SQL Server creates the specified number of partitions in the table and distributes those partitions over the database devices in the table's segment. It builds control pages and page chains for the partitions.

If you decide that you now want to alter the number of partitions in use, you must issue an `unpartition` statement before another `partition` statement for the table. Suppose that you increase the number of partitions to 24. SQL Server recombines the 12 partition page chains into one contiguous chain when the `unpartition` option is issued. It then builds 24 partitions with separate page chains when the new partition is built in the second command.

```
alter table invoice unpartition
alter table invoice partition 24
```

The distribution of partitions is interleaved across devices like this:

inv01	p1, p4, p7, p10, p13, p16, p19, p22
inv02	p2, p5, p8, p11, p14, p17, p20, p23
inv03	p3, p6, p9, p12, p15, p18, p21, p24

You now can use the `sp_helpartition` procedure to view the revised partition. Note that your table uses 3 million pages:

```
sp_helpartition invoice
```

partitionid	firstpage	controlpage
1	1	2
2	393217	393218
3	786433	786434
4	1179648	1179649

QUID PRO QUOS

Not everything is hunky-dory in partition land. You need to review the following list of issues before setting up a partition; they may influence your desire to use partitioning:

- Text and image datatypes work. The text and image column data will not be partitioned, however; they must remain on a single page chain. So this would influence any savings on insert performance.

- Cursor operations will not work the same as prerelease 11 operations. A scan will not return the same results, and an insert will not necessarily position rows in the same order.

- The ALTER TABLE PARTITION N command cannot be issued from a user-defined transaction.

- Any data that was in a table before the ALTER TABLE PARTITION N command will be left in the first partition. On a repartitioned table, this may be an interesting process.

- Full partitions equate to page stealing. There may be some overhead with page stealing.

- You can't add a clustered index to a partitioned table. However, you can un-partition the table, stripe the database, reload the data and add a clustered index to the table.

11.15 Table Loading

Table loading is one of the longer running operations that needs to be tuned up. The following hints can help speed database creation and table loading:

- Use the for load option to create a database if you intend to issue the load database command immediately afterward:

```
create database invdb for load on
inv01=256, inv02=256, inv03=256,
log on
inv04=256, inv05=256
```

This postpones zeroing allocation units until the load is complete. Then, it only needs to do it to untouched units.

- Load tables during off-hours when the server is not busy.

- Use a large 16KB memory pool for faster reads and writes.

- Increase named cache buffers for loading.

- Presort data by using a high-speed sorting tool, such as SYNCSORT for UNIX, in the order of the indexes being built on loaded tables.

- Use *bulk copy* (BCP).

- If you are replacing all the data in a large table, use the truncate table command instead of the delete command. Otherwise, all the pages get logged. With truncate, only the pages deallocated are logged.

11.16 Bulk Copy

Bulk copy is useful in loading and unloading remote or local tables. It also can provide a means to simply place the contents of a table into a memory array.

Bulk copying into a table is fast. Data can be transferred in native form, unlike the character string format required by SQL calls. However, you should adhere to some steps if you want to get the best results. First, drop any indexes and triggers for the table unless it is a very small table. Bulk copy detects the presence of an index and logs all data changes instead of only allocation page changes. Also, you don't want to incur the overhead of updating indexes row by row as the data is inserted into the table. An index or trigger also causes bulk copy to run using a slower set of programs. However, some very large tables with clustered indexes do not take a performance hit. In this example, you only have a single nonclustered index to drop:

```
drop index inv_indx from invoice
```

The second step is to set the "`select into/bulkcopy`" option for the database via the `sp_dboption` procedure. This makes bulk copy legal:

```
sp_dboption invdb, "select into/bulkcopy", true
```

The third step is to establish a batch size. Bulk copy handles input records in "batches" that are transactions. Each batch is a new transaction and must start on a new data page (bad news). So you don't want to set this number too low. An ideal number might be the number of rows that fit on a page or larger. This example uses 300.

The fourth task is to select other `bcp` command options. Options of interest follow. You need to pick terminators for fields and rows that cannot be found in the data being bulk copied.

Option	Specifies
-b	Batch size
-c	I/O is stored in character format (easy to read and clean up data)
-n	I/O is stored in native format (compressed)
-Pxx	sa password
-r	The row terminator character(s), nulls, tabs or strings to be used
-Syy	Server name
-t	The field terminator character(s), nulls, tabs or strings to be used
-Usa	sa administrator user ID

In the following `bcp` command syntax, the `invoice` table is loaded with data from the `indata` file. The input is in character format. Fields are terminated with commas, and rows are terminated with exclamation marks.

```
bcp invdb..invoice in indata -Usa -Pitsok -Sdun_server  -b 300 -t , -r ! -c
```

The fifth task is to set the `trunc log on chkpt` option to keep the transaction log from filling up. If your database has a threshold procedure that automatically dumps the log when it fills, you will save the transaction dump time. Batch size is required for `trunc log on chkpt` to help.

The sixth task is optional. If the table being loaded is partitioned, you can start up one process for each partition. Using the same table supplied in the partitioning example, you would be able to concurrently load all 24 partitions at one time. This has a dramatic effect on bulk copy elapsed time.

PROGRAMMER INTERFACE

Bulk-Library/C provides routines allowing Client-Library and Server-Library applications to use the bulk-copy interface. A high-speed transfer of data from an application program's variable storage to database rows is available for insert, commonly called *bulk copy in*. Selects can perform bulk-copy-out processing, though it doesn't afford a performance gain. In addition, administrators can perform bulk copies by using the bcp utility. This facility is for use with Open Client/Server and Open Server Gateway. Figure 11-4 shows how bcp can be used to bulk copy in rows from `your_table` to copies of the table on remote/local servers 1 and 2.

Several procedures are called to allocate necessary control structures, initialize variables, get properties, bind variables, receive and send in bulk. A nontrivial amount of C programming is necessary to implement bulk-copying capabilities in your own applications.

A gateway server uses the client-side routines to obtain bulk-copy data from the remote server and server-side routines to forward the data to a client. In a

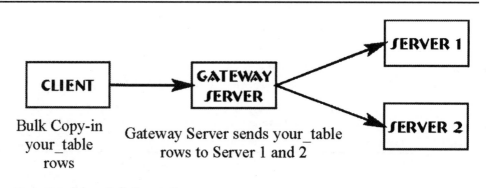

Figure 11-4 Sybase Bulk Copy to Servers

gateway scenario, you can issue two types of requests: *tabular datastream* (TDS) text/image insert and TDS bulk copy. In either case, some hefty coding is required. You must add it to the `srv_language` and `srv_bulk` event handlers. You must synchronize the changes placed in one handler with that in the other. Sybase provides an Open Server example in `ctosdemo.c`.

You should keep these points in mind:

- The size of the TDS packet affects efficiency. A larger packet size improves throughput. To tune packet size, you must allow larger sizes for the server and in the `cs_packet_size` connection property in your program.

- You can make packet-size changes for all users with the server parameters listed here (512 is the default packet size for all parameters):

```
sp_configure "default network packet size", 2048     Default size for
all users

sp_configure "max network packet size",4096     Max size client program
can request

sp_configure "additional network memory",1000     Added memory for
client program using a larger packet size
```

In conclusion, bulk copy should be used to speed table loading. One downside to bulk copy is that you must get a backup of the target table after the copy out is finished. Remember that logging is not in effect for bulk copy. After bulk copy, a table is not in a recoverable state. If bulk copy or your C program fails on the server, you need to rerun. There is no restart capability with bulk copy, such as one a custom load program or third-party tool might provide.

11.17 Indexing

Indexes are not a minor matter. They constitute one of the biggest areas of Sybase tuning. There are many options to choose from, many variables to factor in, myriad sources of statistical data, and even more work than you can imagine. This section attempts to simplify the subject of tuning indexes. Otherwise, it could take volumes to discuss the subject in great detail.

Here is a list of index-related topics that will be discussed in the order shown. If you are familiar with the basics of Sybase indexing, you might want to jump ahead to the tuning hints, where an exhaustive list of tuning suggestions is provided that will streamline your search.

Indexing Topics	
Index Structures	Tuning Indexes with `set statistics io`
Clustered Indexes	Tuning Indexes with `sp_sysmon`
Nonclustered Indexes	Hints for Tuning Indexes
Coverage	

THE INDEX STRUCTURE

The key and pointer to a lower level of the index or to a data page make up an index entry. Entries are stored as rows on pages, similar to data rows. An index B-tree is made up of as many levels as necessary to contain all the index entries. The highest level in the index consists of one root page. The number of intermediate levels varies from 0 to n, depending on how large the table is and how many entries fit on a page or whether the max_rows_per_page option is set (256 is the maximum number of rows for heap tables and clustered indexes). Each intermediate page has chain pointers to the next and previous page at the same level. The keys themselves point down to the next intermediate level page. In a clustered index, the lowest level consists of the data pages themselves. In a nonclustered index, the lowest level is the leaf level. The leaf level contains all the index keys for the table and pointers to the page where rows are stored. This structure should not be confused with the Sybase IQ bitmapped indexes discussed in the next section.

MAX_ROWS_PER_PAGE

You can use the max_rows_per_page parameter to maintain partially filled pages indefinitely. It also is valuable for limiting page-level locking. SQL Server inserts up to only this number of rows on a page. For heap tables and clustered indexes, acceptable values are 0 to 256. For nonclustered indexes, the maximum value for max_rows_per_page is the number of index rows that fit on the leaf page, up to a maximum of 256. So, it won't do any good to choose a number of rows larger than will fit on a leaf page. The nonclustered inv_comp_indx index maximum number of rows can be determined as the following, for example:

```
select (@@pagesize - 32)/minlen
from sysindexes
where name = "inv_comp_indx"
minlen = key size = 40
pagesize = 2048
max_rows_per_page = 50
```

CLUSTERED INDEXES

A table can have only one clustered index. The key is considered the primary key to table data. It does not have to be unique, but it is a good idea to make it unique, even if that means including an Identity column, because duplicate keys create serious performance problems. If duplicate keys cannot be avoided, at least partition the table to reduce contention and increase the rows per page to reduce the amount of overflow processing. Sometimes it also helps to have a larger number of table pages to randomize the keys better.

It is possible not to even have a clustered index on a table. The table then is called a heap table because all rows are inserted at the end of the table instead of at randomized page locations, as with a clustered index.

NONCLUSTERED INDEXES

All RDBMSs support clustered and nonclustered index types. Both types are necessary to satisfy different types of processing requirements. A Sybase table can have up to 249 nonclustered indexes; these are used to access the table quickly by using a key that may be different for each index. Nonclustered indexes improve `select` queries while degrading insert and delete activity. If a nonclustered index is intended to be kept permanently, it should be built as compact and unique as possible. Use numeric fields rather than character fields because they are scanned faster. Nonpermanent indexes can satisfy interim join and sort processing requirements without incurring the overhead of multiple table scans. When they no longer are needed, they can be dropped.

COVERAGE

If a nonclustered index contains all the columns of a table necessary to satisfy a query within its key, the index *covers* the query. In these instances, SQL Server reads only the index leaf pages to produce the result set and leaves the table data alone. Furthermore, the optimizer chooses the smallest index that satisfies this query. This is faster than a clustered index query.

A composite index for this purpose can have up to 16 columns and a maximum of 256 bytes. Nothing is stopping you from building multiple indexes for this purpose. But, keep in mind that although selects benefit from composite indexes, updates suffer. Additional time is needed to update indexes.

Showplan output for a query indicates that an index was used for the query coverage.

TUNING INDEXES WITH `set statistics io`

The `set statistics io` option is a quick way to determine actual I/Os for a query or its caching effectiveness. Here is a list of output fields displayed at query time:

Output	Specifies
Logical reads	Number of pages read from data cache
Physical reads	Number of reads or large I/O reads from disk
Scan count	Number of times an index or table was used in the query or scanned; if zero, then a worktable was used
Total writes	Number of writes to disk (I/Os)

The following query returns the `statistics io` output, which shows that 2000 I/Os were performed. There is a clustered index on the company column.

```
select * from invoice (index inv_comp_indx)
where company = "Dunham Software"
Table: titles  scan count 1, logical reads: 3107, physical reads: 2000
Total writes for this command: 0
```

In this example, the cache hit ratio is equal to the cache hits divided by physical reads. With `statistics io`, the logical reads include physical reads and cache reads combined. Here is the formula for determining the query cache hit ratio:

Query_cache_hit_ratio = (logical reads - physical reads)/physical reads
55 percent = 3107 - 2000/2000

TUNING INDEXES WITH `sp_sysmon`

Another method for tuning indexes is with `sp_sysmon`. The index-management report shown in Figure 11-5 extends your capability to see index activity. This information is more extensive and can be used to get a global picture of activity instead of a snapshot by query, such as `statistics io` gives.

(A) `Ins/Upd Requiring Maint` is the number of insert- and update-related operations that might have resulted in index changes. The `per xact` value gives an indication of the proliferation of indexes requiring update activity.

(B) `Deletes Requiring Maint` is the number delete operations that potentially required modification to indexes. It is important only if it is contributing to many page shrinks, which are expensive.

(C) `Page Splits` occur when a page fills and must be divided into two new pages. The index entries are split between the two new pages, and upward/downward pointers are updated. This is very expensive and an indication that an index needs to be rebuilt by applying a fill factor or that the `max_rows_per_page` should be increased, if possible. The `ascending inserts mode` option also may influence the location of splits.

(D) `Retries` and `Deadlocks` are an indication of serious contention for index pages at the time of the split and should be researched down to the query level.

```
Index Management
----------------
    Nonclustered Maintenance    per sec   per xact    count  % of total
    ------------------------    -------   --------   ------  ----------
      Ins/Upd Requiring Maint     16.0       1.6      15111     n/a    (A)
        # of NC Ndx Maint         12.4       1.3      12333     n/a
        Avg NC Ndx Maint / Op      n/a       n/a    0.81616     n/a
      Deletes Requiring Maint      2.5       0.2       1117     n/a    (B)
        # of NC Ndx Maint          0.3       0.0        252     n/a
        Avg NC Ndx Maint / Op      n/a       n/a    0.22560     n/a
      RID Upd from Clust Split     0.0       0.0          0     n/a
        # of NC Ndx Maint          0.0       0.0          0     n/a
        Avg NC Ndx Maint / Op      0.0       0.0          0     n/a
    Page Splits                    1.3       0.1        399     n/a
      Retries                      0.2       0.0         97     5.1 %(C)
      Deadlocks                    0.0       0.0          7     0.7 %(D)
      Empty Page Flushes           0.0       0.0          7     0.7 %
      Add Index Level              0.0       0.0          0     0.0 %(E)
    Page Shrinks                   0.0       0.0          0     n/a    (F)
```

Figure 11-5 Index Management Output from `sp_sysmon`

Users could be contending for only a few index entries or pages if these numbers are high. It may be a matter of moving batch insert processes to off-hours.

(E) `Add Index Level` counts the new index levels added. It may be a heads-up indicator that some index-rebuild maintenance is going to be needed. The greater the number of levels in an index, the more I/Os and CPU will be incurred when using indexes.

(F) `Page Shrinks` are the inverse of page splits and are very costly. If batch deletes are responsible for these, the processing should be moved to off-hours. If you discover that a table is being deleted row by row or that a large percentage of a table is being deleted, consider dropping and rebuilding indexes to cut down the time and shrink overhead associated with the processing.

HINTS FOR TUNING INDEXES

- Reduce the number of indexes on tables in SMP environments where contention is a problem.

- Reduce the fill factor in `create index` commands in SMP environments. This temporarily reduces contention for data and index pages.

- Use `fillfactor` to allow space for inserts and to reduce splitting. When the reserved space runs out, reload the table with a new `fillfactor` setting.

- To freeze the space reserved in pages, use the `max_rows_per_page` value at table and index create/alter time. This reduces lock contention and improves concurrency. The `sp_chgattribute` procedure is used to alter the existing number of rows. Here is an example of setting `max_rows_per_page` for a table and its index:

```
create table invoice
(company char(30) not null,
 ...
  date datetime not null)
with max_rows_per_page = 40
create unique clustered index inv_comp_indx
on invoice(company)
with max_rows_per_page=60
sp_helpindex inv_comp_indx
```

- If index page splitting is a problem, increase the fill factor. On nonclustered indexes, a page split requires that all the affected data rows be modified to point at the new leaf page after the split. This is very expensive. Splitting all by itself is expensive without this added overhead. It encompasses building two new pages, moving rows and logging the updates. `Fillfactor` also slows fragmentation of indexes. In this example, leaf pages will be allowed to fill to only 70 percent during the building of the `inv_comp_indx` clustered index:

```
create unique clustered index inv_comp_indx
on invoice(company)
with fillfactor=70
```

- Nonunique clustered indexes have overflow pages. Randomized calls to a page must in turn walk the overflow chain to locate the required page. This problem can be solved partially with larger table segments. More rows per page also can help.

- Use a nonclustered index with all the fields used in queries to provide coverage. With such an index, queries can be satisfied via index access. Data pages do not need to be accessed or locked.

- Just as page splits are expensive, page merges are, too. One way to avoid this phenomenon is to defer deletes to off-hours, when concurrency won't suffer from the process.

- Reduce the number of indexes to improve update, insert, and delete performance.

- Assign indexes to their own data cache, devices, and controllers for faster throughput and increased concurrency.

- Use `set forceplan` to make a query use the tables in the order specified in the `from` clause of a query.

- Use the `set table` count to increase the number of tables optimized at one time.

- Use the `INDEX`, `PREFETCH`, or `MRU/LRU` clause in queries to specify an index, I/O size, or cache strategy to be used.

- Use the `sp_cacheconfig` procedure to disable or enable the MRU (fetch-and-discard) caching strategy for a table.

- Create clustered indexes off-hours to avoid locked-out tables. SQL Server locks the table to reorder the pages.

- Create nonclustered indexes off-hours to avoid locking contention. A shared lock is placed on the table, which inhibits updates.

- Rebuild indexes to eliminate fragmentation. To accomplish this on a nonclustered index, drop the indexes and triggers, bulk copy out the data, truncate the table, bulk copy in the data, and rebuild the indexes and triggers. To defragment a clustered index or a coverage nonclusterd index, just drop and create the clustered index.

- Use a 16KB cache pool for tables with clustered indexes and frequent table scans.

- Use the `with sorted_ data_file` clause to increase index-building speed. Input to the index-building process must be presorted. SYNCSORT is probably the fastest way to sort information. Here is an example:

```
create clustered index ind_comp_indx on invoice(company)
with sorted_data_file,
allow_dup_row
```

■ Add an Identity column to nonunique clustered indexes to avoid page overflows. Here is an example:

```
create table invoice
(spid smallint not null,
 company char(30) not null,
 ...
 ident1 numeric(30,0) identity)
go
create unique clustered index inv_ix3 on invoice (spid, ident1)
```

■ Avoid indexing columns with mostly NULLs. They cause poor retrieval performance.

■ Avoid including monotonic data in indexes. High insert environments always should cluster on a key that provides the greatest degree of random-
ness. If this can't be achieved, at least partition the table. These measures
reduce lock and device contention.

■ The optimizer may not choose an access path including an index. To guarantee that an index is used, you can include it in the query. Here is an example:

```
select * from invoice (index inv_state_indx)
where state = "WA"
```

■ Compact indexes are best. Keep the key as small as possible. Avoid storing
numeric data in character datatypes. Use numeric datatypes whenever possible because they compare faster than character datatypes. Compact indexes can be scanned quicker in coverage queries.

■ Use dbcc traceon(302) to debug queries and decide whether an index or join
order for a query will help. It also can help you design better indexes for
your tables.

■ If you have large static fields in your table columns, you might want to en-
code them and use a separate table to translate them to useful display values. The invoice table has a field called part_name, for example. Part_name is
30 bytes of character data, with values such as lawn mover, computer, and gas
choke dist ring. It would be better to assign numbers to all the possible
part types listed. This would be a part_number. Now the data table is more
compact. To display the true names for parts, a separate table is built containing only the part_name and part_number. A lookup in this new table

would retrieve the name when needed. Indexes on `part_number` also would be more compact and would scan faster.

- Varchar columns should be used only when the amount of data in the column varies substantially. Otherwise, there is no savings after accounting for overhead.

- Be sure that the WHERE clause in queries using an index include the leading column. Otherwise, the optimizer may choose to do a table scan.

- You can set the number of times an index page is recycled through the cache area before it is flushed to disk by using the Number of Index Trips parameter. This value can be set higher to improve cache use and lower to improve cache flushing.

- Use the `sp_estspace` procedure on an empty table with indexes built to estimate the size of indexes and their creation times. The procedure is supplied with the number of records for the table, fill factor, and I/O rate.

- Temporary clustered or nonclustered indexes may satisfy a special processing requirement without the need to do multiple table scans. Afterward, these indexes can be dropped.

11.18   *Interactive Query* (IQ) Accelerator

Sybase IQ uses Bit-Wise™ indexes to satisfy ad-hoc and decision-support queries against warehouse databases. This is a Sybase concoction consisting of bitmapped indexes using compression, ad-hoc join strategies, and some other innovations. There are some advantages over plain bitmapped indexes.

Conventional indexes (B-tree, for *balanced-tree*) are good with high-cardinality data (many unique values). These indexes do not operate well with low-cardinality data (few unique values) or ad-hoc queries that cannot find an index to speed processing. You might think the answer is to build all the possible indexes, but this becomes cost prohibitive as disk-storage requirements explode. That is where bitmapping excels. Bitmapped indexes take values for fields and fields within fields and create a map of repeating values. The result uses bit strings to represent the keys. The final product is compressed into a tightly packed and quickly accessed map. Data aggregation has been a problem while satisfying joins using bitmapped indexes, however. Sybase IQ bridged this gap by prejoining the information, thus preoptimizing the results of joins. Also, Sybase IQ can fall through to the conventional B-tree type database indexes if the query optimizer so warrants.

It really isn't an elegant solution for OLTP databases, and you will learn why in this section. You'll also explore some of the ways you can tune Sybase IQ.

Warehouse databases provide a playing field for users who need to issue every select, join and table scan imaginable. A warehouse gives users a place to do this without upsetting the OLTP environment. But warehouses need performance, too. They don't just exist. They are a money-making asset to many businesses. Sybase IQ can help achieve that goal.

The components that make up Sybase IQ include the Sybase IQ Open Server, Sybase IQ system tables, Sybase IQ database tables, indexspaces, indexes, and command set. Users issue Sybase IQ-specific commands, which are filtered and processed using fast indexes. If an index does not exist, is not available, won't satisfy a call, or isn't the fastest access path, the request is passed on to Sybase SQL Server. So, in effect, Sybase IQ adds a software layer between the end user and SQL Server.

With Sybase IQ, it is possible to index every column in a database with multiple types of indexes, each providing a performance boost for given types of queries. This, of course, has an economical limit, determined by the disk space available for the indexes, index building time, or index update time. For these reasons, Sybase IQ isn't ideal for OLTP transactions. Here are some other reasons why not to use Sybase IQ with OLTP.

NOT SUPPORTED BY SYBASE IQ

- The `into` clause, `compute` clause, or `corresponding` keyword of the `union` clause.
- The `convert` function
- Transact-SQL identifier length restrictions (except the maximum of 30)
- Transact-SQL # characters and tempdb
- Transact-SQL local variables
- The `some`, `any` or `all` search condition
- The `match is true`, `is false` and `is unknown` conditions

The datatypes supported by Sybase IQ include char, varchar, tinyint, smallint, uint, int, date, datetime, float, and real. The limitations for these do not appear to be identical to those for Sybase tables, but I could be mistaken.

Consistent user-level commit/rollback doesn't exist between Sybase IQ and SQL Server. Here is an example. An underlying database table consists of 500,000 rows. All this data is loaded into a Sybase IQ indexspace. If the underlying database is altered and 250,000 rows are deleted, you must delete the same rows within Sybase IQ indexspace. Synchronization is not automatic because no physical link exists between the indexspace used by Sybase IQ and an underlying database. This is probably the biggest reason for not using Sybase IQ with OLTP.

You set up Sybase IQ by following the steps in the *Sybase IQ Administration Guide*. The major steps include installing the server and software, running the IQinstall script to install your databases, performing security administration, defining an attached database (if your target database is non-Sybase), and defining indexpaces and indexes. An IQ Create Indexspace template is available that enables you to build most of the index components. However, you need to expand on the template, which by default only creates FASTPROJECTION indexes.

Sybase IQ offers five index types; Table 11-2 shows how you should use these index types. One or more may apply to individual columns or queries.

Tuning Sybase IQ is multifaceted. You have to optimize disk use, index selection, good database design, multiuser access, and memory.

The first thing to attack for performance is the choice of indexes. As Table 11-2 shows, query types work best using the right index. Sybase IQ allows multiple index types on columns and automatically determines the best one to use. But you must make sure that the right types are built and available. Otherwise, the optimizer may choose to bypass Sybase IQ.

The JOINOPTIMIZATION option causes Sybase IQ to perform cost estimations of all join query plans and to select the best plan. The best query plan uses smaller, intermediate join sets. Set this option on with the IQ SET JOIN command. Another way to reduce the cost of ad-hoc joins is to prejoin indexsets. Using prejoined indexsets requires up-front work. Also, if the sets joined do not reference the largest indexset, they will not outperform an ad-hoc join request. The following commands show how to prejoin the invoice and line item tables. In this example, the indexsets are joined on item_nbr, and there is a join relationship of many-to-one, which means that there are many item_nbr(s) in the invoice table to one item_nbr in the item table.

```
IQ CREATE JOINED INDEXSET INVITJOIN1
FOR INVOICE(ITEM_NBR) = ITEM(ITEM_NBR)
MANY>>ONE
```

Each user gets two types of indexspaces: one main and one private. These can be permanent or temporary. The MAIN indexspace is allocated with the IQ CREATE INDEXSPACE command, whereas the private indexspace can be manually or automatically allocated. The private indexspace is used by Sybase IQ to handle internal processing. Both types of indexspaces need to be controlled closely to get the best performance. You will want to control the size and number of segments built because they directly impact performance.

In the area of disk use, you should take full advantage of disk striping. Sybase IQ allows disk striping using the IQ SET DISKSTRIPING ON|OFF|RAWDETECT command and the IQ SET STRIPINGDENSITY NNN command. Striping is best when segments are divided evenly across disk drives. STRIPINGDENSITY lets you control the number of stripes, which is important when different-size devices are used and when you want to place successive segments on different devices.

The IQ SET command is used to override SESSION or SERVER-WIDE defaults. The settings specified will replace existing defaults or exist for the life of a user ses-

TABLE 11-2   **Sybase IQ Index Type Selection**

Query/Column Type	Index Type to Use	Type to Avoid
All columns queried	FASTPROJECTION	
SELECT projection list	FASTPROJECTION	HIGHGROUP HIGHNONGROUP
WHERE clause calculations	FASTPROJECTION	LOWDISK
AVG/SUM argument or	FASTPROJECTION	LOWDISK
COUNT argument	HIGHNONGROUP LOWFAST HIGHGROUP	
MIN/MAX argument	FASTPROJECTION LOWFAST HIGHNONGROUP	LOWDISK
LIKE argument in WHERE clause	FASTPROJECTION	
Ad-hoc JOIN columns	FASTPROJECTION HIGHGROUP	HIGHNONGROUP
Duplicates Not Allowed field	FASTPROJECTION HIGHGROUP LOWFAST LOWDISK	HIGHNONGROUP
COUNT DISTINCT or	FASTPROJECTION	HIGHNONGROUP
SELECT DISTINCT or	HIGHGROUP	
GROUP BY arguments	LOWFAST	
Joined INDEXSET column	FASTPROJECTION HIGHGROUP LOWFAST	HIGHNONGROUP
Range queries	HIGHGROUP HIGHNONGROUP	LOWDISK
Columns used in WHERE clause ad-hoc queries	HIGHGROUP LOWFAST	
Columns used in join predicate	HIGHGROUP or LOWFAST	
Columns that contain a high number of unique values	HIGHNONGROUP	
Columns that contain a high number of unique values and are part of a SELECT GROUP BY, DISTINCT or DISTINCT COUNT	HIGHGROUP	
Columns that contain a low number of unique values and do not already use multiple indexes	LOWFAST	

sion, depending on the syntax used. Several of the parameters specified can be instrumental in tuning Sybase IQ performance. A full description of this command and others are located in the *Sybase IQ Language Reference*. This section deals only with the options shown in Figure 11-6.

Increasing available memory, block sizes, and buffers to values larger than the installation defaults can increase performance, depending on the type of index activity.

Sybase IQ's established default buffer assignments can be increased to provide better buffer hit ratios. One way to increase buffers is with the IQ SET command just discussed. Another way is with the sp_IQAddLogin procedure. In the following example, itemdb will use 5000 main buffers and 2000 private buffers when the next USE is executed. This procedure can be rerun for different indexspaces and users. These settings will be saved in the sysIQ_logins table.

```
sp_IQAddLogin " ", itemdb, " ", 5000, 2000, 1, "", "", "", RW
```

Some other parameters that affect disk performance are MAXCOMPRESSION, BLOCKSIZE, and SIZE. These parameters are set when the indexspace is created (see the next example). You should try to create a SIZE that is equivalent to the number of blocks you want to occupy the first segment (the full size of your indexspace in blocks divided by the number of stripes). BLOCKSIZE must be a power of 2 between 512 and 32,768. It is at it's optimum when it matches the I/O blocking factor for your operating system. MAXCOMPRESSION can be a power of 2 between 2 and 16. In this example, 16 indicates that Sybase IQ will compress data up to a ratio of 16 to 1. Settings in main and private indexspaces must match.

```
IQ CREATE INDEXSPACE FOR yourdb,
PATHNAME="/usr/a3/yourdb":,
SIZE=10000,  BLOCKSIZE=8192, MAXCOMPRESSION=16,
...

where SIZE=number of blocks for the first indexspace segment
     BLOCKSIZE=I/O transfer blocksize in bytes
     MAXCOMPRESSION=maximum compression ratio
```

Buffering requires memory. You want to achieve your desired level of buffering without exhausting real memory; otherwise, operating system paging will degrade performance. The best way to see how many buffers currently are available and being used is with the IQ STATUS command.

Memory is another area of tuning. The *Administration Manual* states that you need one byte of memory for every eight rows of data that are deleted from a table with HIGHGROUP indexes.

The SHMEMMB parameter defines the total amount of shared memory (in megabytes) to use when the indexspace is opened for read-only access. When the UNIX kernel will not allow you to specify a large enough amount of memory per indexspace, you can take advantage of the SYSTEMSHMMAX and SYSTEMSHMSEG options to allocate multiple shared memory segments. An example follows

Option	Description
BLOCKFACTOR	Number of records per block (default 10,000)
BLOCKSIZE	Number of bytes per block (default 500,000)
COMMIT	Number of commits for delete (default 0)
DEFAULTBUFFERS	Number of buffers (default 1,000)
DEFAULTPRIVATEBUFFERS	Number of private buffers (Default 500)
DISKSTRIPING ON | OFF | RAWDETECT	Turn internal disk striping on or off (default RAWDETECT)
ESTIMATEDRECORDCOUNT	Better management of memory during IQ INSERT (default 0)
INSERTNUMMTBUFFERS	Number of buffers to use for multithreaded insert (default 5)
INSERTNUMROWSPERBUFFER	Number of rows per buffer for serial or multithreaded insert (default 10,000)
LIMIT	Maximum number of rows to read from source table (indexset) (default NO LIMIT)
MBSORT	Number of megabytes of memory used by each sort object (default 5MB)
SYSTEMSHMEMMB	Number of megabytes of shared memory used for indexspace read/only access
STRIPINGDENSITY	Number of stripes to create per segment (default 0). The zero default creates as many stripes as there are segments.
SYSTEMSHMMAX	Number of megabytes will match the amount made available when configuring the kernel
MBGROUPBY	Number of megabytes to use for GROUP BY optimization (default 1)
VERTICALGROUPBYOPTIMIZATION	Turn GROUP BY optimization on or off. When on, Sybase IQ will attempt to select the best grouping method (default on)
ROWCOUNT	Processing stops after number of rows (default 0) Default of 0 will return all rows

Figure 11-6 Sybase IQ Tuning Options

that allows shared memory segments of 50MB until a total of 500MB is reached:

```
IQ SET SERVERDEFAULT SYSTEMSHMMAX 500
IQ SET SERVERDEFAULT SYSTEMSHMSEG  50
```

The MBSORT parameter defaults to 5MB, which isn't very much. This is a good parameter to bump up for those types of queries that use sort (ORDER BY or GROUP BY).

IQ DBCC CHECKDB and IQ SHOW INDEXSPACE STATS are the tools to determine how effective your changes to these parameters have been. The array statistics are of particular interest and include the following:

```
NHashtbClears

NHashtbCollisions      < Helpful for hit ratio

NHashtbEntries

NHashtbFinds           < Helpful for hit ratio

NHashtbHits            < Helpful

NHashtbHits1           < Helpful

NHashtbHits2           < Helpful

NHashtbInserts

NHashtbLChain

NHashtbRehash          < HELPFUL
NHashtbMaxEntries
```

11.19   Network Tuning and TDS Packet Sizing

No two network configurations are exactly the same. Yours will have special needs that other administrators won't face. Their experiences may not apply to your particular situation. But cheer up: The rules for network tuning are the same for everyone. These are the areas of importance when tuning the network. They are in order of the easiest to accomplish to the hardest.

- Analyze the network for bottlenecks and overall load.
- Set the default and maximum packet size.
- Add network memory.
- Isolate online applications with different packet requirements.
- Isolate batch applications.
- Increase or upgrade NICs.
- Increase the number of ports.
- Increase the number of network engines.

PACKET OPTIONS

Sybase supports the TCP/IP and SPX/IPX packet communications protocols. The client sends a packet to the server and waits for a reply. Packets can be a fixed size or variable. A delay mechanism is available to allow packets to fill up more before being transmitted—this is called *packet batching*. Packet batching is turned on by default. Some networks run faster with it on, whereas others run faster with it off. You can turn off packet batching by setting the `tcp no delay` `sp_configure` parameter to 1. Packets are transmitted regardless of their size, so be sure to take some benchmarks before and after transmitting.

Tabular datastream (TDS) packets are 512 bytes by default. Try increasing packet sizes if network traffic consists mainly of large query result sets. If the average query returns more than 512 bytes of data during transmission, for example, a larger packet size will perform better. If the system is strictly for *Decision Support System* (DSS), very large sizes may be warranted. For OLTP systems, it is best to leave the `default network packet size` parameter at 512 bytes or to reduce it and force larger packet sizes to be used in individual applications.

Packet sizing is not an exact science. You can determine your need for larger packets from the `sp_sysmon` network reports. You will have to experiment with assorted sizes to arrive at the optimum for your servers and users, though. SQL Server reserves enough memory for all defined users (number of user connections and number of remote connections) to log in using `default network packet size`. Larger sizes require additional network memory assigned with the `additional network memory` parameter.

NETWORK STATISTICS

You can locate bottlenecks in a number of ways. Your users already may be calling to tell you that you have a problem. But they probably don't see the whole picture. If an application is running slowly, it may not be a problem with the network. Your first goal should be to rule out other possible causes. Have your user re-create the bottleneck or report the problem the next time it occurs. At that time, generate the Network I/O Management report with `sp_sysmon`.

The first two things to look for are saturated engines and total network traffic in bytes. If all engines are saturated, you have a bottleneck. If the total traffic in bytes exceeds the hardware capabilities, you have a bottleneck. If both answers are no, you might want to use Showplan to evaluate your user's query. Suppose that you have a bottleneck. You need to determine what processes were running at the time of the bottleneck. A large number of bytes sent could be representative of some heavy batch or query processing, for example. Maybe some replication, backup or bulk-copying processing was in progress. Figure 11-7 shows sample `sp_sysmon` output.

There is the possibility that the transaction volume has exceeded your software/hardware configuration. To avoid being overtaken by growth, you should keep a historical database with statistics. Use a spreadsheet to graph your growth. A well-constructed capacity-planning graph includes two lines: one to identify the activity where hardware must be ordered and one where hardware must be upgraded. This requires that you know the limitations of your hardware (ports, NIC speeds, and so on).

```
Network I/O Management
----------------------
  Total Network I/O Requests    214.3        1.1     16106        n/a
    Network I/Os Delayed          0.0        0.0         0        0.0 %(A)
  Total TDS Packets Received  per sec   per xact     count  % of total
  ------------------------    -------   --------     -----  ----------
    Engine 0                     25.2        0.3      1940      23.8 %
    Engine 1                     25.2        0.2      1940      23.8 %
    Engine 2                     25.5        0.1      1921      23.7 %
    Engine 3                     32.7        0.2      2339      28.7 %
  ------------------------    -------   --------     -----  ----------
  Total TDS Packets Rec'd       108.6        0.7      8140
  Total Bytes Received        per sec   per xact     count  % of total
  ------------------------    -------   --------     -----  ----------
    Engine 0                   1888.0        8.3     37225      31.6 %(B)
    Engine 1                    977.8        7.0     35162      29.8 %(C)
    Engine 2                    479.2        6.3     23152      19.7 %(D)
    Engine 3                    364.2        6.2     22244      18.9 %(E)
  ------------------------    -------   --------     -----  ----------
  Total Bytes Rec'd            3709.2       27.8    117783         (F)
  Avg Bytes Rec'd per Packet      n/a        n/a        27        n/a
  ------------------------------------------------------------------
  Total TDS Packets Sent      per sec   per xact     count  % of total
  ------------------------    -------   --------     -----  ----------
    Engine 0                     25.7        0.2      1950      24.5 %
    Engine 1                     25.3        0.3      1923      24.1 %
    Engine 2                     22.5        0.1      1753      22.0 %
    Engine 3                     32.2        0.2      2340      29.4 %
  ------------------------    -------   --------     -----  ----------
  Total TDS Packets Sent        105.7        0.8      7966
  Total Bytes Sent            per sec   per xact     count  % of total
  ------------------------    -------   --------     -----  ----------
    Engine 0                   1918.5       11.5     77850      45.3 %(G)
    Engine 1                   1172.5       10.1     45069      26.2 %(H)
    Engine 2                    782.9        8.7     27559      16.1 %(I)
    Engine 3                    660.8        4.5     21220      12.4 %(J)
  ------------------------    -------   --------     -----  ----------
  Total Bytes Sent             4534.7       38.8    171698         (K)
  Avg Bytes Sent per Packet       n/a        n/a        38        n/a
```

Figure 11-7 Network I/O Management Output for `sp_sysmon`

(**A**) `Network I/Os Delayed` shows I/O delays and means that you have a serious bottleneck in your network configuration or available hardware bandwidth.

(**B-F**) `Total Bytes Received` is the number of bytes received by each engine. This is a way of determining whether all your engines are load balanced or saturated. `Average Bytes Received Per Packet` helps determine the optimum default packet size. In Figure 11-7, it could be lower than the 512-byte default. If this number is close to or higher than the default packet size, an increase in the default is in order.

(**G-K**) `Total Bytes Sent` is the number of bytes sent by each engine. This is used with `Total Bytes Received` to determine whether engines are load balanced or saturated. `Average Bytes Sent Per Packet` helps determine the optimum default packet size. In Figure 11-7, it could be lower than the 512-byte default. In fact, the report indicates small send and receive packets. This system may be a candidate for turning off packet batching. If this number is close to or higher than the default packet size, an increase in the default is in order.

(B-K) SMP systems that support network affinity migration will distribute the traffic across engines. SQL Server selects an engine for a user during login for the duration of the connection. If all engines show high levels of activity sustained, this could be an indication that more engines are needed. Check the CPU utilization reports.

HINTS FOR TUNING THE NETWORK

- TCP/IP packet batching can improve performance for socket-based networks and those that emulate terminals. It can hurt systems with light network traffic or very small packet sizes.

- The Net-Flex 2 and Compaq Ethernet 16TP are two NICs that use Packet Burst mode. They can greatly improve performance when many packets exist and they are relatively small. To take advantage of this feature, you need to enable Packet Burst mode in both the server and client workstations.

- Use larger packet sizes for tasks that perform large data transfers. Increase network memory to accommodate these changes.

- Use small packets for OLTP and large packets for DSS servers. Here are some sizes you might want to play with:

OLTP servers	256 bytes, 512 bytes and 1KB
DSS servers	1KB, 2KB, 4KB, 8KB and 16KB
Batch applications and BCP	8KB and 16KB
Symmetric replication	8KB and 16KB

- Filter data to avoid large transfers.

- Isolate heavy network users from ordinary users.

- Use stored procedures, views, and triggers to reduce network traffic. Shorter commands are sent to the server because the bulk of the code resides at the server. Complete result sets are returned to the client. Filtering of the result set can be enforced with stored procedures.

- Avoid remote backup systems that transfer data over the network.

- Schedule server-based replication for off-hours.

- The size of the TDS packet affects efficiency. A larger packet size can improve batch-application throughput. To tune packet size, you must allow larger sizes for the server and in the `cs_packet_size` connection property in your program.

▪ You can make packet-size changes for all users with the following server parameters:

```
sp_configure "default network packet size",640
sp_configure "max network packet size",8192
```

If average bytes per packet in `sp_sysmon` reports is within 10 percent of the default packet size configured for your server, increase `"default network packet size"` in 10-percent increments, measuring network I/O for effects. An OLTP system using the installation `"default network packet size"` of 512, for example, sees an average of 500 bytes per packet. You might want to make the following changes:

Additional_netmem_pages = (((large packet connections*8KB)* 3) * 1.20)/2KB

144 = (((10 * 8192) * 3) * 1.2)/2048

```
sp_configure "additional network memory",144     (new settin
```

In addition to making the necessary changes to `sp_configure`, you might want to do the following:

Locate any processes that need larger packet sizes and have the client use the 8192KB packet size for those processes only. This could include batch-maintenance processes.

Use a Performance Monitor (for example, DBAware) to measure packet-size performance using different sizes over time. This can help you select the best default packet size to use. Individual queries with larger packet sizes should be tuned separately using the `"isql Asize"` (UNIX, Windows), `"load isql -Asize"` (Novell), and `"isql /tdspacketsize = size"` commands (VMS).

```
isql A4096
```

Turn off the `rows affected` messages for queries to reduce some network traffic. Use this command:

```
dbcc tune (doneinproc, 0)
```

▪ Larger packet sizes should be requested in Open Client applications with large result sets. You can accomplish this by using `"isql -Usa -Annnnn"`, where `nnnnn` is the packet size. You also can set it in the `ct_con_props()` connection properties function.

▪ Avoid cursors in applications or tune them. They can require individual row or set-of-row transmissions.

▪ TCP is faster than SPX/IPX—even more so with large data transfers.

▪ If your system is out of bandwidth, you can reduce the `"number of user connections"` parameter as an emergency measure while acquiring more NICs and so on. This acts as a governor on the amount of system activity and network connections. Use `sp_configure` with the `"user connections"` value to view and set the maximum concurrent connections. This value usually is computed as the number of workstations plus mirrored devices and background processes. Here's how it looks:

```
1>      sp_configure "number of user connections"
2>      go


name                    min         max         config_value    run_value


user_connections        5           512         290             290

(return status=0)
```

- Provide multiple high-speed NIC cards as needed to handle network loads. Use Fibre (FDDI) or fast Ethernet networks for high-speed or high-volume requirements. See Chapters 6 and 17 for more on network tuning.
- Try running with packet batching off with `"tcp no delay"` set to `1` (`sp_configure`).
- Choose a transport stack that supports attention signals. If a query cancels, all the rows are prevented from being sent back to the client. Instead, these leftover rows are flushed, which reduces network traffic. Novell and Microsoft both support this feature with a software patch.
- Load balance network traffic across separate servers, controllers, multiple network listeners, and engines.
- A SQL Server engine will go to sleep after a blocking network I/O. It could sleep too long (this is called a *latency period*). Try increasing the `sp_configure` `"runnable process search count"` to reduce latency periods. This solution could improve networking at the expense of more CPU.
- If network I/O activity is low or infrequent, you can reduce the `sp_configure` `"i/o polling process count"` value. If it is too high, try increasing the value.

11.20 NetWare Servers

NetWare-based systems have special needs. Many white papers go into extensive detail on tuning Novell dedicated servers and NetWare. This section isn't meant to replace those papers. Instead, it is intended to streamline your efforts by offering you a list of tuning hints.

TUNING HINTS FOR NETWARE SERVERS

- Release 4.01 has better memory management than 3.1.1.
- Use a 64KB block factor when setting up partitions.

- Use Compaq Insight Manager to monitor system hardware, CPU, and EISA bus use.

- Load SQLSRVR with the -P option on dedicated systems.

- The default size of a NetWare buffer is 4KB for both NetWare 3.11 and 4.01. Under NetWare 3.11, this size can be altered by using a "set cache buffer size" equal to a value between 4KB and 16KB.

- Compaq Array Accelerator on the IDA-2 and SMART controllers provide substantial performance for database activities under NetWare. Both controllers have a 4MB mirrored posted write cache. The SMART SCSI Array controller provides load balancing. However, you must perform manual striping across multiple SMART controllers to get the best performance.

- Fast Ethernet II is preferred for its higher transmission rate. Also, Ethernet II can be a prerequisite if you plan to connect to devices in non-Novell networks. Here is an example of the Novell AUTOEXEC.NCF definitions to provide both TCP/IP and SPX/IPX connectivity on a server using a single NIC:

```
LOAD CPQETHER NAME=DSI-IP SLOT=5 FRAME=ETHERNET_II
LOAD CPQETHER NAME=DSI-IPX SLOT=5
BIND IPX TO DSI-IPX NET=SLOW
LOAD TCPIP
BIND IP TO DSI-IP ADDR=509.509.509.1 MASK=FF.FF.FF.1
```

It is best to avoid multiple protocol networks because NetWare has to send out search packets for each frame type. This adds to the network burden. In this case, it would be better to separate the frame types to their own NICs or to replace all the IPX hardware.

- Adjust the following SET parameters. They have the greatest impact on system performance. Here is a list of the important ones:

```
MAXIMUM CONCURRENT DISK CACHE WRITES

DIRTY DISK CACHE DELAY TIME

MAXIMUM CONCURRENT DIRECTORY CACHE WRITES

MAXIMUM DIRECTORY CACHE BUFFERS

MINIMUM DIRECTORY CACHE BUFFERS

READ AFTER WRITE VERIFY = OFF

IMMEDIATE PURGE OF DELETED FILES = ON

MAXIMUM PHYSICAL RECEIVE PACKET SIZE = 1130 (10 Mbps Ethernet)

MAXIMUM PHYSICAL RECEIVE PACKET SIZE = 4202 (16 Mbps Token Ring)

MAXIMUM PHYSICAL RECEIVE PACKET SIZE = 2154 (4 Mbps Token Ring)

CACHE BUFFER SIZE = 16 KB
```

FILE DELETE WAIT TIME = 4 (NetWare 3.11 only)

FILE DELETE WAIT TIME = 1 (NetWare 4.01 only)

MINIMUM FILE DELETE WAIT TIME = 1 (NetWare 3.11 only)

GARBAGE COLLECTION INTERVAL = 1 MIN (NetWare 4.01 only)

MINIMUM PACKET RECEIVE BUFFERS

MAXIMUM PACKET RECEIVE BUFFERS

MINIMUM NUMBER OF CACHE BUFFERS

11.21   Busy Servers

The sp_sysmon output for kernel use reports on SQL Server activities and is the single fastest way to determine whether your server needs more engines (see Figure 11-8). In the sample report, the average engine use is 97.6 percent. Any sustained value of more than 90 percent is an indication of a need for more processing power. At 95 percent and above, you will experience degraded performance. It is recommended that you disable the housekeeping task prior to performing this tuning.

(A) The Engine Busy Utilization average is your quickest indication of a CPU shortage. Once you hit 95 percent, response times begin degrading, as does batch processing. Work normally relegated to the housekeeper task is queuing up because there are no idle times. Intermittent lock-ups probably are really checkpointing activities that are busy flushing dirty pages to disk. A high CPU Yields by Engine count and a high Engine Busy Utilization count could be an indication that nonserver-based processing is locking out the server.

You really don't want to wait for an out-of-CPU condition to arise. Instead, you want to monitor resources over time, keeping a database with your growth history on it. The best tools for this are SQL Monitor and DBAware from Menlo Software. With DBAware, you easily can track engine and server growth and use. Also, you don't want to configure in a new processor if you haven't

```
Kernel Utilization
------------------

   Engine Busy Utilization:
      Engine 0             99.5 %
      Engine 1             98.3 %
      Engine 2             95.3 %
      Engine 3             97.1 %
   ----------          --------------        ----------------
   Summary:            Total: 390.2 %        Average:  97.6 % (A)
...
```

Figure 11-8 Kernel Use Output for sp_sysmon

completely tuned all other aspects of your system first. You may not really need a processor.

 NOTE: You also can use the `select @@cpu_busy` command or the `cpu_busy` percentage returned from `sp_monitor` to see CPU use. However, the `cpu_busy` percentage is not a correct indicator of CPU use.

11.22   SMP Processors

SQL Server's SMP architecture allows any server task to use any available engine. Applications don't need to be altered to run with SMP machines. The server automatically distributes processing and user connections across engines.

The occasion may arise when you need to set affinity. Sometimes, you can improve performance by using CPU affinity, which you force by using the dbcc tune command. Not all operating systems support CPU affinity, however. Those that don't support it ignore the command. Here, `server_first_cpu` specifies the engine the server will think is engine 0. Other engines are bound incrementally based on the engine 0 assignment. Engine 3 would be bound to `server_first_cpu` + 3, for example. If the resulting number is higher than the real number of processors, it wraps.

```
dbcc tune(cpuaffinity, server_first_cpu [, on| off] )
```

- Where `server_first_cpu` is set to -1 to use the default starting CPU number
- Where `server_first_cpu_start` is set to -1 and "`off`" is used to disable the affinity of CPUs
- Where the on| off flag is not specified to display just current affinity settings

Suppose that you have a 4 CPU machine with CPUs numbered 0 through 3. On a 4 engine SQL Server, affinity is set to begin with engine 3 in the following example:

```
dbcc tune(cpuaffinity, 3, "on")
```

Actual Engine	Server CPU
0	1
1	2
2	3
3	0

In addition to CPU affinity, you can use process affinity to force a process to run on an engine. You should use these two techniques sparingly when attempting to balance engine use.

Figure 1-95 shows a `sp_sysmon` report for CPU use in an SMP machine. You quickly can see which processors are running at maximum use and whether the overall machine use is taxed. The following section lists some other things to watch out for in an SMP system.

SMP TUNING HINTS

- Long and frequent locks may be an indication that buffers, registers, memory or devices are locked by an SMP thread. Check the Mutiex statistics (NetWare).

- If the boot processor is underused, changing the configuration to Shared mode may help.

- If the monitor does not show use of the secondary processors, your system is not running SMP-aware programs.

- If all processors are saturated, as they are in the example in Figure 1-95, it is time to add processors.

- If the `sp_sysmon` data cache management value "`spinlock`" is high, using named caches may improve performance for SMP systems.

- The increased throughput of SMP may result in increased lock contention when tables with multiple indexes are updated. Reduce the number of indexes on tables to reduce lock contention.

- If any engines other than engine 0 are underused, it may help to move network I/O off engine 0. SQL Server selects an engine to handle network I/O for user connections. Engine affinity remains assigned until termination of a user connection.

- Set the `sp_configure` parameter "`maximum online engines`" equal to the number of processors (minus one for each nonserver process that must be active concurrently). Be sure to dedicate at least one engine to the operating system.

- Use CPU affinity and process affinity to balance processing.

- Use dataserver affinity to cut overhead associated with the transfer of process information between CPUs. Do not do this on asymmetric multiprocessors because contention between SQL Server and the operating system will degrade performance.

- Increase the preemptive priority of dataserver engines.

- If there is contention for the log semaphore, increase the "`user log cache size`" (ULC) `sp_configure` parameter to improve transaction buffering.

- On SMP systems with high transaction rates, binding the transaction log to its own cache can reduce cache spinlock contention.

- For NT-based systems, see Chapter 8, "Microsoft® Windows NT™ 4.0 Tuning," on using NT's monitor for SMP tuning.

11.23 MPP Processors

Massively parallel processing (MPP) is a name that fits. Processing horsepower has become synonymous with scalability. In a similar fashion, parallel processing is equivalent to scalability.

Traditionally, processors have used one or a few processors to access data, sometimes improving performance by sharing cached memory. MPP blows these methods away. What changed? Well, the hardware vendors extended their reach into the world of parallel processing, which was not new. Next, the operating-system vendors took advantage of running subtasks in parallel. Finally, the RDBMS vendors are getting on the bandwagon.

With MPP, superior data-mining and analysis capabilities are possible. Response times and throughput improve. All areas of processing are being transitioned to parallel processing. Sybase is leading the way with updates (insert, update and delete), utilities (load, backup, restore and create index), and system servers.

Sybase's implementation of MPP is unique. Multiple SQL Server nodes, each harnessing one or more processors, are assigned partitions of data to work on (base and regular realms). Partitioning links performance to the data and its use. The user then can assign processing power where data use demands it. In the event of a node failure, another node picks up the processing. There are three types of partitions:

Hash partitioning	Data is randomized evenly across partitions.
Range partitioning	Data is grouped according to key.
Schema partitioning	Data is partitioned by table.

Because partitioning is defined in a system catalog, it is not necessary to put any code in your application programs to take advantage of MPP. A parallel global optimizer accesses the catalog (probably caching in memory what it finds) and determines the best processing. To see query plans with their enhanced parallel report features, complete these four steps:

1. Run update statistics.
2. `1> sp_pragma "opt_explain", "on"` (turn on explain)
3. `2> sp_pragma "opt_explain", "filename", invoice` (output sent to invoice file)
4. Browse the `$NAVIGATOR/invoice.detail` file.

How does MPP divide up the work? Several processors are given the job of working on a task related to data in their partition. At their conclusion, the results are merged. Think about it: This is no small feat. The results are astounding. If I can believe the Usenet e-mails I have been reading, hours have become minutes and minutes seconds on queries that have been tuned previously.

After you implement a Sybase MPP system, you need to tune it. You do this with the Sybase *MPP Manager* (MPPM) utilities. MPP tuning is outside the scope of this book. For more information, refer to the Sybase documentation *Sybase MPP 11.0 for Sun Ultra Enterprise PDB Cluster Server with Solaris 2.5.1.*

11.24 Symmetric Replication

The Sybase Replication Server has many new acronyms and facilities you should know. Generally, replication is thought of as data propagation between two detached databases. In the Sybase world, the originating database or table (also known as *source*) commonly is called the *primary*. The associated target database or table (also known as *destination*) commonly is called the *replicate*.

Replication provides some easily attained performance benefits. In some—but not all—cases, it can be advantageous to segregate corporate enterprise data from local site specific data. To clarify this point, imagine this example. A large corporation has servers scattered across the United States in almost every state. Each state server has a local database with data representative of the business in the state. Some of the tables are replicated from other states or the corporate headquarters, which is in Los Angeles. The corporate headquarters could replicate changes to each of the individual states by using Sybase replication, or it could send updates to only a few states (intermediaries), which in turn would route updates to their neighboring states. This would reduce communications costs and help "parallelize" the workload.

Suppose that Los Angeles sends updates to New York and Texas. However, the Texas server crashes. Because the replicated tables in New York are fine, Texas-based users can reference them until their server recovers.

What other advantages exist? Locally maintained tables can be accessed much faster than remote tables. Also, communications traffic is relegated to faster *local area network* (LAN) communications for local data rather than slower *wide area network* (WAN) communications.

You can derive quite a few other benefits from asynchronous replication. There is less lock contention because different sites maintain their own copies of tables. Duplicate tables have fewer contenders accessing each copy.

Sybase supports *heterogeneous* database replication, which means that users now can view the whole enterprise. A user viewing up-to-date and in-sync enterprise data is more productive. Sybase's transaction-based replication guarantees that the data is updated more quickly than snapshots, table copies, and other nontransaction-based schemes. Integrity is maintained across multiple replicate databases, even if they are on disparate RDBMSs. All these features improve user performance.

The replication server can process asynchronous procedures that are distributed to replicate databases where they execute. Of tremendous value is the capability to change many rows in a single-procedure execution instead of replicating only one row. Stored procedures using applied functions update information on the primary database and then pass a stored procedure to a replicate database. There, the stored procedure processes, making however many changes to that local database.

Going in the opposite direction, starting with a replicate database, a stored procedure using request functions causes updates to occur on the primary database. Afterward, through normal replication or the previously mentioned applied-function technique, these updates are propagated back to the replicate database.

Entering system commands and those available with *Replication Server Manager* (RSM) enables you to get the basic information necessary to tune the replication environment. Latency is the enemy of replication. The longer updates remain queued up in the replication pipeline, the more likely something will go wrong or someone will become unhappy. Latency can be inherent to the routing chosen, type and speed of communications hardware and software, number of tables, columns and rows being replicated, and number of replicate databases. Also, there may be other factors not mentioned here.

Table 11-3 lists some RSM commands that help you monitor replication. Another aspect of enterprise-wide databases that shouldn't be overlooked is management costs. Sybase has attempted to resolve this with the Sybase Enterprise SQL Server Manager, OmniConnect, and DirectConnect. Designed specifically to deal with the complexities of geographically dispersed databases, users can cut costs by managing many servers, databases, security, performance, backups, and recovery from one location. Another tool called InfoHub is for SQL access to MVS-based nonrelational databases. These tools help to enforce enterprise-wide server standards, too.

TABLE 11-3   Replication Administration Commands

Command	Displays
admin disk_space	Disk partitions accessed by Replication Server
admin show_connections	Connections to Replication Server
admin sqm_readers	Threads reading the inbound queue
admin statistics,md	Statistics about message delivery
admin statistics,mem	Statistics about memory use
admin who	Threads
admin who_is_up and admin who_is_down	Threads that are up or down
admin who,dsi	*Data Server Interface* (DSI) threads
admin who,rsi	*Replication Server Interface* (RSI) threads
admin who,sqm	Queues managed by *Stable Queue Manager* (SQM)
admin who,sqt	Queues managed by *Stable Queue Transaction* (SQT) *Interface*

So what is keeping the world from adopting replication? CIOs don't know whether there is a payback for their users! Users don't know much about the technical or cost aspects of replication! Administrators are afraid of the work it will take to transition to distributed databases! But, even more important, many individuals don't know what key factors should signal their need for replication. Here is a list of some of those factors:

- A consolidated corporate view of distributed data is needed.

- Many of the reasons for client/server computing at distributed sites exist.

- Distributed processing would improve performance.

- Heterogeneous databases need to be synchronized (Sybase provides bidirectional replication between major data sources, including SQL Server, Oracle, DB2, IMS, Informix, VSAM, Lotus Notes, SQL Anywhere and more than 25 target DBMSs).

- Distributed systems need near real-time visibility of consistent data.

- The enterprise is too large to use centralized computing.

- Business units are diversifying.

- Consulting groups are recommending a datamart or data warehouse.

11.25   Asynchronous Queries

A synchronous query will not get a response back until the query is complete. However, asynchronous queries gain control immediately, even though the result set may not be built for a long time. Asynchronous queries essentially are single occurrences of multithreaded tasks. As a programmer, you can enter the world of asynchronous applications by using Client-Library.

Client-Library enables you to develop applications that can use asynchronous processing across all Sybase-supported platforms. Your programs can make server requests while continuing to process other work. As an example, you could issue parallel requests to the server. Asynchronous programs can be canceled midstream, thus eliminating the need to return a set of rows. This eliminates unnecessary network I/O.

HINTS FOR TUNING ASYNCHRONOUS QUERIES

- Avoid Windows DB-Library calls, such as `dbsqlexec()`, that are synchronous. The fact that DB-Library's synchronous interface is not event driven and does not naturally support graphical user interfaces are two reasons why Sybase provides the Client-Library.

■ Use the Sybase Client-Library. The Open Client and Open Server products supply the actual interface to the library services. How do the services work? On systems that poll for I/O (UNIX and MS Windows), each I/O request completes or indicates that it would block the request from taking further action by returning an operating-system-specific return code. The software checks to see whether any blocked I/O has completed and generates an asynchronous notification when an I/O event occurs. On systems that trigger callback routines (VMS, OpenVMS and Macintosh), each I/O request is queued to the operating system and the operating system notifies a callback routine when the requested I/O operation has completed. Finally, on systems that support native threads (MS NT, IBM OS/2, OSF DCE and Novell NetWare) a worker thread is dispatched within the operating system. It blocks further action until the I/O finishes. You should take advantage of the nonblocking calls available in Client-Library, such as dbsql-sok(), dbdataready(), dbpoll(), and dbsqlok().

When do you need an asynchronous application? Boy, that is a good question. If there is a third-party tool or an existing facility that will accomplish the throughput you need, the answer is *never*. But, if you are going to write Open Client applications (maybe to use cursors), you will benefit by planning around asynchronous activities. Anything you build, you also have to maintain, so beware of overbuilding because it leads to overmaintenance.

11.26 Query Optimization

How should you tune your queries? I believe it is important to keep a couple of things in mind when taking on a task as formidable as tuning individual queries. First, use the Pareto principle. That is, 80 percent of the gain will be derived from 20 percent of the work. If you group your queries into those that will yield the greatest return on investments and those that won't, you have completed the first step. Next, you want to look for the most obvious things; things such as table scans and the use of temporary tables are indications that indexes aren't being used. To aid you in your search, use the tools available.

SHOWPLAN and STATISTICS I/O are fundamental sources of information about individual queries. The *Sybase User Guide* and almost every book available on tuning Sybase repeat many of the fundamental things to look for when tuning queries. The following list of hints is compiled from all the things I could find on the subject of query optimization.

There are some excellent third-party tools for reviewing SQL code. They can automate the selection and rewriting of queries to optimize them.

STATIC AND DYNAMIC SQL

Ad-hoc queries essentially are free-form requests for information. A query is considered static SQL. Under the covers, Sybase submits dynamic SQL to satisfy your request, though. So how does the processing flow from the static form of call to a dynamic one?

It begins with the parsing of the SQL statement for syntactic validity. Already, the SQL statement is being sliced, diced, and ordered in the way in which processing must proceed. This makes the syntax output ready for the optimizer to use in determining the best query plan. After choosing a plan, the compiler creates and launches the executable code. A dynamic call uses the executable code as the basis for accessing the database. A SQL that is reusable now is a candidate for being converted to a stored procedure. If the database changes, the recompile facility is used to reoptimize the query plans.

COST-BASED OPTIMIZER

The optimizer examines parsed and normalized queries and prepares a query plan. A *query plan* is a set of steps and access methods that represent the least-costly approach in terms of time. Multiple query plans can exist for a query. They are all compiled and loaded into the procedure cache ready for execution. If the plans are changed, they must be flushed from memory and reloaded.

HINTS FOR TUNING QUERIES

- Use the `set forceplan on` command to make SQL Server join tables in a query in the same order they are listed in your `from` clause.
- Use the `set prefetch` command to enable or disable large I/O for a session.
- Use `sp_cachestrategy` to change cache strategies.
- Use large I/O for *Decision Support Systems* (DSSs).
- Design transactions to release locks and commit as soon as possible.
- Eliminate unnecessary referential integrity constraints.
- Use stored procedures and triggers to shift work to the server and reduce network traffic.
- Use asynchronous queries and programs to use nonblocking calls and allow parallelization of the application.
- Use the minimum locking level that satisfies the application requirements.
- If the subquery is too big, remove the restrictive outer join.
- If a `GROUP BY ALL` query is running too long, upgrade to Sybase 11 where it runs quicker.
- If a subquery `JOIN` is running too long, be sure it is being optimized correctly.
- If a subquery with `JOIN` columns is running long, make sure the join columns have an index or are covered.

- If a query with duplicates in correlation columns is running long, Sybase 11 will run faster because the results are cached in memory.

- Use temporary tables as interim tables for complex joins. This is necessary only when the optimizer won't achieve a better solution than you can engineer.

- Create replicated table environments where ad-hoc queries can run without draining the normal OLTP server.

- Set PowerBuilder AutoCommit to TRUE for a transaction object. The default is FALSE, which is much more resource intensive. Here is the syntax:

```
your_trans_object.AutoCommit = TRUE
```

- Use identity columns to increment a unique key column in a table. They can be nonzero, non-null integers or fractions. They begin with 1 and are incremented automatically when a row is inserted. The largest number is limited by the identity column maximum, which is 38 digits. A major drawback of identity columns is that gaps can crop up between numbers. You would have to query your way through the gaps or use cursoring. Another alternative is to set the sp_configure "identity burning set" value, which sets aside incremental numbers in memory. When they are used up, another group of numbers is set up. This is supposed to solve the gap problem, but because one value services all your tables, a new problem is introduced. If the system crashes or a shutdown with NOWAIT is issued, there is a large gap between the numbers. You should try to standardize the size of identity columns, standardize shutdown policies, avoid rollbacks in long-running transactions, and move processing (math, string manipulation and so on) to the client machine.

- Use SELECT INTO, which is faster than INSERT with a nested SELECT.

- Make transactions small and fast for the most frequent user. If there is a path in the transaction logic that takes longer, design the processing so that it is the exception path.

- Declare cursor intent (READ ONLY or UPDATE).

- Allow subqueries to short-circuit after doing the least amount of work—not the most. Placing the least-restrictive OR clause first in a list of OR clauses is one example. Queries with many ANDS and ORS should be reordered to cause short-circuiting early if the Boolean criteria is not satisfied.

- Use >= in an indexed where clause instead of just >. Here is an example:

```
select * from invoice where amount > 10.00
select * from invoice where amount >= 11.00
```

The first query is much slower than the second because SQL Server must locate the first occurrence of the amount at 10.00 and then scan forward looking for the first value greater than 10.00. If there are many 10.00 amounts, it takes longer.

- Queries with EXISTS and IN clauses are faster than those with NOT EXISTS and NOT IN clauses if the fields referenced are not indexed. This is because all values must be examined for matches with a negative expression. The same is not true of a positive expression.

- Provide a stored procedure with values to variables in order for the optimizer to choose the right path.

- Do not use the count aggregate in a subquery to do an existence check. SQL Server may end up doing a table or index scan. Instead, use the EXISTS or IN clause.

- Avoid putting noncolumn data fields inside a MIN or MAX clause; they can result in a scan. In the following example, the second clause performs a scan of the nonclustered index on the amount field. The max optimization feature is used for the first clause.

```
max(amount*1.20)
max(amount) * 1.20
```

- If you are joining two columns of different datatypes, the column with the type lower in the SQL datatypes hierarchy is converted to match its join partner's datatype. If this column is indexed, SQL Server uses the index only if it is not the one that had its datatype converted. Avoid join problems by building tables with matching datatypes. You also can use the convert function in the query to force the conversion to happen to the other side of the join. In the following example, there is an index on part.part, but invoice.part is the char datatype, whereas part.part is the varchar datatype.

Without convert:
```
select * from invoice, part
where invoice.part = part.part
```

With convert:
```
select * from invoice, part
where convert(varchar(20), invoice.part) = part.part
```

- Along the same lines as the last bullet, avoid incompatible datatypes anywhere they could occur in a query because the optimizer may be impacted.

- Use third-party tools designed to optimize queries, such as Precise SQL.

- Use set showplan on to study query plans and locate areas that need tuning. The most obvious thing to look for is a table scan. The second most obvious thing to look for in showplan output is the use of a worktable.

- Use the `dbcc traceon(3604, 302, 310)` commands to interrogate what the optimizer is doing.

- Use the `set statistics io on` command to see the number of logical and physical I/Os for a query.

- If your application must run at locking level 3, use the `NOHOLDLOCK` clause.

- Perform calculations against literals, not columns, as in this example:

```
lastqtr <; dateadd(dd,getdate(), -90)
```

is better than

```
datediff(dd,lastqtr,getdate()) &gt; 90
```

- The optimizer considers permutations of four tables at a time on multitable joins. If you are using more than four tables, you can set the `set table count` option to increase the number of tables the optimizer considers (the maximum is 8). For eight tables, the syntax follows:

```
set table count 8
```

- Always specify indexes in queries if they are known and if they are known to be the best access path. Review statistics I/O for a query to see whether the index you chose required less I/O than the optimizer. Issue `UPDATE STATISTICS` to keep the optimizer informed of changes.

- Use the `WITH SORTED_DATA_FILE` clause to build clustered indexes using a presorted file.

- Use the LRU option to override the fetch-and-discard MRU caching strategy in queries. Here is an example:

```
select * from invoice (index inv_company prefetch 2 lru)
```

- Always include the leading column for an index in the `where` clause. Otherwise, the optimizer avoids using the index.

- Add SARGs to eliminate or reduce scanning.

- Use `OR` instead of `UNION` when the SARG columns are not indexed. The reverse is true if the SARG columns are indexed.

- Avoid `NOT EQUALS` expressions. The positive expression is less likely to result in scanning.

SURROGATE PRIMARY-KEY GENERATION

Surrogate primary-key generation seems to be an area of great mystery in Sybase. I read the many papers on this and the monotonic solutions and chuckled. The same collision and deadlocking issues exist in every DBMS and

RDBMS I've dealt with. It seems like I've had to use design alternatives the early 80s to resolve this. Identity columns is one approach. Here is a ferent one.

An old-time approach that has been successful for decades involves combining a unique field with the primary-key counter. If the contention being encountered is between users generating keys, add the user ID to the key (USERID+NBR). Each user gets his own primary-key sequencing. If the contention is between companies, locations, or some other qualifier, use that qualifier when building the primary key. It is important that you do your research in determining the item that uniquely identifies the source of contention.

11.27 Sizing SysAudits

Heavy auditing can affect performance because audit records are written to the sybsecurity database. Processes sleep while waiting for audits to process. There are two options for tuning this database. First, place the database on its own device. A device that optimizes sequential writes is best (such as RAID 0). That eliminates some contention. Audit records are queued up in memory. The default size is 41.4KB (100 records). The largest size available is 24MB (65,335 records). You would never need to use the maximum, but a modest increase would improve performance—perhaps something on the order of 1MB, as shown here:

2473 rows = 1,048,576/424

```
sp_configure "audit queue size",2473
```

The rule is to treat the sybsecurity database like any other being tuned. If it is a bottleneck, increase the queue size or provide faster disk-write performance to eliminate contention.

11.28 Read-Only Cursors and Tables

Read-only cursors in Sybase are not a myth, nor should you consider them a waste of time. Some administrators might say it is better to just bypass declaring a cursor's intent. They might believe that only shared page locks will result unless an update is issued. This is not always true. Sybase may choose to set update locks. If it does, unwanted contention may result. Other update and exclusive locks will be locked out. If indexed columns are in the update list generated, even a table scan can occur. Your only alternative is to add the following cursor statement using the for read only syntax.

```
[for {read only | update [of column_name_list]}]
```

The following procedure, for example, uses the read-only setting for the invoice table:

```
create proc invoice_cursor_proc as
select *
from invoice for read only
```

The only downside to using this clause is that your cursor is not for update now. It also means that you need to identify where this coding is required. But, if your goal is to squeeze out unnecessary update locks, for read only cursors can help. Locking isn't the only issue. If you identify those application processes and tables that can be isolated from update, you may be able to isolate read-only tables to their own disk devices. Write I/O slows down everything on a device. Read-only I/O is faster. You could benefit from read-only table isolation. Also, identifying read-only tables may complete a necessary step in preparing for migration of certain tables to a DSS server.

It is equally important to close cursors as soon as you can. If you code the SET CLOSE ON ENDTRANS statement, Sybase automatically closes the cursor at the end of the transaction. Avoid leaving cursors open in error because the locks will degrade performance.

11.29 Optimizing Cursors

Sybase SQL Server is based on handling sets, not row-at-a-time processing. This fact makes for a great tuning opportunity when using Sybase. So, whenever you begin to code a new program, keep this fact in mind.

If your bulk processing of data has caused you to code row-at-a-time SQL processes, you need to identify these and consider conversion to set coding. Figure 11-9 shows how a master table merge would be handled via group-row processing. Although both methods shown are functionally equivalent, the bulk-row processing on the right is much faster than the fetch-row processing on the left. Array fetches can yield reductions of 10 percent to 15 percent in I/Os.

Applications declare cursors in a select statement to process rows individually. The cursor allows each row to be fetched and manipulated, while remembering the location of the next row to be processed. This example shows that one of your best opportunities for tuning applications with cursors is to remove them. They use more memory, locks, and network packets to get the job done. The following section presents a list of tuning hints.

HINTS FOR TUNING CURSOR APPLICATIONS

- Avoid cursors as much as possible; they are expensive and can create application-locking bottlenecks.
- Stored procedures require less memory.
- Use cursor rows n to retrieve n rows at a time.
- Declare cursor read-only intent to reduce locking.
- Use UNION or UNION ALL instead of OR clauses.

Row Processing (slower)	Set Processing (faster)
EXEC SQL DECLARE change_cursor FOR	EXEC SQL UPDATE parts
SELECT new_part_no,	SET part_name =
new_part_name,	
new_part_name,	part_cost =
new_part_cost,	
new_cost	FROM part_updates;
FROM part_updates;	WHERE new_part_name =
parts.part_o;	
EXEC SQL OPEN change_cursor;	EXEC SQL INSERT INTO
WHILE change_cursor_rows_returned	part (part_no, part_name,
part_cost)	
BEGIN	SELECT new_part_no,
new_part_name,	
EXEC SQL FETCH change_cursor INTO	new_part_cost
new_part_no, new_part_name, new_cost;	FROM part_updates
EXEC SQL SELECT part_no, part_name, part_cost	WHERE new_part_no NOT IN
FROM parts	(SELECT part_no FROM
parts);	
WHERE part_no = new_part_no;	
IF not_found THEN	
EXEC SQL INSERT	
INTO parts (part_no, part_name, part_cost)	
VALUES (new_part_no,	
new_part,	
new_cost);	
ELSE	
EXEC SQL UPDATE parts	
SET name = new_part,	
cost = new_cost,	
WHERE part_no = new_part_no;	

Figure 11-9 Row Versus Set Processing

- Reduce network traffic by fetching all the rows that are to be returned to the client application.
- Use column names in the FOR UPDATE clause to reduce locking.
- Leave cursors open across commits and rollbacks. Use the "close on endtran off" setting to leave cursors open.
- Use the ct_cursor(ct_cursor_rows) parameter in Open Client applications to reduce network traffic.
- Maximize TDS packet size.

11.30 Referential Constraints

There is a 16-table limit on referential constraints in Sybase, but you really don't want to drive this feature to the maximum because it costs in performance. If the RDBMS has to maintain integrity across many tables, it can slow update processing. Of course, there might be a valid integrity concern driving the creation of the constraints. But what if the designers overbuilt in this area? Maybe they didn't even need to build additional tables. Perhaps these tables can be collapsed without losing any functionality or performance. Here is an example of some constraints for the `invoice`, `other`, and `other2` tables. After reviewing the use of the `other` and `other2` tables, you discover that they are used sporadically, and the constraints are not critical. Therefore, not only can the constraints be removed, but the tables can be removed and built at the time they are needed from the `invoice` table—even a view will suffice. You can take it even one step further. What if the `other` and `other2` tables only have rows if a certain flag is turned on in the `invoice` field? Suppose that if the `invcol2` field is zero, there are no `other` or `other2` table entries. In those cases, it is not necessary to check for referential integrity. How would you avoid a referential integrity check? The answer is with a trigger.

```
create table invoice
(invcol1 smallint, invcol2 smallint, primary key (invcol1),
constraint invcon1 foreign key (invcol2) references other (othercol1))
go
create table other
(othercol1 smallint, othercol2 smallint, primary key (othercol1))
go
create table other2
(othercol1 smallint, othercol2 smallint, primary key (othercol1))
go
```

As an administrator, you want to be able to review the constraints in use, and if they are prolific, perhaps meet with different application teams to look at alternatives. To get a list of constraints, type the following:

```
sp_helpconstraint invoice
```

11.31   Recovery Interval and the Housekeeper Process

RECOVERY INTERVAL IN MINUTES

The *recovery interval* is the period of time SQL Server waits before writing dirty pages from the cache to disk. This wait reduces I/O because a page may change many times before it is flushed to disk. It will be flushed by the checkpoint routine when the interval is complete, or, if a dirty page moves beyond the wash marker, it is written immediately to disk.

You probably should leave the interval at the default value (5 minutes) if you are weak-hearted. If the interval is too long, response times will deteriorate. If it is too short, it wastes CPU and I/O. During a checkpoint, Sybase SQL Server's data cache is forcibly written to disk. Other database activity is suspended until the disk I/O completes. User response times are a little faster following the checkpoint while the data cache is filled up again. In this example, you set the interval to 10 minutes:

```
sp_configure "recovery interval in minutes",10
```

HOUSEKEEPER TASK

During moments of idle bliss, SQL Server's housekeeper task automatically writes dirty buffers. This improves checkpointing and recovery time because the buffers are flushed for free. It also improves CPU use because system tasks are deferred to a time when they can't interfere with application processes.

System administrators need to configure the "housekeeper free write percent" parameter of sp_configure, which controls the maximum percentage by which the housekeeper task can increase database writes (the default is 1 and disabled is 0). The following command, for example, enables the housekeeper task to increase writes over their normal amount by 20 percent. Depending on the speed of the devices, you can play with this value, adjusting it slowly upward, until it no longer is advantageous to go further.

```
sp_configure "housekeeper free write percent",20
```

When the housekeeper gets its chance to work, it writes dirty buffers. If the batch limit is reached for a device (the default 3 I/Os), it switches to another device. This switching continues in an attempt to avoid overloading any one device. For high-speed disks, the batch limit can be increased. In the following example, the limit is set to 40 for all devices:

```
dbcc tune(deviochar, -1, "40")
```

After the housekeeper is done writing buffers, it checks to see whether more than 100 new log records have been written since the last checkpoint. If so, it triggers another checkpoint. This is why there are statistics called *free checkpoints*. The main parameter that drives housekeeping is "housekeeper free write percent".

Checkpoints issued via the "recovery interval in minutes" setting can degrade online performance because they can interrupt other processes and use cycles that otherwise would go to user processes. It seems like it would be better to set the "recovery interval in minutes" parameter higher than the default and allow the housekeeper task to take care of really busy systems via the free write value. That way, more checkpointing would occur during idle periods. The only question remaining is what values to choose for "recovery interval in minutes", dbcc batch limit and "housekeeper free write percent". The answer is to analyze the recovery-management sp_sysmon output, as shown in Figure 11-10.

```
Recovery Management
-------------------
  Checkpoints                  per sec   per xact    count   % of total
  -----------------------      -------   --------    -----   ----------
    # of Normal Checkpoints    0.01001   0.01112         2   n/a (A)
    # of Free Checkpoints      0.00085   0.00111         4   n/a (B)
  -----------------------      -------   --------    -----
  Total Checkpoints            0.01086   0.01223         6
  Avg Time per Normal Chkpt    0.19984 seconds               (C)
  Avg Time per Free Chkpt      0.00852 seconds               (D)
```

Figure 11-10   Recovery Management Output for sp_sysmon

(A) `# of Normal Checkpoints` is the number of checkpoints caused by the normal checkpoint process. If this number is larger than the free checkpoints, increase the number of checkpoints issued by the housekeeper task.

(B) `# of Free Checkpoints` is the number of checkpoints initiated by the housekeeper task. If this value is very low, increase the housekeeper batch limit value (using `dbcc`). If it is higher than `# of Normal Checkpoints`, increase the "recovery interval in minutes" parameter with `sp_configure`.

(C) `Avg Time per Normal Chkpt` is the average number of seconds a normal checkpoint lasted.

(D) `Avg Time per Free Chkpt` is the average number of seconds a free checkpoint lasted.

Given the numbers in the sample `sp_sysmon`, you might try setting "housekeeper free write percent" to 20, the batch limit to 40 and the recovery interval to 10 minutes. Then, you can get another report and see what effect it had.

11.32   Locking and Deadlocking

Some time ago, I read an e-mail that explained that locking policies were really tied to whether you were an optimist or a pessimist. The e-mail was making the point that if you felt it was unlikely that one user would grab a record that another person was using, you could use an optimistic locking approach. If you felt that there was a high probability of contention, you would implement a pessimistic locking approach. This is a wise assessment. How often we forget that we are the builders of our own nightmare domains and then take up residence in them.

A database and application design that eliminates any opportunity for two users to contend for a resource probably will never have to deal with deadlocks or lockouts. If two users can update a table, for example, that is not usually a problem. But, when two users can update a row, locking begins to get interesting. Now imagine that two users are allowed to update the same column in a row concurrently. You have the beginning of a nightmare scenario. Nevertheless, there are ways to allow this to happen, just as there are ways to design around it.

INITIAL NUMBER OF LOCKS

The formula for computing the `sp_configure` "number of locks" parameter is only good for the initial setting. The memory used by locks becomes part of the "total memory" requirement for SQL Server. In the following example, you graciously allow each user in a pretty large network an average of 40 locks. This increases total memory use by 703 pages.

*Nbr_of_locks = Number of concurrent users and processes * 40*
*20,000 = 500 * 40*
*Lock_memory_pages = Nbr_of_locks * 72 bytes / 2048*
703 = 1,440,000 / 2048

```
sp_configure "number of locks",20000
```

LOCK PROMOTION

To prevent any process from exhausting all available page locks or wasting precious CPU on locking, escalation of page locks to table locks is necessary. This can be accomplished at the table (lowest level), database, or server level (highest level). If a level isn't defined, the next-higher level takes precedence. An example of each follows. The first sp_setpglockpromote command sets the lock *low water mark* (LWM) to 5000, *high water mark* (HWM) to 50,000 and percentage of table locks to 5 percent. If the number of locks incurred is between the low and high water marks and is 5 percent of the database, SQL Server escalates to table locking. This frees page locks and reduces overhead for the remainder of the transaction.

```
sp_setpglockpromote "table", invoice, 5000, 50000, 5
```

The LWM and HWM values establish minimum and maximums before escalation is considered. To achieve the same locking promotion for all tables in the invdb01 database, the following command is issued:

```
sp_setpglockpromote "database", invdb01, 5000, 50000, 5
```

This simplifies the effort of defining promotion, but it potentially introduces a problem. If there are many different table sizes, you can't be certain that the 5 percent of table size always will fall between the LWM and HWM values. Also, 5 percent of a very large table with 1 million pages might be more locks than you defined in sp_configure. You can see the dilemma. Finally, you can define lock promotion server-wide with the following commands:

```
sp_setpglockpromote "server", null, 5000, 50000, 5
```

or use

```
sp_configure "lock promotion lwm",5000
sp_configure "lock promotion hwm",50000
sp_configure "lock promotion pct", 5
```

Keep in mind the fact that escalation will not occur if it would cause a conflict with another process that needs the page or table locked differently. My recommendation is that you establish lock promotions at the table level. You also might provide a server-wide catch-all, in case someone forgot to establish them for a table. If properly defined, they can enhance locking performance.

TUNING LOCKING

Figure 11-11 shows output from the sp_sysmon lock-management report. You can use the report to set server-wide locking settings and identify some applications or locking thresholds that are causing more serious locking problems.

(A) If Total Lock Requests per second is approaching the amount you specified for the "locks" parameter in sp_configure, the red flag should go up. You have a problem. You need to increase the sp_configure "number of locks" value immediately.

(B) If the Avg Lock Contention percentage is more than .2 percent, you have sporadic locking problems—probably with applications. Other values in the report will clue you in to the area of contention. The .2 percent recommendation is valid only if the sp_sysmon sampling was big enough to give an accurate picture of system activity.

(C) Deadlock Percentage is the percentage of total lock requests. I personally don't like deadlocks and think they should be eliminated at any cost. I think the system is expending a lot of resources in performing deadlock detection and correction. Other processes suffer while the deadlock resolution is performed. You may see this differently. Less than .5 percent might be acceptable in some environments. I wouldn't want to have to deal with more than a handful of occurrences of deadlocks. Deadlocks by Lock Type and its totals identify whether the locks are Exclusive Table, Shared Table, Exclusive Intent, Shared Intent, Exclusive Page, Update Page, Shared Page, or Address locks involved in the deadlocks. These fields really just let you know that the application or database design has a problem.

(D) Address Locks are those for index pages.

(E) Last Page Locks on Heaps are counts for the last pages on heap tables. If there is a problem in this area, the table should be partitioned or repartitioned, if possible. Another alternative is to use max_rows_per_page to reduce contention.

(F, G) If Deadlock Searches is high and Average Deadlocks per Search is zero, you should be able to reduce the frequency of deadlock searching.

(H) If Total Lock Promotions is nonzero and deadlocks are significant, lock promotions could be the cause. You might want to increase the LWM, HWM and PCT for lock promotions on tables that have deadlocks.

WHO HAS THE LOCK?

To see who currently has locks and which processes are blocked, use the sp_lock and sp_who procedures, in that order. In the following example, you can see that processes are running that have table locks and page locks. There also is a blocked process, as indicated by the -blk suffix on the locktype.

```
Lock Management
---------------
  Lock Summary              per sec     per xact      count   % of total
  -----------------------   -------    --------      -----   ----------
  Total Lock Requests        5842.0        34.0      358968      n/a    (A)
  Avg Lock Contention           7.9         0.0         888      0.2 %(B)
  Deadlock Percentage           0.0         0.0           0      0.0 %(C)
  Lock Detail               per sec     per xact      count   % of total
  -----------------------   -------    --------      -----   ----------
  Exclusive Table
    Granted                   605.5         3.0       36564    100.0 %
    Waited                      0.0         0.0           0      0.0 %
  ----------------------    -------    --------      -----
  Total EX-Table Requests     605.5         3.0       36564     10.2 %
  Shared Table
    Granted                   487.8         5.0       27303    100.0 %
    Waited                      0.0         0.0           0      0.0 %
  ----------------------    -------    --------      -----
  Total SH-Table Requests     487.8         5.0       27303      7.6 %
  Exclusive Intent
    Granted                   816.3         5.0       49347    100.0 %
    Waited                      0.0         0.0           0      0.0 %
  ----------------------    -------    --------      -----
  Total EX-Intent Requests    816.3         5.0       49347     13.7 %
  Shared Intent
    Granted                   216.0         2.0       13069    100.0 %
    Waited                      0.0         0.0           0      0.0 %
  ----------------------    -------    --------      -----
  Total SH-Intent Requests    216.0         2.0       13069      3.6 %
  Exclusive Page
    Granted                   531.0         5.0       32149    100.0 %
    Waited                      0.0         0.0           0      0.0 %
  ----------------------    -------    --------      -----
  Total EX-Page Requests      531.0         5.0       32149      9.0 %
  Update Page
    Granted                   463.4         4.0       28018      7.8 %
    Waited                      7.7         1.0        1111      0.3 %
  ----------------------    -------    --------      -----
  Total UP-Page Requests      471.1         5.0       29129      8.1 %
  Shared Page
    Granted                    16.0         1.0         975    100.0 %
    Waited                      0.0         0.0           0      0.0 %
  ----------------------    -------    --------      -----
  Total SH-Page Requests       16.0         1.0         975      0.3 %
  Exclusive Address                                                      (D)
    Granted                  1355.3         3.0       89221    100.0 %
    Waited                      0.0         0.0           0      0.0 %
  ----------------------    -------    --------      -----
  Total EX-Address Requests  1355.3         3.0       89221     24.9 %
  Shared Address
    Granted                  1343.0         5.0       81211    100.0 %
    Waited                      0.0         0.0           0      0.0 %
  ----------------------    -------    --------      -----
  Total SH-Address Requests  1343.0         5.0       81211     22.6 %
  Last Page Locks on Heaps                                              (E)
    Granted                   277.7         2.2       16699    100.0 %
    Waited                      0.0         0.0           0      0.0 %
  ----------------------    -------    --------      -----
  Total Last Pg Locks         277.7         2.2       16699      4.7 %
  Deadlocks by Lock Type    per sec     per xact      count   % of total
  ----------------------    -------    --------      -----   ----------
                               0.0         0.0           0      n/a
  Deadlock Detection
    Deadlock Searches          0.3         0.0          32      n/a    (F)
    Searches Skipped           0.0         0.0           0      0.0 %
    Avg Deadlocks per Search   n/a         n/a     0.00000      n/a    (G)
  Lock Promotions                                                      (H)
```

Figure 11-11 Lock Management Output for sp_sysmon

```
1> sp_lock
2> go
spid  locktype    table_id    page  dbname   class

4     Sh_table    140022011   0     invdb01  Non Cursor Lock
5     Sh_page     120022033   180   invdb01  Non Cursor Lock
3     Sh_intent   120022033   0     invdb01  Non Cursor Lock
3     Sh_page_blk 120022033   254   invdb01  Non Cursor Lock
6     Ex_intent   120022033   0     invdb01  Non Cursor Lock
6     Update_page 120022033   254   invdb01  Non Cursor Lock
7     Ex_table    240000383   0     cusdb01  Non Cursor Lock
```

You quickly can determine that the processes in question are not using cursors (Non Cursor Lock). While coming to a resolution of the blocked process, you want to keep cursors in mind as a potential solution. However, one of the many other solutions provided in the following list of tuning hints may well be the one for the job.

The sp_who command indicates a "lock sleep" status for the blocked process and gives the PID of the contender.

HINTS FOR TUNING LOCKING

■ Use the ct_describes cs_version_key function to see key data and detect changes to a column. This will help you implement a column-level locking scheme.

■ Use the max_rows_per_page option to limit the number of rows on a page, which can reduce page contention and deadlocks. The max_rows_per_page value applies to the data pages of an unindexed table or the leaf pages of an index. You can view this value in the maxrowsperpage column of the sysindexes database. The following example forces only one row on each page for the invoice table:

```
create table invoice
(company char(40) not null,
...
date datetime not null,)
with max_rows_per_page=1
```

To change max_rows_per_page for an existing table, use the sp_chgattribute command. This only affects rows added to the table after the change is made. This example increases the number of rows in the prior example to three rows per page. If you want to make your change on all the rows in the table, you can bulk copy the table out using the sp_chgattribute command to change the table and then bulk copy it back in.

```
sp_chgattribute invoice, "max_rows_per_page",3
```

▪ Use CT-Library cursors to reduce locking issues.

▪ Make sure updates and deletes don't scan the table, or they will lock all rows encountered, causing a whirlwind of contention.

▪ Commit or roll back as soon as possible to release exclusive locks. Use small and fast transactions. Never allow user interaction in the middle of a transaction.

▪ Replace mass deletes with `drop`, and `reload` where applicable.

▪ Avoid isolation level-3 locking because shared locks are retained until commit or rollback of the transaction. This kind of locking is needed only when nonrepeatable reads or phantoms have been affecting the results of queries.

▪ If your application must run at locking level 3, use the `NOHOLDLOCK` clause.

▪ Use timestamps and the `tsequal()` function to check for cursored row updates. Compare the timestamp to the one obtained the last time it was read. If it has changed, the record has been modified by another process. To add a timestamp to the `invoice` table, issue the following command:

```
alter table invoice add timestamp
```

Because the new field is null, you must issue updates to all the rows in the table for the timestamp to be given a time/date value.

To use the before and after timestamp comparison, you first must select the row using the `"for browse"` clause. Then, in the update, use the `tsequal` (timestamp equal) function as a `where` clause condition for update. The whole purpose of this technique is to prevent updating a row that already has been changed by another user. The coding is not complicated. The real test of your character is in working out what will happen when a mismatch in timestamps is found. I think the current transaction should be rolled out, or the user should be notified of a change. Good luck with this decision.

Use `sp_lock` and `print_deadlock_info` to get information about deadlocks.

▪ Add the `"at isolation read uncommitted"` clause to the end of a `SELECT` statement to see the uncommitted writes of other ongoing transactions.

▪ Use segments, partitioning, and striping on many disk devices and controllers to reduce contention for rows.

▪ Perform database maintenance such as index creation during off-hours.

▪ Do not turn off deadlock detection (`deadlock checking period = 0`) because it causes spinlock contention. The deadlock-checking period has a minimum default of 500 milliseconds. Increasing its value reduces the amount of overhead with checking. However, it also means a longer delay before deadlocks are detected. If they aren't a problem in your system, increase the value. Use the `sp_sysmon` output to tune this parameter for each server.

■ Provide sufficient indexing to force SQL Server to use page locking instead of table locking. Otherwise, use cursors with frequent commit points to reduce the number of page locks.

■ Use partitions to reduce locking contention on the last page of heap tables.

■ If contention is in one area of a table, use a clustered index to randomize the data across the pages in the table. If the table already has a clustered index, rethink the index key to get better randomization. Sometimes, reversing key fields or using the inverse of a number can produce much better randomization. This also can reduce page overflows for clustered indexes that allow duplicates.

■ Use the `fillfactor` parameter to partially fill pages, which provides better insert performance. Page splits result in exclusive locks on index pages. Regular index maintenance using `fillfactor` can eliminate page splitting or reduce it to acceptable levels.

■ Use the lowest isolation level locking required for an application to work properly.

■ If you need to perform mass updates and deletes on active tables, do so with a stored procedure using a cursor and frequent commits. This will reduce blocking.

■ Set the server, database, or table lock promotion thresholds to prevent mass updates from taking longer than necessary or exhausting available locks.

■ If the `"Total Lock Requests"` per second value in the `sp_sysmon` locking report is approaching the `"number of locks"` `sp_configure` setting, increase the setting.

■ If the `"Avg Lock Contention"` percentage in the `sp_sysmon` locking report is greater than .2 percent, research the cause of contention.

■ If the number of deadlocks in the `sp_sysmon` counts is nonzero, research the cause of deadlocks.

■ If the `"Last Page Locks on Heaps"` in `sp_sysmon` is nonzero, consider partitioning the heap tables or repartitioning them to reduce page contention.

■ If `"Total Lock Promotions"` is nonzero and `deadlocks` is nonzero, there may be a link between lock promotions and the deadlocks. Review changes to the sizes of tables that may be causing the promotion thresholds to trigger too soon and increase table locking, leading to deadlocks.

11.33 Spinlocks

Spinlocks are the fastest locking mechanism in Sybase. They are used for caches (one each), deadlock locks, semaphores, pages, tables and partitions in SMP systems. Their internal workings are pretty simple. First of all, spinlocks are single threaded. If a thread attempts to use a spinlock already in use, it will "spin" until the lock is released. So, spinlocks in Sybase work very much like their counterparts in Microsoft SQL Server (`spin counter`), and Oracle (`spin_count`).

The data cache management summary report from `sp_sysmon` shows the count and percentage of spinlock contention. If this value is greater than 10 percent, you want to look at eliminating contention for the disk-based objects in question. Remember that spinlocks are single threaded. Database resources, such as tables and indexes, will remain locked until the process locking it releases it. You can use segments, partitioning, more devices, and named data caches to resolve the spinlock contention. Even an increase in the size of the default or named cache probably will resolve contention because overall system throughput can be improved. Similarly, giving the transaction log its own device can reduce contention.

Deadlocks are very expensive. Besides locking up multiple tasks, they cause additional system resource use. In the event of an abort, a transaction must be rolled out and rescheduled. Use the `sp_configure "deadlock retries"` to establish the number of attempts to circumvent a deadlock. In addition, deadlock detection will hold spinlocks on memory locks. This is controlled via the `sp_configure "deadlock checking period"`. In high-volume systems, don't set this value to zero. A zero value causes more deadlock checking, which is pure overhead. If anything, you want to set this to a value that reduces deadlock checking.

As of release 11, you have some new `sp_configure` parameters that can influence performance for systems with multiple server engines. Because many processes can hit on resources concurrently, hash memory tables are used to randomize access to resources. Of course, there is then semaphore contention for the memory hash table. So, spinlocks are used to protect access to the hash tables as well as to lock the actual resource. With the new parameters, you can define what ratio of spinlocks is used for the hash memory table versus the actual resource. The ratio determines how many spinlocks will be devoted to protecting the hash tables versus the actual resource. These commands list the current defaults for those settings:

```
sp_configure "address lock spinlock ratio"
```

Sets the ratio of spinlocks used on multiple engine hash tables

```
sp_configure "table lock spinlock ratio"
```

Sets the ratio of spinlocks used on table lock hash tables

```
sp_configure "partition spinlock ratio"
```

Sets the ratio of spinlocks used on partition hash tables

```
sp_configure "page lock spinlock ratio"
```

Sets the ratio of spinlocks used on page lock hash tables

```
sp_configure "user log cache spinlock ratio"
```

Sets the ratio of ULCs to spinlocks used

I'm not a rocket scientist, but I can picture a hashing table with spinlocks controlling table entries. Given the list of spinlock ratios here, the real question is how to know what number of spinlocks will suffice to protect hashing tables. If I understand this accurately, the number of spinlocks for the hash tables must equal the largest number of concurrent accesses to the same resources or hashed entries. Because this value can vary depending on processing, it is a moving target. It might interest you to know that these different hash tables don't all have the same levels of activity, even though they are all very busy entities. It may even be safe to theorize that each type of spinlock activity influences the others. The flow of information in the server is like a conveyor belt in an assembly line. If any of the little rollers that contribute to movement along the conveyor belt has a problem, the whole belt slows down. All spinlock activity could respond similarly. If one activity is faster than the others, the slower one will bring everything down. Thus, you have the term *bottleneck*. The hash tables are listed here in order of most active to least active.

Activity on the Spinlock Conveyor Belt	
Page Lock hash table	More page lock activity than engine address lock activity
Address Lock hash table	More address lock activity than partition lock activity
Partition Lock hash table	More partition lock activity than table lock activity
Table Lock hash table	More table lock activity than user log cache lock activity
User Log cache	More user log activity than . . .

Granted, other spinlock processes probably belong on the theoretical conveyor belt, but they are internal processes over which you have no control. Where is this whole analogy leading? When selecting a ratio for these activities, those with greater activity need more spinlocks for hash tables because there is a greater potential for contention. Also, it would be best to err on the high side because too few could be a real concern. In any event, you can get a quick overview of contention with the sp_sysmon task-management report.

11.34   User Log Cache and Semaphores

As in the other sections, this section takes a look at the sp_sysmon output to use in tuning transaction logging. The report in Figure 11-12 is the transaction management output for sp_sysmon.

There is one *user log cache* (ULC) for each configured user connection. SQL Server uses these caches to hold transaction log records until flushed. This helps to reduce the contention on the log.

```
Transaction Management
----------------------
  ULC Flushes to Xact Log     per sec   per xact     count   % of total
  ----------------------      -------   --------     -----   ----------
       by Full ULC               94.0        1.0      1221     18.5 %(A)
       by End Transaction        77.1        1.0      5345     80.9 %(B)
       by Change of Database      0.0        0.0         0      0.0 %(C)
       by System Log Record       0.3        0.0        44      0.6 %
       by Other                   0.0        0.0         0      0.0 %
  ----------------------      -------   --------     -----
     Total ULC Flushes         171.4        2.0      6610
...
  ULC Semaphore Requests
       Granted                 1101.1        8.4     41000     94.2 %
       Waited                   100.9        2.0      2515      5.8 %(D)
  ----------------------      -------   --------     -----
     Total ULC Semaphore Req   1202.0       10.4     43515
  Log Semaphore Requests
       Granted                   44.5        0.4      7702     65.3 %
       Waited                     55.5        0.3      4084     34.7 %(E)
  ----------------------      -------   --------     -----
     Total Log Semaphore Req    100.0        0.7     11786
...
```

Figure 11-12   Transaction Management Output for sp_sysmon

(A, B) A By Full ULC percentage of more than 25 percent or a By End Transaction percentage of less than 75 percent is an indication that flushing is happening more than once per transaction. Increase the size of the user log cache size (default 2048) by using sp_configure. Here is an example:

```
sp_configure "user log cache size", 4096
```

If the value in the "count" column is consistently less than the defined value for the "user log cache size" parameter, reduce the user log cache size to the value in the "count" column (but no smaller than 2048 bytes).

(C) The By Change of Database percentage is an indication of context switches in multiple database transactions. When this exceeds a few percents, performance is degraded by having multiple databases. These switches also result in added log writes. You might consider recombining databases.

A log cache semaphore is a locking mechanism that prevents multiple tasks from attempting to flush records in a ULC.

(D, E) If the % of Total for "Waited" semaphores (SMP environments) is greater than 25 percent, try increasing the size of the "user log cache size" value. If this does not reduce the percentage considerably, try breaking up the database into multiple databases, each with its own log.

HINTS FOR TUNING TRANSACTIONS AND THE USER LOG CACHE

  ■ A high number of system calls may be an indication of poor application design or nonindexed database access.

■ Watch for context switches, as indicated by the sp_sysmon output "by Change of Database" percentage. These switches result in added logging. You might want to combine multiple databases or reengineer your transactions to eliminate these switches.

■ Make sure that the log is on a device separate from the database.

■ If the percentage of semaphore waits, as indicated in the sp_sysmon report, is greater than 25 percent, try increasing the size of the "user log cache size" parameter with sp_configure. If that does not reduce the percentage considerably, try breaking the database up into multiple databases, each with its own log.

■ A By Full ULC percentage of more than 25 percent or a "by End Transaction" percentage of less than 75 percent is an indication that flushing is happening more than once per transaction. Increase the size of the user log cache size (minimum 2048) by using sp_configure.

11.35 Transaction Logs

Each database has a log. The log is one of the major points of contention in Sybase SQL Server. Your decisions about log tuning will have a large influence on server performance for all users. The major tasks involved in tuning the log follow.

MAJOR LOG-TUNING TASKS

■ Place the log on separate device(s) from the data—or even separate controller(s).

■ Make the syslogs segments large enough to hold the longest transactions.

■ Choose an optimal I/O pool size (2KB, 4KB, or 8KB).

■ Make the log cache large enough for rollbacks and deferred update transactions.

■ Tune the user log cache size.

Log pages are flushed to disk when the log pages are full, a transaction ends or switches databases, a process triggers a ULC write, a group commit is issued ,or the cache runs out of space. A group commit will occur even though the log page is not full, so the log is made up of full and partially full pages. Consequently, a 4KB pool reduces writes by allowing larger pages, but it can help only if the transaction volume matches the need. You can use the sp_sysmon output to determine whether this is true.

The sp_sysmon output for the task-management report is of a broad nature (see Figure 11-13). Most of the information in this report duplicates information you reviewed in other reports. You can use this information to pinpoint an area that needs to be looked at more closely (locking and semaphores, for example). In this section, you will use the report to look into a few logging-related values not covered in other sections of this chapter.

(A) Group Commit Sleeps shows the times a task committed and went to sleep while the log was written to disk. In Figure 11-13, this value is 23.1 percent, which is relatively high. A high number is an indication that a smaller log I/O size would benefit page flushing. Flushing the page wakes up tasks that are sleeping on the group commit.

(B) Last Log Page Writes shows the times a task switched out because it was put to sleep while writing the last log page. In Figure 11-13, this value is 20.5 percent, which is relatively high. If "Avg # Writes per Log Page" also is high, it is an indication that the last page is being rewritten frequently. In that case, a smaller log I/O size would reduce the number of writes.

HINTS FOR TUNING THE LOG

- If "Transaction Log Writes" per second divided by "Transaction Log Alloc" per second from sp_sysmon is greater than 1 and "Transaction Log Writes" per second is more than 50 percent of the log device's rated capacity, a larger log I/O pool should be tried.

- Place the log on a separate device from your data. This is done with the "log on" clause of the create database command.

- Because the log is sequential, the disk head on the log device rarely will need to perform seeks, and you can maintain a high I/O rate to the log. Choose a device based on its track-to-track transfer rate.

- If the sp_sysmon reports indicate a need for a larger I/O pool, do the following. First, use this command to see the cache and I/O sizes for all databases on the server:

```
sp_logiosize "all"
```

Task Management	per sec	per xact	count	% of total
Connections Opened	0.0	0.0	0	n/a
Task Context Switches by Engine				
Engine 0	112.3	0.5	13217	15.0 %
Total Task Switches:	444.2	4.4	88390	
Task Context Switches Due To:				
...				
Group Commit Sleeps	55.2	0.5	7633	23.1 %
Last Log Page Writes	49.8	0.4	6754	20.5 %
...				

Figure 11-13 Task Management Output of sp_sysmon

Now, set the log I/O size for a database to 4KB (the parameter default) with this command:

```
sp_logiosize "default"
```

■ If the syslogs table has its own cache, contention is reduced, especially on SMP systems with high transaction rates. Size the cache to reduce the times log pages must be read again after being flushed from the cache. Triggers using inserted and deleted tables, as well as deferred updates and rollbacks, need to reread the log. Syslogs can be given its own cache with the sp_dboption and sp_bindcache commands. Then, use sp_sysmon reports to tune the newly built cache based on its hit ratio.

■ Use the syslogshold table for information used to set up a threshold process for long-running transactions.

■ Use the "last chance threshold" on the log segment to trigger the sp_thresholdaction stored procedure to issue a dump transaction command, as shown here:

```
create procedure sp_thresholdaction
@dbname varchar(30),
                @segmentname varchar(30),
                @space_left int,
                @status int
                as
                dump transaction @dbname to "/dev/invlog01"
```

You have to decide how hung transactions will be handled because the dump process will not remove them. You can kill them manually; just use sp_who to find those with LOG SUSPEND status. Or you can change the "abort xact when log is full" value to abort the transaction with an 1105 error. These things are mentioned here because they are important to perfor-mance. A hung system is not advantageous.

■ Place the log for a database on its own device. In this example, the invdb01 database was created using this syntax:

```
create database invdb01 on inv01 = 100, inv01 = 40 log on inv01 = 8
```

You then can view it with the following select statement:

```
1> select * from sysusages where dbid=db_id("invdb01")
2> go
```

dbid	segmap	lstart	size	vstart	pad	unreservedpgs
6	2	0	51200	83887104	NULL	2200
6	2	51200	20480	83963904	NULL	4480
6	3	71680	4096	83984384	NULL	1077
6	3	75776	10240	151006208	NULL	8840

■ To provide two separate devices with 100MB each, issue the following command:

```
alter database invdb01 log on inv02 = 100, inv03 = 100
```

■ Finally, issue `sp_dropsegment` to free up the `inv01` device segment for the log and use `sp_extendsegment` to give that space back to the database.

11.36 Triggers

Triggers improve performance in a couple of ways. The first execution causes a copy to be compiled and loaded into memory. Subsequent executions use the built and loaded memory copy.

Because the triggered code and SQL calls all happen on the server, the amount of network traffic also is reduced. There are some things you can do to improve trigger processing.

HINTS FOR TRIGGERS

■ Avoid the chance of update triggers firing in a loop with the `self_recursion` option.

■ A trigger or stored procedure can be revisited for tuning from time to time. The beauty of encapsulation is that it can happen without impacting the rest of your application code.

■ Make sure that the procedure cache is large enough to house all the triggers and other objects used frequently.

11.37 Fault Tolerance

Fault tolerance, failover, and 7x24 are trademarks of the 90s RDBMS. With a little planning and the right hardware, you can have really great recoverability. Sybase provides facilities to make this job a piece of cake compared to some other database vendors. Here is a list of things you should take advantage of; remember that your speed of recovery is a tunable:

■ Partitions make loading and restoring data a parallel operation.

■ Segments speed processing and can be device specific. Therefore, they can be used to divide up the recoverable database by devices.

■ Mirrored databases on separate devices provide device failover. Mirrored updates take longer but can be better than running full-scale backups. Some mirrored RAID devices allow for reading from both devices, which can improve retrieval queries. It is better if the RAID arrays perform both writes to mirrored devices in parallel, too. This is known as *nonserial mode*, and it is dangerous. The trade-off is full failover capability. Here is the mirroring syntax to add a mirror or remove it:

```
disk mirror
name = "original_device", mirror = "mirror_device"
disk unmirror
name="original_device",mode=remove
```

- Hot swap servers allow for complete server swapping in the event of failure.

- Multiple small databases allow fast parallel restore operations. They also give you multiple sets of syslogs, which cause a major reduction is contention.

- Backups are important. But, if you have implemented a nonstandard backup procedure, your recovery could involve laying down layers of restores to get everything back. You need to have the process documented and tested to verify that it works.

- The hardware you chose is equally important. Network cards and RAID arrays are available that will hot swap devices or entire arrays in the event of failure. Many have hot-swap power supplies, in case that fails. The bottom line is that you can buy just about as much fault tolerance as your pocketbook will allow.

11.38   Backup and Recovery

The backup server can perform high-speed online database backup, with loading and recovery in unattended mode triggered by predetermined thresholds. Typically, you will back up to disk or 4-mm or 8-mm tapes. But some other types of media will work, too. Big shops usually have the added overhead of remote backups and hot backup servers. These eat up a lot of local processing power, as well as cause some serious network traffic. There are alternatives for these shops, many of which are running 7x24. Here are some other ways to meet backup and recovery demands for large shops:

- Nonstandard backups don't run regularly. Certain databases are backed up daily, weekly, monthly, quarterly, or yearly, depending on update activity. Others may flip-flop every other night. That's the basic idea of nonstandard backups.

- Replication is a form of backup. A remote site could be a disaster-recovery site. One of the advantages of replication is that updates for transactions are routed only over the network. Also, the atomicity of transactions is maintained.

- Remote backups or hot backup servers should take advantage of 8KB or 16KB packet sizes and Fibre (FDDI) channels to speed processing. Fibre now comes in 100 Mbps to 600 Mbps.

Enhancements in release 11 make it possible to stack dumps on a single tape. This represents a space savings, but it does require you to spin down more tape. It is best to write full tapes in one pass, if possible. Also, some systems have problems with writing more than one file/volume at a time (IBM RS6000 4mm tape device 2GB to 4GB, for example). Of course, those restrictions may no longer exist. It is a good idea to research these problems with vendors first.

To avoid backup problems, use `tar` or `dd` to copy dump files to tape and `dd` to move a dump file from one device to another.

The charter for this book doesn't include how to go about backup and recovery, but the following section provides a list of items Sybase recommends that you back up. Some of the tasks are ones that should use common tuning practices.

HINTS ON TUNING BACKUPS AND COMPLETE RECOVERY

- Master database to standard backups and the source to rebuild the master
- User databases to standard backups and creation source
- Indexes to standard backups and procedures to completely rebuild
- `sp_configure` source
- Log backup (for warm starts)/mirror log
- A master hard-copy list of logins and passwords
- Replication definitions
- Partition, segment, and striping definitions
- Source and BCP copies (character format) for sysdatabases, sysusages, sysdevices, and syslogins tables

  Device numbers are encoded in the `vstart` variable. You might want to collect the sysusage output by device, for example. Here is a command for doing this. Because the device number is encoded in the `vstart` variable, it can be computed as the following:

  device number = vstart divided by 2**24 (2 to the power of 24)

```
select * from sysusages
where vstart/power(2,24) = 0
order by vstart
go
dbid    segmap    lstart    size    vstart    pad     unreservedpgs
--      --        --        --      --        --      --

1       7         0         1024    4         NULL    108
3       7         0         1024    1028      NULL    228
2       7         0         1024    2052      NULL    228
```

  (5 rows affected)

  In this example, you query sysusages for a map of the master device (device 0).

- Hot backup servers for 7x24 shops

Transaction updates are replicated on the duplicate server. In the event of a server failure, the hot backup server swaps into service immediately. This server should be located on different hardware to avoid the possibility that it would become part of a larger failure.

■ Replication can be a form of backup, too. Remote backup sites could be replicated as well, thus providing offsite full disaster-recovery capabilities.

■ Run DBCC consistency checks regularly, or you might be backing up garbage. Do the checks shown in these examples. Run checks on replicated and hot backup site databases from time to time.

```
dbcc checkdb(invdb01)
dbcc checkalloc(invdb01)
dbcc checkcatalog(invdb01)
dbcc checktable(invoice)
dbcc tablealloc(invoice)
```

■ Test your backup and recovery procedures on a test server to be sure they work. Begin by recovering the system, followed by individual databases and indexes. Write up procedures to be used by nontrained personnel.

■ Mirror mission-critical databases.

■ Use nonstandard backups to help alleviate the processing load for backups.

■ Use thresholds to dump things before space becomes critical.

■ Operating system configuration source and backups

11.39   Referring to `sp_configure`

Throughout this chapter, you have looked at the tuning of individual `sp_configure` parameters. The same material won't be repeated here. Instead, Table 11-4 lists all the `sp_configure` parameters, along with their descriptions. If the parameter is one that is important to system performance, it is flagged.

11.40   Coming Soon . . . Messages

Messages are self-contained request packages, with queries and routing information all rolled into one bundle. The neat thing about messages is that after they are handed off, there is no need for the client to stay around, which means there is no dependence on a client connection to the server. The client is free to work on other requests or even to shut down for the day.

A message is routed to its destination where it runs and accumulates the results. Because it has routing information, it then is returned to the sender. If a computer failure is encountered during the processing, the message is queued again for execution or for routing, depending on the point of failure. A user gets the results of the query after the failure is resolved.

TABLE 11-4 Parameters for Sybase `sp_configure`

Release 11 Parameter	Affects Prior Release Name	Performance (Y/N)
address lock spinlock ratio	N/A	Y
additional network memory	N/A	Y
allow sql server async i/o	T1603 (trace flag)	Y
allow remote access	remote access	N
allow nested triggers	nested trigger	Y
allow updates to system tables	allow updates	N
configuration file	N/A	N
cpu grace time	ctimemax	Y
cpu accounting flush interval	cpu flush	Y
deadlock retries	N/A	Y
deadlock checking period	N/A	Y
default fill factor percent	fillfactor	Y
default language id	default language	N
default network packet size		Y
default database size	database size	N
disk i/o structures	cnblkio	N
event buffers per engine	N/A	Y
executable code size	sql server code size	Y
freelock transfer block size	N/A	Y
housekeeper free write percent	N/A	Y
i/o polling process count	cmaxscheds	Y
i/o accounting flush interval	i/o flush	Y
identity grab size	N/A	N
lock shared memory	T1611 (trace flag)	Y
lock promotion LWM	N/A	Y
lock promotion PCT	N/A	Y
lock promotion HWM	N/A	Y
max async i/os per engine	cnmaxaio_engine	Y
max async i/os per server	cnmaxaio_server	Y
max network packet size	maximum network packet size	Y
max engine freelocks	N/A	Y
max number of network listeners	cmaxnetworks	Y
memory alignment boundary	calignment	N
number of extent i/o buffers	extent i/o buffers	Y
number of languages in cache	language in cache	N

TABLE 11-4 **Parameters for Sybase** `sp_configure` **(Continued)**

Release 11 Parameter	Affects Prior Release Name	Performance (Y/N)
number of locks	locks	Y
number of sort buffers	csortbufsize	Y
number of devices	devices	Y
number of index trips	cindextrips	Y
number of remote connections	remote connections	Y
number of messages	cnmsg	N
number of open databases	open databases	Y
number of open objects	open objects	Y
number of languages in cache	cnlanginfo	N
number of mailboxes	cnmbox	N
number of alarms	cnalarm	N
number of pre-allocated extents	cpreallocext	N
number of oam trips	coamtrips	Y
number of user connections	user connections	Y
number of remote logins	remote logins	N
number of remote sites	remote sites	Y
o/s async i/o enabled	N/A	Y
o/s file descriptors	N/A	N
page lock spinlock ratio	N/A	Y
page utilization percent	N/A	Y
partition spinlock ratio	N/A	Y
partition groups	N/A	Y
permission cache entries	cfgcprot	N
print deadlock information	T1204 (trace flag)	N
print recovery information	recovery flags	N
procedure cache percent	procedure cache	Y
recovery interval in minutes	recovery interval	Y
remote server pre-read packets	pre-read packets	UNK
runnable process search count	cschedspins	N
shared memory starting address	mrstart	N
size of auto identity column	N/A	N
sort page count	csortpgcount	Y
sql server clock tick length	cclkrate	N
stack size		Y
stack guard size	cguardsz	N

TABLE 11-4 Parameters for Sybase sp_configure **(Continued)**

Release 11 Parameter	Affects Prior Release Name	Performance (Y/N)
systemwide password expiration	password expiration interval	N
table lock spinlock ratio	N/A	Y
tcp no delay	T1610 (trace flag)	Y
time slice		Y
total data cache size	N/A	Y
total memory	memory	Y
user lock cache spinlock ratio	N/A	Y
user lock cache size	N/A	Y

In many respects, messages are a lot like conventional batch jobs in mainframe applications. They receive execution and routing priorities. They are queued up for execution if the backlog is large enough.

So, you might be asking, "Why bother with them?" The answer is because they solve some problems in computing. It would be possible to have interrupt-free computing, for example. Perhaps someday it would be possible to marry OLTP and DSS (warehouse) computing without impacting performance for either.

Message computing, if it ever becomes a reality, could really change our database world. Sybase has announced its plans to go after this dream.

---

[1]The tpmC benchmarks shown were found at the Transaction Processing Councils Web site at www.tpc.org.

12

Mainframe Coding

12.1 COBOL Compilers/Optimizers

It's an accepted fact that the greatest amount of legacy system code on the mainframe today is written in COBOL. It can make a big difference which release of COBOL and which COBOL optimizer you are using.

Here's what's available. IBM provides **OS/VS COBOL, VS COBOL II, COBOL/370** (now extinct) and **COBOL for MVS and VSE** (see Figure 12-1 for trade-offs). In addition to these, **CA-Realia** and **Micro-Focus COBOL** are mainframe compatible. Also, Computer Associates provides **CA-OPTIMIZE** and **CA-OPTIMIZE II** for OS/VS COBOL and VS COBOL II. The latter tools optimize COBOL further than the standard optimization that comes with the IBM compilers.

Because OS/VS COBOL no longer is supported and VS COBOL II is next to go out the door, many shops face some decisions they didn't expect. Should they convert up to COBOL/370 or should they convert their legacy code to a new language or platform? Some are using this as an impetus to go client/server. However, I believe that most will come forward to COBOL/370. For now, you need to get the best possible performance from COBOL.

I recommend that you get all your live code to COBOL for MVS, along with your year 2000 changes, and that you use the best optimizer available. You will need to test Computer Associates' optimizers to see how they perform for you. Optimization in my programs means between 25 percent and 40 percent CPU reduction. This number is much smaller compared to another optimizer, such as the one IBM supplies at no extra cost.

Sometimes, coding style and data definitions in programs yield CPU savings, and sometimes compiler options do. The following section presents some hints for using COBOL efficiently.

OS/VS Cobol VS Cobol II	COBOL/370	
No 31-bit addressing	32-bit addressing	32-bit addressing
No optimization	Optimized	Optimized
3rd-part optimizer	3rd-party optimizer	No 3rd party optimizer
Runs slowest batch	Runs medium batch	Runs fastest batch*
Runs slowest online	Runs fastest online*	Runs medium online*

*Your shop may experience different results

Figure 12-1   Mainframe COBOL Performance Trade-offs

COBOL RECOMMENDATIONS

- Place the IGZCPAC and IGZCPCO COBPACKS in shared storage. You can do this by sysgenning in CA-IDMS and IMS and adding to LPA. You should not mix OS/VS COBOL and COBOL II programs when processing.

- Use a customized IGZOPT module for IDMS/DC with the options STAE=NO, SSRANGE=NO, and SPOUT=NO.

- Do not write CA-IDMS database procedures in VS COBOL II.

- The block size of VS COBOL II runtime modules should be greater than 3120.

Often, you cannot determine what impact a particular compiler option will have on performance without researching manuals and trade journals. Here are some hints on what to expect with different options:

Compiler Option	Effect on Performance
NUMPROC(PFD)	Faster and more efficient option for numeric comparisons
TRUNC(BIN)	Slowest
TRUNC(STD)	Medium speed
TRUNC(OPT)	Fastest—should be used only when data in fields corresponds to the picture and use
SSRANGE	Makes program run slower
FASTSRT	Faster, but depends on sort product
OPTIMIZE	Fastest
AWO	Some savings on variable-size records
TEST	Slower—not supported for IDMS/DC
CMPR2	Makes code compatible with VS COBOL 2, losing many enhancements, but runs faster

Compiler Option	Effect on Performance
DYNAM	Not supported by IDMS/DC
RESIDENT	Great when used with RENT, slows things a little
RENT	Great when used with RESIDENT, slows things a little
LIBKEEP	Faster
RTEREUS	Faster
AIXBLD	Slower
STAE	Not supported by IDMS/DC
MIXRES	Much Slower

12.2 Computational Variables

Programming guides usually expound on the efficiency of using COMP and COMP-3 in mathematics. This is an accepted convention for COBOL coders. I don't think there is a comprehension of what the bottom-line uses look like for these datatypes, though.

If you compare computational field assignment tuning with other forms of tuning, the return is very small. You can expect to get back only a few percent on these kinds of changes. The chart in Figure 12-2 gives you some idea of the trade-offs in doing certain kinds of operations. The best opportunity lies in

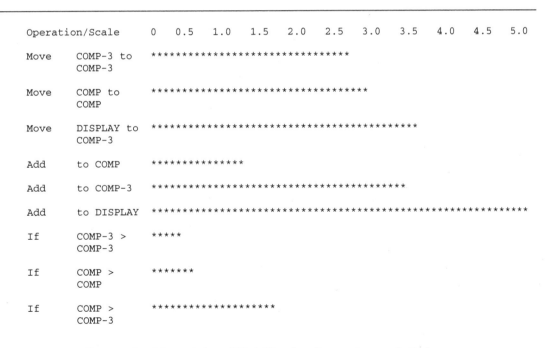

```
Operation/Scale   0    0.5   1.0   1.5   2.0   2.5   3.0   3.5   4.0   4.5   5.0

Move    COMP-3 to   *******************************
        COMP-3

Move    COMP to     *********************************
        COMP

Move    DISPLAY to  *********************************************
        COMP-3

Add     to COMP      ***************

Add     to COMP-3    ****************************************

Add     to DISPLAY   ******************************************************************

If      COMP-3 >     *****
        COMP-3

If      COMP >       *******
        COMP

If      COMP >       *******************
        COMP-3
```

Figure 12-2 Computational Operations and Their Uses (smaller numbers are better)

using COMP in subscripts for table arrays. The numbers were derived from a program that was strobed to get instruction CPU use.

With VS COBOL II, COMP fields automatically are synchronized on full-word boundaries. This used to be a tuning consideration, but now it is handled by the compiler, so don't waste time coding COMP as SYNC.

12.3   Coding Around CA-IDMS Database Deadlocks

One thing to keep in mind when dealing with deadlocks is that they are inherent to the database and application design. A well-designed system will not encounter deadlocks. In CA-IDMS, the most common database design flaw leading to the incorporation of deadlocks is the single OOAK record. Using multiple OOAK records with junction records and indexes generally eliminates these deadlocks. Now take a look at the *deadly embrace*.

The most common form of deadly embrace involves one record type. In Figure 12-3, program A modifies the DEPARTMENT record and is preparing to modify the EMPLOYEE record. Program B has modified the EMPLOYEE record before program A issues a request for it. Program B now attempts to modify the DEPARTMENT record. At this moment, both run units are prevented from finishing their record-locking operations: It is a stalemate. Program B aborts with an nn29 deadlock status code. Program A is allowed to complete, but only after several seconds or minutes have elapsed. The terminal user for program B sees his screen clear, and an abort message (which is very unprofessional) appears; the terminal user for program A experiences a long pause for response (which is very frustrating). Both users are unhappy campers.

If program A had added KEEP EXCLUSIVE to its calls for both the records, the deadlock probably wouldn't have occurred. These calls would have forced a single thread along the path where the programs originally deadlocked. Figure 12-4 shows an example of how the KEEP EXCLUSIVE calls would be coded.

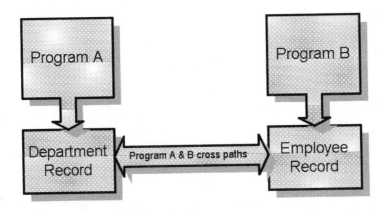

Figure 12-3   The Deadly Embrace

```
OBTAIN KEEP EXCLUSIVE DEPT-RECORD.
OBTAIN KEEP EXCLUSIVE EMPL-RECORD.
MOVE FIELDS to EMPL-RECORD.
MODIFY EMPL-RECORD.
```

Figure 12-4 Sample Code to Prevent Deadlocks

Both records now will be locked out to program B during the update. This also means that the elapsed time for program B will be longer while it waits. However, it won't be as long as the deadlock that resulted in an abort. This isn't enough to solve the problem, though. What if program B was the first to lock the EMPLOYEE record? Wouldn't this cause a deadlock, too? Yes, it could. It therefore is advisable to modify program B to do some things. First, program B must access the DEPARTMENT and EMPLOYEE records in the same order as program A. Second, program B should ready the areas for these two records in retrieval. If program B needs to update the DEPTARTMENT and EMPLOYEE records, it also should add KEEP EXCLUSIVE to its calls to eliminate any more locking conflicts.

What have you learned from this example? Well, when programs will be updating records concurrently, they should issue an "OBTAIN KEEP EXCLUSIVE" for those records and access them in the same path order. This method will eliminate deadlocks.

You can reduce or eliminate deadlocking in other ways. One is to reevaluate who is performing the updates and to provide business measures to prevent multiple user updates. Another way is to use flags that identify a path as available for update. The latter solution is not a very good method because it requires extensive coding and deadlocks still may occur.

Now carry the KEEP EXCLUSIVE solution one step further. You can do this by putting update code (and the KEEP EXCLUSIVE calls) into a common update subprogram. Ideally, this subprogram would be called near the end of the run-unit processing. In this way, the end of the run unit commits all the records automatically. Waiting until the end causes the records to be locked for the minimal amount of elapsed time. You should use an CA-IDMS extended run unit between the calling and called program. All programs accessing these records for update would use the newly created subprogram. This should reduce wait times due to concurrent accesses.

When putting the update processing near the end of the run unit is not convenient, an occasional deadlock will occur. You can force a new run unit in subprograms by not extending run units. The overhead of an additional run unit is the trade-off for not deadlocking or waiting for the mainline program's run unit to end. The advantage of the new run unit is that all locks held by it will be released upon completion. And, if you've coding everything properly, this will be when control is returned to a calling program or dialog. Consequently, a subprogram with its own run unit will hold locks for a much shorter time frame than the calling routine would have. This reduction in the window during which locks are held can greatly reduce deadlocks. I hope these techniques will cure all your deadlocks.

Identifying and cataloging deadlocks is key to resolving as many of these aborts as possible. The CA-IDMS log contains information about a deadlock (see Figure 12-5).

Coding isn't the only solution. Sometimes, smaller database pages help alleviate the number of deadlock abends. In the example in Figure 12-4, this might have been a reasonable solution. Remember that every time a task is put in a wait, the deadlock-detection software is invoked. This is not the case in release 12, in which intervals are used to drive the timing for deadlock detection.

12.4   Single Threading Batch Updates

In batch programs, deadlocks are a bigger issue. If a 29 minor code occurs, the run unit is rolled all the way out. This can account for some serious rollback time. In some instances, conflicting updates are at the beginning of processing. Here is a useful way to deal with the issue when one batch program is deadlocking with another batch program. Keep in mind, though, that the best ways to deal with deadlocks were presented in the preceding section.

```
08.49.09 JOB00268   IDMS DC207005 V5 T24318 DEADLOCK DBKEY 4323434:255 PGRP
010 TASK ADS2 PROG DIAG0006 SUBS    BILLS111
08.49.09 JOB00268   WITH T24328 TASK CODE ADS2 PGM DIAG0015 ECB 00725114
08.49.09 JOB00268   RUN-UNIT 17929480 ROLLED OUT, SSCSTAT 1229
08.49.09 JOB00268   IDMS DC173008 V5 APPLICATION ABORTED. BAD IDMS STATUS
RETURNED; STATUS=1229
08.49.10 JOB00268   IDMS DC466014 V5 ABORT OCCURRED IN DIALOG DIAG0006
PROCESS PM-DIAG0006 VERSION  0001
08.49.10 JOB00268   IDMS DC466015 V5 AT OFFSET 1A84 SOURCE SEQUENCE NUMBER
0000000
```

Descriptions:

TASK = T24318 and T24328 are dialogs deadlocking each other—use with SREPORT for task stats

DIAG0006 and DIAG0015 are deadlocking dialogs

RUNUNIT = 17929480 use with JREPORTs for database activity

SUBS = BILLS111 subschema

OFFSET = 1A84 shows the dialog load module offset for DIAG0006 when abending use the FDBLIST of ADSORPRTS to see the actual line of code in progress at time of deadlock

DBKEY = 4323434:255 which can be computed to be page = 4323434/256 = 16888 and the line index is 255 (which can be SMP space lock)

1229 = 12 major code is store and 29 minor code is deadlock because of the 255 line index indicator it appears these two run-units got a page lock deadlock while attempting to store records at the same time

Figure 12-5   Deadlock Information on the CA-IDMS Log

By placing an ENQUEUE dataset such as the one shown here in the job steps where deadlocking has occurred, a single thread is enforced:

```
//ENQ1      DD DSN=LOCK.DSN,DISP=OLD
```

Only one job step can use the ENQUEUE dataset with DISP=OLD so each job will get the dataset for the duration of the step. This technique is superior to using job scheduling because job scheduling, which submits jobs to the internal reader in a staggered fashion, generally uses a submit time. If something aborts, the staggered submission of jobs now is goofed up.

If your job step runs for hours, it won't be feasible to hold up all other jobs for hours while it completes. In this case, first determine whether all the deadlocking occurs early in the processing. It is possible to use a timed delay to allow each job to have control of the deadlocking database area for a specific time period—for example, 15 seconds. This delay must occur at the beginning of the job step. The Assembler source code in Figure 12-6 is a delay program just for this purpose.

The delay program causes a 15-second wait. During these 15 seconds of elapsed execution time, the ENQ1 dataset is locked. Other jobs with equivalent steps must wait for the delay step to complete. They then begin execution, each in turn, in a cascade fashion. The program is executed like this:

```
//DELAY1     EXEC PGM=DELAY,PARM='SECONDS=015'
//ENQ1       DD DSN=PROD.ENQ1,DISP=(OLD,KEEP,KEEP)
```

12.5 Avoiding Unnecessary *KEEP EXCLUSIVE* Locks

Isn't that terrible of me? Right after sharing with you how significant KEEP EXCLUSIVE is in preventing deadlocks, I'm going to tell you how dreadful it can be. Most of the time, it is harmless to use KEEP EXCLUSIVE. It is not a good idea in one situation, however. If your program must loop through a long set or index looking for one record to update, don't lock all the records with KEEP EXCLUSIVE (see the example in Figure 12-7).

A big problem with the code presented in Figure 12-7 is that KEEP EXCLUSIVE is placed on all GL-records, even when they aren't going to be updated. This added locking during a record scan can lock up the whole database and use extra CPU. The code has been rectified in the example in Figure 12-8, where the KEEP EXCLUSIVE call has been moved to the inner loop. Doing this avoids putting locks on records that are not targeted for update.

You can use the following key methods to deal with deadlocks.

METHODS FOR DEALING WITH CA-IDMS DEADLOCKS

- Adjust the database page size downward to eliminate locking.
- Spend more time on the physical database design to avoid contention.
- Use KEEP EXCLUSIVE where a single path needs to be single threaded.

```
* MVS 370 ASM - DELAY PROGRAM
DELAYX      CSECT
       YREGS
       DC    C'&SYSDATE &SYSTIME'
       DC    C'DELAY VERSION 1.00'
       DS    0F
       ENTRY         DELAY
DELAY  EQU   *
       USING *,R15
       SAVE  (14,12),,DELAY
       DROP  15
       USING DELAY,R15
       L     R8,=A(DELAY)
       USING DELAY,R7
       LA    R0,SAV
       ST    R13,SAVEAREA+4
       ST    R0,8(R13)
       LR    R13,R0
       L     R3,0(R1)
PARSE  LA    R3,1(R3)
       CLI   0(R3),C'='
       BNE   PARSE
       LA    R3,1(R3)
       PACK  PARMIN,0(3,R3)
REPEAT CP    PARMIN(3),=P'0'
       BE    RTN
       STIMER WAIT,TUINTVL=SECOND
       SP    PARMIN(3),=P'1'
       B     REPEAT
RTN    L     R13,SAVEAREA+4
       LM    R14,R12,12(R13)
       XR    R15,R15
       BR    R14
       LTORG
SAVEAREA DC     18F'0'
PARMIN  DS      PL3'0'
SECOND  DC      A(1*1*1000000/30)
        END
```

Figure 12-6 An ASM Delay Program

```
WHILE END-PROCESSING EQ 'N'
REPEAT.
        OBTAIN KEEP EXCLUSIVE NEXT GL-RECORD WITHIN GL-NDX.
        IF DB-END-OF-SET
            MOVE 'Y' TO END-PROCESSING.
        ELSE
        IF GL-IND EQ 'P'
           DO.
               MOVE WK-GL-CODE TO GL-CODE.
               MODIFY GL-RECORD.
               MOVE 'Y' TO END-PROCESSING.
           END.
END.
```

Figure 12-7 A Problem KEEP EXCLUSIVE Loop

```
WHILE END-PROCESSING EQ 'N'
REPEAT.
        OBTAIN NEXT GL-RECORD WITHIN GL-NDX.
        IF DB-END-OF-SET
            MOVE 'Y' TO END-PROCESSING.
        ELSE
        IF GL-IND EQ 'P'
          DO.
                OBTAIN KEEP EXCLUSIVE CURRENT GL-RECORD.
                MOVE WK-GL-CODE TO GL-CODE.
                MODIFY GL-RECORD.
                MOVE 'Y' TO END-PROCESSING.
          END.
END.
```

Figure 12-8 The Corrected KEEP EXCLUSIVE Loop

- Use KEEP LONGTERM NOTIFY only in extreme cases when locks must be kept across pseudo-converses and tasks. Coding is extensive for these.

- Determine why more than one person would be updating records at the same time. Usually, this is tied to an application or database design flaw. Sometimes, this can be solved by users not accessing the same records.

- Use commit logic to release locks.

- Design the application to hold key record locks for the minimal window of time. Lock records just prior to a commit or the end of a run unit.

- Establish the correct sysgen definitions for RULOCKS and SYSLOCKS.

- Use RETRIEVAL NOLOCK in ADSO dialogs whenever possible.

- Use smaller and more restrictive subschemas whenever possible.

12.6   Abendaid Trace for CA-IDMS Applications

Abendaid, from COMPUWARE, is pretty much a standard in most shops today. It is the quickest way to find the cause and a list of solutions for common and uncommon abends. Everyone detests dump reading, even if they are proficient at it.

One day, I was running Strobe on a batch program and saw an interesting line of data. It said that the #XAAIDMS utilized 36 percent of the CPU for the run.

Research isolated this to Abendaid, but it was only when performing its CA-IDMS trace work. Well, I found a whopper tuning opportunity. It turns out that Abendaid was needed only in the test environment. In production, I could turn off the CA-IDMS trace portion and still leave the usual ABEND AID "DIAGNOSTIC INFORMATION" for abends intact. This netted 36 percent CPU. I made it the shop standard, and the savings were phenomenal.

To turn off all the Abendaid stuff, you can put the following DD statement in your JCL. I don't recommend that you do this; I'm just showing you your options here.

```
//ABNLIGNR    DD      DUMMY
```

To turn off just Abendaid CA-IDMS tracing and get a big CPU gain without sacrificing the useful ABEND AID "DIAGNOSTIC INFORMATION", put the following DD statement in your JCL:

```
//ABNLIGNI    DD    DUMMY
```

Your systems programming staff can turn off the CA-IDMS trace facility as the default. I recommend that every shop consider leaving this off in production. The CPU savings is well worth it.

If you don't have Strobe, run some tests with and without the tracing facility. Use the JESMSGS to see changes in CPU on the *task control block* (TCB), which equates to user processing CPU use.

12.7   The Right Language for the Right Job

Most of the time, this tuning suggestion will never help. But there will be that one particular instance when speed is a must. It might be something that is executed millions of times a day. The suggestion is to use a faster executable language. Some math functions will perform much better in FORTRAN, for example, and some bit twiddling is better written in Assembler code.

The performance of Assembly language programs is related directly to the programmer's understanding of the language. Different instruction sets and forms of data provide better performance. Figure 12-9 shows two columns of data that list the relative performance from fastest to slowest for Assembler data and instruction types. One thing particularly helpful to know is that the MVCL instruction becomes more expensive as more data is moved.

To illustrate this point, I've included a sample Assembler program that takes over some of the math previously performed in a COBOL program. The math function is one with which many people are familiar: the sum of the squares.

Fastest	Data Types	Instructions
|	Bit	(RR, RX, SI, SS for bit only)
|	Binary	RR(register to register)
|		RX(register to storage, indexed)
to		RS(register to storage, no index)
|	Character	SS(storage to storage)
|	Decimal	SS(storage to storage)
|	All types	SI(storage to immediate)
	Floating Point	(RR, RX)
Slowest		

Figure 12-9   Relative Performance ASM Datatypes and Instructions

This math formula is commonly used to compute the distance along one side of a triangle. In practice, geographers and cartographers use it to measure the distance between two points. Figure 12-10 shows the original COBOL source program that computes the sum of the squares. Figure 12-11 shows a COBOL and Assembler solution that uses the faster assembler for math functions. Both solutions give the same result, but the one in Figure 12-11 clearly is faster.

Be sure to statically link the SOTSASM program with the calling program. Otherwise, a performance penalty will be associated with dynamic loading. Normally, you would not be able to deduce something such as dynamic loading. That is another reason to use a monitoring tool such as Strobe for tuning, which will show overhead associated with processing outside of your program.

Once incorporated, the savings at runtime are determined by reviewing the JES statistics in your job. Figure 12-12 shows the before and after numbers for comparison of the two methods. Where is the payback, you might ask? This only shows a savings of a few seconds. The payback is in the 500 million computations performed each day using the formula. Given that many executions, you save several CPU hours of time each month.

12.8 Computing Your Savings

Sometime after management says "GO," you will implement your first tuning change. You must cost-justify your efforts. Data-processing services have a computed value that is defined judiciously, primarily to bill departments for resource use. You need to get your hands on these numbers. Use them to estimate your savings. Figure 12-13 shows you an example of what they generally look like. They are coupled to your company's cost of operating its hardware (processors, networks, printers, and so on) and its software services (programming, operations, systems programming and, so on).

```
PERFORM       1000-GET-SOTS THRU
              1000-GET-SOTS-EXIT      UNTIL
              (WS-SUM-OF-SQUARES      LESS   THAN 2000 OR
              WS-N-TIMES  GREATER THAN  +10).
********
1000-GET-SOTS
********
DIVIDE 3 INTO WS-VERT  GIVING
      WS-VERT  ROUNDED.
DIVIDE 3 INTO WS-HORZ  GIVING
      WS-HORZ  ROUNDED.
COMPUTE WS-SUM-OF-SQUARES =
      (WS-VERT  * WS-VERT) +
      (WS-HORZ * WS-HORZ).
ADD +1 TO WS-N-TIMES.
********
1000-GET-SOTS-EXIT.
********
          EXIT.
```

Figure 12-10 A COBOL Sum of the Squares Example

```
—COBOL—

PERFORM       1000-GET-SOTS THRU
              1000-GET-SOTS-EXIT        UNTIL
              (WS-SUM-OF-SQUARES        LESS   THAN 2000 OR
              WS-N-TIMES GREATER THAN  +10).
********
1000-GET-SOTS
********
CALL 'SOTSASM' USING  WS-VERT
                      WS-HORZ
                      WS-SUM-OF-SQUARES
                      WS-WORK.

ADD +1 TO WS-N-TIMES.
********
1000-GET-SOTS-EXIT.
********

                      EXIT.

—ASSEMBLER—

* NAME: SOTSASM
* R4-7        EQU 4-7    WORK
* R8          EQU 8      WS-VERT
* R9          EQU 9      WS-HORZ
* R10         EQU 10     WS-SUM-OF-SQUARES
* R11         EQU 11     WS-WORK
* R12         EQU 12     BASE
* R13         EQU 13     SAVE
*
SOTSASM       CSECT      *
              USING      *,15              ADDRESSABILITY
              B          L0001             JUMP OVER CONSTANTS
              DC         C' '
              DC         CL8'SOTSASM'      MODULE NAME
              DC         C'V1'             RELEASE
              DC         C'  10.00'        ASSEMBLY TIME
              DC         C' 02/02/94'      ASSEMBLY DATE
              DC         C' DUN'           OWNER
              DC         C' JAD'           AUTHOR
S0001         DC         0D'0'
              DC         (72)X'00'
L0001         DC         0H'0'
              STM        14,12,12(13)      SAVE REGISTER CONTENTS
              LR         R12,15            LOAD BASE ADDRESS
              DROP       15                DROP TEMPORARY BASING
              USING      SOTSASM,R12       ADDRESSABILITY
              LR         11,1              R11 -> PARM LIST
              LR         10,0              R10 -> SAVE REGISTER 0
              SR         0,0               LENGTH OF DYNAMIC SAVE
              LA         1,S0001           R1 -> STATIC SAVE AREA
              ST         0,0(1)            SAVE LENGTH IN WD1
              ST         13,4(1)           CHAIN SAVE AREAS
              ST         1,8(13)           *
              LR         13,1              R13 -> NEW SAVE AREA
              LR         1,11              R1 -> PARM LIST
              LR         0,10              R0 -> ORIGINAL CONTENTS
* REG EQUATES
R0            EQU        0
R1            EQU        1
R2            EQU        2
R3            EQU        3
R4            EQU        4
R5            EQU        5
R6            EQU        6
```

Figure 12-11 A COBOL and Assembler Dual-Program Solution

```
R7              EQU       7
R8              EQU       8
R9              EQU       9
R1              EQU       10
R11             EQU       11
R12             EQU       12
R13             EQU       13
R14             EQU       14
R15             EQU       15
                LM        R8,R11,0(R1)          GET PARM LIST
                USING     SOTSWRK,R11
                CLC       SOTSLIT,=CL7'SOTSASM'
                BNE       ERRETURN
DIVIDE1         DS        0H
                USING     VERTDIFF,R8
                ZAP       0(8,R7),0(5,R8)
                SRP       0(8,R7),001(0),0   MULTIPLY BY 10
                MVC       0(1,R6),=X'3C'     STORE 3
                DP        2(6,R7),0(1,R6)    DIVIDE BY 3
                ZAP       0(8,R7),2(5,R7)
                SRP       0(8,R7),64-1(0),5
                ZAP       0(5,R9),3(5,R7)    SAVE REG FOR MULT
DIVIDE2         DS        0H
                USING     HORZDIFF,R9
                ZAP       0(8,R7),0(5,R9)
                SRP       0(8,R7),001(0),0   MULTIPLY BY 10
                DP        2(6,R7),0(1,R6)    DIVIDE BY 3
                ZAP       0(8,R7),2(5,R7)
                SRP       0(8,R7),64-1(0),5
                ZAP       0(5,R9),3(5,R7)    SAVE REG FOR MULT
SUMTHEM         DS        0H
                ZAP       0(16,R7),0(5,R9)   R9 FROM DIVIDE
                MP        6(10,R7),0(5,R9)   MULT VERT
                ZAP       0(16,R6),0(5,R8)   R8 FROM DIVIDE
                MP        6(10,R6),0(5,R8)   MULT HORZ
                AP        7(9,R6),7(9,R7)  ADD SUM OF SQUARES
                USING     SOTSSUM,R10
                UNPK      0(8,R10),7(9,R6)PUT IN DISPLAY OUTPUT
                OI        7(R10),X'F0'          FIX THE SIGN
* RETURN TO CALLER
NORMEND         DS        0H
                LR        11,(15)
                LR        10,(0)
                LR        1,13        R1 -> DYNAMIC SAVE AREA
                L         13,4(13)        R13 -> PREVIOUS SAVE AREA
                L         14,12(13)         RESTORE RETURN ADDRESS
                LR        15,11    R15 -> RETURN CODE
                LR        0,10     R0 -> REASON CODE
                LM        1,12,24(13)     RESTORE REGISTER CONTENTS
                MVI       12(13),X'FF'    FLAG SAVE AREA
                BR        14                --MVS/370 EXIT-->
ERRETURN        DS        0H
                MVC       6(1,R11),BADRC    AN ERROR HAS OCCURRED
                B         NORMEND
                LTORG
BADRC           DC        C'0'
SOTVERT         DSECT
VERTDIFF        DS        5P                   S9(8) COMP-3
SOTHORZ         DSECT
HORZDIFF        DS        5P                   "
SOTSUM          DSECT
SUMOFSQR        DS        8C                   DISPLAY NUMERIC
SOTSWRK         DSECT
SOTLIT          DS        CL6
SOTRC           DS        CL1
                END       SOTSASM
```

Figure 12-11 A COBOL and Assembler Dual-Program Solution (Continued)

12.9 CA-IDMS Retrieval Lock = NO (Retrieval Nolock)

In IDMS, the Dialog Options menu of the ADS Generator has an option called Retrieval Lock. Normally, this is set to YES. You can set it to NO if the dialog and the dialogs or programs linked to don't do database updates and provided that the subschemas implicitly ready the areas in retrieval or the dialog explicitly readies the areas in retrieval. The advantage of doing this is that SELECT locks are turned off.

Locking is one of the major overheads in CA-IDMS online. An average reduction of 10 percent CPU in dialogs where this facility is turned off is not uncommon. It may take a little reengineering of subschemas and READY statements, but it's worth it.

12.10 CA-IDMS Extended Statistics

You can issue the ACCEPT verb to collect statistics in your own programs. There is an excellent write-up in the *CA-IDMS Programmer's User Guide*. One important fact isn't clear, though. When you want to get extended statistics, they

Method	CPU Time Sec(s)
Using Cobol	4.76
Using Cobol/Assembler Combination	2.82

Figure 12-12 Comparing Assembler to COBOL (10KB executions)

Billable		Prime-Shift-Rate	Non-Prime-Rate
Processing Services	CPU Hour	$600.00	$300.00
	Tape Drive Hour	$60.00	$30.00
	Print Lines (1000)	$0.10	$0.05
Disk Storage	Track/day	$0.0010	$0.0005
IDMS Online	CPU Min	$6.00	$3.00
DB2 Online	CPU Min	$6.00	$3.00
Programming	Programmer Hour	$35.00	$35.00
	Sr. Pgmr Hour	$40.00	$40.00
	Analyst Hour	$45.00	$45.00
	Sr. Analyst Hour	$50.00	$50.00
Data Admin.	DB Admin. Hour	$55.00	$55.00
	Sr. DB Admin. Hr	$60.00	$60.00
Consulting	General	$75.00	$75.00
	Year 2000	$200.00	$300.00
Printing	Laser (page)	$0.01	$0.01
Microfiche/film	et cetera		

Figure 12-13 IS Internal Charge-Back Service Rate Table

are available only to online programs in *Central Version* (CV) or to local batch mode programs. These statistics are not available to batch programs running in CV mode. Apparently, there wasn't enough room to pass this information through the SVC. Be cognizant of this fact.

12.11 Hot-Key Lookups and Saving the Prior Record Obtained

There are a million places in programs to use this feature, and the savings are really astounding. This tuning change will work with DB2, CA-IDMS and, for that matter, any database on the mainframe or PC. One of the most overlooked performance gains is one of the most obvious. If you keep the last record obtained in a save area and then compare the key with the next one being requested, you can eliminate unneeded database calls. Considering that an indexed database call could entail three I/Os internally, this can really add up.

Suppose that a program has to put 2 header lines of data and 12 detail lines on a display screen. Each detail line contains 5 columns of data. Each field/column of data is coming from a different database record (worst-case scenario). If 3 of the 5 fields/columns are displaying data that repeats on each line, the same records probably are being obtained repetitively. Under the covers, nested down in the workings of the program, are repetitive calls to the database for information such as tax rate, dictionary lookups, attributes of assorted types and lots of other static information.

If you could eliminate 20 to 30 database calls per transaction, the result might be a large elapsed time and CPU gain for the giant volume of transactions affected. This is especially true for those top 10 programs identified in Chapter 1. Figure 12-14 shows an example of eliminating database calls without using a save record.

I call this a *hot-key lookup* because the prior EMP-REC that was obtained will still be available in working storage if the key hasn't changed. Most of the time, this is a safe way to eliminate database calls. However, if other processing could corrupt the contents of your record, you will need to save it in a record-save area for comparison later. Figure 12-15 shows you how to modify this routine to do this.

```
IF WK-EMP-ID NE   SPACES
      DO.
      IF WK-EMP-ID NE EMP-ID OF EMP-REC        ☜ Hot Key Test
      DO.
      MOVE WK-EMP-ID TO EMP-ID OF EMP-REC.
      OBTAIN CALC EMP-REC.
      END.
MOVE EMP-NAME TO WS-EMP-NAME.
END.
```

Figure 12-14 Database Hot-Key Lookups

```
IF WK-SAVE-EMP-ID NE  SPACES
    DO.
    IF WK-SAVE-EMP-ID NE EMP-ID OF EMP-REC
        DO.
        MOVE WK-SAVE-EMP-ID TO EMP-ID OF EMP-REC.
        OBTAIN CALC EMP-REC.
        MOVE EMP-REC TO WK-SAVE-EMP-REC.
        END.
    MOVE EMP-NAME TO WS-EMP-NAME.
    END.
```

Figure 12-15 Saving the Last-Used Record

Database calls use thousands of instructions, whereas a hot-key or saved-record lookup is in the tens of instructions. Other system overhead, such as concurrency, locking and system programs called jack up the savings even higher. I've seen dialogs in which this technique was employed for every record obtained, and an 80 percent CPU reduction was realized. If you apply this to the top 20 online programs in your shop, your users will love you.

12.12   The Notorious Subroutine Calls

You might have seen some of these calls while wading through code. The program performs the same tasks every time through the loop, even though it doesn't need to. The best example of this is where generalized skeletons for online screens (shell programs) are created. The goal is to simplify the screen code building to the point at which the programmer doesn't even need to think. The fallout is that every program does everything, all the time, whether or not it is warranted.

Of course, the code is working. Why fool with it, right? Well, this is just another area to realize a great savings for a small investment of your time. My favorite programs set an end-of-search indicator. When you see these, you know you're hot on the trail to a big savings. To top it off, if this type of program is used as a prototype for 100 other programs, propagating your tuning change becomes a manufacturing process. Each time you repeat it, you get another savings.

Figure 12-16 contains repetitive code that always is executed, when it actually needs to be executed only for a valid GL-TYPE = "P".

Notice that seven routines are called to do work before the program checks to see whether this is even the record that needs to be worked on. This is easy to fix: Just move the calls for the seven subroutines ahead of the "CALL SCRNOUT" line. That way, they aren't invoked unless they need to be. In many instances, those seven subroutines call seven more, and those make database calls. The overall effect is refreshing to see.

The result is a 75-percent savings in processing. Response times are even greater than the CPU savings. You don't have to be a rocket scientist to use techniques like these.

```
MOVE 'N' TO END-PROCESSING.
WHILE NOT END-PROCESSING
REPEAT.
        OBTAIN NEXT GL-REC      WITHIN GL-NDX.
        CALL FORMAT.                    ☞   Don't do this if not a
                                            record match
        CALL UNPACK.                    ☞           "
        CALL TIMESTMP.                  ☞           "
        CALL DATESTMP.                  ☞           "
        CALL USERNOTE.                  ☞           "
        CALL GETACCT1.                  ☞           "
        CALL GETACCT2.                  ☞           "
        !*    Check for hit
        IF GL-TYPE = 'P'
            CALL SCRNOUT.
        ELSE
            MOVE 'Y TO END-PROCESSING.
        END.
```

Figure 12-16   Repeating Work Unnecessarily

12.13   The Notorious String Search

Almost as common but not so obvious is the byte-manipulation work going on. Here is an example of a program that determines the length of a string:

```
! GET LENGTH OF RECORD
MOVE 150 TO WS-LEN.
WHILE  COMP-NAME(WS-LEN) EQ SPACES OR
       COMP-NAME(WS-LEN) EQ LOW-VALUES
    REPEAT.
        SUBTRACT +1 FROM WS-LEN.
    END.
```

Assuming that the ADSO language has no built-in function for deriving the length, this seems like a reasonable bit of code. However, what if it is executed 4 million times a day?

If the record is kept in a save record similar to the examples in section 12.11, you might alleviate some of the overhead. But Figure 12-17 hosts a simpler solution to cut the processing time.

The additional code can potentially eliminate three-fourths of all the loops through the comparisons. Bytes don't need to be compared if prior tests resulted in a reject. This is a simple binary-halving routine. Depending on the nature of the data in COMP-NAME, it can be tweaked further. If you customize the routine based on the data, I guess you could call it *smart stringing*.

12.14   Custom Nonbinary Search Routines

You can implement binary search routines in several ways. I will discuss a more traditional routine in the chapters covering mainframe and PC-caching routines. Here, I'll discuss a technique you can use when you must obtain optimum performance at any cost. Suppose that you want to build the fastest possible nonbinary search routine for your application. The key is only 4 bytes in length, but there are thousands of keys. You know that the keys start with the letters A through Z and that keys beginning with the letters A, D, G, J, M, P, and S are accessed the most. Building a smart data-search routine is one way to achieve your tuning goal.

Using the design in Figure 12-18, you would provide the code necessary to access your hypothetical data, giving precedence to the most-used keys.

```
! GET LENGTH OF RECORD
IF      SUBSTR(COMP-NAME,15,1) EQ SPACES OR
        SUBSTR(COMP-NAME,15,1) EQ LOW-VALUES
        MOVE 14 TO WS-LEN.
ELSEIF  SUBSTR(COMP-NAME,32,1) EQ SPACES OR
        SUBSTR(COMP-NAME,32,1) EQ LOW-VALUES
        MOVE 31 TO WS-LEN.
ELSEIF  SUBSTR(COMP-NAME,75,1) EQ SPACES OR
        SUBSTR(COMP-NAME,75,1) EQ LOW-VALUES
        MOVE 74 TO WS-LEN.
ELSE    MOVE 150 TO WS-LEN.
WHILE   COMP-NAME(WS-LEN) EQ SPACES OR
        COMP-NAME(WS-LEN) EQ LOW-VALUES
        REPEAT.
          SUBTRACT +1 FROM WS-LEN.
        END
```

Figure 12-17 A Fast String Search

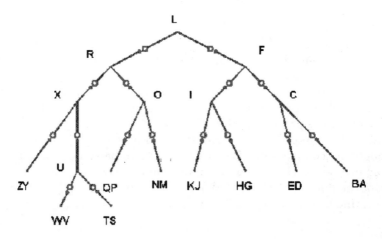

Figure 12-18 A Hypothetical Data-Access Path

You only need to compare the first byte of each key to reach the bottom of the data-search hierarchy. Pseudocode to process the example looks something like this:

```
IF REQUEST-BYTE1 <  L
    IF REQUEST-BYTE1  < F
        IF REQUEST-BYTE1 < C
            then read A & B table entries from table position 1
        ELSE then read C, D & E table entries from table position 55
    ELSE
        IF REQUEST-BYTE1 < I
            then read G & H table entries from table position 159
        ELSE then read I, J & K table entries from table position
        222
ELSE IF REQUEST-BYTE1 < R
    IF REQUEST-BYTE1 < O ... and so on
```

By saving the data positions of the most-used keys, you quickly can position within the data. The first record beginning with the letter I is occurrence 222, for example. Your program performs tests against your REQUEST-BYTE1 key and the letters searched most often. If the key matches the letter I, your table search begins at position 222. This technique is valid for use with tables, databases or files.

Also, you want to code your customized routines to take advantage of hot keys. That is, the last key requested may match the current request. In those cases, it is unnecessary to do a lookup. Customized search routines afford maximum speed because they conform to data-use trends. If you want to take this approach one step further, you can design the algorithm to be self-modifying. The algorithm learns how data is accessed on a user or cyclical basis and modifies itself accordingly. The ensuing processing is spellbinding: A lookup actually occurs prior to the request for data.

12.15 Measuring Your Success

Two products can help you adequately benchmark your results. In the world of CA-IDMS, **Hiperstation,** by Peregrin Systems, enables you to script multiple transactions for use in stress, volume, and concurrency testing without human intervention. You can install this tool in TSO, IMS DC, or CICS. The TSO foreground connection works great with a cross-domain VTAM connection to CA-IDMS. This makes it an all-around useful transaction-processing facility. Here's a brief dissertation on how it works. You record transaction scripts by executing your transactions in recording mode. Then, you can replay them from 1 to n times at 0-to-n-second intervals on 0 to n terminals.

In DB2, IBM's *Teleprocessing Network Simulator* (TPNS) acts as a transaction driver to fully drive any SQL scenario. Both these tools enable you to see the true impact of a tuning change. Scoping out a change with individual transactions is fine for verifying that the code is more efficient, but to really see the impact to the system as a whole, you need to stress it with dozens of user IDs. This becomes a critical decision when your tuning change is swapping one resource for another; you could introduce a new bottleneck.

12.16   MVS LPA/ELPA

There isn't much to say about the *link pack area* (LPA)—just that all the frequently executed programs belong there and that you need to work closely with the Systems Programming department to identify new candidates for this facility. It reduces loading of programs from JOBLIBS, STEPLIBS, and LOAD/ATTACH Assembler macro calls used by online DBMSs. This is not an area for gigantic gains, but keep it in mind for your all-encompassing tuning project.

12.17   The Notorious Loop (S322 Abend Variety)

How do you normally deal with an S322 abend (CPU time-out)? Do you use trace or program displays to determine how to resolve these looping programs? Well, here is a new approach. With Strobe, you can capture the lines of code looping in the production run. You can determine the exact lines of code within a few minutes. This can eliminate the need to copy production databases to test ones, recompile programs and who knows how many other tasks to re-create the problem in test mode.

Strobe can be turned on before the program begins execution or after it is running. In a few minutes, it collects enough samples to report back to you with the hexadecimal offsets of lines of code that were looping. You can see from the output of the Performance Profile report in Figure 12-19 that most of the time is CPU rather than elapsed.

To further refine the search for the cause of the loop, you review Strobe reports. As shown in Figure 12-20, the loop is in a call to subprogram BILLPGM3 from BILLPGGM1.

Resource	Usage		
SESSION TIME	9 MIN 58.54 SEC		
CPU TIME	8 MIN 54.42 SEC	☜	mostly CPU
WAIT TIME	0 MIN 0.00 SEC		
STRETCH TIME	1 MIN 4.12 SEC		

Figure 12-19 Strobe Output for a Tight Loop

The final step in the search is to see CPU use by offsets with load modules (see Figure 12-21). The offset at 7540 was cross-referenced with the production compile listing, and the most heavily used instructions were determined to be part of a single paragraph. That paragraph was executed using a "PERFORM UNTIL", but the values in the until clause could never be satisfied. The search for the cause of the loop has ended. As long as this correction is being made to resolve the loop, it also is a good time to optimize the program using compiler directives, such as OPTIMIZE.

12.18 CA-ADS Generation

A big 30 percent CPU gain is possible if you're not using executable code in your ADS dialogs. The Dialog Options screen in *Application Dialog System Generator* (ADSG) enables you to define a dialog with symbol tables and diagnostics. Using SYMBOL TABLES=Y prevents executable-code generation. At runtime, the dialog is interpreted one line at a time; this eats up a lot of CPU time.

```
STROBE* PERFORMANCE PROFILE          BILLJ110          02/18/94          PAGE    4
                   ** PROGRAM SECTION USAGE SUMMARY **
MODULE   SECTION   SECTION  FUNCTION  CPU TIME PERCENT    TIME HISTOGRAM  MARGIN OF ERROR:  1.72%
  NAME     NAME     SIZE      SOLO      TOTAL       .00.00   25.00   50.00   75.00  100.00


BILLPGM3 BILLPGM3 66785                          100.00   100.00   ******************************
                                                 ------   ------
PROGRAM BILLPGM1   TOTALS                         100.00   100.00
```

Figure 12-20 Strobe Output for a Tight Loop

```
STROBE* PERFORMANCE PROFILE          BILLJ110       2/18/94             PAGE    5
                    ** PROGRAM USAGE BY PROCEDURE **

MODULE - BILLPGM3                      SECTION - BILLPGM3
LINE PROCEDURE  STARTING  INTERVAL  CPU TIME PERCENT TIME PERCENT  CPU TIME HISTOGRAM  MARGIN OF ERROR: 1.72%
NUMBER  NAME    LOCATION   LENGTH       SOLO          TOTAL         00   11.00   22.00   33.00   44.00

                000000    16832    .00          .00          - .
                0051C0       64   15.60        15.60          .**********
                005200       64    9.07         9.07          .*****
                005240       64   10.58        10.58          .******
                005280     2240    .00          .00          - .
                005B40       64    5.52         5.52          .***
                005B80      320    .00          .00          - .
                005CC0       64    8.45         8.45          .****
                005D00     2112    .00          .00          - .
                007540       64   42.12        42.12          .******************************
                008580       64    8.66         8.66          .*****
                0085C0    24833    .00          .00          - .
                                  ------       ------
SECTION  BILLPGM3   TOTALS        100.00       100.00
```

Figure 12-21 Strobe Output for a Tight Loop

Figures 12-22 and 12-23 show two examples of turning off symbol and diagnostic tables in your dialogs during normal production-source migrations.

Of course, there is a valid reason to turn SYMBOL TABLES on while testing dialogs: to use the online debugger. However, once you go to production, you shouldn't need the debugger. If you move whole dictionaries from TEST to PROD, you might inadvertently move a bunch of dialogs with SYMBOL TABLES turned on to production. Oops! That would cause the production system to crawl. The examples provided will help you avoid this mistake.

The trade-offs between the two methods shown follow:

- UCF batch jobs have a tendency to become bottlenecked if more than one is running (refer to Figure 12-22).

- The ADSOBGEN program (refer to Figure 12-23) generates a dialog load module, but it does not cause the NEWCOPY indicator in central version to be switched on, as does UCF batch (refer to Figure 12-22). Consequently, ADSOBGEN runs in roughly half the time of the UCF batch routine.

```
//UCFB     EXEC PGM=UCFBTCH,REGION=1M
//STEPLIB DD DSN=IDMSPROD.CV5.LOADLIB,DISP=SHR
//SYSCTL  DD DSN=IDMSPROD.CV5.SYSCTL,DISP=SHR
//SYSLST  DD SYSOUT=*
//SYSIPT  DD *
SIGNON PRODMIGR
MIGRPASS
DCUF SET DICTNAME BILLPROD
DCUF SIMULATE
ADSG
BILLD0001                                    ➥    Dialog Name
%PF13
%TAB N%ENTER                                 ➥    Turn Off Symbol Tables
%PF10
&MEMBER
%PF13
%TAB %TAB N%ENTER                            ➥    Turn Off Diagnostic Tables
%PF10
%CLEAR  %CLEAR  %CLEAR
DCUF SIMULATE OFF
BYE
```

Figure 12-22 Turning Off Symbol and Diagnostic Tables (UCFBTCH)

```
//ADSOBGEN EXEC PGM=ADSOBGEN,REGION=4M
//STEPLIB DD DSN=IDMSPROD.CV5.LOADLIB,DISP=SHR
//        DD DSN=IDMSPROD.LOADLIB,DISP=SHR
//CDMSLIB DD DSN=IDMSPROD.CV5.LOADLIB,DISP=SHR
//        DD DSN=IDMSPROD.LOADLIB,DISP=SHR
//SYSCTL  DD DSN=IDMSPROD.CV5.SYSCTL,DISP=SHR
//SYSLST  DD SYSOUT=*
//SYSIPT  DD *
 SIGNON USER IS PRODMIGR PASS IS PRODPASS DBNAME=BILLDICT.
 GENERATE FROM SOU MOD DIALOG=BILLD0001 VER=1 DIAG TAB=N SYM TAB=N .
```

Figure 12-23 Turning Off Symbol and Diagnostic Tables (ADSOBGEN)

There is one more step when turning off symbol and diagnostic tables for ADSO dialogs: getting a list of the candidate dialogs. In Figure 12-24, a Culprit reporting routine gives you a list of candidate dialogs.

The Culprit routine produces a report of all dialogs in a dictionary that have symbol tables or diagnostics tables turned on (see Figure 12-25).

12.19   FDR from Innovation Data Processing

This product is pretty widespread. Whether you are performing standard or nonstandard backups, compresses of PDS files or reorganizations of VSAM and IAM files, FDR is the fastest and most advanced method. This tool claims to outperform DFDSS V2.5 and greatly save on CPU. The most important thing to note is that these activities usually are in the top 20 CPU burners in most mainframe shops. The greatest thing you can do to relieve the amount of processing for these activities is to use nonstandard backups. Most shops consider nonstandard backups to mean doing different packs every other day. That isn't true. A complete implementation of nonstandard backups categorizes files into daily, weekly, monthly, and quarterly backups. These files should reside on volumes and storage groups and should be defined according to their specific activity and need for recovery. The same idea applies to the frequency of file compresses and reorganizations. The road to making these utility runs nonstandard can be a little bumpy, but when you get to your destination, you will have saved a lot of CPU.

12.20   DB2 Table Access from CA-IDMS

Many shops today have what I call *competing databases*. The evolution that took place, bringing multiple DBMSs under one datacenter roof, is not important. The important thing now is their peaceful coexistence.

One of the greatest causes of CPU use is the proliferation of redundant data. In Chapter 17, you will look at collapsing redundant systems into a better model of information processing for your enterprise. For now, take a look at ways to access the same data from multiple telecommunications drivers.

A traditional approach to accessing data that resides in multiple DBMSs is extracting and copying. Propagation is a much more complex issue. Other ways to get at data include the popular LU6.0 and LU6.2 programs. These programs are used to ship requests for packets of data to a foreign DBMS and then wait for the results. This is not an easy approach to implement. Finally, there is software that promotes warehousing.

12.21   IDMS/Gateway

A relatively new series of tools is coming on the market as I write this book. I've only just heard about these tools that have direct access; I haven't seen them in action. The tools are available from Vegasoft through TACT (The A Consulting Team, Inc.). See Appendix D for vendor addresses.

```
//* SYMBOL OR DIAGNOSTIC SWITCH TURNED ON REPORT
//*
//*          Report is 132 bytes wide by 55 lines / page
//*          but it can fit on an 80 column screen for easy viewing.
//*
//*          It is possible to use this routine to generate control
//*          cards which are input to a standard UCFBATCH
//*          routine which will perform the dialog regens, while
//*          turning off the tables. The savings computation is
//*          only an estimate. This should run once for each dict
//****************************************************************
//STEP010 EXEC CULPRIT
//STEPLIB  DD   DSN=IDMSPROD.CV5.LOADLIB,DISP=SHR
//         DD   DSN=IDMSPROD.LOADLIB,DISP=SHR
//SYSCTL   DD   DSN=IDMSPROD.CV5.SYSCTL,DISP=SHR
//SYSIN    DD *
 DATABASE DBNAME=BILLDICT
 PRO USER=BILLUSER PW=BILLPASS
 IN 10000 DB SS=IDMSNWKA   $DICT SUBSCHEMA
 PATH01 OOAK-012 PROG-051 PROGCMT-050
 PATH- LOADHDR-156
 REC CMT-050    403 9
 REC SYMB-TABLES        409 1
 REC DIAG-TABLES        411 1
 010 LENGTH
 010 WORK-AMT
 010 REVISED-SIZE
 010 SYMB-IND ' '
 010 DIAG-IND ' '
 010 GOOD-PATH      'N'
 010 WDIALOG '                '               $STORE DBKEY
 01SORT PROG-NAME-051
 010OUT 132   LP=55
 SELECT PROG-051 MAINLINE-051 GT 0
 SELECT PROG-051 DIALOG-051 GT 0
 013       YOUR COMPANIES NAME HERE
 01H1   1  ' '
 01H2   35 'ADS DIALOG -SYMBOL OR DIAGNOSTIC TABLE TURNED ON REPORT'
 01H3   55 'TABLES FOUND'
 01H3   75 'D-I-A-L-O-G       S-I-Z-E      I-N     B-Y-T-E-S'
 01H4   45 'ADS DIALOG
 01H4   55 'S=SYMB D=DIAG'
 01H4   75 'CURRENT'
 01H4  105 'EST. W/OUT TABLES'
 01H5   1  ' '
 0151   45 PROG-NAME-051    SZ=8
 0151   55 SYMB-IND     SZ=1
 0151   60 DIAG-IND     SZ=1
 0151   75 LOADHDR-SYMTABLEN-156   SZ=8
 0151  105 REVISED-SIZE     SZ=8
 017       IF PATH-ID NE '01'        020             $TEST FOR PATH 01
 017       MOVE 'N' TO GOOD-PATH                     $INIT PATH SWITCH
 017       MOVE PROG-NAME-051 TO WDIALOG             $PROG TO WORK
 017       MOVE 'CALC' TO CALL-TYPE                  $CALC CONSTANT TO WORK
 017       MOVE 'LOADHDR-156' TO CALL-REC            $LOADHDR TO WORK
 017       CALL DB-EXIT(CALL-TYPE,CALL-REC, WDIALOG  8)$GET RECORD
 017       IF IDMS-STATUS NE '0000'       010        $STATUS NOT OK
 017       IF PROG-NAME-051 NE LOADHDR-MODNAME-156 010      $NOT A MATCH
```

Figure 12-24 Reporting on Dialogs with Symbol and Diagnostics On

```
017        MOVE 'Y' TO GOOD-PATH                    $DID GET IT
017        IF LOADHDR-SYMTABLEN-156 EQ  0    003  $ SYMB-TABLE ?
017        COMPUTE LOADHDR-SYMTABLEN-156 - LOADHDR-MODLEN-156 WORK-AMT
017        B  004
017003     MOVE LOADHDR-MODLEN-156 TO WORK-AMT    $NO SYMB-TABLE
017004     IF DIAG-TABLES NE 'D' 005               $NO DIAG TABLE
017        COMPUTE  WORK-AMT - 1458  REVISED-SIZE $SUBTRACT AVG DIAG
017        B  030
017005     MOVE  WORK-AMT TO REVISED-SIZE         $AMT WITHOUT DIAG
017        B  030                                  $BRANCH TO 30
017010     CALL DB-EXIT ('DBKEY ' 'PROG-051 ' DBKEY-ALPHA(PROG-051))
017        DROP                                     $REPOSITION & OUT
017020     IF GOOD-PATH NE 'Y' DROP                 $CAME THRU 10?
017030     MOVE ' ' SYMB-IND                        $INIT BYTES
017        MOVE ' ' DIAG-IND
017        IF SYMB-TABLES EQ 'S'  AND DIAG-TABLES EQ 'D' 100 $BOTH ON
017        IF SYMB-TABLES EQ 'S'  AND DIAG-TABLES EQ ' ' 200 $SYMB ONLY
017        IF DIAG-TABLES  EQ 'D' AND SYMB-TABLES EQ ' ' 300 $DIAG ONLY
017        IF SYMB-TABLES NE 'S'  AND DIAG-TABLES NE 'D'  DROP $NEITHER
017100     MOVE SYMB-TABLES TO SYMB-IND
017        MOVE DIAG-TABLES TO DIAG-IND
017        TAKE 1
017200     MOVE SYMB-TABLES TO SYMB-IND
017        MOVE ' ' TO DIAG-IND
017        TAKE 2
017300     MOVE DIAG-TABLES TO DIAG-BYTE
017        MOVE ' ' TO SYMB-BYTE
017        TAKE 3
```

Figure 12-24 Reporting on Dialogs with Symbol and Diagnostics On (Continued)

```
REPORT NO. 01      YOUR COMPANIES NAME HERE      01/01/90 PAGE      1

ADS DIALOG - SYMBOL OR DIAGNOSTIC TABLE TURNED ON REPORT
```

ADS DIALOG	TABLES FOUND S=SYMB D=DIAG		D-I-A-L-O-G S-I-Z-E CURRENT	I-N EST.	B-Y-T-E-S W/OUT TABLES
BILLD050	S	D	90,356		63,396
BILLD200	S		71,656		40,172
BILLD375	S	D	114,944		54,396
BILLD486	S		143,284		27,060
BILLD827		D			23,832

Figure 12-25 Output from Culprit Run

IDMS/Gateway is a tool that allows ADS/O and DC-COBOL applications to access all data in mainframe CICS, as well as DB2, Sybase, and Oracle on the PC (products available from TACT).

12.22 IDMS/DB2 and ADS/DB2

These tools offer complete mainframe DB2 table access to CA-IDMS DC-COBOL and ADS programs. This is a quantum leap for several hundred shops that have both these DBMSs. Both release 12 CA-IDMS SQL and DB2 SQL commands can coexist in the same program. Both dynamic and static SQL commands are supported. Figure 12-26 gives you a simple example of the syntax (products available from TACT). Figure 12-27 lists some CA-IDMS R12 and R14 performance enhancements.

12.23   DB-CICSLINK and CA-Visual Objects

The **DB-CICSLINK** (product available from TACT) tool allows CA-IDMS programs and dialogs with CICS 3.1 through 3.3. It eliminates relinking programs and recompiling.

On another front, Computer Associates announced **CA-Visual Objects**, which will allow database connectivity between CA-IDMS, DB2, Oracle, and so on. Computer Associates will be a major competitor in the database connectivity race. Someday, you may even see some kind of a standard emerge for connectivity that enables all software on all platforms to perform universal database calls.

12.24   IPCP (Interprogram Control Processor) from Software Diversified Services

With this product, you can eliminate some of the downtime for CICS applications. IPCP gives you an automated way to open, close, allocate, and deallocate files from the CICS region without shutting down or operator intervention. This is an ideal way to handle those special batch updates or reorganizations of databases.

IPCP is accessed in batch programs with parameters (see Figure 12-28). Or you can access it online. IPCP also processes standard CEMT commands from the batch utility program. If CICS needs to restart after a failure, IPCP automatically handles the files that were being tracked by it before the failure.

```
PROGRAM: BILLINV1
EXEC SQL                                              ☜   CA-IDMS SQL
              SELECT COMPANY INTO :COMPANY
              FROM IDMS.CUSTOMER
              WHERE COMPNAME = :COMPNAME
END-EXEC.

MOVE COMP-INV-DATE TO INVDATE.
MOVE COMP-INV-NUM   TO INVNUM.

EXEC DB2                                              ☜   DB2 SQL
              SELECT INVOICE INTO :INVOICE
              FROM DB2.INV
              WHERE INVKEY = :INVKEY
END-EXEC
```

Figure 12-26 DB2 and CA-IDMS SQL in a DC-COBOL Program

- ESA Dataspace support. The system scratch area can be assigned to a virtual area eliminating any I/O. User databases can also be assigned to ESA.
- Support for unlinked user indexes which can be added, changed, deleted, or maintained without changing the database structure.
- Indexes that allow duplicates can be sorted in DB-KEY order.
- DMCL's can be changed dynamically.
- Files can be allocated and deallocated dynamically.
- There is a new lock manager which can reduce CPU by 60%.
- Areas can be expanded without unload/reload of data.
- Separate logical and physical database definitions in the dictionary will greatly reduce the amount of time doing subschema compiles.
- DISPLAY ALL interruptable in IDD to prevent taking too long.
- Full relational database and SQL support across CA-IDMS relational and DB2 relational databases.
- Nucleus and major control blocks are XA eligible.
- Extensions to multi-tasking for database functions.
- Communications and remote data access enhancements.
- Run scratch manager modules in multi-tasking mode.
- 24-hour support—DynamicLINE, LTERM and PTERM definitions and security defintions.
- Dynamic resource allocation of RLE, RCE and DPE control blocks.
- An improved SQL algorithm.

Figure 12-27 Other CA-IDMS R12 Enhancements

```
//STEP010        EXEC PGM=IPCPBTCH,REGION=8M
//IPCPDS         DD DSN=IPCP.COMDLIB,DISP=SHR
//AUDIT          DD SYSOUT=*
//SYSIN          DD *
  CEMT SET TRANSACTION(BIL1) DISABLED        ↩  Disable CICS trans
    NOUP LIST=BILLLST1                       ↩  Execute FileClose/Dealloc
//STEP020        EXEC PGM=BILLUPDT,REGION=8M
//BILFIL1        DD DSN=PRODVS.BILL,DISP=SHR
//SYSPRINT       DD SYSOUT=*
//STEP030        EXEC PGM=IPCPBTCH,REGION=8M
//IPCPDS         DD DSN=IPCP.COMDLIB,DISP=SHR
//AUDIT          DD SYSOUT=*
//SYSIN          DD *
  OKUP LIST=BILLLST2                         ↩  Execute File Alloc/Open
    CEMT SET TRANSACTION(BIL1) ENABLED       ↩  Enable CICS trans
```

Figure 12-28 IPCP Batch Execution

CA-DADS (*Dynamic Allocate Deallocate Subsystem*), from Computer Associates, is another product available to you for this kind of processing savings. You really need to evaluate which tool will fit your needs best. It is important to reduce batch windows and eliminate downtime for online users. Doing so leverages your investment in applications and personnel.

12.25   DB2 Database Warehousing

Here are some products that aid in managing database warehouses. IBM provides **Datahub**, which enables DBAs to control the creation of warehouse tables. Prism Solutions provides **Prism Warehouse Manager**, which works with VSAM, QSAM, IMS, DB2, Oracle, Sybase, and Red Brick Systems. Data is transformed from several sources into a single target information database while maintaining the structural components of the data. The target is on the mainframe of a client/server system. IBM also provides **Data Propagator**, **Data Joiner,** and **Data Guide** to help propagate data to different databases and platforms. The biggest tuning options open to those involved in data warehousing, distribution, replication, and propagation are first to reduce the number of times updates need to be applied to target databases. Second, reduce the number of times databases or their updates are transmitted across a wide area network.

12.26   Reducing Table Conversion and Loading
for Multiple DBMSs

Other than the tools and methods already mentioned in previous chapters on buffering and database tuning, there are a few products you should keep in mind.

Bridge/Fastload, from Bridge Technology, is one such tool. Consider this tool when you need to load DB2, DB2/2, or DB2/6000 databases rapidly. This tool completely bypasses the conventional DB2 logging and performs fast loading of tables.

Another product is **DEC DB Integrator** from Digital. As a user of multiple database managers, such as DB2, you now can use Sybase and Oracle to view the data from multiple database systems concurrently without the overhead of table unloading/loading and datatype conversions.

12.27   Speeding Up QMF Queries

Another way to get performance from QMF queries is to convert them to a faster processing language and tune up the SQLs. The following two tools can help you if you decide that it is cost-justified for your shop.

Platinum **Compile/QMF** converts QMF queries to COBOL. The **Rocket Compiler** converts the queries to COBOL II or C language.

12.28 DB2 Column Sizes

DB2 columns should match the datatype for which they were intended. Columns containing only numeric data, for example, should be defined as numeric to save on space and processing time.

DB2 builds a 2-byte prefix on columns defined as varchar. DB2 computes the offset to the next column after it encounters a varchar column. Therefore, these should be placed after all other columns to reduce mandatory offset computations.

12.29 DB2 Update Logging

DB2 maintains both active and archive log files. When the active log fills, DB2 automatically offloads it to a *mass storage system* (MSS) or an archive log tape. Archive logs can contain up to 1000 datasets. In addition, DB2 can be set up to perform single (2 to 53 active files at one time) or dual logging (4 to 106 active log files at one time). Each of these datasets is a single extent VSAM *linear dataset* (LDS). The point is that logging represents a substantial part of the overhead for DB2. The decision you make whether to use single or dual logging can impact overall response.

DB2 logs a range of updated columns in a fixed-length row. DB2 determines which is the first-affected column and the last-affected column. All columns between these two columns (inclusive) are logged. Therefore, you should analyze your update activity and try to place groups of updated columns as close together as possible. This reduces the amount of data that must be logged.

To get a list of columns, issue the following command:

```
SELECT * FROM SYSIBM.SYSCOLUMNS
```

12.30 Optimizing DB2 Access at Reorganization Time

A DB2 database is made up of a set of DB2 data-related objects, including storage groups, tablespaces, tables, indexes, and views. Each of these objects has its own peculiar tuning properties. You can use segmented tablespaces, for example, to place multiple tables in a single tablespace. Or, you can assign different DASD volumes to a particular storage group. Keep in mind that DB2 uses the volumes in order of assignment, regardless of their relationship to the head of the string on the channel. A tablespace can contain one or more datasets containing tables, and these datasets can be placed across volumes and channels for performance. You can adjust the size of pages in tablespaces to improve read and write performance. Also, you can create partitioned indexes on a table in a partitioned tablespace and divide it into multiple index spaces, or you can build clustering indexes that match the order of records in a base table. You have many general tuning opportunities.

DB2's distribution of free space and the insertion of rows can result in a degradation of performance that is related to rows that are out of clustering sequence. You can obtain the ratio of rows clustered in insertion order to those not from the performance reports discussed in Chapter 1. When the clustering ratio is less than 85 percent (a rule of thumb), you will want to reorganize the table placing the rows in their natural clustering order and allow for sufficient free space to reduce the clustering problems.

Tables with variable-length rows are more susceptible to out-of-clustering sequence problems. During update, if a row does not fit on its target page, DB2 creates a pointer to another page where the row is stored. From that point on, DB2 does not return the row to its original target page, even if space becomes available. Consequently, there is more occasion to perform reorganizations.

Another illustration of the effect of free space on performance is noncontiguous leaf pages and multilevel indexes. Constant update activity leaves leaf pages in disarray and increases the number of index levels. Sequential index-access performance degrades geometrically as these situations escalate. Again, a reorganization is the solution. And, again, free space must be reevaluated to reduce the future impact of noncontiguous leaf pages. Note that loading records in descending order instead of ascending order eliminates the page splitting that occurs. This page splitting can cause poor space usage and many additional levels. Use the standard free space formulas provided in Figure 12-29 when resizing your tables and indexes.

12.31   DB2 Read-Only Tables

Some tables will not require any update. Document, dictionary, cross-reference, history, formulas, and other static datatypes can be candidates for special tuning considerations. You can turn on locking at the table or tablespace by using LOCKSIZE TABLESPACE or LOCKSIZE TABLE. You can optimize tables and indexes at the time of load, and free space is unnecessary. Consider the use of a simple nonpartitioned tablespace to reduce the number of space-map pages required. Also, these types of tables are ideal for compression.

12.32   Segmented and Partitioned Tablespaces

Here are a few ways to achieve better segmented tablespace performance:

- Use segmented tablespaces when concurrent access to multiple tables requires fewer open datasets.
- Segmented tablespaces offer a performance gain when used with tables displaying common-access properties.
- Segment size should be optimized for I/O.

Some common methods for achieving performance with partitioned tablespaces follow:

TABLE CALCULATIONS

Constants	Formulas
#records = 100K	usable page size = 4074 * .95 = 3870
avg rec = 80 bytes	records/pg = FLOOR(3870/80) = 48
pg size = 4k	pages used = 2 + CEILING(100k/48) = 2086
PCTFREE = 5% each pg	total pages = FLOOR(2086 * 21/20) = 2190
FREEPAGE = 20 (1 in 20 free)	estimated kbytes = 2190 * 4 = 8760

INDEX CALCULATIONS

Constants and Variables

k=keylength
p=PCTFREE
n=avg # dup keys or 1 if none

Formulas

s=availabl space (100-p)/100
m=subpages/page
*entries/page = FLOOR(s * n * 4050/(k+(4*n))) for index with one subpage/page*
*entries/page = FLOOR(s * n * (4067 -m * (k +21))/(k + (4 *n)))*

for index with more than one subpage/page, assuming sizes of
4050 and 4067

Example

k = 10
m = 1
n = 1
s = (100-10)/100 = 0.9
entries/pg = FLOOR(4050 *.9/(10 +4)) = 260
leaf pgs 1st = CEILING(100k/260) = 385
non-leaf pgs 2nd = CEILING(385/260) = 2
non-leaf pgs 3rd = CEILING(2/260) = 1
Total all levels = 388
*Total space = 4 * (388 + 2) = 1560*

Figure 12-29 DB2 Free Space Formulas

- Place historical data in a separate partition with less PCTFREE and FREESPACE defined.

- Run parallel jobs against multiple partitions to achieve smaller batch-processing windows.

- Use partitions to distribute corporate data by division or batch-processing cycle, thus reducing the time to process the data in batches and queries.

- Use partitions to isolate data based on its need to be updated or backed up.

- Use a separate partition for data that is not mission-critical and may even be deleted or dropped frequently.

12.33   DB2 Resource Limits

The *Resource Limit Specification table* (RLST) enables you to enforce a time limit for execution of DML SQL requests before termination. You can do this by using the START RLIMIT command. Resource limits should be established above the natural average query time limit but below the time necessary to cause performance degradation and unacceptable deadlock levels for the general consensus of users.

12.34   DB2 Deadlocking

DB2 indexes are the most common cause of deadlocking. Index pages contain many more entries than table pages and are all locked with a page lock. Consequently, update activity has more occasion to deadlock. Subpages can alleviate some of the contention encountered. Subpage 1 is accepted as the best choice where inserts are predominant.

12.35   CA-IDMS Transaction Statistics

One of the ways you can determine where your CPU is being used is by collecting CA-IDMS transaction statistics. The *COBOL DB/DC Reference Guide* gives you documentation on collecting both batch and online statistics. If you want to run a prototype of every DML call to see what each individual call uses in CPU time on your M/F processor, however, you need to do it with an online program. The statistics block for IDMS/DC has user and system CPU time collection. Combined, these two statistics represent the entire CPU time for a DML call. These two fields are scaled to ten-thousandths of a second ($10**-4$ second).

Appendix E supplies a sample COBOL program for collecting these statistics. Figure 12-30 shows you a comparison of CPU costs for respective *Data Manipulation Language* (DML) calls under IDMS releases 5.7 and 10.2. I was unable to get these statistics for the new releases 12.0 and 12.1, but I hope to have them for a next edition. Be careful when collecting transaction statistics; they can fill the log with messages. If your charge-back system uses the log files, the effect of grossly larger logging files can impact the production charge-back jobs.

If you decide to collect DC transaction statistics in your programs, you need to issue the following DCMT commands to turn on statistics before running your programs. This prevents a 3815 or 3850 error-status code when attempting to accept statistics—that is, provided that statistics are not left on all the time in your systems.

`DCMT VARY STAT TRAN ON`	Turns on statistics
`DCMT VARY STAT INT 1`	Sets statistic interval
`DCMT VDP STAT01 COBOL PROGRAM ENABLE`	Builds *program dynamic element* (PDE)

I find that it is much easier to collect statistics by using Strobe. However, there will be occasions when transaction statistics and even displays to the printer will help isolate the CPU use in a task or dialog thread.

Machine Cobol DML Command	Release 5.7 (IBM 3083 Model E) Standard CA-IDMS Buffering IDMS CPU Time	Release 10.2 on 136 Mips DB-Megabufs IDMS CPU Time
BIND RECORD	0.0009	0.000076
ACCEPT RECORD DBKEY	0.0009	0.000091
ACCEPT SET DBKEY	0.0009	0.000091
ACCEPT SET DBKEY NEXT	unknown	0.000091
ERASE	0.0009	0.000108
READY AREA	0.0012	0.000092
IF SET EMPTY	0.0014	0.000082
GET RECORD	0.0015	0.000091
OBTAIN CALC	0.0033	0.000091
FIND CALC	0.0029	0.000091
OBTAIN USING DBKEY	0.0020	0.000091
FIND USING DBKEY	unknown	0.000091
OBTAIN CURRENT RECORD	0.0019	0.000082
FIND CURRENT RECORD	unknown	0.000082
OBTAIN CURRENT IN SET (chain)	unknown	0.000091
FIND CURRENT IN SET (chain)	unknown	0.000091
OBTAIN CURRENT IN AREA	0.0019	0.000099
FIND CURRENT IN AREA	unknown	0.000099
MODIFY RECORD	0.0021	0.000100
OBTAIN OWNER IN SET	0.0023	0.000091
OBTAIN NEXT IN SET (calc-via)	0.0027	0.000100
FIND NEXT IN SET (calc-via)	unknown	0.000100
OBTAIN FIRST IN SET (calc-via)0.0031	0.000091	
FIND FIRST IN SET (calc-via)	unknown	0.000091
OBTAIN PRIOR IN SET (calc-via)	0.0027	0.000100
FIND PRIOR IN SET (calc-via)	unknown	0.000100
OBTAIN LAST IN SET (calc-via)	unknown	0.000091
FIND LAST IN SET (calc-via)	unknown	0.000091

Figure 12-30 IDMS DML CPU Use

Machine Cobol DML Command	Release 5.7 (IBM 3083 Model E) Standard CA-IDMS Buffering IDMS CPU Time	Release 10.2 on 136 Mips DB-Megabufs IDMS CPU Time
OBTAIN FIRST IN NDX (sys owned)	n/a	0.000097
FIND FIRST IN NDX (sys owned)	n/a	0.000097
OBTAIN LAST IN NDX (sys owned)	n/a	0.000097
FIND LAST IN NDX (sys owned)	n/a	0.000097
OBTAIN NEXT IN NDX (sys owned)	n/a	0.000097
FIND NEXT IN NDX (sys owned)	n/a	0.000097
BIND Plus FINISH	0.0049	0.000199
CONNECT	0.0053	0.000108
DISCONNECT	0.0053	0.000108
MODIFY	0.0021	0.000100
STORE (no set membership)	0.0144	0.000100
COMMIT (varies with updates)	unknown	0.000100

Figure 12-30   IDMS DML CPU Use (Continued)

Notice that many of the DML verbs in release 10.2 have the same CPU time, which otherwise would have different times. This is because with DB-Megabuf, many calls are satisfied out of the buffer. In fact, to more clearly resolve the differences in CPU time, you would have to execute tens of thousands of calls instead of the 100 for each verb that your benchmark did. Feel free to experiment on your own. If you get more expert numbers for use in design reviews and tuning situations, by all means, use your own numbers. They only represent a scale for calculating the cost of transactions at review time.

12.36   IDMSTABX Tuning for CA-IDMS System-Owned Indexes

The REBUILD FROM INDEX option of IDMSTABX (the index-building utility) enables you to reorganize an existing system-owned index. The first step of the utility process creates a work file (the SYS002 DD), which contains three control cards and images of all the unloaded index entries. The second step is a SORT, which typically takes place only to reorder the control cards. Therefore, it is in your best interest to change the order of the first three cards without sorting the entire file. This can save a great deal of runtime. Figure 12-31 shows how to accomplish this manipulation in your IDMSTABX JCL.

12.37 DB2 Lock Tuning

The duration of tablespace locks is determined by the ACQUIRE and RELEASE options of BIND. In general, these options are acquired when a plan is allocated, a resource is used, a resource is released at commit time, or a resource is released at PLAN or PACKAGE deallocation time.

```
//* SORT CONTROL CARDS
//SORT0001   EXEC PGM=SORT,PARM='STOPAFT=3',REGION=1M
//SYSIN      DD DSN=IDMSTABX.SYSPCH,DISP=(OLD,DELETE,KEEP)
//SYSOUT     DD SYSOUT=*
//SORTIN     DD DSN=IDMSTABX.SYS002,DISP=OLD
//SORTOUT    DD DSN=SORT0001.SORTOUT,
//              DISP=(,CATLG,DELETE),
//              SPACE=(TRK,(100,10),RLSE),
//              UNIT=WORK,LRECL=80
//SYSUDUMP   DD SYSOUT=W
//* APPEND REMAINDER OF FILE
//SORT0002   EXEC PGM=SORT,PARM='SKIPREC=3',REGION=20
//SYSIN      DD *
   SORT FIELDS=COPY
//SYSOUT     DD SYSOUT=*
//SORTIN     DD DSN=IDMSTABX.SYS002,DISP=(OLD,DELETE,KEEP)
//SORTOUT    DD DSN=SORT0001.SORTOUT,DISP=MOD,
//              UNIT=WORK,LRECL=080
//SYSUDUMP   DD SYSOUT=W
```

Figure 12-31 TABX Sort Time Reduction

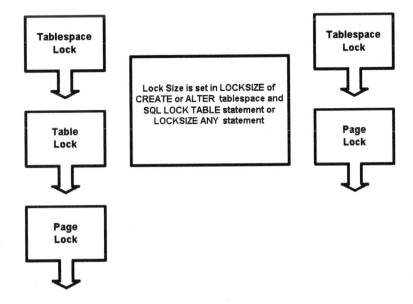

Figure 12-32 A DB2 Locking Diagram

The duration of page locks is set in the ISOLATION option. Usually, the locks are acquired when the page is accessed. Figure 12-32 provides a reference for the order of locking.

12.38 DB2 Query I/O Parallelism

The diagram in Figure 12-33 exemplifies the way parallel I/O is processed in a DB2 query and reduces the overall elapsed time. On the left, I/O is serialized. On the right, I/O is run parallel. The elapsed time is reduced by using parallel I/O processing.

12.39 DB2 Sequential-Key Contention

Sequential keys take several shapes. The most common is a next-number table. To reduce access contention, you can use several programming techniques:

- Use multiple next-number tables to reduce contention.
- Use random keys for row inserts.
- Invert the key (9-s complement) or reverse key byte order before store and retrieve operations to force randomization.
- Access a key just prior to issuing a commit.

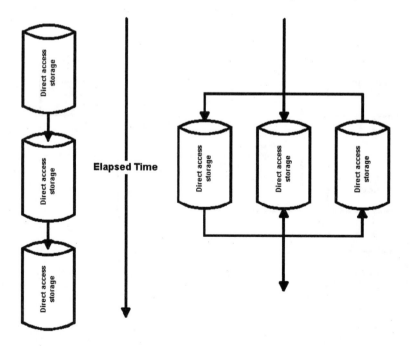

Figure 12-33   DB2 Parallel I/O

- Partition the table into smaller pieces based on key use.
- Use a check digit in front of keys to force partial randomization.

12.40 MVS Paging

As the amount of database activity migrates away from disk volumes and into memory tables, the paging rate increases. When the paging rate reaches 3000 pages/second on page packs, it is time to increase the available real memory on the operating system. The best way to avoid a problem in this area is to involve systems programming in changes that impact paging. Systems programming can monitor the resources and help make the best decisions affecting paging rates.

12.41 Optimizing Tape Performance

Improved data recording compression (IDRC) is an enhancement that nets you between 2:1 and 3:1 on mainframe tape data storage. Because this compression is now in the hardware, there is a savings in CPU and elapsed time. This means that you can turn off *Fast Dump / Restore* (FDR) compression.

You can optimize block sizes for tapes in two ways. The first is to manually increase the blocking of files to reduce EXCPs. The second is to set BLKSIZE=0, where *Space Management System* (SMS) is employed. SMS automatically chooses the optimum block size for output files.

With hardware enhancements come added benefits. Expect a 2:1 gain in storage and access times when you convert your 18-track tape units to 36-track units.

12.42 COBOL Open and Close

This is a minor point, but you should group file open and close statements to reduce multiple loading of the I/O drivers. The *Return on Investment* (ROI) on this tuning hint is small. It isn't going to be a savings you can clout. The best way to deal with this is to make it a shop standard where you work. As applications become more complex, it isn't always possible to close files at the same moment. So, you also need to bend on the rule. Here are examples of open and close verbs for multiple files:

OPEN	CLOSE		
OPEN INPUT	BILL1	CLOSE	BILL1
	BILL2		BILL2
	BILL3		BILL3
OUTPUT	BILL4		BILL4
	BILL5.		BILL5.

12.43   COBOL REWRITE Verb

It is possible to open a QSAM/SAM file for input and output. After reading a record, you can modify the record and store it back to the same sequential file location by using the COBOL REWRITE verb. There are limitations, but this method avoids the extra I/O overhead of copying the output to another file. Restart is a bit tricky for these files.

12.44   JES MSGLEVEL(1,0)

The JES MSGLEVEL(1,0) parameter eliminates allocation and disposition JES messages from your output job listings. These can represent from 10 percent to 25 percent of the SYSOUT produced in utilities and compile listings. These messages may be redundant or unused in many job classes in your shop. You can implement this parameter in three ways. You can place it on a job card. You can apply it to a specific class of jobs that run in an initiator. Or, you can apply it to all jobs. The savings can be measured in elapsed time, CPU, lines-of-print and kilobytes of spool reduced. This message parameter is a way to achieve a global savings quickly.

12.45   Managing Jobs

ThruPut Manager, from MVS Solutions, Inc., is a very unique tool. There are five base components. Each one provides a number of management and tuning features worth mentioning. The five integrated components are Job Classing Services, TM/Job Binding Services, TM/Dataset Contention Services, Job Setup Services and TM/Robotic Setup Services. Figure 12-34 highlights some of the key performance-related features.

- Assign jobs to classes based upon use of a IMS, DB2, or IDMS region. Jobs can be deferred if a region is not available. And, jobs can be bound to a CPU where a software is licensed. Test and production database usage can be assigned to different job classes that may have differing dispatching.

- The number of batch jobs using a database region can be limited. When the maximum is reached, other jobs automatically will be held and released to survive within assigned limits.

- Tape drive usage can be controlled to avoid too many jobs from starting, if they would exceed a predefined limit for tape units available.

- Restrict the number of concurrent FDR backups running.

- Limit the number of nonproduction database jobs running.

- Restrict jobs from starting that would have dataset conflicts.

- Automatic recall for HSM or FDRABR migrated datasets.

Figure 12-34   Some of the Performance Uses for ThruPut Manager

---

12.46   CICS/ESA 2.3.1

Using RETURN IMMEDIATE in programs provides a significant performance improvement over EXEC CICS START. A savings in the range of 50 percent to 75 percent in response time can be realized. There is a drawback, however; you cannot use RETURN IMMEDIATE with terminals other than the initiating one.

12.47   Reorganizing Large DB2 Tables with Alternate Indexes

One of the problems with multimillion row DB2 tables is that index building can be slow. If you allow the indexes to be built during reorganization, the time spent is astronomical. If you drop the indexes prior to the reorganization and then create them afterward, the DSNDB07 area tends to run out of space. So what is the solution? Well, try this. Unload the data by using DSNT1AUL. Next, drop and re-create the indexes after a load/replace using an empty file as input. Finally, perform a second load/replace using the output of the first step as input (sorted in clustering sequence). This should avoid the DSNDB07 problem.

12.48   Purging CA-IDMS Records

Many customized procedures can reduce windows of outage for online databases. It can be advantageous to document all these procedures. One common example is when there is a need to purge scores of CA-IDMS records. This can force the database administrator to sit down with the applications programmer to discuss ways to reduce outages. Consequently, using one of the many sequential prefetch buffering utilities can find a way into standard purge processes. Large DMCL buffer assignments are an alternative if one of the prefetch utilities is not available.

To purge a large number of records spread out randomly across an area, first sweep the area, locating target records putting their db-keys on file. Next, sort the file in db-key order so that the purge can be accomplished with a single sweep of the area. Finally, erase the records taking advantage of the sorted file and tools such as Fast Access or DB-Megabuf. The database needs to be offline only for the final step. Obviously, the last step should happen during off-peak hours.

12.49   Reducing Paper Costs

In an effort to stem the rising costs of paper use in large corporations, most have begun to use tools to place reports online in an effort to reduce paper and printing costs. The biggest benefit is not the tremendous savings in paper costs, however; it is the immediate availability of information. No longer do users have to wait for the paper-jam turnaround. One company put all its master file-data online and, as a result, reduced its manufacturing turnaround time. This shocked management, which didn't expect this result. They finished their annual production backlog ahead of time and had to turn their attention toward new products and services. **Control-D** and **Dispatch** are two competing products in this arena.

12.50   CA-IDMS Integrated Index Tuning

It is not the intention of this book to repeat the contents of any CA-provided manual here. Those books have all the necessary information on the creation of index SR7/8 records, updates, and purges and all the formulas for index administration. Therefore, only the key steps to successful index-performance maintenance are presented here:

1. Gather current statistics for the index.
2. Review the schema for the index to determine the type of index (symbolic key, db-key or unsorted).
3. Determine the length of the key.
4. Determine the number of I/Os to access a target record.
5. Determine the number of users contending for records per second.
6. Determine the total number of index entries.
7. Determine the desired number of levels in an index tree.
8. Determine the number of SR8 entries.
9. Determine the size of SR8 records.
10. Determine the cost of compression.
11. Determine the number of bytes in the index.
12. Determine the page size for the index.
13. Determine the number of displacement pages, if necessary.
14. Determine the total number of pages in the index.
15. Determine the area and how many files to use.
16. Prepare a worksheet, program, or TSO CLIST to automate this process when repeated in the future.

12.51   Client/Server Philosophy

Quite often, you hear reasons why client/server development or installation is to be avoided. A higher cost ratio often is cited as the cause. Another reason for avoiding or postponing this technology is the perception that it isn't needed. Figure 12-35 provides a list of productivity and performance rationales for taking another look at this technology, though. These guidelines were compiled over a two-year period to satisfy my own curiosity about the benefits of client/server. Some of the items represent tangible tuning reasons for choosing client-based applications.

Now, I realize that it is possible to debate some of the benefits listed here in light of arguments favoring mainframe-equivalent capabilities. However, this list does present some basic reasons for moving toward client/server.

PC software development is evolving at a much higher rate than mainframe and is cross-platform independent. What does this mean to you? At some point, it may no longer be competitive for your company to build mainframe software. It

- Locate the processing as close to the user as possible.
- Link users to best-of-breed PC software products.
- Provide open systems solutions for scalability.
- Target reusability found in the best object technology.
- Distribute transaction volumes across platforms.
- Invest in new avenues that match technology with the core competency of the company.
- Capitalize on existing networks.
- Be able to absorb developers from the college PC software market.
- Benefit from a fully implemented EMAIL solution with PC FAX and world-wide WANs.
- Exploit cut-n-paste, *Dynamice Data Exchange* (DDE), and *Object Linking and Embedding* (OLE) in mission-critical applications.
- Utilize *advanced intelligent networks* (AIN) to tie processors to phone switches in new ways.
- Match GUI advances to business needs.
- Utilize graphic flow processing in applications.
- Converge media technology like CD-ROM, images, and rewritable optical with applications.
- Position the company at the forefront of major technological advances.
- Fuel smarter and more insightful software decisions.
- Add new software strengths to existing legacy systems.
- Trade client/server risks for mainframe risks.
- Utilize cost effective optical media for microfiche, manual, report, and document distribution.
- Get on board with massively parallel processors.
- Gain form the benefits of RISC processing.
- Give users the freedom to use PC-based end user tools to view data.
- Provide the best tools for users to clean up dirty data before it goes to mainframe.

Figure 12-35   Client/Server Productivity and Performance Gains

- Provide best-of-method processing techniques for the business operations.
- Migrate development off the mainframe.
- Decrease the distance between the developer and end user with RAD PC tools.
- Convert mainframe to a repository accessed by the best PC development tools.
- Tie PC publishing tools to a publishing-oriented business.
- Tie PC music tools to a music-oriented business.
- Tie PC media tools to a media-oriented business.
- Map technology closely to business processes.
- Increase processing independence and avoid corporate data center outages.
- Investigate the use of royalty-free software to reduce licensing burdens.
- Centralize world-wide data administration around client/server.
- Define world-wide application life cycle standards embracing client/server.
- Define a new standard for world-wide applications.
- Capitalize on the use of the Internet/Intranet(s).
- Expand types of services available to in-house and out-of-house users.
- Utilize events, triggers, and robotic processing at end-user workstations.
- Provide high-powered CAD/CAM workstations and features tied to corporate data.
- Client/server is network centric.
- Client/server facilities data collection is real time.
- Client/server allows for a solution tailored to the individual.

Figure 12-35   Client/Server Productivity and Performance Gains (Continued)

will be time to branch into client/server or take a beating. This concept is not easy to grasp. Try to picture what technology means to your business. If your technology were two decades older than that used by everyone else, would you be able to compete? Well, at the rate client/server and personal computer technologies are growing, the mainframe soon will be two decades behind current PC trends. This fact is amplified by the ever-growing importance of information. Experts tell us that information will play the most important role in business by the year 2000.

Chapter 16 introduces some tuning opportunities for Xbased and client/server programmers. Because literally thousands of software packages exist that contribute to tuning in some fashion, it isn't possible to cover them all in this text. So some choice mainstream tuning tools and topics will be presented to whet your appetite.

13

Mainframe Sorts

13.1 SYNCSORT Tuning

SYNCSORT is a remarkable product from SYNCSORT Incorporated. It has a built-in memory manager that looks at the available virtual memory and determines the best way to perform sorts. If there is enough available memory, all sorting is performed in memory. SYNCSORT overrides the JCL REGION= parameter. Also, if you do not supply any SORTWK files, the product allocates the minimal number required to perform the processing.

With the focus on data warehousing, SYNCSORT also can reformat and aggregate data before it is handed off to bulk loading facilities. With its multi-output feature, it can create two or more output files in a single pass at the input.

The DCB=BUFNO=nn parameter is not required with the SYNCSORT product, because it has its own physical I/O routines.

SYNCSORT outperforms other sorting products (vendors not mentioned for legal reasons) easily. So, you're asking, "What can I do to tune SYNCSORT?" Well, first look at some runtime statistics where I modified SORTWK files.

Small Sort

Number of SORTWKs	Elapsed Time (sec)	CPU Time (sec)
4	05.90	0.18
8	08.54	0.22

As you can see, small volume sorts don't need to have a lot of SORTWK files. This is because the sorting is being performed in memory and the additional SORTWK files add up as extra file-allocation time. The message TURNAROUND SORT PERFORMED was found in the message output, which confirmed that sorting occurred in memory.

In a medium-size test, the number of SORTWK files begins having an impact on resources used. The elapsed time drops nearly by half with 10 SORTWK files.

Medium Sort (600 K Records)

Number of SORTWK Files	Elapsed Time (min)	CPU Time (sec)
4	2.40.96	11.61
8	2.16.82	11.27
10	1.22.18	10.05

Finally, a large sort continues the trend for savings when more SORTWK files are used. The following statistics are for a 1.2 million record sort. Instead of showing elapsed time, EXCPS are shown. The EXCP count dropped with additional SORTWK files; this is where the savings comes from.

Large Sort (1.2 M records)

Number of SORTWK Files	EXCPS	CPU Time (sec)
5	13,159	11.44
10	12,661	11.33

So, as is now apparent, the main tool available to you for leveraging tuning of sorts is the SORTWK. You can do a few other things to improve sorting. Figure 13-1 shows a list of things that will improve sort performance.

You will find that SYNCSORT is a *smart sorting* tool, because it automatically discerns so many factors from the operating system by itself.

UNIX VERSION OF SYNCSORT

The same kinds of sort, merge, and copy capabilities are available with the UNIX, version of SYNCSORT. It can be invoked from the UNIX sort command, the shell commands syncsort or sort, or with SORT and MERGE from Micro Focus Cobol programs. You can use the following options to tune resource use and view statistics:

/DATASIZE	Optimizes data sizes
/MEMORY	Specifies the amount of virtual memory
/STATISTICS	Provides statistics
/WORKSPACE	Specifies a directory or combination of directories for a scratch directory or temporary files

- SYNCSORT recommends using CYLINDER allocation rather than tracks or blocks for SORTWK files. Here is an example.

```
//SORTWK01    DD    SPACE=(CYL,(20,20)),UNIT=WORK
```

- SORTLIB does not need to be in job JCL if the library has been added to LPA. This is a good idea because most shops perform hundreds of thousands of sorts per year.
- The primary allocation for sort should be large enough to handle the most frequent volume of data processed. Secondary extents cause additional overhead.
- Batch sorts will automatically release unused sort space after the input phase has completed.
- SYNCSORT handles buffering internally. It isn't necessary to add BUFNO definitions to sort steps.
- Here is the formula for calculating the cylinders of space needed for both primary and secondary SORTWK space allocations. These should always be allocated using cylinders.

$$TotalNumberofTracks = \frac{A \times B \times 1.3}{C}$$

where: A is number of records to sort, B is the average record length, C is track bytes (46,476 for 3380 track/56,664 for 3390 track capacity), 1.3 is a SYNCSORT constant

$$TotalNumberofCylinders = \frac{TotalTracks}{15}$$

$$PrimarySORTWKAlloc = \frac{TotalCylinders}{SORTWKs}$$

$$SecondarySORTWKAlloc = \frac{TotalCyls}{.10}$$

- SYNCSORT will dynamically allocate up to 4 SORTWK files. For sorts less than 5000 records, programmers should not have to put SORTWK files in their JCL.
- If you have designated 10 SORTWKs and only 9 volumes are available, SYNCSORT will attempt to put these on different volumes. However, if they are not available, it will double them up on the same volumes.
- SYNCSORT will avoid, if possible, using the volumes which were allocated for SORTWKs to do its allocations for SORTIN and SORTOUT files.

Figure 13-1 Sort Recommendations

■ If you allocate more SORTWK files than are necessary, the additional over-head of allocation causes your job to use more resources than necessary. This can result in an increase of a few seconds. However, adding additional SORTWK files on a very large sort can cut CPU and wall clock time in half. There is no preset ideal number of SORTWK files. The correct tuning method is to review the output in the JES message log statistics and adjust your numbers accordingly.

■ MAXSORT is special. When your sorts are so large that there isn't enough work pack space to perform them, then MAXSORT provides a method that involves multiple runs to create work files. These are concatenated into the sort output phase. Since this requires different JCL, it is advised that you consult the MAXSORT manual for more details.

■ Review job output messages. Sorts that get the message "TURNAROUND SORT PERFORMED" had their sort done in memory. These job steps can have all SORTWKs removed provided this is a normal record load for the sort per-formed.

Figure 13-1   Sort Recommendations (Continued)

SyncSort UNIX can help cut Oracle sort and aggregation (externally) time by 60 to 80 percent, depending on the data and type of operation. Syncsort Incor-porated is a company with incredible sort products. You can find company con-tact information in Appendix D.

13.2   IBM's VS Cobol II Release 4 and SYNCSORT's SYNCSORT/Cobol

With the IBM announcement that OS/VS Cobol 2.4 no longer will be supported after June of 1994, many shops have been migrating their code to VS Cobol II and COBOL/370. COBOL/370 is a little bit of a leading-bleeding-edge leap for many shops. So, the jump to VS Cobol II probably will be more prevalent.

There are some super savings in using VS Cobol II. There's 31-bit addressing (via AMODE=31, RMODE=ANY). Also, if you go forward to VS Cobol Release level 4, there are significant performance enhancements for internal sorts. This is great news. Prior to that, you only had two ways to improve internal sorts. One was to break the input and output phases into two programs and perform the sort externally with a faster sorting product. The other was to use the product SYNCSORT/Cobol. I prefer the latter product just because SYNCSORT is so ef-ficient.

13.3 SAS Sort Tuning

I've mentioned two of SYNCSORT Inc's products: SYNCSORT and SYNC-SORT/Cobol. Well, there is another one. It is SYNCSORT A SAS Sort Accelerator. Because SORT and sas routines both can fall in the top 20 CPU users for most shops, these are areas where you can get the biggest savings. Consider these as first things to do when tuning. By substituting PROC SYNCSORT in place of the usual PROC SORT, you invoke SYNCSORT's super efficient routines, giving you a savings in I/O, CPU, and elapsed time.

SAS provides an excellent manual for programmers that describes techniques for tuning SAS applications. It is called *SAS Programming Tips* (ISBN-1-55544-431-8). Encapsulating that base of knowledge here is beyond the scope of this book.

14

CA-IDMS 12.x and 14.0 System Tuning

14.1 The Special Design Needs of Network Databases

Poor performance with CA-IDMS databases can be attributed to excessive database calls (both external and internal), buffering, physical implementation deficiencies, or improper placement within a distributed database environment. Let me add a small dissertation on the distributed database and then abandon the subject. CA-DDS (*distributed database system*) is a tool that can help you deploy your data to satellite divisions. Multiple concurrent updates then can be applied to several divisional databases that comprise the corporate (enterprise) database network. The data stored in these separate division databases has been normalized to the divisional needs. Users from different divisions can be granted access to other divisions with which they conduct business. A view of the data from all the divisions would represent the composite corporate database. The difference is that each division manages its own data autonomously. A distributed database environment offers marked advantages, such as security, disaster recovery, and redundant network access paths, to name a few. A side effect can be better performance.

A *database management system* (DBMS) is only as powerful as its capability to access data. This makes the connectivity of data the pivotal point for performance. Many articles and handouts written regarding CA-IDMS database design stress pointers, indexing, and clustering as the key methods for improving performance. They still are. In fact, they will be the focus of this section.

The mapping of a logical model into a physical database is an exercise in trade-offs. Do you want to optimize performance and sacrifice some of the flexibility your logical model delivered? If so, you may have a database that looks like an airplane, except without wings. A physical database that supports all future changes also can run like a stuffed pig. Either way, you could win and lose at the same time.

If your database was designed using a tool such as BACHMAN Data Analyst (from the Re-Engineering Product Set), you probably began with a logical database design that was normalized using an *entity relationship model* (ERM). Repeating attribute values have been eliminated from entities, nonkeyed attributes are dependent on an entity's entire key, partial-keyed attributes have been resolved, and of course, there no dependencies exist between an entity's nonkeyed attributes (transitive dependencies). Simply, you have achieved third normal form, if you're lucky. If all this sounds unfamiliar to you, then STOP EVERYTHING! Your database may never have been normalized at design time. A design that has been normalized provides a good foundation for performance.

If you suspect a poor design, you might want to consider reengineering your database. The process involves decomposing (reverse engineering) the current database into its respective logical model, normalizing it, and reapplying the physical design constraints. The results can give new life to a system. Even if you apply only a piece of the final product for performance purposes, your system will benefit.

Your next line of attack is to address individual performance problems. Table 14-1 provides a tuning-decision chart for CA-IDMS database users. The chart is a standalone source for quickly identifying your tuning options, based on some symptom of poor performance you identify.

TABLE 14-1   CA-IDMS Design Tuning Decision Chart

SYMPTOM	SOLUTION
The database is too large to maintain or the logical model is apt to change frequently.	Implement foreign keyed records.
Referential integrity is the biggest issue.	Combine records or use direct pointers.
Sequential processing will be used most.	Implement a set or index.
Random processing will be used most.	Implement an index or CALC keyed record.
Sporadic changes in the application require additions of ever more intermediate VIA record levels.	Use a bill of material set design.
There are multiple relationships between two records.	Define multiple sets before considering more records.
Disconnect or modify results in a set walk; erase causes unwanted logical deletions; or last and prior obtains are not permitted.	Add a prior pointer.
Obtain owner results in sets longer than six occurrences.	Convert to a user-defined index set or add a junction via record.

TABLE 14-1   CA-IDMS Design Tuning Decision Chart (Continued)

SYMPTOM	SOLUTION
CALC-to-CALC processing results in too much physical I/O.	Convert one record to VIA and access it with a new CALC record or with a new system-owned index based upon the key.
Records participate in a set stored with CURRENT DATE, TIME, or NEXT NUMBER	Use a descending key.
The set to be accessed has mixed ascending and descending key fields.	Use integrated indexes and not sorted sets.
Heavy CALC and VIA overflows are present	Consider larger pages, more pages in the area, or reorganization. Also, consider putting records in separate areas.
Heavy SR8 splitting (more SR8s), and/or spawning (more levels) is present.	Define larger SR8s, more SR8s or regular index rebuilds. Consider additional free space within SR8s.
Heavy fragmentation of variable-length records is present.	Consider database reorganization, free space setting and page size used.
There are multiple access strategies to the record.	Optimize storage and retrieval for the most utilized path.
A group of records accessed most of the time.	Use VIA clustering of records.
There are more than 12 records in every sorted chain set, and all records are retrieved during processing.	Use a sorted index set.
Too many records are being clustered together, or there are too many SR8s for a user-mode index.	Try a system-owned index by combining the keys of records found in the path.
The set path cannot be collapsed anymore.	Combine multiple record occurrences into a single larger record.
The database data must be ported across multiple platforms, or clustering is too great.	Use a foreign key design similar to a relational table, or break out lower level VIAs into their own database areas.
Records have lots of blank spaces and/or are large.	Consider compression (IDMSCOMP/IDMSDCOM or PRESSPACK) and variable length records.
Index performance is degrading.	Recalculate SR8 size for optimization and reorganize the index.
Random retrieval is not performing fast enough.	Try CALC records or supply a complete key value on a sorted index.
Partial key lookups aren't performing fast enough.	Use a sorted index with a generic partial key search.
The index retrieval results in a partial area sweep.	Use index records with db-key as the sort key.
Database areas contain too many record occurrences to perform recoveries or maintenance. Buffer conflicts are high, too.	Break records out into their own respective areas, or if this cannot be done, break them into logical key ranges per area. Consider the use of the distributed database product or your own APPC routines.

TABLE 14-1   CA-IDMS Design Tuning Decision Chart (Continued)

SYMPTOM	SOLUTION
Deadlocks are out of the ordinary.	Use or remove KEEP EXCLUSIVE locking as appropriate to resolve the abends. Lock records that create bottlenecks for short periods of time, by putting them in their own subprogram, with its own run-unit. Use smaller pages for CALC records. Use commit logic. Use retrieval-only subschemas for retrieval-only paths. Use NOLOCK retrieval in qualified ADSO dialogs.
Online update volumes exceed the design capabilities of the DBMS.	Switch high volume updates to batch processing, or use methods other than the database to achieve throughput.
Index retrieval transaction runs too long.	Use better index loading techniques and reload indexes to collapse out extra index levels.
Index orphan count is high (mixed index and non-indexed access is present)	Run a customized program to sweep the index and offload the data. Then rebuild the index in reverse order. Be sure to use schema definitions that allow for index growth. See Appendix H for a sample program code used to capture SR8 statistics.
Index compression/decompression is suspected of high CPU usage.	Reduce size of SR8s, the size of keys, or turn off compression to avoid index sweeps.
Index update transactions run too long.	Free pages and page space for SR8s may be insufficient. Check SR8 split and spawn counts. Also, check buffering. Release SR8 locks with frequent commits.
Deadlocks on index transactions are high.	Space is too tight on index owner's page or displacement wasn't used for bottom-level SR8s.
Obtain owner results in a set walk.	Add an owner pointer.
The set path is long and uses too many calls.	Analyze the database structure for opportunities to collapse the number of records in the path making the path shorter.
The index retrieval results in a complete area sweep.	Consider using OBTAIN NEXT WITHIN AREA and utilize a prefetch buffering tool.

After applying the solutions in this chart to your day-to-day performance problems, you will be one step ahead. Remember that the issues of maintenance, multiple path updates, multiple path retrievals, ownership, backup, and recovery, as well as multiple user security all have to be considered in your design decisions. Aren't database tradeoffs *FUN*?

14.2   Integrated Indexing for CA-IDMS

There are nine major steps to creating high-performance indexes in CA-IDMS. They are detailed here, along with some key questions and concerns to keep in mind.

1. Define the access requirements and the supporting index definitions.

   a. Were one or more indexes really required?

   b. Were key fields the best possible choices?

   c. Can access be obtained directly, without walking any records or using an index?

   d. With large indexes, separate areas for index and target records are advised.

2. Define the order of index loading.

   a. SR8s must be loaded uniformly for best performance.

   b. Future splits should involve only the last member added to an index instead of a group of members.

   c. Future splits should occur on adjacent free space on the SR8's page or next page.

   d. Records must be presorted for initial load and added in index-key or db-key order.

   e. Set currency should be established on the last record in the set prior to insertion of a NEXT-ordered unsorted set.

   f. Set currency should be established on the first record in the set prior to insertion of a PRIOR-ordered set.

   g. Members stored via the index using db-key have no special processing concerns.

   h. An ascending index with DUPLICATES LAST should be loaded as ascending.

   i. An ascending index with DUPLICATES FIRST should be loaded as descending.

   j. A descending index with DUPLICATES FIRST should be loaded descending.

   k. A descending index with DUPLICATES LAST should be loaded ascending.

   l. Insertions at the right end of an SR8 (highest ascending key or lowest descending key) affect processing by causing all levels of the index to be updated. Internal SR8 manipulation is minimal, however.

   m. Insertions at the left end of an SR8 (lowest ascending key or highest descending key) normally involve the current SR8 level only. Internal SR8 manipulation involves calculating the number of members and offsets.

3. Define the order of the target records.

   a. If records are stored as CALC or hashed, the index key order should be used when building the index.

   b. It may be faster to sweep the target records with a user-written program collecting the index key and db-key. This file can be presorted for optimum index building.

4. Define the DMCL buffers, XA-buffering or dataspace buffering of indexes.

   a. Placing the entire database areas into DB-Megabuf dataspaces prior to index loading can greatly speed up the building process.

   b. For standard DMCL buffering, be sure to provide one buffer page for the SMP page and top-level index, as well as five buffer pages for each other index level and 40 pages for the index set owner.

5. Reserve space for updates and future growth.

   a. Allow space on index pages, and within SR8s, at index building time.

   b. Leave enough room on pages for insertion of new SR8s.

   c. The page reserve never should exceed 30 percent of the page size, or it will render SMP useless and cause area sweeps looking for space.

   d. Use a page reserve at load time, or if a page reserve is not used, run IDMSXPAG with the SMI BASED ON clause to allot space for SR8 splits.

   e. Increase the maximum number of entries per SR8 specified in the SCHEMA INDEX BLOCK CONTAINS clause. This schema change implies subschema regeneration, also.

6. Displace VIA members away from the index.

   a. Place the index owner and member records into separate areas.

   b. Displace member records using the LOCATION MODE VIA clause in the schema.

7. Displace bottom-level SR8s.

   a. Specify a displacement value in index-set definitions to force bottom-level SR8s to locate on a different page than upper level SR8s.

8. Define index compression.

   a. Compression occurs in bottom-level SR8s only. The overhead of compression/decompression must be weighed against any improvement in space utilization and EXCP(s) used.

9. Handle the orphans.

   a. Random updates can result in orphans that no longer point up a level in the index tree. Added I/O and CPU result from orphan repositioning. Orphans are adopted into the index structure as the index is walked. Make a point to perform regular maintenance to eliminate orphans.

Appendix H contains some sample program excerpts for the explicit purpose of gathering SR8 statistics. Feel free to add these to your programs. In addition, the *CA-IDMS Database Reference Guide* includes an appendix with a complete set of index calculations.

SQL INDEX COVERAGE

Just as you will find in other RDBMSs, CA-IDMS can perform query coverage. If all the columns in a SQL query list and `where` clause exist in an index, only SR8 leaf pages are processed. This avoids actual I/O to the target table and commonly is termed *coverage*.

Another consideration in queries involves the columns used in the `where` clause. For a keyed or sequential index scan to be chosen by the optimizer as the access path, the far left-hand index columns must be part of the `where` clause. An index on columns A, B, and C, for example, is used if the `where` clause contains A, A and B, or A and B and C. If this rule is not satisfied, an index leaf page scan is performed. This is a more intensive a scan than the full- and partial-keyed ones.

Presspack, from Computer Associates Inc., also can be used to achieve a higher level of performance for database records. Given the situation that many of your record occurrences possess common strings of data, the compression from Presspack can result in many more records being stored on a database page. This has serious implications. If now, you are able to get 600 records into a database buffer with a single DML call, as opposed to 40, as before, imagine the reduction in I/Os. This tool should be considered at database design time. Keep in mind that there is a CPU penalty, though. When the overhead of compression exceeds the combined savings of `EXCP(s)` and disk space, it might not be wise to compress a given record.

14.3   CA-IDMS Subschema Tuning

CA-IDMS employs run-unit locking at the record level. This locking is advantageous when concurrency is an issue. If a subschema contains many records that are not required for retrievals or updates, however, additional unnecessary implicit locking may be present. The natural course of action to eliminate unnecessary implicit locking is to customize subschemas for application programs.

There are two approaches to tuning subschemas. The first is to attack the size of subschemas used by the longest-running batch programs, longest-running online programs and most-executed programs. Second is to attack the largest subschemas. Breaking up global subschemas can greatly improve performance. As much as 30 percent CPU savings can be realized, depending on the proliferation of records and sets within subschemas.

The process of determining which records and sets are needed in an application path and then matching these to the ones used in subschemas can be very tedious. I recommend that you start by limiting your endeavor to tuning the top 10 batch and online CPU-intensive applications. If you are successful, you can determine whether to continue with additional programs.

14.4   Using XA Storage

This section presents some CA-IDMS release 12 enhancements that will result in better memory use and paging.

- Release 12.0 has many sysgen and tuning improvements.
- Define an XA reentrant program pool and storage pool to SYSTEM in sysgen.
- Relink your Cobol and Assembler programs with AMODE=31 and RMODE=ANY.
- Change TASK statements in the sysgen to specify LOCATION=ANY.
- Turn off ADSO features that relocate storage to the scratch area.
- Make sure that there is sufficient real storage to back up the XA environment you sysgen. Ideally, all active programs are loaded (BLDL) only at one time. Otherwise, paging and CDMSLIB EXCP(s) deteriorate the system performance. This brings up an interesting point that I often take for granted. When was the last time the libraries in the CDMSLIB and user-defined LOAD-LISTs were ordered to reduce loading time? In the example in Figure 14-1, the TEMP.LOADLIB is used to test new software. However, it may not have been removed after its useful life and now is introducing additional loading costs.
- If you are using VS Cobol II in the CA-IDMS/DC environment, there are some peculiarities. Figure 14-2 shows the best compile and link parameters

```
//CDMSLIB DD DSN=IDMSPROD.CV5..LOADLIB,DISP=SHR      * CV DEPENDENT LIB
//    DD  DSN=IDMSPROD.MBUF.LOADLIB,DISP=SHR         * DB-MEGA LIB
//    DD  DSN=IDMSPROD.TEMP.LOADLIB,DISP=SHR         * TESTING NEW SOFT
//    DD  DSN=IDMSPROD.RHDCCSA.LOADLIB,DISP=SHR      * SCR MGR
//    DD  DSN=IDMSPROD.CV5.LOADLIB,DISP=SHR          * INSTALL LIB
//    DD  DSN=CUST.SUBS,DISP=SHR                     * CUST SUBS LIB
//    DD  DSN=CUST.UTST.LOADDC,DISP=SHR              * CUST STAGE 1
//    DD  DSN=CUST.STST.LOADDC,DISP=SHR              * CUST STAGE 2
//    DD  DSN=CUST.PROD.LOADDC,DISP=SHR              * CUST STAGE 3
```

Figure 14-1   CDMSLIB Tuning and BLDLs

Online Compile:
```
//COBOLII  EXEC PGM=IGYCRCTL,REGION=8M,
//    PARM=('SOURCE,OPT,XREF,DATA(31)')
```

Online Link:
```
//LINKOFF  EXEC PGM=IEWL,REGION=512K,
//PARM='LET,LIST,MAP,XREF,AMODE=31,RMODE=ANY'
```

Figure 14-2   VS Cobol II Compile and Link Parameters

for a CA-IDMS/DC program that is using the VS Cobol II compiler. Note the OPT (optimize) and AMODE=31 (working storage above line) tuning options.

■ XA pools are used to fully exploit 31-bit addressing. Table 14-2 gives you a good idea of the use of pools.

14.5   Using XA Scratch Areas

The scratch area acts as a database-like work area for many tools in CA-IDMS. See Chapter 2, "Mainframe Blocking and Buffering," for an example of putting scratch in VIO to eliminate waiting and reduce single threading. You also have the option of putting the scratch area in memory (preferred).

To allow local mode access to an XA memory scratch area, for example, add the following statements to the SYSIDMS statement in your JCL. It may be necessary to increase the size of subpool 255, depending on the amount of memory needed to hold the scratch area.

XA_SCRATCH=ON   Puts scratch in XA

SQL_INTLSORT=ON/OFF

USERCAT=OFF   Avoids extra catalog calls

TABLE 14-2   CA-IDMS/DC Pool Use

BELOW 16 MEGABYTES	ABOVE 16 MEGABYTES

24 Bit Program Pool
< 16 Megabytes
- nonreentrant programs
  - multiple copies loaded
- quasi-reentrant OS/VS Cobol
  programs
    - one copy of program
    - multiple copies in working
      storage for different users
	31 Bit XA-Program Pool
	> 16 Megabytes
	- multiple concurrent program execution
	- VS Cobol II programs, dialogs and
	  specially written ASM programs
	- variable subschemas (VIBLs)

24 Bit Reentrant Pool
< 16 Megabytes
- Release 10.2 nucleus modules
	31 Bit XA-Reentrant Pool
	> 16 Megabytes
	- reentrant programs, dialogs
	  and subschemas
	  - Release 12.0 nucleus modules

24 Bit Storage Pool < 16 Megabytes - anything remaining which hasn't gone to 31 bit addressing	31 Bit XA-Storage Pool > 16 Megabytes - VS Cobol II working storage and linkage variables
- OS/VS Cobol working storage and linkage variables	- most prolific control blocks and work records

- assorted left over control blocks
  and work records
- file I/O because IBM still does it
  that way
- RHDCUXIT and called exits	

In your DMCL, you specify a new area named DDLOCSCR and assign sufficient buffers for it.

14.6   Journal Tuning

Here is a list of assorted techniques for improving journal and journal-offload performance within CA-IDMS:

■ Turning on Journal Run Unit Quiesce Levels reduces journal I/O during peak hours, writes journal blocks that contain more information and performs fewer journal swaps and offloads.

■ Place journals on high-speed volumes where there is little contention. Journals may be candidates for the 3390 DASD fast-write feature.

■ Turn on the journal-fragmentation feature. This can result in a faster warm start. It is ideal for large journal files.

■ You can improve journal archive performance by adding the following control statements to the SYSIDMS parameters in the archive JCL:

```
IDMSQSAM=ON

QSAMAREA=ARCHIVE.JOURNAL

QSAMBUF#=30
```

Try QSAMBUF# values between 30 and 90. Another setting is the BUFFERS nn clause of the archive-journal utility. However, it will improve only condensed processing. This type of buffering is an alternative to prefetch. Prefetch can have a negative performance impact on queries with subselects. QSAM buffering does one track at a time. If you want to trace what is happening, you can use the BUFFERSTAT parameter on the SYSIDMS statement, or you can add the following parameter to the other QSAM ones listed:

```
QSAMTRACE=ON
```

14.7   Multitasking

I'm going to be blunt about this facility: This is a mixed brew. Some shops experience better throughput, whereas others don't. I think it is a great plus for shops with extra processors. As a rule of thumb, don't use this if your CPU already is depleted. If you're brave and want to cautiously attempt to exploit this facility, however, here are some useful points:

■ As of releases 12 and 14, things have changed drastically. Multitasking is really paying off for shops at release 14. Some see as high as 15 percent improvement.

- Types of processing have been subdivided into families called *MPMODES*. There are six MPMODES: DRIVER, LOADER, USER, DB, DC and ANY. You can have one TCB for each, except ANY, which is unlimited. The main *gotcha* is the number of TCBs you define. As the number increases, the time to process work becomes elongated. ADS, VS COBOL II, OS/VS COBOL, Assembler, and the CA-IDMS system itself will degrade as the number of TCBs goes up. But, in the right environment, overall throughput is increased.

- OS/VS COBOL and Assembler performance degrade if defined with ANY on the program statement in the sysgen. If left to default to USER MPMODE, these will run as before. The degradation is caused by multiple copies of programs being loaded where concurrent execution is occurring.

- Because old OS/VS COBOL routines potentially can prevent you from deriving the full benefit of multitasking, you might want to consider converting your inventory to VS COBOL II. A list of automated code-conversion tools to do the job follows:

  Instant COBOL II, from Software Diversified Services

  CA-Migrate/COBOL, from Computer Associates International

  MHtran-2 and **Translate/RW** (MVS and VSE versions), from Prince Software Products, Inc.

  MAP (Migration Assistance Program), **COBOL to COBOL/COBOL II**, from Computer Task Group

  CCCA and COBOL Report Writer Release 4, from IBM ·

  See Appendix D for vendor information. As a general rule, you can expect a slight CPU increase for converting from OS/VS COBOL to VS Cobol II.

- Multitasking online commands

  The DCMT DISPLAY SUBTASKS command yields a display similar to this:

  ```
  *** DISPLAY SUBTASKS (ALL) REQUEST ***

                       TASK        DISPATCH      WAKEUP

  NAME       NUMBER    STATUS      COUNT         COUNT

  MAINTASK   0001      IDLE        10,000        5,000

  SUBT0001   0002      BUSY        20,001        10,000

  SUBT0002   0002      IDLE        200,000,000   1,100,000
  ```

- The DCMT DISPLAY SUBTASK 2 command yields a display similar to this:

  ```
  *** SUBTASK DISPLAY —TIMES ARE IN .0001 SECONDS ***
                        NAME      SUBT0003

                        NUMBER    0004

                        STATUS    BUSY
  ```

```
            COUNT WAKEUPS          902,000
      COUNT TASK DISPATCHES        1,100,000
         USER MODE CPU TIME        58,000
       SYSTEM MODE CPU TIME        555,00
    COUNT TIMES FAST POSTED        123,000
      COUNT TIMES OS POSTED        00
    COUNT FOUND WORK PASS 1        902,000
    COUNT FOUND WORK PASS 2        00
 COUNT TIMES POSTEXIT RESUMED      888,888
```

- The DCMT DISPLAY MPMODES command yields a display similar to this:

```
*** MULTITASK ENVIRONMENT, MPMODE TABLE ***
```

NAME	REQUEST COUNT	WAIT COUNT
ANY	1,000,000	00
DC	1,000,000	5,000
DB	1,000,000	10,000
USER	20	00
LOADER	5,000	00

- MAX TASKS is one of the most useful tuning tools when using multitasking. You need to reduce the MAX TASKS at first until you determine how to deal with individual bottlenecks associated with increased concurrency. If you don't solve your bottlenecks, there is a good chance you will forfeit the greatest gain you could have derived.

  Concurrency causes new bottlenecks on database areas. If you can isolate which dialogs and programs are causing bottlenecks, you can test solutions. Reducing the task priority for transactions that cause bottlenecks will help some. A better solution is to find ways to improve speed for these transactions. Look at caching for database areas with the greatest contention.

- CPU use by multitasking CV systems can increase by 10 to 40 percent. Depending on processor use, you may have to include database segmentation in your plan to implement multitasking. "Well, I never promised you a rose garden." This increase in CPU use is why there is no potential benefit for using multitasking on an already saturated mainframe.

- APAR CS78328 enables you to determine the amount of CPU that CA-IDMS needs versus the amount it used. The values captured with this patch can be input in the following formula to determine effectiveness. An effectiveness of 50 percent means that half of the time, the system was waiting for the CPU.

```
(SYS-CPU + USER-CPU + OTHER-CPU)   /10000
----------------------------------------   =   ELAPSED * 1.04858
Percentage of Effectiveness
```

14.8 Database Segmentation Versus Distributed Database Processing

Large database users have to weigh the trade-offs of segmenting databases as opposed to using distributed database processing. It is much easier and less costly to implement segmented databases than to adopt a distributed database solution. Distributed tools aren't cheap, although the setup is pretty straight-forward. LU6.2 home-grown applications are complicated and require a great deal of coding, testing and debugging. If you embark on this, document every-thing and create generalized programs you can clone later to expand your sys-tem connections. The typical development time for a custom LU 6.2 program written in Assembler is 25 weeks.

14.9 ESA Batch LSR

Typically, VSAM files are buffered using parameters supplied at cluster-definition time or within the execution JCL. This type of buffering is known as *nonshared resource* (NSR). However, another type of buffer called *local shared resource* (LSR) can far exceed the performance possible with NSR buffering. Even though LSR was designed to allow buffers to be shared by different address spaces (tasks) in the operating system, they prove to be most effective in boosting performance for individual tasks. Here are some other benefits of LSR buffers:

- The batch LSR subsystem enables programs using VSAM NSR buffers to switch to LSR buffers without changing code.

- LSR buffers don't aren't overlaid and are useful with online random processing.

- To implement LSR buffers, you must modify your JCL to include BLSR buffer definitions and the number of buffers defined.

Not every DBMS or RDBMS has a facility to use LSR buffers. You can write a general-purpose LSR routine in Assembler using less than 250 lines of code. You must issue two main macros in Assembler to allocate the buffers for data and index-cluster components.

14.10 *Resource Control Element* (RCE), *Resource Link Element* (RLE) and *Dispatch Priority Element* (DPE) Control-Block Tuning

Some of CA-IDMS's control-block chains fluctuate automatically as needed. Others are an integral part of the sysgen, requiring that administrators define initial and secondary numbers of control blocks to be allocated. Such is the case with RCE, RLE and DPE control blocks. The numbers of these blocks used are related directly to the number of active tasks and retained resources allocated to those active tasks. You want to try to establish reasonable settings in the sysgen. You can do this by assessing their peak usage and allocating enough control blocks to satisfy this usage in primary allocations. Here is a display from Performance Monitor that you can use to ascertain the correct settings:

```
         _Storage Pool Summary
Pools        # Times              Pools
Genned       Sys  SOS             SOS
2            0                    0

             Genned               HWM
RLE          5900                 4102    ☞ should be < genned value
RCE          5300                 3991    ☞      "
DPE          1000                 510     ☞      "
Stack        800                  594     ☞      "
```

You can see the same information by using the DCMT DISPLAY STAT SYS command. The output of the command follows:

```
INTERNAL:   RLEs    RCEs      DPEs    Stack
            4102    3991      510     594 HWM
            5900    5300      1000    800 Sysgen Threshold
```

14.11 Release 12.0 Sysgen Options

Here are the main release 12.0 sysgen options that can impact performance:

- The *deadlock detection interval* specifies the elapsed time before detection is performed. This is supposed to reduce CPU, but I would test it.
- The *journal fragment interval* is the elapsed time before the system writes out a dummy journal record used to speed up warm start.
- The *journal-transaction level* is the number of active run units that must coexist before journal writes are deferred.
- *Nojournal retrieval* turns off BGIN and ENDJ checkpointing for retrieval-only run units.
- The *queue journal before* option limits queue record journaling to before images. This reduces I/O at the expense of roll forward for queue records. Roll back still works fine.
- Resource limits for tasks result in an increase in CPU. I recommend that you do not use these limits unless you have an overwhelming problem controlling online programs.
- *Max tasks* is nothing new. It is a good idea to revisit tuning this number frequently or to set it differently for peak and off-peak hours.

- Set *page release* to off to eliminate the overhead of freeing virtual pages.
- Turn *storage protection* on at the system and off at the program. In release 14.2, I've seen a 40-percent drop in overall CPU use by CV when doing this. You can see the same thing. Strobe pinpoints the CPU overhead in RHDC-STGP (a storage-protect program).
- The *scratch* area is in XA storage, eliminating all I/O.
- Multiple XA storage pools can be defined to contain system, user, shared and database storage.
- This is nothing new, but RETRIEVAL NOLOCK and UPDATE NOLOCK should be specified.
- Programs should be defined as residing in a dictionary and loadlib, which together are referenced in a LOADLIST that reduces CPU use by limiting the search-library list.
- Specify NODYNAMIC on loadlists.

The RUNUNITS for loader, security, signon, msgdict, queue and systest/dest should be monitored with timed displays for 24 hours a day for one month. Take the highest levels of use and increase the preallocated sysgen value by 10 percent. Run units issue a single BIND and FINISH sequence during their lives. If the system activity exceeds the preallocated run units, the system allocates new ones. These new run units issue BIND and FINISH journal sequences unnecessarily. Without the DC Performance Monitor, you can see the number of additional run units (overflows) in the following manner:

DCMT DIS MEM MAP

RHDCOS00 B8228	63A0	GLBLDM53	1D008	DMSDBIO	AAD98	IDMSDBMS
OPT D5380	D1D70	CCE	D20E0	SCAAREA	D3760	RUA
CSA E0340	D5C90	NLT	DEC40	DDT	DFD20	LTT
PTT 116C80	F4370	QDT	111680	TDT	1117C0	PDT
TRCEBUFS 269FC0	269000	TCA	269020	DCEAREA	269040	TCEAREA
MPMODTBL 2A7640	2A6C60	ECBLIST	2A71E0	RCA	2A75E0	RLEAREA
RCEAREA 2E50A0	2BAD5C	DPEAREA	2DDC4C	ILEAREA	2E45C4	SCT
CSVCAREA 39B200	2EAE60	PGMPOOL	2F2000	RENTPOOL	324000	RHDCD04W
RHDCD05V 3A0800	39B800	RHDCD0ZU	39EA00	RHDCD07Q	3A0200	RHDCRUSD
RHDCLGSD 466000	3A1000	PMONCIOD	3A1A00	PMONCROL	3A8000	STGPOOL

```
XALODBUF    7B5000  ABENDSTG  7BD000  HIADDR    7BD320  EREAREA
B7AAB0
ESE         B8F0E0  SVC240    FD21F0  XAPGMPL   EF00000 XARENTPL
F6D0000
XASTGPL     FCAC000
V05  ENTER NEXT TASK CODE:
```

The RUA address is D5380. Next, you will want to display memory at this address:

DCMT DIS MEM D5380 1000

```
<ADDR>    <OFFSET>                    <HEX>                    <CHARACTER>
000D5380  00000000  00070054 00001940 000D5398 0000026C  *..........Q...%*
000D5390  00000010  000D55E4 00000694 02C9C4D4 E2D5E6D2  *...U..M.IDMSNWK*
000D53A0  00000020  E2404040 40404040 40404040 40404040  *S             *
000D53B0  00000030  40800001 001112F8 00000000 000D55E8  *......8.......Y*
000D53C0  00000040  FFFFFFC4 00000328 00000328 00000055  *...D...........*
000D53D0  00000050  00000000 00000000 24C4C4D3 C4C3D9E4  *........DDLDCRU*
```

Use the DSECT reference to chase the RUH control blocks down off the RUA address. Inside each RUA is the RUHALLOC (number of times the run unit has been used), RUHFREES (number of times a commit has been issued for this run unit) and RUHOVEL (run-unit overflows minus additional run-units). These numbers can be used to determine whether sysgenned run-unit options are too large or too small.

With the Performance Monitor, the number of run-unit overflows is easily viewable (see the Total Ovrflw and Current Ovrflw columns in Figure 14-3).

Turn off statistics in sysgen. This is something you don't want to leave on when you aren't actively tuning.

```
IDMS/R PM-R10.2   Cullinet Software, Inc. V05            14:49:49.85
CMD—>                                                    Window : 02
                                                         Refresh: 10
02 System Run Unit Summary                    >
     Rual Sysgen  Total    Total    Current Current
     Type Number  Alloc    Ovrflw   Alloc   Ovrflw   Dbname      Nodename
  _  LOADER  1    4574     32       1       0        CUSTDB01
  _  LOADER  1    1168     5        1       0        CUSTDICT
  _  LOADER  1    10027    200      1       0        ORDRDICT
  _  SIGNON  1    305      3        1       0
  _  MESSAGE 1    3019     19       1       0
  _  LOADER  1    8644     58       1       0
  _  QUEUE   1    827      88       1       0
```

Figure 14-3 Run-Unit Overflows with Performance Monitor

14.12   DDLDCLOD Area Tuning

The CA-IDMS dictionary load area is the location from which *Application Development System Online* (ADSO) modules and *online mapping* (OLM) screens are loaded. It is in your best interest to perform the best possible tuning of the load area. Here is a hint on the way to go about it:

Use Culprit to determine the average module size (LOADHDR-MODLEN-156 in the LOADHDR-156 record PIC S9(8) COMP) of entities in the load area. Use this information to size the pages in the load area to prevent page overflows. Even though ESA buffer pools make it convenient to load modules once per cycle of CV, this initial loading process is faster and reduces CV restart overloading.

14.13   Release 12.0 Journal Tuning

Release 12 introduced a new option for tuning journals. I've already covered a lot of separate issues that impact tuning throughout this book (see Chapter 12, "Mainframe Coding"). New in release 12.0 is the capability to use dataspaces for journaling. This reduces the time for rollback.

14.14   FDR Backups

How many shops use *Fast Dump Restore* (FDR) to take backups? My bet is a lot of them. There are quite a few options within FDR to improve performance. Here is one that helped me. Backups should use the compress option to save on tape storage:

```
DUMP DATASET(INCLUDE(IDMSPROD.DB01*))    -
OUTDDNAME(OUTDD1) -
ALLDATA(*)   -
CANCELERROR -
COMPRESS    -          ☞ compression saves output media space
SHARE
```

14.15   Tuning CA-IDMS Utility Proclib JCL

The procedure library for CA-IDMS generally is tuned in most shops. Here is a reminder to review your proclib jcl for utilities that use sequential files and buffer them. Good examples are the LADERMAN's IDMS dictionary migration and IDMS UNLOAD/RELOAD utilities. SCHEMA, SUBSCHEMA and DCML files (especially print files) with EXCP counts of more than 100 should be buffered. CULPRIT and EZTREIVE retrieval JCL should use DB-Megabuffs to reduce EXCPS. Database restructures should use DB-MEGABUFF's new SEQUENTIAL PREFETCH option. By doing so, you greatly reduce runtime. Figure 14-4 shows typical output statistics for this utility. The output statistics show that I/Os normally would be 722. But, because of prefetch, there was a 91-percent hit rate, eliminating 650 I/Os.

14.16 OLQBATCH JCL

One of the things you can do to speed up OLQ in batch is provide a copy of the scratch area in memory. Figure 14-5 shows the JCL to do this. Any mechanism that improves scratch-area use will provide the same result. Placing the scratch area in a hiperspace or dataspace, for example, would yield desirable results. The key is to get the area into memory where I/O is eliminated.

14.17 Subschema Sizing

Back in the release 10 days of CA-IDMS, subschema tuning yielded huge savings in CPU use. This was because the extra records in subschemas usually equated to extra lock-table synchronization. Under the covers, CA-IDMS was chasing more records. The problem with tuning subschemas is the amount of manpower necessary to make the changes. It can be quite demanding on DBA(s) and programmers.

JES Messages:

```
+DB905246 SEQ PRE-FETCH BUFFERS: MAX STORAGE N/A
+DB905247 SEQ PRE-FETCH BUFFERS: MAX TRACKS
+DB905249 FILE: X12CUST  SEQ BUFFER ALLOCATED
+DB905250 SEQUENTIAL BUFFER POOL NOW:      50K
```

Output Statistics:

```
3 JAN 96 19:25                   DB-MEGABUF SEQUENTIAL PROCESSING
              JOB: DBAJEFF1 DMCL: XCUSDMCL COXATAB: COXSTAB
              I/O STATISTICS AT FILE CLOSE
FILE        BLOCKS     SEQ-BUFFER-ALLOCATION  I/O    IDMS I/O   SEQ I/O HIT%   EXCP
NAME        ALLOCATED  C/T SZ  #  MAX SIZE    TYPE   REQUESTS   EXCPS          SAVE
XCUST01     720        TRK 1   2  98K READ    722    69         91%     650
TOTALS                         98K READ    722    69         91%     650
          DBAJEFF1   STARTUP:  3 JAN 96 19:25   SHUTDOWN:  3 JAN 96 19:26
```

Figure 14-4 DB-Megabuff Sequential Prefetch Statistics

```
//STEP1    EXEC PGM=IDMSINIT
//STEPLIB    DD DSN=PRODIDMS.LOADLIB,DISP=SHR
//SYSLST     DD  SYSOUT=*
//SYSUDUMP   DD  SYSOUT=*
//DSCRDB     DD DSN=&SCRATCH,DISP=(,PASS),UNIT=WORK,
//            SPACE=(4276,(10000))
//SYSIPT     DD *
   PROCESS=AREA,DMCL=SCRDMCL
   AREA=DDLDCSCR
//STEP2    EXEC PGM=OLQBATCH,REGION=6M
//STEPLIB    DD DSN=PRODIDMS.LOADLIB,DISP=SHR
//DSCRDB     DD DSN=&SCRATCH,DISP=(OLD,PASS)
//........rest of OLQBATCH JCL like database for local processing
```

Figure 14-5 Virtual Scratch Area for OLQBATCH

NOTE: Remember the reports gathered in Chapter 1, "Statistics Collection." Locate the 10 highest CPU (by volume) transactions. Now, concentrate your efforts on minimizing the number of records, sets and areas in their subschemas. This can return from 15 to 25 percent CPU, if they were very large to begin with. I personally wouldn't bother with the rest of the subschemas in my shop.

14.18   DC Limits

DC Limits provide a means to limit processing. The associated cost of computing when a limit is reached, however, often doesn't justify the feature. My experience is that these definitions can add overhead to the overall system. If you've lived without them so far, it may be wise to continue in that mode. Limits aren't for everybody. On the other hand, if you are running out of CPU power and currently have limits turned on, you might want to consider turning them off to get a small return.

14.19   CA-IDMS Release 14.0 Performance Enhancements and Tuning

This chapter was given the number of 14 to correlate with CA-IDMS release 14. Whether the release comes too late or just in time for customers weary of waiting for CA-IDMS enhancements, it is a turning point for this DBMS. I was a veteran employee of Cullinane Database Systems, which changed its name to Cullinet Software and was later purchased by Computer Associates. There were many enhancements in the works during the transition. To my memory, the enhancements in release 14.0 were not among them. That means these enhancements are really the product of imagination and engineering at the hands of Computer Associates. I believe this represents a product turning point. You can expect CA-IDMS to continue its tradition of growth and perhaps remain in the ranks of world-class RDBMSs.

This was a landmark performance release. Extended multitasking and support of IBM's Parallel Sysplex technology are big ones. Many of the CA-IDMS tools now support the use of ESA dataspaces and XA database buffers. If you don't do anything else, at least consider switching to release 14 to unload some of the third-party software you purchased to do these things for you.

Some minor adjustments to the cost-based algorithm of the optimizer were made in this release. They enforce new rules for index access that benefit SQL where statistics are not available.

In the sections that follow, I will address CA-IDMS SQL tuning opportunities and briefly discuss the use of IBM Parallel Sysplex. You also can take advantage of the SQL catalog tables as described in Appendix P.

14.20   CA-IDMS SQL Bulk Transfer

One of the benefits of using the CA-IDMS SQL option is the bulk transfer capability. This is a Computer Associates extension to the ANSI-SQL Standard. With a single SELECT, FETCH or INSERT, you can return as many rows as you want. To accomplish this, you must declare a host variable array to hold the rows, open a cursor and issue a SQL command with the BULK clause. See Figure 14-6, where the first 1000 ZIP code rows are returned to the bulk array. Using bulk transfer provides two benefits. First, the resources used are minimized. Second, bulk transfer can reduce the coding required for processing voluminous table rows.

Bulk FETCH returns as many rows as you request in the ROWS parameter. If ROWS is not supplied, FETCH returns as many rows as will fit in the bulk array. If the array is filled by a FETCH request, SQLCODE is set to zero. FETCH positions the cursor on the last row returned. So, subsequent FETCHS get the next batch of rows. Unlike FETCH, SELECT returns the same rows each time the command is issued.

A compiled CA-IDMS SQL program is called an RCM. It is linked with an access module used by the optimizer to select the best access strategy. The optimizer uses the type of statements, selection criteria, and statistics (from the update-statistics utility) in the data dictionary to choose an access strategy.

```
EXEC SQL   BEGIN DECLARE SECTION   END-EXEC.
01 BULK-ARRAY.
    02 BULK-OCCURS OCCURS 1000 TIMES.
        03 ZIP            PIC   X(5).
        03 ZIP-PLUS-4     PIC   X(4).
01 BULK-ARRAY-LEN         PIC   S9(4) VALUE 1000.
EXEC SQL END DECLARE SECTION   END-EXEC.
  .
EXEC SQL
    DECLARE ZIP CURSOR FOR
    SELECT ZIP, ZIP-PLUS-4
    FROM ZIPCODE
END-EXEC.
  .
MOVE INPUT-DIV-CODE TO DIV-CODE.
  .
EXEC SQL
    OPEN ZIP
END-EXEC.
  .
FETCH-PARAGRAPH.
EXEC SQL
    FETCH ZIP
    BULK :BULK-ARRAY ROWS :BULK-ARRAY-LEN
END-EXEC.
    IF SQLCODE=100 AND SQLCNRP=0
MOVE 'Y' TO END-FETCH
DISPLAY 'NO ROWS RETURNED'
    ELSE IF SQLCODE=100 AND SQLCNRP  > 0
MOVE 'Y' TO END-FETCH
DISPLAY 'RETURNED ' SQLCNRP ' ROWS'
    ELSE IF SQLCODE=0
MOVE 'N' TO END-FETCH
DISPLAY 'THERE ARE MORE ROWS TO FETCH'
  .
    ...get more rows...
```

Figure 14-6   CA-IDMS SQL Bulk Transfer

14.21 CA-IDMS SQL Runtime Directives

Runtime directives are specified as parameters in your JCL. Supplied on the SYSIDMS DD statement, they look like this:

```
//SYSIDMS DD *
DMLTRACE=ON
//*
```

Table 14-3 lists the directives that impact your runtime performance.

These parameters offer some tuning opportunities for your CA-IDMS applications. Look-ahead and prefetch are obvious I/O savings areas, whereas tracing can enable you to determine where DML and SQL calls can be tuned.

14.22 CA-IDMS SQL Joins

Table procedures in CA-IDMS SQL are not equivalent to those used in other RDBMSs. A table procedure can enable the programmer or DBA to navigate complex non-SQL network databases or remote databases to acquire information at the time a SQL call is issued. To allow the optimizer a means of determining access paths for JOIN calls using table procedures, CA-IDMS provides some syntax at key-creation time for estimating the I/Os used in the call. In the following example, the estimated row and I/O counts influence decisions by the optimizer:

```
CREATE PRIMARY KEY ITEM_KEY ON INV.ITEM
(INV_NUM, ITEM_NUM)
ESTIMATED ROWS 1
ESTIMATED IOS  5;
```

TABLE 14-3 CA-IDMS Runtime Directives

DIRECTIVE	DESCRIPTION
DMLTRACE=ON/OFF(default)	Traces DML requests of program
IDMSQSAM=ON/OFF(default)	Activates QSAM look-ahead for database
QSAMAREA=area/first used(default)	Identifies area for look-ahead
QSAMBUF#=nnn	Overrides BUFNO= in JCL and specifies the number of QSAM buffers to use
QSAMTRACE=ON/OFF(default)	Traces look-ahead reads
SQLTRACE=ON/OFF(default)	Traces all SQL requests
PREFETCH=ON(default)/OFF	Prefetch is activated when sequential area sweeps are detected
XA-SCRATCH=ON/OFF(default)	Determines whether scratch space will be allocated from XA storage

14.23 CA-IDMS EXPLAIN PLAN

Just like other RDBMSs, CA-IDMS relational enables you to issue an `explain` command that influences the access-path strategy for SQL optimization. The following command requires security to the access module, the SQL statement, and schema ownership or table create/insert privileges on the table the SQL statement employs; additionally, you must have use authority for the `pinv_access` where the results reside:

```
explain access module pinvac01
module pinvup01
into table pinv_access
```

This `explain` plan returns the access strategy for the SQL in RCM `pinvup01` in table `pinv_access`. If no table is supplied, the output defaults to the `access_plan` table.

`Explain` for a `select` statement is different than `explain` for a whole RCM. Here is an example of issuing `explain` for a `select` statement:

```
explain statement
'select p.prod_id, p.prod_cost
from product p, item i
where p.prod_id = i.prod_id'
statement number 1;
```

The access strategy is linked to this particular statement by the `statement number 1` identifier. No location was supplied for the access plan, so it defaults to `plan_table`.

You can build your own command center for performing `explain` plans. A TSO list can be used to run `explain` on all your tables. The output can be piped to a file or database where you can issue `find` commands to locate potential table scans or to locate particular hints in the output.

Other query-tuning opportunities to watch for follow:

- Non-SQL database access that can be controlled by using views
- Avoiding NOT, OR, IN and EXISTS in queries
- Nested operations, especially perserve
- Indexes that should be rebuilt regularly
- Table reorganization
- Separation of tables and indexes into their own areas
- Use of QSAM versus PREFETCH buffers
- Using dataspaces
- Reviewing queries with UNION, GROUP BY, ORDER BY and DISTINCT

- Elimination of SORTS

- Reducing the number of outer JOINS

14.24 CA-IDMS UPDATE STATISTICS

Statistics are used by the optimizer to determine the optimum access strategy to CA-IDMS relational tables. The Update Statistics utility generates new statistics and a new access strategy. The statistics are stored in the DDLDML area and are not viewable. Whenever you modify a SQL database in R12 or a SQL or non-SQL database in R14, remember to issue this command. Here is a sample command:

```
update statistics for table your_schema.your_table
area your_segment.your.area
sample nn
```

where nn = sample percentage of rows used to generate statistics.

At code-generation time, the optimizer creates run trees. Run-tree directives go to IDMSHLDB. The optimizer also creates pseudocode for calculations and data conversions. These particular directives go to IDMSEXP; they are very similar to the old XDEs used in the ADSO command stacks but are considerably faster.

Here are some important facts about the optimizer. In release 12, the update statistics work for SQL databases. They will not work for network databases, though. You can specify the estimated occurrences (EST OCC) clause of the schema record statement and the estimated pages (EST PAG) clause of the schema area statement to force the optimizer to work better. You should use large numbers for the estimated pages and small numbers for the estimated occurrence settings to improve performance. If you suspect that these parameters might help, check for TABLE SCAN, SET SCAN OWNER TO MEMBER and SET SCAN MEMBER TO OWNER access strategy messages by the optimizer. In release 14, the UPDATE STATISTICS command works for both SQL and network databases, at which time you probably will be able to remove these clauses from the schema.

If you want to see what happens while SQL and non-SQL tables are being accessed (for example, table procedures), you can issue the following debugging commands. If you are using table procedures, using the first two commands enables you to view the SQL and associated DML calls together. This can make it easy to analyze what is happening. You should use the DBUGAMC setting only at the request of CA technical support, because it generates a truckload of output.

SQLTRACE=ON	Enables SQL call tracing
DMLTRACE=ON	Enables network call tracing
DEBUGAMC=ON	For tech support use only

14.25   CA-IDMS with IBM's Parallel Sysplex

IBM's Parallel Sysplex technology has put a real twist on multiprocessing. Many shops have multiple *central versions* (CVs) running on a single box. However, each of these CVs has to maintain its own ESA/XA buffer areas that cache *most recently used* (MRU) database pages. If a CV needs to access data in a common database or replicated database on another CV, it must issue costly I/O. Shared cache is an alternative. With shared cache, multiple CVs can access common information without incurring the I/O otherwise required.

How does it work? When database pages (equivalent to blocks, for this description) are retrieved or updated, they update the shared cache. Local CV buffers also are updated. If a page is needed, the DBMS looks in the local buffers and then the shared cache. If the page is not found, a disk retrieval is performed and the cycle restarts.

Shared cache tuning is possible, too. You can create multiple shared caches to load balance the activity. Here are the DMCL definitions for adding two shared caches—one for each of two databases:

```
ALTER DMCL PRODCV05
      FILE BILLING1
            SHARED CACHEB1;
      FILE ORDER1
            SHARED CACHEO1;
```

After the shared cache is implemented, you can use the following DCMT commands to dynamically modify the shared cache for these two database files:

```
DCMT VARY FILE BILLING1 SHARED CACHE NO
DCMT VARY FILE ORDER1 SHARED CACHE CACHEO1
DCMT DIS SHARED CACHE
DCMT DIS STATISTICS FILE ORDER1
```

The first command removes the BILLING1 file from shared cache use. The second command assigns the CACHEO1 area to use with file ORDER1. You can use this method to implement and manage the shared cache areas instead of or with the DMCL compiler. You can use the last two commands to display statistics for the cache areas and files. You can use the buffer hits columns in output displays to determine your hit ratio using the shared cache. You can monitor your adjustments this way or with any of the CA-IDMS Performance Monitors that provide buffer statistics.

Automatic routing of database-retrieval requests to underloaded CVs is another feature of sysplex processing. This is one way to get proper load balancing, and if it means just defining another CV region to extend your load, that is quite significant. Remember that each of these CVs also will be sharing data in caches.

IBM DFSMS OPTIMIZER (DFSMSOPT)

There are two sides to every coin. If CA-IDMS is using IBM Sysplex, it probably is a good idea to optimize Sysplex operations. You can do this in several ways. One way is to tune the Sysplex. Another is to tune file access for the Sysplex. DFSMSopt is an IBM facility that collects and processes statistics from each system in a Sysplex and stores them in a database. The database is used to generate reports about the following:

- Storage hardware
- Subsystem use
- Volumes
- Datasets
- Device skew
- I/O bottlenecks
- I/O-intensive windows of time

The reports are used for capacity planning and system tuning of the *storage management system* (SMS), which governs the use of disk devices and load balancing. The *Hierarchical Storage Manager* (HSM), which is used to archive datasets, also can benefit from the use of database statistics. The HSM Monitor/Tune can automatically tune DFHSM and FDSMShsm through threshold-based triggers and issue NetView alerts and hierarchical storage management.

Because the database files that are read into the shared cache used by CA-IDMS probably are under the control of SMS, it is advantageous to tune the SMS system, too. Use the I/O Bottleneck and Intensive Windows reports to isolate problem areas in database access that could be attributed to SMS performance.

14.26   LPA Library Considerations

Several installation programs for CA-IDMS are eligible for inclusion in the MVS LPA (*link pack area*), which causes the programs to remain resident in memory and reduces the instruction path required to call them. A list of candidates follows:

```
RHDCSCRM

RHDCSCRN

RHDCLINR

RHDCOS00

RHDCCSA

RHDCBANR
```

RHDCUXIT is also a candidate. However, the user exits linked in with it must be reentrant. Most shops have accounting, security, and some home-grown ones linked into this program. So be careful.

14.27   IDMS Server and OpenIngres Enterprise Access

Only a handful of shops can benefit by the following tips. These tips apply to using OpenIngres connectivity to CA-IDMS. You might be contemplating this when the announced replication capabilities of ASG-Replicator (from Allen Systems Group) become commonplace. In any event, here they are:

- Use the DIRECT EXECUTE IMMEDIATE 'EXPLAIN STATEMENT' in CA-OpenIngres Enterprise Access to evaluate calls.
- Tweak the SYSCA.ACCESSIBLE_TABLES list to reduce catalog lookup time.

15

Mainframe Multilevel Caching

15.1 The Cost of Database Calls

When your mainframe application program issues a request for database services, a long sequence of events follows. Consider a CA-IDMS database call. The following events unfold after your application program issues a *Data Manipulation Language* (DML) call:

1. First, your program calls a common database routine. That program must save registers and stack data. It then checks the call parameters passed to it for correctness. Finally, it issues a vector call to the main DBMS routine. This routine also must save registers and stack data.

2. The DBMS looks at the currency tables or uses the CALC algorithm to calculate the DB-KEY. After any other edits pass successfully, the main DBMS routine calls the *database I/O* (DBIO) program. The DB-KEY and the buffer lock are passed to DBIO. This program again must save registers and check for correct parameters.

3. DBIO finds the area/file junction control block for the requested page.

4. DBIO calculates the *relative byte number* (RBN) and gets the FC59 (*file control block*) for the I/O.

5. When DBIO looks at the buffer pool, other third-party vendor XA and ESA buffer pool managers are called in to do their thing. They, too, have to save and restore registers and check setup arguments.

6. If a page is not found in the buffer pool, the Buffer Manager checks the available pool. If a page isn't available, DBIO calls MVS to do the actual I/O read. If the buffer pool is full, a forced write is issued or a wait ECB is

issued. If the page was in the buffer pool, DBIO checks the page locks. If the use is SHR, it uses it. If the use is EXCL, the task must wait.

7. Finally, the physical page is retrieved. Control works its way backward up the long chain of subprograms to the DBMS, where the Locking Manager is called to update the record locks. Journaling gets control as needed for updates and sometimes even for retrievals.

8. Along the return path FREEMAINS, register restores, and return codes are being handled. Finally, the program's working storage is updated with the record.

It is easy to see why the addition of XA and ESA storage-caching routines can greatly reduce the overhead of database calls. However, often overlooked are the second-, third- and fourth-layer caching routines that can be built within your applications to even further reduce the overhead of database instruction paths.

For the sake of this book, first caching routines are considered those provided with the DBMS or extended through the use of XA buffers, ESA buffers and hiperpools by third-party vendors. Second-level caching is considered that accomplished by comparing the last record used with the current record requested. Third-level caching is considered memory tables containing a complete set, partial set, or most-used set of records that are searched before resorting to a database call. Fourth-level caching is when you can intelligently apply the user's business and use trends to the caching that is occurring. Later chapters will look at fourth-level caching. Experience has shown that the instruction path for obtaining a record via second- and third-level caching is 25 percent to 50 percent faster than getting a record out of the XA buffer pools.

This chapter will provide you with the knowledge necessary to use second- and third-level caching, which you can tailor for your needs. If you implement more than one level of caching, it is termed *multilevel* caching. Figure 15-1 shows a view of multilevel caching with four levels.

15.2 Second-Level Caching (Simplest)

In CA-IDMS, there are three ways to accomplish second-level caching. The first is to compare the key of the current record with the key of the last record obtained. Of course, this is valid only for keyed records. If the keys match, the record currently in the program's working storage matches the one being re-

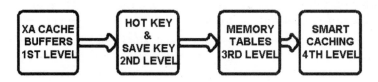

Figure 15-1 Multilevel Caching

quested. No call must be issued. For an example of this, see Section 12.11 on hot keys in Chapter 12, "Mainframe Coding."

The second method is very similar to the hot-key method described in Chapter 6, "Microsoft SQL Server 6.5 Tuning," and can be used with it. The only difference is that the db-key of the last record of each type is kept in a working storage save-key. In CA-IDMS, you do this by defining a save-key with PIC S9(8) COMP in working storage. When the record is obtained the first time, its db-key is moved to the save area db-key. Later, when iterative calls for the same record are made, the record is obtained by using the save db-key. db-key calls are almost twice as fast as symbolic key record calls.

Of course, it stands to reason that if you need the same record more than once, it would be wiser to save the entire record's data than issuing another database call. This is the basis of the third method of accomplishing a second-level cache.

Figures 15-2 and 15-3 show examples of saving the db-key of a record and the entire record.

15.3 Third-Level Caching with Memory Tables

Memory table caching is the next best way to prevent the overhead associated with database calls. Often, your online application will have pageable screens. As each screen is filled with several columns of data, many database calls may be issued to the same records. Generally, there is some piece of data that must be used over and over on output lines. An example is DEPARTMENT. If you were listing employees on a screen, several may have the same DEPARTMENT. However, similar department fields may not be clustered, so a hot-key solution like the one in section 15.2 won't eliminate the database calls. Instead, your application

---

Dictionary element for key save area

```
RECORD ELEMENT IS CUST-SAVE-DB-KEY VERSION 1
PICTURE IS  S9(8)
USAGE IS COMP
ELEMENT LENGTH IS 4
.
```

Saving the db-key

```
MOVE WRK-NUMBER TO CUST-NUMBER.
OBTAIN CUST-REC WITHIN CUST-INDEX USING CUST-NUMBER.
ACCEPT DB-KEY INTO CUST-SAVE-DB-KEY OF CUST-WKREC
        FROM  CUST-REC CURRENCY.
```

Recalling the same record

```
OBTAIN CUST-REC DB-KEY IS CUST-SAVE-DB-KEY OF CUST-WKREC.
```

Figure 15-2 Saving the db-keys of CA-IDMS Records

Saving the entire record for future reference

```
MOVE WRK-NUMBER TO CUST-NUMBER.
OBTAIN CUST-REC WITHIN CUST-INDEX USING CUST-NUMBER.
MOVE CUST-REC TO CUST-SAVE-REC
```

Recalling the save data

```
IF WRK-NUMBER EQ CUST-NUMBER OF CUST-REC
    DO.
              MOVE CUST-SAVE-REC TO CUST-REC.
    END.
```

Figure 15-3   Saving the Entire Database Record

---

needs to save several DEPARTMENT records and be able to look them up quickly. This mandates the use of an array. Many programmers never consider this additional programming effort because it is not in the original estimate for development, and they do not understand the cost these database calls will incur later in production. This kind of development typically occurs later to resolve hot spots for the sake of tuning.

The code provided in Figure 15-4 satisfies the need to look up many records from a table array that are scanned sequentially. A mainline ADSO dialog that is going to display data found in the array while paging must be coded. In addition, three new programs were added to handle the memory array loading of static data, obtaining addressability to the memory array and auditing the array when problems are encountered. Figures 15-4 through 15-7 show the sample programs. It is important to define the memory array as an ADSO global work record to reduce the memory array loading to one time (preloaded one time) and to limit the number of times GET STORAGE requests are issued to obtain addressability to the array. The design shown enables GET STORAGE to occur only once per execution of the mainline routine. You will need to review the code in the examples to get a feel for the processing.

Figure 15-4's source uses a global common cache area that is loaded automatically when the first user attempts to execute the program. Subsequent accesses are satisfied out of the array. Consequently, no EXCPS are needed for all subsequent accesses.

The cost of setting up these routines might seem high, but if you make the programs general enough, you can reuse them on several systems for which performance is an issue. And the code is simple enough to port to any DBMS. This technique would work with IMS, DB2, CICS and so on.

The primary use for a high-speed online caching routine is for applications that perform so many transactions that they effectively are bottlenecked with themselves. The sample application is an airline-ticket system. It is conceivable that this might be a valid use for this coding technique.

```
!****************************************************************
!*  PREMAP NAME:  TICKMAIN-PREMAP (TICKETS ONLINE)
!****************************************************************
IF FIRST-TIME AND GLOBAL1-STATUS NE 'LOAD OK ' ! TABLE NOT FOUND
   DO.
   CALL GETTABLE.                     ! TRY TO GET TABLE
   IF GLOBAL1-STATUS NE 'LOAD OK '   ! TABLE NOT BUILT
      DO.
      LINK TO PROGRAM 'MEMPGM1'.      ! BUILD TABLE
      CALL GETTABLE.                  ! TRY TO GET TABLE
      END.
   IF GLOBAL1-STATUS EQ 'STGNOTOK'   ! GET TABLE FAILED
      DISPLAY MSG TEXT IS 'GETSTG REQUEST FAILED FORM MEMORY1'.
   END.

DEFINE SUBROUTINE GETTABLE.
LINK TO PROGRAM 'MEMPGM2' USING (SUBSCHEMA-CONTROL,
                                 GLOBAL1-RECORD).
GOBACK.
```

Figure 15-4   A Mainline Program Using Memory Table Data

15.4   Third-Level Caching with Sorted Tables

Now take a look at the differences between sequential and sorted table caching. The next example uses a memory table that changes dynamically as the mixture of records changes. Each user gets his own memory table. In this way, each user has his own up-to-date personal cache area that changes as the nature of the work he performs changes. Because there is no sharing of the cache data between users, there is no collision to worry about. Collisions cause data flushing, which mean less-than-perfect cache performance.

15.5   Third-Level Caching with Hashed Tables

This book doesn't present an example for third-level caching with hashed tables, but basically the same mechanisms exist, as for sorted tables. The difference is the method of storing and retrieving the records from the memory table. Because CA enables you to access the standard CA-IDMS CALC routine, you could incorporate it into the memory routine, or you could be inventive and build your own routine. I suggest that you avoid heavy mathematics. The CPU overhead cancels out any savings from using a memory-based table at some point.

15.6   Smart Caching

I've been hyping *smart caching* since the beginning of the book. Now the time has come to explain how to use it in your own applications. The program

```
                IDENTIFICATION DIVISION.
                PROGRAM-ID.    MEMPGM1.
                AUTHOR.        JOHN DOE
                INSTALLATION.  TICKETS ONLINE
                DATE-COMPILED.
                ************************************************************
                * GET STORAGE FOR THE TICK-CODE MEMORY TABLE AND LOAD TABLE*
                ************************************************************
                ENVIRONMENT DIVISION.
                IDMS-CONTROL SECTION.
                PROTOCOL.    MODE IS IDMS-DC  .
                             IDMS-RECORDS MANUAL.
                CONFIGURATION SECTION.
                SOURCE-COMPUTER. IBM-370.
                SPECIAL-NAMES.
                INPUT-OUTPUT SECTION.
                FILE-CONTROL.
                I-O-CONTROL.
                DATA DIVISION.
                FILE SECTION.
                SCHEMA SECTION.
                DB TICKSUB1 WITHIN TICKSCHM VERSION 1.
                ************************************
                WORKING-STORAGE SECTION.
                ************************************
                01  WS-BEGIN                       PIC X(8) VALUE '<WS HERE'.
                01  WS-CNT                          PIC S9(5) COMP-3.
                01  COPY IDMS SUBSCHEMA-RECNAMES.
                01  COPY IDMS SUBSCHEMA-SSNAME.
                01  COPY IDMS SUBSCHEMA-SETNAMES.
                01  COPY IDMS SUBSCHEMA-AREANAMES.
                01  COPY IDMS TICK-RESV-RECORD.
                01  COPY IDMS SUBSCHEMA-CTRL .
                01  WS-END                          PIC X(8) VALUE '<WS END '.
                ************************************
                LINKAGE SECTION.
                ************************************
                01  GLOBAL1-RECORD.
                    05  GLOBAL1-ARRAY
                        OCCURS 10000 TIMES.
                        10  GLOBAL1-TICK-RESV      PIC 9(4).
                    05  GLOBAL1-STATUS             PIC X(8).
                    05  GLOBAL1-END                PIC X.
                01  MEMTBL1-RECORD.
                    05  MEMTBL1-ARRAY
                        OCCURS 10000 TIMES.
                        10  MEMTBL1-TICK-RESV      PIC 9(4).
                    05  MEMTBL1-STATUS             PIC X(8).
                    05  MEMTBL1-END                PIC X.

                ************************************
                PROCEDURE DIVISION.
                ************************************

                ***************
                1000-MAIN-LINE.
                ***************
                    MOVE  'MEMPGM1'   TO PROGRAM-NAME.
                    MOVE  'TICKSUB1'  TO SUBSCHEMA-SSNAME.
```

Figure 15-5   A Program to Load a Memory Table

```
      BIND  RUN-UNIT     FOR SUBSCHEMA-SSNAME.
      BIND               TICK-RESV-RECORD.
      READY TICK-RESV-AREA USAGE-MODE IS RETRIEVAL.
      PERFORM 2000-GETSTG THRU
            2000-EXIT
      OBTAIN FIRST TICK-RESV-RECORD WITHIN TICK-RESV-NDX
      IF MEMTBL1-STATUS NOT EQUAL 'STGNOTOK'
          PERFORM 3000-INIT-N-LOAD THRU 3000-EXIT
                  VARYING WS-CNT FROM +1 BY +1
                  UNTIL WS-CNT EQUAL +10000
          MOVE 'LOAD OK' TO MEMTBL1-STATUS
      FINISH.
      DC RETURN.
      GOBACK.
***********
1000-EXIT.
***********
      EXIT.
***********************
2000-GETSTG.
***********************
      FREE STORAGE STGID 'TICK'.
      GET STORAGE FOR MEMTBL1-RECORD TO MEMTBL1-END
          WAIT
          KEEP
          LONG
          SHARED
          STGID 'TICK'
          VALUE IS LOW-VALUE
      ON ANY-ERROR-STATUS
          MOVE 'STGNOTOK' TO MEMTBL1-STATUS.

      IF ERROR-STATUS = '3201' OR
          ERROR-STATUS = '3202'
          GET STORAGE FOR MEMTBL1-RECORD TO MEMTBL1-END
          NOWAIT
          KEEP
          LONG
          SHARED
          STGID 'TICK'
          VALUE IS LOW-VALUE
      ON ANY-ERROR-STATUS
          MOVE 'STGNOTOK' TO MEMTBL1-STATUS.
      IF DB-STATUS-OK
          MOVE 'STG OK ' TO MEMTBL1-STATUS.
2000-EXIT.
      EXIT.


*****************************
3000-INIT-MENH-DATA.
*****************************
      IF DB-END-OF-SET
          MOVE LOW-VALUES TO TICK-NUMB (WS-CNT).
      ELSE
          MOVE LOW-VALUES TO TICK-NUMB (WS-CNT)
          MOVE TICK-NUMB OF TICK-RESV-RECORD
            TO TICK-NUMB (WS-CNT)
          OBTAIN NEXT TICK-RESV-RECORD WITHIN TICK-RESV-NDX.
3000-EXIT.
      EXIT.
```

Figure 15-5   A Program to Load a Memory Table (Continued)

```
         IDENTIFICATION DIVISION.
         PROGRAM-ID.      MEMPGM2.
         AUTHOR.          JOHN DOE
         INSTALLATION.    TICKETS ONLINE
         DATE-COMPILED.
         ********************************************************
         * GET MEMORY1 STORAGE TABLE AND MOVE IT THE GLOBAL1 RECORD *
         ********************************************************
         ENVIRONMENT DIVISION.
         IDMS-CONTROL SECTION.
         PROTOCOL.      MODE IS IDMS-DC  .
                        IDMS-RECORDS MANUAL.
         CONFIGURATION SECTION.
         SOURCE-COMPUTER. IBM-370.
         SPECIAL-NAMES.
         INPUT-OUTPUT SECTION.
         FILE-CONTROL.
         I-O-CONTROL.
         DATA DIVISION.
         FILE SECTION.
         *************************************
         WORKING-STORAGE SECTION.
         *************************************
         *************************************
         LINKAGE SECTION.
         *************************************
         01   COPY IDMS SUBSCHEMA-CTRL .
         01   MEMTBL1-RECORD.
              05   MEMTBL1-ARRAY
                   OCCURS 10000 TIMES.
                   10  MEMTBL1-TICK-RESV      PIC 9(4).
              05   MEMTBL1-STATUS             PIC X(8).
              05   MEMTBL1-END                PIC X.
         01   GLOBAL1-RECORD.
              05   GLOBAL1-ARRAY
                   OCCURS 10000 TIMES.
                   10  GLOBAL1-TICK-RESV      PIC 9(4).
              05   GLOBAL1-STATUS             PIC X(8).
              05   GLOBAL1-END                PIC X.
         *************************************
         PROCEDURE DIVISION USING SUBSCHEMA-CTRL,
                            GLOBAL1-RECORD.
         *************************************

         ****************
         1000-MAIN-LINE.
         ****************
             GET STORAGE FOR MEMTBL1-RECORD TO MEMTBL1-END
                 WAIT
                 KEEP
                 LONG
                 SHARED
                 STGID 'TICK'
             ON ANY-ERROR-STATUS
                 MOVE 'STGNOTOK' TO MEMTBL1-STATUS.
             IF DB-STATUS-OK
                 MOVE 'STG OK  ' TO MEMTBL1-STATUS.
             MOVE MEMORY1-RECORD
               TO GLOBAL1-RECORD.
             GOBACK.
         ***********
         1000-EXIT.
         ***********
             EXIT.
```

Figure 15-6 A Program to Retrieve a Memory Table

```
IDENTIFICATION DIVISION.
PROGRAM-ID.    MEMPGM3.
AUTHOR.        JOHN DOE
INSTALLATION.  TICKETS ONLINE
DATE-COMPILED.


****************************************************************
* DISPLAY CONTENTS OF MEMORY TABLE ON SCREEN (LINE MODE)    *
****************************************************************
ENVIRONMENT DIVISION.
IDMS-CONTROL SECTION.
PROTOCOL.     MODE IS IDMS-DC  .
              IDMS-RECORDS MANUAL.
CONFIGURATION SECTION.
SOURCE-COMPUTER. IBM-370.
SPECIAL-NAMES.
INPUT-OUTPUT SECTION.
FILE-CONTROL.
I-O-CONTROL.
DATA DIVISION.
FILE SECTION.
**************************************
WORKING-STORAGE SECTION.
**************************************
01  WS-SCRN-DATA                    PIC 9(4).
    WS-SCRN-DATA-END                PIX X.
**************************************
LINKAGE SECTION.
**************************************
01  GLOBAL1-RECORD.
    05   GLOBAL1-ARRAY
         OCCURS 10000 TIMES.
         10  GLOBAL1-TICK-RESV      PIC 9(4).
    05   GLOBAL1-STATUS             PIC X(8).
    05   GLOBAL1-END                PIC X.
01  MEMTBL1-RECORD.
    05   MEMTBL1-ARRAY
         OCCURS 10000 TIMES.
         10  MEMTBL1-TICK-RESV      PIC 9(4).
    05   MEMTBL1-STATUS             PIC X(8).
    05   MEMTBL1-END                PIC X.
**************************************
PROCEDURE DIVISION.
**************************************

****************
1000-MAIN-LINE.
****************
    GET STORAGE FOR MEMTBL1-RECORD TO MEMTBL1-END
        WAIT
        KEEP
        LONG
        SHARED
        STGID 'TICK'
    ON ANY-ERROR-STATUS
        MOVE 'STGNOTOK' TO MEMTBL1-STATUS.
    IF MEMTBL1-STATUS NOT EQUAL 'STGNOTOK'
        PERFORM 2000-WRITE-SCRN THRU 2000-EXIT
            VARYING WS-CNT FROM +1 BY +1
            UNTIL WS-CNT EQUAL +10000 OR
            MEMTBL1-TICK-CODE (WS-CNT) EQUAL SPACES.
    GOBACK.
***********
1000-EXIT.
***********
    EXIT.
****************
2000-WRITE-SCRN.
****************
    MOVE MEMTBL1-TICK-RESV (WS-CNT)
        TO WS-SCRN-DATA.
    WRITE LINE TO TERMINAL WAIT
      FROM WS-SCRN-DATA TO WS-SCRN-DATA-END.
***********
2000-EXIT.
***********
    EXIT.
```

Figure 15-7 A Program to Display a Memory Table Online (Auditing)

examples provided in Figures 15-5 through 15-7 are the basis for the smart-caching example I will describe. These program examples already establish a memory table. They preload the table with commonly used records in sorted order. Believe it or not, very little else remains to be done to implement a smart-caching system. I'll explain.

To look up a record in the current memory table, it is necessary only to issue a COBOL search command. This will perform a binary search on the table, which is very efficient. It is even more efficient if the table in memory is defined in COBOL using the `indexed by` definition as opposed to a standalone `occurs` clause.

If a user requests a record that is not in the current memory table, you would code a request to get the record from disk (I/O is incurred if the record is not in the buffer). To insert this new record into your table, you need to make a slot available. You can do this in two ways. The first method is to start at one end of the table and read entries, shifting them over one as you go. This leaves a blank spot to insert your new record based on its sort key. This method requires very little coding. You only need to check to see whether the current key in the memory table is higher or lower than your new one. The second step is a little harder to envision, but it reaps additional performance savings. You keep a counter in the memory table of the times an entry has been accessed. As you look for the correct place to insert your record, you check the counter. Each entry has a counter. You pick an entry with a very low counter to insert the new entry and eject an old entry. In this way, only the heaviest hit entries gravitate into the table.

At this point, you have a memory table initially loaded with entries from a sorted file. As use progresses, the table gravitates toward a more useful set of entries. Now comes the best part: smart caching. For your application to be smart, it must save the entries kept in the table somewhere. The ideal place is another database. You only need to save the type of record and key of the record currently held in the memory table. Why do this? Well, you want the table to be preloaded with these entries the next time the application starts processing. That way, the performance will be closer to optimum at startup.

What if the records in the memory table vary by time of day, day of week, processing cycle or even by user? That is the beauty of smart caching. You have complete control over how the table initially is loaded. When you save the table entries (at time intervals or by using some other criteria), you can store them away based on the criteria. You might save the keys in the memory table hourly to a database by user ID, for example. Then, when the user runs the application the next time, the memory table routines initially load the memory table based on information for that particular user and the hour of day the processing occurs. You even could refresh the user's memory table hourly based on the entries stored away, or you might prefer to merge the information in the save area with a dynamically changing memory table. There is no predetermined set of rules governing the way you use smart caching. It is only important to remember that your goal is to take repetitive calls out of some business activity that already is occurring.

The flushing, reinitialization, updating and customization of the memory-caching routines provide an extra level of performance not available in conventional *least recently used* (LRU) and *most recently used* (MRU) buffer caching algorithms. For this reason, smart caching will become the next-generation caching facility.

Smart caching is caching tied to the pattern in which a business or user manipulates data. Figure 15-8 gives you some idea of the savings from avoiding extra instructions nested in the many software layers.

I tried smart caching with a large online application. In my tests, each user was given an independent memory table. Each user employ an additional 75KB of memory. Because the number of users on this system was extensive, the system-wide memory use increased from a 15MB high-water mark to 20MB. See the statistics in the PMAM (CA-IDMS Performance Monitor) display screen in Figure 15-9; notice the size of pool number 131.

Comparison of Instruction Paths

Without Smart Caching	With Smart Caching
IDMSDBMS instructions	Smart Driver Instructions
+ IDMSDBIO instructions	+ 1 Link and DBMS Storage Mgmt
+ Buffering Product instructions	+ Less Operating System Overhead
+ Links and DBMS System Overheads	0———5,000———15,000->
+ Operating System Overheads	
0———5,000—15,000—25,000—>	

Figure 15-8 Smart Caching Versus Regular Buffering Products

```
IDMS/R PM-R10.2        Cullinet Software, Inc. V1           10:52:54.7
CMD—>                                                       Window: 0
                                                            Refresh: 1
02    Storage Pool Detail
Pool Total    Storage  High    SOS    SOS   Cushn  Pages    Release  Pages  Pfix
ID   Storage  In_Use   Water   Count  Now   Size   Released Count    Pfixed Count
0    4480KB   1772KB   4092KB                128KB  6877K             3850K
131  27MB     20MB     20MB                  77824  22M               8905K
01 Realtime Monitor Menu

  PFkey  Description                             PFkey  Description
_  PF1   System Run Unit Summary          _  PF2   Scratch Manager Detail
_  PF3   Communication Line Detail        _  PF4   Active User Task Detail
_  PF5   Active System Task Detail        _  PF6   Run Unit Detail
_  PF7   Lterm Resource Usage Summary     _  PF8   Buffer I/O Summary
_  PF9   Storage Pool Detail              _  PF10  Program Pool Detail
_  PF11  Database Overview                _  PF12  Run Unit Overview
_  PF13  Task + Prog Pool Overview        _  PF14  Storage Pool Overview
_  PF15  Database I/O Driver Detail       _  PF16  Journal Detail
```

Figure 15-9 Performance Monitor Storage Pool Detail

Effectively, I traded 5MB of memory for the savings that smart caching could generate. In this example, that savings was 20 million database calls per week. The savings also netted 11-percent CPU—a by-product of reducing database calls. This savings was over and above the savings already realized by using a premiere CA-IDMS XA buffering product.

What this says is that *smart caching is superior to other forms of caching*. It also says that there is a double benefit for adding it to applications that already benefit from vendor-supplied buffering products.

Now imagine the impact of taking the 10 most heavily used online database transactions in your system and implementing smart caching in them. CPU drops like a rock. Elapsed time also drops like a rock. Users phone in to say they love it. Information Services management publicizes new service levels. You get a big fat raise at the end of the year. Yes, you could be the $10 million winner. Well, there are a few quid pro quos. Each increase in memory for caching results in a little higher paging rate. There is a point of diminishing return. So be cautious with this technique and use it sparingly.

15.7   Selecting the Best Caching Routines

I think it's safe to assume that smart caching isn't the best solution for every tuning problem. For some problems, smart caching is too robust, and for others, it might be just a Band-Aid. Several other caching vehicles are available. Some tools can be purchased and easily installed. Others must be built, tested, and maintained. Figure 15-10 shows the relative processing elapsed times of differing techniques. The chart shows entries in order of processing speed. The fastest method is a smart cached memory table, and the slowest is the conventional IDMS batch CV mode. Most of the methods shown for achieving more rapid execution will port to other mainframe database environments. This chart is geared at mainframe-based database systems. The underlying technique, though, is portable to other platforms.

15.8   CA-PMO & CA-Quick Fetch

Computer Associates has two outstanding products that do for *partitioned dataset* (PDS) libraries what other caching software does for databases. You can expect a quick payback on these.

The first is **CA-PMO,** which places PDS directories into virtual storage for both load libraries and nonload libraries. MVS has *library lookaside* (LLA) and *virtual lookaside facility* (VLF) caching mechanisms. But the features and savings in Computer Associate's products extend this savings. For example, PMO automatically refreshes modules that have been updated. This usually is done with a batch job in LLA and requires the whole library to be refreshed. That results in lost potential savings because all module-use counts are reset. Figure 15-11 shows a cost-savings screen. Use this screen to quickly assess whether the product is cost-justified.

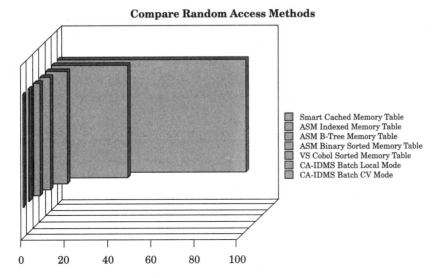

Figure 15-10   CA-IDMS Cached Record Techniques

Second, there is **CA-Quick Fetch**, which eliminates DASD loads by managing the caching of frequently used program load modules. This is the VLF zone in MVS. However, Quick Fetch is self-tuning and handles all your libraries, not just link-list ones, like VLF.

One of the key tuning tasks is to constantly monitor and change the LLA and VLF `parmlib` entries. This isn't necessary with PMO and Quick Fetch, which are self-tuning. You have the option of turning off LLA and VLF when PMO/QF are in place and operational. This results in an additional performance gain.

IBM *Partitioned dataset extended* (PDSE) libraries use indexed directories, and if SMS is functioning, the directory can be loaded into a dataspace. This should enhance performance for PDSE libraries. However, LLA will not work with PDSE libraries, and there are other known deterrents to their common use. You need to evaluate whether you can achieve better performance with PDSE libraries or standard PDS libraries.

15.9   What Is Data in Memory (DIM)?

Data in memory (DIM) is referred to in the following sections. You can think of DIM as just another way of caching. Placing commonly used data for retrieval and update in ESA memory is one way to reduce overhead associated with concurrent or repetitive access of files and records. The following sections evaluate some of the advanced features of ESA you can capitalize on and the ways in which to implement them.

```
PMO. 4.2 (Active)        Sys=IPOX  08AUG94.10.00.00  PMO Active Time = 0.400 days
                         D5 Performance and Cost Savings (Cumulative)
Start: 08AUG94.00.00.00    End: 08AUG94.10.00.00

                       LNKLST         Private      --------------Total------------
                       Cumulative     Cumulative      Cumulative      Per Hour
Library Searches       300,000        1,200,000       1,500,000       1,500.000
Resolved by PMO        200,000          800,000       1,000,000       1,000.000
Pct of Library Searches     66               66              66              66
Elapsed Time Saved       1.00H            2.00H           3.00H           0.30H
CPU Time Saved          10.0M            30.0M           40.0M           4.00M
EXCPs Saved            150,000          750,000         900,000          90,000
Money Saved on:
Elapsed Time       $   100.00     $   200.00      $   300.00      $    30.00
CPU Time           $   100.00     $   200.00      $   300.00      $    30.00
EXCPs              $    50.00     $   100.00      $   150.00      $    15.00

Total              $   350.00     $   500.00      $   750.00      $    75.00
```

Figure 15-11   Performance and Cost-Savings Screen in PMO

Appendix I, "Hiperspace and Dataspace Reference Manuals," contains a list of references that will be helpful if and when you embark on your first data-in-memory endeavor. These materials specifically apply to the use of hiperspaces, dataspaces, data-in-virtual, and hiperbatch. *Virtual I/O* (VIO) is covered in another section of the book. Each of these techniques provides an effective way to reduce EXCPS and elapsed time by placing data in memory. Each technique has its own benefits and issues, which are explored in the following sections. Keep in mind that it may be necessary to know Assembler programming to effectively use some of these features.

15.10   What is Hiperbatch?

High-performance batch (hiperbatch) uses *high-performance spaces* (hiperspaces) to reduce the elapsed time for both QSAM and VSAM file access. An entire dataset is copied into a hiperspace in an initial job step, and then it can be accessed without any I/O operations in all subsequent job steps. A new term to become familiar with is *data lookaside facility* (DLF). Hiperbatch uses DLF objects. DLF system definitions define the specific datasets under the control of hiperbatch and which hiperspace(s) these datasets will occupy. Each dataset gets a DLF object. The first sequential processing for a qualified dataset causes a DLF object to be built comprising one or more hiperspaces. The dataset is loaded into the object. Any subsequent access to the dataset actually uses the hiperspace.

HIPERBATCH SYSTEM REQUIREMENTS
(MVS/SP 3.3 AND ABOVE)

Hiperbatch requires *expanded storage* (ESTOR is backed by real memory) and VSAM NSR buffers. The amount depends on the number and size of DLF objects to be stored. A DLF object is an object that holds files for hiperbatch processing. Datasets stored in DLFs are limited to 6GB for QSAM and 4GB for VSAM. Because the underlying hiperspaces have a 2GB limitation, this means that from 1 to n of such hiperspaces may be required for very large files. There are some consequences. One is that hiperspace storage is not tallied in your job step region use, which means that job accounting won't see it. Using very large amounts of expanded memory can have some serious paging impacts on a mainframe. This technique is best used for small or medium files that are reused heavily in the same batch window. The HBAID utility identifies candidates.

HIPERBATCH DLF DEFINITIONS

Several key steps are involved in the building of hiperspaces and DLF objects for hiperbatch.

Steps for Defining DLFs

1. Decide whether to use retained or temporary DLF objects. Temporary objects flush after the last job finishes using the object. Because there may be interim periods of nonuse, it may be necessary to use a program that opens the dataset and keeps it open for the entire period during which it is supposed to survive. This can be done with an Assembler program and the STIMER macro. An alternative approach is to define retained DLFs.

2. Provide the COFDLFxx parmlib member. The CONEXIT keyword of this member specifies the DLF exit name (required). COFXDLF1 is the recommended name.

3. Provide the MAXEXPB keyword, which defines the maximum expanded storage hiperbatch can use.

4. Provide the PCTRETB keyword, which defines the percentage of expanded storage defined with the MAXEXPB, keyword which can be retained for passing DLFs between job steps.

5. Modify the system command to point at the COFDLFxx parmlib member.

Hiperbatch Access Considerations   To delete a DLF that has been retained, supply a DISP=(NEW,KEEP,DELETE) or DISP=(OLD,DELETE) in your JCL. This removes the DLF when an abort occurs or when processing using the DLF is done, respectively.

When the dataset and DLF definitions are complete, you are ready to run a job that reads the entire dataset. This automatically loads it to the hiperspace. Subsequent jobs read and write to the hiperspace. You will not see I/O stats for their file access.

It is possible to modify the list of allowable datasets defined with DLF. There are consequences to making these kinds of changes while any of the previously defined datasets are in use.

Consequences of Modifying DLF While Datasets Are in Use

■ Modifying the definitions pertaining to an in-use DLF dataset can result in back-level data being used by jobs.

■ Removing the definition pertaining to an in-use DLF dataset can result in one job using the DASD-based dataset and another using a hiperspace dataset. Changes to the DASD dataset will not be reflected in requests targeted at the hiperspace dataset.

■ Another consideration to keep in mind is that IEBGENER and DFSORT are not supported. Consequently, you need to use some other utility to initially load the files into storage.

You can use a utility called HBAID (*Hiperbatch Aid*) on MKTTOOLS to identify candidate datasets you have; these are datasets with concurrent access.

DLF Commands   DLF offers some operator facilities to aid you in using hiperbatch (see Figure 15-12). Only the operator commands are summarized here. You will want to read the manuals and prepare conscientious procedures for your implementation.

15.11 What are Hiperspaces?

High-performance spaces (hiperspaces) are one means of implementing *data in memory* (DIM). Data moved to hiperspaces is addressable one block at a time (a 4-KB page). The pages reside in *expanded memory* (ESTOR) or *auxiliary memory* (AUX) for scroll-type spaces and in ESTOR alone for cache-type spaces. Each hiperspace can occupy up to 2GB.

Command	Purpose
DISPLAY DLF	Lists current DLFs, hiperspaces and data sets.
MODIFY DLF	When used with the STATUS subcommand, the effectiveness of MAXEXPB and PCTRETB keywords can be seen.
START DLF	Fires up DLF. This can be accomplished by adding the startup command to the COMMNDxx parmlib member.
STOP DLF	Shuts down DLF after all activity is quiesced.
MODIFY DLF,MODE=QUIESCE	Quiesces activity.
MODIFY DLF,MODE=NORMAL	Restarts activity after a quiesce.
MODIFY DLF,MODE=DRAIN	Stops activity.
COFDMON	Invoke DLF monitor which shows performance statistics.

Figure 15-12 DLF Operator Facility Commands

You get to choose what type of retention you want for pages allocated to hiperspaces. Selecting CASTOUT=YES results in the hiperspace pages being flushed when inactive. Conversely, CASTOUT=NO keeps pages indefinitely, with the only exception being when storage is reconfigured. Retaining pages indefinitely has the marked advantage of better performance.

Hiperspace memory is not shown on your job-accounting statistics. Therefore, you have to find some way of charging back its use. Also, it is important to note that even though hiperspaces use expanded memory, they can be paged out to a page pack if not enough expanded memory is available.

Because hiperspaces act on data at a page level, this facility lends itself to performance solutions for sequential file processing.

15.12 What Are Dataspaces?

Dataspaces, like hiperspaces, have a 2-GB size limit and are not reflected in your job-accounting statistics. However, they have the advantage of being byte-addressable and can occupy CSTOR (real memory), as well as *expanded memory* (ESTOR) and *auxiliary memory* (AUX). Dataspace use is becoming very popular. It can be found in many vendor-supplied products, such as Batch Pipes (from IBM). Dataspaces are also integrated into many of the subsystem components of the MVS operating system.

Byte addressability means that individual records can be moved to and from dataspaces, making it the method of choice for direct table access. You need to write your programs in Assembler, and more important, provide a hashing routine. The easiest of these probably would be a binary search routine. That, of course, implies that you load the dataspace in sorted record order. A dataspace accessible by only one user is known as SCOPE=SINGLE (private dataspace). A shared dataspace is termed SCOPE=ALL or SCOPE=COMMON, which makes data available to several address spaces concurrently. The latter can be created only with a supervisor state or PSW key 0 through 7.

ESA dataspaces, like XA buffers, require real memory to support the direct addressability of data. In the event of a shortage of real memory, the system can page out portions of your dataspace. This can influence your performance. When the paging rates exceed 20 to 25 pages per second, this can be an indicator of excessive paging. You may need to have more expanded storage to support ESA hiperspaces and dataspaces.

You should be at MVS/ESA 3.1 or higher to use dataspaces, and if you are using data in virtual, the ICF catalog facility is a must.

DATASPACE ACCESS LISTS (ALS)

The *access list* consists of a table of definitions that provides security. Each dataspace is assigned a *space token* (STOKEN). The STOKEN is tied to an *access list entry* (ALE). Two types of access lists exist. The first access list is called *Dispatchable Unit* (DU-AL). If you wrote your own problem-program to perform dataspace updates and retrieval, it could access only entries that it built.

However, if a program in supervisor state has built some other dataspaces and has given your program an *access list entry token* (ALET) for those dataspaces, your program now can share them. A program running in supervisor state (or PSW key 0-7) is the way to make dataspaces available to multiple jobs or programs in different address spaces.

The ALET value stored in the access list is loaded into the *access register* (AR) to get addressability to a dataspace.

ACCESS REGISTERS (ARS) AND NEW INSTRUCTIONS

Access Register (AR) mode enables a program to access up to 16 (2GB) dataspaces concurrently. When executing in this mode, your program supplies a *general-purpose register* (GPR) and *access register* (AR) to locate the data within a dataspace. The speed of processing instructions is very fast because *dynamic address translation* (DAT) is used to execute them, and DAT is performed by the hardware.

A program can run in Primary or AR mode. In Primary mode, the program can access data in its own address space. In AR mode, it can access a dataspace. The following instructions are used to switch modes:

```
SAC     512     AR Mode
SAC     0       Primary Mode
```

Several other new instructions exist for dealing with ARs. The following sections present a list of instructions and some examples of their use.

DATASPACE INSTRUCTIONS

LAM	2,2,DSP2ALET	Loads multiple ARs from storage
DSP2ALET	DS CL8	Dataspace ALET
STAM	2,2,DSP2ALET	Loads storage location from multiple ARs
CPY	6,7	Copies contents of AR 7 to AR 6
LAE	12,0	Loads ALET and address into AR/GPR
EAR	9,9	Copies contents of AR 9 to GPR 9
SAR	9,9	Copies contents of GPR 9 to AR 9

EXAMPLE: CREATING A DATASPACE

```
DSPSERV         CREATE,              x
                NAME=dspname,        x
                STOKEN=dsptoken,     x
                BLOCKS=dspblks,      x
                ORIGIN=dsporig
```

EXAMPLE: DELETING A DATASPACE

```
DSPSERV        DELETE,              x
               STOKEN=dsptoken
```

EXAMPLE: ADDING DATASPACE TO ACCESS LIST

```
ALESERV        ADD,                 x
               STOKEN=dsptoken,     x
               ALET=dspalet
```

EXAMPLE: REMOVING DATASPACE FROM ACCESS LIST

```
ALESERV        DELETE,              x
               ALET=dspalet
```

EXAMPLE: EXTENDING THE SIZE OF A DATASPACE

```
DSPSERV        EXTEND,              x
               STOKEN=dsptoken,     x
               BLOCKS=dspmore
```

EXAMPLE: RELEASING SPACE IN A DATASPACE

```
DSPSERV        RELEASE,             x
               STOKEN=dsptoken
```

EXAMPLE: VIEWING DATASPACE STORAGE

```
SNAPX          DSPSTOR
```

An example of a dataspace program to build a sorted record table in memory is supplied.

A SAMPLE DATASPACE LOAD PROGRAM

Figure 15-13 provides some code you can use to load a dataspace. You must supply your own input file, record size, and block size. You will need to create your own program to read the dataspace. It is advised that the input file be sorted

on a key field so that you can use a binary-keyed search routine to look up data
in the dataspace.

```
                PRINT   NOGEN
   *            SAMPLE LOAD PROGRAM
   ENTRY        LOAD
   LOAD         DS      0D
                USING LOAD,12
                LR      12,15
                LR      15,13
                LA      13,SAVREGS
                ST      15,4(,13)
                ST      13,8(,15)
                B       *+76
   R0           EQU     0
   R1           EQU     1
   R2           EQU     2
   R3           EQU     3
   R4           EQU     4
   R5           EQU     5
   R6           EQU     6
   R7           EQU     7
   R8           EQU     8
   R9           EQU     9
   R10          EQU     10
   R11          EQU     11
   R12          EQU     12
   R13          EQU     13
   R14          EQU     14
   R15          EQU     15
                LA      R11,4095(,R12)              BASE
                LA      R11,1(,R11)
                USING   LOAD+4096,R11               BASE+1
                B       ALOC1
                DC      C'DATASPACE LOAD'           IDENTIFICATION
   ALOC1        DS      0H
                SAC     512
                SYSSTATE ASCENV=AR
                LAE     R12,0                       SET BASE REG AR
                BASR    R12,0                       SET BASE REG GPR
                USING   *,R12
                DS      0H
                SAC     0
                SYSTATE ASCENV=P
                OPEN    (LOADIN,INPUT),MODE=31      OPEN INP FILE
                MODESET KEY=ZERO
                LA      R1,ECB1
                SYSEVENT TRANSWAP                   GOING NON-SWAPPABLE
                LTR     R15,R15
                BE      ALOC2
                LR      R10,R15
                MODESET KEY=NZERO
                WTO 'LOAD FAILED - UNABLE TO GO NON-SWAPPABLE',ROUTCDE=11
```

Figure 15-13 A Sample Dataspace Load Program Source

```
                ABEND 100,DUMP
ALOC2           WAIT    ECB=ECB1                                NONSWAPPABLE
                SAC     512
                SYSTATE ASCENV=AR
                DSPSERV CREATE,NAME=MYSPACE,STOKEN=MYTOKEN,                  X
                BLOCKS=20,ORIGIN=MYORIGIN,                                   X
                SCOPE=COMMON,TYPE=BASIC
                LTR     R15,R15                                 ALLOCATE WORKED?
                BE      ALOC3                                   YES
                MODESET KEY=NZERO
                WTO 'LOAD FAILED - UNABLE TO ALLOC DATASPACE',ROUTCDE=11
                ABEND 200,DUMP
ALOC3           L       R8,MYORIGIN                             BEGIN OF DATASPACE
                ALESERV ADD,STOKEN=MYTOKEN,ALET=MYALET,AL=PASN
                LTR     R15,R15                                 ADD ALET WORKED?
                BE      LOAD1
                MODESET KEY=NZERO
                WTO 'ADD ALET FAILED',ROUTCDE=11
                ABEND 300,DUMP
LOAD1           SAC     0
                SYSSTATE ASCENV=P
                MODESET KEY=NZERO
                L       R15,READ1
                BASSM R5,R15
                L       R5,=F'512'                              LRECL LENGTH
                L       R7,R5
                LA      R4,WORK1
                MVCL    R4,R6                                   XFER DATA TO WORK
FIELD
                SAC     512
                SYSSTATE ASCENV=AR
                MODESET KEY=ZERO
                L       R9,R5                                   LEN IN R9
                MVCL    R8,R4                                   WORK REC TO DATASPACE
                B       LOAD1
READ1           DC      A(X'00000000'+READ2)                   24BIT MODE
READ2           GET     LOADIN
                LR      R7,R1
                BSM     0,R5
CLOSE           MODESET KEY=NZERO
                L       R15,=A(X'80000000'+CLOSE1)
                BSM     0,R15
CLOSE1          CLOSE   (LOADIN),MODE=31
                L       R13,4(,R13)
                L       R14,12(,R13)
                LM      R0,R12,20(R13)
                BR      R14                                     FINISHED
SAVEREGS        DS      16F
WORK1           DS      CL512
LOADIN          DCB     DDNAME=LOADIN,DSORG=PS,MACRF=GL,EODAD=CLOSE
                LTORG
                END
```

Figure 15-13 A Sample Dataspace Load Program Source (Continued)

15.13   What is MVS *Data in Virtual* (DIV)?

Data in virtual (DIV) is a facility that makes it possible to access and update random blocks (pages) of memory in a hiperspace. DIV comes with several services to program its use.

DIV BASIC SERVICE COMMANDS

ACCESS	MAP	UNMAP
IDENTIFY	SAVE	UNACCESS
MAP	RESET	UNIDENTIFY

Again, you must write your programs in Assembler. And, because you are working with a hiperspace, the rules of hiperspaces apply. Typically, this facility supports working with a range of pages in a file that has been loaded into a hiperspace.

16

PC and Client/Server Caching

16.1 Caching Methods

There are three distinct worlds to deal with on the PC: DOS, Windows, and UNIX. DOS affords many tuning opportunities, which were covered in Chapter 3, "PC Files and Buffers." Windows prior to the NT version was rather limited for tuning. Other than some memory settings, background clicks, and the size of a swap file, you didn't have much control. Several ways to tune UNIX are covered throughout the book. Also covered in prior chapters was SMARTDRV. However, it is about to be revisited for comparison with other PC-caching techniques.

To exemplify some of the forms of caching available to you on the PC, two CA-Clipper programs have been created. These programs compare six discrete random-access methods.

PC CACHING METHODS TESTED

1. SMARTDRV

2. RAMDISK

3. Sequential memory table

4. Nested If-Else logic array

5. Binary-searched memory table

6. Standard database access

The benchmark wasn't completely fair. It should be clear in your mind that sequential memory tables and If-Else logic arrays are really effective only for small numbers of records. For this test, five entries were used. They scream, "But what do you do with large databases?" The binary-searched memory table turned out to be the fastest method for large tables; it provided tight control over memory use and avoided interference from other files being accessed concurrently. The next-best fit for really large databases is SMARTDRV. You should try to use the maximum number of buffers. You are limited only by your available memory. See the results for yourself in Table 16-1.

The programs used to perform the tests are provided here so that you can scrutinize the coding and perhaps apply the techniques in your own database system design.

 NOTE: Figure 16-1 contains the source to run tests 1, 2, 3, 4 and 6. Figure 16-2 contains the test 5 source.

TABLE 16-1   **Random-Access Testing**

SEARCH METHOD	RUN TIME
Standard Database Search	7 minutes 27 seconds (50,000 requests) (no buffers)
RAMDISK Method	1 minute 46 seconds (50,000 requests) (4000 record database)
Binary Memory Table Search	1 minute 31 seconds (50,000 requests) (4000 record table)
SMARTDRV Method	49 seconds (50,000 requests) (4000 record database)
Sequential Memory Array Search	30 seconds (50,000 requests) (5 entry table)
IF-ELSE Logic Array Search	18 seconds (50,000 requests) (5 entry logic array)

```
CLEAR SCREEN
SET CONSOLE OFF
SET PRINTER ON
SET PRINT TO TUNECLIP

? 'TEST1 - GET 5 RANDOM RECORDS 10000 TIMES with SMARTDRV'
USE D:\ZIPSCUT1\ZIPTABLE INDEX D:\ZIPSCUT1\ZIPNDX2
PUBLIC ZIPTBL[5]
PUBLIC ZIP_1, ZIP_2, ZIP_3, ZIP_4, ZIP_5
STORE 00000 TO CNT
? 'TEST1 - START TIME: '+TIME()
DO WHILE CNT < 10000
    STORE '11111' TO ZIP_ABBREV
    SEEK ZIP_ABBREV
    STORE '33333' TO ZIP_ABBREV
    SEEK ZIP_ABBREV
    STORE '22222' TO ZIP_ABBREV
    SEEK ZIP_ABBREV
    STORE '44444' TO ZIP_ABBREV
    SEEK ZIP_ABBREV
    STORE '55555' TO ZIP_ABBREV
    SEEK ZIP_ABBREV
    CNT = CNT + 1
ENDDO
? 'TEST1 -   END TIME: '+TIME()
!! F: DRIVE IS A RAMDISK TO DOS
? 'TEST2 - GET 5 RANDOM RECORDS 10000 TIMES WITH RAMDISK'
STORE 00000 TO CNT
USE F:\ZIPTABLE INDEX F:\ZIPNDX2
SEEK ZIP_ABBREV
? 'TEST2 - START TIME: '+TIME()
DO WHILE CNT < 10000
    STORE '11111' TO ZIP_ABBREV
    SEEK ZIP_ABBREV
    STORE '33333' TO ZIP_ABBREV
    SEEK ZIP_ABBREV
    STORE '22222' TO ZIP_ABBREV
    SEEK ZIP_ABBREV
    STORE '44444' TO ZIP_ABBREV
    SEEK ZIP_ABBREV
    STORE '55555' TO ZIP_ABBREV
    SEEK ZIP_ABBREV
    CNT = CNT + 1
ENDDO
? 'TEST2 -   END TIME: '+TIME()
? 'TEST3 - GET 5 RECORDS 10000 TIMES FROM MEMORY TABLE ARRAY'
STORE 00000 TO CNT
STORE '0000' TO ZIPNUM
STORE '11111' TO ZIPTBL[1]
STORE '33333' TO ZIPTBL[2]
STORE '22222' TO ZIPTBL[3]
STORE '44444' TO ZIPTBL[4]
STORE '55555' TO ZIPTBL[5]
? 'TEST3 - START TIME: '+TIME()
DO WHILE CNT < 10000
    STORE 1 TO CNT2
    DO WHILE CNT2 < 5
IF    ZIPTBL[CNT2] = '11111'
        STORE '1111' TO ZIPNUM
      ELSEIF ZIPTBL[CNT2] = '33333'
```

Figure 16-1 Statistics Program for Tests 1 through 4 and 6

```
                    STORE '2222' TO ZIPNUM
                ELSEIF ZIPTBL[CNT2] = '22222'
                    STORE '3333' TO ZIPNUM
                ELSEIF ZIPTBL[CNT2] = '44444'
                    STORE '4444' TO ZIPNUM
                ELSEIF ZIPTBL[CNT2] = '55555'
                    STORE '5555' TO ZIPNUM
                ENDIF
                CNT2 = CNT2 + 1
          ENDDO
          CNT = CNT + 1
     ENDDO
     ? 'TEST3 -    END TIME: '+TIME()
     ? 'TEST4 - GET 5 RANDOM RECORDS 10000 TIMES FROM IF/ELSE LOGIC'
     ? 'TEST4 - START TIME: '+TIME()
     STORE '11111' TO ZIP_1
     STORE '33333' TO ZIP_2
     STORE '22222' TO ZIP_3
     STORE '44444' TO ZIP_4
     STORE '55555' TO ZIP_5
     STORE '0000'    TO ZIPNUM
     STORE 00000 TO CNT
     DO WHILE CNT < 10000
         IF ZIP_1 <> '11111'
             IF ZIP_1 <> '33333'
                 IF ZIP_1 <> '22222'
                     IF ZIP_1 <> '44444'
                         IF ZIP_1 <> '55555'
                             STORE '5555' to ZIPNUM
                         ENDIF
                     ELSE
                     STORE '4444' TO ZIPNUM
                     ENDIF
                 ELSE
                 STORE '3333' TO ZIPNUM
                 ENDIF
             ELSE
             STORE '2222' TO ZIPNUM
             ENDIF
         ELSE
         STORE '1111' TO ZIPNUM
         ENDIF
         IF ZIP_2 <> '11111'
             IF ZIP_2 <> '33333'
                 IF ZIP_2 <> '22222'
                     IF ZIP_2 <> '44444'
                         IF ZIP_2 <> '55555'
                             STORE '5555' to ZIPNUM
                         ENDIF
                     ELSE
                     STORE '4444' TO ZIPNUM
                     ENDIF
                 ELSE
                 STORE '3333' TO ZIPNUM
ENDIF
             ELSE
             STORE '2222' TO ZIPNUM
             ENDIF
         ELSE
         STORE '1111' TO ZIPNUM
         ENDIF
```

Figure 16-1 Statistics Program for Tests 1 through 4 and 6 (Continued)

```
  IF ZIP_3 <> '11111'
     IF ZIP_3 <> '33333'
        IF ZIP_3 <> '22222'
           IF ZIP_3 <> '44444'
              IF ZIP_3 <> '55555'
                    STORE '5555' to ZIPNUM
              ENDIF
           ELSE
           STORE '4444' TO ZIPNUM
              ENDIF
        ELSE
        STORE '3333' TO ZIPNUM
           ENDIF
     ELSE
     STORE '2222' TO ZIPNUM
        ENDIF
  ELSE
  STORE '1111' TO ZIPNUM
  ENDIF
  IF ZIP_4 <> '11111'
     IF ZIP_4 <> '33333'
        IF ZIP_4 <> '22222'
           IF ZIP_4 <> '44444'
              IF ZIP_4 <> '55555'
                    STORE '5555' to ZIPNUM
              ENDIF
           ELSE
           STORE '4444' TO ZIPNUM
              ENDIF
        ELSE
        STORE '3333' TO ZIPNUM
           ENDIF
     ELSE
     STORE '2222' TO ZIPNUM
        ENDIF
  ELSE
  STORE '1111' TO ZIPNUM
  ENDIF
  IF ZIP_5 <> '11111'
     IF ZIP_5 <> '33333'
        IF ZIP_5 <> '22222'
           IF ZIP_5 <> '44444'
              IF ZIP_5 <> '55555'
                    STORE '5555' to ZIPNUM
                 ENDIF
              ELSE
              STORE '4444' TO ZIPNUM
              ENDIF
           ELSE
           STORE '3333' TO ZIPNUM
              ENDIF
        ELSE
        STORE '2222' TO ZIPNUM
ENDIF
  ELSE
  STORE '1111' TO ZIPNUM
  ENDIF
  CNT = CNT + 1
ENDDO
? 'TEST4 -    END TIME: '+TIME()
RETURN
```

Figure 16-1 Statistics Program for Tests 1 through 4 and 6 (Continued)

```
**********************************
* PROGRAM: TUNECLI2
* WILL LOAD A SORTED DATABASE FILE TO
* A SORTED MEMORY TABLE AND PERFORM
* 50,000 BINARY SEARCHES FOR STATS
**********************************
***
*** SET UP ENVIRONMENT
***
SET CONSOLE OFF
SET PRINTER ON
SET PRINT TO TUNECLI2
STORE .T. TO PRINT_FLAG
SET BELL OFF
SET SCOREBOARD OFF
SET DECIMALS TO 0
SET TYPEAHEAD TO 100
SET COLOR TO W+/B, GR+/RB, B
***
*** BUILD MEMORY TABLE
***
CLEAR SCREEN
? 'TEST1 - LOAD 4000 DB ENTRIES INTO SORTED MEMORY ARRAY'
USE D:\ZIPSCUT1\ZIPTABLE INDEX D:\ZIPSCUT1\ZIPNDX2
GOTO TOP
STORE 0001 TO SLICE_HIGH
PUBLIC ZIPSMRT[5]
STORE SPACE(6)  TO ZIPSMRT[1]
STORE SPACE(6)  TO ZIPSMRT[2]
STORE SPACE(6)  TO ZIPSMRT[3]
STORE SPACE(6)  TO ZIPSMRT[4]
STORE SPACE(6)  TO ZIPSMRT[5]
PUBLIC ZIPTBL[5000]
DO WHILE .NOT. EOF() .AND. SLICE_HIGH < 3999
   STORE ZIPABBREV TO ZIPTBL[SLICE_HIGH]
   SKIP +1
   @ 5,10 SAY ZIPTBL[SLICE_HIGH]+STR(SLICE_HIGH)
   SLICE_HIGH = SLICE_HIGH + 1
ENDDO
***
*** SET TEST VALUES
***
***
*** PERFORM TEST
***
SLICE_SAVE = SLICE_HIGH
SLICE_LOW  = 0000
SLICE_FILE = 0000
CNT        = 00001
11111_CNT = 1
33333_CNT = 1
22222_CNT = 1
44444_CNT = 1
44444_CNT = 1
? 'TEST1 - FIND 5 RECORDS 10000 TIMES USING BINARY MEMORY SEARCH'
? 'TEST1 - STARTED '+TIME()
DO WHILE CNT < 10000
   STORE .F. TO BINSRCHED
```

Figure 16-2 Statistics Program for Test 5

```
          STORE 11111_CNT TO CNT3
          STORE '11111' TO ZIP_SEARCH
          STORE CNT3 TO 11111_CNT
          DO BINSRCH
          STORE .F. TO BINSRCHED
          STORE 33333_CNT TO CNT3
          STORE '33333' TO ZIP_SEARCH
          STORE CNT3 TO 33333_CNT
          DO BINSRCH
          STORE .F. TO BINSRCHED
          STORE 22222_CNT TO CNT3
          STORE '22222' TO ZIP_SEARCH
          STORE CNT3 TO 22222_CNT
          DO BINSRCH
          STORE .F. TO BINSRCHED
          STORE 44444_CNT TO CNT3
          STORE '44444' TO ZIP_SEARCH
          STORE CNT3 TO 44444_CNT
          DO BINSRCH
          STORE .F. TO BINSRCHED
          STORE 44444_CNT TO CNT3
          STORE '55555' TO ZIP_SEARCH
          STORE CNT3 TO 44444_CNT
          DO BINSRCH
          CNT = CNT + 1
ENDDO
? 'TEST1 - ENDED '+TIME()
RETURN


PROCEDURE BINSRCH
DO PULL
IF BINSRCHED
   RETURN
ENDIF
DO WHILE .NOT. BINSRCHED
   SLICE_FILE = ((SLICE_HIGH - SLICE_LOW) / 2) + SLICE_LOW
   IF SLICE_FILE <= 1 .OR. SLICE_FILE >= SLICE_SAVE
      STORE .T. TO BINSRCHED
      LOOP
   ENDIF
   IF ZIPTBL[SLICE_FILE] > ZIP_SEARCH
      SLICE_HIGH = SLICE_FILE
   ELSEIF ZIPTBL[SLICE_FILE] = ZIP_SEARCH
      STORE .T. TO BINSRCHED
      DO PUSH
   ELSE
      SLICE_LOW  = SLICE_FILE
   ENDIF
ENDDO
SLICE_HIGH = SLICE_SAVE
SLICE_LOW  = 0000
SLICE_FILE = 0000
RETURN

PROCEDURE PUSH
STORE ZIPSMRT[4] TO ZIPSMRT[5]
STORE ZIPSMRT[3] TO ZIPSMRT[4]
STORE ZIPSMRT[2] TO ZIPSMRT[3]
```

Figure 16-2 Statistics Program for Test 5 (Continued)

```
STORE ZIPSMRT[1] TO ZIPSMRT[2]
STORE ZIPTBL[SLICE_FILE] TO ZIPSMRT[1]
RETURN

PROCEDURE PULL
IF ZIP_SEARCH = ZIPSMRT[CNT3]
      STORE .T. TO BINSRCHED
      RETURN
ENDIF
STORE 1 TO CNT3
DO WHILE CNT3 < 6
   IF ZIP_SEARCH = ZIPSMRT[CNT3]
      STORE .T. TO BINSRCHED
      RETURN
   ENDIF
   CNT3 = CNT3 + 1
ENDDO
RETURN
```

Figure 16-2 Statistics Program for Test 5 (Continued)

17

Communications and Networking

Not everyone reading this section is going to come into this with a knowledge of communications. It is a trade with as much technical jargon as the database industry itself, so I will spend the next few paragraphs familiarizing newcomers with some of the terms you can expect to see throughout this chapter. If you already are acquainted with these terms, you should jump to section 17.1 now.

The term *telecommunications* has been around for several decades. The definition has evolved from "telephone-only communications" to a more global role that encompasses telephone, microwave, radio, and satellite communications. Today, you hear the term *network* being substituted for telecommunications and vice versa. It is easy to see why this could happen. At one time, networks were limited to two or more stations residing in an office or building. Now, they could represent stations and peripheral devices around the globe, as in a *wide area network* (WAN). Even WAN could be renamed *world-access network* instead of wide area network. So when should you use the telecommunications and network labels? Nobody has the perfect answer. But here is my proposition. The *telecommunications* term should be retired. It really applies to the state of communications when transmission was limited to telephone technology, as the "tele" prefix implies. The term *communications*, without the prefix, is still valid. It is best used to differentiate the type of technology employed in transmitting a signal (for example, satellite communications). Today, however, everything dealing with connecting stations, channels, servers, and computers should be considered modern-day networking and labeled as such.

Cell Relay: This is a way to transmit data through carrier services that use 53-byte cells. This form of relay is faster than frame relay. The *Asynchronous Transfer Mode* (ATM) protocol uses cell relay.

Ethernet: A network topology defined in IEEE specification 802.3. Ethernet networks transmit data at 10 Mbps over assorted cable types. Fast Ethernet is a term applied to 100 Mbps technology, which is the next generation for Ethernet.

EISA: *Extended Industry Standard Architecture* is an I/O bus specification for 8-, 16-, and 32-bit data movement. It also supports bus mastering on 16- and 32-bit buses. This is a much faster and preferable bus speed. Here is a list of maximum speeds attainable using different bus architectures:

- ISA   10 Mbps
- EISA   66 Mbps
- Micro Channel IBM   160 Mbps
- PCI   264 Mbps

PCI: The Peripheral Component Interconnect bus supports 32-bit bus-mastered data transfer.

Full duplex: This mode of transmission allows simultaneous sending and receiving of data packets. It therefore is twice as fast as half-duplex.

Hub: This is a plug-n-play box that enables you to plug 4, 8, or 16 10BASE-T ports (Ethernet) or 8 to 64 Fast Ethernet users into a central routing device. Hub devices can be cascaded, which allows scaling to the number of users and locals needed. Quality hubs provide pushbutton cascading, automatic speed sensing, and LED displays of port status. These devices usually are stackable, which means that you can add another device by plugging it into an existing one. Once connected, usually via a DB9 connector, the hubs work as a single integrated unit.

Switch: Switches are a means to introduce 100BaseTX (Fast Ethernet) hardware into an existing 10BaseTX (Ethernet) network. A two-port 10/100 switch can have your existing 10BaseTX devices on one port and newer 100BaseTX devices on the other switch. Typically, when the older and slower Ethernet devices have been replaced, the 10BaseTX port automatically runs at the higher 100Mbps speed.

LAN: A *local area network* hooks workstations, servers, and shared peripherals together. LAN networks have distance restrictions and require matching software and hardware to set up the network.

NIC: A *network interface controller* is a hardware expansion card used to connect two network devices.

Token Ring: Defined in IEEE Specification 802.5, these networks employ a ring. Speeds of 4 Mbps or 16 Mbps are possible.

UTP: *Unshielded twisted pair* is a type of wire connection that does not use an outer shielding on the cable.

Sometimes, good performance is more a matter of making the right choices than tweaking parameters. When it comes to communications, this is often the case. Performance and scalability of any network environment are related directly to networking protocols and software packages selected. The best way to understand which protocols are available and how they differ is to take a look at the standards.

The *International Organization for Standardization* (ISO) has provided a model for *Open Systems Interconnection* (OSI), which enables hardware and software to communicate. The model decomposes data communications into layers, each with specific functions in the overall communications structure. There are seven layers; number one is the physical layer and number seven is the application layer. This model provides a means for categorizing features in standards and setting boundaries for functionality. In theory, the model enables protocols within a layer to change without impacting other layers. However, it is an idealistic representation that seldom maps perfectly to the real-world implementation of protocols. Notice that several protocols span more than one layer in Table 17-1.

Just because a protocol may reside at the same layer as another protocol does not mean that it will have the same features or performance as the other protocol. A TCP/IP network, for example, can support millions of users on hundreds of thousands of hosts, whereas a NetBEUI network is lucky to handle 20 users.

Here are some general tuning tips that apply to most network operating software. First, try to load as few *network loadable modules* (NLMs), procedures, and protocol stacks as necessary. This method saves on memory and multiprotocol packet collisions. It may be wise to rearchitect your network to standardize on the best protocol. Use high-speed routers and fiber backbones where they gain the most for your network. Believe it or not, 22-gauge wire gets better transmission distance than smaller gauge 24 and 26 without repeaters.

17.1   TCP/IP

TCP/IP is fast becoming the best network for your money. It is highly routable and scalable to millions of users and thousands of hosts. The Internet is proof of this. Also, companies are rapidly building Internet/intranet networks. For remote communications, employees working from home can connect to work using a standard ISP provider. Instead of paying $600/month for a dedicated line, they can get unlimited Internet access for $200/year. That's a whopping savings of $7000/year per employee. The only catch is security. You need a very good firewall to prevent illegal entry into your business. Fortunately, firewalls are available.

TCP/IP works well with wire or fiber, too. An interoffice backbone can handle any amount of traffic. With the large number of Web development tools offering interconnectivity with databases, it won't be long before everyone is doing this —and even the mainframe is accessible using TCP/IP.

Linking TCP/IP networks to the mainframe can present some interesting bottlenecks. TCP/IP, put simply for the purposes of this book, is the capability to access host databases from the PC or UNIX platforms. It is the networking protocol. Instead of providing you with an in-depth understanding of the mechanics, I will present you with some vendor-supplied products that enhance performance.

First, there is **SNS/TCPaccess 2.0** from Interlink. These interoperability specialists provide an integration product that guarantees fewer bottlenecks

TABLE 17-1   OSI Layers and Residents

OSI LAYER	RESIDENTS (protocols)
(7) Application layer uses protocols to talk to other layers. This layer selects services for each end user application.	Novell e-mail Novell NetWare Core Protocol NCP UNIX e-mail, telnet, schedulers, databases X.400 e-mail protocol X.500 network directory sharing services
(6) Presentation layer converts data between application and communications formats. It also handles encryption	Novell NetWare Core Protocol NCP UNIX telnet Apple Filing Protocol AFP MS LAN Mgr Server Messaging Blocks SMB
(5) Session layer performs session management tasks like beginning, ending, and restarting sessions	Novell NetWare Named Pipes, NetBIOS Novell NetWare Core Protocol NCP Simple Mail Transfer Protocol SMTP File Transfer Protocol FTP Simple Network Management Protocol SNMP UNIX telnet

(4) Transport layer handles security and end-to-end control of messages exchanged between users.	Novell Sequenced Packet Exchange SPX
	Novell NetWare Core Protocol NCP
	NetBios NetBEUI
	Transmission Control Protocol TCP
	Dynamic Host Configuration Protocol
	   DHCP
	Internet User Datagram Protocol UDP
	BanyanVines Interprocess Comm Protocol
	   VIPC

(3) Network layer handles the interconnection of sub-networks and routing of packets between them (a.k.a hops)...	Novell Internetwork Packet Exchange IPX Internet Protocol IP
(2) DataLink layer builds packets specific to an access method and provides error detection for each subnetwork.	Ethernet Fiber Distributed Data Interface FDDI Asynchronous Transfer Mode ATM Novell LAN drivers Open Datalink Interface ODI Network Driver Interface Spec NDIS UNIX LAN drivers, MAC Network Interface Controller NIC drivers ARCNET
(1) Physical layer deals with the software-to-hardware exchange, for bit-by-bit transmission.	Network Interface Controller NIC, adapters, for wire, radio, fiber optics, etc.

while delivering reduced CPU consumption. Just read the fact sheet on this product:

- High-speed bidirectional file-transfer capabilities
- Bidirectional printing
- Thousands of concurrent sessions
- High-performance resource sharing even with mixed workloads
- Low CPU consumption
- Access to host applications in both environments
- Support for FDDI fiber-optic LANS (100 megabits/second)

ProView from Network Telemetrics, Inc. can proactively measure SNA/LAN PC response times for hosts and servers:

- Measures response times verifying service levels
- Charts trends and pinpoints bottlenecks
- Keeps data in a DB2/2 database for easy query

TCP/IP is usually pretty fast. If connections are backlogged, you can adjust the operating system parameter TCPWINDOW upward.

TCP/IP VERSUS SNA

TCP/IP has some advantages over the conventional SNA protocol. Besides requiring less control-packet information during transmission, TCP/IP is full duplex, which eliminates the need for line turnaround (switch direction) and polling. Communications channels can achieve greater throughput.

TCP/IP CONNECT TIME WITH ORACLE SQL*NET

Connect time for TCP (Ethernet) users from client-to-host can seem forever. You can do a few things to improve connect times. First, place the TCP address directly in the tsnames.or file. This can reduce hostname resolution by 1000 percent. Second, the prespawned server option of SQL*NET eliminates process startup time when connecting a client to the server.

TCP WITH MICROSOFT SQL SERVER

Using named pipes as the *interprocess communications* (IPC) method on top of Microsoft TCP/IP is preferred because features such as integrated security and adjustable packet size are available only with named pipes. The capability to adjust packet size greatly enhances performance tuning. You can find instructions for setting this up in *Article ID: Q107647 of the Microsoft Knowledge Base* (available over the Internet).

WINDOWS 95 ENHANCEMENTS

Pretty much everything went 32-bit in Windows 95, including network client, file- and printer-sharing routines, protocols, and network card drivers. To be able to take advantage of the faster 32-bit architecture, you must have a computer with *Extended Industry Standard Architecture* (EISA) or *Peripheral Component Interconnection* (PCI) and a network adapter card. Besides 32-bit capabilities, the network client runs a NetWare *virtual loadable module* (VLM), moves drivers to extended memory, and performs *packet bursts* (concurrent packet transmissions). A large number of relatively small packets are handled best with packet bursts. Typically, you need to enable packet-burst mode in both server and workstation. Also, you need special network cards that take advantage of this feature; two such cards are the Compaq Ethernet 16TP Controller and the NetFlex (including NetFlex-2 and NetFlex-3).

17.2 NetBEUI

The *NetBIOS Extended User Interface* (NetBEUI) is suitable for small networks with less than 25 workstations. It will not support routing of packets to other networks.

17.3 IPX/SPX

The *Internet Packet Exchange / Sequenced Packet Exchange* (IPX/SPX) protocols are considered common in Novell networks (NetWare 2.*x* through 4.*x*). Now, it is gaining popularity with Windows 95/NT. NetBEUI is limited in that it cannot be routed across networks, but IPX/SPX can. You can use this for small to medium networks of up to 400 workstations. In a Windows 95/NT system, you need to make only a few decisions when setting up a network. First, you must choose a frame type (packet structure) that is compatible with your entire network. Second, you can select the maximum number of connections. The number you choose will affect the amount of processor and memory use. If you set maximum connections equal to zero, for example, an unlimited number of sessions can connect. This would cause a memory shortage and possibly a system crash.

TCP/IP can outperform IPX/SPX with an eight-percent improvement. TCP/IP also allows connectivity to a wide range of dissimilar platforms, such as UNIX servers/workstations, RISC, DOS, and Windows—whereas IPX/SPX generally is found on Novell NetWare-based systems. If Novell is the vehicle of choice, you should take advantage of database-, file- and printer-sharing services.

17.4 Banyan VINES

Banyan VINES supports large networks with many servers. Its claim to fame is being able to access devices without network addresses. The software is not used widely, however. That could change with the release of StreetTalk for Windows NT 7.5, which now enables TCP/IP support for client-to-server connections as well as server-to-server connections. In addition, this new release provides guaranteed logon, which means that if a server is down, the logon fails over to an available server.

17.5 DEC PATHWORKS

Digital Equipment Corporation's (DEC) Pathworks enables you to interconnect heterogeneous clients in a client/server network, resulting in simultaneous access to Windows, UNIX, and OS/2 workstations. It can support large networks.

17.6 Release 12.0 CA-IDMS Sysgen Telecommunications Tuning

Tuning CA-IDMS telecommunications performance usually is overlooked. Administrators have a tendency to take for granted the communications world—mainly because it is somebody else's job. But you need to contact that somebody and pass on the following suggestions:

- Compaction condenses redundant data in 3270 datastreams.
- PERMREADBUF permanently allocates read buffers for 3270 terminals.
- Set the RPL count to 1/3 times the number of active terminals as determined with DCUF SHOW USER ALL commands issued during peak hours. This is a starting number that must be adjusted up or down to optimize throughput.
- Put the VTAM printers on their own line.

Request parameter lists (RPLs) determine the number of concurrent requests that are handled. Too few RPLs will bottleneck terminal responses.

In some instances, the tuning must occur in the CA-IDMS sysgen. One such option is the RPL count. Figure 17-1 shows how to arrive at the RPL count and compaction performance by using DCMT display commands. The same information is displayed using the Performance Monitor in Figure 17-2.

17.7 TPX from Computer Associates

TPX (*Terminal Productivity Executive*), from Computer Associates, offers a multiple-session manager, ACL/E (a nifty language that can be used to program robotics screen processing), session switching, automatic time-out processing, VTAM pass-through printing, and advanced data compression for 3270 datastreams, all of which represent time savings.

TPX has some standard performance parameters. By entering the D STOR and D STORXA commands, the administrator of TPX can get storage-use statistics to analyze whether below-the-line and XA storage are being used effectively. Here is a list of useful statistics returned from the D STOR command:

GET LINE NAMES

```
DCMT  DIS   LINE
***  DISPLAY LINES (ALL) REQUEST ***
     DRIVER  TYPE AND/OR   APPL/TABLE   NUMBER OF
 LINE-IDSTATUS  MODULE  ACCESS METHOD   DD/OTHDRPTERMS
 ────    ─────  ────    ─────────       ──────
 CONSOLE INSRV  RHDCD04WWTO      CONSOLE 1
 VTAM05  INSRV  RHDCD05VVTAM 3270        IDMSPRD5212
 UCF05   INSRV  RHDCD0ZUUCF      RHDCFSTB13

 V5  ENTER NEXT TASK CODE:
```

GET RPL COUNT

```
DCMT DIS MEM PLE VTAM05 200

 <ADDR>    <OFFSET> <HEX>                                              <CHARACTER>
 000F4508  00000000 E5E3C1D4  F5F34040  40404040  40404040  *VTAM05          *
 000F4518  00000010 40404040  40404040  001102F0  000F45E8  *    ...0...Y *
 000F4528  00000020 00274C50  0039B818  00003128  0089D384  *...&.......ILD*
 000F4538  00000030 00000000  006C9988  0089D2B8  000006C4  *.....%RH.IK...D*
 000F4548  00000040 F5E57000  00000000  002DFFEC  15000000  *5V.............*
 000F4558  00000050 000F452C  000F452C  00000000  000F45D0  *..............*
 000F4568  00000060 00000000  0087EFBA  0035F8CA  000F4EB8  *....G....8...+.*
 000F4578  00000070 000F6638  0000012F  00000048  00000000  *...............*
 000F4588  00000080 08C9C4D4  E2E3E2E3  F5000800  00000000  *.IDMSPRD5......*
 000F4598  00000090 00000000  00010005  00000000  0089D334  *...........IL.*
 000F45A8  000000A0 0089D3F4  00000000  0089D734  0000000   *.IL4....IP.....*
 000F45B8  000000B0 00000000  0089D434  00004383  00000000  *.....IM...C....*
 RPL performance
 000F45C8  000000C0 00000000  00000000                      *........        *
 V5  ENTER NEXT TASK CODE:

x'00' is VTAM APPLID = VTAM05
x'80' is VTAM ACBNAME = IDMSPRD5
x'B8' is largest number of concurrent terminal I/O requests = 00004383 = 17283
decimal RPL requests
x'BC' is the number of times an application had to wait because no RPL was
available = 00000000 meaning no waits
```

GET COMPACTION PERFORMANCE

```
DCMT DIS LINE VTAM05
*** PHYSICAL LINE DISPLAY ***
PLINE-ID VTAM05
STATUS INSRV
MODULE 5V
COMPACT  39.60%        [wes] compaction performance
APPL-ID IDMSPRD5
LTERM-ID   PTERM-ID  TYPE/M   STATUS   TERM-ID    FES-ID  UCF-STAT UCF-MODE
LTV5L101   PTV5L101  3287 2   DISCON   TPXAI001
LTV5L102   PTV5L102  3287 2   DISCON   TPXAB009
LTV5U101   PTV5U101  3287 2   DISCON   TPXAA004
LTV5L103   PTV5L103  3277 2   INSRV    TPXAT003
LTV5L104   PTV5L104  3277 2   INSRV    TCPAN002
LTV5L105   PTV5L105  3277 2   INSRV    TCPAN005
```

Figure 17-1 DCMT RPL-Related Commands

■ Open ACBs versus total ACBs

■ Terminals logged on

■ Percentage of DSA and slot storage used

■ Number of free-space fragments

■ Number of slot requests overflowing into DSA or larger slot areas

You can modify the use of storage TPX in two panels that enable you to alter settings. Figure 17-3 shows the options table detail panel, and Figure 17-4 shows the above-the-line storage-allocation panel. In addition, the overall

```
IDMS/R PM-R10.2        Cullinet Software, Inc. V05          14:26:08.91
CMD->                                                       Window : 02
                                                            Refresh: 10
02 Communication Line Detail                                                  >
 Line      Write   Total   Read    Total   Line    RPL  Waits    Total RPLs
 Name      Errors  Writes  Errors  Reads   Status  Gen  On RPL   Requested
CONSOLE    0       0       0       0       INSRVC  0    0        0
VTAM05     0       8676    0       8427    INSRVC  5    0        17283
UCF05      0       5851    0       1341    INSRVC  0    0        0
```

Figure 17-2 PMRM Communications Line RPL Displays

```
Command ===>                              Panelid   -
TEN0101
                                          Userid    -    TPXAD-
MIN
                                          Terminal  -
VTL50101
System Options Table:   SYS1PROD          Date      -
05/05/95
                                          Time      -
00:30:33
Performance Parameters
- - - - - - - - - - - - - - - - - -


VTAM Authorized Path Facility:      N
Large Message Processing Option:    Y
Rtasks:                             1
Load profiles at startup:           Y
Broadcast Pacing:                   300
Maximum Sessions:                   00300           (1)
Maximum TPX Users:                  00300           (2)
TPX Save Areas:                     300
Receive-Any Count:                  050

Can be updated dynamically using the TPXOPER Reload Command
```

(1) Set maximum sessions to 0 for no limit on signons
(2) Set maximum TPX users to 0 for no limit on signons

Figure 17-3 TPX The Systems Options Table Detail Panel

```
Command ===>                                   Panelid   -    TEN0101
                                               Userid    -    TPXADMIN
                                               Terminal  -    VTL50101
System Options Table:     SYS1PROD             Date      -    05/05/95
                                               Time      -    00:30:33
Storage Allocated (above 16m line)
- - - - - - - - - - - - - - - - - - - - - -

XA Storage:            7170      K
DXA Percentage:          20      %

Pool#  Size  Percent    Pool#  Size  Percent    Pool#  Size   Percent
- - - - - - - - - - - - --- - - - - - - - - - - - - - - - - - - - -
etc.

                  XA Slot Percentage Total = 100 %
```

Figure 17-4   TPX The Storage-Allocation Panel

storage use should be kept around 70 percent. You can control this number by adjusting the region size in the startup for TPX.

Finally, you can use the D STATS command for TPX to display useful tuning information for individual terminals and users, such as message volumes, average message size, and compression percentages. Use these values to analyze VTAM ITLIM packet tuning.

17.8   NetSpy Network Performance Monitor
from Computer Associates

SMF statistics are created by this real-time monitor, which collects VTAM traffic and response time data for TSO, CA-IDMS, IMS, and CICS. A big benefit of this tool is that it provides you with tuning recommendations. A full discussion of this popular tool is beyond the scope of this book. The key question to ask yourself is, "Am I using the best possible VTAM/NCP monitor for tuning my network?"

17.9   Network Performance Monitor (NPM)
for MVS/XA from IBM

Host and network response times, buffer pool levels, load versus response times, and a TPNS interface are some of the highlights of IBM's tool for network analysts. Don't overlook Big Blue when researching support products: This one will do the job.

A list of other programs that aid in network analysis and performance follows.

VTAM Performance Analysis and Reporting System (VTAMPARS).   This product is from IBM and offers the same types of features as NPN, only for VS1 operating systems.

3270 Optimizer/CICS and 3270 Superoptimizer/CICS. These products are from BMC Software; they are yet another pair of products with 3270 traffic statistics. The Superoptimizer compresses both inbound and outbound datastreams, whereas the optimizer does only outbound. Interestingly, compression generally saves in CPU and elapsed time. Encryption and decryption can end up adding to both CPU and elapsed time, however.

Network Performance Analyze (NPA). This product is from Quintessential Solutions and is for use with WANs in an MS-DOS environment.

IBM Token-Ring Network Trace and Performance Program. This program is from IBM; it captures token-ring traffic by users and overall in the PC/MS-DOS environment.

17.10   Blast from US Robotics

I've seen this one, and I'm sold on it. Blast is the tool for PC-to-PC transfers and PC-to-mainframe file transfers. The mainframe emulation enables the scripting of mainframe sessions. The remote PC feature gains access to the keyboard, disk, screen and printer on another PC.

Terminal emulation includes VT100, IBM3101, ANSI, TTY, and a host of others. The product works with PC DOS, UNIX V & SCO, Xenix, IBM RS/6000, IBM mainframes, Apple Macintosh, DEC VAX, and so on. Protocols such as XMODEM, YMODEM, ZMODEM, KERMIT, FTP, TCP/IP, and AUTOPOLLING are supported.

You need to make a handful of tuning decisions to benefit from the full functionality of the product:

- Make sure that Blast is being used on the sending and receiving computer for optimum performance.
- Better line quality makes for faster transfers. Dedicated lines are best. Higher quality lines are necessary to use larger packet sizes.
- The @PAKTSZ parameter enables you to select larger packets for faster transfers.
- Blast enables you to choose the best compression option for the kind of work you are doing.
- KERMIT is freeware for mainframe, but it is slow.
- MODEM is fastest among X/Y/Zmodem selection.
- BHOST is a Blast facility that runs on a target PC. You should set the fastest modem rate you can (a maximum of 115 Kbaud) and the RTS/CTS pacing, screen-scaling ratio, display scan interval, compression buffer and file-buffer parameters for best throughput.

Here is a subset of the statistics provided by the product:

- Total number of packets sent or received and their sizes

- Elapsed transfer time

- Number of retries during transfer

- Number of bytes transferred
- Line quality

Another product with a similar name is **DataBlaster**, from Bus-Tech Incorporated. This is a bidirectional file-transfer program. Yet another product is **Outbound**, from FireSign Computer Company. It's always nice to have multiple vendors from which to choose. Half the fun is exploring the products available.

17.11   LAN Software Selection

It is a really good idea to get your company to standardize on a single LAN gateway, such as IRMA, ATTACHMATE, or DI3270. This standardization can reduce software and maintenance costs. I would choose the most popular brand name with the greatest functionality. Otherwise, you will pay again when you decide to switch brands.

Fault tolerance is another issue with LANs. Some network software products enable you to redirect your network sessions in the event of a LAN failure. This means having redundant network connection definitions and physical routers. No data is lost, and sessions continue uninterrupted by the failure. The best software reestablishes the original connection after repairs are instituted.

STAR TOPOLOGY

When stations are connected to a central node, this is known as a *star network*. This is frequently the case with time-sharing systems. The central node becomes a single point of failure, which is a pitfall in this design. If this node fails, the whole network goes down.

RING TOPOLOGY

A *ring network* has all stations connected serially in a circle. The stations can ship tokens (packets) along the circle, or a polling system can collect messages. In either case, software must be able to balance the work between stations; otherwise, one station could usurp the resources. With proper hardware, you can define multiple rings, which provides a backup ring in case of failure. Transfer of control passes from one token (station) in the case of its failure.

BUS TOPOLOGY

Finally, there is the *bus topology*, in which nodes are connected to a common communications resource, such as a channel. Because data doesn't need to be retransmitted, as in star and ring topologies, some of the delay time is eliminated.

17.12 VTAM Versus TSO Foreground

My experience has been that using VTAM-based teleprocessing monitors as front ends to database management systems always outperforms using TSO. TSO appears to use more memory and CPU than custom VTAM front ends.

17.13 Client/Server

Many of the key tuning issues with client/server applications surround the network. Figure 17-5 shows a list of key issues you should deal with when tuning this arena. Industry use of client-based applications have been growing at a phenomenal rate. There is a great deal of information that isn't even available for general publication yet.

Note the number of issues that revolve around the network and its operation. Based on this list, it is paramount that you have top-notch network personnel working on client/server-based systems.

You can use Computer Associates' **Paramount/XP** capacity application modeler to determine the effects that hardware and software changes will have on client/server applications. There has been a surge in products entering the market aimed at the needs of client/server users. It is beginning to look like these types of applications may be our future legacy database systems.

CAPACITY	SCALABILITY	RELIABILITY
THREAD LENGTHS	HIGH VOLUMES	CONNECTIVITY
LOAD BALANCING	CPU SPEED	I/O RATES
MEMORY	NETWORK	TRAFFIC RATES
CLASS LIBRARIES	DEPLOYMENT	
TIERED DESIGNS	CHANGE CONTROL	
QUALITY ENGINEERING	CONSULTING COSTS	

Figure 17-5 Client/Server Tuning Issues

17.14   ATM

Asynchronous Transfer Mode (ATM), which began as WAN technology that transmits up to 2GB of data per second, has not gained wide acceptance. It offers many desirable advancements, such as cell relay switching to provide faster switching and packet throughput and collisionless point-to-point connections. This protocol is almost ready for LAN-based networks. It still needs to adopt the various physical hardware modes available to other technologies.

17.15   FDDI

Fiber Distributed Data Interface (FDDI) is basically fiber optics. The lure of fiber optics is the 100 Mbps transmission rate (200 Mbps with full duplex Ethernet), which I hear will have a new upper limit soon. Because this technology requires you to rewire, it is best saved for a backbone that needs that extra *umph*. Based on token ring technology, FDDI supports two rings of cable. The second ring provides network backup in case of failure. Some advantages that FDDI provides follow:

- Avoids extreme electromagnetic disturbance
- Provides immunity to damage from lightning-induced currents
- Provides high-speed interbuilding links
- Supports high-security applications
- Supports very long-distance high-speed applications

17.16   Frame Types

Frames are basically data structures that map to specific protocol packet requirements. With Novell NetWare 3.11 and 4.01 comes a decision of which Ethernet frame type to use. If you currently are using a mixture of 802.3, 802.2 and Ethernet II types, you should seriously consider standardizing on one type. Multiple frame types results in added network packet traffic. NetWare sends out search packets for each frame type in use. In addition to network traffic, CPU cycles and additional memory are used.

One thing to remember when choosing a topology is that some lend themselves to mixing types of cable. Ring networks (IEEE 802.4 and IEEE 802.5), for example, can mix cables because each station's connection to the next station is unique. An Ethernet connection can't do this, however, because all stations are connected to the same cable.

17.17   Novell NetWare and UNIXWare

Before I jump into a discussion of Novell NetWare, I thought it might be helpful to give the novice some valuable information. First, Novell is bigger than a breadbasket. It requires a trained professional (a Novell engineer). Any company that uses Novell has one of those people. Before you do anything, find that person. Also, the Novell manuals (an impressive set) offer extensive information about setup. They don't provide as much information about tuning as I'd like to see, though. Here are some of the basic line commands you can enter from any workstation. Even if you aren't the network administrator, some of these commands will help you gather information.

Novell Command	Function
ATTACH	Attaches a server
CASTOFF	Turns off broadcasts from other stations/servers
CASTON	Turns on broadcasts from other stations/servers
CHKVOL	Displays LAN disk space
FILER	Uses Network File Manager
FIND	Displays all files here and now
FLAG	Shows network drive file flags
FLAGDIR	Shows network drive subdirectory flags
GRANT	Grants access rights
LDISCAN	Runs inventory scan (outside Windows)
LISTDIR	Lists directories here and now
LOGIN/LOGOUT	Signs on and off the network
NFOLIO	Tutors on infobases
NVER	Displays network version
PCON	Reconfigures print jobs
PCONSOLE	Goes to printer console
PSTAT	Displays printer status
RENDIR	Renames a directory
REVOKE	Revokes access rights
SETPASS	Sets network password
SLIST	Lists servers found
SYSCON	Goes to network console
SYSTIME	Displays current date and time
USERLIST	Lists users on LAN and times signed on

NETWARE

The most significant change you can make to a server-based system is to increase memory. By doing so, you also can increase parameters, which enables more concurrent processing. Keep this in mind while tweaking the following parameters. Also, if you allow too many concurrent processes, you take the chance of a system stalling or crashing. You can tune the typical Novell Net-Ware environment by adjusting several parameters:

- `DIRTY DISK CACHE DELAY TIME`

- `MINIMUM & MAXIMUM DIRECTORY CACHE BUFFERS`

- `MINIMUM CACHE BUFFERS`

- `MAXIMUM CONCURRENT DIRECTORY CACHE WRITES`

- `MAXIMUM CONCURRENT DISK CACHE WRITES`

- `READ AFTER WRITE VERIFY=OFF (DIRECTFS only)`

- `IMMEDIATE PURGE OF DELETED FILES=ON (DIRECTFS only)`

- `MAXIMUM PHYSICAL RECEIVE PACKET SIZE`

- `CACHE BUFFER SIZE`

- `FILE DELETE WAIT TIME=1MIN`

- `MINIMUM FILE DELETE WAIT TIME=1MIN`

- `GARBAGE COLLECTION INTERVAL=1MIN`

- `MINIMUM & MAXIMUM PACKET RECEIVE BUFFERS`

One of the problems that plagues NetWare is memory fragmentation. This can be caused by performing administrative tasks on the server, which you should avoid. You can schedule the server for periodic restarts to refresh memory. These precautions will reduce fragmentation problems. Some general tuning tips for NetWare servers follow:

- Use the latest version of NetWare.
- Apply the latest revisions.
- Avoid loading unnecessary NLMs that can cause fragmentation.
- Use a 64KB block factor when setting up NetWare partitions.
- Limit controller duplexing and database mirroring to cut CPU overhead.
- Use more memory to reduce bottlenecks.
- Standardize on one network protocol and frame type.
- Optimize the tuning parameters mentioned earlier in this section.
- Use *symmetric multiprocessing* (SMP) to get more CPU power.
- For databases, use the database-optimization techniques described in other chapters.

UNIXWARE

You may want to use some of the following general tuning tips to simplify the UNIXWare tuning effort. This is by no means everything you can do; it simply highlights things that should not be overlooked.

- Use *asynchronous I/O* (AIO) with raw devices or file systems. Databases such as Sybase automatically take advantage of AIO.

- Adjust the SVMMLIM and HVMMLIM parameters, which identify the maximum amount of memory available to a user. Determine the maximum use and set these values just a little larger.

- Increase the SHMMAX parameter until only one shared memory segment is being allocated, which is more efficient than multiple segments. The ipcs -b UNIX command indicates the number of segments allocated.

- Avoid unnecessary swapping. The sar -r and sar -w commands display the free memory for the system. This value is shown in 4KB pages. When it drops below 400KB, swapping occurs. You can resolve this by increasing the SHMMAX parameter or increasing real memory.

- For Intel Pentium processors, take advantage of the 4MB PSE memory paging. You can do this by using the PSE_PHYSMEM kernel parameter. For Sybase to use this memory area, set both PSE_PHYSMEM and the SHMMAX parameter equal to the SP_CONFIGURE memory setting in Sybase.

- Adjust the NPROC parameter to 50 greater than MAXUP to give operating system processes room to run. NPROC specifies the maximum concurrent processes allowed to run and acts as a governor on the system. Reduce this number if resources are exhausted.

17.18   100/200 Mbit Fast Ethernet

This technology is not that simple; there is a lot more to it than meets the eye. First, there are two standards to choose from, namely 100BASE-T and 100VG-AnyLAN. Second, 100BASE-T has three possible topologies: 100BASE-TX, 100BASE-T4, and 100BASE-FX, each depending on different cabling and duplexing. 100BASE-TX uses two pairs of UTP cable: 100BASE-T4 is a three-wire setup, and 100BASE-FX uses fiber-optic cable. The 100VG-AnyLAN uses four pairs of UTP wire; it differs from the other technology because packets can be prioritized. Thus, the server can be given priority over user workstations. This little discussion only begins to scratch the surface about 100 Mbit requirements and differences. Many more esoteric rules and limitations exist. The hardware upgrades require users to do their homework and choose which option is best. The following are some trade-offs associated with each of these topologies.

100BASE-TX

- Full duplex operation (transmit and receive concurrently) for throughput to 200 Mbps
- Half-duplex operation for throughput to 100 Mbps
- Network diameter = 205 meters, Lobe length = 100 meters

100BASE-FX

- Lobe length of two kilometers for full-duplex setup fiber optics
- Network diameter = 400+ meters, Lobe length = 2000 meters
- Full-duplex operation for throughput to 200 Mbps

100VG-ANYLAN

- Collisionless transmission to increase application performance
- Server priority over workstation
- Network diameter = 2500 meters, Lobe length = 100 meters
- 100 Mbps

My wish-list network, given the ones reviewed in this chapter, would have to be 100BASE-FX. You can never go wrong with more speed and newer technology. After you spend the dollars and own the best that money can buy, who is going to complain? Besides, I've seen 100BASE-TX PCI adapter cards for only $67.99.

18

Advanced Techniques

18.1 Roadmaps

During the life cycle for corporate systems, many files are created and redundancy flourishes. As the number of new programs and files increases, it often is impossible to determine whether a file or process already exists that will satisfy new requests.

In essence, a *roadmap* is a complete analysis of where the master file and database data exist and are used. The roadmap contains all the process models (workflows) for the entire corporation (or subsidiary, on a smaller scale). All its derivative files (file mutations) and processes (parallel processes) are mapped onto a single large chart (the corporate roadmap). During this analysis, you must identify the originator (the owner) of all master files and databases, as well as their flow, which inevitably spawns redundant offspring. At the conclusion of this long and arduous process, you will possess a picture of the proliferation of data in all segments of your business.

Figure 18-1 shows a roadmap of where the purchase-order data is used in a fictitious business. Notice that several organizations are using pieces of the original master file in mutated states. Several processes are being played out to achieve all the states of the data. Also, the batch window of processing has become elongated to accomplish the redundant processing of data. This presents a tuning window of opportunity.

Ideally, in the reengineering of a system such as this, all the mirrored files will be collapsed into a single file. The original master file update now will call subroutines to achieve all the individual updates to satisfy the many requirements that already exist for the data. The consolidation of processing and files will generate a runtime savings, however. The result will be a single master

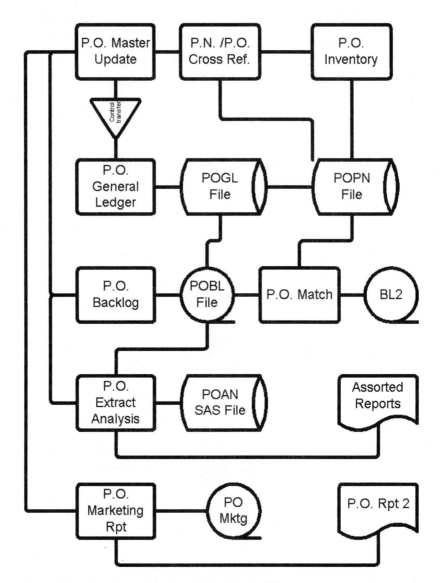

Figure 18-1   A Roadmap of Purchase Order File Proliferation

file, a single mainline process and reports. Figure 18-2 shows the collapsed pur-chase-order structure.

To attack the roadmap and reengineering of your business units, for the sake of streamlining batch windows and saving on maintenance dollars, you must have the highest commitment from *Information Systems* (IS) management. In some instances, the Board of Directors must approve a reengineering project. The cost can be enormous, but the savings can be astronomical. The cost may double or triple the IS budget. The result can take two to three years for payback. Ultimately, the cost of processing and maintenance can be cut by 50 percent or more.

The roadmap approach requires an initial exhaustive analysis. The collection of all systems, master files, processes, and interdependencies will help you discover where collapsing the system structure will yield the biggest return. It is not uncommon to find major master files replicated 20 times in large companies.

18.2   Reengineering and Reverse Engineering

This book isn't meant to be the master document for reengineering. The subject is broad. It will suffice to mention here some of the improvements you can make

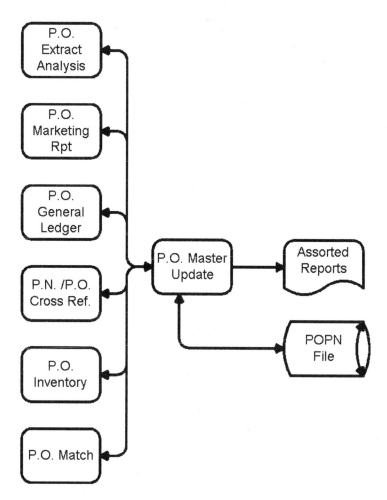

Figure 18-2 Collapsed Purchase Order Work/Data Flow

and some of the tools available to get the job done.

Reengineering and reverse engineering can put new life into old systems and enable you to achieve substantial performance rewards.

An applications system will evolve into an aberration over time. Often, it is obsolete on the day it is delivered. Much of the analytical information used to design the *logical data model* (LDM) and transpose it to the *physical data model* (PDM) was supposition. Knowing what you know today, you could build the system again and do it better. Knowing the cost and amount of time the initial effort instituted, however, you don't dare.

I say *dare*. Why, you ask? Because the second system will outperform the first. You will gain in four key areas. And, it won't cost as much as you think.

- New functionality

- Improved performance

- Next-generation software tools and platforms

- Resolution of known deficiencies

Although your applications system may have stagnated, the industry hasn't (see Figure 18-3). The products, services, and techniques you thought were state of the art at the system's inception now are considered naive. A reengineered system that incorporates the latest trends, however, still will cost less than abandoning the design for something new. If you continually reverse engineer a system and incorporate improvement, it ultimately will become the industry leader in its arena.

18.3 RAD

What can I say about *rapid application development* (RAD) that you don't already know? It is a method like so many popularized in the 1980s and 1990s. I'm not an advocate for any of today's processes. I think they still are evolving and getting better. I have evaluated RAD, however, and can attest to its sound approach. The different aspects of RAD are used by every organization, although not always in unison or in the same order. Appendix B, "Rapid Application Development (RAD)," gives you my synopsis on the RAD approach to development.

18.4 Life Cycle

A vast number and range of tools dealing with software life-cycle management are available. When you start looking at these, you will want to keep the points in Figure 18-4 in mind. If you find a tool that accommodates all these elements, buy it. These are the hot buttons for getting the most out of your software-management dollars. What does life-cycle management have to do with performance? Only this: A complete software solution avoids unnecessary duplication of coding. It eliminate errors. It enables you to avoid buying multiple tools to ac-

Product	Company	Supported Databases
ERwin	Logic Works	DB2
	1060 Route 206,	Gupta SQL/DB
	Princeton, NJ 08540	Informix
	(609) 243-0088	Ingres
		MS SQL Server
		Sybase SQL Server
S-Designor	SDP Technologies	DB2
	One Westbrook Corporate	Oracle
	Center	Informix
	Suite 805,	Sybase
	Westchester, IL 60154	Ingres
		RDB
		AS/400
		SQL Server
		SQL Base
		Paradox
Bachman Re-engineering	Bachman	DB2
Product Set	(617) 354-1414	CA-IDMS
		and others

Figure 18-3 Vendors of Valuable Reengineering Tools

complish the same goals and then having to maintain them. It reduces the cost of administration. All these things are tied to the method chosen to maintain software.

18.5 Open Sizing

Open systems/sizing is more than a question of using UNIX or finding hardware or software independence. And developing client/server applications is far from a no-brainer. Instead, it is a massively complex series of decisions, which when answered, could be the basis for the greatest savings in information systems. Get real! We're talking 30- to 80-percent reductions in IS costs. Granted, UNIX is the wave for open sizing today. Things such as the SPEC1170 standards to allow interconnection between a variety of UNIX operating systems will help produce a wide customer base.

A typical businesspartner solution using UNIX might be a DB2 host data repository with OS/2 client machines and IBM RS/6000 UNIX servers connected to the

Revision Archival

Revision Editing, Compiling and Debugging

Storage of Source Without Duplication

Checkin/out Security by Level

Revision Merging for Parallel Development

Vertical Platform Software Management

Distributed Software Management

Self Training

GUI Front End

Self Documenting

Change Control Signoff/Forms Incorporated

Email Interface

Defect Management Tracking Incorporated

Support for all languages and compilers

Total Integration of Facilities

Figure 18-4   Life Cycle Hot Buttons

host via TCP/IP. Much software can be used with this arrangement. You might develop using the Sybase relational database software, for example.

In the world of software development, a house divided against itself cannot stand. Success with UNIX-based systems depends on choosing this platform for the right reasons. UNIX-based systems provide easy portability to several platforms, run several times faster than equivalent DOS or Windows systems, require cheaper hardware, require cheaper software, and provide for cheaper manageability of enterprise data on UNIX.

Don't underestimate your need for corporate acceptance of new platforms. Unless information management is wildly in favor of a new direction for systems incorporating UNIX, any plans to move in that direction will be squashed. After you get the go-ahead, you need to adopt some proven philosophies for successful UNIX development efforts, such as the following.

UNIX-BASED DEVELOPMENT PHILOSOPHIES

- Quality should never be sacrificed.
- Enterprise data is cheaper to manage than division data.
- Shelfware should be mandated for all solutions.
- Shelfware never should be modified.

- End users should be responsible for shelfware acquisitions.
- PC-based reporting is cheaper than mainframe reporting.
- File-based reporting reduces paper costs.
- Tightly integrated systems cost more to maintain than bridges.
- In-house reviews of competitive shelfware reduce costly mistakes.
- Broad-based in-house training eliminates costly delays.
- Programmer productivity is higher on workstations than network terminals.
- Parallel processors such as the NCR3600 with UNIX process quickly.

You can measure your success with open systems and downsizing in several ways. First and foremost is the basic cost of hardware and software. Almost of equal importance is the number of software defects and requests for enhancement. If you track the number of lines of codes supported at the mainframe versus the PC/server and the number of defects (or enhancements) per line of code, you should be able to compare costs over a given period of time (by platform). If the downsized platform uses functions instead of lines of code, you must correlate the number of lines of code in a function.

18.6 Right Sizing

Right sizing is a mystery. Does the industry consider this a method for placing your applications on the right *hardware platform*, or does it consider it building your *software* for the right platform? This term presents some real semantics problems, but one thing is certain: Both methods reap big savings. Take your least-used mainframe applications and supporting software (database management systems and vendor tools) and move them to a smaller processor, for example. The immediate benefit can be millions of dollars saved for scaled software licensing. You can achieve this kind of move without any development.

18.7 Trend Software: The Next Generation

At a recent PC user group meeting, I saw several products demonstrated that use new methods of processing, such as associations, attachment of elements, triggers, event- and time-driven processing, *dynamic link libraries* (DLLs), *dynamic data exchange* (DDE), and *object linking and embedding* (OLE)—which includes in-place activation, linking, embedding, drag-and-drop, uniform data transfer, automation, monikers, compound files, classes, objects, encapsulation, inheritance, abstraction, and polymorphism. I also saw methods such as remembrance, behavioral models, business modulation, substitution, knowbotics, language recognition, acceptance, notification (or messaging), prompting (or conversing), watching, listening, repairing, and simulation. Wow! That's a lot of new techno-jargon. Each of these methods could translate into more efficient processing for your customer base.

I could devote an entire chapter to each of these methods. Instead, I've decided to give just one example of a trigger in the next section.

18.8   Oracle WebServer Option

Oracle is in the running with the best of the Web development tools. The complete series of integrated products includes Oracle7 Server, Oracle Media Server, Oracle TextServer, Oracle PowerBrowser, Oracle Media Server, Oracle Web Agent, and HTTP Server with its *Web request broker* (WRB). Each tool provides features that no available individual Web-based solution seems to be able to match. And here, it is all integrated. You can invoke database-stored procedures from your Web application, for example, and you can pull in audio and video files from the database.

Most notable is the capability to track visitors' access patterns to your Web site. On subsequent visits, you could produce a database-generated list of items that most interest potential visitors. That is pretty close to trendware, isn't it?

18.9   Triggers

Triggers are provided in every *relational database management system* (RDBMS) of which I am aware. Triggers provide a simple means to invoke a procedure at the target server, gather information and return it to the client machine, often using bulk data movement. Here is an example of an ANSI/ISO SQL3 standard trigger:

```
CREATE TRIGGER reorg BEFORE UPDATE ON parts
FOR EACH ROW
BEGIN
IF part.qty_list > part.maximum THEN
INSERT INTO dbareorg
VALUES (part.qty, SYSDATE);
ENDIF;
END;
```

Triggers are driven by events, date and time, or other means. This trigger creates an entry in a *database-administrator* (DBA) owned database when the number of parts maintained in a relational database exceeds some maximum quantity.

The trigger, in effect, becomes a tuning mechanism to notify the DBA that relational table maintenance is required. This can be an alternative approach to running extensive table reports frequently to monitor performance.

The downside in this example is that not all RDBMSs support true triggers.

The idea to grasp is that many of the repetitive tasks (proficient and deficient) that you perform each day (personal and business processes) escape your attention because you are focused on a single goal. So you avoid time management for small tasks that appear to be tangent to your goal. The new processing features in Windows-based tools, which focus on connectivity and pushbutton ease, are all centered around reducing the element of time spent on these menial tasks.

That brings me to my main point. When these new methods are exhausted, vendors and developers will see the next plateau of processing they can attack as they creep ever closer to true artificial intelligence. I think that next plateau will be *trend software.*

I have been leaning more toward conceptual ideas in databases lately. One of the ideas that keeps resurfacing is trends. You can think of *trends* as business processes that repeat. Trends are tied to time periods, events, or business practices and often are overlooked during the data logical modeling process. Here are some practical examples.

It doesn't make sense to keep records in a database if they are no longer accessed. Likewise, why compress data that is used every one ten-thousandth of a second? With some knowledge of how you use data over the short, medium, long, or special term, your software can make educated processing decisions for you. Now look at a few examples that will save many IS dollars if implemented.

If a customer order record is being closed because it has reached the end of its life cycle, it is logical to assume that it now will be archived. Either the archival process is encompassed in the order-closing process, or it is triggered to take place somehow. The reverse is true, too. A record that is archived easily can be recalled to the database somehow.

Here's another example: The addition of order #120000 means that the database is now at 75-percent utilization. This causes the batch updates, index reorganizations, and backups to trigger automatically. A message is sent to the capacity-planning department that a threshold has been reached.

Figure 18-5 shows some immediate areas where trend-software techniques would be beneficial.

Performance trends, such as dynamic *Extended Architecture* (XA) buffer assignments, can be tied to the time of day, day of week, and other learned trends. You are lucky if the performance-software products you see today enable you to dynamically change the tuning parameters. But to learn the business trends of your systems and have them adjust automatically in unattended mode is asking a lot. The next generation of products probably will do these things and more. So why don't you incorporate this automation into your next design model? This work should be part of the application system you are building. Of course, it is done behind the scenes and out of plain sight of your business-partners. But, none the less, it has to be done. The question often overlooked is, "Why not automate everything?"

Implementing triggers to control all the elements of data administration and performance based on normal business *trends* is probably the basis of the next generation of application and database development products. Trend software has every possibility of becoming the next line of smart products. The key is timing. Because events are tied to other events, times of the day, week, month,

TREND EVENT	RESULTING ACTIONS
BACKUPS	Backups are self adjusting based on update load trends
ARCHIVAL	Records and files archive automatically based upon business rules and trends
ANALYSIS	Reports are generated automatically based upon activity trends
TUNING	Record and file placement is dependent upon trend of usage
REDESIGN	Database and file design adjusts automatically based upon based upon
BUSINESS PROCESS	Business events trigger other business events automatically
LOAD LEVELING	Parallel processing and multitasking will self adjust based on trends
CAPACITY PLANNING	When certain levels have reached capacity, planning functions are automatic
PURGING	Business and usage rules drive the purging of unneeded records and files
COMPRESSION	Business and usage rules drive the compression of records or files
ENCRYPTION	Business and usage rules drive the encryption of records or files
FUZZY LOGIC	Systems that can respond quickly to changes
SECURITY	Business templates and triggers enforce security automatically
SMART TRIGGERS	Triggers are tied to a user's habits or business procedures and principles
PROCEDURE SUPPORT	Code can process on Client or Server tied to database or application
RECURSION SUPPORT	Ability of a procedure to execute itself
RULE BASED OPT	Just like it sounds...Optimization based on rules
DATA BASED OPT	Just like it sounds...Optimization automated based on data
REPEAT-CORRECTIONS	Whenever record A gets corrected, the trend is to build B and C
REPEAT-INSERTIONS	Whenever record A is inserted, it is generally followed by going to screen
REPEAT-DELETIONS	Whenever record A is deleted, it is generally followed by going to screen C
REPEAT-UPDATES	Whenever record A is updated, it is generally followed by another update
SMART CACHING	Automatic multilevel cache building based on trend data usage

Figure 18-5 Trends Toward Automation

or business cycle, they all can be triggered to happen automatically. You already can see some of these trends. What you don't see are data-engineering products to incorporate the smarts into the development cycle. Why not? If you don't automate it, somebody will have to perform this task. That's an extra body for which you'll need to pay a salary.

Trends have to be the most advanced methods of gaining performance that are yet untapped. You don't need to wait for tools to simplify the use of trends. Instead, be ingenious about incorporating trend analysis into your logical and physical data models and programming. And yet, trends are only one aspect of artificial software intelligence in the path of software technology's rapid growth.

18.10 Database Alerts

Alerts are becoming very common. In Oracle, you can define alerts to notify you of resource shortages or databases running out of space. With the WebServer option, you can track an individual's personal preferences as he or she browses a home page on the Internet. Later, when that person revisits the home page, a customized screen can present items of interest based on his or her previous visits. Buying habits can become part of the database. Alerts are one of the features that help to adapt applications and extend their functionality. Alerts also provide a way to notify administrators of performance issues.

18.11 *Total Quality Management* (TQM)

How software quality is defined and achieved is the subject of TQM. In today's information development society, a menagerie of quality controls exists. The new breed of quality-control terms and processes is gaining momentum throughout the computing industry. Some companies are embracing TQM, whereas others skim from the science or ignore it entirely (see Appendix M, "Total Quality Management Terms and Procedures").

One area in which tuning can adopt some of the rhetoric and get into the act is in that of defect management. Currently, most shops track reported software bugs, enhancement requests, and so on. Often, this information is logged into tools such as IBM's Information Management System (INFOMAN) or Allen System's Groups IMPACT. All that is required to begin defect management is to add measurement fields to these logging routines that identify the root cause of software failures. After many problems have been logged, it is possible to chart the percentage of problems that are repeat problems. It also is possible to identify which systems have the greatest number of problems. If 20 problems a week occur in one system and it is determined that these problems are all due to insufficient disk space, for example, it might be worthwhile for a company to address this problem. The *return on investment* (ROI) is the alleviated downtime for applications and regained employee hours.

Ideally, a shop would identify other aspects of TQM that would provide immediate benefits. Several of the processes involved in the quality-assurance methods guarantee fault-resistant software, which can reduce development, testing and maintenance costs.

18.12   Workflow Technology

Has the end-user community lead us astray? Many of the quid pro quos that were the basis for building the legacy systems of today were based on assumptions made decades ago in businesses. A long time ago, someone mapped the business needs to automation. As a result, today businesses may be automating the wrong things. That is where workflow technology can pay off. It's smart to revisit every aspect of your business, review it, measure it, and determine the bottlenecks.

Simply speaking, workflow technology reengineers what your business does before you apply automation (computers) to it. This eliminates many steps in your business before you automate steps that shouldn't even exist. You don't want to automate a bad process! Figure 18-6 contains a list of workflow tools that can help.

Processing is evolving in the direction of the human brain's capabilities and limitations. Each mini-revolution in the computer age can be linked to a fun-

Company	Tool(s)
Action Technologies Inc.	Action Workflow Manager
	Action Workflow Analyzer
Delrina Technology	FormFlow
Digital Equipment Corp.	TeamLinks
FileNet Corp.	Visual WorkFlo
Holosofx	Workflow-BPR
IBM	Flowmark
ICL	PowerFlow
Imara Research	Imara Workflow
Intelus Corp.	ProcessFlo
UES Inc.	KI Shell
ViewStar Corp.	Workflow Toolkit
Workgroup Systems	a la mode Workgroup

Figure 18-6   Workflow Products

damental function of the brain and the methods used to deal with information (thus, information systems). To speculate in the broadest sense, an in-depth analysis of daily thoughts as they relate to individual and business events would yield a long list of prospects for brain-like intelligence in software and hardware systems. People have grown accustomed to being participants in the building process, or anticipation process, of new software functionality.

18.13   *Artificial Lifeforms* (ALIFE)

I was being a couch potato watching television one day when a show about artificial lifeforms aired on public television. This show focused on programmers who wrote programs to simulate a robot attempting to walk under a bar. They defined parameters that made the task effectively impossible. The ALIFE program ran all night trying millions of solutions to the problem. The programmers went home where they had real lives. The next day, the programmers were able to look at the methods the program found to accomplish the goal. In this particular instance, the ALIFE program evolved into a different-looking creature to accomplish its goal. This kind of evolution is a lot more plausible than the human kind. At that moment, something clicked in my little brain. Why couldn't ALIFE be used to manage databases?

Artificial lifeforms are not really sentient beings; they merely are programs designed to emulate the capabilities of living creatures. These capabilities currently revolve around eating, burning energy, being born, dying, seeing, hearing, smelling, jumping, walking, running, adapting, evolving, and the ever-popular problem solving, to name a few. The list of possible traits is limited only to peoples' imaginations and understanding of their own remarkable designs. Along these lines, I have a dream.

My dream is a program that will get all the tuning information available and modify system parameters, always looking for better performance. The program could save successful configurations and maybe even discover anomalies people didn't know existed. Maybe, after the ALIFE program had evolved through several million variations, it would discover some bizarre aberration causing performance to double or triple, surprising the software vendor.

If we ever get little droids like R2-D2 to do work for us, I'm certain that ALIFE programming is going to be at the heart of their existence. It is very promising in every aspect of robotics and automation.

18.14   Nanotechnology

This might sound a bit bizarre, but I guarantee you it's for real. Nanotechnology is entering our world. The semiconductor technology of today is doubling storage densities every 18 months. With each improvement comes a radical boost in processor performance. Eventually, semiconductor advancements will hit a wall, though. You already might have read trade journal articles discussing the maximum number of microns this type of technology can support. That is where nanotechnology will take over.

Discoveries already are making scientific history. At Sandia National Laboratories, smart micromachines as small as human blood cells already are being manufactured. Several computer designers are doing extensive research. IBM Zurich, for example, created a nanocalculator using carbon molecules on atom-sized grooves etched in copper. Other scientists have produced micropumps the size of bacteria. This blossoming industry is in hot pursuit of assemblers, the term being applied to nanofactories capable of building virtually anything. An assembler could build a super-computer chip or even a jet engine. One use for assemblers is damaged cell repair. Nanotechnology already has been used to produce human insulin from bacteria in the body. Personally, I'd like to see this technology used to eradicate the need for diabetics to take insulin shots or blood sugar tests. If they can create a micromachine to measure blood sugar and then gauge the automatic production of insulin, it would pretty much do the job.

The impact this technology could have on tuning is enormous. To begin with, it may beckon in a new era of database machines. Tuning may be artificial intelligence based and grown into the database machine. Speeds could be literally millions or billions of times of even the speeds touted for the year 2000. There is a downside. Micromachines are at least two decades away, and their actual use may be limited by the motivations driving the designers.

If you want to learn more about nanotechnology, try searching the Internet. Several sites have information. Eric Drexler is considered the founding father of this technology and is chairman of the Foresight Institute.

FOOD FOR THOUGHT

The Internet is getting slow. I don't know whether you've noticed it, too. Even ISDN is only going to buy time for a few fortunate telecommuters. The Internet Engineering Task Force and the World Wide Web Consortium are investigating ways of creating a single connection to retrieve multiple objects. This will improve future browser performance. But the problem is more extensive. As multimedia expands, it will suck more performance out of transmission bandwidth. Let's face it. A small movie clip can be several megabytes of data. Now imagine full movie transmissions, radio, and television on the Internet.

If the Internet represents to the world what blood does to our body, the doctors of the Internet are at work everywhere. Long-distance phone companies already have Fibre backbones going all over the world. However, these backbones are very weak when crossing oceans, mountains, and deserts.

Those companies with the most at stake are investing in solutions. MCI recently upgraded its 45-Mbps DS-3 Internet backbone to 622-Mbps OC-12 (Internet 2 technology). Several universities are switching to this higher bandwidth. A new company called Teledesic Corporation is planning to send up 840 satellites in a medium earth orbit dedicated to providing high-speed TPC/IP communications to every part of the globe. Even in the depths of Africa, the jungles of Yucatan, or the mountain tops in Tibet, these satellites will provide the backbone for heavy-duty Web surfing. This all will begin happening in the year 2000. Whose idea was this? None other than Bill Gates and Craig McCaw, two of the wealthiest techies in our computer domain. I'm thankful they are spearheading this push for Web power. I'm certain they will be rewarded for their efforts. They may even end up controlling the communications world. More power to them.

Another concern is the speed from the long-distance carrier to a home or business. What good is Fibre if you have to transmit over wire the last 10 miles? The solution appears to be another opportunity for local carriers. The first city to provide complete Fibre access will be Anaheim, California. It figures that the place where Disney made dreams come true would be the first to get this. At a cost of around $90 million, the 300,000 residents of Anaheim will be able to hook up by the year 2004. The rest of the world probably will follow as commerce widens on the Net.

But this technology also is scary. Remember all those biblical prophecies in the Book of Revelations about the last times and the mark of the beast? What about the need to have a mark to buy and sell? Once the whole globe goes online, it would be a short hop to instigate a global buy-and-sell system. Who knows what the future holds? You and I live in the present. We live in the computer era, and performance and empowerment are the name of the game.

CONCLUSION

I would like to conclude by encouraging you to be part of the intelligence-in-software building process. Be creative in your tuning efforts. Be entrepreneurial in exploiting the full potential of your creativity.

Be willing to share your discoveries. The Internet is a great forum for ideas. I would love to hear about tuning solutions that could be incorporated into future editions of my book. I'm equally concerned about correcting any errors in future editions. I'm only one writer, and I depend on the experience and dedication of many other people. I hope this text and any future editions will be a blessing to you.

Subject:	*Database Performance Tuning Handbook*
E-mail address:	jdunham@announce.com
Home-page address:	www.announce.com/~jdunham

Cobol Coding Considerations

Suggestion	Reason
Place most used variables at the beginning of working storage.	To minimize paging.
Unreferenced variables and literals.	Cobol optimizers will remove these and report on them.
COMP & COMP SYNC.	Provides the fastest math computations where display of products is seldom seen.
Sign all COMP variables.	To avoid extra sign processing.
COMP-3	Is best for decimal math.
Use the same number decimals in all variables involved in math.	To avoid extra decimal processing.
Use the same COMP types for FROM and TO fields in moves.	To avoid mixed format conversions.
Avoid moving spaces to fields which can be initialized in working storage.	To avoid repetitive processing.
Combine file opens into a single statement.	To eliminate redundant I/O routine loading.
Indexing is faster than subscripts.	Saves 60% CPU utilization on subscript work.
Move unnecessary statements outside of loops where they are repeated.	To reduce CPU usage.
Check the prior keyed table or database record before issuing the call for another record.	Many types of processing request the same record several times in a row.
Terminate searches as soon as the table element or record is obtained or exceeded in value.	This is one of the best methods for saving CPU and I/O.

Suggestion	Reason
Use binary or indexed tables for large tables with 100 or more entries.	To reduce lookup time.
Code all new routines and all old date routines to handle CENTURY. The year 2000 is closing rapidly and studies have shown that the absence of century will slow processing	Saves retrofitting dates later.
Use GROUP moves.	Saves over several individual field moves.
When to use COMPUTE.	Use COMPUTE when there are more than two levels of math to perform. Avoid ON SIZE ERROR coding to avoid extra CPU usage.

B

RAD (Rapid Application Development)

KEY STEPS IN THE RAD PROCESS

Project Definition:	Objectives, scope, data interfaces and conceptual model defined.
Conceptual Solution:	Object oriented model of application and prototype prepared.
Development:	Code reusable objects, design and load databases, test programs.
Business Partners:	Business partners to prepare test plan, training, and facilities acquisition.
Deliverables:	Independent deliverables are tested.
Implementation:	Full scale production databases are loaded.
	Facilities are installed.
	Training is completed.
Evaluation Phase:	Post analysis to determine if objectives met.

KEY PLAYERS AND THEIR ROLES

Executive Sponsor: Business unit executive with signature power for all aspects of the RAD project. Also acts as an ambassador.

Project Manager: Builds the RAD team and environment. Also, handles scheduling.

User Manager: Assigns user representatives to tasks. Oversees implementation.

Users: Business partners understanding the business and the objectives and responsible for testing the solution.

Software Developer: Designs and builds the software solution.

SAR and PS Command Syntax on SYSTEM 5 and UNIX Systems

As a prelude to presenting the command syntax for these two important UNIX tuning commands, let me say that UNIX is relatively easy to learn. Many college books and/or college computer lab assistants can quickly enlighten you on the basics for UNIX commands. Also, you can use the MAN (manual command) to get the syntax for any supported command.

SAR Command Syntax

NAME

sar - system activity reporter (UNIX Posix)

SYNOPSIS

```
sar [ -ubdycwaqvmpgrkxDSAC ] [ -o file] t [ n ]
sar [ -ubdycwaqvmpgrkxDSAC ] [ -s time] [ -e time ] [ -i sec ]
    [ -f file ]
```

DESCRIPTION

sar, in the first instance, samples cumulative activity counters in the operating system at n intervals of t seconds, where t should be 5 or greater. If t is specified with more than one option, all headers are printed together and the output may be difficult to read. If the sampling interval is less than 5, the activity of sar itself may affect the sample. If the -o option is specified, it saves the samples in `file` binary format. The default value of n is 1. In the second instance, with no sampling interval specified, `sar` extracts data from a previously recorded `file`, either the one specified by the `-f` option or, by default, the standard system activity daily data file `/var/adm/sa/sadd` for the current day `dd`. The starting and ending times of the report can be bounded via the `-s` and `-e time` arguments of the form `hh` [`:mm` [`:ss`]]. The `-i` option selects records at `sec` second intervals. Otherwise, all intervals found in the data file are reported.

In either case, subsets of data to be printed are specified by option.

SYNTAX

-u   Report CPU utilization (the default):

%usr	portion of time running in user mode
%sys	portion of time running in system mode
%wio	portion of time idle with some process waiting for block I/O
%idle	portion of time idle

When used with -D,

%sys   split into percent of time servicing requests from remote machines (remote) and all other system time (local). If you are using a 3B2 Computer with a co-processor, the CPU utilization (default) report will contain the following fields: %usr, %sys, %idle, scalls/s; where scalls/s is the number of system calls, of all types, encountered on the co-processor per second.

-b   Report buffer activity:

bread/s, bwrit/s	transfers per second of data between system buffers and disk or other block devices
lread/s, lwrit/s	accesses of system buffers
%rcache, %wcache	cache hit ratios (1 minus bread/lread) as a percentage
pread/s, pwrit/s	transfers via raw (physical) device mechanism

When used with -D, buffer caching is reported for locally-mounted remote resources

-d   Report activity for each block device, e.g., disk or tape drive, with the exception of XDC disks and tape drives. When data is displayed, the device specification `dsk-` is generally used to represent a disk drive. The device specification used to represent a tape drive is machine dependent. The activity data reported:

%busy   portion of time device was busy servicing a transfer request

avque   average number of requests outstanding during that time

r+w/s   number of data transfers from or to device

blks/s   number of bytes transferred in 512 byte units

avwait   average time in milliseconds that transfer requests wait idly on queue

avserv   average time to be serviced (which for disks includes seek, rotational latency, and data transfer)

-y   **Report TTY device activity:**

rawch/s   input character rate

canch/s   input character rate processed by canon

outch/s   output character rate

rcvin/s   receive rate

xmtin/s   transmit rate

mdmin/s   modem interrupt rate

-c   **Report system calls:**

scall/s   system calls of all types; sread/s, swrit/s, fork/s, exec/s - specific system calls

rchar/s   characters transferred by read system calls

wchar/s   characters transferred by write system calls

When used with -D,

the system calls are split into incoming, outgoing, and strictly local calls; no incoming or outgoing fork and exec calls are reported.

-w   **Report system swapping and switching activity:**

swpin/s, number of transfers and 512 byte units transferred for
bswin/s   swapins

swapot/s number of transfers and 512 byte units transferred for swapouts

bswot/s   (including initial loading of some programs)

pswch/s   process switches

-a   **Report use of file access system routines:**

iget/s

namei/s

dirblk/s

-q   **Report average queue length while occupied, and % of time occupied:**

runq-sz,   size of run queue of processes in memory and runnable
%runocc

swpq-sz,   these are no longer reported by sar
%swpocc

-v   **Report status of process, i-node, file tables:**

proc-sz   process table entries/size (evaluated once at sampling point)

inod-sz   inod table entries/size

file-sz   file table entries/size

lock-sz   lock table entries/size

ov   overflows that occur between sampling points for each table

-m   **Report message and semaphore activities:**

msg/s,   primitives per second
sema/s

-p   **Report paging activities:**

atch/s   page faults per second that are satisfied by reclaiming a page currently in memory (attaches per second)

pgin/s   page-in requests per second

ppgin/s   pages paged-in per second

pflt/s   page faults from protection errors per second (illegal access to page) or copy-on-writes

vflt/s   address translaction page faults per second (valid page not in memory)

slock/s   faults per second caused by software lock requests requiring physical I/O

-g   **Report paging activities:**

pgout/s   page-out requests per second

ppgout/s   pages paged-out per second

pgfree/s   pages per second placed on the free list by the page stealing daemon

%5ipf   the percentage of S5 inodes taken off the freelist by iget which had reusable pages associated with it. These pages are flushed and cannot be reclaimed by processes. Thus, this is the percentage of igets with page flushes.

-r   Report unused memory pages and disk blocks:

freemem   average pages available to user processes

freeswap   disk blocks available for page swapping

-k   Report kernel memory allocation (KMA) activities:

sml_mem   memory pool reserves and allocations for small requests—the amount of memory in bytes KMA has for the small pool

alloc   the number of bytes allocated to satisfy small memory requests

fail   number of requests for small memory amounts that failed

lg_mem   memory pool reserves and allocations for the large memory pool

alloc   analogous to small pool

fail   analogous to small pool

ovsz_alloc   the amount of memory allocated for oversize requests

fail   the number of oversize requests which could not be satisfied because oversized memory is allocated dynamically (there is no pool)

-x   Report remote file sharing (RFS) operations:

open/s   number of opens per second by clients (incoming) and server (outgoing)

create/s   number of creates per second by clients (incoming) and server (outgoing)

lookup/s   number of lookups per second by clients (incoming) and server (outgoing)

readdir/s   number of directory reads per second by clients (incoming) and server (outgoing)

getpag/s   number of get pages per second by clients (incoming) and server (outgoing)

putpage/s   number of put pages per second by clients (incoming) and server (outgoing)

..others

-D   Report remote file sharing activity:

When used in combination with -u, -b, or -c, it causes sar to produce the remote file sharing version of the corresponding report. -Du is assumed when only -D is specified.

-A   **Report all data:**

Equivalent to specifying -udqbwcayvmpgrkxSDC.

-c   **Report remote file sharing data caching overhead:**

snd-inv/s   number of invalidation messages per second sent by your machine as a server.

snd-msg/s   total outgoing RFS messages sent per second.

rcv-inv/s   number of invalidation messages received from the remote server.

rcv-msg/s   total number of incoming RFS messages received per second.

dis-bread/s   number of read messages that would be eligible for caching (if caching had not been turned off because of an invalidation message). This indicates the penalty incurred because of the invalidation message.

blk-inv/s   number of pages removed from the client cache in response to cache invalidation messages.

Files

/var/adm/sa/sadd

daily data file, where dd are digits representing the day of the month

See Also

sag (1G), sar (1M)

ps(1)   386/ix **ps**(1)

NAME

ps - report process status

SYNOPSIS

ps [options]

DESCRIPTION

_p_s prints certain information about active processes. Without _o_p_t_i_o_n_s, information is printed about processes associated with the controlling terminal. Output consists of a short listing containing only the process ID, terminal identifier, cumulative execution time, and the command name. Otherwise, the information that is displayed is controlled by the selection of _o_p_t_i_o_n_s.

_O_p_t_i_o_n_s accept names or lists as arguments. Arguments can be either separated from one another by commas or enclosed in double quotes and separated from one another by commas or spaces. Values for _p_r_o_c_l_i_s_t and _g_r_p_l_i_s_t must be numeric.

The _o_p_t_i_o_n_s are given in descending order according to volume and range of information provided:

- **-e**   Print information about every process now running.

- **-d**   Print information about all processes except process group leaders.

- **-a**   Print information about all processes most frequently requested: all those except process group leaders and processes not associated with a terminal.

- **-f**   Generate a full listing. (See below for significance of columns in a full listing.)

- **-1**   Generate a long listing. (See the following text.)

- **-n _n_a_m_e**
Valid only for users with a real user id of root or a real group id of sys. Takes argument signifying an alternate system _n_a_m_e in place of /unix.

- **-t _t_e_r_m_l_i_s_t**
List only process data associated with the terminal given in _t_e_r_m_l_i_s_t. Terminal identifiers may be specified in one of two forms: the device's file name (e.g., tty04) or, if the device's file name starts with tty, just the digit identifier (e.g., 04).

- **-p _p_r_o_c_l_i_s_t.**
List only process data whose process ID numbers are given in _p_r_o_c_l_i_s_t.

- **-u _u_i_d_l_i_s_t**
List only process data whose user ID number or login name is given in _u_i_d_l_i_s_t. In the listing, the numerical user ID will be printed unless you give the -f option, which prints the login name.

- **-g _g_r_p_l_i_s_t**
List only process data whose process group leader's ID number(s) appears in _g_r_p_l_i_s_t. (A group leader is a process whose process ID number is identical to its process group ID number. A login shell is a common example of a process group leader.)

Under the -**f** option, _**p**_**s** tries to determine the command name and comments given when the process was created by examining the user block. Failing this, the command name is printed as it would have appeared without the -**f** option, in square brackets.

The column headings and the meaning of the columns in a _**p**_**s** listing are given in the following text; the letters f and l indicate the option (full or long, respectively) that causes the corresponding heading to appear; all means that the heading always appears. Note that these two options determine only what information is provided for a process; they do not determine which processes will be listed.

F (l)	Flags (hexadecimal and additive) associated with the process
00	Process has terminated: process table entry now available.
01	A system process: always in primary memory.
02	Parent is tracing process.
04	Tracing parent's signal has stopped process: parent is waiting [_p_t_r_a_c_e(2)].
08	Process is currently in primary memory.
10	Process currently in primary memory: locked until an event completes.
S (l)	The state of the process:
O	Process is running on a processor.
S	Sleeping: process is waiting for an event to complete.
R	Runnable: process is on run queue.
I	Idle: process is being created.
Z	Zombie state: process terminated and parent not waiting.
T	Traced process stopped by a signal because parent is tracing it.
X	SXBRK state: process is waiting for more primary memory.
UID (f,l)	The user ID number of the process owner (the login name is printed under the -**f** option).
PID (all)	The process ID of the process (this datum is necessary in order to kill a process).
PPID (f,l)	The process ID of the parent process.
C (f,l)	Processor utilization for scheduling.
PRI (l)	The priority of the process (higher numbers mean lower priority).
NI (l)	Nice value, used in priority computation.

ADDR (l)   The physical memory address of the first page of the user block. If the user block is swapped out, ADDR is shown as 0.

SZ (l)   The size (in pages or clicks) of the swappable process's image in main memory.

WCHAN (l)   The address of an event for which the process is sleeping, or in SXBRK state (if blank, the process is running).

STIME (f)   The starting time of the process, given in hours, minutes, and seconds. (A process begun more than twenty-four hours before the _p_s inquiry is executed is given in months and days.)

TTY (all)   The controlling terminal for the process (the message, ?, is printed when there is no controlling terminal).

TIME (all)   The cumulative execution time for the process.

COMMAND(all)   The command name (the full command name and its arguments are printed under the -f option).

A process that has exited and has a parent, but has not yet been waited for by the parent, is marked <defunct>.

FILES

/dev

/dev/sxt/*

/dev/tty*

/dev/xt/*   terminal ("tty") names searcher files

/dev/kmem   kernel virtual memory

/dev/swap   the default swap device

/dev/mem   memory

/etc/passwd   UID information supplier

/etc/ps_data   internal data structure

/unix   system name list

SEE ALSO

getty(1M), kill(1), nice(1)

WARNING

Things can change while _p_s is running; the snapshot it gives is only true for a split second, and it may not be accurate by the time you see it. Some data printed for defunct processes is irrelevant. If no `_t_e_r_m_l_i_s_t,` `_p_r_o_c_l_i_s_t, _u_i_d_l_i_s_t,` or `_g_r_p_l_i_s_t` is specified, `_p_s` checks `_s_t_d_i_n, _s_t_d_o_u_t,` and `_s_t_d_e_r_r` in that order, looking for the controlling terminal, and will attempt to report on processes associated with the controlling terminal. In this situation, if `_s_t_d_i_n, _s_t_d_o_u_t,` and `_s_t_d_e_r_r` are all redirected, `_p_s` will not find a controlling terminal, so there will be no report.

On a heavily loaded system, `_p_s` may report an `_l_s_e_e_k(2)` error and exit. `_p_s` may seek to an invalid user area address; having obtained the address of a process' user area, `_p_s` may not be able to seek to that address before the process exits and the address becomes invalid.

`ps -ef` may not report the actual start of a tty login session, but rather an earlier time, when a getty was last respawned on the tty line.

Vendors and Products
(in alphabetical order by vendor)

Vendors:	Products:
Aberdeen Group, Inc. (617) 723-7890	Market Research Reports
Action Technologies, Inc. Alameda, CA	Action Workflow Manager Action Workflow Analyzer
Aladdin Publishing Company 1265 Helberta #4 Redondo Beach, CA 70277 (310) 798-6488	Clip SQL—allows use of Gupta SQL Base and IBM DB2 with CA-Clipper
Allen Systems Group (813) 649-1300 or (804) 424-7013	Fast Access, XADC Tracer—use IDMS journal data to load DB2
Andyne Computing Limited 552 Princess Street Kingston, ON, Canada K7L1C7 (613) 549-4355	GQL 4.1 (Graphic Query Language)
Aonix 595 Market Street San Francisco, CA 94105 (415) 543-0900	Object ADA OOPS development
Aris Corporation (800) 431-ARIS	DFRAG and Virtual DBA for Oracle
Asymetrix Corporation (800) 448-6453 or (206) 637-1500	Asymetrix Info Designer (CASE tools for Access, Sybase, Oracle, Foxpro and Paradox)
Bachman Information Systems, Inc. (617) 354-1414	Data Analyst and Re-Engineering Product Set Bachman/Analyst, Bachman/DBA, Bachman/Database Designer Kits

Vendors:	Products:
Baltic Advanced Technologies Peldu 26/28 Riga, LV-1050 Latvia	OptStyle for Delphi
BGS Systems, Inc. 128 Technology Center Waltham, MA 02254 (617) 890-0000	Crystal Performance Evaluator for CICS Crystal Performance Evaluator for DB2
Boole & Babbage 3131 Zanker Road San Jose, CA 95134-1933 (408) 526-3000	CICS Manager (identify system problems for DB2) STOPX37/II—stops xx37 type storage abends Hiper-Cache—reduces batch excps Command/Post—Distributed database management Command/MQ—Systems management Mainview—Server performance
Borland Software, Inc. Scotts Valley, CA (800) 331-0877 or (408) 461-9000 (800) 336-6464	Paradox & Paradox for Windows dBase IV & V and dBase for Windows
BMC Software P.O. Box 100 Sugar Land, TX 77487 (800) 841-2031	Data Migrator for IMS/DB2 (fast migration of IMS data to DB2 tables) Recover Plus for DB2 Data Packer for DB2 Copy Plus for DB2 Snapshot Copy for DB2 Catalog Manager for DB2 Change Manager for DB2 DASD Manager for DB2 Load Plus for DB2 Unload Plus for DB2 Reorg Plus for DB2 V3.3 Extended Buffer Manager for DB2 Opertune for DB2 (dynamic tuning of DB2 subsystem) Data Optimizer by DataTools Inc (distributed by BMC) SQL-Back Track by DataTools Inc 3270 Optimizer CICS Journal Manager Plus for CICS Recovery Manager Plus for CICS Recovery Plus for CICS/VSAM Recovery Plus for VSAM Application Restart Control (AR/CTL) for IMS Backup and Verification for VSE (IMS) Batch Control Facility for IMS BMP Restart for IMS Change Accumulation Plus for IMS Database Integrity Plus for IMS Data Packer/IMS for IMS Delta IMS for IMS Extended Terminal ASSIST (ETA) for IMS

Vendors:	Products:
	Fast Reorg Facility for IMS
	Image Copy Plus for IMS
	LoadPlus for IMS
	Local Copy Plus for IMS
	Pointer Checker Plus for IMS
	Prefix Resolution Plus for IMS
	Q:Manager IMS for IMS
	Recovery Plus for IMS
	Reorg Plus for VSE for IMS
	Secondary Index Utility for IMS
	Unload Plus for IMS
	TRIMAR DEDB Secondary Index Facility for IMS
	TRIMAR Fast Path Analyzer for IMS
	TRIMAR Fast Path Online Utilities for IMS
	TRIMAR Fast Path Unload/Reload for IMS
	TRIMAR Fast Recovery Utility for IMS
	TRIMAR Online DEDB Image Copy for IMS
	TRIMAR Restart Control Facility for IMS
Bradmark Technologies, Inc. 4265 San Felipe, Ste. 800 (800) 621-2808	DBGENERAL Performance Monitor, Server Manager for Oracle, Sybase and Microsoft SQL SQLab for Oracle
Bridge Technology (617) 424-6266	Bridge/Fastload
Bus-Tech Inc. (800) BTI-7577	Data Blaster—bi-directional file transfer
Candle Corporation 2425 Olympic Blvd. Santa Monica, CA 90404 (310) 829-5800	Omegamon for MVS Omegamon for IMS !DB/Dasd for DB2 !DB/SMU for DB2 Omegamon for DB2
Case Methods Development (214) 644-8173	CASE/Framework Synergy (CASE tools for SQLBase, DB2, Sybase, DB2 and ORACLE) Synergy (Case tool for SQLBase, Oracle, Sybase and DB2)
CASEware Technology (801) 782-0404	DDL to Xbase Converter Tool
CDW Software (713) 780-2382	CDW/Batch, CDW/SuperLoad, CDW/SuperReorder, CDW/SuperReorg
C.W. Kreimer & Associate, Inc. 5001 Baum Blvd., Suite 530 Pittsburg, PA 15213-1851	APPtitude Seminars CA-Clipper & CA-Visual Objects Training
Chen & Associates (504) 928-5765	ER-Modeler Package, Reverse-DBMS, Normalizer (ER/Case for DB2, Sybase, SQL Server, Oracle, CA-Ingres, Adabas, CA-Datacom, HP Image, Focus, FoxPro, Paradox and others)

Vendors:	Products:
Cogito Limited	DB-Allocate DB-Megabuf Plus DB-Synchro DB-Buffer Plus
Communications Horizons (212) 724-0150	RaSQL/X—get btrieve files accessed from CA-Clipper
Computer Associates World Wide Headquarters 711 Stewart Avenue Garden City, N.Y. 11530-4787 (800) 645-3003 or (516) 227-3300	CA-IDMS/R, CA-ADS, CA-IDMS Performance Monitor CA-Ramis/Server (for use with CA-IDMS, DB2, Xbase) CA-QbyX (for use with CA-IDMS, DB2 etc.) CA-DDS, CA-Migrate/Cobol, CA-IDMS Press-pack CA-Realia Cobol & CA-Realia II Workbench FASTDASD CA-Ret, CA-dBFast, CA-Realizer, CA-Clipper CA-Visual-Express—ODBC to IDMS SQL or network databases in a client/server environment CA-DADS, CA-Visual Objects, CA-Open Road, CA-Plink OO DB-Delivery Insight for DB2—shows time waiting for I/O CA-Endevor change control CA-In2uitive for DB2 CA-Explore for VSE, VM, VTAM, CICS and SQL/DS (performance monitors) GoalPlex CA-NETSPY, CA-TPX, CA-TPX/ACLE, CA-Paramount/XP CA-PMO (PDS directory caching) CA-Quick Fetch (PDS load library caching)
Computer Concepts Corporation 80 Orville Drive Bohemia, NY 11716	d.b.Express is a user tool for graphic display of CA-Clipper database fields
Computer Systems Advisers (800) 537-4262	Silverrun Workbench (Design for DB2, Informix, Ingres, Oracle, Rdb, Sybase, Microsoft SQL Server, dBase IV)
Computer Task Group 800 Deleware Ave. Buffalo, NY 14209 (716) 887-7221	Cobol to Cobol/Cobol II MAP (Migration Assistance Program)
COMPUWARE 31440 Northwestern Highway P.O. Box 9080 Farmington Hills, MI 48333-9080 (810) 737-7300	FILE-AID (edit DB2 and IMS data in SPF fashion) ABEND-AID, XPEDITER, Conversion-XPERT, DBA-XPERT, QA Center, EcoTools, EcoNet, Fault-XPERT
CorVu North America, Inc. (800) 610-0769	Query, MSS, DSS, Executive Alerts and Report Writing Tools

Vendors:	Products:
CPU Computer Information Systems, Inc. Newton, MA	Robo Response—measures actual response times
Data Access Corporation 14000 SW 119 Ave. Miami, FL 33186 (305) 238-0012	Visual DataFlex 4GL OOP Development for Multiple Platforms
DataSoft (Pty) Ltd. via COMPUSTAT 2741-512502	ODBC Express
D. Appleton Co., Inc. (214) 869-1066	Model Pro (IDEFIX Data Models for DB2, Ingres, Oracle, SQLBase, Sybase and others), IDEF/Leverage
DBopen (201) 792-6645	DBexplain for DB2
Delrina Technology Toronto, Canada	FormFlow
Digital Equipment Corp. Maynard, MA	TeamLinks
Diversified Software Systems, Inc. 18630 Sutter Blvd. Morgan Hill, CA 95037 (408) 778-9914	JOB/SCAN
Easel Corporation 25 Corporate Drive Burlington, MA 05803 (617) 221-2100	Synchrony Object Studio
Eden Systems (317) 848-9600 or (800) 288-9510	ES RE/Vision (for OS/VS Cobol to VS Cobol II conversion)
Embarcadero Technologies Inc (415) 834-3131	DBArtisan (Oracle, Sybase, MS SQL space Management) Call limits for users and objects
Eventus (800) 871-4871	ADHAWK SQL LAB, SQL STUDIO, MONITOR for Oracle
Executive Software (800) 829-4357	Diskeeper for Windows NT (defragmenter)
Extend Systems (800) 235-7576 or (406) 587-7575	Advantage XBase Server ExtendBase (faster Xbase and CA-Clipper indexing)
Expetune Pty, Ltd. Level 50 Aust Tel 0418372999 Intl Tel +6119416781	Strobe Rules Based Tuning for IMS, CA-IDMS, DB2, ADABAS
FileNet Corp. Costa Mesa, CA	Visual WorkFlo
Fire Sign Computer Company (800) 825-7228	Outbound—unattended UNIX, PC server file transfers

Vendors:	Products:
French Technology Press Office, Inc. (312) 222-1235	O2 (object oriented DBMS)
General Software Incorporated (GENESOFT) (703) 760-7804	Data Base Designer (DBD) (Expert design system for DB2, SQL/DS and others)
Gupta 1060 Marsh Rd. Menlo Park, CA 94025 (800) 876-3267 or (415) 321-9500	Gupta SQLBase Server (for DOS, Windows, OS/2, UNIX) Gupta SQL Network (too much to list) SQL Windows Corporate Edition 5.0 Database Support for (Gupta SQLBase Server, IBM DB2, IBM AS/400, IBM OS/2 Database Manager, Oracle, Sybase SQL Server, Microsoft SQL Server, Informix, CA-Ingres, Cincom Supra, HP ALLBASE/SQL, dBASE, Paradox, Oracle, Rdb) Flowmark
HLS Technologies, Inc. (714) 434-9411	Avoid Bind—eliminates unnecessary rebinding of DB2 programs when compiling
Holistic Systems, Inc. (617) 238-0213	HOLOS OLAP and Mulidimensional database system
Holosofx Manhattan Beach, CA	Workflow-BPR
Hyperact, Inc 3437 335th Street West Des Moines, IA 50266 (515) 987-2910	MemDB Delphi Native Database Engine Hyperterp Delphi script SiteXtras
ICL Irvine, CA	PowerFlow
Imara Research Toronto, Canada	Imara Workflow
Innovation Data Processing Corporate Headquarters 275 Paterson Avenue Little Falls, NJ 07424 (201) 890-7300	FDR FDR REORG FDRABR IAM (allows 20GB files, compression and buffering)
Information Builders (800) 969-INFO or (212) 736-4433	Enterprise Data Access (EDA)/SQL SMARTMODE for DB2—query analyzer/ governor prevents runaway DB2 requests
Infotel Corporation (800) 543-1982 or (813) 264-2090	Infopak (for DB2 table compression) MasterReorg (for DB2) Inform2, Inforeorg, Infoscope, Infoscan, Infocopy, Infotrace, Infocypher, Infoload, Inforecovery tools for DB2
Innovative Computer Technologies, Inc. (905) 336-1333	Diskview Performance Monitor (DPM) for DEC VAX
Integrated Development Corporation	SmartMem (reduced CA-Clipper program memory usage)

Vendors:	Products:
Intel Corporation	Pentium
Intelus Corp. Rockville, MD	ProcessFlo
Interlink Computer Sciences (800) 422-3711	SNS/TCP access 2.0 Interlink
International Business Machines Corporation P.O. Box 50020 San Jose, CA 95150 — Old Orchard Road Armonk, NY 10504 (914) 765-1900	DB2, DB2 Performance Monitor, SQL/DS, SPUFI, QMF OS/2 CICS, CICSPARS CICS/MVS, MVS/XA, MVS/ESA, MVS/SA CMS, VM, CMF CSP IMS, IMS DC, IMS DC Monitor, IMSPARS ISPF, TSO/E SAA MS—automatic placement of datasets needing performance VTAM, VSAM, TPNF, DFDSS RACF RMF—can show if I/O response avg better than guideline OS/VS Cobol, VS Cobol II, Cobol/370 CCCA (Cobol and CICS Converion Aid)— 5785-ABJ IBM Cobol Report Writer Release 4 (for OS/VS Cobol to VS Cobol II conversion) CICS/VS Performance Analysis Reporting System/MVS (CICSPARS) Network Performance Monitor (NPM) MVS/XA DFP (for catalog constraint and storage relief) Token Ring Network Trace and Performance Program DFSMS/MVS 1.1
International DB2 User Group (IDUG) (312) 527-6777 (voice mail)	The user group provides many presentations on performance
Intersolv (800) 777-8858	Excelerator for Windows, Excelerator II (SSADM for DB2, DB2/2 and Oracle)
KnowledgeWare Atlanta, GA (800) 338-4130	Application Development Workbench (ADW) (design through development for DB2, IMS, CA- IDMS, VSAM and SQL type databases) ObjectView provides PC gateways to dBase, FoxPro, Btrieve, Paradox and CA-Clipper
Landmark Systems Corporation 8000 Towers Cresent Drive Vienna, VA 22180-2700 (800) 488-7990	CICS, MVS, DB2 and VTAM Performance Monitor NaviGate NaviGraph

Vendors:	Products:
Logic Works 1060 Route 206 Princeton, NJ 08540	ERwin/DBF ERX SQL (ER design & development for Xbase and SQL databases)
Macro 4, Inc. (800) 766-6224	The Performance Analyzer 1.5 for AS/400 systems
MAK Software Consultants (800) 625-7547	Object Skipjack
Mercury Interactive Corporation (800) TEST-911	LoadRunner for Sybase and Oracle system load testing
Menlo Software 744 College Avenue Menlo Park, CA 94025-5204 (415) 324-1286	DBAware—monitor for Oracle and Sybase
MetaWare, Inc. 2161 Delaware Avenue Santa Cruz, CA 95060 (408) 429-6382	High C++ (32 bit C compiler)
Microsoft Corporation Redmond, WA (800) 426-9400 or (206) 882-8080	MS-DOS Windows and Windows 95 FoxPro Microsoft SQL Server FoxPro Connectivity Kit
Microway Inc (508) 746-7341	NDP CIC++ (32 bit C compiler) NDP FORTRAN (32 bit Fortran compiler)
MVS Solutions, Inc. 200-D Konrad Crescent Markham, ON Canada L3R8T9 (905) 940-9404	Job Classing Services Job Setup Services TM/Job Binding Services TM/Dataset Contention Services TM/Robotic Setup Services
Neon Systems Incorporated (800) 505-6366	Enterprise Direct (LAN-based DBMS access) Shadow Direct (high-speed ODBC to many RDBMS)
Netron Corporation (416) 636-8333	Netron/Cap (Case Cobol tool for CA-Datacom, CA-IDMS, CA-VAX/DB, Rdb, CA-Ingres, Sybase, VAX DBMS, HP Allbase/SQL, Image, DB2, DB2/2, IMS, SQL/DS, Informix and Oracle)
Network Telemetrics, Inc. 27001 Agroura Rd., Suite 280 Calabasis Hills, CA 91301-5339 (818) 878-7300	ProView (SNA/LAN Tuning)
Objectivity Incorporated 800 El Camino Real Menlo Park, CA 94025 (415) 688-8000	Objectivity/DB

Vendors:	Products:
Opus Software GmbH, Switzerland Im Kratten 32 8623 Wetzikon 01 930 76 36	Opus DirectAccess RDD for Delphi-to- MS Access
On-Line Resources Inc. 20540 E. Arrow Highway, Suite N2 Covina, CA 91724 (818) 332-8879	FAST GET is a mouse driven menu for CA- Clipper
OOPSOFT INC (888) OOPSOFT	Object Express (OOPS)
OpenLink Software, Inc. 10 Burlington Mall Rd. Suite 265 Burlington, MA 01803 (617) 273-0900	OpenLink High Performance ODBC Driver
OpenTech (214) 776-0771	Shrink—stack, compress and recycle datasets to reclaim tapes
Oracle Corporation (415) 506-4806	Oracle7 (for OS/2, UNIX, VMS, MVS, VM and others) Oracle CASE (with several CASE tools)
Peregrine Systems, Inc. 1959 Palomar Oaks Way, Carlsbad, CA 92009 (619) 431-2400	Hiperstation
Pervasive Software, Inc. formerly Btrieve Technologies (512) 794-1719 (800) BTRIEVE	Btrieve, Btrieve 6 Scalable SQL Client Server in a Box
Performance Awareness Corporation Raleigh, NC	Pre-Vue-X is an X-Windows system performance measurement tool
Planning Sciences, Inc. 26 West Dry Creek Circle Suite 250 Denver, CO 80120 (303) 794-8701	Gentia, GentiaDB
Platinum Technolody, Inc. USA or Canada (800) 442-6861	Platinum Catalog Facility (PCF) Platinum Relational Catalog Query (RC/QUERY) Platinum Relational Catalog Migrator (RC/MIGRATOR) Platinum Relational Catalog Update (RC/UPDATE) Platinum Relational Catalog Secure (RC/SECURE) Platinum Compare Facility Platinum Database Analyzer (PDA) Platinum Plan Analyzer (PPA) Platinum SQL-Ease, SeQueL to Platinum Platinum Recovery Analyzer

Vendors:	Products:
	Platinum Package/It
	Platinum Pipeline (PIP)
	Platinum Utilities (PUT)
	Platinum Quick Copy
	Platinum Data Compressor
	Platinum Rapid Reorg
	Platinum Fast Load, Platinum Fast Unload
	Platinum Tools for Windows NT
	Platinum Fast Index
	Platinum Fast Recover
	Platinum Guide/Online (PG/O)
	Platinum Compile/QMF
	Platinum Governor Facility
	Platinum Integrator
	Platinum Batch Processor (PBP)
	Platinum DB-Vision—monitor Oracle performance
	Platinum Data Transport move data (IMS or VSAM to DB2) and sequential files to SQL Server, Sybase, Oracle, DB2/2
Popkin Software and Systems (212) 571-3434	System Architect (Case design for DB2, Informix, Oracle, CA-Ingres, DB2/400, Progress, Xbase, Interbase, Microsoft SQL Server or Sybase)
Precise Software Solutions Inc. 50 Braintree Hill Office Park, Suite 110 Braintree, MA 02184 (617) 380-3300	Precise/SQL Oracle Tuning Monitor
Prince Software Products 900D Lake St. Ramsey, NJ 07446 (201) 934-0022	MHtran-2/MVS, (OS/VS Cobol to VS Cobol II conversion) MHtran-2/VSE, for VSE Translate/RW/MVS (OS/VS Cobol Report Writer conversion to VS Cobol II) Translate/RW/VSE for VSE Conversion Services for Cobol
Programart Corporation University Place 124 Mount Auburn Street Cambridge, MA 02138-9536 (617) 661-3020	STROBE APMPower
Programmer's Warehouse: Reseller 8283 N. Hayden Road Suite 195 Scottsdale, AZ 85258 (602) 443-0580	Bandit (report writer for CA-Clipper)
Q+E Software (800) 876-3101	MultiLink/VE
QDB Solutions (617) 577-9206	QDB/Analyzer (Xbase data metrics)
QUALITAS	386MAX

Vendors:	Products:
Quark Research Corporation 234 Kimberly Rd. Newington, CT 06111 (203) 666-3870	PDQ XBASE is a high performance SQL engine using 32 bit processing
Quarterdeck (800) 683-6696	WinProbe 95 system performance and resource fragmentation
Quintessential Solutions Inc (619) 280-1628	Network Performance Analyze (NPA) for WANs
Rational 2800 San Tomas Expressway Santa Clara, CA 95051-0951 (408) 496-3600	Object Transition by Design
Ravel Software, Inc. 2674 N. First St, #200 San Jose, CA 95134 (408) 955-0244	Migration 2000—upsize from Gupta SQLBase, Sybase, FoxPro, Foxbase, BTRIEVE, CA-Clipper, etc. to Oracle
RDS (800) 841-3127 or (717) 763-9510	SMF/Xpress (DB2 performance monitor) SQL/Xpress (Prototype SQL queries for performance) Vista Performance Workbench (VPW)
Recital Corporation Danvers, MA	Visual Recital is an open systems product with compatability to xBase, Oracle, Ingres, Sybase, Informix and DB2/6000
Relational Architects International 33 Newark Street Hoboken, NJ 07030 (201) 420-0400	Smart/Restart for DB2, Smart/CAF, Smart/QBF Smart/Monitor for DB2 Thread/STOPPER for DB2 Thread/SENTRY for DB2
Responsive Systems (908) 972-9416	Scalpel for DB2 (buffer pool sizing and analysis) Buffer Pool Tool for DB2 buffer tuning Scalpel/XPERT form MXG and SMF DASD Performance Analyzer Coupling Facility Sizing Module
Revelation Technologies (800) 262-4747 or (203) 973-1000	DB2, Netware SQL SQL Server Bonds
Rochester Software Connection Incorporated (507) 288-5922	ShowCase ShowCase Gateway WindowLink
Rocket Software (508) 875-4321	Rocket Compiler (for DB2 QMF conversion)
SAS Institute, Inc. SAS Circle, Box 8000 Cary, NC 27512-8000	SAS SAS/DB2 SAS/SQL-DS "SAS Programming Tips, A Guide to Efficient Processing" ISBN-1-55544-431-8
SDP Technologies, Inc. (708) 947-4250	S-Designor

Vendors:	Products:
Sequiter Software, Inc. (403) 437-2400	CodeBase 6—access dBase IV or FoxPro RDD speeds access and supports Client/Server
SMART Corporation 1-415-988-8996	SMART DB workbench for transitioning from legacy databases to Oracle
Softbase Systems, Inc. 1-800-669-7076	DGF (Data Generation Facility) for DB2
Softech (316) 729-9315	DBFtrieve—get to Btrieve from CA-Clipper, FoxPro and dBase for Windows
Softlanding (604) 360-0188	UNIX Base Linux 17 (vendor)
Software Diversified Services 5155 East River Road, Suite 411 Minneapolis, MN 55421-9927 (512) 571-9000 or (800) 443-6183	VSAM Express SuperTools Instant Cobol II (for OS/VS Cobol to VS Cobol conversion)
Software Engineering of America, Inc. 2001 Marcus Ave. Lake Success, New York 11042 (516) 328-7000 (800) 272-7322	PDSFAST FASTGENR (IEBGENER replacement)
Software Publishing Corporation 3165 Kifer Rd. Santa Clara, CA 95056 (408) 450-7314	Superbase V2.0 (Super Basic Language access to Xbase)
Software Pursuits 1420 Harbor Bay Parkway Suite 200 Alameda, CA 94501 (510) 769-4900 (800) 367-4823	SPI/Cache (moves data to memory in VM systems)
Softworks (800) 727-4422 or (301) 856-1892	Capacity Plus for DB2
SQLlBench 770-9533	SQLBench Performance Evaluation for INFORMIX, Oracle, Sybase, DB2 and NT SQL Server
Star Quest (800) 763-0050	StarSQL Pro ODBC-to-DRDA driver
Succinct Software (713) 893-8780	Flex DASD
SuccessWare International 27349 Jefferson Avenue, Suite 110 Temecula, CA 92590 (909) 699-9657	HiPer SIx (Rushmore Search Indexing RDD for CA-Clipper) SIx Driver v3.0—speedy Xbase RDD APOLLO for Delphi—Speedy Xbase RDD Mach SIx
Sybase, Inc. 1-800-8-SYBASE PowerSoft Products Division 1-800-937-7693 or 1-800-925-0072	Sybase SQL Server, SQL Toolset, SQL Anywhere, Sybase Replicator Server, Replication Agents for Oracle and DB2 (the Watcom products), PowerBuilder, (Expressway 1-103), Sybase IQ

Vendors:	Products:
Sylvain Faust, Inc. 880 boul de la Carriere Suite 130 Hull, Quebec Canada J8Y 6T5	SQL-Programmer 2.0—programmer productivity for Sybase, Oracle and Microsoft SQL Server
Symantec Corporation 175 West Broadway Eugene, OR 97401 (800) 441-7234	dbANYWHERE (superior 3-tier client/server solution)
Syncsort, Inc. 50 Tice Boulevard Woodcliff Lake, NJ 07675 (201) 930-8200	Syncsort (for MVS and UNIX) Syncgenr
SysData Int'l (800) 937-4734 or (201) 795-9400	DL/2 IMS to DB2 Transparency Quickstart-batch appl checkpoint restart and automatically recovers from deadlocks and abends
TechnoSolutions (360) 260-9710	SQL Navigator for Oracle
The Database Solutions Company (800) 933-7668	DBTune for Oracle—tunes by optimizing the data structure while leaving the logical structure unchanged
Tone Software Corporation (800) 833-8663 or (714) 991-9460	DCC-Compact (for DB2 table compression)
Transarc Corporation The Gulf Tower 707 Grant Street Pittsburg, PA 15219 (412) 338-4400	Distributed Computing Environment (DCE) open-systems Encina-Distributed application development and deployment AFS&DFS file systems for scalability
Trilogy Technology Intl. (800) 585-8668	OpenPath RDA/ODBC connectivity to Sybase, Oracle and Informix etc.
Trinzic Corporation 101 University Avenue Palo Alto, CA 94301 (617) 891-6500	Trinzic InfoHub (in conjunction with Sybase OmniSQL will allow users to access CA-IDMS, IMS, VSAM, ADABAS and DB2 databases using Sybase front-end)
UES Inc. Dayton, OH	KI Shell
Unelko Corporation (800) 542-6424 or (602) 991-727	Bridgit
Unikix Technologies Billerica, MA	Kix Scan Processing rates for UNIX and potential bottlenecks
Vegasoft. Inc.	IDMS/Gateway IDMS/DB2 ADS/DB2 DB-CICSLINK

Vendors:	Products:
Make Requests for Cogito and Vegasoft products from TACT (The A Consulting Team, Inc.) 200 Park Avenue South Suite 901 New York, NY 10003 (212) 979-8228 (800) 433-TACT	
In Brazil contact Tecom Sistema Ltda RJ—Rua Jeronimo de Lecmos 162 CEP 20560, Brasilia 011-55-21-577-1322	
In Finland contact Vegasoft Oy, P.O. Box 45 00921 Helsinki, Finland 011-358-0-349-2468	
In France contact Relasoft S.A, "Le Sextant" 2 Rue Des Yoyageurs, B.P. 8347, 95804 Cergy—Pontoise Cedex France 011-33-1-30.32.20.22	
In Germany contact Dr. Holtmann + Partner GMBH Tibarg 32C 22459 Hamburg, Deutschland 011-49-40-25-18-139	
In Holland contact Lync Products B.V. Postbus 3003 2280 MG Rijswijk, Holland 011-31-(0)70-398 88 39	
Veritas Software (415) 335-8000	SmartSync (recovery accelerator for Oracle)
Viasoft (800) 525-7775 or (602) 952-0050	ESW Reengineering (Cobol code re-engineering)
ViewStar Corp. Alameda, CA	Workflow Toolkit
WebinTool Jian Hu Roslin Institute (Edinburgh) Roslin, Midlothian EH259PS UK	General Purpose WWW-to-SQL database interface
Workgroup Systems Edmond, OK	a la mode Workgroup
XDB Systems Incorporated (800) 488-4948	XDB-Server (for OX/2) XDB-Link

CA-IDMS DML Command CPU Benchmark Program

```
ID DIVISION.
        PROGRAM-ID.      BENCHMRK.
        AUTHOR.          JEFF DUNHAM
        DATE-WRITTEN.    11/01/95.


        ****************************************************************
        *     PROGRAM TITLE: GATHER DML COMMAND CPU BENCHMARKS
        *             DESC: PERFORM SELECTED CALLS IN IDMS DC,
        *                   COLLECT STATS AND OUTPUT TO A DC REPORT
        *                   THIS ROUTINE MUST DO 100 CALLS OF A
        *                   GIVEN TYPE TO GET ADEQUATE BENCHMARKS
        *                   STATISTICS. YOU WILL NEED TO DIVIDE BY
        *                   100 TO SEE REAL TIME IN 10/THOUSANDTHS.
        *                   A FEW CALLS HAVE ADDITIONAL CALC CALL
        *                   OVERHEAD WHICH NEEDS TO BE REMOVED.
        *                   INCREASE THE NUMBER OF CALLS AND SIZE
        *                   OF COUNTERS FOR BETTER RESOLUTION.


        ****************************************************************
        ENVIRONMENT DIVISION.
        INPUT-OUTPUT SECTION.
        IDMS-CONTROL SECTION.
        PROTOCOL.  MODE IS IDMS-DC
```

```
                        IDMS-RECORDS MANUAL INCREMENTED BY 05.
        DATA DIVISION.
        SCHEMA SECTION.
        DB WORLDSUB WITHIN WORLDCHM.
        *****************************
        WORKING-STORAGE SECTION.
        *****************************
        01  FILLER      PIC X(14)      VALUE 'SUBSCHEMA-CNTL'.
        01  COPY IDMS SUBSCHEMA-CTRL.
        01  FILLER      PIC X(16)      VALUE 'SUBSCHEMA-SSNAME'.
        COPY IDMS SUBSCHEMA-NAMES.
        01  FILLER      PIC X(16)      VALUE 'CUSTOMER'.
        COPY IDMS RECORD CUSTOMER.
        01  FILLER      PIC X(16)      VALUE 'INVOICE'.
        COPY IDMS RECORD INVOICE.
        01  FILLER      PIC X(16)      VALUE 'BILLING'.
        COPY IDMS RECORD BILLING.
        01  FILLER      PIC X(16)      VALUE 'EMPLOYEE'.
        COPY IDMS RECORD EMPLOYEE.
        01  FILLER      PIC X(16)      VALUE 'SECURITY'.
        COPY IDMS RECORD SECURITY.
        01  FILLER      PIC X(16)      VALUE 'BILLING-OOAK'.
        COPY IDMS RECORD BILLING-OOAK.
        01  FILLER      PIC X(16)      VALUE 'EMPLOYEE-OOAK'.
        COPY IDMS RECORD EMPLOYEE-OOAK.
        01  FILLER      PIC X(16)      VALUE 'SECURITY-OOAK'.
        COPY IDMS RECORD SECURITY-OOAK.
        01  FILLER      PIC X(16)      VALUE 'ZIPCODE-OOAK'.
        COPY IDMS RECORD ZIPCODE-OOAK.
        01  FILLER      PIC X(16)      VALUE 'SALES-OOAK'.
        COPY IDMS RECORD SALES-OOAK.
        01  FILLER      PIC X(16)      VALUE 'PROJECT-OOAK'.
        COPY IDMS RECORD PROJECT-OOAK.
        01  FILLER      PIC X(16)      VALUE 'DEPARTMENT-OOAK'.
        COPY IDMS RECORD DEPARTMENT-OOAK.
        01  FILLER      PIC X(16)      VALUE 'COUNTRY-OOAK'.
        COPY IDMS RECORD COUNTRY-OOAK.
        01  FILLER      PIC X(16)      VALUE 'LANGUAGE-OOAK'.
        COPY IDMS RECORD LANGUAGE-OOAK.
        01  FILLER      PIC X(16)      VALUE 'PROJECT        '.
        COPY IDMS RECORD PROJECT.
        01  FILLER      PIC X(16)      VALUE 'DEPARTMENT        '.
```

```
COPY IDMS RECORD DEPARTMENT.
01  FILLER        PIC X(16)      VALUE 'COUNTRY     '.
COPY IDMS RECORD COUNTRY.
01  FILLER        PIC X(16)      VALUE 'LANGUAGE      '.
COPY IDMS RECORD LANGUAGE.
01  FILLER        PIC X(16)      VALUE 'HISTORY      '.
COPY IDMS RECORD HISTORY.
01  FILLER        PIC X(16)      VALUE 'ORGANIZATION      '.
COPY IDMS RECORD ORGANIZATION.
01  FILLER        PIC X(16)      VALUE 'ZIPCODE      '.
COPY IDMS RECORD ZIPCODE.
01  FILLER        PIC X(16)      VALUE 'MAILCODE      '.
COPY IDMS RECORD MAILCODE.
01  LOOP-CNT       PIC S9(8) COMP-3.
01  REC-ID.
    05 REC-LIT      PIC X(4) VALUE 'TEMP'.
    05 REC-NUM      PIC 9(4).
01  WORK1-CPU       PIC S9(10) COMP-3.
01  WORK2-CPU       PIC S9(10) COMP-3.
01  STATISTICS-BLOCK.
    05 USER-ID      PIC X(32).
    05 LTERM-ID     PIC X(8).
    05 PROG-CALL    PIC S9(8) COMP.
    05 PROG-LOAD    PIC S9(8) COMP.
    05 TERM-READ    PIC S9(8) COMP.
    05 TERM-WRITE   PIC S9(8) COMP.
    05 TERM-ERROR   PIC S9(8) COMP.
    05 STORAGE-GET  PIC S9(8) COMP.
    05 SCRATCH-GET  PIC S9(8) COMP.
    05 SCRATCH-PUT  PIC S9(8) COMP.
    05 SCRATCH-DEL  PIC S9(8) COMP.
    05 QUEUE-GET    PIC S9(8) COMP.
    05 QUEUE-PUT    PIC S9(8) COMP.
    05 QUEUE-DEL    PIC S9(8) COMP.
    05 GET-TIME     PIC S9(8) COMP.
    05 SET-TIME     PIC S9(8) COMP.
    05 DB-CALLS     PIC S9(8) COMP.
    05 MAX-STACK    PIC S9(8) COMP.
    05 USER-TIME    PIC S9(8) COMP.
    05 SYS-TIME     PIC S9(8) COMP.
    05 WAIT-TIME    PIC S9(8) COMP.
    05 PAGES-READ   PIC S9(8) COMP.
```

```
        05  PAGES-WRIT      PIC S9(8) COMP.
        05  PAGES-REQ       PIC S9(8) COMP.
        05  CALC-NO         PIC S9(8) COMP.
        05  CALC-OF         PIC S9(8) COMP.
        05  VIA-NO          PIC S9(8) COMP.
        05  VIA-OF          PIC S9(8) COMP.
        05  RECS-REQ        PIC S9(8) COMP.
        05  RECS-CURR       PIC S9(8) COMP.
        05  FILLER          PIC X(4).
        05  FRAG-STORED     PIC S9(8) COMP.
        05  RECS-RELO       PIC S9(8) COMP.
        05  TOT-LOCKS       PIC S9(8) COMP.
        05  SEL-LOCKS       PIC S9(8) COMP.
        05  UPD-LOCKS       PIC S9(8) COMP.
        05  STG-HI-MARK     PIC S9(8) COMP.
        05  FREESTG-REQ     PIC S9(8) COMP.
        05  SYS-SERV        PIC S9(8) COMP.
        05  RESERVED        PIC X(40).
        05  USER-SUPP-ID    PIC X(8).
        05  BIND-DATE       PIC S9(7) COMP-3.
        05  BIND-TIME       PIC S9(8) COMP.
        05  TRANSTAT-FLGS   PIC S9(8) COMP.
    01  WORK-DBKEY          PIC S9(8) COMP.
    01  WORK-DATE           PIC X(8).
    01  WORK-TIME           PIC X(8).
    01  WORK-USER           PIC X(8).
    01  WORK-TASK           PIC X(8).
    01  REPORT-DATA-80.
        05  CALL-TYPE       PIC X(24).
        05  LITERAL-2       PIC X(14) VALUE '   TOTAL CPU: '.
        05  S-CPU-TOTAL     PIC 9(8).
        05  LITERAL-3       PIC X(14) VALUE 'ERROR STATUS: '.
        05  STATCODE        PIC X(14).
        05  FILLRD          PIC X(4).
    *****************************
    LINKAGE SECTION.
    *****************************
    * WE MAKE THE ASSUMPTION THAT IDMS-STATUS IS A FOREGONE        *
OVERHEAD
    * ON ALL DATABASE CALLS WHICH CANNOT BE AVOIDED.
    *****************************
    PROCEDURE DIVISION.
    *****************************
```

```
 1000-MAINLINE.
       BIND TRANSACTION STATISTICS
           ON ANY-STATUS NEXT SENTENCE.
 * BIND RUN-UNIT
       PERFORM 2000-STATISTICS THRU 2000-EXIT.
       MOVE 'BIND RUN-UNIT' TO CALL-TYPE.
       PERFORM 1001-BRU         THRU 1001-EXIT
          VARYING LOOP-CNT FROM 1 BY 1
          UNTIL LOOP-CNT EQUAL 100.
       PERFORM 3000-STATISTICS THRU 3000-EXIT.
       BIND RUN-UNIT DBNAME 'WORLDDB '.
 * BIND RECORD
       PERFORM 2000-STATISTICS THRU 2000-EXIT.
       MOVE 'BIND RECORD' TO CALL-TYPE.
       PERFORM 1002-BR          THRU 1002-EXIT
          VARYING LOOP-CNT FROM 1 BY 1
          UNTIL LOOP-CNT EQUAL 4.
       PERFORM 3000-STATISTICS THRU 3000-EXIT.
 * READY AREA
       PERFORM 2000-STATISTICS THRU 2000-EXIT.
       MOVE 'READY AREA ' TO CALL-TYPE.
       PERFORM 1003-RA          THRU 1003-EXIT.
       PERFORM 3000-STATISTICS THRU 3000-EXIT.
 * OBTAIN CALC
       MOVE 'MAIN' TO RSPON-ID OF CUSTOMER
       PERFORM 2000-STATISTICS THRU 2000-EXIT.
       MOVE 'OBTAIN CALC' TO CALL-TYPE.
       PERFORM 1004-OC          THRU 1004-EXIT
          VARYING LOOP-CNT FROM 1 BY 1
          UNTIL LOOP-CNT EQUAL 10.
       PERFORM 3000-STATISTICS THRU 3000-EXIT.
 * GET RECORD
       MOVE 'MAIN' TO RSPON-ID OF CUSTOMER
       OBTAIN CALC CUSTOMER.
       PERFORM 2000-STATISTICS THRU 2000-EXIT.
       MOVE 'GET RECORD' TO CALL-TYPE.
       PERFORM 1005-GR          THRU 1005-EXIT
          VARYING LOOP-CNT FROM 1 BY 1
          UNTIL LOOP-CNT EQUAL 10.
       PERFORM 3000-STATISTICS THRU 3000-EXIT.
 * FIND CALC
```

```
                 PERFORM 2000-STATISTICS THRU 2000-EXIT.
                 MOVE 'FIND CALC' TO CALL-TYPE.
                 PERFORM 1006-FC         THRU 1006-EXIT
                    VARYING LOOP-CNT FROM 1 BY 1
                    UNTIL LOOP-CNT EQUAL 10.
                 PERFORM 3000-STATISTICS THRU 3000-EXIT.
          * OBTAIN FIRST IN SET
                 MOVE 'ORDR' TO RSPON-ID OF BILLING
                 OBTAIN CALC BILLING
                 OBTAIN FIRST EMPLOYEE-OOAK WITHIN BILLING-AREA
                    ON ANY-STATUS NEXT SENTENCE.
                 OBTAIN FIRST SECURITY-OOAK WITHIN BILLING-AREA
                    ON ANY-STATUS NEXT SENTENCE.
                 OBTAIN FIRST ZIPCODE-OOAK WITHIN BILLING-AREA
                    ON ANY-STATUS NEXT SENTENCE.
                 OBTAIN FIRST BILLING-OOAK WITHIN BILLING-AREA
                    ON ANY-STATUS NEXT SENTENCE.
                 OBTAIN FIRST SALES-OOAK WITHIN WORLD-AREA
                    ON ANY-STATUS NEXT SENTENCE.
                 OBTAIN FIRST PROJECT-OOAK WITHIN BILLING-AREA
                    ON ANY-STATUS NEXT SENTENCE.
                 OBTAIN FIRST DEPARTMENT-OOAK WITHIN WORLD-AREA
                    ON ANY-STATUS NEXT SENTENCE.
                 OBTAIN FIRST COUNTRY-OOAK WITHIN WORLD-AREA
                    ON ANY-STATUS NEXT SENTENCE.
                 OBTAIN FIRST LANGUAGE-OOAK WITHIN WORLD-AREA
                    ON ANY-STATUS NEXT SENTENCE.
                 PERFORM 2000-STATISTICS THRU 2000-EXIT.
                 MOVE 'OBTAIN FIRST IN SET' TO CALL-TYPE.
                 PERFORM 1007-OFIS       THRU 1007-EXIT
                    VARYING LOOP-CNT FROM 1 BY 1
                    UNTIL LOOP-CNT EQUAL 10.
                 PERFORM 3000-STATISTICS THRU 3000-EXIT.
          * OBTAIN LAST IN SET
                 PERFORM 2000-STATISTICS THRU 2000-EXIT.
                 MOVE 'OBTAIN LAST IN SET' TO CALL-TYPE.
                 PERFORM 1008-OLIS       THRU 1008-EXIT
                    VARYING LOOP-CNT FROM 1 BY 1
                    UNTIL LOOP-CNT EQUAL 10.
                 PERFORM 3000-STATISTICS THRU 3000-EXIT.
          * FIND LAST IN SET
                 PERFORM 2000-STATISTICS THRU 2000-EXIT.
```

```
        MOVE 'FIND LAST IN SET' TO CALL-TYPE.
        PERFORM 1009-FLIS        THRU 1009-EXIT
           VARYING LOOP-CNT FROM 1 BY 1
           UNTIL LOOP-CNT EQUAL 10.
        PERFORM 3000-STATISTICS THRU 3000-EXIT.
* FIND FIRST IN SET
        PERFORM 2000-STATISTICS THRU 2000-EXIT.
        MOVE 'FIND FIRST IN SET' TO CALL-TYPE.
        PERFORM 1010-FFIS        THRU 1010-EXIT
           VARYING LOOP-CNT FROM 1 BY 1
           UNTIL LOOP-CNT EQUAL 10.
        PERFORM 3000-STATISTICS THRU 3000-EXIT.
* OBTAIN NEXT IN SET
        OBTAIN FIRST EMPLOYEE-OOAK WITHIN BILLING-AREA
           ON ANY-STATUS NEXT SENTENCE.
        PERFORM 2000-STATISTICS THRU 2000-EXIT.
        MOVE 'OBTAIN NEXT IN SET' TO CALL-TYPE.
        PERFORM 1011-ONIS        THRU 1011-EXIT
           VARYING LOOP-CNT FROM 1 BY 1
           UNTIL LOOP-CNT EQUAL 100.
        PERFORM 3000-STATISTICS THRU 3000-EXIT.
* OBTAIN PRIOR IN SET
        PERFORM 2000-STATISTICS THRU 2000-EXIT.
        MOVE 'OBTAIN PRIOR IN SET' TO CALL-TYPE.
        PERFORM 1012-OPIS        THRU 1012-EXIT
           VARYING LOOP-CNT FROM 1 BY 1
           UNTIL LOOP-CNT EQUAL 100.
        PERFORM 3000-STATISTICS THRU 3000-EXIT.
* FIND NEXT IN SET
        PERFORM 2000-STATISTICS THRU 2000-EXIT.
        MOVE 'FIND NEXT IN SET' TO CALL-TYPE.
        PERFORM 1013-FNIS        THRU 1013-EXIT
           VARYING LOOP-CNT FROM 1 BY 1
           UNTIL LOOP-CNT EQUAL 100.
        PERFORM 3000-STATISTICS THRU 3000-EXIT.
* FIND PRIOR IN SET
        PERFORM 2000-STATISTICS THRU 2000-EXIT.
        MOVE 'FIND PRIOR IN SET' TO CALL-TYPE.
        PERFORM 1014-FPIS        THRU 1014-EXIT
           VARYING LOOP-CNT FROM 1 BY 1
           UNTIL LOOP-CNT EQUAL 100.
        PERFORM 3000-STATISTICS THRU 3000-EXIT.
```

```
* OBTAIN CURRENT RECORD TYPE
      PERFORM 2000-STATISTICS THRU 2000-EXIT.
      MOVE 'OBTAIN CURRENT RECORD' TO CALL-TYPE.
      PERFORM 1015-OC         THRU 1015-EXIT
          VARYING LOOP-CNT FROM 1 BY 1
          UNTIL LOOP-CNT EQUAL 10.
      PERFORM 3000-STATISTICS THRU 3000-EXIT.
* FIND CURRENT RECORD
      PERFORM 2000-STATISTICS THRU 2000-EXIT.
      MOVE 'FIND CURRENT RECORD' TO CALL-TYPE.
      PERFORM 1016-FC         THRU 1016-EXIT
          VARYING LOOP-CNT FROM 1 BY 1
          UNTIL LOOP-CNT EQUAL 10.
      PERFORM 3000-STATISTICS THRU 3000-EXIT.
* OBTAIN CURRENT IN SET
      PERFORM 2000-STATISTICS THRU 2000-EXIT.
      MOVE 'OBTAIN CURRENT IN SET' TO CALL-TYPE.
      PERFORM 1017-OCIS        THRU 1017-EXIT
          VARYING LOOP-CNT FROM 1 BY 1
          UNTIL LOOP-CNT EQUAL 10.
      PERFORM 3000-STATISTICS THRU 3000-EXIT.
* FIND CURRENT IN SET
      PERFORM 2000-STATISTICS THRU 2000-EXIT.
      MOVE 'FIND CURRENT IN SET' TO CALL-TYPE.
      PERFORM 1018-FCIS        THRU 1018-EXIT
          VARYING LOOP-CNT FROM 1 BY 1
          UNTIL LOOP-CNT EQUAL 10.
      PERFORM 3000-STATISTICS THRU 3000-EXIT.
* OBTAIN CURRENT IN AREA
      PERFORM 2000-STATISTICS THRU 2000-EXIT.
      MOVE 'OBTAIN CURRENT IN AREA' TO CALL-TYPE.
      PERFORM 1019-OCIA        THRU 1019-EXIT
          VARYING LOOP-CNT FROM 1 BY 1
          UNTIL LOOP-CNT EQUAL 50.
      PERFORM 3000-STATISTICS THRU 3000-EXIT.
* FIND CURRENT IN AREA
      PERFORM 2000-STATISTICS THRU 2000-EXIT.
      MOVE 'FIND CURRENT IN AREA' TO CALL-TYPE.
      PERFORM 1020-FCIA        THRU 1020-EXIT
          VARYING LOOP-CNT FROM 1 BY 1
          UNTIL LOOP-CNT EQUAL 50.
      PERFORM 3000-STATISTICS THRU 3000-EXIT.
```

```
* OBTAIN FIRST IN NDX SET
      PERFORM 2000-STATISTICS THRU 2000-EXIT.
      MOVE 'OBTAIN FIRST IN NDX' TO CALL-TYPE.
      PERFORM 1021-OFIN         THRU 1021-EXIT
         VARYING LOOP-CNT FROM 1 BY 1
         UNTIL LOOP-CNT EQUAL 25.
      PERFORM 3000-STATISTICS THRU 3000-EXIT.
* OBTAIN NEXT IN NDX SET
      PERFORM 2000-STATISTICS THRU 2000-EXIT.
      MOVE 'OBTAIN NEXT IN NDX' TO CALL-TYPE.
      PERFORM 1022-FFIN         THRU 1022-EXIT
         VARYING LOOP-CNT FROM 1 BY 1
         UNTIL LOOP-CNT EQUAL 25.
      PERFORM 3000-STATISTICS THRU 3000-EXIT.
* OBTAIN LAST IN NDX SET
      PERFORM 2000-STATISTICS THRU 2000-EXIT.
      MOVE 'OBTAIN LAST IN NDX' TO CALL-TYPE.
      PERFORM 1023-OLIN         THRU 1023-EXIT
         VARYING LOOP-CNT FROM 1 BY 1
         UNTIL LOOP-CNT EQUAL 25.
      PERFORM 3000-STATISTICS THRU 3000-EXIT.
* FIND FIRST IN NDX SET
      PERFORM 2000-STATISTICS THRU 2000-EXIT.
      MOVE 'FIND FIRST IN NDX' TO CALL-TYPE.
      PERFORM 1024-FFIN        THRU 1024-EXIT
         VARYING LOOP-CNT FROM 1 BY 1
         UNTIL LOOP-CNT EQUAL 25.
      PERFORM 3000-STATISTICS THRU 3000-EXIT.
* FIND NEXT IN NDX SET
      PERFORM 2000-STATISTICS THRU 2000-EXIT.
      MOVE 'FIND NEXT IN NDX' TO CALL-TYPE.
      PERFORM 1025-FNIN         THRU 1025-EXIT
         VARYING LOOP-CNT FROM 1 BY 1
         UNTIL LOOP-CNT EQUAL 25.
      PERFORM IDMS-STATUS.
      PERFORM 3000-STATISTICS THRU 3000-EXIT.
* FIND LAST IN NDX SET
      PERFORM 2000-STATISTICS THRU 2000-EXIT.
      MOVE 'FIND LAST IN NDX' TO CALL-TYPE.
      PERFORM 1026-FLIN        THRU 1026-EXIT
         VARYING LOOP-CNT FROM 1 BY 1
         UNTIL LOOP-CNT EQUAL 25.
```

```
            PERFORM 3000-STATISTICS THRU 3000-EXIT.
* IF SET EMPTY
            PERFORM 2000-STATISTICS THRU 2000-EXIT.
            MOVE 'IF SET EMPTY' TO CALL-TYPE.
            PERFORM 1027-ISE        THRU 1027-EXIT
                VARYING LOOP-CNT FROM 1 BY 1
                UNTIL LOOP-CNT EQUAL 10.
            PERFORM 3000-STATISTICS THRU 3000-EXIT.
* STORE RECORD
            MOVE 'DOE' TO EMP-ID OF EMPLOYEE.
            OBTAIN CALC EMPLOYEE
            MOVE 'STORE RECORD' TO CALL-TYPE.
            PERFORM 2000-STATISTICS THRU 2000-EXIT.
            PERFORM 1028-SR         THRU 1028-EXIT
                VARYING LOOP-CNT FROM 1 BY 1
                UNTIL LOOP-CNT EQUAL 100.
            PERFORM 3000-STATISTICS THRU 3000-EXIT.
* DISCONNECT RECORD
            PERFORM 2000-STATISTICS THRU 2000-EXIT.
            MOVE 'DISCONNECT REC (+ CALC)' TO CALL-TYPE.
            PERFORM 1030-DR         THRU 1030-EXIT
                VARYING LOOP-CNT FROM 1 BY 1
                UNTIL LOOP-CNT EQUAL 100.
            PERFORM 3000-STATISTICS THRU 3000-EXIT.
* CONNECT RECORD
            PERFORM 2000-STATISTICS THRU 2000-EXIT.
            MOVE 'CONNECT REC (+ CALC)' TO CALL-TYPE.
            PERFORM 1029-CR         THRU 1029-EXIT
                VARYING LOOP-CNT FROM 1 BY 1
                UNTIL LOOP-CNT EQUAL 100.
            PERFORM 3000-STATISTICS THRU 3000-EXIT.
* MODIFY RECORD
            MOVE 'DOE' TO EMP-ID OF EMPLOYEE.
            OBTAIN CALC EMPLOYEE
            PERFORM 2000-STATISTICS THRU 2000-EXIT.
            MOVE 'MODIFY RECORD' TO CALL-TYPE.
            PERFORM 1031-MR         THRU 1031-EXIT
                VARYING LOOP-CNT FROM 1 BY 1
                UNTIL LOOP-CNT EQUAL 100.
            PERFORM 3000-STATISTICS THRU 3000-EXIT.
* ERASE RECORD
            PERFORM 2000-STATISTICS THRU 2000-EXIT.
```

```
      MOVE 'ERASE REC (+ CALC)' TO CALL-TYPE.
      PERFORM 1032-ER           THRU 1032-EXIT
          VARYING LOOP-CNT FROM 1 BY 1
          UNTIL LOOP-CNT EQUAL 100.
      PERFORM 3000-STATISTICS THRU 3000-EXIT.
* OBTAIN OWNER IN SET
      PERFORM 2000-STATISTICS THRU 2000-EXIT.
      MOVE 'OBTAIN OWNER IN SET' TO CALL-TYPE.
      PERFORM 1033-OOIS         THRU 1033-EXIT
          VARYING LOOP-CNT FROM 1 BY 1
          UNTIL LOOP-CNT EQUAL 10.
      PERFORM 3000-STATISTICS THRU 3000-EXIT.
* FIND OWNER IN SET
      PERFORM 2000-STATISTICS THRU 2000-EXIT.
      MOVE 'FIND OWNER IN SET' TO CALL-TYPE.
      PERFORM 1034-FOIS         THRU 1034-EXIT
          VARYING LOOP-CNT FROM 1 BY 1
          UNTIL LOOP-CNT EQUAL 10.
      PERFORM 3000-STATISTICS THRU 3000-EXIT.
* ACCEPT SET DBKEY
      PERFORM 2000-STATISTICS THRU 2000-EXIT.
      MOVE 'ACCEPT SET DBKEY' TO CALL-TYPE.
      PERFORM 1035-ASK          THRU 1035-EXIT
          VARYING LOOP-CNT FROM 1 BY 1
          UNTIL LOOP-CNT EQUAL 10.
      PERFORM 3000-STATISTICS THRU 3000-EXIT.
* ACCEPT RECORD DBKEY
      PERFORM 2000-STATISTICS THRU 2000-EXIT.
      MOVE 'ACCEPT RECORD DBKEY' TO CALL-TYPE.
      PERFORM 1036-ARK          THRU 1036-EXIT
          VARYING LOOP-CNT FROM 1 BY 1
          UNTIL LOOP-CNT EQUAL 10.
      PERFORM 3000-STATISTICS THRU 3000-EXIT.
* ACCEPT SET NEXT DBKEY
      PERFORM 2000-STATISTICS THRU 2000-EXIT.
      MOVE 'ACCEPT SET NEXT DBKEY' TO CALL-TYPE.
      PERFORM 1037-ASNK         THRU 1037-EXIT
          VARYING LOOP-CNT FROM 1 BY 1
          UNTIL LOOP-CNT EQUAL 10.
      PERFORM 3000-STATISTICS THRU 3000-EXIT.
* COMMIT TEST
      PERFORM 2000-STATISTICS THRU 2000-EXIT.
```

```
              MOVE `COMMIT ` TO CALL-TYPE.
              PERFORM 1038-COMMIT      THRU 1038-EXIT
                  VARYING LOOP-CNT FROM 1 BY 1
                  UNTIL LOOP-CNT EQUAL 100.
              PERFORM 3000-STATISTICS THRU 3000-EXIT.
              FINISH.
              GOBACK.
          1000-EXIT.
              EXIT.


          1001-BRU.
              BIND RUN-UNIT DBNAME `WORLDDB `.
              FINISH.
          1001-EXIT.
              EXIT.


          1002-BR.
              BIND PROJECT
                  ON ANY-STATUS NEXT SENTENCE.
              BIND DEPARTMENT
                  ON ANY-STATUS NEXT SENTENCE.
              BIND COUNTRY
                  ON ANY-STATUS NEXT SENTENCE.
              BIND LANGUAGE
                  ON ANY-STATUS NEXT SENTENCE.
              BIND HISTORY
                  ON ANY-STATUS NEXT SENTENCE.
              BIND CUSTOMER
                  ON ANY-STATUS NEXT SENTENCE.
              BIND BILLING
                  ON ANY-STATUS NEXT SENTENCE.
              BIND INVOICE
                  ON ANY-STATUS NEXT SENTENCE.
              BIND EMPLOYEE
                  ON ANY-STATUS NEXT SENTENCE.
              BIND SECURITY
                  ON ANY-STATUS NEXT SENTENCE.
              BIND INVOICE
                  ON ANY-STATUS NEXT SENTENCE.
              BIND BILLING-OOAK
                  ON ANY-STATUS NEXT SENTENCE.
              BIND EMPLOYEE
```

```
          ON ANY-STATUS NEXT SENTENCE.
     BIND SECURITY
          ON ANY-STATUS NEXT SENTENCE.
     BIND ZIPCODE
          ON ANY-STATUS NEXT SENTENCE.
     BIND EMPLOYEE-OOAK
          ON ANY-STATUS NEXT SENTENCE.
     BIND SECURITY-OOAK
          ON ANY-STATUS NEXT SENTENCE.
     BIND ZIPCODE-OOAK
          ON ANY-STATUS NEXT SENTENCE.
     BIND DEPARTMENT-OOAK
          ON ANY-STATUS NEXT SENTENCE.
     BIND SALES-OOAK
          ON ANY-STATUS NEXT SENTENCE.
     BIND PROJECT-OOAK
          ON ANY-STATUS NEXT SENTENCE.
     BIND COUNTRY-OOAK
          ON ANY-STATUS NEXT SENTENCE.
     BIND LANGUAGE-OOAK
          ON ANY-STATUS NEXT SENTENCE.
     BIND ORGANIZATION
          ON ANY-STATUS NEXT SENTENCE.
     BIND MAILCODE
          ON ANY-STATUS NEXT SENTENCE.
 1002-EXIT.
     EXIT.


 1003-RA.
     READY WORLD-AREA            USAGE-MODE UPDATE.
     READY WORLD2-AREA           USAGE-MODE UPDATE.
     READY WORLD3-AREA           USAGE-MODE UPDATE.
     READY BILLING-AREA          USAGE-MODE UPDATE.
     READY ..........ETC         USAGE-MODE UPDATE.
 1003-EXIT.
     EXIT.


 1004-OC.
     MOVE 'DOE' TO EMP-ID OF EMPLOYEE.
     OBTAIN CALC EMPLOYEE .
     MOVE 'JOHNSON' TO EMP-ID OF EMPLOYEE.
     OBTAIN CALC EMPLOYEE .
```

```
        MOVE 'JONES' TO EMP-ID OF EMPLOYEE.
        OBTAIN CALC EMPLOYEE .
        MOVE 'DAVIDSON ' TO EMP-ID OF EMPLOYEE.
        OBTAIN CALC EMPLOYEE .
        MOVE 'COSTNER' TO EMP-ID OF EMPLOYEE.
        OBTAIN CALC EMPLOYEE .
        MOVE 'NESS' TO EMP-ID OF EMPLOYEE.
        OBTAIN CALC EMPLOYEE .
        MOVE 'ARMSTRONG' TO EMP-ID OF EMPLOYEE.
        OBTAIN CALC EMPLOYEE .
        MOVE 'COPPER' TO EMP-ID OF EMPLOYEE.
        OBTAIN CALC EMPLOYEE .
        MOVE 'BAKER' TO EMP-ID OF EMPLOYEE.
        OBTAIN CALC EMPLOYEE .
        MOVE 'LOVELACE' TO EMP-ID OF EMPLOYEE.
        OBTAIN CALC EMPLOYEE .
   1004-EXIT.
        EXIT.


   1005-GR.
        GET CUSTOMER .
        GET CUSTOMER .
        GET CUSTOMER .
        GET CUSTOMER .
        GET CUSTOMER .
        GET CUSTOMER .
        GET CUSTOMER .
        GET CUSTOMER .
        GET CUSTOMER .
        GET CUSTOMER .
   1005-EXIT.
        EXIT.


   1006-FC.
        MOVE 'DOE' TO EMP-ID OF EMPLOYEE.
        FIND CALC EMPLOYEE .
        MOVE 'JOHNSON' TO EMP-ID OF EMPLOYEE.
        FIND CALC EMPLOYEE .
        MOVE 'JONES' TO EMP-ID OF EMPLOYEE.
        FIND CALC EMPLOYEE .
        MOVE 'DAVIDSON ' TO EMP-ID OF EMPLOYEE.
        FIND CALC EMPLOYEE .
```

```
        MOVE 'COSTNER' TO EMP-ID OF EMPLOYEE.
        FIND CALC EMPLOYEE .
        MOVE 'NESS' TO EMP-ID OF EMPLOYEE.
        FIND CALC EMPLOYEE .
        MOVE 'ARMSTRONG' TO EMP-ID OF EMPLOYEE.
        FIND CALC EMPLOYEE .
        MOVE 'COPPER' TO EMP-ID OF EMPLOYEE.
        FIND CALC EMPLOYEE .
        MOVE 'BAKER' TO EMP-ID OF EMPLOYEE.
        FIND CALC EMPLOYEE .
        MOVE 'LOVELACE' TO EMP-ID OF EMPLOYEE.
        FIND CALC EMPLOYEE .
    1006-EXIT.
        EXIT.


    1007-OFIS.
        OBTAIN FIRST INVOICE WITHIN INV-SET
            ON ANY-STATUS NEXT SENTENCE.
        OBTAIN FIRST PROJECT WITHIN PROJ-SET
            ON ANY-STATUS NEXT SENTENCE.
        OBTAIN FIRST DEPARTMENT WITHIN DEPT-SET
            ON ANY-STATUS NEXT SENTENCE.
        OBTAIN FIRST COUNTRY WITHIN CTRY-SET
            ON ANY-STATUS NEXT SENTENCE.
        OBTAIN FIRST EMPLOYEE WITHIN EMPL-SET
            ON ANY-STATUS NEXT SENTENCE.
        OBTAIN FIRST SECURITY WITHIN SECU-SET
            ON ANY-STATUS NEXT SENTENCE.
        OBTAIN FIRST CUSTOMER WITHIN CUST-SET
            ON ANY-STATUS NEXT SENTENCE.
        OBTAIN FIRST LANGUAGE WITHIN LANG-SET
            ON ANY-STATUS NEXT SENTENCE.
        OBTAIN FIRST BILLING WITHIN BILL-SET
            ON ANY-STATUS NEXT SENTENCE.
        OBTAIN FIRST HISTORY WITHIN HIST-SET
            ON ANY-STATUS NEXT SENTENCE.
    1007-EXIT.
        EXIT.


    1008-OLIS.
        OBTAIN LAST INVOICE WITHIN INV-SET
            ON ANY-STATUS NEXT SENTENCE.
```

```
          OBTAIN LAST PROJECT WITHIN PROJ-SET
             ON ANY-STATUS NEXT SENTENCE.
          OBTAIN LAST DEPARTMENT WITHIN DEPT-SET
             ON ANY-STATUS NEXT SENTENCE.
          OBTAIN LAST COUNTRY WITHIN CTRY-SET
             ON ANY-STATUS NEXT SENTENCE.
          OBTAIN LAST EMPLOYEE WITHIN EMPL-SET
             ON ANY-STATUS NEXT SENTENCE.
          OBTAIN LAST SECURITY WITHIN SECU-SET
             ON ANY-STATUS NEXT SENTENCE.
          OBTAIN LAST CUSTOMER WITHIN CUST-SET
             ON ANY-STATUS NEXT SENTENCE.
          OBTAIN LAST LANGUAGE WITHIN LANG-SET
             ON ANY-STATUS NEXT SENTENCE.
          OBTAIN LAST BILLING WITHIN BILL-SET
             ON ANY-STATUS NEXT SENTENCE.
          OBTAIN LAST HISTORY WITHIN HIST-SET
             ON ANY-STATUS NEXT SENTENCE.
     1008-EXIT.
          EXIT.


     1009-FLIS.
          FIND LAST INVOICE WITHIN INV-SET
             ON ANY-STATUS NEXT SENTENCE.
          FIND LAST PROJECT WITHIN PROJ-SET
             ON ANY-STATUS NEXT SENTENCE.
          FIND LAST DEPARTMENT WITHIN DEPT-SET
             ON ANY-STATUS NEXT SENTENCE.
          FIND LAST COUNTRY WITHIN CTRY-SET
             ON ANY-STATUS NEXT SENTENCE.
          FIND LAST EMPLOYEE WITHIN EMPL-SET
             ON ANY-STATUS NEXT SENTENCE.
          FIND LAST SECURITY WITHIN SECU-SET
             ON ANY-STATUS NEXT SENTENCE.
          FIND LAST CUSTOMER WITHIN CUST-SET
             ON ANY-STATUS NEXT SENTENCE.
          FIND LAST LANGUAGE WITHIN LANG-SET
             ON ANY-STATUS NEXT SENTENCE.
          FIND LAST BILLING WITHIN BILL-SET
             ON ANY-STATUS NEXT SENTENCE.
          FIND LAST HISTORY WITHIN HIST-SET
             ON ANY-STATUS NEXT SENTENCE.
```

```
1009-EXIT.
    EXIT.


1010-FFIS.
    FIND LAST INVOICE WITHIN INV-SET
        ON ANY-STATUS NEXT SENTENCE.
    FIND LAST PROJECT WITHIN PROJ-SET
        ON ANY-STATUS NEXT SENTENCE.
    FIND LAST DEPARTMENT WITHIN DEPT-SET
        ON ANY-STATUS NEXT SENTENCE.
    FIND LAST COUNTRY WITHIN CTRY-SET
        ON ANY-STATUS NEXT SENTENCE.
    FIND LAST EMPLOYEE WITHIN EMPL-SET
        ON ANY-STATUS NEXT SENTENCE.
    FIND LAST SECURITY WITHIN SECU-SET
        ON ANY-STATUS NEXT SENTENCE.
    FIND LAST CUSTOMER WITHIN CUST-SET
        ON ANY-STATUS NEXT SENTENCE.
    FIND LAST LANGUAGE WITHIN LANG-SET
        ON ANY-STATUS NEXT SENTENCE.
    FIND LAST BILLING WITHIN BILL-SET
        ON ANY-STATUS NEXT SENTENCE.
    FIND LAST HISTORY WITHIN HIST-SET
        ON ANY-STATUS NEXT SENTENCE.
1010-EXIT.
    EXIT.


1011-ONIS.
    OBTAIN NEXT EMPLOYEE WITHIN EMPL-SET
        ON ANY-STATUS NEXT SENTENCE.
1011-EXIT.
    EXIT.


1012-OPIS.
    OBTAIN PRIOR EMPLOYEE WITHIN EMPL-SET
        ON ANY-STATUS NEXT SENTENCE.
1012-EXIT.
    EXIT.


1013-FNIS.
    FIND NEXT EMPLOYEE WITHIN EMPL-SET
        ON ANY-STATUS NEXT SENTENCE.
```

```
1013-EXIT.
    EXIT.


1014-FPIS.
    FIND PRIOR EMPLOYEE WITHIN EMPL-SET
        ON ANY-STATUS NEXT SENTENCE.
1014-EXIT.
    EXIT.


1015-OC.
    OBTAIN CURRENT EMPLOYEE-OOAK
        ON ANY-STATUS NEXT SENTENCE.
    OBTAIN CURRENT SECURITY-OOAK
        ON ANY-STATUS NEXT SENTENCE.
    OBTAIN CURRENT ZIPCODE-OOAK
        ON ANY-STATUS NEXT SENTENCE.
    OBTAIN CURRENT BILLING-OOAK
        ON ANY-STATUS NEXT SENTENCE.
    OBTAIN CURRENT SALES-OOAK
        ON ANY-STATUS NEXT SENTENCE.
    OBTAIN CURRENT PROJECT-OOAK
        ON ANY-STATUS NEXT SENTENCE.
    OBTAIN CURRENT DEPARTMENT-OOAK
        ON ANY-STATUS NEXT SENTENCE.
    OBTAIN CURRENT COUNTRY-OOAK
        ON ANY-STATUS NEXT SENTENCE.
    OBTAIN CURRENT LANGUAGE-OOAK
        ON ANY-STATUS NEXT SENTENCE.
1015-EXIT.
    EXIT.


1016-FC.
    FIND CURRENT EMPLOYEE-OOAK
        ON ANY-STATUS NEXT SENTENCE.
    FIND CURRENT SECURITY-OOAK
        ON ANY-STATUS NEXT SENTENCE.
    FIND CURRENT ZIPCODE-OOAK
        ON ANY-STATUS NEXT SENTENCE.
    FIND CURRENT BILLING-OOAK
        ON ANY-STATUS NEXT SENTENCE.
    FIND CURRENT SALES-OOAK
        ON ANY-STATUS NEXT SENTENCE.
```

```
      FIND CURRENT PROJECT-OOAK
          ON ANY-STATUS NEXT SENTENCE.
      FIND CURRENT DEPARTMENT-OOAK
          ON ANY-STATUS NEXT SENTENCE.
      FIND CURRENT COUNTRY-OOAK
          ON ANY-STATUS NEXT SENTENCE.
      FIND CURRENT LANGUAGE-OOAK
          ON ANY-STATUS NEXT SENTENCE.
  1016-EXIT.
      EXIT.


  1017-OCIS.
      OBTAIN CURRENT WITHIN INV-SET
          ON ANY-STATUS NEXT SENTENCE.
      OBTAIN CURRENT WITHIN PROJ-SET
          ON ANY-STATUS NEXT SENTENCE.
      OBTAIN CURRENT WITHIN DEPT-SET
          ON ANY-STATUS NEXT SENTENCE.
      OBTAIN CURRENT WITHIN CTRY-SET
          ON ANY-STATUS NEXT SENTENCE.
      OBTAIN CURRENT WITHIN EMPL-SET
          ON ANY-STATUS NEXT SENTENCE.
      OBTAIN CURRENT WITHIN SECU-SET
          ON ANY-STATUS NEXT SENTENCE.
      OBTAIN CURRENT WITHIN CUST-SET
          ON ANY-STATUS NEXT SENTENCE.
      OBTAIN CURRENT WITHIN LANG-SET
          ON ANY-STATUS NEXT SENTENCE.
      OBTAIN CURRENT WITHIN BILL-SET
          ON ANY-STATUS NEXT SENTENCE.
      OBTAIN CURRENT WITHIN HIST-SET
          ON ANY-STATUS NEXT SENTENCE.
  1017-EXIT.
      EXIT.


  1018-FCIS.
      FIND CURRENT WITHIN INV-SET
          ON ANY-STATUS NEXT SENTENCE.
      FIND CURRENT WITHIN PROJ-SET
          ON ANY-STATUS NEXT SENTENCE.
      FIND CURRENT WITHIN DEPT-SET
          ON ANY-STATUS NEXT SENTENCE.
```

```
              FIND CURRENT WITHIN CTRY-SET
                  ON ANY-STATUS NEXT SENTENCE.
              FIND CURRENT WITHIN EMPL-SET
                  ON ANY-STATUS NEXT SENTENCE.
              FIND CURRENT WITHIN SECU-SET
                  ON ANY-STATUS NEXT SENTENCE.
              FIND CURRENT WITHIN CUST-SET
                  ON ANY-STATUS NEXT SENTENCE.
              FIND CURRENT WITHIN LANG-SET
                  ON ANY-STATUS NEXT SENTENCE.
              FIND CURRENT WITHIN BILL-SET
                  ON ANY-STATUS NEXT SENTENCE.
              FIND CURRENT WITHIN HIST-SET
                  ON ANY-STATUS NEXT SENTENCE.
          1018-EXIT.
              EXIT.


          1019-OCIA.
              OBTAIN CURRENT WITHIN BILLING-AREA
                  ON ANY-STATUS NEXT SENTENCE.
              OBTAIN CURRENT WITHIN WORLD-AREA
                  ON ANY-STATUS NEXT SENTENCE.
          1019-EXIT.
              EXIT.


          1020-FCIA.
              FIND CURRENT WITHIN BILLING-AREA
                  ON ANY-STATUS NEXT SENTENCE.
              FIND CURRENT WITHIN WORLD-AREA
                  ON ANY-STATUS NEXT SENTENCE.
          1020-EXIT.
              EXIT.


          1021-OFIN.
              OBTAIN FIRST CUSTOMER WITHIN CUST-NDX
                  ON ANY-STATUS NEXT SENTENCE.
              OBTAIN FIRST ORGANIZATION WITHIN ORGN-NDX
                  ON ANY-STATUS NEXT SENTENCE.
              OBTAIN FIRST MAILCODE WITHIN MAIL-NDX
                  ON ANY-STATUS NEXT SENTENCE.
              OBTAIN FIRST ZIPCODE WITHIN ZIP-NDX
                  ON ANY-STATUS NEXT SENTENCE.
```

```
1021-EXIT.
    EXIT.


1022-FFIN.
    OBTAIN FIRST CUSTOMER WITHIN CUST-NDX
        ON ANY-STATUS NEXT SENTENCE.
    OBTAIN FIRST ORGANIZATION WITHIN ORGN-NDX
        ON ANY-STATUS NEXT SENTENCE.
    OBTAIN FIRST MAILCODE WITHIN MAIL-NDX
        ON ANY-STATUS NEXT SENTENCE.
    OBTAIN FIRST ZIPCODE WITHIN ZIP-NDX
        ON ANY-STATUS NEXT SENTENCE.
1022-EXIT.
    EXIT.


1023-OLIN.
    OBTAIN LAST CUSTOMER WITHIN CUST-NDX
        ON ANY-STATUS NEXT SENTENCE.
    OBTAIN LAST ORGANIZATION WITHIN ORGN-NDX
        ON ANY-STATUS NEXT SENTENCE.
    OBTAIN LAST MAILCODE WITHIN MAIL-NDX
        ON ANY-STATUS NEXT SENTENCE.
    OBTAIN LAST ZIPCODE WITHIN ZIP-NDX
        ON ANY-STATUS NEXT SENTENCE.
1023-EXIT.
    EXIT.


1024-FFIN.
    FIND FIRST CUSTOMER WITHIN CUST-NDX
        ON ANY-STATUS NEXT SENTENCE.
    FIND FIRST ORGANIZATION WITHIN ORGN-NDX
        ON ANY-STATUS NEXT SENTENCE.
    FIND FIRST MAILCODE WITHIN MAIL-NDX
        ON ANY-STATUS NEXT SENTENCE.
    FIND FIRST ZIPCODE WITHIN ZIP-NDX
        ON ANY-STATUS NEXT SENTENCE.
1024-EXIT.
    EXIT.


1025-FNIN.
    FIND NEXT CUSTOMER WITHIN CUST-NDX
        ON ANY-STATUS NEXT SENTENCE.
```

```
                 FIND NEXT ORGANIZATION WITHIN ORGN-NDX
                    ON ANY-STATUS NEXT SENTENCE.
                 FIND NEXT MAILCODE WITHIN MAIL-NDX
                    ON ANY-STATUS NEXT SENTENCE.
                 FIND NEXT ZIPCODE WITHIN ZIP-NDX
                    ON ANY-STATUS NEXT SENTENCE.
        1025-EXIT.
              EXIT.


        1026-FLIN.
                 FIND LAST CUSTOMER WITHIN CUST-NDX
                    ON ANY-STATUS NEXT SENTENCE.
                 FIND LAST ORGANIZATION WITHIN ORGN-NDX
                    ON ANY-STATUS NEXT SENTENCE.
                 FIND LAST MAILCODE WITHIN MAIL-NDX
                    ON ANY-STATUS NEXT SENTENCE.
                 FIND LAST ZIPCODE WITHIN ZIP-NDX
                    ON ANY-STATUS NEXT SENTENCE.
        1026-EXIT.
              EXIT.


        1027-ISE.
              IF FNSC-MENT-SET EMPTY
                 NEXT SENTENCE.
              IF PROJ-SET EMPTY
                 NEXT SENTENCE.
              IF DEPT-SET EMPTY
                 NEXT SENTENCE.
              IF CTRY-SET EMPTY
                 NEXT SENTENCE.
              IF EMPL-SET EMPTY
                 NEXT SENTENCE.
              IF SECU-SET EMPTY
                 NEXT SENTENCE.
              IF CUST-SET EMPTY
                 NEXT SENTENCE.
              IF LANG-SET EMPTY
                 NEXT SENTENCE.
              IF BILL-SET EMPTY
                 NEXT SENTENCE.
        1027-EXIT.
              EXIT.
```

```
1028-SR.
    MOVE LOOP-CNT TO REC-NUM.
    MOVE REC-ID TO EMP-ID OF EMPLOYEE.
    STORE EMPLOYEE.
1028-EXIT.
    EXIT.


1029-CR.
    MOVE LOOP-CNT TO REC-NUM.
    MOVE REC-ID TO EMP-ID OF EMPLOYEE.
    OBTAIN CALC EMPLOYEE.
    CONNECT EMPLOYEE TO UGSC-EMPL-SET.
1029-EXIT.
    EXIT.


1030-DR.
    MOVE LOOP-CNT TO REC-NUM.
    MOVE REC-ID TO EMP-ID OF EMPLOYEE.
    OBTAIN CALC EMPLOYEE.
    DISCONNECT EMPLOYEE FROM UGSC-EMPL-SET.
1030-EXIT.
    EXIT.


1031-MR.
    MODIFY EMPLOYEE.
1031-EXIT.
    EXIT.


1032-ER.
    MOVE LOOP-CNT TO REC-NUM.
    MOVE REC-ID TO EMP-ID OF EMPLOYEE.
    OBTAIN CALC EMPLOYEE.
    ERASE EMPLOYEE.
1032-EXIT.
    EXIT.


1033-OOIS.
    OBTAIN OWNER WITHIN INV-SET
        ON ANY-STATUS NEXT SENTENCE.
    OBTAIN OWNER WITHIN PROJ-SET
        ON ANY-STATUS NEXT SENTENCE.
    OBTAIN OWNER WITHIN DEPT-SET
```

```
                    ON ANY-STATUS NEXT SENTENCE.
            OBTAIN OWNER WITHIN CTRY-SET
                    ON ANY-STATUS NEXT SENTENCE.
            OBTAIN OWNER WITHIN EMPL-SET
                    ON ANY-STATUS NEXT SENTENCE.
            OBTAIN OWNER WITHIN SECU-SET
                    ON ANY-STATUS NEXT SENTENCE.
            OBTAIN OWNER WITHIN CUST-SET
                    ON ANY-STATUS NEXT SENTENCE.
            OBTAIN OWNER WITHIN LANG-SET
                    ON ANY-STATUS NEXT SENTENCE.
            OBTAIN OWNER WITHIN BILL-SET
                    ON ANY-STATUS NEXT SENTENCE.
            OBTAIN OWNER WITHIN HIST-SET
                    ON ANY-STATUS NEXT SENTENCE.
        1033-EXIT.
            EXIT.


        1034-FOIS.
            FIND OWNER WITHIN INV-SET
                    ON ANY-STATUS NEXT SENTENCE.
            FIND OWNER WITHIN PROJ-SET
                    ON ANY-STATUS NEXT SENTENCE.
            FIND OWNER WITHIN DEPT-SET
                    ON ANY-STATUS NEXT SENTENCE.
            FIND OWNER WITHIN CTRY-SET
                    ON ANY-STATUS NEXT SENTENCE.
            FIND OWNER WITHIN EMPL-SET
                    ON ANY-STATUS NEXT SENTENCE.
            FIND OWNER WITHIN SECU-SET
                    ON ANY-STATUS NEXT SENTENCE.
            FIND OWNER WITHIN CUST-SET
                    ON ANY-STATUS NEXT SENTENCE.
            FIND OWNER WITHIN LANG-SET
                    ON ANY-STATUS NEXT SENTENCE.
            FIND OWNER WITHIN BILL-SET
                    ON ANY-STATUS NEXT SENTENCE.
            FIND OWNER WITHIN HIST-SET
                    ON ANY-STATUS NEXT SENTENCE.
        1034-EXIT.
            EXIT.
```

```
1035-ASK.
    ACCEPT WORK-DBKEY FROM INV-SET CURRENCY
        ON ANY-STATUS NEXT SENTENCE.
    ACCEPT WORK-DBKEY FROM PROJ-SET CURRENCY
        ON ANY-STATUS NEXT SENTENCE.
    ACCEPT WORK-DBKEY FROM DEPT-SET CURRENCY
        ON ANY-STATUS NEXT SENTENCE.
    ACCEPT WORK-DBKEY FROM CTRY-SET CURRENCY
        ON ANY-STATUS NEXT SENTENCE.
    ACCEPT WORK-DBKEY FROM EMPL-SET CURRENCY
        ON ANY-STATUS NEXT SENTENCE.
    ACCEPT WORK-DBKEY FROM SECU-SET CURRENCY
        ON ANY-STATUS NEXT SENTENCE.
    ACCEPT WORK-DBKEY FROM LANG-SET CURRENCY
        ON ANY-STATUS NEXT SENTENCE.
    ACCEPT WORK-DBKEY FROM BILL-SET CURRENCY
        ON ANY-STATUS NEXT SENTENCE.
    ACCEPT WORK-DBKEY FROM HIST-SET CURRENCY
        ON ANY-STATUS NEXT SENTENCE.
    ACCEPT WORK-DBKEY FROM CUST-SET CURRENCY
        ON ANY-STATUS NEXT SENTENCE.
1035-EXIT.
    EXIT.


1036-ARK.
    ACCEPT WORK-DBKEY FROM SECURITY CURRENCY
        ON ANY-STATUS NEXT SENTENCE.
    ACCEPT WORK-DBKEY FROM BILLING CURRENCY
        ON ANY-STATUS NEXT SENTENCE.
    ACCEPT WORK-DBKEY FROM PROJECT CURRENCY
        ON ANY-STATUS NEXT SENTENCE.
    ACCEPT WORK-DBKEY FROM DEPARTMENT CURRENCY
        ON ANY-STATUS NEXT SENTENCE.
    ACCEPT WORK-DBKEY FROM COUNTRY CURRENCY
        ON ANY-STATUS NEXT SENTENCE.
    ACCEPT WORK-DBKEY FROM SECURITY CURRENCY
        ON ANY-STATUS NEXT SENTENCE.
    ACCEPT WORK-DBKEY FROM LANGUAGE CURRENCY
        ON ANY-STATUS NEXT SENTENCE.
    ACCEPT WORK-DBKEY FROM BILLING CURRENCY
        ON ANY-STATUS NEXT SENTENCE.
    ACCEPT WORK-DBKEY FROM HISTORY CURRENCY
```

```
                    ON ANY-STATUS NEXT SENTENCE.
              ACCEPT WORK-DBKEY FROM CUSTOMER CURRENCY
                    ON ANY-STATUS NEXT SENTENCE.
          1036-EXIT.
              EXIT.


          1037-ASNK.
              ACCEPT WORK-DBKEY FROM INV-SET NEXT CURRENCY
                    ON ANY-STATUS NEXT SENTENCE.
              ACCEPT WORK-DBKEY FROM PROJ-SET NEXT CURRENCY
                    ON ANY-STATUS NEXT SENTENCE.
              ACCEPT WORK-DBKEY FROM DEPT-SET NEXT CURRENCY
                    ON ANY-STATUS NEXT SENTENCE.
              ACCEPT WORK-DBKEY FROM CTRY-SET NEXT CURRENCY
                    ON ANY-STATUS NEXT SENTENCE.
              ACCEPT WORK-DBKEY FROM EMPL-SET NEXT CURRENCY
                    ON ANY-STATUS NEXT SENTENCE.
              ACCEPT WORK-DBKEY FROM SECU-SET NEXT CURRENCY
                    ON ANY-STATUS NEXT SENTENCE.
              ACCEPT WORK-DBKEY FROM LANG-SET NEXT CURRENCY
                    ON ANY-STATUS NEXT SENTENCE.
              ACCEPT WORK-DBKEY FROM BILL-SET NEXT CURRENCY
                    ON ANY-STATUS NEXT SENTENCE.
              ACCEPT WORK-DBKEY FROM HIST-SET NEXT CURRENCY
                    ON ANY-STATUS NEXT SENTENCE.
              ACCEPT WORK-DBKEY FROM CUST-SET NEXT CURRENCY
                    ON ANY-STATUS NEXT SENTENCE.
          1037-EXIT.
              EXIT.


          1038-COMMIT.
              COMMIT.
          1038-EXIT.
              EXIT.


          2000-STATISTICS.
              ACCEPT TRANSACTION STATISTICS NOWRITE INTO STATISTICS-BLOCK.
              MOVE ZEROES TO WORK1-CPU, WORK2-CPU.
              ADD USER-TIME TO WORK1-CPU.
              ADD SYS-TIME TO WORK1-CPU.
          2000-EXIT.
              EXIT.
```

```
3000-STATISTICS.
    ACCEPT TRANSACTION STATISTICS NOWRITE INTO STATISTICS-BLOCK.
    ADD USER-TIME TO WORK2-CPU.
    ADD SYS-TIME TO WORK2-CPU.
    SUBTRACT WORK1-CPU FROM WORK2-CPU GIVING S-CPU-TOTAL.
    MOVE ERROR-STATUS TO STATCODE.
    WRITE PRINTER FROM REPORT-DATA-80 LENGTH 80.
3000-EXIT.
    EXIT.


4000-EXIT.
    EXIT
```

12 Rules of Relational Database (a simplified version)

Rule	Description
Representation of information	All data is represented logically in tables.
Guaranteed logical accessibility	All data is accessible logically using a combination of table name, key name, key value and column.
NULL Support	Null values represent missing information and are not to be confused with empty, blank, or zero filled data. They also are not necessarily equal.
Dynamic online catalog	The definition of data is represented in the same manner as data so that it can be relationally accessed.
Comprehensive data sub-language	A unique language (today we call this SQL) which is supported along with several other programming languages to achieve data definition, view, and manipulation.
Updatable views	All views that can theoretically exist and be updated.
High-level insert, update and delete	Both base and derived relations can be handled as singular requests and apply to retrieval, insert, update, and deletion of data.
Physical data independence	Program and terminal activities are preserved when changes are made in storage representations or access methods*.
Logical data independence	Program and terminal activities are preserved when changes are made to base tables.
Integrity independence	Integrity constraints must be definable in the unique sub-language and stored in the catalog.

Rule	Description
Distribution independence	The unique sub-language must support database distribution while preserving program and terminal activities.
Nonsubersion	A relational system which performs low-level processing of records (one-at-a-time) cannot supplant the integrity rules in effect in high-level, (many-at-a-time) record processing by a relational language.
Relational Table Database	Defined as a rectangular array of columns and rows, where columns are homogenous, non-grouped, uniquely named data items (attributes) and rows are not duplicated. It is also important to impose the property that column and row order within the array is immaterial.

* The rules for achieving 1st through 4th normal found can be found in the chapter on logical database design.

G

Object Technology

Concept	Description
Encapsulation:	Data and I/O are hidden from the user and developer.
Classification:	Each object is an instance of a class.
Inheritance:	Sub-classes automatically inherit the characteristics of the owning class.
Polymorphism:	Messages sent to different sub-classes can be handled differently.

Capturing Statistics for SR8 Integrated Indexes Within Your Program

1. Define the following IDD record.

```
ADD REC DB-STAT-EXTENDED.
    03      SR8-SPLITS          PIC S9(8) USA COMP.
    03      SR8-SPAWNS          PIC S9(8) USA COMP.
    03      SR8-STORES        . PIC S9(8) USA COMP.
    03      SR8-ERASES          PIC S9(8) USA COMP.
    03      SR7-STORES          PIC S9(8) USA COMP.
    03      SR7-ERASES          PIC S9(8) USA COMP.
    03      BIN-SEARCH-TOT      PIC S9(8) USA COMP.
    03      LVL-SEARCH-TOT      PIC S9(8) USA COMP.
    03      ORPHAN-ADOPTIONS    PIC S9(8) USA COMP.
    03      LVL-SEARCH-BEST     PIC S9(8) USA COMP.
    03      LVL-SEARCH-WORST    PIC S9(8) USA COMP.
    03      FILL032             PIC X(32) USA DISPLAY.
```

2. Copy the DB-STAT-EXTENDED record into your program.

```
WORKING-STORAGE SECTION.
COPY IDMS DB-STATISTICS.        ☞ Required standard statistics record
COPY DB-STAT-EXTENDED.          ☞ Extended Index statistics record
```

3. Code the call for statistics in your program at a useful location.

```
PROCEDURE DIVISION.
MOVE 0995 TO DML-SEQUENCE.
CALL 'IDMS' USING SUBSCHEMA-CTRL
                              IDBMSCOM (71)
                              DB-STATISTICS
                              DB-STAT-EXTENDED.
```

4. Code displays for standard statistics as follows.

```
EXHIBIT NAMED DATE-TODAY.
EXHIBIT NAMED TIME-TODAY.
EXHIBIT NAMED PAGES-READ.
EXHIBIT NAMED PAGES-WRITTEN.
EXHIBIT NAMED PAGES-REQUESTED.
EXHIBIT NAMED CALC-TARGET.
EXHIBIT NAMED CALC-OVERFLOW.
EXHIBIT NAMED VIA-TARGET.
EXHIBIT NAMED VIA-OVERFLOW.
EXHIBIT NAMED LINES-REQUESTED.
EXHIBIT NAMED RECS-CURRENT.
EXHIBIT NAMED CALLS-TO-IDMS.
EXHIBIT NAMED FRAGMENTS-STORED.
EXHIBIT NAMED RECS-RELOCATED.
EXHIBIT NAMED LOCKS-REQUESTED.
EXHIBIT NAMED SEL-LOCKS-HELD.
EXHIBIT NAMED UPD-LOCKS-HELD.
EXHIBIT NAMED RUN-UNIT-ID.
EXHIBIT NAMED TASK-ID.
EXHIBIT NAMED LOCAL-ID.
```

5. Code displays for extended SR8 statistics as follows.

```
EXHIBIT NAMED SR8-SPLITS.
EXHIBIT NAMED SR8-SPAWNS.
EXHIBIT NAMED SR8-STORES.
EXHIBIT NAMED SR8-ERASES.
EXHIBIT NAMED SR7-STORES.
EXHIBIT NAMED SR7-ERASES.
EXHIBIT NAMED BIN-SEARCH-TOT.
EXHIBIT NAMED LVL-SEARCH-TOT.
EXHIBIT NAMED ORPHAN-ADOPTIONS.
EXHIBIT NAMED LVL-SEARCH-BEST.
EXHIBIT NAMED LVL-SEARCH-WORST.
```

Hiperspace and Dataspace Reference Materials

Source	From	Cost*	Description
G225-4500-05	IBM	3.95	IBM's MVS/ESA Software Newsletter, First Qtr, 1991 Hiperspace—Down to Earth, Bob Rogers
G321-5421-00	IBM	3.10	VM Data Spaces and ESA/XC Facilities, SJ30-1
GC24-3404-00	IBM	35.00	MVS/ESA Data-In-Memory Concepts and Facilities
GC28-1200-00	IBM	3.25	MVS/ESA Application Development Guide: HIPERBATCH
GC28-1214-01	IBM	5.25	IBM BatchPipes/MVS Introduction Ver 1 Rel 1
GC28-1359-02	IBM	5.80	MVS/ESA General Information
GC28-1468-00	IBM	17.00	MVS/ESA Application Development Guide Ver 5
GC28-1639-04	IBM	4.00	MVS/ESA Appl Dev Gd: Callable Services for High-Level Languages Ver 4
GC28-1644-05	IBM	7.75	MVS/ESA Appl Dev Guide: Assembler Language Programming
GC28-1652-04	IBM	4.00	MVS/ESA Application Development Guide Ver 4
GC28-1673-00	IBM	1.90	MVS/ESA Application Development Guide: HIPERBATCH
GC28-1821-03	IBM	6.25	MVS/ESA Application Development Guide
GC28-1822-04	IBM	8.60	MVS/ESA Application Development Macro Guide
GC28-1822-04	IBM	8.60	MVS/ESA Application Development Macro Reference

Source	From	Cost*	Description
GC28-1828-05	IBM	8.15	MVS/ESA SPL: Initialization and Tuning (system performance with VIO)
GC28-1831-03	IBM	7.65	MVS/ESA System Modifications
GC28-1832-03	IBM	7.65	MVS/ESA IPCS
GC28-1852-02	IBM	10.75	MVS/ESA SPL: Application Development Guide
GC28-1854-04	IBM	8.25	MVS/ESA Applicaton Development : Extended Addressability
GT00-7794	IBM	5.80	IBM's MVS/ESA Software Newsletter, Third/Fourth Qtr, 1992 Hiperspace—Down to Earth II
LY28-1456-01	IBM	6.10	MVS/ESA Component Diagnosis: Data-In-Virtual
LY28-1568-01	IBM	9.15	MVS/ESA Component Diagnosis: Real Storage Manager
LY28-1843-01	IBM	22.75	MVS/ESA Diagnosis: Using Dumps and Traces
SC33-0887-00	IBM	10.00	CICS/ESA Shared Data Tables Guide V 3.3
Classroom	Amdahl		Data Space/Hiperspace, 4.5 days, Course Code:MEAP, 1-800-233-9521
Classroom	IBM		MVS/ESA Data-in-Memory Performance Solutions, 1-800-IBM-TEACH
Video	CSR		Data Space/Hiperspace, 3 hrs, Course Code: 34678, 1-800-SRA-1277

* Prices are subject to change by the vendor.

J

CA-Clipper Command Benchmark Comparison

Each of the clipper commands or command pairs was executed 10,000 times and the before and after time was captured. The resulting statistics were adjusted to remove the overhead associated with the DO-WHILE loop and loop counter. The commands and their respective execution times are shown in the table below. The source used to create the statistics in this table is also included at the end of the appendix.

Clipper Command	Execution Elapsed Time *
STRING(MEMORY(0))	413
USE file	102
SEEK index key	6
DO-WHILE	3
@ SAY	3
SET COLOR	1
STORE VARIABLE	1
SUBSTRING VARIABLE	1
SUBSTRING MONTH(DATE)	1
LTRIM VARIABLE	1
STRING VARIABLE	1
SET KEY	0.1
DO/RETURN pair	0.1
RELEASE VARIABLE	0.1

Clipper Command	Execution Elapsed Time *
SELECT file id	0.1
IF/ENDIF pair	0.1
CLEAR GETS	0.1

* All times are in seconds to perform 10,000 executions on a 386 DX25 machine with FASTOPEN and SMRTDRV in effect.

Sample Statistics Collection Program

```
CLEAR SCREEN
SET CONSOLE OFF
SET PRINTER ON
SET PRINT TO OUTPUT
? 'COLLECT STATS ON 10,000 EXECUTIONS OF COMMON CLIPPER
COMMANDS'
? 'ALL TIMES MUST HAVE -DO WHILE- TIME SUBTRACTED'
****************************
STORE 00000 TO CNT
? 'DO WHILE/BUMP COUNTER COMMANDS START TIME : '+TIME()
DO WHILE CNT < 10000
   CNT = CNT + 1
ENDDO
? 'DO WHILE/BUMP COUNTER COMMANDS END TIME : '+TIME()
****************************
STORE 00000 TO CNT
? 'RELEASE VAR COMMAND START TIME : '+TIME()
DO WHILE CNT < 10000
   XYZ = '  '
   RELEASE XYZ
   CNT = CNT + 1
ENDDO
? 'RELEASE VAR COMMAND END TIME : '+TIME()
****************************
STORE 00000 TO CNT
STORE '12345' TO ABC
? 'SUBSTRING VAR COMMAND START TIME : '+TIME()
DO WHILE CNT < 10000
   STORE SUBSTR(ABC,1,3) TO XYZ
   CNT = CNT + 1
ENDDO
? 'SUBSTRING VAR COMMAND END TIME : '+TIME()
****************************
```

```
STORE 00000 TO CNT
?  'RELEASE VAR COMMAND START TIME : '+TIME()
DO WHILE CNT < 10000
   XYZ = '   '
   RELEASE XYZ
   CNT = CNT + 1
ENDDO
?  'RELEASE VAR COMMAND END TIME : '+TIME()
****************************
STORE 00000 TO CNT
STORE '12345' TO ABC
?  'SUBSTRING VAR COMMAND START TIME : '+TIME()
DO WHILE CNT < 10000
   STORE SUBSTR(ABC,1,3) TO XYZ
   CNT = CNT + 1
ENDDO
?  'SUBSTRING VAR COMMAND END TIME : '+TIME()
****************************
STORE 00000 TO CNT
?  'SUBSTRING MONTH/DATE COMMAND START TIME : '+TIME()
DO WHILE CNT < 10000
   STORE SUBSTR(CMONTH(DATE()),1,3) TO XYZ
   CNT = CNT + 1
ENDDO
?  'SUBSTRING MONTH/DATE COMMAND END TIME : '+TIME()
****************************
STORE 00000 TO CNT
STORE '12345' TO ABC
?  'LTRIM VAR START TIME : '+TIME()
DO WHILE CNT < 10000
   STORE LTRIM(ABC) TO LIT1
   CNT = CNT + 1
ENDDO
?  'LTRIM VAR END TIME : '+TIME()
****************************
STORE 00000 TO CNT
STORE 123 TO TEMP1
?  'STR VAR COMMAND START TIME : '+TIME()
DO WHILE CNT < 10000
   STORE STR(TEMP1) TO TEMP2
   CNT = CNT + 1
ENDDO
```

```
? 'STR VAR COMMAND END TIME : '+TIME()
*****************************
STORE 00000 TO CNT
? 'STR(MEMORY(0)) COMMAND START TIME : '+TIME()
DO WHILE CNT < 10000
   STORE STR(MEMORY(0)) TO MEM1
   CNT = CNT + 1
ENDDO
? 'STR(MEMORY(0)) COMMAND END TIME : '+TIME()
*****************************
STORE 00000 TO CNT
? 'SET KEY COMMAND START TIME : '+TIME()
DO WHILE CNT < 10000
   SET KEY 28 TO HELP
   CNT = CNT + 1
ENDDO
? 'SET KEY COMMAND END TIME : '+TIME()
*****************************
STORE 00000 TO CNT
? 'DO/RETURN COMMAND START TIME : '+TIME()
DO WHILE CNT < 10000
   DO COMMAND2
   CNT = CNT + 1
ENDDO
? 'DO/RETURN COMMAND END TIME : '+TIME()
*****************************
STORE 00000 TO CNT
? 'SET COLOR COMMAND START TIME : '+TIME()
DO WHILE CNT < 10000
   SET COLOR TO R+/N, R+/N, W+
   CNT = CNT + 1
ENDDO
? 'SET COLOR COMMAND END TIME : '+TIME()
*****************************
STORE 00000 TO CNT
? '@ SAY COMMAND START TIME : '+TIME()
DO WHILE CNT < 10000
   @ 20,20 SAY 'SAY TEST'
   CNT = CNT + 1
ENDDO
? '@ SAY COMMAND END TIME : '+TIME()
*****************************
```

```
STORE 00000 TO CNT
SELECT A
USE D:\PALYCUT1\AGETABLE INDEX D:\PALYCUT1\AGENDX2
?  'SELECT COMMAND START TIME : '+TIME()
DO WHILE CNT < 10000
   SELECT A
   CNT = CNT + 1
ENDDO
?  'SELECT COMMAND END TIME : '+TIME()
****************************
STORE 00000 TO CNT
?  'USE COMMAND START TIME : '+TIME()
DO WHILE CNT < 10000
   USE D:\PALYCUT1\AGETABLE INDEX D:\PALYCUT1\AGENDX2
   CNT = CNT + 1
ENDDO
?  'USE COMMAND END TIME : '+TIME()
****************************
STORE 00000 TO CNT
   STORE 'ACADIA' TO AGE_ABBREV
?  'SEEK COMMAND START TIME : '+TIME()
DO WHILE CNT < 10000
   SEEK AGE_ABBREV
   CNT = CNT + 1
ENDDO
?  'SEEK COMMAND END TIME : '+TIME()
****************************
STORE 00000 TO CNT
?  'IF COMMAND START TIME : '+TIME()
DO WHILE CNT < 10000
   IF AGE_ABBREV = 'ACADIA'
   ENDIF
   CNT = CNT + 1
ENDDO
?  'IF COMMAND END TIME : '+TIME()
****************************
STORE 00000 TO CNT
?  'STORE COMMAND START TIME : '+TIME()
DO WHILE CNT < 10000
   IF AGE_ABBREV = 'ACADIA'
```

```
            STORE 'ACADIA' TO AGE_ABBREV
       ENDIF
       CNT = CNT + 1
ENDDO
?   'STORE COMMAND END TIME : '+TIME()
****************************
STORE 00000 TO CNT
?   'CLEAR GETS COMMAND START TIME : '+TIME()
DO WHILE CNT < 10000
       CLEAR GETS
       CNT = CNT + 1
ENDDO
?   'CLEAR GETS COMMAND END TIME : '+TIME()
RETURN
```

——CA-Realia PC Cobol Version——

```
        IDENTIFICATION DIVISION.
    PROGRAM-ID. COMPTEST.
    ENVIRONMENT DIVISION.
    CONFIGURATION SECTION.
    SOURCE-COMPUTER. IBM-PC.
    OBJECT-COMPUTER. IBM-PC.
    INPUT-OUTPUT SECTION.
    FILE-CONTROL.
    DATA DIVISION.
    FILE SECTION.
    WORKING-STORAGE SECTION.
    01   DOS-COMMAND         PIC X(121).
    01   FILE-HANDLE         PIC S9(4) COMP-5.
    01   FILE-NAME           PIC X(79).
    01   FILE-ACCESS-MODE    PIC S9(4) COMP-5.
    01   READ-COUNT          PIC S9(4) COMP-5.
    01   BUFFER              PIC X(80).
    01   NBR-TIMES           PIC 9(12)
USAGE IS COMP.
    01   COMP0001            PIC S9(12)V99
                USAGE IS COMP.
```

```
        01  COMP0001B              PIC S9(12)V99
USAGE IS COMP.
        01  COMP0001-3             PIC S9(12)V99
USAGE IS COMP-3.
        01  COMP0001-3B            PIC S9(12)V99
USAGE IS COMP-3.
        01  DISPLAY4               PIC S9(12)V99
VALUE +123456.99.
        01  COMP0004-3             PIC S9(12)V99
USAGE IS COMP-3.
     PROCEDURE DIVISION.
     100-START-OF-PROGRAM.
    PERFORM 100-OPEN-FILE THRU 100-EXIT.
           PERFORM 200-READ-RECORDS
      THRU 200-EXIT 20 TIMES.
    CALL 'DOS_CLOSE_FILE' USING FILE-HANDLE.
    STOP RUN.
     100-OPEN-FILE.
    MOVE 'C:\IN1.TXT' TO FILE-NAME.
    MOVE 0 TO FILE-ACCESS-MODE.
            CALL 'DOS_OPEN_FILE' USING FILE-HANDLE
    FILE-NAME
    FILE-ACCESS-MODE
    MOVE 1 TO READ-COUNT.
     100-EXIT.
         EXIT.
     200-READ-RECORDS.
   MOVE 80 TO READ-COUNT.
   CALL 'DOS_READ_FILE' USING FILE-HANDLE
BUFFER READ-COUNT.
    PERFORM 300-TEST
       THRU 300-TEST-EXIT.
     200-EXIT.
         EXIT.
     300-TEST.
    PERFORM 600-INIT-IT THRU 600-EXIT.
    DISPLAY 'MOVE COMP TO COMP 10000 TIMES'.
    PERFORM 400-TYPE-0 THRU 400-TYPE-0-EXIT
      UNTIL NBR-TIMES > 10000.
    PERFORM 600-INIT-IT THRU 600-EXIT.
    DISPLAY 'ADD TO COMP 10000 TIMES'.
    PERFORM 400-TYPE-1 THRU 400-TYPE-1-EXIT
```

```
    UNTIL NBR-TIMES > 10000.
PERFORM 600-INIT-IT THRU 600-EXIT.
DISPLAY 'DISPLAY ADD TO COMP-3 10000 TIMES'.
PERFORM 400-TYPE-2 THRU 400-TYPE-2-EXIT
    UNTIL NBR-TIMES > 10000.
PERFORM 600-INIT-IT THRU 600-EXIT.
DISPLAY 'MOVE COMP-3 TO COMP-3 10000 TIMES'.
PERFORM 400-TYPE-3 THRU 400-TYPE-3-EXIT
    UNTIL NBR-TIMES > 10000.
PERFORM 600-INIT-IT THRU 600-EXIT.
DISPLAY 'MOVE DISPLAY TO COMP-3 10000 TIMES'.
PERFORM 400-TYPE-4 THRU 400-TYPE-4-EXIT
    UNTIL NBR-TIMES > 10000.
PERFORM 600-INIT-IT THRU 600-EXIT.
DISPLAY 'IF COMP-3 > COMP-3 10000 TIMES'.
PERFORM 400-TYPE-5 THRU 400-TYPE-5-EXIT
    UNTIL NBR-TIMES > 10000.
PERFORM 600-INIT-IT THRU 600-EXIT.
DISPLAY 'IF DISPLAY > COMP-3 10000 TIMES'.
PERFORM 400-TYPE-6 THRU 400-TYPE-6-EXIT
    UNTIL NBR-TIMES > 10000.
PERFORM 600-INIT-IT THRU 600-EXIT.
DISPLAY 'IF COMP > COMP-3 10000 TIMES'.
PERFORM 400-TYPE-7 THRU 400-TYPE-7-EXIT
    UNTIL NBR-TIMES > 10000.
PERFORM 600-INIT-IT THRU 600-EXIT.
DISPLAY 'ADD TO DISPLAY 10000 TIMES'.
PERFORM 400-TYPE-8 THRU 400-TYPE-8-EXIT
    UNTIL NBR-TIMES > 10000.
PERFORM 600-INIT-IT THRU 600-EXIT.
DISPLAY 'IF COMP > COMP 10000 TIMES'.
PERFORM 400-TYPE-9 THRU 400-TYPE-9-EXIT
    UNTIL NBR-TIMES > 10000.
    300-TEST-EXIT.
EXIT.
    400-TYPE-0.
MOVE COMP0001 TO COMP0001B.
MOVE COMP0001B TO COMP0001.
MOVE COMP0001 TO COMP0001B.
MOVE COMP0001B TO COMP0001.
MOVE COMP0001 TO COMP0001B.
MOVE COMP0001B TO COMP0001.
```

```
            MOVE COMP0001 TO COMP0001B.
            MOVE COMP0001B TO COMP0001.
            MOVE COMP0001 TO COMP0001B.
            MOVE COMP0001B TO COMP0001.
            MOVE COMP0001 TO COMP0001B.
            MOVE COMP0001B TO COMP0001.
            PERFORM 500-BUMP-IT.
              400-TYPE-0-EXIT.
                  EXIT.
              400-TYPE-1.
            ADD +13.31 TO COMP0001.
            ADD +13.31 TO COMP0001.
            ADD +13.31 TO COMP0001.
            ADD +13.31 TO COMP0001.
            ADD +13.31 TO COMP0001.
            ADD +13.31 TO COMP0001.
            ADD +13.31 TO COMP0001.
            ADD +13.31 TO COMP0001.
            ADD +13.31 TO COMP0001.
            ADD +13.31 TO COMP0001.
            ADD +13.31 TO COMP0001.
            ADD +13.31 TO COMP0001.
            PERFORM 500-BUMP-IT.
              400-TYPE-1-EXIT.
            EXIT.
              400-TYPE-2.
            ADD +13.31 TO COMP0001-3.
            ADD +13.31 TO COMP0001-3.
            ADD +13.31 TO COMP0001-3.
            ADD +13.31 TO COMP0001-3.
            ADD +13.31 TO COMP0001-3.
            ADD +13.31 TO COMP0001-3.
            ADD +13.31 TO COMP0001-3.
            ADD +13.31 TO COMP0001-3.
            ADD +13.31 TO COMP0001-3.
            ADD +13.31 TO COMP0001-3.
            ADD +13.31 TO COMP0001-3.
            ADD +13.31 TO COMP0001-3.
            PERFORM 500-BUMP-IT.
              400-TYPE-2-EXIT.
                  EXIT.
              400-TYPE-3.
            MOVE COMP0001-3 TO COMP0001-3B.
```

```
          MOVE COMP0001-3B TO COMP0001-3.
          MOVE COMP0001-3 TO COMP0001-3B.
          MOVE COMP0001-3B TO COMP0001-3.
          MOVE COMP0001-3 TO COMP0001-3B.
          MOVE COMP0001-3B TO COMP0001-3.
          MOVE COMP0001-3 TO COMP0001-3B.
          MOVE COMP0001-3B TO COMP0001-3.
          MOVE COMP0001-3 TO COMP0001-3B.
          MOVE COMP0001-3B TO COMP0001-3.
          MOVE COMP0001-3 TO COMP0001-3B.
          MOVE COMP0001-3B TO COMP0001-3.
          PERFORM 500-BUMP-IT.
             400-TYPE-3-EXIT.
                 EXIT.
             400-TYPE-4.
          MOVE DISPLAY4 TO COMP0004-3.
          MOVE COMP0004-3 TO DISPLAY4.
          MOVE DISPLAY4 TO COMP0004-3.
          MOVE COMP0004-3 TO DISPLAY4.
          MOVE DISPLAY4 TO COMP0004-3.
          MOVE COMP0004-3 TO DISPLAY4.
          MOVE DISPLAY4 TO COMP0004-3.
          MOVE COMP0004-3 TO DISPLAY4.
          MOVE DISPLAY4 TO COMP0004-3.
          MOVE COMP0004-3 TO DISPLAY4.
          MOVE DISPLAY4 TO COMP0004-3.
          MOVE COMP0004-3 TO DISPLAY4.
          PERFORM 500-BUMP-IT.
             400-TYPE-4-EXIT.
                 EXIT.
             400-TYPE-5.
          IF COMP0001-3 > COMP0001-3B
          PERFORM 500-BUMP-IT
             ELSE
          IF COMP0001-3 > COMP0001-3B
          PERFORM 500-BUMP-IT
             ELSE
          IF COMP0001-3 > COMP0001-3B
          PERFORM 500-BUMP-IT
             ELSE
          IF COMP0001-3 > COMP0001-3B
          PERFORM 500-BUMP-IT
             ELSE
```

```
    IF COMP0001-3 > COMP0001-3B
PERFORM 500-BUMP-IT
  ELSE
  IF COMP0001-3 > COMP0001-3B
PERFORM 500-BUMP-IT.
  PERFORM 500-BUMP-IT.
    400-TYPE-5-EXIT.
        EXIT.
    400-TYPE-6.
  IF DISPLAY4 > COMP0004-3
PERFORM 500-BUMP-IT
  ELSE
  IF DISPLAY4 > COMP0004-3
PERFORM 500-BUMP-IT
  ELSE
  IF DISPLAY4 > COMP0004-3
PERFORM 500-BUMP-IT
  ELSE
  IF DISPLAY4 > COMP0004-3
PERFORM 500-BUMP-IT
  ELSE
  IF DISPLAY4 > COMP0004-3
PERFORM 500-BUMP-IT
  ELSE
  IF DISPLAY4 > COMP0004-3
PERFORM 500-BUMP-IT.
  PERFORM 500-BUMP-IT.
    400-TYPE-6-EXIT.
        EXIT.
    400-TYPE-7.
  IF COMP0001 > COMP0001-3
PERFORM 500-BUMP-IT
  ELSE
  IF COMP0001 > COMP0001-3
PERFORM 500-BUMP-IT
  ELSE
  IF COMP0001 > COMP0001-3
PERFORM 500-BUMP-IT
  ELSE
  IF COMP0001 > COMP0001-3
PERFORM 500-BUMP-IT
  ELSE
```

```
   IF COMP0001 > COMP0001-3
PERFORM 500-BUMP-IT
  ELSE
  IF COMP0001 > COMP0001-3
PERFORM 500-BUMP-IT.
  PERFORM 500-BUMP-IT.
   400-TYPE-7-EXIT.
       EXIT.
   400-TYPE-8.
  ADD +13.31 TO DISPLAY4.
  ADD +13.31 TO DISPLAY4.
  ADD +13.31 TO DISPLAY4.
  ADD +13.31 TO DISPLAY4.
  ADD +13.31 TO DISPLAY4.
  ADD +13.31 TO DISPLAY4.
  ADD +13.31 TO DISPLAY4.
  ADD +13.31 TO DISPLAY4.
  ADD +13.31 TO DISPLAY4.
  ADD +13.31 TO DISPLAY4.
  ADD +13.31 TO DISPLAY4.
  ADD +13.31 TO DISPLAY4.
  PERFORM 500-BUMP-IT.
   400-TYPE-8-EXIT.
       EXIT.
   400-TYPE-9.
  IF COMP0001 > COMP0001B
PERFORM 500-BUMP-IT
  ELSE
  IF COMP0001 > COMP0001B
PERFORM 500-BUMP-IT
  ELSE
  IF COMP0001 > COMP0001B
PERFORM 500-BUMP-IT
  ELSE
  IF COMP0001 > COMP0001B
PERFORM 500-BUMP-IT
  ELSE
  IF COMP0001 > COMP0001B
PERFORM 500-BUMP-IT
  ELSE
  IF COMP0001 > COMP0001B
PERFORM 500-BUMP-IT.
```

```
       PERFORM 500-BUMP-IT.
         400-TYPE-9-EXIT.
             EXIT.
         500-BUMP-IT.
       ADD +1 TO NBR-TIMES.
         500-BUMP-IT-EXIT.
             EXIT.
         600-INIT-IT.
       MOVE +2489 TO COMP0001
COMP0001B
COMP0001-3
COMP0001-3B
DISPLAY4
COMP0004-3.
         MOVE +1 TO NBR-TIMES.
           600-EXIT.
         EXIT.
```

────── VS Cobol II (Mainframe) Version ──────

```
       IDENTIFICATION DIVISION.
               PROGRAM-ID.   COMPTEST.
               AUTHOR. FREDERICK.
                   DATE-WRITTEN. 01/01/96.
               ENVIRONMENT DIVISION.
               CONFIGURATION SECTION.
               SOURCE-COMPUTER. IBM-3090.
               OBJECT-COMPUTER. IBM-3090.
               INPUT-OUTPUT SECTION.
               FILE-CONTROL.
                   SELECT FILE-IN ASSIGN TO SYS001.
               DATA DIVISION.
               FILE SECTION.
               FD  FILE-IN
                   LABEL RECORDS ARE STANDARD
                   BLOCK CONTAINS 0 RECORDS
                   RECORDING MODE IS F
                   DATA RECORD IS IN-DATA.
               01  IN-DATA          PIC X(80).
               WORKING-STORAGE SECTION.
               01  EOF                              PIC X .
                   88  NOT-EOF                      VALUE 'N'.
```

```
        88  YES-EOF                          VALUE 'Y'.
   01  INPUT-AREA.
        02  PGMR-CODE                        PIC X
                OCCURS 73 TIMES.
        02  FILLER7                          PIC X
                OCCURS 7 TIMES.
   01  NBR-TIMES                             PIC 9(12)
                                                 USAGE IS COMP.

   01  COMP0001                              PIC S9(12)V99
                                                 USAGE IS COMP.

   01  COMP0001B                             PIC S9(12)V99
                                                 USAGE IS COMP.

   01  COMP0001-3                            PIC S9(12)V99
                                                 USAGE IS COMP-3.

   01  COMP0001-3B                           PIC S9(12)V99
                                                 USAGE IS COMP-3.

   01  DISPLAY4                              PIC S9(12)V99
                                             VALUE +123456.99.

   01  COMP0004-3                            PIC S9(12)V99
                                                 USAGE IS COMP-3.

PROCEDURE DIVISION.
100-START-OF-PROGRAM.
    PERFORM 100-OPEN-FILE THRU 100-EXIT.
    PERFORM 200-READ-RECORDS
        THRU 200-EXIT UNTIL EOF EQUAL 'Y'.
    CLOSE FILE-IN.
    STOP RUN.
100-OPEN-FILE.
    OPEN INPUT FILE-IN.
    MOVE 'N' TO EOF.
100-EXIT.
    EXIT.
200-READ-RECORDS.
    READ FILE-IN INTO INPUT-AREA AT END MOVE 'Y' TO EOF.
    PERFORM 300-TEST
        THRU 300-TEST-EXIT.
200-EXIT.
    EXIT.
*
*   CHECK FOR TEST TO PERFORM
*
300-TEST.
```

```
                        PERFORM 600-INIT-IT THRU 600-EXIT.
                        DISPLAY 'MOVE COMP TO COMP 10000 TIMES'
                        PERFORM 400-TYPE-0 THRU 400-TYPE-0-EXIT
                          UNTIL NBR-TIMES > 10000.
                        PERFORM 600-INIT-IT THRU 600-EXIT.
                        DISPLAY 'ADD TO COMP 10000 TIMES'
                        PERFORM 400-TYPE-1 THRU 400-TYPE-1-EXIT
                          UNTIL NBR-TIMES > 10000.
                        PERFORM 600-INIT-IT THRU 600-EXIT.
                        DISPLAY 'ADD TO COMP-3 10000 TIMES'
                        PERFORM 400-TYPE-2 THRU 400-TYPE-2-EXIT
                          UNTIL NBR-TIMES > 10000.
                        PERFORM 600-INIT-IT THRU 600-EXIT.
                        DISPLAY 'MOVE COMP-3 TO COMP-3 10000 TIMES'
                        PERFORM 400-TYPE-3 THRU 400-TYPE-3-EXIT
                          UNTIL NBR-TIMES > 10000.
                        PERFORM 600-INIT-IT THRU 600-EXIT.
                        DISPLAY 'MOVE DISPLAY TO COMP-3 10000 TIMES'
                        PERFORM 400-TYPE-4 THRU 400-TYPE-4-EXIT
                          UNTIL NBR-TIMES > 10000.
                        PERFORM 600-INIT-IT THRU 600-EXIT.
                        DISPLAY 'IF COMP-3 > COMP-3 10000 TIMES'
                        PERFORM 400-TYPE-5 THRU 400-TYPE-5-EXIT
                          UNTIL NBR-TIMES > 10000.
                        PERFORM 600-INIT-IT THRU 600-EXIT.
                        DISPLAY 'IF DISPLAY > COMP-3 10000 TIMES'
                        PERFORM 400-TYPE-6 THRU 400-TYPE-6-EXIT
                          UNTIL NBR-TIMES > 10000.
                        PERFORM 600-INIT-IT THRU 600-EXIT.
                        DISPLAY 'IF COMP > COMP-3 10000 TIMES'
                        PERFORM 400-TYPE-7 THRU 400-TYPE-7-EXIT
                          UNTIL NBR-TIMES > 10000.
                        PERFORM 600-INIT-IT THRU 600-EXIT.
                        DISPLAY 'ADD TO DISPLAY 10000 TIMES'
                        PERFORM 400-TYPE-8 THRU 400-TYPE-8-EXIT
                          UNTIL NBR-TIMES > 10000.
                        PERFORM 600-INIT-IT THRU 600-EXIT.
                        DISPLAY 'IF COMP > COMP 10000 TIMES'
                        PERFORM 400-TYPE-9 THRU 400-TYPE-9-EXIT
                          UNTIL NBR-TIMES > 10000.
                300-TEST-EXIT.
                    EXIT.
```

```
400-TYPE-0.
    MOVE COMP0001 TO COMP0001B.
    MOVE COMP0001B TO COMP0001.
    MOVE COMP0001 TO COMP0001B.
    MOVE COMP0001B TO COMP0001.
    MOVE COMP0001 TO COMP0001B.
    MOVE COMP0001B TO COMP0001.
    MOVE COMP0001 TO COMP0001B.
    MOVE COMP0001B TO COMP0001.
    MOVE COMP0001 TO COMP0001B.
    MOVE COMP0001B TO COMP0001.
    MOVE COMP0001 TO COMP0001B.
    MOVE COMP0001B TO COMP0001.
    PERFORM 500-BUMP-IT.
400-TYPE-0-EXIT.
    EXIT.
400-TYPE-1.
    ADD +13.31 TO COMP0001.
    ADD +13.31 TO COMP0001.
    ADD +13.31 TO COMP0001.
    ADD +13.31 TO COMP0001.
    ADD +13.31 TO COMP0001.
    ADD +13.31 TO COMP0001.
    ADD +13.31 TO COMP0001.
    ADD +13.31 TO COMP0001.
    ADD +13.31 TO COMP0001.
    ADD +13.31 TO COMP0001.
    ADD +13.31 TO COMP0001.
    ADD +13.31 TO COMP0001.
    PERFORM 500-BUMP-IT.
400-TYPE-1-EXIT.
    EXIT.
400-TYPE-2.
    ADD +13.31 TO COMP0001-3.
    ADD +13.31 TO COMP0001-3.
    ADD +13.31 TO COMP0001-3.
    ADD +13.31 TO COMP0001-3.
    ADD +13.31 TO COMP0001-3.
    ADD +13.31 TO COMP0001-3.
    ADD +13.31 TO COMP0001-3.
    ADD +13.31 TO COMP0001-3.
    ADD +13.31 TO COMP0001-3.
```

```
          ADD +13.31 TO COMP0001-3.
          ADD +13.31 TO COMP0001-3.
          ADD +13.31 TO COMP0001-3.
          PERFORM 500-BUMP-IT.
     400-TYPE-2-EXIT.
          EXIT.
     400-TYPE-3.
          MOVE COMP0001-3 TO COMP0001-3B.
          MOVE COMP0001-3B TO COMP0001-3.
          MOVE COMP0001-3 TO COMP0001-3B.
          MOVE COMP0001-3B TO COMP0001-3.
          MOVE COMP0001-3 TO COMP0001-3B.
          MOVE COMP0001-3B TO COMP0001-3.
          MOVE COMP0001-3 TO COMP0001-3B.
          MOVE COMP0001-3B TO COMP0001-3.
          MOVE COMP0001-3 TO COMP0001-3B.
          MOVE COMP0001-3B TO COMP0001-3.
          MOVE COMP0001-3 TO COMP0001-3B.
          MOVE COMP0001-3B TO COMP0001-3.
          PERFORM 500-BUMP-IT.
     400-TYPE-3-EXIT.
          EXIT.
     400-TYPE-4.
          MOVE DISPLAY4 TO COMP0004-3.
          MOVE COMP0004-3 TO DISPLAY4.
          MOVE DISPLAY4 TO COMP0004-3.
          MOVE COMP0004-3 TO DISPLAY4.
          MOVE DISPLAY4 TO COMP0004-3.
          MOVE COMP0004-3 TO DISPLAY4.
          MOVE DISPLAY4 TO COMP0004-3.
          MOVE COMP0004-3 TO DISPLAY4.
          MOVE DISPLAY4 TO COMP0004-3.
          MOVE COMP0004-3 TO DISPLAY4.
          MOVE DISPLAY4 TO COMP0004-3.
          MOVE COMP0004-3 TO DISPLAY4.
          PERFORM 500-BUMP-IT.
     400-TYPE-4-EXIT.
          EXIT.
     400-TYPE-5.
          IF COMP0001-3 > COMP0001-3B
               PERFORM 500-BUMP-IT
          ELSE
```

```
    IF COMP0001-3 > COMP0001-3B
        PERFORM 500-BUMP-IT
    ELSE
    IF COMP0001-3 > COMP0001-3B
        PERFORM 500-BUMP-IT
    ELSE
    IF COMP0001-3 > COMP0001-3B
        PERFORM 500-BUMP-IT
    ELSE
    IF COMP0001-3 > COMP0001-3B
        PERFORM 500-BUMP-IT
    ELSE
    IF COMP0001-3 > COMP0001-3B
        PERFORM 500-BUMP-IT.
    PERFORM 500-BUMP-IT.
400-TYPE-5-EXIT.
    EXIT.
400-TYPE-6.
    IF DISPLAY4 > COMP0004-3
        PERFORM 500-BUMP-IT
    ELSE
    IF DISPLAY4 > COMP0004-3
        PERFORM 500-BUMP-IT
    ELSE
    IF DISPLAY4 > COMP0004-3
        PERFORM 500-BUMP-IT
    ELSE
    IF DISPLAY4 > COMP0004-3
        PERFORM 500-BUMP-IT
    ELSE
    IF DISPLAY4 > COMP0004-3
        PERFORM 500-BUMP-IT
    ELSE
    IF DISPLAY4 > COMP0004-3
        PERFORM 500-BUMP-IT.
    PERFORM 500-BUMP-IT.
400-TYPE-6-EXIT.
    EXIT.
400-TYPE-7.
    IF COMP0001 > COMP0001-3
        PERFORM 500-BUMP-IT
    ELSE
```

```
        IF COMP0001 > COMP0001-3
            PERFORM 500-BUMP-IT
        ELSE
        IF COMP0001 > COMP0001-3
            PERFORM 500-BUMP-IT
        ELSE
        IF COMP0001 > COMP0001-3
            PERFORM 500-BUMP-IT
        ELSE
        IF COMP0001 > COMP0001-3
            PERFORM 500-BUMP-IT
        ELSE
        IF COMP0001 > COMP0001-3
            PERFORM 500-BUMP-IT.
        PERFORM 500-BUMP-IT.
    400-TYPE-7-EXIT.
        EXIT.
    400-TYPE-8.
        ADD +13.31 TO DISPLAY4.
        ADD +13.31 TO DISPLAY4.
        ADD +13.31 TO DISPLAY4.
        ADD +13.31 TO DISPLAY4.
        ADD +13.31 TO DISPLAY4.
        ADD +13.31 TO DISPLAY4.
        ADD +13.31 TO DISPLAY4.
        ADD +13.31 TO DISPLAY4.
        ADD +13.31 TO DISPLAY4.
        ADD +13.31 TO DISPLAY4.
        ADD +13.31 TO DISPLAY4.
        ADD +13.31 TO DISPLAY4.
        PERFORM 500-BUMP-IT.
    400-TYPE-8-EXIT.
        EXIT.
    400-TYPE-9.
        IF COMP0001 > COMP0001B
            PERFORM 500-BUMP-IT
        ELSE
        IF COMP0001 > COMP0001B
            PERFORM 500-BUMP-IT
        ELSE
        IF COMP0001 > COMP0001B
            PERFORM 500-BUMP-IT
```

```
         ELSE
         IF COMP0001 > COMP0001B
             PERFORM 500-BUMP-IT
         ELSE
         IF COMP0001 > COMP0001B
             PERFORM 500-BUMP-IT
         ELSE
         IF COMP0001 > COMP0001B
             PERFORM 500-BUMP-IT.
         PERFORM 500-BUMP-IT.
400-TYPE-9-EXIT.
         EXIT.
500-BUMP-IT.
         ADD +1 TO NBR-TIMES.
500-BUMP-IT-EXIT.
         EXIT.
600-INIT-IT.
         MOVE +2489 TO COMP0001
                      COMP0001B
                      COMP0001-3
                      COMP0001-3B
                      DISPLAY4
                      COMP0004-3.
         MOVE +1 TO NBR-TIMES.
600-EXIT.
         EXIT.
```

Cobol Soundex Program

```
IDENTIFICATION DIVISION.
        PROGRAM-ID.             SNDXPR1.
        ****************************************************************
        * SOUNDIT PROGRAM MODIFIED AS FOLLOWS:                    *
        *                                                         *
        *       06/05/90 - DATE PROTECT ROUTINES REMOVED          *
        *       12/12/90 - ADD SPECIAL CHAR CORRECTIONS           *
        ****************************************************************
        AUTHOR.                 JEFFREY A. DUNHAM
        INSTALLATION.           COPYRIGHT, 1990



        DATE-WRITTEN.           12/12/90.
        REMARKS.                THIS IS THE DBMS SOUNDIT PGM
                                THIS PROGRAM IS CALLED BY ANY
                                DBMS APPLICATION PROGRAM AND
                                BUILDS THE SOUNDIT KEY.
            EJECT
        ****************************************************************


        **   CREATE SOUNDIT KEY                                   **


        ****************************************************************
```

```
ENVIRONMENT DIVISION.
INPUT-OUTPUT SECTION.
FILE-CONTROL.
DATA DIVISION.
FILE SECTION.
WORKING-STORAGE SECTION.
*
01  FILLER                      PIC X(50)    VALUE
    '** WORKING STORAGE FOR SOSOUNDX BEGINS HERE =>'.
01  N                       PIC 9(4)    COMP VALUE ZERO.
01  M                       PIC 9(4)    COMP VALUE ZERO.
01  O                       PIC 9(4)    COMP VALUE ZERO.
01  SNDX-WORK-AREA.
    05  SNDX-WK-LIT             PIC X(50)    VALUE
    '** DBMS SOUNDIT WORK AREA BEGINS HERE  ======>'.
  03  SNDX-WK-OUTPUT-GRP.
    05  SNDX-WK-OUTPUT-KEY    PIC X OCCURS 1000 TIMES.
  03  SNDX-WK-KEY-LEN-GRP.
    05  SNDX-WK-INPT-KEY-LENGTH PIC 9(4).
    05  SNDX-WK-OUPT-KEY-LENGTH PIC 9(4).
  03  SNDX-WK-INPUT-GRP.
    05  SNDX-WK-INPUT-KEY      PIC X OCCURS 1000 TIMES.
*
  01  SNDX-QUICK-INIT-GRP.
*    12345678901234567890123456789012345678901234567890
    05  SNDX-GRP1              PIC X(50) VALUE
    '00000000000000000000000000000000000000000000000000'.
    05  SNDX-GRP2              PIC X(50) VALUE
    '00000000000000000000000000000000000000000000000000'.
    05  SNDX-GRP3              PIC X(50) VALUE
    '00000000000000000000000000000000000000000000000000'.
    05  SNDX-GRP4              PIC X(50) VALUE
    '00000000000000000000000000000000000000000000000000'.
    05  SNDX-GRP5              PIC X(50) VALUE
    '00000000000000000000000000000000000000000000000000'.
    05  SNDX-GRP6              PIC X(50) VALUE
    '00000000000000000000000000000000000000000000000000'.
    05  SNDX-GRP7              PIC X(50) VALUE
    '00000000000000000000000000000000000000000000000000'.
    05  SNDX-GRP8              PIC X(50) VALUE
    '00000000000000000000000000000000000000000000000000'.
    05  SNDX-GRP9              PIC X(50) VALUE
```

```
                '00000000000000000000000000000000000000000000000000'.
        05    SNDX-GRP10              PIC X(50) VALUE
                '00000000000000000000000000000000000000000000000000'.
        05    SNDX-GRP11              PIC X(50) VALUE
                '00000000000000000000000000000000000000000000000000'.
        05    SNDX-GRP12              PIC X(50) VALUE
                '00000000000000000000000000000000000000000000000000'.
        05    SNDX-GRP13              PIC X(50) VALUE
                '00000000000000000000000000000000000000000000000000'.
        05    SNDX-GRP14              PIC X(50) VALUE
                '00000000000000000000000000000000000000000000000000'.
        05    SNDX-GRP15              PIC X(50) VALUE
                '00000000000000000000000000000000000000000000000000'.
        05    SNDX-GRP16              PIC X(50) VALUE
                '00000000000000000000000000000000000000000000000000'.
        05    SNDX-GRP17              PIC X(50) VALUE
                '00000000000000000000000000000000000000000000000000'.
        05    SNDX-GRP18              PIC X(50) VALUE
                '00000000000000000000000000000000000000000000000000'.
        05    SNDX-GRP19              PIC X(50) VALUE
                '00000000000000000000000000000000000000000000000000'.
        05    SNDX-GRP20              PIC X(50) VALUE
                '00000000000000000000000000000000000000000000000000'.
   *

   LINKAGE SECTION.
   *

   01   SNDX-AREA.
        03   SNDX-OUTPUT-GRP.
          05    SNDX-OUTPUT-KEY        PIC X OCCURS 1000 TIMES.
        03   SNDX-KEY-LEN-GRP.
          05    SNDX-INPUT-KEY-LENGTH   PIC 9(4).
          05    SNDX-OUTPUT-KEY-LENGTH  PIC 9(4).
        03   SNDX-INPUT-GRP.
          05    SNDX-INPUT-KEY         PIC X OCCURS 1000 TIMES.
        03   SNDX-FILL-GRP.
          05    SNDX-FILL              PIC X OCCURS 1000 TIMES.
   *

   PROCEDURE DIVISION USING SNDX-AREA.
   *
   *
   *     PERFORM SOUNDIT REDUCTION OF INPUT KEY CREATING 4 BYTE
   *     OUTPUT KEY. IF ROUTINE FAILS THEN PLACE THE RETURN CODE
```

```
*      IN SNDX-OUPUT-KEY FIELD OF ZZZZ. IF EVERYTHING IS OK THEN
*      RETURN THE OUTPUT KEY IN THE SNDX-OUTPUT-KEY FIELD.
*
 10-MAIN.
      MOVE 1 TO N.
      PERFORM 30-ZERO THRU 30-ZERO-EXIT.
      MOVE SNDX-INPUT-KEY (1) TO SNDX-WK-OUTPUT-KEY (1).
      MOVE SNDX-INPUT-KEY (1) TO SNDX-WK-INPUT-KEY (1).
      MOVE 2 TO N.
      MOVE 2 TO O.
      PERFORM 20-KEY-CONVERT THRU 20-KEY-CONVERT-EXIT UNTIL
          N GREATER THAN SNDX-INPUT-KEY-LENGTH OR
          O GREATER THAN SNDX-OUTPUT-KEY-LENGTH.
      IF SNDX-WK-OUTPUT-KEY (1) EQUAL '0' AND
         SNDX-WK-OUTPUT-KEY (2) EQUAL '0' AND
         SNDX-WK-OUTPUT-KEY (3) EQUAL '0' AND
         SNDX-WK-OUTPUT-KEY (4) EQUAL '0' AND
         SNDX-WK-OUTPUT-KEY (5) EQUAL '0' AND
         SNDX-WK-OUTPUT-KEY (6) EQUAL '0' AND
         SNDX-WK-OUTPUT-KEY (7) EQUAL '0' AND
         SNDX-WK-OUTPUT-KEY (8) EQUAL '0' AND
         SNDX-WK-OUTPUT-KEY (9) EQUAL '0' AND
         SNDX-WK-OUTPUT-KEY (10) EQUAL '0' THEN
         MOVE 'Z' TO SNDX-WK-OUTPUT-KEY (1)
         MOVE 'Z' TO SNDX-WK-OUTPUT-KEY (2)
         MOVE 'Z' TO SNDX-WK-OUTPUT-KEY (3)
         MOVE 'Z' TO SNDX-WK-OUTPUT-KEY (4).
      MOVE 1 TO N.
      PERFORM 40-MOVE THRU 40-MOVE-EXIT.
      GOBACK.
 10-MAIN-EXIT.
      EXIT.


 20-KEY-CONVERT.
      COMPUTE M = N - 1.
      IF SNDX-INPUT-KEY (N) EQUAL
        ('A' OR 'E' OR 'H' OR 'I' OR 'O' OR 'U' OR 'W' OR 'Y') OR
         SNDX-INPUT-KEY (N) EQUAL ' ' THEN
         MOVE SNDX-WK-INPUT-KEY (M) TO SNDX-WK-INPUT-KEY (N)
         ADD 1 TO N
         GO TO 20-KEY-CONVERT-EXIT.
      IF SNDX-INPUT-KEY (N) EQUAL
```

```
                ('B' OR 'F' OR 'P' OR 'V')
            IF SNDX-INPUT-KEY (N) EQUAL SNDX-WK-INPUT-KEY (M) THEN
                MOVE SNDX-WK-INPUT-KEY (M) TO SNDX-WK-INPUT-KEY (N)
                ADD 1 TO N
                GO TO 20-KEY-CONVERT-EXIT
            ELSE
                MOVE SNDX-INPUT-KEY (N) TO SNDX-WK-INPUT-KEY (N)
                MOVE '1' TO SNDX-WK-OUTPUT-KEY (O)
                ADD 1 TO O
                ADD 1 TO N
                GO TO 20-KEY-CONVERT-EXIT.
        IF SNDX-INPUT-KEY (N) EQUAL
            ('C' OR 'G' OR 'J' OR 'K' OR 'Q' OR 'S' OR 'X' OR 'Z')
            IF SNDX-INPUT-KEY (N) EQUAL SNDX-WK-INPUT-KEY (M) THEN
                MOVE SNDX-WK-INPUT-KEY (M) TO SNDX-WK-INPUT-KEY (N)
                ADD 1 TO N
                GO TO 20-KEY-CONVERT-EXIT
            ELSE
                MOVE SNDX-INPUT-KEY (N) TO SNDX-WK-INPUT-KEY (N)
                MOVE '2' TO SNDX-WK-OUTPUT-KEY (O)
                ADD 1 TO O
                ADD 1 TO N
                GO TO 20-KEY-CONVERT-EXIT.
        IF SNDX-INPUT-KEY (N) EQUAL
            ('D' OR 'T')
            IF SNDX-INPUT-KEY (N) EQUAL SNDX-WK-INPUT-KEY (M) THEN
                MOVE SNDX-WK-INPUT-KEY (M) TO SNDX-WK-INPUT-KEY (N)
                ADD 1 TO N
                GO TO 20-KEY-CONVERT-EXIT
            ELSE
                MOVE SNDX-INPUT-KEY (N) TO SNDX-WK-INPUT-KEY (N)
                MOVE '3' TO SNDX-WK-OUTPUT-KEY (O)
                ADD 1 TO O
                ADD 1 TO N
                GO TO 20-KEY-CONVERT-EXIT.
        IF SNDX-INPUT-KEY (N) EQUAL
            ('L')
            IF SNDX-INPUT-KEY (N) EQUAL SNDX-WK-INPUT-KEY (M) THEN
                MOVE SNDX-WK-INPUT-KEY (M) TO SNDX-WK-INPUT-KEY (N)
                ADD 1 TO N
                GO TO 20-KEY-CONVERT-EXIT
            ELSE
```

```
                    MOVE SNDX-INPUT-KEY (N) TO SNDX-WK-INPUT-KEY (N)

                    MOVE '4' TO SNDX-WK-OUTPUT-KEY (O)

                    ADD 1 TO O

                    ADD 1 TO N

                    GO TO 20-KEY-CONVERT-EXIT.

            IF SNDX-INPUT-KEY (N) EQUAL

                ('M' OR 'N')

                IF SNDX-INPUT-KEY (N) EQUAL SNDX-WK-INPUT-KEY (M) THEN

                    MOVE SNDX-WK-INPUT-KEY (M) TO SNDX-WK-INPUT-KEY (N)

                    ADD 1 TO N

                    GO TO 20-KEY-CONVERT-EXIT

                ELSE

                    MOVE SNDX-INPUT-KEY (N) TO SNDX-WK-INPUT-KEY (N)

                    MOVE '5' TO SNDX-WK-OUTPUT-KEY (O)

                    ADD 1 TO O

                    ADD 1 TO N

                    GO TO 20-KEY-CONVERT-EXIT.

            IF SNDX-INPUT-KEY (N) EQUAL

                ('R')

                IF SNDX-INPUT-KEY (N) EQUAL SNDX-WK-INPUT-KEY (M) THEN

                    MOVE SNDX-WK-INPUT-KEY (M) TO SNDX-WK-INPUT-KEY (N)

                    ADD 1 TO N

                    GO TO 20-KEY-CONVERT-EXIT

                ELSE

                    MOVE SNDX-INPUT-KEY (N) TO SNDX-WK-INPUT-KEY (N)

                    MOVE '6' TO SNDX-WK-OUTPUT-KEY (O)

                    ADD 1 TO O

                    ADD 1 TO N

                    GO TO 20-KEY-CONVERT-EXIT.

    * HANDLE NUM 0 - 9 CAN USE GE AND LE ALSO

            IF SNDX-INPUT-KEY (N) EQUAL

                ('0' OR '1' or '2' or '3' or '4' or '5' or '6' or '7'
                '8' or '9')

                MOVE SNDX-INPUT-KEY (N) TO SNDX-WK-INPUT-KEY (N)

                MOVE SNDX-INPUT-KEY (N) TO SNDX-WK-OUTPUT-KEY (O)

                ADD 1 TO O

                ADD 1 TO N.

                GO TO 20-KEY-CONVERT-EXIT.

    * DROP SPEC CHARS

            MOVE ' ' TO SNDX-WK-INPUT-KEY (N) .

            ADD 1 TO N .

      20-KEY-CONVERT-EXIT.
```

```
        EXIT.


0099-ERR1.
    GO TO 0099-ERR2.
0099-ERR1-EXIT.
    EXIT.


30-ZERO.
    MOVE SNDX-QUICK-INIT-GRP TO SNDX-WK-OUTPUT-GRP.
30-ZERO-EXIT.
    EXIT.


40-MOVE.
    MOVE SNDX-WK-OUTPUT-GRP TO SNDX-OUTPUT-GRP.
40-MOVE-EXIT.
    EXIT.


40-ADJACENT.
    IF SNDX-INPUT-KEY (N) EQUAL SNDX-WK-INPUT-KEY (N) THEN
        MOVE ' ' TO SNDX-WK-INPUT-KEY (N)
    ELSE
        MOVE SNDX-INPUT-KEY (N) TO SNDX-WK-INPUT-KEY (N).
40-ADJACENT-EXIT.
    EXIT.


0099-ERR2.
    MOVE 'Z' TO SNDX-OUTPUT-KEY (1).
    MOVE 'Z' TO SNDX-OUTPUT-KEY (2).
    MOVE 'Z' TO SNDX-OUTPUT-KEY (3).
    MOVE 'Z' TO SNDX-OUTPUT-KEY (4).
    GOBACK.
0099-ERR2-EXIT.
```

Total Quality Management Terms

Total Quality Management (TQM) is the more encompassing label usually given Statistical Quality Control (SQC).

Software Quality Assurance (SQA) is how software quality is defined and achieved.

Software Configuration Management (SCM) is all the things affecting change during the life cycle.

Software Process Improvement (SPI) is basically a smarter way of handling the software life cycle.

Software Engineering Institute (SEI) is a federally funded research and development center within the Carnegie Mellon University devoted to advancing software engineering.

Capability Maturity Model (CMM) is a model showing organizations progressing through 5 stages as their processes improve. This model places its emphasis on organization maturity instead of others which emphasize improving the process or individuals involved in the process.

Software Engineering Process Group (SEPG) is a team within organizations to deal with SPI.

Software Productivity Research (SPR) is a model which competes with CMM. This model differs based upon productivity of individuals and paradigms affecting behavior. These are key elements in the overall model overlooked by CMM. Evolving leadership is a key to the success of evolving processes.

Key Process Areas (KPA).

Software Engineering Self-Assessment Test (SESAT) is a way of determining your maturity level.

Metrics are measurements.

Activities

NORMAL ACTIVITIES INCLUDE

- Identify the SEPG group
- Measure the company's maturity level
- Educate the SEPG team, management, technical staff and users
- Decide on commitment level to SPI
- Choose activities appropriate to maturity and commitment levels which will wipe out defects, and improve processes or the individuals involved in the processes.

Activities with payback which can alleviate defects and improve performance

- Peer reviews
- Requirements code and design inspections
- Capture causes of defects and classify them
- Assign work to reduce defects
- Measuring SPI costs versus quality savings (ROI)

CMM Maturity Levels

- Initial (chaotic)
- Repeatable (project management or process discipline)
- Defined (institutionalized)
- Managed (quantified)
- Optimizing (process improvement)
- Add sharpening skills for employees
- Provide an environment where skill transfer is optimized

Best Database Software Sites in the World

This list is taken from the Power Link (authors) home page `http://announce.com/~jdunham/power.htm`. With any luck, this Internet site will still be around when you access it and will have been kept up-to-date.

The Power Link is an expressway to Internet DBMS sites. This listing is in order by DBMS product or related subject.

ADABAS

`http://www.ozemail.com.au/%7Eexpetune/`	(Tools) Expetune Pty Ltd
`news:comp.databases.adabas`	(Usenet Newsgroup) Issues related to ADABAS

BTRIEVE

`http://www.btrieve.com/`	Pervasive Software Inc (formerly Btrieve Technologies)
`http://www.btrieve.com/product/index.htm`	Products
`http://www.btrieve.com/product/produc_2.htm`	Scalable SQL
`http://www.btrieve.com/product/produ_23.htm`	Inscribe
`http://www.btrieve.com/product/produ_10.htm`	Btrieve 6
`http://www.btrieve.com/product/produ_19.htm`	ODBC Interface
`http://www.daaccess.com/`	Data Access Home Page

http://www.daaccess.com/dataflex/tdf01.html/	DataFlex
http://www.daaccess.com/dataflex/s_and_t/white.html	Technical White Papers

BOOKS

http://www.amazon.com/	AMAZON.COM Books
http://www.hotline.com.au/	Australias Hotline Books
http://www.cis.ie/marketplace/micromail/	Micromail Computer Books and Software
http://marketplace.com/0/obs/obshome.html/	The Online Bookstore
http://www.osborne.com/	Osborne McGraw-Hill Books
http://www.coriolis.com/	Coriolis Books
http://www.idg.books.com/online_bookshelf/	IDG Books
http://www.wrox.com/	Wrox Press
http://www.aw.com/	Addison Wesley
http://www.awl.com/corp/subjects.html#cse	Computer Science and Engineering
http://www.awl.com/corp/subjects.html#computing	Computing and Applications
http://www.aw.com/Delphi	Component Design: Extending Delphi 32-bit
http://www.prenhall.com/	Prentice Hall
http://www.wiley.com/	John Wiley and Sons
http://www.mcp.com/sams/	SAMS Books
http://www.sybex.com/sams/	Sybex USA
http://www.mispress.com/	MIS Press
http://www.bf.rmit.edu.au/~orafaq/books.html	Oracle FAQS (books)
http://www.mcp.com/421208311953/cgi-bin/bag?isbn=0-672-30512-7&last=/bookstore	*DB2 Developer's Guide*, 2nd Edition
http://www.almaden.ibm.com/redbooks/	IBM Redbooks Home Page
http://204.146.47.71:80/data/db2/support/servinfo/	DB2 Product and Service Technical Library
http://www.research.digital.com/SRC/personal/Paul_McJones/System_R	System R History

`http://www.nta.no/brukere/olea/db2book`	*Understanding DB2 for OS/2* by Ole Jorgen Anfidsen
`http://www.mcp.com/421208311953/cgi-bin/ bag?isbn=0-672-30512-7&last=/bookstore`	*DB2 Developer's Guide* by Craig Mullins
`http://www.amazon.com/exec/obidos/ Subject=SAS/`	*DB2Guide to Sas/DB2* by Diane E. Brown
`http://www.illumine.com/`	The Illuminations Oracle Bookstore
`http://www.wiley.com:80/compbooks/catalog/ 04.html`	Wiley Publishing Computer Books
`http://www.bookaisle.com/cgi-eba/ addlogo.exe?Template=main.htm+Retailer =dsilink`	Book Aisle
`http://www.eznet.com/%7Ealanm/prog.htm`	Custom Foxpro Database Programming
`http://rampages.onramp.net/~silver/fox.htm`	FoxPro Programmer Reference
`http://dev3.info.apple.com/mdg/html/ MicrosoftFoxProv.2.6.html`	Microsoft FoxPro v. 2.6 (Macintosh Developer's Guide)
`http://www.borland.com/delphi/books/`	Delphi Supporting Books
`http://members.aol.com/drbobnl/menubook.htm`	Delphi Book Review from Dr. Bob
`http://super.sonic.net/delphisig/books.html`	Delphi North Bay SIG
`http://www.borland.com/Product/biblio/ bibdelph.html`	Borland Delphi Book List 1
`http://www.borland.com/Product/biblio/ bibdel2.html`	
`http://www.borland.com/Product/biblio/ bibpas.html`	Borland Delphi Book List 2 Borland Pascal Book List
`http://www.coriolis.com/`	*Delphi 2 Database Applications* by Richard Haven
`http://www.coriolis.com/`	*Delphi 2 Multi-media Adventure Set* by Scott Jarol, Dan Haygood

`http://www.coriolis.com/`	*Delphi Programming Explorer* by Jeff Duntemann, Jim Mischel, Don Taylor
`http://www.coriolis.com/`	*Developing Custom Delphi Components* by Ray Konopka
`http://www.cs.vu.nl/~jprins/tp.html#BOOKS`	Turbo Pascal Programmers Page
`http://www.idgbooks.com/online_bookshelf/`	*Delphi Programming for Dummies* by Ruben King
`http://www.idgbooks.com/online_bookshelf/`	*Delphi Programming Problem Solver* by Ruben King
`http://www.idgbooks.com/online_bookshelf/`	*Delphi 2 Secrets* by Tom Swan
`http://www.idgbooks.com/online_bookshelf/`	*Foundations of Delphi Programming* by Tom Swan
`http://www.idgbooks.com/online_bookshelf/`	*Learn Delphi Database Programming Today* by Jeff Cogswell
`http://www.idgbooks.com/online_bookshelf/`	*Learn Delphi Today* by Jeff Cogswell, Tom Swan
`http://www.iscinc.com/CGI/delphres.cgi`	ISC's Database of Delphi Resources
`http://www.jamsa.com/`	*Delphi Programmer's Library* by Kris Jamsa
`http://www.mcgraw-hill.com/`	*Delphi In-Depth* by Cary Jensen, Loy Anderson
`http://www.mcp.com/1615134622715/que/que_text.html`	*Building Delphi Database Applications* by Paul Kimmel
`http://www.mcp.com/1615134622715/que/que_text.html`	*Building Internet Applications with Delphi 2.0* by Davis Chapman
`http://www.mcp.com/1615134622715/que/que_text.html`	*Delphi By Example* by Blake Watson
`http://www.mcp.com/sams/`	*Delphi Developer's Guide* by Xavier Pacheco, Steven Teixeira

`http://www.mcp.com/sams/`	*Delphi Unleashed* by Charlie Calvert
`http://www.mcp.com/sams/`	*Essential Delphi* by Michelle Manning
`http://www.mcp.com/sams/`	*Teach Yourself Database Programming with Delphi in 21 Days* by Gurewich(s)
`http://www.mcp.com/1615134622715/que/ que_text.html`	*Using Delphi* by Matcho, Faulkner
`http://www.mispress.com/`	*Delphi, A Developer's Guide* by Vince Kellen, Bill Todd
`http://www.mispress.com/`	Delphi Database Development
`http://www.mispress.com/`	*Programming Delphi Custom Components* by Fred Bulback
`http://www.mispress.com/`	*Teach Yourself Delphi* by Devra Hall
`http://www.prenhall.com/`	*Developing with Delphi* by Ford
`http://www.prenhall.com/`	*The Way of Delphi 2: Reusing Objects, Components, Properties and Events* by G. Entsminger
`http://www.sybex.com/`	*Mastering Delphi* by Marco Cant
`http://www.sybex.com/`	*Mastering Delphi 2 for Windows* by Marco Cant
`http://www.vmedia.com/home.html`	*Delphi for Windows Power Toolkit* by Harold Davis
`http://www.webcom.com/~optimax/delbooks.html`	The Delphi Resource Center
`http://www.wiley.com/compbooks/`	*Developing Windows Applications Using Delphi* by Paul Penrod
`http://www.wrox.com/`	*Beginning Delphi 2.0* by Peter Wright

`http://www.wrox.com/`	*Instant Delphi Programming* by Dave Jewell
`http://www.wrox.com/develop/delphi/books.htm`	*The Revolutionary Guide to Delphi 2* by Long, McNab, Winning, Hinks, Wako, and Swart
`http://www.xmission.com/~tclay/revlist.htm`	Delphi Book Reviews

CA PRODUCTS

`http://www.cai.com/products/img.htm`	Home Page for Information Mgmt White Papers from Computer Associates
`http://host.telescan.com/Stocks/Corporate_Snapshot.html?Symbol=SYBS`	Computer Assc Intl Inc Stock Chart (CA)

CA-CLIPPER

`http://www.cai.com/`	Computer Associates Home Page
`http://www.wdb.com/ems/lists/clputilp.htm`	Clipper Programming Tools and Their Producers
`news:comp.lang.clipper`	(Usenet Newsgroup) Clipper and Visual Objects Programming Languages
`news:fido.clipper`	(Usenet Newsgroup) Clipper DBMS and Language
`news:fido.ger.clipper`	(Usenet Newsgroup) Alles xu Clipper
`news:fido7.clipper`	(Usenet Newsgroup) Clipper DBMS
`news:fido7.clipper.fileecho`	(Usenet Newsgroup) Clipper database related files
`news:relcom.comp.dbms.clipper`	(Usenet Newsgroup) Clipper database development system

CA-DATACOM

`http://www.cai.com/products/addbm/datacom.htm`   CA-DATACOM Database Home Page

CA-DB

`http://www.cai.com/products/addbm/db.htm`   CA-DB Database Home Page

CA-IDMS

`http://www.cai.com/products/addbm/idms.htm`   CA-IDMS Database Home Page

`http://allensysgroup.com/`   (Tools) Allen Systems Group, Inc.

`http://allensysgroup.com/catalog/product/idms/idms.htm`   CA-IDMS Tools

`http://www.ozemail.com.au/%7Eexpetune/`   (Tools) Expetune Pty Ltd

`http://www.tact.com/`   (Tools) TACT Software Home Page

`http://www.announce.com/~jdunham/index.html`   CA-IDMS Tuning

`http://www.hslinc.com/iuaindex.html`   CA-IDMS Information User Association Home Page

`news:bit.listserv.idms-l`   (Usenet Newsgroup) CA-IDMS Discussions

CA-INGRES

`http://www.cai.com/`   Computer Associates Home Page

`http://www.cai.com/products/ingres.htm`   CA-OpenIngres/OpenRoad Database

`http://www.cai.com/products/addbm/oidir/oidir.htm`   CA-OpenIngres Product Direction

`http://www.cai.com/products/inglet/index.htm`   CA Inquire Ingres Newsletters

`http://www.naiua.org/`   North American Ingres User Association

`http://www.naiua.org/faqs.html`   The Ingres FAQS Page

`http://www.naiua.org/open_road.html`	Open Road Information and Resources
`http://www.naiua.org/ingres_world.html`	Ingres World Home Page
`http://www.naiua.org/iua_list.html`	World-Wide User Group List
`http://www.pcug.org.au/~sranson`	Australian Capital Territory IUG
`http://endeavor.informatik.tu-chemnitz.de/FGDB/USG/GIUA/GIUA001.htm`	German IUG
`http://www.naiua.org/miua.html`	Midwest IUG
`http://www.mbcc.mass.edu/neiua/index.html`	New England IUG
`http://www.naiua.org/ingres/naiua.html`	North America IUA
`http://igubu.saix.net/iugsa/`	South African IUG
`http://www.itu.ch/RUBIS`	Switzerland IUG
`http://www.tnc.com/`	TNC Home Page
`http://www.tnc.com/ingres/other_rdbms.html`	Other RDBMS Resources
`http://www.tnc.com/ingres/previous_worlds.html`	1994 and 1995 Ingres World Technical Papers
`http://www.leeds.ac.uk/ucs/docs/beg12/beg12.html`	Getting Started with Ingres
`http://iamwww.unibe.ch/~scg/FreeDB/FreeDB.59.html`	Ingres and Perl
`http://wonder.lancs.ac.uk/`	Online Training Materials for Ingres
`http://www.bmc.com/products/pat/amo/brpa158b.html`	Patrol Knowledge Modules for CA-OpenIngres and CA-Ingres
`http://www.compumedia.com/~kkirk/raid.html`	RAIDs with Databases
`http://www.cs.mu.oz.au/%7Eyuan/Ingres/ingres.html`	Super Link for Ingres at Melborne University (Willian Yuan)
`http://www.cs.mu.oz.au/~yuan/Ingres/ingres.html`	Ingres—The Intelligent Reference
`http://iamwww.unibe.ch/~scg/FreeDB/FreeDB.5.html`	University Ingres
`http://www-mtl.mit.edu/CIDM/memos/94-5/section3.3.html`	Ingres Caching and Data Access

`http://www.well.com/user/ideamen/trace.html`	Ingres and OpenIngres Trace Points
`http://wonder.lancs.ac.uk/TeachYourself.html`	Teach yourself Ingres
`http://www.essex.ac.uk/cs/software/risc/ingres.html`	Ingres on RISC Platforms
`http://www.liv.ac.uk/middleware/html/ingres.html`	UCSG Accessing Ingres Data
`http://enfo.com/Wqms/Ingres/Intro.html`	Ingres Database System
`http://www.pmel.noaa.gov/epic/doc/ingres-manage.html`	Ingres Database Management on UNIX
`http://www.cms.dmu.ac.uk/Courses/Common/Ingres/Creating-Tables.html`	Montfort University— Creating Ingres Tables on UNIX
`http://bmw.mbcc.mass.edu/neiua/`	NEIUA Home Page
`http://www.ri.bbsrc.ac.uk/webintool.html`	(Tools) WebinTool
`http://www.aberdeen.com/pubpg.htm`	(Articles) Aberdeen Group Inc., Market Research Reports
`http://www.ovum.com/`	(Articles) Ovum Limited
`http://www.andyne.com/`	(Tools) GQL (Graphic Query Language) from Andyne
`http://host.telescan.com/Stocks/Corporate_Snapshot.html?Symbol=ADYNF`	Andyne Computing Ltd Stock (ADYNF) NASDAQ
`http://www.gentia.com/`	(Tools) Gentia/GentiaDB from Planning Sciences Inc.
`http://host.telescan.com/Stocks/Corporate_Snapshot.html?Symbol=PLNSY`	Andyne Computing Ltd Stock (PLNSY) NASDAQ
`http://www.holossys.com/`	(Tools) Holos from Holistic Systems
`http://www.transarc.com/afs/transarc.com/public/www/Public/Partners/ask-ingres-windows4gl.html`	(Tools) The ASK Group's Windows4GL(™) and ASK Openroad(™)
`http://www.wustl.edu/packages/ingres/`	(Tools) Washington University's Archives
`ftp://ftp.adc.com/pub/ingres/Ingres-FAQ.1`	(FTP) Ingres FAQS from ADC
`news:comp.databases.ingres`	(Usenet Newsgroup) Issues related to the Ingres products

`news:comp.databases`	(Usenet Newsgroup) comp.databases
`news:comp.lang.pascal.delphi`	(Usenet Newsgroup) comp.lang.pascal.delphi
`news:alt.computer.consultants`	(Usenet Newsgroup) Computer Consultants

DB2 FAMILY

`http://www.ibm.com/`	IBM Corporation Home Page
`http://www.software.hosting.ibm.com/data/db2`	DB2 Product Family and Technical Papers
`http://www.software.ibm.com/data/db2/db26000.html`	DB2 for AIX/6000
`http://www.software.ibm.com/software/data.html`	DataGuide, Visualizer and Multimedia Manager
`http://www.software.ibm.com/data/drda.html`	Distributed Relational Database Architecture (DRDA)
`http://www.software.ibm.com/db2/db2pe.html`	DB2 Parallel Edition for AIX
`http://www.software.ibm.com/data/db2/stmate.html`	DB2 Estimator for Windows
`http://www.software.ibm.com/db2/db2hp.html`	DB2 for HP/UX
`http://www.software.ibm.com/data/db2/db22.html`	DB2 for OS/2
`http://www.software.ibm.com/db2/db2v2.html`	DB2 Version 2
`http://www.software.ibm.com/db2/db2mvs.html`	DB2 for MVS/ESA
`http://www.software.ibm.com/data/db2/db2wfac2.html`	DB2 World Wide Web Connection
`http://www.software.ibm.com/data/db2/sdkv2.html`	DB2 SDK V 2
`http://www.developer.ibm.com/`	IBM Solution Developer Support
`http://www.software.ibm.com/db2/db2tech/db2cert.html`	IBM DB2 Professional Certification Program from IBM
`http://www.software.ibm.com/software/data.html`	Data Management

`http://www.software.ibm.com/is/sw-servers/` `database/index.html`	IBM Database Server
`http://www.software.ibm.com/data/dbtools/`	DB Tools Index
`http://www.software.ibm.com/data/dbtools/` `db2n1b02.html`	Performance Monitor for MVS Database 2
`htt://www.neonsys.com/`	Shadow Direct from Neon Systems Inc.
`http://www.infotelcorp.com/`	MasterReorg by Infotel Corporation
`http://www.starquest.com/`	StarSQL Pro ODBC-to- DRDA driver by Star Quest
`ftp://ps.boulder.ibm.com/ps/products/`	(FTP) Personal Products
`ftp://ps.boulder.ibm.com/ps/products/db2/info/`	(FTP) DB2 for OS/2 Newsletter
`ftp://ps.boulder.ibm.com/ps/products/db2/` `fixes/us/db22v12/`	(FTP) DB2 Service Pack
`http://www.webcom.com/raberd/db2mail.html`	DB2 Mail List Subscription
`http://lscftp.kgn.ibm.com/pps/products/` `db2.html`	DB2 Parallel Edition for the RS/6000
`http://www.announce.com/~jdunham/dunham.html`	DB2 Tuning
`http://www.idug.org/`	International DB2 User Group (IDUG)
`http://www.idug.org/regional/rugrost.html`	DB2 Regional User Groups
`http://www.mdug.org.au/Melbourne`	DB2 Users' Group (MDUG)
`http://www.cai.com/products/addbm/db2.htm`	(Tools) Computer Associates DB2 Products
`http://www.platinum.com`	(Tools) Platinum Enhancement Products
`http://www.bmc.com/`	(Tools) BMC Software
`http://www.sqlbench.com/`	(Tools) SQLBench
`http://stls1dv7.stl.ibm.com/`	DB2 Insider's OnRamp
`http://204.146.47.71/qa/www/drt/b_TENG.html`	IBM Database Roundtable
`http://w3.stl.ibm.com/db2/html/db2home.html`	DB2 Home Page (IBM Database 2 for MVS/ESA)
`http://stls1dv7.stl.ibm.com/users/m60/www/`	DB2 Performance Site
`http://www.jcc.com/sql_stnd.html`	SQL Standards Home Page
`http://www.sqlbench.com/`	(Tools) SQLBench

`http://www.inquiry.com/techtips/` `thesqlpro/questindex.html`	Ask the SQL Pro
`http://www.thomsoft.com/`	(Tools) Aonix Software Home Page
`http://www.thomsoft.com/products/index.html`	Products
`http://www.thomsoft.com/products/Ada/ada.html`	ADA
`http://www.thomsoft.com/products/Ada/per.html`	PerfoRMAx Monitor
`http://www.idug.org/reference_lib/mullins.html`	Tools for a Comprehensive DB2 Environment
`http://www.ibm.com/News/CeBIT95/db2.html`	DB2 News Page from IBM
`http://www.boole.com/`	(Tools) Boole & Babbage Home Page
`http://www.webcom.com/raberd/homepage.html`	Ron Rabe's Home Page
`http://www.indiana.edu/~dbateam/db2/db2.html`	DB2 Information and Resources Indiana Univ
`http://members.gnn.com/JoeDB2/db2main.html`	Joe Geller's DB2 Page
`http://info.acm.org/~ryevich/homepage.html`	(Consultants) Richard Yevech
`http://www.ozemail.com.au/%7Eexpetune/`	(Tools) Expetune Pty Ltd
`http://www.comvista.com/net/www/cgidata.html`	Database CGIs
`http://www.mfi.com/softwareguide/` `DB2-Solutions/`	DB2 Family Solutions Directory on Internet
`http://www.almaden.ibm.com/`	IBM Almaden Web Farm

`http://host.telescan.com/Stocks/`
`Corporate_Snapshot.html?Button`
`+Report&Symbol=IBM`
	International Business Machines Corp Com Stock Chart (IBM)

`http://www.candle.com/`	(Tools) Candle Corporation Home Page
`http://www.compuware.com/`	(Tools) COMPUWARE Home Page
`http://www.legent.com/products/dbprods/` `db2home.html`	(Tools) LEGENT Home Page
`http://www.relarc.com`	Relational Architects Intl Home
`http://www.mfi.com/softwareguide/` `DB2-Solutions/`	DB2 Solutions
`http://www.dataspace.com.au/resource.html`	(Consultants) Dataspace Consulting

`http://www.netcom.com/~llyon/home.html`	(Consultants) RDE Systems
`http://www.fyi-systems.com`	(Consultants) FYI Systems
`http://www.triton.co.uk`	(Consultants) Triton
`http://www.responsivesystems.com`	(Consultants) Responsive Systems
`http://tile.net/news/db21.html`	(Usenet List) bit.listserv.db2-l
`news:bit.listserv.db2-l`	(Usenet Newsgroup) DB2 Database Discussion List
`news:comp.databases.ibm-db2`	(Usenet Newsgroup) Problem resolution with DB2 database products
`news:alt.computer.consultants`	(Usenet Newsgroup) Computer Consultants
`news:ibm.globenet.db2mvs.compusrv`	(Usenet Newsgroup) IBM DB2/MVS GLOBNET
`news:bit.listserv.cics-l`	(Usenet Newsgroup) bit.listserv.cics-l
`news:ibm.dialog.db2geo`	(Usenet Newsgroup) ibm.dialog.db2-l
`news:ibm.globenet.db2annce.compusrv`	(Usenet Newsgroup) ibm.globenet.db2annce. compusrv
`news:ibm.globenet.db2beta.cforum`	(Usenet Newsgroup) ibm.globenet.db2beta. cforum
`news:ibm.globenet.db2beta.compusrv`	(Usenet Newsgroup) ibm.globenet.db2beta. compusrv
`news:ibm.globenet.dcaf.cforum`	(Usenet Newsgroup) ibm.gblobnet.dcaf.cforum
`news:ibm.globenet.dbasemgr.compusrv`	(Usenet Newsgroup) ibm.globnet.dbasemgr. compusrv
`news:comp.databases`	(Usenet Newsgroup) comp.database
`news:ibm.globenet.gentech.cforum`	(Usenet Newsgroup) ibm.globnet.gentech.cforum

`news:bit.listserv.ibm-main`	(Usenet Newsgroup) IBM Mainframe Newsgroup

DBASE

`http://www.borland.com`	Borland Software Home Page
`http://www.borland.com/VdBASE/index.html`	Visual dBASE Home Page
`http://www.borland.com/VdBASE/vdbnet.html`	Visual dBASE Internet Sources
`http://www.borland.com/VdBASE/vdbprod.html`	Visual dBASE Product Information
`http://www.borland.com/VdBASE/papers/`	Visual dBASE Technical White Papers
`http://www.borland.com/VdBASE/papers/vdbfox/vdbfox.html`	Visual dBASE 5.5 for FoxPro Users
`http://www.borland.com/VdBASE/vdbprev/db5dos/db5dos.html`	Visual dBASE Previous Versions
`http://www.borland.com/techsupport/VdBASE/`	Visual dBASE Technical Support
`http://www.borland.com/VdBASE/papers/dwintro/dw1intro.html`	dBASE 5.0 for Windows Introduction
`http://www.borland.com/VdBASE/vdbprev/db5dos/ddeva/dd1toc.html`	dBASE 5.0 for Windows Evaluator's Guide
`http://www.borland.com/feedback/listserv.html`	Listserver
`http://www.borland.com/sqllinks/sql25fac.html`	SQL Links Version 2.5 Factsheet
`http://www.borland.com/sqllinks/sql30fac.html`	SQL Links Version 3.0 Factsheet
`http://www.borland.com/feedback/newsgrps.html`	Borland Product Feedback
`http://www.borland.com/feedback/ftp.html`	(FTP) Sites List
`http://host.telescan.com/Stocks/Corporate_Snapshot.html?Button+Report&Symbol=BII`	Borland Intl Inc Com Stock Chart (BII) PACIFIC
`http://host.telescan.com/Stocks/Corporate_Snapshot.html?Button+Report&Symbol=BORL`	Borland Intl Inc Com Stock Chart (BORL) NASDAQ

`news:comp.database.xbase.misc`	(Usenet Newsgroup) Discussion of xBase (dBase-like) products
`news:fido.ger.dbase`	(Usenet Newsgroup) DBASE, CLIPPER
`news:maus.lang.clipper`	(Usenet Newsgroup) DIE dBase-kompatible Datenbank
`news:z-netz.sprachen.dbase`	(Usenet Newsgroup) CLIPPER,DBXL und kompatible
`news:comp.databases`	(Usenet Newsgroup) comp.databases

DELPHI

`http://www.borland.com/delphi/`	Delphi Home Page
`http://www.borland.com/delphi/delcomp/`	Delphi Companion Products
`http://www.borland.com/delphi/delnet.html`	Internet Sources for Delphi
`http://www.borland.com/techsupport/delphi/inforecs/delpages.html`	Delphi Related Web Sites
`http://www.borland.com/delphi/delprod.html`	Product Information Library
`http://www.borland.com/delphi/news/`	Delphi In The News
`http://www.borland.com/delphi/papers/`	White Papers
`http://www.borland.com/delphi/press/`	Press Releases
`http://www.borland.com/feedback/ftp.html`	FTP Site
`http://www.borland.com/feedback/listserv.html`	List Servers/Mailing Lists
`http://www.borland.com/techsupport/delphi/`	Delphi Technical Support
`http://www.borland.com/techsupport/delphi/whatsnew.html`	What's New
`http://www.borland.com/techsupport/delphi/devcorner/index.html`	Developers Corner
`http://www.borland.com/techsupport/delphi/devcorner/techtips.html`	Tech Tips
`http://www.borland.com/techsupport/delphi/techdocs/index.html`	Technical Documents

http://www.borland.com/techsupport/delphi/ inforecs/index.html	Information Resources
http://www.borland.com/techsupport/delphi/ downloads/index.html	Delphi Downloads
http://www.borland.com/techsupport/delphi/ delphi_bugs.html	Bug Reports
http://www.borland.com/techsupport/delphi/ techdocs/bds.html	Search
http://www.borland.com/delphi/papers/ survival/pi-cnvd1.html	*A Survival Guide to Migrating Applications to Delphi 2.0* by P. Illes
http://www.mistral.co.uk/gbamber/index.html	Gordon Bamber Code Corner
http://www.teleport.com/~cwhite/tsexamp.html	Delphi Station
http://www.ans.com.au/~ali/ delphi.html#CodeExamples	Code Examples by Ali Goktogan
http://www.wi.fh-flensburg.de/fbw/wi/ mueller/delphi/downld/dedown.html	Mueller Download Site
http://www.mindspring.com/~addg/	Atlanta Delphi Developers Group ADDG
http://www.launch.com/delphi_sig.html	Austin Delphi Users' Group
http://www.aisd.com/delphiug.html	Bangalore Delphi Users' Group
http://www.shoresoft.com/html/ctdug/sites.htm	CT Delphi Users Group
http://www.3-D.org/	Delphi Developers of Dallas
http://super.sonic.net/delphisig/index.html	Delphi North Bay SIG
http://rainbow.rmii.com/%7Ebillt/debug.html	Denver Borland Users' Group (DeBUG)
http://oeonline.com:80/~dsamoylo/delphi/	Detroit Area Delphi
http://macroent.com/~hadp/	Houston Association of Delphi Professionals
http://www.flash.net/~ronbr/sigdelfi/ sigdelfi.htm	Houston Delphi SIG
http://www.bigcreek.com/delphi/	Central Iowa Delphi Users' Group
http://www.sound.net/~cyclone/delphi/ delphi.htm	Kansas City Delphi Users' Group
http://www.iscinc.com/nydug.html	New York Delphi Users' Group

`http://www.ocdelphi.org/`	Orange County Delphi Users' Group
`http://www.phillydelphi.com/`	Philly Delphi Users' Association
`http://www.nauticom.net/users/kfarra/padug.html`	Pittsburgh Area Delphi Users' Group
`http://205.138.107.3:80/delphi/slc/`	Salt Lake City Delphi Users' GroupG
`http://www.sddug.slctnet.com`	San Diego Delphi Users' Group
`http://www.webcom.com/~tokpela/d2/d2.html`	San Fransisco Bay Area Users' Group
`http://www.hooked.net/users/maldewin/delphi/`	Silicon Valley Computer Society
`http://www.shadow.net/~datachem/sfddg11.html`	Southeast Florida Database Developers' Group
`http://www.netpath.net/delphi.html`	South Eastern Delphi Developers' Group
`http://www.swanlake.com/delphi/index.html`	Triangle Area Delphi Users' Group
`http://cpcug.org/user/delphi/`	Washington DC Delphi Users' Group
`http://www.dkw.com/Delphi.htm`	Calgary Delphi Users' Group
`http://mers.com/tdug.html`	The Toronto Delphi Users' Group
`http://www.geocities.com/SiliconValley/8314/delphi.htm`	Bem-Vindo ? Delphi Brasil
`http://www.mclink.it/mclink/delphi/index.htm`	Delphi Team Roma, Italy
`http://members.aol.com/ddguk/webpage/index.htm`	U.K. Delphi Developers' Group
`http://www.rcai.demon.co.uk/delphi.htm#odug`	Oxfordshire U.K. Delphi Users' Group
`http://pro1.taynet.co.uk/users/CharlottesWeb/`	Scottish Delphi Users' Group
`http://www.hobby.nl/hcc/gg/pa/pa.html`	Netherlands HCC Pascal Gebruikergroep

`http://criticalmass.com/concord/`	**Critical Mass Communications Newsgroup Archives**
`http://www.plexon.com/dp32db1.html`	**Borland Delphi Client/Server Suite 2.0 by Lance Devin**
`http://www.kallista.com/TechPapers/DelphiSQL/DelphiSQL.htm`	**Using Delphi with Microsoft SQL Server 6.0**
`http://www.hyperact.com/hypera37.html`	**(Tools) MemDB Delphi Native Database Engine**
`http://www.platinum.com`	**(Tools) Platinum Enhancement Products**
`http://www.highlander.com/`	**(Tools) Highlander Software (Europe)**
`http://www.sequiter.com/`	**(Tools) CodeBase 6 from Sequiter**
`http://www.sequiter.com/products/info.htm`	**Product Information**
`http://www.sequiter.com/products/60pas.htm`	**Shatter Delphi's Database Performance**
`http://www.sequiter.com/products/60feat.htm`	**CodeBase features**
`http://www.adam.co.za/`	**(Tools) CompuStat Home Page**
`http://www.adam.co.za/odbcexpress/index.htm`	**ODBC Express**
`http://www.opus.ch/ODA/default.htm`	**(Tools) Opus DirectAccess RDD**
`http://www.dnai.com/~amisys/titan.html`	**(Tools) Titan RDD**
`http://www.batsoft.com/`	**(Tools) OptStyle from Baltic Advanced Technologies**
`http://www.oopsoft.com/`	**(Tools) Object Express by OOPSOFT**
`http://www.ts.umu.se/~jola/EFLIB/`	**(Tools) EFLIB from Simtel**
`http://www.algonet.se/~synchron`	**(Tools) Programmer's Heaven CD-ROM**
`http://host.telescan.com/Stocks/Corporate_Snapshot.html?Button+Report&Symbol=BII`	**Borland Intl Inc Com Stock Chart (BII) PACIFIC**

`http://host.telescan.com/Stocks/`
`Corporate_Snapshot.html?Button`
`+Report&Symbol=BORL`
	Borland Intl Inc Com Stock Chart (BORL) NASDAQ

`news:alt.lang.delphi`	(Usenet Newsgroup) Delphi Language
`news:alt.comp.lang.borland-delphi`	(Usenet Newsgroup) Borland Delphi
`news:comp.lang.pascal.delphi.advocacy`	(Usenet Newsgroup) Contentious Issues Related to Delphi
`news:comp.lang.pascal.delphi.announce`	(Usenet Newsgroup) Announcements
`news:comp.lang.pascal.delphi.components.misc`	(Usenet Newsgroup) Component Issues
`news:comp.lang.pascal.delphi.components.usage`	(Usenet Newsgroup) Previously Written Components
`news:comp.lang.pascal.delphi.` `components.writing`	(Usenet Newsgroup) Writing Components
`news:comp.lang.pascal.delphi.databases`	(Usenet Newsgroup) Database Aspects of Borland Delphi
`news:comp.lang.pascal.delphi.misc`	(Usenet Newsgroup) General Issues with Borland Delphi
`news:comp.sources.delphi`	(Usenet Newsgroup) Delphi and Object Pascal Source Code
`news:alt.computer.consultants`	(Usenet Newsgroup) Computer Consultants
`http://www.universal.nl/jobhunt`	(Job Placement) Employment Contacts Worldwide (Nederlands)

FOXPRO

`http://www.microsoft.com`	Microsoft Home Page
`http://www.microsoft.com/minshare`	MS Local User Groups
`http://www.wdb.com/ems/lists/foxutilv.htm`	FoxPro Programming Tools and Their Producers

`http://host.telescan.com/Stocks/`
`Corporate_Snapshot.html?Button`
`+Report&Symbol=MSFT`
	Microsoft Corp Com Stock Chart (MSFT) NASDAQ

`http://www.transformation.com/mfug/`	**Groupe d'Utilisateurs FoxPro de Montreal Montreal FoxPro Users' Group**

`http://198.105.232.4:80/isapi/`
`redir.dll?Target=%2Fsupport`
`%2Fnews%2Ffoxpro.htm`
	Microsoft FoxPro and Visual FoxPro Newsgroups

`http://206.126.103.22/B/bmc/foxpage.htm`	**BMC FoxPage**
`http://206.126.103.22/B/bmc/usergrp.htm#Canada`	**FoxPro User Groups**
`http://www.access.digex.net/~psii/tour.html`	**Visual FoxPro Guided Tour**
`http://www.actgroup.com/vfpconf/`	**The 1996 Visual FoxPro Users Conference— Home Page**
`http://www.belcon.com/foxword/foxword.html`	**FoxWord Report Capture**
`http://www.foxweb.com/`	**FoxWeb: Home Page**
`http://www.imginfo.com/fudg/index.html`	**The FoxPro Users' and Developers' Group**
`http://www.microsoft.com/catalog/` `products/visfoxp/default.htm`	**(Tools) Microsoft Visual FoxPro 3.0**
`http://www.ping.be/%7Eping0150/vfp.html`	**(Tools) Visual FoxPro**
`http://www.sover.net/%7Emarketd/`	**Market Data FAQ Center**
`http://www.state.sd.us/people/colink/` `foxpage.htm`	**State FoxPro Page**
`http://www.state.sd.us/people/colink/` `fox_ug2.htm`	**FoxPro User Groups (2)**
`http://www.transformation.com/foxpro/` `index.html`	**Visual FoxPro Yellow Pages**
`http://www.transformation.com/foxpro/` `group.html`	**Visual FoxPro User Group List**
`http://www.transformation.com/foxpro/` `classtra.html`	**Visual FoxPro Training**
`news:fido7.foxpro`	**(Usenet Newsgroup) FoxPro DBMS**
`news:relcom.comp.dbms.foxpro`	**(Usenet Newsgroup) FoxPro database development system**

`news:comp.databases.xbase.fox`	(Usenet Newsgroup) comp.databases.xbase.fox
`news:comp.databases.xbase.misc`	(Usenet Newsgroup) comp.databases.xbase.misc
`news:microsoft.public.fox.vfp.xplat`	(Usenet Newsgroup) microsoft.public. fox.vfp.xplat
`news:microsoft.public.fox.fox2x.xplat`	(Usenet Newsgroup) microsoft.public. fox.fox2x.xplat
`news:microsoft.public.fox.fox2x.mac-specific`	(Usenet Newsgroup) microsoft.public. fox.fox2x.mac-specific
`ftp://ftp.hop.man.ac.uk/sys/ftp/foxpro/`	(FTP) ftp://ftp.hop.man.ac.uk/ sys/ftp/foxpro/
`ftp://ftp.iinet.com.au/pub/msdos/foxpro/`	(FTP) ftp://ftp.linet.com.au/ dos/foxpro/
`ftp://ftp.microsoft.com/developr/fox/`	(FTP) ftp://ftp.microsoft.com/ developr/fox/

HPC & TUNING

`http://www.cica.indiana.edu/iu_hpc/index.html`	CICA Indiana University Home Page
`http://www.compaq.com/toc.html`	Compaq Computers Table of Contents
`http://www.cait.wustl.edu/cait/infosys.html/`	Center for Appl of Info Tech META List
`http://www.lpac.ac.uk/`	London Parallel Applications Centre
`http://www.lpac.ac.uk/SEL-HPC/Articles/ GeneratedHtml/db.rel.html/`	LPAC High Performance Computing Archives
`http://www.nc.ihost.com/`	Network Computer Coalition Home Page
`http://www.sun.com/`	Sun Microsystems Home Page

`http://tuxedo.novell.com/`	BEA Systems Inc Home Page
`http://cuiwww.unige.ch/`	Database Papers from University of Geneva
`http://www-ccs.cs.umass.edu/db.html`	Database Systems Laboratory at Univ of Mass, Amherst
`http://www.announce.com/~jdunham/index.html`	DB2 Tuning
`http://www.programart.com/`	Programart Home Page
`http://www.win400.com/`	Best Business Engineering and Software Tools Site
`http://www.internic.net/ds/dspg01.html`	Internic Database Services Page
`http://unix.hensa.ac.uk/unix.html`	HENSA University Parallel Computing
`http://titan.ecs.fullerton.edu/%7Ehalr/aibest.html`	The Best of Artificial Intelligence Sites
`news:aus.computers.parallel`	(Usenet Newsgroup) aus.computers.parallel
`news:aus.computers.sun`	(Usenet Newsgroup) aus.computers.sun
`news:aus.computers.ibm-pc`	(Usenet Newsgroup) aus.computers.ibm-pc
`news:wu.cait.3-tier`	(Usenet Newsgroup) Center for the Application of Information Technologys
`news:uk.org.epsrc.hpc.discussion`	(Usenet Newsgroup) IPSRC High Performance Computing Discussion
`news:uk.org.epsrc.hpc.news`	(Usenet Newsgroup) IPSRC High Performance Computing News
`news:utexas.cc.hpcf.sysmod`	(Usenet Newsgroup) System modification reports for HPCF machines
`news:utexas.cc.hpcf.system`	(Usenet Newsgroup) System modifications for HPCF machines

ftp://ftp.cs.city.ac.uk//papers/93/
sarc93-5.ps.Z

PRIMA: A Parallel
Relational Database
Machine

Architecture by D. Bolton,
J.A. McCann, P.E. Osmon,
A. Valsamidis, N. Williams
and X. Zhao

ftp://tr-ftp.es.berkeley.edu/pub/
tech-reports/csd/csd-94-801/all.ps

Characterization of
Contention in Real
Relational Databases
by Vigyan Singhal, and
Alan Jay Smith

ftp://lbdsun.epfl.ch/pub/er94a.ps.Z

Extracting an Entity
Relationship Schema from
a Relational Database
through Reverse
Engineering
by Martin Andersson

ftp://ftp.icsi.Berkeley.edu/pub/
techreports/1994/tr-94-013.ps.Z

Processing Joins With
User-Defined Functions by
Volker Gaede and Oliver
Guenther

ftp://s2k-ftp.cs.berkeley.edu/pub/
tech-reports/s2k/s2k-92-13/all.ps

Predicate Migrations:
Optimizing Queries with
Expensive Predicates by
Joeseph Hellerstein

ftp://ftp.csri.toronto.edu/
csri-technical-reports/254/

Performance Prediction of
Relational Database
Management Systems by
William Hyslop

ftp://cs.utexas.edu/pub/techreports/
tr92-10.ps.Z

A Multi-Resolution
Relational Data Model by
Robert L. Read, Donald S.
Fussell, and Avi.
Silberschtaz

http://www.cs.city.ac.uk/bibliography/cs/
database?TCU/SARC/1993/18

"

`ftp://ftp.cs.city.ac.uk/vol/ftp/root/` `papers/93/sarc93-18.txt`	Distributed Memory Multi-Processor Architecture for Relational Database Systems by J.A. McCann, P.E. Osmon, D. Bolton, N. Williams, A. Valsamidis, and X. Zhao
`http://www.cs.unibo.it/~ciaccia`	Parallel Independent Grid Files Based on a Dynamic Declustering Method Using Error Correcting Codes by Paolo Ciaccia
`ftp://ftp.cs.unibo.it/pub/techreports/` `ABSTRACTS/94.txt`	"
`ftp://ftp.cs.unibo.it/pub/techreports/` `ParallelGridFiles.ps.gz`	"
`http://www.cs.mu.oz.au/tr_db/mu_94_31.ps.gz`	Towards optimal storage design for efficient query processing in relational database systems by Evan Harris
`http://www.cs.mu.oz.au/tr_db/mu_94_08.ps.gz`	Optimal clustering of elations in a a database system by Evan Harris and Kotagiri Ramamohanarao
`http://www.cs.mu.oz.au/tr_db/mu_93_23.ps.gz`	Multiple paths join for nested relational databases by Hong-Cheu Liu and Kotagiri Ramamohanarao
`ftp://ftp.uni-mannheim.de/info/rumdoc/` `rum3994.ps.Z`	Oracle on the KSR-1 Parallalel Computer by Heinz Kredel, Robert Schumacher, and Erich Strohmaier
`http://www.cs.columbia.edu/~mauricio/` `papers/pdis94.ps`	Predictive Load Balancing of Parallel Hash-Joins over Heterogeneous Processors in the Presence of Data Skew by H. Dewan, M. Hernandez, K. Mok, and S. Stolfo

`http://www.cs.wisc.edu/~mmehta/` `papers/vldb95.ps`	Managing Intra-Operator Parallelism in Parallel Database Systems by Manish Mehta and David J. DeWitt
`http://www.cs.wisc.edu/~mmehta/papers/` `thesis.ps`	Resource Allocation in Parallel Shared-Nothing Database Systems by Manish Mehta
`http://www.cs.wisc.edu/~mmehta/papers/` `vldb94.ps`	Meeting Response-Time Goals for a Multi-Class Workload by Kurt Brown, Manish Mehta, Michael Carey, and Miron Livy
`http://www.cs.wisc.edu/~mmehta/papers/de93.ps`	Batch Scheduling in Parallel Database Systems by Manish Mehta, Valery Soloviev, and David DeWitt
`http://www.cs.wisc.edu/~mmehta/papers/` `vldb93.ps`	Dynamic Memory Allocation for Multiple-Query Workloads by Manish Mehta and David J. DeWitt
`http://www.cs.wisc.edu/~poosala/tech/` `abst.sigmod95.ps`	Balancing Histogram Optimality and Practicality for Query Result Size Estimation by Yannis Ioannidis and Viswanath Poosala

`http://www.comp.vuw.ac.nz/Publications/`
`tr-94.html#CS-TR-94-20`
`ftp://ftphost.comp.vuw.ac.nz/doc/`
`vuw-publications/CS-TR-94/CS-TR-94-20.ps.gz`
	Efficient Retrieval of Structured Spatial Information from a Large Database by Eric K. Jones and Aaron Roydhouse

`http://www.cs.utexas.edu/users/schwartz/` `#dinesh-thesis`	Making Database Optimizers More Extensible by Dinesh Das
`ftp://ftp.cs.utexas.edu/pub/predator/` `das-thesis.ps`	`"`

`ftp://ftp.cs.utexas.edu/pub/predator/` `icde-11.ps`	Prairie: A Rule Specification Framework for Query Optimizers by Dinesh Das and Don Batory
`http://www.cs.utexas.edu/users/schwartz/` `#icde-11`	"
`http://www.insa-lyon.fr/Labos/LISI/theme2/` `texte/icde96.ps.Z`	Towards the reverse engineering of denormalized databases by J-M. Petit, F. Toumani, J-F. Boulicaut, and J. Kouloumdjian
`http://web.cs.ualberta.ca/~database/` `publications/ozsu/cikm95/cikm95.ps`	Experimenting with Temporal Relational Databases by I. Goralwalla, A.U. Tansel, and M.T. Ozsu
`http://bluebox.uwaterloo.ca/~pwyan/` `papers/icde94.ps`	Performing group-by before join by Weipeng P. Yan and P. Larson
`ftp://ftp.cs.unibo.it/pub/techreports/` `ABSTRACTS/94.txt`	Dynamic Allocation of Signature Files in Multiple-Disk Systems by Paolo Ciaccia
`ftp://ftp.cs.unibo.it/pub/techreports/` `MultiDiskSignatureFiles.ps.gz`	"
`ftp://ftp.cs.unibo.it/pub/techreports/` `ABSTRACTS/95.txt`	Optimal Multi-Block Read Schedules for Partitioned Signature Files by Paolo Ciaccia
`ftp://tr-ftp.cs.berkeley.edu/pub/` `tech-reports/csd/csd-94-796/`	Indexes for User Access to Large Video Databases by Lawrence A. Rowe, John S. Boreczky, and Charles A. Eads
`http://www.cs.bham.ac.uk/~anp/papers.html`	Architectural Support for Data Mining by Martin L. Holsheimer, and Marcel Kersten
`ftp://ftp.cwi.nl/pub/CWireports/AA/CS-R9429`	"

`ftp://ftp.research.att.com/dist/db/` `att-db-93-9.ps.Z`	Parallel pointer-based join techniques for object-oriented data bases by D. Lieuwen, D. DeWitt, and M. Mehta
`http://web.cs.ualberta.ca/~database/` `publications/ozsu/distdb/short.ps`	Distributed Database Systems: Where Are We Now? by M. T. Ozsu, and P. Valduriez
`ftp://ftp.cs.utexas.edu/pub/techreports/` `tr95-09.ps.Z`	Enhancing Query Plans for Many-Way Joins by Roberto J. Bayardo
`http://web.cs.ualberta.ca/~database/` `publications/ozsu/handbook/handbook`	Distributed and Parallel Database Systems by M.T. Ozsu and P. Valduriez
`http://www.execsoft.com`	Diskeeper by Executive Software
`http://www.quarterdeck.com`	WinProbe 95 by Quarterdeck
`http://www.rab-conferences.com`	Raid Advisory Board

INFORMIX

`http://www.informix.com`	Informix Home Page
`http://www.informix.com/informix/corpinfo/` `zines/whiteidx.htm`	White Papers
`http://www.illustra.com/cgi-bin/` `Webdriver?Mlval=homeIllustra/`	Informix Temporary Page
`http://www.illustra.com/cgi-bin/` `Webdriver?Mlval=about`	Illustra
`http://www.openpath.com/`	(Tools) OpenPath RDA/ODBC from Trilogy
`http://www.platinum.com`	(Tools) Platinum Enhancement Products
`http://www.sqlbench.com/`	(Tools) SQLBench

`http://host.telescan.com/Stocks/`
`Corporate_Snapshot.html?Button`
`+Report&Symbol=IFMX`
	Informix Corp Com Stock Chart (IFMX) NASDAQ

`news:comp.databases.informix`	(Usenet Newsgroup) Informix DBMS software discussions

INTERBASE

news:relcom.fido.su.su.dbms.interbase

(Usenet Newsgroup)
FIDOnet, Borland
Interbase Workgroup
Servers

MAGAZINES

http://www.cuj.com/

C/C++ Users Journal

http://www.advisor.com/

Databased Advisor
Magazine Home Page

http://www.advisor.com/av.htm

Access/Visual Basic Advisor

http://www.advisor.com/db.htm

Databased Advisor
Magazine

http://www.advisor.com/pa.htm

PowerBuilder Advisor
Magazine

http://www.advisor.com/fa.htm

FoxPro Advisor Magazine

http://www.dbmsmag.com

DBMS Magazine Online

http://www.dbmsmag.com/pcappdev.html

Client/Server and Host
Application Dev Tools
Buyer's Guide

http://www.dbmsmag.com/buyguide.html

DBMS 1996 Buyer's Guide
and Client Server Source-
book

http://www.dbmsmag.com/pcdbms.html#P192

DBMS 1996 Buyer's
Guide —Database Servers
and Host DBMSs

http://www.idbmsmag.com/intsys.html

Internet Systems Magazine

http://www.platinum.com/edge/edge.htm

Platinum Software Edge
Online Industry News

http://www.sdmagazine.com

Software Development
Online Magazine

http://www.samag.com

Sys Admin Magazine

http://www.dciexpo.com/

Database & Client/Server
International Expo

http://www.oramag.com/

Oracle Magazine

http://www.informant.com/oracle/oi_index.HTM

Oracle Informant Magazine

http://www.informant.com/paradox/pi_index.HTM

Paradox Informant
Magazine

`http://www.informant.com/delphi/di_index.HTM`	Delphi Informant Magazine
`http://www.sybase.com/inc/sybmag`	Sybase Magazine
`http://www.compuware.com/uni_mag/uni_mag.htm`	UNIFACE Magazine
`http://www.vbonline.com/vb-mag/`	Visual Basic Online Magazine
`http://www.arry.nl/DBM/default.htm`	Database Magazine (Dutch)
`http://www.array.nl/Release/default.htm`	Software Release (Dutch)
`http://www.corelmag.com/PAGES/ONLINE/online.htm`	Corel Magazine Online
`http://www.infoworld.com/`	InfoWorld
`http://techweb.cmp.com/`	TechWeb Home Page
`http://techweb.cmp.com/cw/current/`	Communications Week
`http://techweb.cmp.com/crn/current/`	Computer Reseller News
`http://techweb.cmp.com/crw/current/`	Computer Retail Week
`http://techweb.cmp.com/ebn/current/`	Electronic Buyer's News
`http://techweb.cmp.com/hpc/current/`	Home PC
`http://techweb.cmp.com/techweb/inf/current/`	Informatiques
`http://techweb.cmp.com/iw/current/`	Info Week
`http://techweb.cmp.com/ia/current/`	Interactive Age
`http://techweb.cmp.com/ng/current/`	NetGuide
`http://techweb.netguide.com/`	NetGuide Live
`http://techweb.cmp.com/nc/current/`	Network Computing
`http://www.winmag.com/`	Windows Magazine
`http://www.dmreview.com`	DM REVIEW
`http://www.ntsystems.com`	NT Systems
`http://www5.zdnet.com/`	ZD Net from Ziff Davis
`http://www5.zdnet.com/anchordesk/`	Anchor Desk
`http://www5.zdnet.com/complife/`	Computer Life
`http://www5.zdnet.com/cshopper/`	Computer Shopper
`http://www5.zdnet.com/familypc/`	Family PC
`http://www5.zdnet.com/intweek/`	Inter@active Week
`http://www.underground-online.com/`	Internet Underground
`http://www.pcmag.com/iu/iuser.htm`	Internet User
`http://www.zdnet.com/macuser/`	Mac User
`http://www.macweek.com/`	Mac Week

`http://www.zdnet.com/pccomp/`	PC Computing
`http://www.pcmag.com/`	PC Magazine
`http://www.pcweek.com/`	PC Week
`http://www.zdnet.com/wsources/`	Windows Sources
`http://www.zdnet.com/yil/`	Yahoo Internet Life
`http://www.zdimag.com/`	ZD Internet Magazine
`http://www.zdnet.com/zdeurope/`	International Magazines
`http://www.zdnet.com/clifeuk/`	Computer Life (U.K.)
`http://www.zdnet.com/pcdirf`	PC Direct (France)
`http://www.zdnet.com/pcdiruk/`	PC Direct (U.K.)
`http://www.zdnet.com/pcdirger/`	PC Direkt (Germany)
`http://www.zdnet.com/pcexpert/`	PC Expert (France)
`http://www.zdnet.com/pcmaguk/`	PC Magazine (U.K.)
`http://www.zdnet.com/pcpro/`	PC Professionell (Germany)
`http://www.zdnet.com/planet/`	Pl@net (Germany)
`http://www.zdu.com/`	ZD Net University
`http://www.euro.net/sala/home.html`	Net Info (Europe)
`http://www.dbpd.com`	DATABASE PROGRAMMING AND DESIGN
`http://www.doit.com/delphi/Undu.html`	The Unofficial Delphi Newsletter
`http://www.pinpub.com/level3/l3ndelph.htm`	Delphi Developer from Pinnacle Publishing
`http://www.cobb.com/ddj/index.htm`	Delphi Developers Journal
`http://ourworld.compuserve.com:80/homepages/DelphiMagazine/`	Delphi Magazine
`http://www.vbonline.com/vb-mag/`	Visual Basic Online
`http://www.byte.com/`	Byte Magazine
`http://www.pennant.com/delphi.html`	Delphi Connection Magazine

MS ACCESS

`http://www.microsoft.com`	Microsoft Inc Home Page
`http://www.microsoft.com/msaccess/default.htm`	Access Home Page

`http://www.microsoft.com/minshare`	MS Local User Groups
`http://www.microsoft.com/accessdev/`	Developer Forum
`http://www.microsoft.com/accessdev/` `accinfo/adtsumm.htm`	Developer's Toolkit
`http://www.microsoft.com/msaccess/internet/` `ia/default.htm`	Internet Assistant
`http://www.microsoft.com/msaccess/` `ProductInfo/Brochure/default.htm`	Data Sheet
`http://www.microsoft.com/msaccess/` `productInfo/experttools/ureldes/ureldes.htm`	Designing Relational Databases
`http://www.microsoft.com/kb/deskapps/` `access/q89586.htm MS Access as a DDE Server`	
`http://www.symantec.com/dba/dbawpr1.html`	(Tools) Symantec dbANYWHERE
`ftp://ftp.symantec.com/public/`	(FTP) Symantec FTP site
`ftp://ftp2.symantec.com/public/`	(FTP) Symantec FTP site #2

`http://host.telescan.com/Stocks/`
`Corporate_Snapshot.html?Button`
`+Report&Symbol=MSFT`
	Microsoft Corp Com Stock Chart (MSFT) NASDAQ

`http://www.nova.edu/Inter-Links/cica/` `access.html`	Inter-Links Microsoft Access Files
`http://tinker.winsite.com/win3/` `access/WinCam.One`	Microsoft Access Files
`http://www.innovision1.com/msadp`	Digital Dreamshop's Microsoft Access Developer's Pages
`news:comp.databases.access`	(Usenet Newsgroup) Issues related to the MS Access
`news:comp.os.ms-windows`	(Usenet Newsgroup) MS Windows
`news:comp.databases`	(Usenet Newsgroup) comp.databases
`news:comp.lang.basic.visual`	(Usenet Newsgroup) Visual Basic
`news:alt.computer.consultants`	(Usenet Newsgroup) Computer Consultants

MICROSOFT SQL SERVER

http://www.microsoft.com/SQL/	Microsoft SQL Server Home Page
http://www.microsoft.com/minshare	MS Local User Groups
http://www.microsoft.com/catalog/products/ sqlserver/default.htm	Microsoft SQL Server Product Specifications
http://www.embarcadero.com/	(Tools) DBArtisan from Embarcadero Tech. Inc.
http://www.sfi-software.com/	(Tools) Sylvain Faust Incorporated Home Page
http://www.symantec.com/dba/dbawpr1.html	(Tools) Symantec dbANYWHERE
http://www.platinum.com	(Tools) Platinum Enhancement Products
http://host.telescan.com/Stocks/ Corporate_Snapshot.html?Button +Report&Symbol=MSFT	Microsoft Corp Com Stock Chart (MSFT) NASDAQ
news:comp.databases.ms-sqlserver	(Usenet Newsgroup) Microsoft SQL Server
news:bit.databases.mssql-1	(Usenet Newsgroup) Microsoft SQL Server List
http://www.tpc.org/	(Benchmarks) TPC Council

MSS & DSS

http://www.arborsoft.com	Arbor Home Page
http://www.arborsoft.com/products/prodtoc.html	Products & ESSBASE
news:comp.databases.olap	Analytical Processing, Multidimensional DBMS, EIS, DSS
http://www.pidoinfo.se/places.htm	What is OLAP, DSS, EIS?
http://clever.net/dbd/olap	OLAP, DSS and EIS Development
http://www.access.digex.net/~grimes/olap	Online Analytical Processing (OLAP)
http://www.tekptnr.com/tpi/tdwi	The Data Warehousing Institute
http://pwp.starnetinc.com/larryg/index.html	The Data Warehousing Information Center

`http://www.syncsort.com/`	SYNCSORT Home Page
`http://www.holossys.comn/`	HOLOS OLAP and Multi-dimensional database system from Holistic Systems Inc

NEWS

`http://www.nytsyn.com/`	New York Times Home Page
`http://www.wired.com/news/`	Wired Magazine/News
`http://www.newspage.com/`	NewsPage - 25,000 News Articles Daily
`http://www.news.com/Categories/Index/` `0,3,2,00.html?ntb.cmptng`	c/net NEWS.COM (Computing)

OBJECTIVITY/DB

`http://www.objectivity.com/`	Objectivity Home Page
`http://www.objectivity.com/Objy/products.html`	Products and Technology
`http://www.objectivity.com/ODB/whtpaper.html`	White Papers

ORACLE

`http://www.oracle.com`	Oracle Corporation Home Page
`http://www.uk.oracle.com`	Oracle Europe Home Page
`http://www.oracle.com/products/`	Oracle - Products
`http://www.oracle.com/products/oracle7/` `server/whitepapers/html/index.html`	Oracle7 Enterprise Server Whitepapers
`http://www.oracle.com/products/tools/`	Oracle Client/Server Development Tools
`http://www.oracle.com/products/rdb/html/` `index.html`	Oracle Rdb Products
`http://www.oracle.com/products/` `applications/html/`	Oracle Applications
`http://www.oracle.com/products/tools/html/` `des2k.html`	Designer 2000 Product
`http://www.oracle.com/products/tools/html/` `dev2k.html`	Developer 2000 Product

`http://www.oracle.com/cgi-bin/search.cgi`	Oracle Search Online
`http://www.alliance.oracle.com/`	Alliance Online
`http://www.oracle-users.com/`	Oracle User Resource Inc. (ECO 97 Boston)
`http://www.ioug.org/`	IOUG Americas Alliance User Groups
`http://www.aa.gov.au/aNZORA.html`	ANZORA Oracle User Group Australia
`http://www.cois.com/houg`	HOUG Home Page
`http://www.hk.super.net/~hkoug/`	Hong Kong Oracle Users Group Home Page
`http://www.rtt.in.net/inoug/inoug.htm`	Indiana Oracle Users Group Homepage
`http://www.oracle.co.jp/`	Oracle Japan Home Page
`http://www.ugn.com/sfoug1.htm`	SFOUG South Florida Oracle User Group
`http://sunsite.www.unc.edu/ncoug`	NCOUG North Carolina Oracle User Group
`http://www.crtnet.com/voug`	VOUG Virginia Oracle User Group
`http://www.state.me.us/bis/dba/msoug/msoug.htm`	MSOUG Maine State Oracle User Group
`http://www.dbcorp.ab.ca/coug`	COUG Calgary Oracle User Group
`http://www.ougf.fi/eoug/eoug.html`	EOUG European Oracle User Group
`http://www.menlosoftware.com/`	Menlo Software's Home Page
`http://govt.us.oracle.com/`	Welcome to Oracle Government Page
`http://www.bf.rmit.edu.au/`	Research FAQ sheets from Royal Melbourne Institute of Technology
`http://www.jcc.com/`	JCC Home Page
`http://www.jcc.com/cgi-bin/jcc_search_engine`	JCC Search Engine
`http://www.tpc.org/`	(Benchmarks) TPC Council
`http://www.syncsort.com/`	(Tools) SYNCSORT UNIX Home Page

http://www.compuware.com/	(Tools) ECOTools from Compuware
http://www.sfi-software.com/	(Tools) Sylvain Faust Incorporated Home Page
http://www.precisesoft.com/	(Tools) Precise/SQL Oracle Monitor by Precise Software Solutions Inc
http://www.adra.com/prodts-2.htm#cadra	(Alliance Partner) Adra Systems (CADRA)
http://www.brite.com/html/netscape/product.html	(Aliance Partner) Brite Voice Systems (Voice Recognition)
http://www.openlinksw.com/docs/product.html	(Tools) OpenLink Software (ODBC Drivers)
http://www.openpath.com/	(Tools) OpenPath RDA/ODBC from Trilogy
http://www.sequent.com/	(Platforms/Tools) Sequent Computer Systems
http://www.pyramid.com/products/products.html	(Platforms) Pyramid Products
http://www.ncr.com/	(Platforms) NCR
http://www.unibol.com/	(Alliance Partner) Unibol Home Page (Oracle Migration Technology Initiative)
http://kayak.npac.syr.edu:1963/NPAC	Oracle 7 Database Server
http://www.mcs.com/~hugo/oracle.html	The SSC Oracle Page
http://www.intellimatch.com/oracle/	IntelliMatch Jobs
http://www.wustl.edu/packages/clips2sybase/	(Tools) Washington University's Archives
http://www.unravel.com/	(Tools) Ravel Software Solutions
http://www.openvision.com/	(Tools) Open Vision Technologies (AXXiON NetBackup)
http://www.sqlbench.com/	(Tools) SQLBench
http://www.aris.com/	(Tools) DFRAG and Virtual DBA by Aris Software

`http://www.smartdb.com/`	(Tools) SMART DB by Smart Corporation
`http://www.merc-int.com/`	(Tools) LoadRunner by Mercury Interactive
`http://www.corvu.com/`	(Tools) CorVu North American (CorVU)
`http://www.avanco.com/`	(Consultants) Avanco Intl
`http://www.csac.com/`	(Consultants) Computer Systems Authority
`http://www.symantec.com/dba/dbawpr1.html`	(Tools) Symantec dbANYWHERE
`http://www.platinum.com`	(Tools) Platinum Enhancement Products
`http://www.thomsoft.com/`	(Tools) Aonix Software Home Page
`http://www.thomsoft.com/products/index.html`	Products
`http://www.thomsoft.com/products/Ada/ada.html`	ADA
`http://www.thomsoft.com/products/Ada/per.html`	PerfoRMAx Monitor
`http://www.datatools.com`	(Tools) Data Optimizer from DATATOOLS
`http://www.eventus.com/`	(Tools) ADHAWK from Eventus
`http://www.bradmark.com/`	(Tools) DBGENERAL Server Manager, Monitor from BRADMARK
`http://www.technosolutions.com/`	(Tools) SQL Navigator from TechnoSolutions
`http://www.veritas.com/`	(Tools) SmartSync form Veritas Software
`http://host.telescan.com/Stocks/Corporate_Snapshot.html?Button+Report&Symbol=ORCL`	Oracle Systems Corp Com Stock Chart (ORCL) NASDAQ
`http://host.telescan.com/Stocks/Corporate_Snapshot.html?Button+Report&Symbol=BVSI`	Brite Voice Systems Corp Com Stock Chart (BVSI) NASDAQ
`news:comp.databases.oracle.marketplace`	(Usenet Newsgroup) comp.databases.oracle. marketplace

`news:comp.databases.oracle.misc`	(Usenet Newsgroup) comp.databases.oracle.misc
`news:comp.databases.oracle.tools`	(Usenet Newsgroup) comp.databases.oracle.tools
`news:comp.databases.oracle.server`	(Usenet Newsgroup) comp.databases. oracle.server
`news:comp.databases.oracle`	(Usenet Newsgroup) SQL database products of Oracle Corporation
`news:fido7.rdbms.oracle`	(Usenet Newsgroup) Oracle DBMS
`news:reclom.comp.dbms.oracle`	(Usenet Newsgroup) Oracle database discussions
`news:slac.database.oracle`	(Usenet Newsgroup) Discussion of the use of Oracle at SLAC
`news:alt.computer.consultants`	(Usenet Newsgroup) Computer Consultants

PARADOX

`http://www.borland.com/`	Borland Software Home Page
`ftp://ftp.borland.com/`	Directory of ftp.borland.com
`http://netserv.borland.com/paradox/papers/`	Paradox Technical White Papers
`http://netserv.borland.com/paradox/pdxprev/pdx45dos/`	Paradox 4.5 for DOS
`http://netserv.borland.com/techsupport/paradox/`	Paradox Technical Support
`http://www.borland.com/`	Welcome to Borland Online
`http://www.borland.com/paradox/`	Paradox 7 Home Page
`http://www.borland.com/paradox/cobb/`	Inside Paradox for Windows Master Index
`http://www.borland.com/paradox/pdxintro.html`	Introduction to Paradox 7

`http://www.borland.com/paradox/pdxprev/pdx5win/`	Paradox 5.0 for Windows
`http://www.borland.com/techsupport/paradox/pdox7/pdx7upd.html`	Paradox 7 for Windows 95
`http://members.aol.com/sck333/homepage/sck333.htm`	Paradox for Windows (PW) Developers
`http://netaccess.on.ca/~dmartens/paradox/pdoxpage.htm#TT`	The Paradox Page
`http://www.sonic.net/~richw/paradox.html`	What is Paradox?
`http://www.wdn.com/ems/lists/pdxutilv.htm`	Paradox Programmer's Products and Their Producers
`http://www.wdn.com/ems/lists/pdxutilp.htm`	Paradox Programmer's Tools and Their Producers
`news:asu.group.paradox`	(Usenet Newsgroup) Discussion for Paradox users at ASU
`news:comp.databases.paradox`	(Usenet Newsgroup) Borland's database for DOS and MS Windows
`news:uiuc.sw.paradox`	(Usenet Newsgroup) All about the Paradox database package
`news:fido7.dbms.borland`	(Usenet Newsgroup) DBMS by Borland
`news:reclcom.fido.su.dbms.borland`	(Usenet Newsgroup) FIDOnet, about DBMS by Borland
`news:comp.ai`	(Usenet Newsgroup) comp.ai
`news:comp.databases`	(Usenet Newsgroup) comp.databases
`news:comp.databases.ibm-db2`	(Usenet Newsgroup) comp.databases.ibm-db2
`news:alt.computer.consultants`	(Usenet Newsgroup) alt.computer.consultants

PROGRESS

`http://www.progress.com`	Progress Software Home Page

`http://www.progress.com/V8/V8.html`	Progress Version 8
`http://www.progress.com/WhitePapers/` `whitepapers.html`	Progress White Papers
`http://www.progress.com/`	Progress Software Home Page
`http://www.progress.com/Demos/demodisk.html`	Progress Downloadable Demo
`http://www.progress.com/Product/product.html`	Progress Software Corporate Information
`http://www.progress.com/Product/` `v7overview.html`	Version 7 Product Overview
`http://www.progress.com/Support/`	Progress Software Technical Services
`http://www.progress.com/Support/customers.html`	On-Line Support Services
`http://www.progress.com/webtools/webtools.htm`	Internet Freeware
`http://danae.marques.co.za/users/progress.htm`	Progress Professionals South Africa
`http://web.idirect.com/%7Eipcn/`	(Consulting) Independent Progress Consulting Network (IPCN)
`http://www.mdn.com/people/Phillip_Laird/` `skippy.html`	(Consulting) Progress Programmers Overseas
`http://www.ozemail.com.au/%7Epfred/` `progress.html`	Progress RDBMS Australian Home Page
`http://www.peg.com/`	Progress E-Mail Group Home Page
`http://www.peg.com/cgi-bin/pdir?faq`	FAQ Subject Index
`http://www.well.com/user/allegro/vapug.html`	(Consulting) Allegro Consultants, Ltd.
`http://www.westnet.com/~gsmith/pperform.htm`	Progress Performance FAQ
`http://host.telescan.com/Stocks/` `Corporate_Snapshot.html?Symbol=PRGS`	Progress Software Com Stock Chart (PRGS) NASDAQ
`news:comp.databases.progress`	(Unsenet Newsgroup) The Progress 4GL and RDBMS

RAID

`http://www.raid-advisory.com/`	Raid Advisory Board (RAB)

http://www.adjile.com/	(Vendor) Adjile Systems
http://www.amdahl.com/	(Vendor) Amdahl Inc
http://www.andataco.com/	(Vendor) Andataco Inc
http://www.artecon.com/raid	(Vendor) Artecon Inc
http://www.boxhill.com/	(Vendor) BoxHill Systems Corp
http://www.ciprico.com/	(Vendor) Ciprico Inc
http://www.cmsenh.com/	(Vendor) CMS Enhancements Inc
http://www.clariion.com/	(Vendor) CLARiiON Advanced Storage Solutions (Data General)
http://www.compaq.com/	(Vendor) Compaq
http://www.conley.com/	(Vendor) Conley
http://www.cyberstorage.com/	(Vendor) CyberStorage Systems
http://www.conner.com/	(Vendor) Conner (Seagate)
http://www.storage.digital.com/	(Vendor) Digital Equipment Corp
http://www.wdc.com/	(Vendor) Western Digital
http://www.fcpa.com/	(Vendor) Fujitsu
http://www.datastor.com/	(Vendor) DataStor Inc
http://www.dpt.com/	(Vendor) Distributed Processing Technology
http://www.eccs.com/	(Vendor) ECCS Inc
http://www.emc.com/	(Vendor) EMC Inc
http://www.eurologic.com/	(Vendor) Eurologic Systems Ltd
http://www.hitachi.com/	(Vendor) Hitachi Inc
http://www.storage.ibm.com/	(Vendor) IBM Corp
http://www.micronet.com/	(Vendor) Micronet Technology
http://www.mti.com/	(Vendor) MTI
http://www.micropolis.com/	(Vendor) Micropolis Pte Ltd
http://www.nstor.com/	(Vendor) nStor
http://www.openstore.com/	(Vendor) Open Storage Solutions

`http://www.seagate.com/`	(Vendor) Seagate
`http://www.storagedimensions.com/`	(Vendor) Storage Dimensions Corp
`http://www.storage.com/`	(Vendor) Storage Computer
`http://www.streamlogic.com/`	(Vendor) StreamLogic
`http://www.symbios.com/`	(Vendor) Symbios Logic
`http://www.raidtec.com/`	(Vendor) Raidtec Corporation

RDB

`http://www.dec.com`	Digital Equipment Corp Home Page
`http://www.wustl.edu/packages/clips2sybase/`	(Tools) Washington University's Archives
`http://www.thomsoft.com/`	(Tools) Aonix Software Home Page
`http://www.thomsoft.com/products/index.html`	Products
`http://www.thomsoft.com/products/Ada/ada.html`	ADA
`http://www.thomsoft.com/products/Ada/per.html`	PerfoRMAx Monitor
`http://host.telescan.com/Stocks/Corporate_Snapshot.html?Button+Report&Symbol=DEC`	Digital Equipment Corp Chart (DEC) NYSE
`http://host.telescan.com/Stocks/Corporate_Snapshot.html?Button+Report&Symbol=DEC-A`	Digital Equipment Corp Chart (DEC-A) NYSE
`news:comp.databases.rdb`	(Usenet Newsgroup) The Rdb DBMS from DEC
`news:vmsnet.databases.rdb`	(Usenet Newsgroup) vmsnet.databases.rdb

RMS

`http://www.thomsoft.com/`	(Tools) Aonix Software Home Page
`http://www.thomsoft.com/products/index.html`	Products
`http://www.thomsoft.com/products/Ada/ada.html`	ADA
`http://www.thomsoft.com/products/Ada/per.html`	PerfoRMAx Monitor

SQLBASE

http://www.gupta.com

Centura Software Home Page

http://host.telescan.com/Stocks/
Corporate_Snapshot.html?Button
+Report&Symbol=CNTR

Centura Software Corp Com Stock Chart (CNTR) NASDAQ

news:comp.databases.gupta

(Usenet Newsgroup) Gupta SQL Windows client-server development

SYBASE

http://www.sybase.com

Sybase Incorporated Home Page

http://www.sybase.com/products/

Sybase Products

http://www.sybase.com/products/system11/

Sybase System 11

http://www.sybase.com/products/system11/
sqlsrv11.html

Sybase SQL Server 11

http://www.sybase.com/products/system11/
sqlserver11_whitepaper.html

Sybase SQL Server 11 White Paper

http://www.sybase.com/products/internet/
webworks.html

Open for Business on the Net

http://www.sybase.com/products/system11/
migration/index.html

Migration Resource Guide

http://www.sybase.com/Offerings/Whitepapers/

Sybase White Papers

http://www.sybase.com/Offerings/Samples/
Linux/index.html

Sybase Open Client/C for LINUX

http://www.tpc.org/

(Benchmarks) TPC Council

http://ftp.sybase.com/

(FTP) ftp.sybase.com

http://reality.sgi.com/pablo/Sybase_FAQ/

Sybase FAQ Index from Silicon Graphics

http://ptoon.ccit.arizona.edu/Sybase/
SybaseTuning.HTML

Topher's Top 10 from Arizona EDU

http://www.acs.ncsu.edu/Sybase/

NC University Sybase Archives

http://sybase.pnl.gov:2080/Sybase/.Sybase.html

PNNL Sybase Information Repository

http://www.platinum.com

(Tools) Platinum Enhancement Products

http://www.sfi-software.com/	(Tools) Sylvain Faust Incorporated
http://www.sqlbench.com/	(Tools) SQLBench
http://www.openpath.com/	(Tools) OpenPath RDA/ODBC from Trilogy
http://www.tiac.net/users/sqltech/	(Tools) SQL Technologies Inc
http://www.strategy.com/press/prs_syb.htm	MicroStrategy: Sybase Warehouse Works Initiative Press Release
http://www.adp.unc.edu/info/sybase.html	Sybase SQL Developers from ADP
http://www.cis.ohio-state.edu/hypertext/faq/usenet/sybase-faq/faq.html	Ohio State University FAQs
http://moray.stanford.edu:7000/misc/dbgsybase.html	Stanford University's Sybase on DBG Machines
http://ccs-www.cs.umass.edu/db.html	University of Massachusetts Univ Computer Laboratory
http://www.cornut.fr	Eclipse Query (Sybase) Shareware Tool
http://arch-http.hq.eso.org/bfrasmus/wdb/wdb.html	A Web interface to SQL Databases
http://www.wustl.edu/packages/clips2sybase/	(Tools) Washington University's Archives
http://www.symantec.com/dba/dbawpr1.html	(Tools) Symantec dbANYWHERE
ftp://ftp.symantec.com/public/	(FTP) Symantec FTP site
ftp://ftp2.symantec.com/public/	(FTP) Symantec FTP site #2
http://www.thomsoft.com/	(Tools) Aonix Software Home Page
http://www.thomsoft.com/products/index.html	Products
http://www.thomsoft.com/products/Ada/ada.html	ADA
http://www.thomsoft.com/products/Ada/per.html	PerfoRMAx Monitor
http://host.telescan.com/Stocks/Corporate_Snapshot.html?Button+Report&Symbol=SYBS	Sybase Inc Com Stock Chart (SYBS) NASDAQ
news:comp.databases.sybase	(Usenet Newsgroup) Sybase products

`news:osu.sybase`	(Usenet Newsgroup) Sybase
`news:sybase.server.bugsnews.oahu`	(Usenet Newsgroup) Sybase bugs
`news:alt.computer.consultants`	(Usenet Newsgroup) Computer Consultants

TITANIUM

`http://www.mdbs.com/`	Micro Data Base Systems Inc Home Page
`http://www.mdbs.com/mproduct.html`	Products and Services
`http://www.mdbs.com/titanium.html`	Titanium Client/Server Databaese Engine
`http://www.mdbs.com/guru.html`	Guru 4GL Expert-System-Enhanced Database Programming Environment

UNIX

`news:comp.infosystems.www.servers.unix`	(Usenet Newsgroup) comp.infosystems. www.servers.unix
`news:aus.computers.linux`	(Usenet Newsgroup) aus.computers.linux
`news:brasil.unix`	(Usenet Newsgroup) brasil.unix
`news:ca.unix`	(Usenet Newsgroup) ca.unix
`news:comp.sources.unix`	(Usenet Newsgroup) comp.sources.unix
`news:comp.std.unix`	(Usenet Newsgroup) comp.std.unix
`news:comp.unix.aix`	(Usenet Newsgroup) comp.unix.aix
`news:comp.unix.solaris`	(Usenet Newsgroup) comp.unix.solaris
`news:comp.unix.sco.misc`	(Usenet Newsgroup) comp.unix.sco.misc

news:comp.unix.sco.announce	(Usenet Newsgroup) comp.unix.sco.announce
news:comp.unix.programmer	(Usenet Newsgroup) comp.unix.programmer
news:comp.unix.pc-clone.32bit	(Usenet Newsgroup) comp.unix.pc-clone-32bit
news:comp.unix.bsd.misc	(Usenet Newsgroup) comp.unix.bsd.misc
news:comp.unix.large	(Usenet Newsgroup) comp.unix.large
news:comp.unix.misc	(Usenet Newsgroup) comp.unix.misc
news:comp.unix.sys5.misc	(Usenet Newsgroup) comp.unix.sys5.misc
news:comp.unix.unixware.announce	(Usenet Newsgroup) comp.unix.unixware. announce
news:comp.unix.xenix.misc	(Usenet Newsgroup) comp.unix.xenix.misc
news:hannover.uni.comp.unix	(Usenet Newsgroup) hannover.uni.comp.unix
news:kiel.computer.unix	(Usenet Newsgroup) kiel.computer.unix
news:sanet.unix.talk	(Usenet Newsgroup) sanet.unix.talk
news:slac.announce.unixhub	(Usenet Newsgroup) slac.announce.unixhub
news:slac.newusers.unix	(Usenet Newsgroup) slac.newusers.unix
news:su.computers.unix	(Usenet Newsgroup) su.computers.unix
news:swnet.unix	(Usenet Newsgroup) swnet.unix
news:tn.unix	(Usenet Newsgroup) tn.unix
news:tnn.os.unix	(Usenet Newsgroup) tnn.os.unix
news:tw.bbs.comp.unix	(Usenet Newsgroup) tw.bbs.comp.unix

```
news:uw.unix
```
(Usenet Newsgroup)
uw.unix

```
news:uw.unix.sysadmin
```
(Usenet Newsgroup)
uw.unix.sysadmin

```
news:za.unix.misc
```
(Usenet Newsgroup)
za.unix.misc

WWW SPECIFIC

```
http://www.webcom.com/
```
Web Database Integration
White Paper

```
http://www.vpe.com/
```
Internet Development
Toolkit from VPE

```
http://grigg.chungnam.ac.kr/~uniweb/
documents/www_dbms.html
```
WWW DBMS Gateways

```
http://isms.software.ibm.com/celdemo.html
```
DB2 WWW Connection
Demos

```
http://isms.software.ibm.com/db2wdoc.htm
```
DB2 WWW Connection

```
http://isms.software.ibm.com/faq.html
```
DB2 WWW Connection
FAQs

```
http://cscsun1.larc.nasa.gov/~beowulf/db/
all_products.html
```
NASA Products

```
http://www.stars.com/Vlib/Providers/
Database.html
```
Web Developer's Virtual
Database Library

```
http://www.webcompare.com/
```
WebCompare

```
http://www.comvista.com/net/www/cgidata.html
```
Database CGIs

```
http://www.ix.de/ct/Artikel/96/06/Jo.html
```
Artikel 96

```
http://www.cyberdrive.net
```
(Tools) Cyberdrive Limited

```
http://www.starnine.com/webstar/webstar.html
```
(Tools) Webstar 2.0 from
Quarterdeck

```
http://www.servers.apple.com/
```
(Tools) Apple Internet Web
Solution

```
http://browserwatch.iworld.com/
```
(Tools) All Internet
Browsers

```
http://host.telescan.com/Stocks/
Corporate_Snapshot.html?Button
+Report&Symbol=NSCP
```
Netscape Comm Corp Com
Stock Chart (NSCP)
NASDAQ

CALCSPAC.SQL Procedure for Oracle Table Extents

Note: Script obtained from comp.databases.oracle

```
--
-- calcspac.sql
--
-- This sql proc estimates the initial amount of space required by a
-- non-clustered table in an Oracle database.  When using these esti-
-- mates, keep in mind the following sources of inaccuracy:
--   1.  The space used by updates and deletes does not free up immedi-
ately.
--   2.  Trailing null columns and length bytes are not stored.
--   3.  Inserts, updates, and deletes cause fragmentation and chained
--       row pieces.
--
-- This procedure assumes that there is a table with a sample set of
-- data already created.  It allows you to specify the number of rows
-- the actual table would grow to.
--
```

```
—  Inputs:
—   table name
—   table owner
—   number of rows
—
—  This procedure was taken from chapter 8 of the Oracle7 Server
—  Administrator Guide.
—
—  Feb 1, 1996 - Robert Walters          walterba@norand.com
—
set serveroutput on
set verify off
set feedback off


prompt Estimate Space Used by a table.
prompt
prompt Method based on instructions in chapter 8 of Oracle7 Server Ad-
ministrators Guide
prompt
prompt Add 10% to any results to give room for error.
prompt
accept owner            prompt "Enter Table Owner (default user) : "
accept table            prompt "Enter Table Name : "
accept numrows   number prompt "Estimate of total number of rows (0 for
existing count) : "


declare

  — Step 1.  Calculate Total Block Header Size
  —
  — block_header_part_a = fixed_header + variable_trans_header

  block_header_part_a                         number := 0;


  — fixed_header = 57 bytes
  fixed_header                          constant number := 57;


  — variable_trans_header = 23 * I
  —                           where I is the INITRANS for the table.

  variable_trans_header                      number := 0;
  variable_trans_header_overhead      constant number := 23;
```

```
— block_header_part_b = table_directory + row_directory

block_header_part_b                           number := 0;


— table_directory = 4 bytes

table_directory                    constant number := 4;


— row_directory = 2 * number_of_rows_per_block

row_directory                                 number := 0;
row_directory_overhead             constant number := 2;


— total_block_header = block_header_part_a + block_header_part_b

total_block_header                            number := 0;

— Step 2:  Calculate available data space per data block.
—
— available_data_space = (block_size - total_block_header) -
—                                   free_space_overhead
—
— free_space_overhead  = (block_size - block_header_part_a)*(pct-
free/100)

available_data_space                          number := 0;
free_space_overhead                           number := 0;
pctfree_                                      number := 0;
block_size                                    number := 0;


— Step 3:  Calculate combined data space.

average_row_data                              number := 0;


— Step 4:  Calculate total average row size.
—
— avg_row_size = row_header + F + V + average_row_data
— F = number of columns which store 250 bytes or less  * 1
— V = number of columns which store more than 250 byes * 3

avg_row_size                                  number := 0;
row_header                         constant number := 3;
```

```
F                                             number := 0;
F_overhead                        constant number := 1;
V                                             number := 0;
V_overhead                        constant number := 3;
min_avg_row_size                  constant number := 9;


— Step 5:  Calculate average rows per block
—
— number_of_rows_per_block = available_data_space / avg_row_size
—
— but since the number of rows per block is used in
— available_data_space, we must solve the above equation for
— number_of rows per block.
—
— number_of_rows_per_block =
—                     [(block_size - total_block_header) -
—                     free_space_overhead] / avg_row_size
—
— number_of_rows_per_block =
—                     [(block_size - (block_header_part_a +
—                                 block_header_part_b)) -
—                     free_space_overhead] / avg_row_size
—
— number_of_rows_per_block =
—                     [(block_size - (block_header_part_a +
—                                 table_directory +
—                                 row_directory)) -
—
—                     free_space_overhead] / avg_row_size
—
— number_of_rows_per_block =
—                     [(block_size - (block_header_part_a +
—                                 table_directory +
—                                 (row_directory_overhead *
—                                  number_of_rows_per_block))) -
—                     free_space_overhead] / avg_row_size
—
— avg_row_size * number_of_rows_per_block =
—                     (block_size - (block_header_part_a +
—                                 table_directory +
—                                 (row_directory_overhead *
—                                  number_of_rows_per_block))) -
—                     free_space_overhead
```

```
  -
  -  avg_row_size * number_of_rows_per_block =
  -                                           block_size -
  -                                           block_header_part_a -
  -                                           table_directory -
  -                                           (row_directory_overhead *
  -                                            number_of_rows_
  -                                            per_block) -
  -                                           free_space_overhead
  -
  -  (avg_row_size * number_of_rows_per_block) +
  -  (row_directory_overhead * number_of_rows_per_block)  =
  -                                           block_size -
  -                                           block_header_part_a -
  -                                           table_directory -
  -                                           free_space_overhead
  -
  -  (avg_row_size + row_directory_overhead) * number_of_rows_per_block =
  -                                           block_size -
  -                                           block_header_part_a -
  -                                           table_directory -
  -                                           free_space_overhead
  -
  -  number_of_rows_per_block  =
  -
  -  block_size - block_header_part_a - table_directory -
  -  free_space_overhead
  -  ────────────────────────────────────────
  -                      (avg_row_size + row_directory_overhead)
  -
number_of_rows_per_block                    number := 0;


  -   Step 6:  Calculate Number of Blocks and Bytes
  -
  -  number_of_blocks = number_of_rows / number_of_rows_per_block;

number_of_blocks                            number := 0;
number_of_rows                              number := 0;


  -  number_of_bytes = number_of_blocks * block_size

number_of_bytes                             number := 0;


  -
```

```
begin

  dbms_output.put_line ('.');
  dbms_output.put_line ('Analyzing '|| upper(nvl ('&&owner',user)) ||
'.' ||

                                      upper('&&table') || '.');
  dbms_output.put_line ('.');

  -  Analyze the table to get the most current information

  dbms_ddl.analyze_object (type => 'TABLE',
                          schema => upper (nvl ('&&owner',user)),
                          name   => upper ('&&table'),
                          method => 'ESTIMATE');

  -  Get information about the table from the data dictionary.

  select ini_trans * variable_trans_header_overhead,
         num_rows,
         pct_free,
         avg_row_len
  into   variable_trans_header,
         number_of_rows,
         pctfree_,
         average_row_data
  from   all_tables
  where  table_name = upper ('&&table')
  and    owner      = upper (nvl ('&&owner',user));

  select to_number(value)
  into   block_size
  from   v$parameter
  where  name = 'db_block_size';

  if nvl (&&numrows, 0) <> 0 then
    number_of_rows := &&numrows;
  end if;

  - Step 1.  Calculate Total Block Header Size

  block_header_part_a := fixed_header + variable_trans_header;
  dbms_output.put_line ('  Block header part A    = ' ||
```

```
                                         to_char(block_header_part_a));

    — Step 2:  Calculate available data space per data block.
    —
    free_space_overhead  := ceil ((block_size - block_header_part_a)
                                   *(pctfree_/100));
    dbms_output.put_line ('  Free space overhead    = ' ||
                                   to_char(free_space_overhead));


    — Step 3:  Calculate combined data space. (obtained from analyze com-
mand.)

    — Step 4:  Calculate total average row size.
    —
    — F = number of columns which store 250 bytes or less  * 1

    select count(*) * F_overhead
    into    F
    from    all_tab_columns
    where   owner      = upper (nvl ('&&owner', user))
    and     table_name = upper ('&&table')
    and     ((data_type in ('NUMBER','DATE'))
        or (data_type in ('CHAR','VARCHAR2','RAW') and
            data_length <= 250));


    dbms_output.put_line ('  No. columns <= 250 (F) = ' ||
                                        to_char(F));


    — V = number of columns which store more than 250 byes * 3

    select count(*) * V_overhead
    into    V
    from    all_tab_columns
    where   owner      = upper (nvl ('&&owner',user))
    and     table_name = upper ('&&table')
    and     ((data_type in ('LONG','LONG RAW'))
        or (data_type in ('CHAR','VARCHAR2','RAW') and
            data_length > 250));


    dbms_output.put_line ('  No. columns > 250 (V)  = ' ||
                                        to_char(V));


    avg_row_size := row_header + F + V + average_row_data;
```

```
      dbms_output.put_line ('  Average row size       = ' ||
                                        to_char(avg_row_size));


   — Step 5:  Calculate average rows per block


   — block_size - block_header_part_a - table_directory -
free_space_overhead

     — ————————————————————————————————

     —                    (avg_row_size + row_directory_overhead)

     —


   number_of_rows_per_block := floor (
      (block_size - block_header_part_a - table_directory -
free_space_overhead)/
                      (avg_row_size + row_directory_overhead));


   dbms_output.put_line ('  No. rows per block     = ' ||

to_char(number_of_rows_per_block));


   —  Step 6:  Calculate Number of Blocks and Bytes

   dbms_output.put_line ('.');
   number_of_blocks := ceil (number_of_rows / number_of_rows_per_block);

   dbms_output.put_line ('  No. of blocks          = ' ||
                                        to_char(number_of_blocks));


   number_of_bytes := number_of_blocks * block_size;

   dbms_output.put_line ('  No. of bytes           = ' ||
                                        to_char(number_of_bytes));

end;
/
set verify on
set feedback on
```

CA-IDMS SQL System Tables

The relational tables in the CA-IDMS catalog which contain definitions (metadata) derived from the DDL syntax can be useful in identifying all of your user tables, indexes, referential constraints, schemas, files, segments, areas, buffers and optimization.

SYSTEM TABLE NAME	DESCRIPTION
SYSTEM.AM	ACCESS MODULE
SYSTEM.AMDEP	ACCESS MODULE TABLE or VIEW
SYSTEM.AREA	AREA within SEGMENT
SYSTEM.BUFFER	DMCL BUFFER
SYSTEM.COLUMN	TABLE COLUMN
SYSTEM.CONSTKEY	REFERENTIAL CONSTRAINT FOREIGN KEY
SYSTEM.CONSTRAINT	REFERENTIAL CONSTRAINT
SYSTEM.DBNAME	DBNAME ENTRY
SYSTEM.DBSEGMENT	DBNAME TABLE SEGMENT
SYSTEM.DBSSC	DBNAME TABLE SUBSCHEMA
SYSTEM.DBTABLE	DBNAME TABLE
SYSTEM.DMCL	DMCL
SYSTEM.DMCLAREA	DMCL AREA
SYSTEM.DMCLFILE	DMCL FILE
SYSTEM.DMCLSEGMENT	DMCL SEGMENT
SYSTEM.FILE	FILE in SEGMENT

SYSTEM TABLE NAME	DESCRIPTION
SYSTEM.FILEMAP	AREA-to-FILE by PAGE RANGE
SYSTEM.INDEX	INDEX
SYSTEM.INDEXKEY	INDEX KEY COLUMN
SYSTEM.JOURNAL	DMCL JOURNAL FILE
SYSTEM.LOADHDR	LOAD MODULE
SYSTEM.ORDERKEY	LINKED CONSTRAINT SORT KEY
SYSTEM.SCHEMA	SCHEMA
SYSTEM.SECTION	* OPTIMIZER TREE STRUCTURE
SYSTEM.SEGMENT	SEGMENT
SYSTEM.SYMBOL	LOGICAL SYMBOL
SYSTEM.SYNTAX	CREATE-and-ALTER TABLE SYNTAX
SYSTEM.TABLE	TABLE
SYSTEM.VIEWDEP	VIEW for TABLE or other VIEW

* Unreadable without some kind of legend

With CA-IDMS Release 14, viewing this information became much easier. You can issue DISPLAY and PUNCH commands for all the tables listed. For example, the command **DISPLAY ALL VIEW** would provide a list of all views. Also, you get a bunch of SELECTS for the system tables at install time in source library member LISTCAT.

The display below shows a SELECT of index statistics from SYSTEM.INDEX. This particular display is for an index supporting the system tables. Note the many statistics for SR8s, leaf pages, clustering, duplicate keys and filling of index blocks that can be used to adjust index parameters.

```
                OCF 12.0 ONLINE IDMS NO ERRORS        DICT=SYSTEM       1/40
CONNECT TO SYSTEM;

*+ Status = 0

SELECT UNIQUE, CLUSTER, COMPRESS, IXBLKLENGTH, IXBLKCONTAINS, AVGMEM-
ROWS,

AVGMEMPAGES, AVGAMEMCLUSCNT, AVGBMEMCLUSCNT, AVGCMEMCLUSCNT, AVGDMEM-
CLUSCNT,

AVGEMEMCLUSCNT, AVGSR8ROWS, LONGESTSR8, SECLONGSR8, NUMLONGSR8,
AVGSR8PAGES,

MAXSR8PAGES, AVGSR8LEAFS, AVGSR8LEVELS, AVGASR8CLUSCNT, AVGBSR8CLUSCNT,

AVGCSR8CLUSCNT, AVGDSR8CLUSCNT, AVGESR8CLUSCNT, NUMUNIQKEYS, NUMNUL-
LKEYS,

NUMLONGKEYS, AVGDUPSPERKEY, AVGPAGESPERKEY

FROM SYSTEM.INDEX

WHERE TABLE = 'TABLE' AND
```

```
      NAME = 'IX-TABLE';
*+
*+ UNIQUE  CLUSTER  COMPRESS  IXBLKLENGTH  IXBLKCONTAINS     AVGMEMROWS
*+ ———  ———-  ————  ————-  ————-    ———
*+ Y       N        Y                1440            30  3.3000000E+01
*+
*+   AVGMEMPAGES  AVGAMEMCLUSCNT  AVGBMEMCLUSCNT  AVGCMEMCLUSCNT
*+   ————-  ————    ————    ————
*+  0.0000000E+00  3.6000000E+01   3.6000000E+01   3.6000000E+01
*+
*+ AVGDMEMCLUSCNT  AVGEMEMCLUSCNT    AVGSR8ROWS   LONGESTSR8   SEC-
LONGSR8
*+ ————    ————      ———     ———     ———
*+  3.6000000E+01   3.3000000E+01   3.0000000E+00            3
0
*+
*+ NUMLONGSR8   AVGSR8PAGES  MAXSR8PAGES    AVGSR8LEAFS
AVGSR8LEVELS
*+  ———    ———-   ———-    ———
*+          1  1.0000000E+00            0  2.0000000E+00
1.0000000E+00
*+
*+ AVGASR8CLUSCNT  AVGBSR8CLUSCNT  AVGCSR8CLUSCNT  AVGDSR8CLUSCNT
*+ ————    ————    ————    ————
*+  1.0000000E+00   1.0000000E+00   1.0000000E+00   1.0000000E+00
*+
*+ AVGESR8CLUSCNT  NUMUNIQKEYS  NUMNULLKEYS  NUMLONGKEYS  AVGDUPSPERKEY
*+ ————    ———-   ———-   ———    ———-
*+  1.0000000E+00           33            0            0  0.0000000E+00
*+
*+ AVGPAGESPERKEY
*+ ————
*+  1.0000000E+00
*+
*+ 1 row processed
```

IDMSBCF Space Report

The IDMSBCF space reports are relatively new. They provide information similar to that found in the conventional IDMSDUMP and IDMSDBAN utilities. To see for yourself, a sample run is shown here.

JCL

```
000011 //PRNTSP    EXEC PGM=IDMSBCF,REGION=2048K,COND=(4,LT)
000012 //STEPLIB   DD DSN=YOUR.CV.DEPENDENT.LOADLIB,DISP=SHR
000013 //          DD DSN=YOUR.INSTALL.LOADLIB,DISP=SHR
000014 //SYSLST    DD SYSOUT=*
000015 //SYSPRINT  DD SYSOUT=*
000016 //SORTMSG   DD SYSOUT=*
000017 //SYSPCH    DD DUMMY
000018 //SYSJRNL   DD DUMMY
000019 //J1JRNL    DD DUMMY
000020 //J2JRNL    DD DUMMY
000021 //SYSUDUMP  DD SYSOUT=*
000022 //SYSIDMS   DD *
000023 DMCL=R120DMCL
000024 /*
000025 //SYSIPT    DD *
000026 CONNECT TO SYSTEM;
PRINT SPACE FOR SEGMENT EMPDEMO FULL;
```

Output

```
AREA          EMPDEMO.EMP-DEMO-REGION     Distribution of USED Space Report
 Maximum                                        Percent of
 Record Type   Length      Occurrences    Total Space Used      Total Used
    SR7          40              1               40                0.10
    SR8        1,396            3            3,152                8.56
    SR415        196           74           14,504               39.39
    SR420         60           86            5,160               14.01
    SR425         36          150            5,400               14.66
    SR460         40           68            2,720                7.38
 Space Inv.    4,244            1            4,244               11.52
 Overhead         32           50            1,600                4.34
               *** NO logically deleted records found ***
                                    AVAILABLE Space Distribution Re-
port
                                    AVAIL           NUMBER
                                    SPACE          OF PAGES
 AREA          EMPDEMO.INS-DEMO-REGION
 PAGE SIZE          4,276
       PAGES       75,101 THRU        75,125
                                          91-100%               19
                                          81-90 %                4
                                          71-80 %                0
                                          61-70 %                0
                                          51-60 %                0
                                          41-50 %                1
                                          31-40 %                0
                                          21-30 %                0
                                          11-20 %                0
                                          00-10 %                0
                                          SMPS                   1
                                          TOTAL                 25
       FILE    EMPDEMO.INSDEMO
       PAGES       75,101 THRU        75,125
       BLOCKS           1 THRU        25
 Total Space Allocated                    106,900
 Total Space Available   (Percent)         94,140
 (88.06%)
 Total Space Used                          12,760
 Logically Full Pages                           0
 Total Space Unusable    (Percent)              0   (  0.00%)
```

```
AREA        EMPDEMO.INS-DEMO-REGION      Distribution of USED Space Report
            Maximum                                          Percent of
Record Type Length       Occurrences    Total Space Used     Total Used
   SR400        44            74             3,256              25.51
   SR405       316             3               708               5.54
   SR430       308             2               616               4.82
   SR435       148             4               592               4.63
   SR445       652             6             2,544              19.93
Space Inv.   4,244            1             4,244              33.26
Overhead        32            25              800               6.26
             *** NO logically deleted records found ***
```

SCO Unix Tuning

SCO UNIX has a handy configure utility which simplifies tuning. Unlike other UNIX operating systems which require messing around with C code, SCO is a lot like working with Windows NT.

Below is a list of parameters used for tuning SCO UNIX.

Configure Parameter	Description	Min	Max	Bytes/ Sec(s)
AGEINTERVAL	nbr ticks to age process pages			
BDFLUSHR	buffer flush period	1	300	sec
BFREEMIN	nbr freelist buffers	1	100	
CFLCKREC	nbr of system record locks	1	n	28
CTBUFSIZE	tape buffer size	32	256	1024
DMAABLEBUF	nbr DMA buffers	4	128	1024
DO387CR3	80387 math coprocessor setting			
EVDEVS	max event devices per system			
EVDEVSPERQ	max event devices per queue			
EVQUEUES	max open event queues			
GPGSHI	page stealing high water mark	1	n	
GPGSLO	page stealing low water mark	1	n	
KDBSYMSIZE	symbol table size	10000		100000
MAXBUF	max cache buffers			
MAXFC	max freelist pages added	1	n	
MAXPMEM	max pages of memory			

Configure Parameter	Description	Min	Max	Bytes/ Sec(s)
MAXSC	max swapped pages	1	n	
MAXSLICE	max user process time slice ticks	15	60	
MAXUMEM	max user memory pages	1	8192	
MAXUP	max user processes	8	64	
MINARMEM	min user memory pages	1	n	
MINASMEM	min system memory pages	1	n	
MINASMEM	nbr free pages			
MSGSEG	nbr msg segments			
MSGSSZ	msg segment size			
NAUTOUP	automatic update interval			sec
NBLKn	nbr block buffers	4	4 K	
NBUF	nbr cache buffers			1024
NCALL	timeout table size			
NCLIST	char list buffers	1		#terminals*1064
NDISK	nbr disk drives on system	100	600	1076
NEMAP	max I/O mappings			
NFILE	open file table entries	100	600	12
NGROUPS	max nbr groups			
NHBUF	nbr hash queues	**2	**2	
NINODE	nbr inode table entries	100	400	
NLOG	nbr log devices	1	n	
NMOUNT	nbr of mount table entries			
NMPBUF	nbr large I/O buffers (16 KB)	0	16	
NMPHEADBUF	nbr cluster buffer headers	0	600	
NOFILES	max open files per process	1	n	
NPBUF	nbr PIO buffers	1	n	52
NPROC	nbr process table entries	50	400	
NQUEUE	nbr queues for streaming			
NQUEUE	nbr of queues			
NREGION	nbr region table entries			36
NREGION	region table size			
NSSINODE	must be >= NINODE			
NSTREAM	nbr of open streams	64	n	
NSTRPUSH	nbr processes on a stream			
PRFMAX	max profiler symbols			
PUTBUFSZ	console buffer size			
SEMMAP	semaphore map size	1	n	8
SEMMNI	nbr active semaphore identifiers	1	n	32
SEMMNS	nbr of semaphores			

Configure Parameter	Description	Min	Max	Bytes/ Sec(s)
SEMMNU	nbr semaphore undo structures			
SEMMSL	max semaphores per SEMMNI			
SEMOPM	max semaphore operations per call	1	n	8
SEMUME	max nbr entries per undo structure			
SEMVMX	max semaphore value	1	32 K	
SHMALL	max active memory segments			
SHMMAX	max shared memory segement size		n	
SHMMIN	min shared memory segment size		n	
SHMMNI	max nbr shared memory identifiers		n	52
SHMSEG	shared memory segments/process		15	
SPTMAP	mfree map size			
SSCACHEENTS	nbr name cache entries	1	1024	
SSHASHQS	nbr name cache hash entries	1	1021	prime#
SSOFBIAS	open files in cache bias	0	256	
STREVENT	nbr stream events			
STRMSGSZ	max stream msg size			
ULIMIT	largest user file size	512	1 GB	512
VHNDFRAC	vhand paging daemon threshold	1	24	

Index

SOFTWARE AND INFORMATION LICENSE

The software and information on this diskette (collectively referred to as the "Product") are the property of The McGraw-Hill Companies, Inc. ("McGraw-Hill") and are protected by both United States copyright law and international copyright treaty provision. You must treat this Product just like a book, except that you may copy it into a computer to be used and you may make archival copies of the Products for the sole purpose of backing up our software and protecting your investment from loss.

By saying "just like a book," McGraw-Hill means, for example, that the Product may be used by any number of people and may be freely moved from one computer location to another, so long as there is no possibility of the Product (or any part of the Product) being used at one location or on one computer while it is being used at another. Just a book cannot be read by two different people in two different places at the same time, neither can the Product be used by two different people in two different places at the same time (unless, of course, McGraw-Hill's rights are being violated).

McGraw-Hill reserves the right to alter or modify the contents of the Product at any time.

This agreement is effective until terminated. The Agreement will terminate automatically without notice if you fail to comply with any provisions of this Agreement. In the event of termination by reason of your breach, you will destroy or erase all copies of the Product installed on any computer system or made for backup purposes and shall expunge the Product from your data storage facilities.

LIMITED WARRANTY

McGraw-Hill warrants the physical diskette(s) enclosed herein to be free of defects in materials and workmanship for a period of sixty days from the purchase date. If McGraw-Hill receives written notification within the warranty period of defects in materials or workmanship, and such notification is determined by McGraw-Hill to be correct, McGraw-Hill will replace the defective diskette(s). Send request to:

Customer Service
McGraw-Hill
Gahanna Industrial Park
860 Taylor Station Road
Blacklick, OH 43004-9615

The entire and exclusive liability and remedy for breach of this Limited Warranty shall be limited to replacement of defective diskette(s) and shall not include or extend any claim for or right to cover any other damages, including but not limited to, loss of profit, data, or use of the software, or special, incidental, or consequential damages or other similar claims, even if McGraw-Hill has been specifically advised as to the possibility of such damages. In no event will McGraw-Hill's liability for any damages to you or any other person ever exceed the lower of suggested list price or actual price paid for the license to use the Product, regardless of any form of the claim.

THE McGRAW-HILL COMPANIES, INC. SPECIFICALLY DISCLAIMS ALL OTHER WARRANTIES, EXPRESS OR IMPLIED, INCLUDING BUT NOT LIMITED TO, ANY IMPLIED WARRANTY OF MERCHANTABILITY OR FITNESS FOR A PARTICULAR PURPOSE. Specifically, McGraw-Hill makes no representation or warranty that the Product is fit for any particular purpose and any implied warranty of merchantability is limited to the sixty day duration of the Limited Warranty covering the physical diskette(s) only (and not the software or information) and is otherwise expressly and specifically disclaimed.

This Limited Warranty gives you specific legal rights; you may have others which may vary from state to state. Some states do not allow the exclusion of incidental or consequential damages, or the limitation on how long an implied warranty lasts, so some of the above may not apply to you.

This Agreement constitutes the entire agreement between the parties relating to use of the Product. The terms of any purchase order shall have no effect on the terms of this Agreement. Failure of McGraw-Hill to insist at any time on strict compliance with this Agreement shall not constitute a waiver of any rights under this Agreement. This Agreement shall be construed and governed in accordance with the laws of New York. If any provision of this Agreement is held to be contrary to law, that provision will be enforced to the maximum extent permissible and the remaining provisions will remain in force and effect.